Children's
Literature
Review

Guide to Gale Literary Criticism Series

When you need to review criticism of literary works, these are the Gale series to use:

If the author's death date is:

You should turn to:

After Dec. 31, 1959
(or author is still living)

CONTEMPORARY LITERARY CRITICISM

for example: Jorge Luis Borges, Anthony Burgess,
William Faulkner, Mary Gordon,
Ernest Hemingway, Iris Murdoch

1900 through 1959

TWENTIETH-CENTURY LITERARY CRITICISM

for example: Willa Cather, F. Scott Fitzgerald,
Henry James, Mark Twain, Virginia Woolf

1800 through 1899

NINETEENTH-CENTURY LITERATURE CRITICISM

for example: Fedor Dostoevski, Nathaniel Hawthorne,
George Sand, William Wordsworth

1400 through 1799

LITERATURE CRITICISM FROM 1400 TO 1800
(excluding Shakespeare)

for example: Anne Bradstreet, Daniel Defoe,
Alexander Pope, François Rabelais,
Jonathan Swift, Phillis Wheatley

SHAKESPEAREAN CRITICISM

Shakespeare's plays and poetry

Antiquity through 1399

CLASSICAL AND MEDIEVAL LITERATURE CRITICISM

for example: Dante, Homer, Plato, Sophocles, Vergil,
the Beowulf Poet

Gale also publishes related criticism series:

CHILDREN'S LITERATURE REVIEW

This series covers authors of all eras who write for the preschool
through high school audience.

SHORT STORY CRITICISM

This series covers the major short fiction writers of all nationalities
and periods of literary history.

ISSN 0362-4145

volume 16

Children's Literature Review

Excerpts from Reviews,
Criticism, and Commentary
on Books for Children
and Young People

Gerard J. Senick
Editor

Melissa Reiff Hug
Associate Editor

 *Gale Research Inc.*
Book Tower
Detroit, Michigan 48226

STAFF

Gerard J. Senick, *Editor*

Melissa Reiff Hug, *Associate Editor*

Susan Miller Harig, *Senior Assistant Editor*

Motoko Fujishiro Huthwaite, *Assistant Editor*

Sharon R. Gunton, *Contributing Editor*

Jeanne A. Gough, *Permissions & Production Manager*

Lizbeth A. Purdy, *Production Supervisor*
Kathleen M. Cook, *Production Coordinator*
Cathy Beranek, Suzanne Powers, Kristine E. Tipton, Lee Ann Welsh, *Editorial Assistants*

Linda M. Pugliese, *Manuscript Coordinator*
Maureen A. Puhl, *Senior Manuscript Assistant*
Donna Craft, Jennifer E. Gale, *Manuscript Assistants*

Victoria B. Cariappa, *Research Supervisor*
Maureen R. Richards, *Research Coordinator*
Mary D. Wise, *Senior Research Assistant*
Joyce E. Doyle, Kevin B. Hillstrom, Karen D. Kaus, Eric Priehs, Filomena Sgambati, Laura B. Standley, *Research Assistants*

Janice M. Mach, *Text Permissions Supervisor*
Kathy Grell, *Text Permissions Coordinator*
Mabel E. Gurney, *Research Permissions Coordinator*
Josephine M. Keene, *Senior Permissions Assistant*
Eileen H. Baehr, H. Diane Cooper, Anita L. Ransom, Kimberly F. Smilay, *Permissions Assistants*
Melissa Ann Brantley, Denise M. Singleton, Sharon D. Valentine, Lisa M. Wimmer, *Permissions Clerks*

Patricia A. Seefelt, *Picture Permissions Supervisor*
Margaret A. Chamberlain, *Picture Permissions Coordinator*
Pamela A. Hayes, Lillian Tyus, *Permissions Clerks*

Mary Beth Trimper, *Production Manager*
Darlene K. Maxey, *External Production Associate*

Arthur Chartow, *Art Director*
Linda A. Davis, *Production Assistant*

Laura Bryant, *Production Supervisor*
Louise Gagné, *Internal Production Associate*

CONTENTS

PREFACE

As children's literature has evolved into both a respected branch of creative writing and a successful industry, literary criticism has documented and influenced each stage of its growth. Critics have recorded the literary development of individual authors as well as the trends and controversies that resulted from changes in values and attitudes, especially as they concerned children. While defining a philosophy of children's literature, critics developed a scholarship that balances an appreciation of children and an awareness of their needs with standards for literary quality much like those required by critics of adult literature. *Children's Literature Review (CLR)* is designed to provide a permanent, accessible record of this ongoing scholarship. Those responsible for bringing children and books together can now make informed choices when selecting reading materials for the young.

Scope of the Series

Each volume of *CLR* contains excerpts from published criticism on the works of authors and illustrators who create books for children from preschool through high school. The author list for each volume is international in scope and represents the variety of genres covered by children's literature—picture books, fiction, folklore, nonfiction, poetry, and drama. The works of approximately fifteen authors of all eras are represented in each volume. Although earlier volumes of *CLR* emphasized critical material published after 1960, successive volumes have expanded their coverage to encompass criticism written before 1960. Since many of the authors included in *CLR* are living and continue to write, it is necessary to update their entries periodically. Thus, future volumes will supplement the entries of selected authors covered in earlier volumes as well as include criticism on the works of authors new to the series.

Organization of the Book

An author section consists of the following elements: author heading, author portrait, author introduction, excerpts of criticism (each followed by a bibliographical citation), and illustrations, when available.

- The **author heading** consists of the author's full name followed by birth and death dates. The portion of the name outside the parentheses denotes the form under which the author is most frequently published. If the majority of the author's works for children were written under a pseudonym, the pseudonym will be listed in the author heading and the real name given on the first line of the author introduction. Also located at the beginning of the introduction are any other pseudonyms used by the author in writing for children and any name variations, including transliterated forms for authors whose languages use nonroman alphabets. Uncertainty as to a birth or death date is indicated by question marks.

- An **author portrait** is included when available.

- The **author introduction** contains information designed to introduce an author to *CLR* users by presenting an overview of the author's themes and styles, occasional biographical facts that relate to the author's literary career, a summary of critical response to the author's works, and information about major awards and prizes the author has received. Where applicable, introductions conclude with references to additional entries in biographical and critical reference series published by Gale Research Inc. These sources include past volumes of *CLR* as well as *Authors in the News, Contemporary Authors, Contemporary Literary Criticism, Dictionary of Literary Biography, Nineteenth-Century Literature Criticism, Something about the Author, Something about the Author Autobiography Series, Twentieth-Century Literary Criticism,* and *Yesterday's Authors of Books for Children.*

- **Criticism** is located in three sections: **author's commentary** and **general commentary** (when available) and within individual **title entries,** which are preceded by **title entry headings.** Criticism is arranged chronologically within each section. Titles by authors being profiled are highlighted in boldface type within the text for easier access by readers.

The **author's commentary** presents background material written by the author or by an interviewer. This commentary may cover a specific work or several works. Author's commentary on more than one work appears after the author introduction, while commentary on an individual book follows the title entry heading.

The **general commentary** consists of critical excerpts that consider more than one work by the author being profiled. General commentary is preceded by the critic's name in boldface type or, in the case of unsigned criticism, by the title of the journal.

Title entry headings precede the criticism on a title and cite publication information on the work being reviewed. Title headings list the title of the work as it appeared in its country of origin; titles in languages using nonroman alphabets are transliterated. If the original title is in a language other than English, the title of the first English-language translation follows in brackets. The first available publication date of each work is listed in parentheses following the title. Differing U.S. and British titles of works originally published in English follow the publication date within the parentheses.

Title entries consist of critical excerpts on the author's individual works, arranged chronologically by publication date. The entries generally contain two to six reviews per title, depending on the stature of the book and the amount of criticism it has generated. The editors select titles that reflect the entire scope of the author's literary contribution, covering each genre and subject. An effort is made to reprint criticism that represents the full range of each title's reception—from the year of its initial publication to current assessments. Thus, the reader is provided with a record of the author's critical history. Publication information (such as publisher names and book prices) and parenthetical numerical references (such as footnotes or page and line references to specific editions of works) have been deleted at the editor's discretion to provide smoother reading of the text.

Entries on authors who are also illustrators will occasionally feature commentary on selected works illustrated but not written by the author being profiled. These works are strongly associated with the illustrator and have received critical acclaim for their art. By including critical comment on works of this type, the editors wish to provide a more complete representation of the author's total career. Criticism on these works has been chosen to stress artistic, rather than literary, contributions. Title entry headings for works illustrated by the author being profiled are arranged chronologically within the entry by date of publication and include notes identifying the author of the illustrated work. In order to provide easier access for users, all titles illustrated by the subject of the entry will be boldfaced.

CLR also includes entries on prominent illustrators who have contributed to the field of children's literature. These entries are designed to represent the development of the illustrator as an artist rather than as a literary stylist. The illustrator's section is organized like that of an author, with two exceptions: the introduction presents an overview of the illustrator's styles and techniques rather than outlining his or her literary background, and the commentary written by the illustrator on his or her works is called illustrator's commentary rather than author's commentary. Title entry headings are followed by explanatory notes identifying the author of the illustrated work. All titles of books containing illustrations by the artist being profiled as well as individual illustrations from these books are highlighted in boldface type.

• Selected excerpts are preceded by **explanatory notes,** which provide information on the critic or work of criticism to enhance the reader's understanding of the excerpt.

• A complete **bibliographical citation** designed to facilitate the location of the original book or article follows each piece of criticism.

• Numerous **illustrations** are featured in *CLR*. For entries on illustrators, an effort has been made to include illustrations that reflect the characteristics discussed in the criticism. Entries on major authors who do not illustrate their own works may also include photographs and other illustrative material pertinent to the authors' careers.

Other Features

• A list of **authors to appear in future volumes** follows the preface.

• An **appendix** lists the sources from which material has been reprinted in the volume. It does not, however, list every book or periodical consulted for the volume.

• The **cumulative index to authors** lists authors who have appeared in *CLR* and includes cross-references to *Authors in the News, Contemporary Authors, Contemporary Literary Criticism, Dictionary of Literary Biography, Nineteenth-Century Literature Criticism, Something about the Author, Something* *about the Author Autobiography Series, Twentieth-Century Literary Criticism,* and *Yesterday's Authors of Books for Children.*

- The **cumulative nationality index** lists authors alphabetically under their respective nationalities. Author names are followed by the volume number(s) in which they appear. Authors who have changed citizenship or whose current citizenship is not reflected in biographical sources appear under both their original nationality and that of their current residence.

- The **cumulative title index** lists titles covered in *CLR* followed by the volume and page number where criticism begins.

Acknowledgments

No work of this scope can be accomplished without the cooperation of many people. The editors especially wish to thank the copyright holders of the criticism included in this volume, the permissions managers of many book and magazine publishing companies for assisting us in securing reprint rights, and the staffs of the Kresge Library at Wayne State University, the University of Michigan Library, the Detroit Public Library, and the Wayne Oakland Library Federation (WOLF) for making their resources available to us. We are also grateful to Anthony J. Bogucki for his assistance with copyright research.

Suggestions Are Welcome

In response to various suggestions, several features have been added to *CLR* since the series began, including author entries on retellers of traditional literature as well as those who have been the first to record oral tales and other folklore; entries on prominent illustrators featuring commentary on their styles and techniques; entries on authors whose works are considered controversial or have been challenged; occasional entries devoted to criticism on a single work by a major author; explanatory notes that provide information on the critic or work of criticism to enhance the usefulness of the excerpt; more extensive illustrative material, such as holographs of manuscript pages and photographs of people and places pertinent to the authors' careers; a cumulative nationality index for easy access to authors by nationality; and occasional guest essays written specifically for *CLR* by prominent critics on subjects of their choice.

Readers are cordially invited to write the editor with comments and suggestions for further enhancing the usefulness of the *CLR* series.

AUTHORS TO APPEAR IN FUTURE VOLUMES

Aardema, Verna (Norberg) 1911-
Adams, Harriet S(tratemeyer)
   1893?-1982
Adams, Richard 1920-
Adler, Irving 1913-
Ahlberg, Janet 1944- and Allan 1938-
Anderson, C(larence) W(illiam)
   1891-1971
Arrick, Fran
Arundel, Honor (Morfydd) 1919-1973
Asbjörnsen, Peter Christen 1812-1885
   and Jörgen Moe 1813?-1882
Asch, Frank 1946-
Avery, Gillian 1926-
Avi 1937-
Aymé, Marcel 1902-1967
Bailey, Carolyn Sherwin 1875-1961
Ballantyne, R(obert) M(ichael)
   1825-1894
Banner, Angela 1923-
Bannerman, Helen 1863-1946
Barrett, Judi(th) 1941-
Baumann, Hans 1914-1985
Beatty, Patricia Robbins 1922-
   and John 1922-1975
Beckman, Gunnel 1910-
Behn, Harry 1898-1973
Belloc, Hilaire 1870-1953
Berenstain, Stan(ley) 1923- and
   Jan(ice) 1923-
Berger, Melvin H. 1927-
Berna, Paul 1910-
Beskow, Elsa 1874-1953
Bianco, Margery Williams 1881-1944
Bishop, Claire Huchet
Blake, Quentin 1932-
Blos, Joan W(insor) 1928-
Blumberg, Rhoda 1917-
Blyton, Enid 1897-1968
Bodecker, N(iels) M(ogens) 1922-
Bodker, Cecil 1927-
Bonham, Frank 1914-
Brancato, Robin F(idler) 1936-
Branscum, Robbie 1937-
Breinburg, Petronella 1927-
Bridgers, Sue Ellen 1942-
Bright, Robert 1902-
Brink, Carol Ryrie 1895-1981
Brinsmead, H(esba) F(ay) 1922-
Brooke, L(eonard) Leslie 1862-1940
Brown, Marc Tolon 1946-
Browne, Anthony (Edward Tudor)
   1946-
Bryan, Ashley F. 1923-
Buff, Mary 1890-1970 and Conrad
   1886-1975

Bulla, Clyde Robert 1914-
Burch, Robert (Joseph) 1925-
Burgess, Gelett 1866-1951
Burgess, Thornton W(aldo) 1874-1965
Burkert, Nancy Ekholm 1933-
Burnett, Frances Hodgson 1849-1924
Butterworth, Oliver 1915-
Caines, Jeannette (Franklin)
Carlson, Natalie Savage 1906-
Carrick, Carol 1935- and Donald 1929-
Chambers, Aidan 1934-
Chönz, Selina
Christopher, Matt(hew F.) 1917-
Ciardi, John (Anthony) 1916-1986
Clapp, Patricia 1912-
Clarke, Pauline 1921-
Cohen, Barbara 1932-
Colby, C(arroll) B(urleigh) 1904-1977
Colman, Hila
Colum, Padraic 1881-1972
Cone, Molly 1918-
Conrad, Pam 1947-
Coolidge, Olivia E(nsor) 1908-
Coolidge, Susan 1835-1905
Cooney, Barbara 1917-
Courlander, Harold 1908-
Cox, Palmer 1840-1924
Crane, Walter 1845-1915
Cresswell, Helen 1934-
Crompton, Richmal 1890-1969
Cunningham, Julia (Woolfolk) 1916-
Curry, Jane L(ouise) 1932-
Dalgliesh, Alice 1893-1979
Daly, Maureen 1921-
Danziger, Paula 1944-
Daugherty, James 1889-1974
D'Aulaire, Ingri 1904-1980 and Edgar
   Parin 1898-1986
De la Mare, Walter 1873-1956
De Regniers, Beatrice Schenk 1914-
Dickinson, Peter 1927-
Dillon, Eilís 1920-
Dillon, Leo 1933- and Diane 1933-
Dodge, Mary Mapes 1831-1905
Domanska, Janina
Drescher, Henrik
Duncan, Lois S(teinmetz) 1934-
Duvoisin, Roger 1904-1980
Eager, Edward 1911-1964
Edgeworth, Maria 1767-1849
Edmonds, Walter D(umaux) 1903-
Epstein, Sam(uel) 1909- and Beryl
   1910-
Ets, Marie Hall 1893-
Ewing, Juliana Horatia 1841-1885
Farber, Norma 1909-1984

Farjeon, Eleanor 1881-1965
Field, Eugene 1850-1895
Field, Rachel 1894-1942
Fisher, Dorothy Canfield 1879-1958
Fisher, Leonard Everett 1924-
Flack, Marjorie 1897-1958
Forbes, Esther 1891-1967
Forman, James D(ouglas) 1932-
Freedman, Russell 1929-
Freeman, Don 1908-1978
Fujikawa, Gyo 1908-
Fyleman, Rose 1877-1957
Gantos, Jack 1951-
Garfield, Leon 1921-
Garis, Howard R(oger) 1873-1962
Garner, Alan 1935-
Gates, Doris 1901-
Gerrard, Roy 1935-
Giblin, James Cross 1933-
Giff, Patricia Reilly 1935-
Ginsburg, Mirra 1919-
Goble, Paul 1933-
Godden, Rumer 1907-
Goodall, John S(trickland) 1908-
Goodrich, Samuel G(riswold)
   1793-1860
Gorey, Edward (St. John) 1925-
Gramatky, Hardie 1907-1979
Greene, Constance C(larke) 1924-
Grimm, Jacob 1785-1863 and Wilhelm
   1786-1859
Gruelle, Johnny 1880-1938
Guillot, René 1900-1969
Hader, Elmer 1889-1973 and Berta
   1891?-1976
Hague, Michael 1948-
Hale, Lucretia Peabody 1820-1900
Haley, Gail E(inhart) 1939-
Hall, Lynn 1937-
Harnett, Cynthia 1893-1981
Harris, Christie (Lucy Irwin) 1907-
Harris, Joel Chandler 1848-1908
Harris, Rosemary (Jeanne) 1923-
Hayes, Sheila 1937-
Haywood, Carolyn 1898-
Head, Ann 1915-
Heide, Florence Parry 1919-
Heine, Helme
Heinlein, Robert A(nson) 1907-
Highwater, Jamake (Mamake) 1942-
Hoberman, Mary Ann 1930-
Hoff, Syd(ney) 1912-
Hoffman, Heinrich 1809-1894
Holland, Isabelle 1920-
Holling, Holling C(lancy) 1900-1973
Hughes, Langston 1902-1967

Hunter, Mollie 1922-
Hurd, Edith Thacher 1910-
 and Clement 1908-
Hyman, Trina Schart 1939-
Ipcar, Dahlov (Zorach) 1917-
Iwasaki, Chihiro 1918-1974
Jackson, Jesse 1908-1983
Janosch 1931-
Johnson, Crockett 1906-1975
Johnson, James Weldon 1871-1938
Jones, Diana Wynne 1934-
Judson, Clara Ingram 1879-1960
Juster, Norton 1929-
Kelly, Eric P(hilbrook) 1884-1960
Kennedy, (Jerome) Richard 1932-
Kent, Jack 1920-1985
Kerr, (Anne-)Judith 1923-
Kerr, M. E. 1927-
Kettelkamp, Larry (Dale) 1933-
King, (David) Clive 1924-
Kipling, Rudyard 1865-1936
Kjelgaard, Jim 1910-1959
Kraus, Robert 1925-
Krauss, Ruth (Ida) 1911-
Krumgold, Joseph 1908-1980
La Fontaine, Jean de 1621-1695
Lang, Andrew 1844-1912
Langton, Jane (Gillson) 1922-
Latham, Jean Lee 1902-
Lattimore, Eleanor Frances 1904-1986
Lavine, Sigmund A(rnold) 1908-
Leaf, Munro 1905-1976
Lenski, Lois 1893-1974
Levy, Elizabeth 1942-
Lightner, A(lice) M. 1904-
Lipsyte, Robert 1938-
Lofting, Hugh (John) 1866-1947
Lunn, Janet 1928-
MacDonald, George 1824-1905
MacGregor, Ellen 1906-1954
Mann, Peggy
Marshall, James 1942-
Martin, Patricia Miles 1899-1986
Maruki, Toshi 19??-
Masefield, John 1878-1967
Mayer, Marianna 1945-
Mayne, William (James Carter) 1928-
Mazer, Norma Fox 1931-
McCaffrey, Anne (Inez) 1926-
McGovern, Ann
McKee, David (John)
McKillip, Patricia A(nne) 1948-
McNeer, May 1902-
Meader, Stephen W(arren) 1892-1977
Means, Florence Crannell 1891-1980
Meigs, Cornelia 1884-1973

Merrill, Jean (Fairbanks) 1923-
Miles, Betty 1928-
Milne, Lorus 1912- and Margery 1915-
Minarik, Else Holmelund 1920-
Mizumura, Kazue
Mohr, Nicholasa 1935-
Molesworth, Mary Louisa 1842-1921
Morey, Walt(er Nelson) 1907-
Mowat, Farley (McGill) 1921-
Munsch, Robert 19??-
Naylor, Phyllis Reynolds 1933-
Neufeld, John (Arthur) 1938-
Neville, Emily Cheney 1919-
Nic Leodhas, Sorche 1898-1969
North, Sterling 1906-1974
Norton, Andre 1912-
Ofek, Uriel 1926-
Ormondroyd, Edward 1925-
Oxenbury, Helen 1938-
Parish, Peggy 1927-
Peck, Robert Newton 1928-
Perl, Lila
Perrault, Charles 1628-1703
Petersen, P(eter) J(ames) 1941-
Petersham, Maud 1890-1971 and
 Miska 1888-1960
Picard, Barbara Leonie 1917-
Pierce, Meredith Ann 1958-
Platt, Kin 1911-
Politi, Leo 1908-
Price, Christine 1928-1980
Pyle, Howard 1853-1911
Rackham, Arthur 1867-1939
Rawls, Wilson 1919-
Reiss, Johanna 1932-
Reeves, James 1909-1978
Richards, Laura E(lizabeth) 1850-1943
Richler, Mordecai 1931-
Robertson, Keith (Carlton) 1914-
Rockwell, Anne 1934- and Harlow
 19??-1988
Rodgers, Mary 1931-
Rollins, Charlemae Hill 1897-1979
Ross, Tony 1938-
Rounds, Glen H(arold) 1906-
Salinger, J(erome) D(avid) 1919-
Sanchez, Sonia 1934-
Sandburg, Carl 1878-1967
Sandoz, Mari 1896-1966
Sawyer, Ruth 1880-1970
Scarry, Huck 1953-
Scoppettone, Sandra 1936-
Scott, Jack Denton 1915-
Sebestyen, Ouida 1924-
Seton, Ernest Thompson 1860-1946

Sewell, Anna 1820-1878
Sharmat, Marjorie Weinman 1928-
Sharp, Margery 1905-
Shepard, Ernest H(oward) 1879-1976
Shotwell, Louisa R(ossiter) 1902-
Sidney, Margaret 1844-1924
Silverstein, Alvin 1933- and Virginia
 B(arbara Opshelor) 1937-
Sinclair, Catherine 1800-1864
Skurzynski, Gloria (Joan) 1930-
Sleator, William (Warner) 1945-
Slobodkin, Louis 1903-1975
Smith, Jessie Willcox 1863-1935
Snyder, Zilpha Keatley 1927-
Spence, Eleanor (Rachel) 1928-
Sperry, Armstrong W. 1897-1976
Spykman, E(lizabeth) C. 1896-1965
Starbird, Kaye 1916-
Steele, William O(wen) 1917-1979
Stevenson, James 1929-
Stolz, Mary (Slattery) 1920-
Stratemeyer, Edward L. 1862-1930
Streatfeild, (Mary) Noel 1895-1986
Taylor, Sydney 1904?-1978
Taylor, Theodore 1924-
Tenniel, Sir John 1820-1914
Thiele, Colin 1920-
Thomas, Joyce Carol 1938-
Thompson, Julian F(rancis) 1927-
Titus, Eve 1922-
Tolkien, J(ohn) R(onald) R(euel)
 1892-1973
Trease, (Robert) Geoffrey 1909-
Tresselt, Alvin 1916-
Treviño, Elizabeth Borton de 1904-
Turkle, Brinton 1915-
Twain, Mark 1835-1910
Udry, Janice May 1928-
Unnerstad, Edith (Totterman) 1900-
Uttley, Alison 1884-1976
Vining, Elizabeth Gray 1902-
Waber, Bernard 1924-
Wahl, Jan 1933-
Ward, Lynd 1905-1985
White, T(erence) H(anbury) 1906-1964
Wiese, Kurt 1887-1974
Wilkinson, Brenda 1946-
Worth, Valerie 1933-
Wyeth, N(ewell) C(onvers) 1882-1945
Yates, Elizabeth 1905-
Yonge, Charlotte M(ary) 1823-1901
Yorinks, Arthur 1953-
Zemach, Harve 1933-1974 and Margot
 1931-
Zion, Gene 1913-1975

Readers are cordially invited to suggest additional authors to the editors.

Children's
Literature
Review

(Sir) J(ames) M(atthew) Barrie

1860-1937

Scottish dramatist and author of fiction.

The following entry presents criticism of Peter Pan.

Barrie has earned enduring fame for his creation of *Peter Pan; or, The Boy Who Would Not Grow Up* (1904), the world's most popular play for children. He is lauded as a genius who expressed his love of children and mothers as well as a reluctance to mature through this, his best-known work, which is considered a most original exploration of the ramifications of eternal youth. A combination of fairy, adventure, and pirate story featuring a magical boy who lives on the island of Never Land with both human and fantasy characters, it appeals on many levels—literary, mythical, autobiographical, and psychological. Frequently regarded as Barrie's celebration of perpetual innocence, *Peter Pan* is now seen as his rejection of it. Peter Pan is often interpreted as a tragic figure who, despite his apparent freedom, is trapped by his inability to love others and to accept the passage of time.

Inspired by several sources, especially R. M. Ballantyne's *The Coral Island* and Robert Louis Stevenson's *Treasure Island*, *Peter Pan* is often compared to Lewis Carroll's *Alice* books for its ingenuity. The character of Peter Pan—who combines charm, innocence, and valor with selfishness and cruelty—has become part of popular culture and is acknowledged as a symbol of continual youth. The play about him, a British theatrical institution which has run consistently since its first production, is credited with popularizing the then-growing interest in childhood and fantasy. Barrie is recognized for his exceptional insight into both a child's mind and a mother's heart as well as for his ability to access the unconscious. Though he used such timeless dreams of children and storytellers as flying, fighting without incurring injury, and transcending both time and death, Barrie chiefly explored the conflict of growing up and losing innocence, a topic of particular relevance to himself.

Throughout his life, Barrie had a need to remain a child in his mother's eyes. Margaret Ogilvy deeply mourned the sudden death of her adolescent son David, and Barrie's lifelong attempts to replace his older brother in their mother's affections prevented him from achieving emotional maturity. A veneration for mother figures and an interest in boys who cannot or will not grow up permeate not only *Peter Pan* but also many of Barrie's adult novels and plays. His desire to produce a play for children exploring these topics was sparked by his relationship with the family of Arthur Llewelyn Davies, consisting of the unsuccessful barrister, his beautiful wife Sylvia with whom Barrie fell in love, and their five young sons—George, Jack, Peter, Michael, and Nicholas. It was for the entertainment of these boys that *Peter Pan* evolved.

The literary history of *Peter Pan* is one of the most complex in children's literature. It begins with *The Boy Castaways of Black Lake Island* (1901), a book of photographs taken by Barrie of the three eldest Llewelyn Davies boys and Barrie's large dog Porthos engaged in adventures with imaginary pirates and Indians; the only text, allegedly written by four-year-old Peter, consists of elaborate chapter headings detailing the excitement. The character of Peter Pan first appeared in print

in several chapters of the adult novel *The Little White Bird* (1902). While strolling through London's Kensington Gardens with a little boy named David, the narrator—a persona of Barrie—tells him about the elusive Peter Pan who escapes from being a human when he is seven days old, wins the hearts of all the female fairies, and lives in the garden at night. A young girl, Maimie Mannering, stays behind after the gates are closed, becomes Peter's friend, and helps him care for lost children. The chapters concerning Peter were later reprinted as a separate book, *Peter Pan in Kensington Gardens* (1906).

With the dramatization of *Peter Pan* in 1904, Barrie produced "that terrible masterpiece" as Peter Llewelyn Davies later termed it. Joining the charismatic hero in the play are Wendy, John, and Michael Darling; their parents, the loving Mrs. Darling and her somewhat childish husband; Nana, the Newfoundland dog who acts as the family's nanny; assorted fairies, most notably Peter's devoted companion Tinker Bell; the Lost Boys; Indians; pirates; and Peter's nemesis, the villainous antihero Captain Hook, whom children often consider as popular as the play's main character. Peter Pan flies with the Darling children to Never Land, where Wendy assumes the role of wife/mother, and all of them become immersed in a series of thrilling adventures. After Hook jealously steals Wendy away to be his mother, Peter vanquishes him and sets free the captive Darling children and the Lost Boys. When the children return home, Peter chooses to stay on the island and remain forever young. Barrie added a sequel to *Peter Pan* in 1908. *An Afterthought; or, When Wendy Grew Up* features Peter's sad surprise at finding an adult Wendy when he returns after many years to ask her to do spring cleaning for him. Although she has grown up and can no longer fly, she sends her daughter Jane with Peter, and in later years Jane sends her daughter Margaret, with the cycle always continuing. This sequel, which was performed only once in honor of the play's American producer, was included as part of Barrie's novelization of *Peter Pan* titled *Peter and Wendy* (1911; also published as *Peter Pan and Wendy*). In 1957, it was separately published as *When Wendy Grew Up: An Afterthought*. Barrie finally published the play *Peter Pan* in 1928 as part of a collection of his dramas.

Over the years, the play *Peter Pan* and its related works have been the focus of much critical commentary, especially in the area of Freudian interpretation; reviewers first lionized *Peter Pan*, then demoted it, and are currently evaluating it from a more balanced perspective. While Barrie has often been faulted for his sentimentality, he is consistently praised for his perceptive characterizations, adventurous and exciting plot, and particularly for his exceptional understanding of the child's mind. The vast majority of critics agree with Roger Lancelyn Green that *Peter Pan* is not only "the best play for children ever written" but also "one of the few supreme contributions to children's literature."

(See also *Twentieth-Century Literary Criticism*, Vol. 2; *Contemporary Authors*, Vol. 104; and *Dictionary of Literary Biography*, Vol. 10: *Modern British Dramatists, 1900-1945*.)

AUTHOR'S COMMENTARY

[*The following excerpt is taken from Barrie's 1928 preface to the play* Peter Pan. *The dedication is addressed to the five sons of Arthur and Sylvia Llewelyn Davies—George, Jack, Peter, Michael, and Nicholas—who are given numbers from one to five, which correspond to their order of birth.*]

Some disquieting confessions must be made in printing at last the play of *Peter Pan;* among them this, that I have no recollection of having written it. . . . What I want to do first is to give Peter to the Five without whom he never would have existed. I hope, my dear sirs, that in memory of what we have been to each other you will accept this dedication with your friend's love. The play of Peter is streaky with you still, though none may see this save ourselves. A score of Acts had to be left out, and you were in them all. We first brought Peter down, didn't we, with a blunt-headed arrow in Kensington Gardens? I seem to remember that we believed we had killed him, though he was only winded, and that after a spasm of exultation in our prowess the more softhearted among us wept and all of us thought of the police. There was not one of you who would not have sworn as an eye-witness to this occurrence; no doubt I was abetting, but you used to provide corroboration that was never given to you by me. As for myself, I suppose I always knew that I made Peter by rubbing the five of you violently together, as savages with two sticks produce a flame. That is all he is, the spark I got from you.

We had good sport of him before we clipped him small to make him fit the boards. Some of you were not born when the story began and yet were hefty figures before we saw that the game was up. . . . What was it that made us eventually give to the public in the thin form of a play that which had been woven for ourselves alone? Alas, I know what it was, I was

losing my grip. One by one as you swung monkey-wise from branch to branch in the wood of make-believe you reached the tree of knowledge. Sometimes you swung back into the wood, as the unthinking may at a cross-road take a familiar path that no longer leads to home; or you perched ostentatiously on its boughs to please me, pretending that you still belonged; soon you knew it only as the vanished wood, for it vanishes if one needs to look for it. A time came when I saw that No. 1, the most gallant of you all, ceased to believe that he was ploughing woods incarnadine, and with an apologetic eye for me derided the lingering faith of No. 2; when even No. 3 questioned gloomily whether he did not really spend his nights in bed. There were still two who knew no better, but their day was dawning. In these circumstances, I suppose, was begun the writing of the play of Peter. That was a quarter of a century ago, and I clutch my brows in vain to remember whether it was a last desperate throw to retain the five of you for a little longer, or merely a cold decision to turn you into bread and butter.

This brings us back to my uncomfortable admission that I have no recollection of writing the play of *Peter Pan*, now being published for the first time so long after he made his bow upon the stage. You had played it until you tired of it, and tossed it in the air and gored it and left it derelict in the mud and went on your way singing other songs; and then I stole back and sewed some of the gory fragments together with a pen-nib. That is what must have happened, but I cannot remember doing it. I remember writing the story of *Peter and Wendy* many years after the production of the play, but I might have cribbed that from some typed copy. I can haul back to mind the writing of almost every other assay of mine, however forgotten by the pretty public; but this play of Peter, no. . . . It does seem almost suspicious, especially as I have not the original MS. of *Peter Pan* (except a few stray pages) with which to support my claim. I have indeed another MS., lately made, but that 'proves nothing.' I know not whether I lost that original MS. or destroyed it or happily gave it away. I talk of dedicating the play to you, but how can I prove it is mine? How ought I to act if some other hand, who could also have made a copy, thinks it worth while to contest the cold rights? Cold they are to me now as that laughter of yours in which Peter came into being long before he was caught and written down. There is Peter still, but to me he lies sunk in the gay Black Lake.

Any one of you five brothers has a better claim to the authorship than most, and I would not fight you for it, but you should have launched your case long ago in the days when you most admired me, which were in the first year of the play, owing to a rumour's reaching you that my spoils were one-and-six-pence a night. This was untrue, but it did give me a standing among you. You watched for my next play with peeled eyes, not for entertainment but lest it contained some chance witticism of yours that could be challenged as collaboration; indeed I believe there still exists a legal document, full of the Aforesaid and Henceforward to be called Part-Author, in which for some such snatching I was tied down to pay No. 2 one halfpenny daily throughout the run of the piece. (pp. 3-5)

Notwithstanding other possibilities, I think I wrote Peter, and if so it must have been in the usual inky way. Some of it, I like to think, was done in that native place which is the dearest spot on earth to me, though my last heart-beats shall be with my beloved solitary London that was so hard to reach. I must have sat at a table with that great dog waiting for me to stop, not complaining, for he knew it was thus we made our living, but giving me a look when he found he was to be in the play, with his sex changed. (p. 6)

Some say that we are different people at different periods of our lives, changing not through effort of will, which is a brave affair, but in the easy course of nature every ten years or so. I suppose this theory might explain my present trouble, but I don't hold with it; I think one remains the same person throughout, merely passing, as it were, in these lapses of time from one room to another, but all in the same house. If we unlock the rooms of the far past we can peer in and see ourselves, busily occupied in beginning to become you and me. Thus, if I am the author in question the way he is to go should already be showing in the occupant of my first compartment, at whom I now take the liberty to peep. Here he is at the age of seven or so with his fellow-conspirator Robb, both in glengarry bonnets. They are giving an entertainment in a tiny old washing-house that still stands. . . . This washing-house is not only the theatre of my first play, but has a still closer connection with Peter. It is the original of the little house the Lost Boys built in the Never Land for Wendy, the chief difference being that it never wore John's tall hat as a chimney. (pp. 6-7)

Here is that boy again some four years older, and the reading he is munching feverishly is about desert islands; he calls them wrecked islands. He buys his sanguinary tales surreptitiously in penny numbers. I see a change coming over him; he is blanching as he reads in the high-class magazine, *Chatter-box*, a fulmination against such literature, and sees that unless his greed for islands is quenched he is for ever lost. With gloaming he steals out of the house, his library bulging beneath his palpitating waistcoat. I follow like his shadow, as indeed I am, and watch him dig a hole in a field at Pathhead farm and bury his islands in it; it was ages ago, but I could walk straight to that hole in the field now and delve for the remains. I peep into the next compartment. There he is again, ten years older, an undergraduate now and craving to be a real explorer, one of those who do things instead of prating of them, but otherwise unaltered; he might be painted at twenty on top of a mast, in his hand a spy-glass through which he rakes the horizon for an elusive strand. I go from room to room, and he is now a man, real exploration abandoned (though only because no one would have him). Soon he is even concocting other plays, and quaking a little lest some low person counts how many islands there are in them. I note that with the years the islands grow more sinister, but it is only because he has now to write with the left hand, the right having given out; evidently one thinks more darkly down the left arm. Go to the keyhole of the compartment where he and I join up, and you may see us wondering whether they would stand one more island. This journey through the house may not convince any one that I wrote Peter, but it does suggest me as a likely person. I pause to ask myself whether I read *Chatterbox* again, suffered the old agony, and buried that MS. of the play in a hole in a field.

Of course this is over-charged. Perhaps we do change; except a little something in us which is no larger than a mote in the eye, and that, like it, dances in front of us beguiling us all our days. I cannot cut the hair by which it hangs.

The strongest evidence that I am the author is to be found. I think, in a now melancholy volume, . . . *The Boy Cast-aways*. . . . This record is supposed to be edited by the youngest of the three, and I must have granted him that honour to make up for his being so often lifted bodily out of our adventures by his nurse, who kept breaking into them for the fell purpose of giving him a midday rest. No. 4 rested so much at this period

that he was merely an honorary member of the band, waving his foot to you for luck when you set off with bow and arrow to shoot his dinner for him; and one may rummage the book in vain for any trace of No. 5. (pp. 7-8)

Published to whet your memories. Does it whet them? Do you hear once more, like some long-forgotten whistle beneath your window . . . the not quite mortal blows that still echo in some of the chapter headings?—'Chapter II, No. 1 teaches Wilkinson (his master) a Stern Lesson—We Run away to Sea. Chapter III, A Fearful Hurricane—Wreck of the ''Anna Pink''—We go crazy from Want of Food—Proposal to eat No. 3—Land Ahoy.' Such are two chapters out of sixteen. Are these again your javelins cutting tunes in the blue haze of the pines; do you sweat as you scale the dreadful Valley of Rolling Stones, and cleanse your hands of pirate blood by scouring them carelessly in Mother Earth? (pp. 9-10)

The illustrations (full-paged) in *The Boy Castaways* are all photographs taken by myself; some of them indeed of phenomena that had to be invented afterwards, for you were always off doing the wrong things when I pressed the button. (p. 10)

The Boy Castaways has sixteen chapter-headings. . . . These headings anticipate much of the play of *Peter Pan,* but there were many incidents of our Kensington Gardens days that never got into the book, such as our Antarctic exploits when we reached the Pole in advance of our friend Captain Scott and cut our initials on it for him to find, a strange foreshadowing of what was really to happen. In *The Boy Castaways* Captain Hook has arrived but is called Captain Swarthy, and he seems from the pictures to have been a black man. This character, as you do not need to be told, is held by those in the know to be autobiographical. You had many tussles with him (though you never, I think, got his right arm) before you reached the terrible chapter (which might be taken from the play) entitled 'We Board the Pirate Ship at Dawn—A Rakish Craft—No. 1 Hew-them-Down and No. 2 of the Red Hatchet—A Holocaust of Pirates—Rescue of Peter.'. . . The scene of the Holocaust is the Black Lake (afterwards, when we let women in, the Mermaids' Lagoon). The pirate captain's end was not in the mouth of a crocodile though we had crocodiles on the spot. . . . I think our captain had divers deaths owing to unseemly competition among you, each wanting to slay him single-handed. (pp. 11-12)

The dog in *The Boy Castaways* seems never to have been called Nana but was evidently in training for that post. He originally belonged to Swarthy (or to Captain Marryat?), and the first picture of him, lean, skulking, and hunched (how did I get that effect?), 'patrolling the island' in the monster's interests, gives little indication of the domestic paragon he was to become. We lured him away to the better life, and there is, later, a touching picture, a clear forecast of the Darling nursery, entitled 'We trained the dog to watch over us while we slept.' (p. 12)

They do seem to be emerging out of our island, don't they, the little people of the play, all except that sly one, the chief figure, who draws farther and farther into the wood as we advance upon him? He so dislikes being tracked, as if there were something odd about him, that when he dies he means to get up and blow away the particle that will be his ashes.

Wendy has not yet appeared, but she has been trying to come ever since that loyal nurse cast the humorous shadow of woman upon the scene and made us feel that it might be fun to let in a disturbing element. Perhaps she would have bored her way in at last whether we wanted her or not. It may be that even Peter did not really bring her to the Never Land of his free will, but merely pretended to do so because she would not stay away. Even Tinker Bell had reached our island before we left it. It was one evening when we climbed the wood carrying No. 4 to show him what the trail was like by twilight. As our lanterns twinkled among the leaves No. 4 saw a twinkle stand still for a moment and he waved his foot gaily to it, thus creating Tink. (p. 13)

The rebuffs I have got from all of you! They were especially crushing in those early days when one by one you came out of your belief in fairies and lowered on me as the deceiver. My grandest triumph, the best thing in the play of *Peter Pan* (though it is not in it), is that long after No. 4 had ceased to believe, I brought him back to the faith for at least two minutes. We were on our way in a boat to fish the Outer Hebrides . . . , and though it was a journey of days he wore his fishing basket on his back all the time, so as to be able to begin at once. His one pain was the absence of Johnny Mackay, for Johnny was the loved gillie of the previous summer who had taught him everything that is worth knowing (which is a matter of flies) but could not be with us this time as he would have had to cross and re-cross Scotland to reach us. As the boat drew near the Kyle of Lochalsh pier I told Nos. 4 and 5 it was such a famous wishing pier that they had now but to wish and they should have. No. 5 believed at once and expressed a wish to meet himself (I afterwards found him on the pier searching faces confidently), but No. 4 thought it more of my untimely nonsense and doggedly declined to humour me. 'Whom do you want to see most, No. 4?' 'Of course I would like most to see Johnny Mackay.' 'Well, then, wish for him.' 'Oh, rot.' 'It can't do any harm to wish.' Contemptuously he wished, and as the ropes were thrown on the pier he saw Johnny waiting for him, loaded with angling paraphernalia. I know no one less like a fairy than Johnny Mackay, but for two minutes No. 4 was quivering in another world than ours. When he came to he gave me a smile which meant that we understood each other, and thereafter neglected me for a month, being always with Johnny. As I have said, this episode is not in the play; so though I dedicate *Peter Pan* to you I keep the smile, with the few other broken fragments of immortality that have come my way. (pp. 15-16)

J. M. Barrie, "To the Five: A Dedication to 'Peter Pan'," in his The Plays of J. M. Barrie. *Charles Scribner's Sons, 1928, pp. 3-16.*

A. T. QUILLER-COUCH

Heaven, I am ready to believe, lies about the infancy of a few born to die young; but we must find another word for the mysterious country of which most children's birth is but a dream and a forgetting. The glimpses they yield us of it, the glimpses we ourselves remember, are of a country very different from the heaven revealed to grown-ups or constructed by them out of their theologies. . . . Indeed, an angel may now and then find himself astray there, but really it is not heaven at all. You can call it the Land of Romance, or the Woods of Westermain, or the Country east of the Sun and west of the Moon, or simply Fairyland. It contains hosts of fairies, at all events, and one of its lords is Pan, he of the merry pipes and also of the hoof which, when he strikes it on the ground, sends all things scurrying in "panic."

This is the country which Mr. Barrie locates within the railings of Kensington Gardens after lock-up time [in *The Little White Bird*]. He provides it with a capital Pan—Peter Pan—who has

only to be read about to be believed in; he tells us in detail what the fairies do and what the birds; and he is quite clear about his geography. Indeed, he takes us from spot to spot with an air of knowledge so thorough that every child will believe him. . . . (pp. 49-50)

But though many children may read this book and believe it, it does not look to me like a book written for children, and it looks even less like a book written for grown-ups. You may say, and plausibly, that it was written by a fairy for fairies; or, still better, that it was written by a contrite fairy for fairy changelings; but I should prefer to call it a book written by the child inside Mr. Barrie for the children we used to be. (p. 50)

There has always been an elfin touch in Mr. Barrie's writing. . . . When you or I invent our stories of men and women, we step around them and pull them about, and ask ourselves, "Will this do?" "Does this balance?" "This may be all very pretty in itself, but it seems to injure the general effect. Hadn't it better come out?"—distracting questions, which take us outside of the task, and are apt to end in that dreadful one, "Is it, after all, worth while?" I suspect that we are foolishly trying all the while to do that which the critics demand of Mr. Barrie. But Mr. Barrie seems to sit down and forget all this; he has his idea and straightway begins to enjoy himself. He plays with it, he embroiders it, he adds a jewel here and sews in a feather there; the task absorbs him, and each moment of the task absorbs him. I will venture a guess that if ever he produces the book or play which the critics have made up their minds he ought to write, it will be done at white heat, almost at a stretch, when, his genius having given him the simple idea, circumstances happen to allow him no time to play with it. He may not be happy while the compulsion lasts, but, if the critics mean anything, he will make *them* happy.

And I mean to be happy too; but I shall miss the elf with his adorable waywardness, and especially that adorable trick by which he takes logic a little way and then, with a duck of the head, is gone, has dived into truth by a short cut, and smiles back at his venerable but staggered companion. He is infinitely childlike, and I have called him "the child in Mr. Barrie"; he can tell us a hundred things about children; but he is, after all, not a real child, but an elf trying wistfully to get back and be

Barrie's birthplace: Lilybank in the Tenements, Kirriemuir, Scotland. The washhouse in the foreground is the original of the little house which the Lost Boys built for Wendy in Never Land.

one. Why he should desire it so urgently I cannot tell. There are numbers of children in the world, and to most of us it would seem a more distinguished thing altogether to be a genius, and be called Peter Pan, and to have written a book like a Christmas tree, and decorated it with whimsies and trembling tears and shining thoughts and laughter. (pp. 50-1)

A. T. Quiller-Couch, "Mr. J. M. Barrie's New Novel, 'The Little White Bird'," in The Bookman, *London, Vol. XXIII, No. 134, November, 1902, pp. 49-51.*

THE ILLUSTRATED LONDON NEWS

Two ideas underlie Mr. Barrie's delightful new fantasy, *Peter Pan; or, The Boy Who Wouldn't Grow Up*—the child's passion for make-believe, and the average little girl's maternal instinct. Harping on these two strings, the playwright himself makes-believe unflaggingly in an artfully artless, go-as-you-please play which has all the pretty inconsequence of an imaginative child's improvisation, all the wild extravagance of a youngster's dream. . . . [The] latest Barrie heroine—Wendy Darling—loves "mothering" people, and so quickly accepts her mysterious boy-visitor's invitation to quit her comfortable nursery and tend the lost little lads who live motherless in Never Never Never Land. There, in a glorious underground home, Wendy and Peter imitate most piquantly grown-up parents; there, thanks to Mr. Barrie's intuition, all the romantic fancies of youthful brains about friendly Redskins and villainous pirates are thrillingly materialised; till Peter's band, unlike their gallant captain, yearn for their mothers' arms, and in childhood's beautiful confidence creep back home.

"'Peter Pan' at the Duke of York's," in The Illustrated London News, *Vol. CXXVI, No. 3429, January 7, 1905, p. 5.*

MAX BEERBOHM

Peter Pan; or, adds Mr. Barrie, *The Boy Who Wouldn't Grow Up.* And he himself is that boy. That child, rather; for he halted earlier than most of the men who never come to maturity—halted before the age when soldiers and steam-engines begin to dominate the soul. To remain, like Mr. Kipling, a boy, is not at all uncommon. But I know not anyone who remains, like Mr. Barrie, a child. It is this unparalleled achievement that informs so much of Mr. Barrie's later work, making it unique. This, too, surely, it is that makes Mr. Barrie the most fashionable playwright of his time.

Undoubtedly, *Peter Pan* is the best thing he has done—the thing most directly from within himself. Here, at last, we see his talent in its full maturity; for here he has stripped off from himself the last flimsy remnants of a pretence to maturity. (p. 13)

[The] man of genius is that rare creature in whom imagination, not ousted by logic in full growth, abides, uncramped, in unison with full-grown logic. Mr. Barrie is not that rare creature, a man of genius. He is something even more rare—a child who, by some divine grace, can express through an artistic medium the childishness that is in him.

Our dreams are nearer to us than our childhood, and it is natural that *Peter Pan* should remind us more instantly of our dreams than of our childish fancies. One English dramatist, a man of genius, realised a dream for us; but the logic in him prevented him from indulging in that wildness and incoherence which are typical of all but the finest dreams. Credible and orderly are the doings of Puck in comparison with the doings of Peter Pan. Was ever, out of dreamland such a riot of inconsequence

and of exquisite futility? Things happen in such wise that presently one can conceive nothing that might not conceivably happen, nor anything that one would not, as in a dream, accept unhesitatingly. Even as in a dream, there is no reason why the things should ever cease to happen. What possible conclusion can inhere in them? The only possible conclusion is from without. The sun shines through the bedroom window, or there is a tapping at the bedroom door, or—some playgoers must catch trains, others must sup. Even as you, awakened, turn on your pillow, wishing to pursue the dream, so, as you leave [The Duke of York Theatre], will you rebel at the dream's rude and arbitrary ending, and will try vainly to imagine what other unimaginable things were in store for you. For me to describe to you now in black and white the happenings in *Peter Pan* would be a thankless task. One cannot communicate the magic of a dream. . . . You must go to the Duke of York's, there to dream the dream for yourselves.

The fact that Mr. Barrie is a child would be enough, in this generation which so adores children, to account for his unexampled vogue. But Mr. Barrie has a second passport. For he, too, even pre-eminently, adores children—never ceases to study them and their little ways, and to purr sentimental pæans over them, and finds it even a little hard to remember that the world really does contain a sprinkling of adults. In fact, his attitude towards children is the fashionable attitude, struck more saliently by him than by anyone else, and with more obvious sincerity than by the average person. It is not to be wondered at that his preoccupation with children endears him to the community. The strange thing is the preoccupation itself. It forces me to suppose that Mr. Barrie has, after all, to some extent, grown up. For children are the last thing with which a child concerns itself. A child takes children as a matter of course, and passes on to more important things—remote things that have a glorious existence in the child's imagination. A little boy does not say "I am a child", but "I am a pirate", or "a greengrocer", or "an angel", as the case may be. A little girl does not say "I am a little girl, and these are my dolls, and this is my baby-brother", but "I am the mother of this family". She lavishes on her dolls and on her baby-brother a wealth of maternal affection, cooing over them, and . . . stay! that is just Mr. Barrie's way. I need not, after all, mar by qualification my theory that Mr. Barrie has never grown up. He is still a child, absolutely. But some fairy once waved a wand over him, and changed him from a dear little boy into a dear little girl. Some critics have wondered why among the characters in *Peter Pan* appeared a dear little girl, named in the programme "Liza (the Author of the Play)". Now they know. Mr. Barrie was just "playing at symbolists". (pp. 13-14)

Max Beerbohm, "The Child Barrie," in The Saturday Review, *London, Vol. 99, No. 2567, January 7, 1905, pp. 13-14.*

THE OUTLOOK

[*Peter Pan*] is like a breath of fresh air. It is not to be judged by the ordinary standards of the drama. It is a bit of pure phantasy by the writer who, since the death of Robert Louis Stevenson, has most truly kept the heart and mind of a child. *Peter Pan* . . . is for the imaginative, the eternally youthful, and the pure in heart. To all others, as much of the dramatic criticism of the play shows, it is a sealed book, lacking coherence, dramatic construction, and seriousness. Boys and girls of all ages will love it because it is a boy's mind turned inside out and put on the stage. Everything in it happens precisely as it would happen in a world made by a healthy boy of imagination. All the best things come true; there is a real wonderland to which you actually fly; there you build a house precisely as you would in an actual country; there are Indians; above all, there are pirates as ferocious, as picturesquely wicked, and as full of malevolence to children as the pirates you used to dream of were; there is a fascinating crocodile who has swallowed a clock which ticks audibly; there is a lion whom you subdue by looking at him and when he retreats you calmly cut off his tail; there are tremendous combats in which childish ingenuity and simplicity are more than a match for the brute force of grown men; . . . and, last of all, there is an enchanting vision of the tops of trees, of Peter Pan at home in the indestructible domain of childhood, surrounded by fairy lights. Hardened sinner, weary playgoer, ennuied society man and woman, disillusioned pursuer of money, however you may have gone astray, you come out of the theater rested and refreshed. For two hours you have believed in fairies. You have been a child again. And nothing . . . could be better for the average theatergoer than to be carried back to the faith, innocence, credulity, and joy of childhood. (pp. 645-46)

> *A review of "Peter Pan," in* The Outlook, *Vol. 81, No. 12, November 18, 1905, pp. 645-46.*

ALFRED NOYES

Most "grown-ups" nowadays have at least a sense of loss at Christmastide—the sort of sense which Mr. Kipling's pioneer felt, of something "lost behind the mountains"; the sense of a whisper from the Never-never land, *Come and find me!* "David went to look for donkeys," says Mr. Kipling, with alliterative inaccuracy, "and he found a kingdom"; and, though it was really Saul who went according to the Scriptures, the statement may apply figuratively to any of us. The most successful searcher for donkeys at the present day is Mr. Barrie. You may take the most obtuse donkey in London before his footlights, and Mr. Barrie will discover you a kingdom in him, the kingdom of boyhood. A view of life so large, and a touch of satire so gentle that you are awakened only to the infinite pathos of our small errors under the everlasting stars; those are two of the possessions of the author of *Peter Pan;* and his arrival at his astonishingly wide kingdom is an exquisite illustration of a very ancient and beautiful phrase about the width and height and wonder of the kingdom of little children.

Now Santa Claus is in a terrible predicament. His tricks are not subtle enough for the modern child. . . . But what a delightful curtain-raiser to *Peter Pan* one can imagine if Mr. Barrie would give us a plea for Santa Claus, after the manner of his plea for the ancient family of the Clown! Personally, I believe that Santa Claus is only one of the highly coloured disguises of Peter Pan. Remove that ragged white beard and you will find a smooth-faced young messenger from the Never-never land—the land from which all pleasant surprises, all happy chances, all childish miracles descend. Nay, even if you seemed to disclose only the blushing countenance of an indignant parent, you might be sure that this also was only another disguise of that immortal and Protean youth. For Peter Pan partakes of the nature of the universal Pan. . . .

This universality of Peter is the answer to an objection which I once heard raised against the play—that it is too much of a mixture; that Red Indians jostle pirates, and that fairies rub shoulders with crocodiles. But the story is *not* an adventure story for children so much as the story of the adventures of an actual child's mind; and, as for Peter, you cannot shut him out from anywhere. Close the doors and he will fly in through the window or drop down the chimney. (p. 107)

To be a pirate or to smoke cigars . . .—those are legitimate aspirations of boyhood. But they are comprehended by boyhood; and they must not be mistaken for a desire to grow up to anything more or less than the heights of that boyhood.

Now Stevenson grew up. With reference to *Treasure Island,* Margaret Ogilvy once told her son, "consolingly, that she could not thole pirate stories"; but now that her son has written one himself the comparison becomes too inviting to be resisted. Stevenson wrote about pirates with a kind of romantic regret; he put in masterly grown-up touches. . . . At the end of his life you find him almost in distress because he has been writing so much for boys! He was, in fact, a man writing for boys and yearning to lose himself in boyhood; while Barrie is a boy, in triumphant possession of his kingdom, writing for men. Stevenson, in the *Child's Garden,* asks whether his lot does not seem hard to you in summer time, "when I should like so much to play, to have to go to bed by day"? Might not that be the lyrical cry of the dying man himself? Does he not say at the end of all—"it is but a child of air, that lingers in the garden there"? Does he not say of the leaden soldier who had been buried and could not relate what he had seen underground, "I must lay him on the shelf, and make up the tale myself!" Sooner would the author of *Peter Pan* make the very tables and chairs relate it. Stevenson surveyed all these things from the outside, with the eye of an artist, and wrote about them in a classic style. Barrie gets right inside them with the universal Peter Pan, and simply talks to you in a language that winks and twinkles like wet eyelashes over the birth of a divinely beautiful smile at all human foibles and vanities. Stevenson, in his very *Child's Garden,* could say:

> The eternal dawn beyond a doubt
> Will break o'er hill and plain,
> And put all stars and candles out
> Ere we be young again!

Barrie sets all London laughing at the absurdities of the modern "problem play," by simply bringing it into contact with the pure childhood of *Alice-sit-by-the-fire.* (pp. 107-10)

Margaret Ogilvy should have read Stevenson first and her son afterwards; for Barrie begins where Stevenson ended. There is none of that terrible sadness in the author of *Peter Pan.* He calmly proposes to restore the dead to life, to give you back the glory of youth, and to make you young again. Moreover, *he does it!* And I think he succeeds because he has passed through all that sadness and suffering, passed straight through it into the Never-never land, snatched up an exquisite secret of happiness, and returned with it to London to make other people happy.

In the first scene of *Peter Pan,* I think there must be a sort of fairy philosophy behind the fact that Peter himself is represented as being quite miserable about the loss of his own shadow, and blissfully happy when he finds it again. The whimsical humour of it sets you laughing and congratulating yourself that at any rate you *do* possess a shadow. As the play develops, you begin to congratulate yourself on the possession of all sorts of things which hitherto you took quite as a matter of course. (p. 110)

It is impossible and unnecessary to tell the story of the play here. Roughly, it is built upon some such framework as this. Peter Pan comes in through a bedroom window, teaches the children, who are in bed there, to fly—anyone can fly who has faith—and induces them to go off through the window with him on a visit to the Never-never land. On their arrival there they find the bold young companions of Peter Pan awaiting them. These are the lost children, children who have been dropped out of perambulators by careless nurses, children who have strayed away from their homes and never returned. They are all there in the Never-never land, that beautiful distant country of story-books, a country of pirates and Redskins, and all adventurous delights. They have some thrilling escapes. They come into conflict with the pirates, whom they defeat by a clever ruse of Peter's, and terrify so vastly that those murderous villains all jump into the sea and abandon their ship. The three truants, and eventually all the lost children, decide to return home and seek their mothers. There is a wonderful scene in the bedroom of the three truants when they first appear. For their mother, who is waiting there, turns her head away after her first glimpse of them; and, in her fear lest it should be only another dream, she will not look at them till they creep up to her and prove their reality by touching and kissing her. Then the other lost children have to find *their* mothers; and there is another wonderful scene, where a crowd of fashionable ladies enters to claim them, and the children discover their right mothers by certain beautiful tests, one of which, for instance, is the lovely shining light that comes into a mother's eyes when she looks upon her own child.

Round that framework Mr. Barrie has written one of the most exquisite plays of our time. Like all masterpieces of art it is a revelation and an incarnation of things eternal. It embodies a personality so completely that you might almost vow you had a section of the author's soul before you on the stage, like a house from which the front wall had been removed. The father and mother, for instance, represent his parental thoughts and feelings, and the other characters with their adjuncts all take a perfect symbolical meaning in this regard, as they live and move and interact. The rooms and scenes in which they play their parts are as the cells, or partitions, of his brain. The dog completes the picture with a purely physical tug at your heartstrings. He represents the dumb animal qualities of affection. Looked at from this point of view the action of the play takes new lights and colours. We see . . . not fictitious adventures *for* boys, but the actual adventures *of* the Soul of Boyhood in the world of Romance. What pirates these are, for instance, pirates that might have stepped straight out of the red and yellow illustrations of an old broad-sheet ballad; pirates of the imagination and the soul; not earthly, but ideal pirates, who wear boat-cloaks and big boots and blood-spotted bandages round the head. Each of them is the delightful essence and consummation of a thousand conventions. The captain, with an iron hook instead of a hand, is so great an object of terror to his crew that he has only to offer them a shake of that formidable and mysterious claw to make them scream like women. The crew is properly compact of villainous boldness and wild superstition, a mixture which leads directly to their defeat by the valour and cleverness of a Boy. It is the last word on pirates. It is the story of piracy reduced to its simplest terms; stripped of unnecessary details and realities, and made eternal as boyhood. For "grown-ups" it has an exquisite humour. It is like a delicious and subtle parody of all the pirate stories that ever were written, and yet it is as real and vivid as *Treasure Island*. The very song which the pirates sing is pirate-song reduced to its simplest terms. There is no reference to drink or the devil or a dead man's chest: they simply assert in chorus "a pirating we go"! But the effect is marvellous. (pp. 110-14)

On the rest of the play, with its deep human appeal, I cannot help but think that another book—*Margaret Ogilvy* . . .—is the best commentary. At the beginning of this article I said that

Barrie succeeded in restoring the dead to life and in giving you back your lost youth, not because he ignored, but because he had passed through all that sadness of loss which Stevenson voiced; and, certainly, the little girl who wanted to "mother" all the lost children in the Never-never land draws a golden mist of April sunlight between you and the stage if you happen to think at that moment of Margaret Ogilvy. . . . Also in that beautiful last scene where the children test their mothers, is there not something of reminiscence, too? And Peter Pan, that Protean little fellow, whose mother *had* forgotten him in another child, what a wonderful depth his picture takes if you remember one of the most poignant and perfect passages in all modern literature, the passage that describes how a certain little boy tried to comfort his mother for the loss of her other son.

> My sister, who was then passing out of her teens, came to me with a very anxious face and wringing her hands, and she told me to go ben to my mother and say to her that she still had another boy. I went ben excitedly, but the room was dark, and when I heard the door shut and no sound come from the bed, I was afraid, and I stood still. I suppose I was breathing hard, or perhaps I was crying, for after a time I heard a listless voice that had never been listless before say, 'Is that you?' I think the tone hurt me, for I made no answer, and then the voice said more anxiously, 'Is that you?' again. I thought it was the dead boy she was speaking to, and I said in a little lonely voice, 'No, it's no him, it's just me.' Then I heard a cry and my mother turned in bed, and though it was dark knew that she was holding out her arms.

That is exactly how you are made to feel by parts of *Peter Pan*! There are even some almost farcical elements in the play, such as the repentant father's occupation of the dog-kennel, which remind one strangely of another passage in *Margaret Ogilvy:* "I suppose I was an odd little figure; I have been told that my anxiety to brighten her gave my face a strained look and put a tremor into the joke (I would stand on my head in the bed, my feet against the wall, and then cry excitedly, 'Are you laughing, mother?')."

This peculiar impression of reminiscence is almost startling when Peter, rushing forward to the front of the stage, with exquisite simplicity asks the audience whether they believe in fairies; and implores them, if they do, to clap their hands, for their assent will save a certain best-beloved fairy from dying. There was always the same unfailing reply; but, as a recent writer has said, it was a "Yes" that had tears in it as well as laughter. The whole play is so Protean that it is impossible to analyse impressions like these; but perhaps they may all be explained (and especially the test of the shining light) by yet another passage from that classic of our generation, *Margaret Ogilvy:* "For when you looked into my mother's eyes you knew, as if He had told you, why God sent her into the world— it was to open the minds, of all who looked, to beautiful thoughts. And that is the beginning and end of literature." And that, let us add, is what Barrie has done and is still doing, consistently. Peter Pan not only makes you love him, but he makes you love the world at large. (p. 114)

Alfred Noyes, "The Boy Who Wouldn't Grow Up," in The Bookman, *London, Vol. XXIX, No. 171, December, 1905, pp. 107-15.*

A. B. WALKLEY

There has always been much of the frank and trusting simplicity of the child in Mr. Barrie's work. . . . It was certain, therefore, in advance that when he set himself to write a play for children and about children he would give us of his very best, his most fanciful, and his most tender. *Peter Pan* is from beginning to end a thing of pure delight. (p. 209)

The whole affair is a delicious frolic, touched with the lightest of hands, full of quiet wisdom and sweet charity, under its surface of wild fun, and here and there not without a place for a furtive tear. (p. 213)

> *A. B. Walkley, "'Peter Pan',"* in his Drama and Life, *Methuen & Co., 1907, pp. 209-13.*

THE NEW YORK TIMES

So that Peter Pan may not quite slip back into the Never-Never Land . . . , Mr. Barrie has put the whole fairy make-believe into a book. It is not just the story of how Peter played with the fairies beside the Serpentine and navigated the Round Pond in Kensington Gardens in a bird's nest with his shirt for a sail. That has been in a book before. Here it is all as you used to see it through the big window with bright lights along the window sill. . . .

Mr. Barrie makes you quite see it all and feel all the fever and joy of combat and quite wonderful adventures. And he makes you hear Peter's voice—that wonderful voice with the sharp thrill of happiness in it that hurts when you listen to it after you are grown up and are no longer gay and innocent and heartless and cannot fly. It is exactly like the double notes of a violin that always makes you cry. And in the end it is all just as sad as it is beautiful. . . .

[Mr. Barrie has also included] all sorts of other lovely things that only Mr. Barrie could say even if any body else could think of them.

They are the kind of lovely things one dreams about, not the kind of things one spoils with a critic's foolish praise or blame. It is enough that Mr. Barrie has put Peter into a book for fear a play would not hold him long enough. Only curmudgeons can fail to bless Mr. Barrie for doing it.

> *"Peter Pan, with Wendy Grown Up,"* in The New York Times, *October 22, 1911, p. 650.*

THE ATHENAEUM

Peter Pan has become for the latest generation what *Alice in Wonderland* was for a former. The foundations of Lewis Carroll's book were laid so deep that not even a generation and a half have prevailed to assail them. Elderly people still repeat tags from *Alice,* which has passed into the traditions of the language. Will *Peter Pan* do so? If the theme had remained embodied and embedded in the play, we should have had doubts. . . . But the translation of the fantasy into fiction [in *Peter and Wendy*] has made a difference, and has more or less brought *Peter Pan* into the competitive plane with *Alice.* There could hardly, we must say at once, be a greater contrast of inventive and imaginative equipment. Mr. Barrie's ingenuity is as great as Lewis Carroll's, but it is exercised in another *milieu.* His notion of humour is as sharp, but less straightforward; it delights in oddities, in out-of-the-way corners, in surprises, and, it must be confessed, in sentimentalities. We experience rather a shock at the constant alternations of farce and sentiment; we are no sooner attuned to the one than the other trips it up. This is one of Mr Barrie's methods of versatility. Some of the most delicious humour is found side by side with a rather overstrained interpretation of child-life. It is all a curious medley, but the rendering is deft and fresh beyond belief. The author's interest seems to have remained intact, as integral

and sincere as that of his audience. Read, for example, the fight with the pirates, and consider if it could be improved in any way, or the conversations in the nursery, or the adventure in the lagoon. Children will enjoy this book as much as they did the play, and it will survive even the play.

> *A review of "Peter and Wendy,"* in The Athenaeum, *No. 4385, November 11, 1911, p. 588.*

LITERARY DIGEST

Perhaps it is no more incredible that Peter Pan should be held between the covers of a book [*Peter and Wendy*] than for him to fly in and out of the nursery window, but no one would have dared attempt to catch the elusive spirit except Mr. Barrie, and certainly no one could have imprisoned the sprite so tenderly as this same wonderful writer. Books of such convincing imagery elude any attempt at criticism or description; we feel the fascination, but to attempt to explain would be a profanation. . . . We wonder enviously how Mr. Barrie gets his insight into the mother-heart, the child's fancy, and the grown-up's longing.

His style as well as his material is utterly unlike anything we know, and is touched with whimsical fancies and spiritual comprehension. . . . Imagine the pirate horde, the redskins and the mermaids, the make-believe feasts and the very real battles, for they are real when Barrie describes them. . . .

The world should be very thankful for a writer who can create such delightful and exquisite nonsense.

> *A review of "Peter and Wendy,"* in Literary Digest, *New York, Vol. 43, No. 20, November 11, 1911, p. 866.*

GILBERT K. CHESTERTON

In one way Mr. Barrie is unlucky among the men of genius of our time; he is unlucky in his very good luck. He has the two elements of real artistic greatness—simple elements enough, but both every noble ones; he is original and he is popular. Being popular, in the just sense of that exalted term, means giving the people what they want; a thing every inch as essential and idealistic in art as it is in politics. But if popularity means giving the people what they want, originality means having it to give. If the people had it, they could not be said to want it. Originality is the power of going behind the common mind, discovering what it desires as distinct from what it says it desires, satisfying the sub-consciousness. Few modern writers have enjoyed so much as Mr. Barrie this high pleasure of giving people what they wanted, but did not expect. *Peter Pan* is perhaps the one perfect example of this element in contemporary art; it is our nearest approach to a legend. There is something almost anonymous about its popularity; we feel as if we had all written it. It is made out of fragments of our own forgotten dreams, and stirs the heart with sleepy unquiet, like pictures from a previous existence. But this very quality, as of a fairy-cap fitting everyone, as it is Mr. Barrie's peculiar glory, so it is his peculiar danger or mistake. A thing like *Peter Pan* is so obviously our natural food that most of us tend to swallow it whole; to enjoy without attempting to criticise. For this as well as other reasons the new prose version he has published, *Peter and Wendy,* is valuable as giving an opportunity for a maturer judgment of the work, when we have grown accustomed to its remarkable combination of universality and novelty.

For, while there is no modern writer whose romantic clairvoyance more disarms criticism, there is also no author whose quaint and somewhat chaotic thoughts more require criticism to keep them at their best. There runs through Mr. Barrie's extraordinary mind an element of the perverse amounting to the discordant; something that can only be described as an impish bathos. Bits of his books seem to have got in by mistake out of other books: whole scenes and groups of figures, excellent in themselves, will be so out of focus as to be at once gigantic and invisible. He cannot be uniformly nonsensical, like a steady, sensible fellow. Quick-witted, and even cunning, as he is, he has a curious faculty of making quite a small mistake so that it looks like a big mistake. The value and meaning of that excellent play, **What Every Woman Knows,** lay in the character of John Shand, with his solemn worldliness and innocent egotism. It did not depend particularly on the little joke at the end about women being made from man's funny-bone and not his rib. The idea simply was to bring the curtain down on a man's first attempt at laughter; and, as a matter of fact, a bad joke was even more artistically appropriate than a good one. But by this mysterious maladroitness that runs across Mr. Barrie's cleverness, he contrived to give most of the critics and spectators a notion that the whole four acts turned on this Adamic elbow-joint. He left them with the notion that this anatomical fact was really all that every woman knows; and many journals almost confined themselves to the criticism that the joke was not good enough. In the same way the horrible death of Sentimental Tommy on a spike is theoretically quite defensible; but there is something nameless in the way it is done (or perhaps in the way the rest of the book is done) that makes the reader simply feel that the thing does not belong to the story at all. That iron spike is of another material; it is like an iron spike in a chair of carved wood. It is the same in that episode of the barber-baronet in the delightful romp of **When a Man's Single**; one does not know whether to take it seriously or not. But, curiously enough, it was in his greatest and most famous work, **Peter Pan,** that the most startling instances occurred of this violation of the congruity of nonsense, this knack of allowing trifles to stand in the light of triumphs. The scene of the dog who put the children to bed, pretty and popular as it was, was a great mistake. Such things could only happen if the children were in fairy-land already; and this extracts all the thrill and thought out of the escape into fairyland. The front scene, so to speak, the human interior, should have been not only ordinary, but even dull. For it is on those dull, rainy mornings, or hot, empty afternoons that both children and men look out of the window for Peter Pan.

In this respect, the story in book-form is vastly better; the miraculous dog is, comparatively speaking, a sleeping dog, and we are permitted to let him lie. The opening scenes are more domestic and less pantomimic. Again, the new illustrations by Mr. F. D. Bedford . . . have a certain mixture of solid impossibility and exact detail, which is the thing that children love most. . . .

But all these incidental improvements are dwarfed by an essential improvement which never appeared (so far as I saw it; and I saw it three times) in the play. At the end of the story Mr. Barrie put (or ought to have put) a really vital question to Peter Pan. Is it better to be a Pagan god or a Christian man? Is it better to grow up, to drink the wine of Cana and the vinegar of Calvary; or is it better to be irresponsible for eternity? At the end of the play the challenge was frankly shirked. Wendy was to visit Peter once a year; without reference to the fact that she would be ninety at the end of what Peter would regard as a half-holiday. In this book the challenge is accepted. Wendy grows up and has a little daughter, and the god of youth

cheerfully transfers his attentions to the daughter. That is good, clean, philosophical courage. But I shall be always one of those who wish that Peter, when the choice was offered him, had gone to school and married and died.

Gilbert K. Chesterton, "Peter Pan as a Novel," in *The Nation, London, Vol. X, No. 7, November 18, 1911, p. 314.*

ALFRED NOYES

Peter Pan exists. That is the first and last thing to be said about him, and it is the highest praise of Mr. Barrie's genius. Peter Pan exists as a very few other characters in fact or fiction exist. He is independent of print and paper. Artists may come and go, but they cannot hold or bind him. He refuses to be captured, and Mr. Barrie aids and abets him in his elusiveness. (p. 131)

[This] is the great, the supreme test—does the character live beyond the book? And this test is answered by Peter Pan. He has been staged, sculptured, painted, sung in verse and prose, and by the genius of Mr. Barrie he has transcended it all as, I cannot but think, an immortal personality in the annals of fairyland.

In *Peter and Wendy* Mr. Barrie has not made the mistake of capturing his discovery, and delivering him over to his readers, bound hand and foot. In spite of all that has gone before, the reader devours the book greedily, and on page two hundred and sixty-seven he is left still hungry for more. It is with infallible art that Mr. Barrie approaches the perilous task of this delightful narrative of "specimen days" in the life of Peter Pan. . . . We follow the delightful magic thread of the tale through a purple forest of adventure. On all sides we are surrounded by infinite possibilities; yet we are kept cunningly to the matter in hand. It is this that distinguishes the story of Peter Pan from all other creations of the kind. In *Robinson Crusoe,* for instance, we are distinctly limited and it was only by an oversight of the author that the shipwrecked mariner was able to divest himself of all his clothes, swim out to the wreck in the offing, and fill his pockets with ship's biscuits. Incidents of that kind do happen in a dream, and they happen in this modern tale of a dream-island, but only with the sanction of the rare genius that controls the happenings. Mr. Barrie knows the map of his dream-island—and never loses his way in it. He leaves that delightful adventure to the reader, and gives him room enough to wander from earth to heaven. For the map of his Never-land is the map of a child's mind—"always an island more or less, with astonishing splashes of colour here and there, and coral reefs and rakish-looking craft in the offing, and savages and lonely lairs. . . . On these magic shores children at play are for ever beaching their coracles. We too have been there; we can still hear the sound of the surf, though we shall land no more."

That is Mr. Barrie's version of the "Ode on Immortality"; and though the deep note be only perceptible to the grown-up, and even to him only as a distant sea-murmur, like the sound of a most delicate and ethereal shell, it is always there. . . . But Mr. Barrie will not consent to the theory that the gleaming magic must fade into the light of common day. The addition to the legends that concludes this book of *Peter and Wendy* is one of the most enchanting in the history of fairy-land. (pp. 131-32)

[The] whole of the chapter entitled "When Wendy Grew Up" tugs at the heart, and is a masterpiece of that pathos which trembles into smiles. No man living has written anything finer; and it defies criticism. . . . It is obviously a little piece of immortality. It is a book that goes on for ever, in every sense of the word; and its hero can never grow up or grow old "so long as children are gay and innocent and heartless." To understand this book, as all children under ninety will understand it, is to love it and never forget it. To criticise it, in the ordinary sense of the word, would be like dissecting a man's heart. There are pages in it that can only be described as the most sensitive in modern literature. (p. 132)

*Alfred Noyes, in a review of "Peter and Wendy,"
in* The Bookman, *London, Vol. XLI, No. 243, December, 1911, pp. 131-32.*

WILLIAM LYON PHELPS

In the year 1904 came *Peter Pan*, and it had a *succès fou*. This is no spring flower, or hothouse plant; it is a hardy perennial, and will delight thousands of spectators after we shall have all made our exit from the planet. It is one of the most profound, original, and universal plays of our epoch. No London Christmas would be complete without it. It is just as appealing in 1920 as it was in 1904, and there is no reason why it should not produce the same effect in 2020. It is the rapture of children, the joy of old age; and it ought to take its place with *Robinson Crusoe, Gulliver's Travels, The Pied Piper Story, Alice in Wonderland*, and other classics founded on some eternal principle of youth.

At all events, in this play, Mr. Barrie created a character, a personality; Peter Pan is an addition to literature and an addition to humanity. He is a real person—already proverbial—and it seems incredible that he can ever be forgotten. (p. 31)

[The] play *Peter Pan*, with all its objective pictures and thrilling climaxes, is really a tour of the inside of a child's mind. The play, supposedly written by a child, is a child's view of the world; the tick-tock crocodile, the pirate smoking cigarettes like a candelabra, the fairies and the flying are all romantically true to life. Yet it is nowhere invertebrate; it is not a series of pretty pictures, it is emphatically a play, and no one but a great dramatist could have produced it. (p. 32)

William Lyon Phelps, "J. M. Barrie," in his Essays on Modern Dramatists, *The Macmillan Company, 1921, pp. 1-66.*

PATRICK BRAYBROOKE

[With] the immortal *Peter Pan* . . . , Barrie has for all time established himself as the child's good fairy. . . . (p. 114)

Peter Pan is above everything else a fairy tale, but it is a fairy tale which is totally unlike the usual type of such story. For in *Peter Pan*, more than in perhaps any other of Barrie's works, we have a combination of mortals and fairies. Peter Pan himself is both a fairy and a mortal. . . .

The great difference between *Peter Pan* and other fairy stories is that in the latter the people who come in contact with the fairy are not really mortals at all, they are not surprised when the troll turns the prince into a pig. . . . (p. 117)

Wendy and Michael are two of the most ordinary children possible, they have a certain belief in fairies, they apparently dislike having to go to bed (as all good children do). . . .

Peter Pan does not suffer by being dramatised, in fact it really gains, for it is almost impossible to imagine Barrie writing anything that would not do well for the stage. . . . For year by year Peter thrills whole multitudes of children, he makes them laugh while their parents would, if no one were looking, cry, he takes them to the old land of mother love, he takes them

back, back to the pirate ship and the villainous Captain Hook. . . . (p. 118)

Year by year this most lovely play of childish adventure carried out with a deep philosophy transports us to the Never, Never Land, where are all the lost boys.

If a play has the outstanding success that *Peter Pan* has, it is obvious that it must contain something that appeals to successive types of people. For a revival cannot make its appearance year after year unless there is some lasting charm in it that remains constant through a long period, though the outside world changes and customs alter almost daily. (pp. 118-19)

[With] *Peter Pan* the reason of its extraordinary success is that it deals with a theme that is everlastingly charming. Childhood and its curious philosophy of acceptance of what it is told never loses its fresh delight. . . . *Peter Pan* deals with the ordinary child at its very best, it deals with that remarkable love of adventure that children have, when they imagine the fairy king is in the nursery cupboard and that the way to fairyland lies through the wood at the end of the drive. (pp. 119-20)

One very good reason then for the enormous success of *Peter Pan* is that it is a charming picture of the child's mind, for nearly all children in their imagination go through the strange adventures that Wendy and Michael do. . . . *Peter Pan* is not only a play it is a religion, it is, in a pictorial way, the portrait of childish faith, that faith which sees in fairies something that is eternally beautiful and eternally just out of sight.

It is of course a mistake to imagine that in *every* way Peter Pan is a lovable character. He is not, he is at times selfish, his very wish not to grow up, has a certain suggestion of selfishness in it. But if so it merely indicates that Barrie does understand the child's mind, for children are selfish, but in a different way to grown ups, children are selfish without being aware of the fact, grown ups are always entirely aware of it. Some critics have seen in *Peter Pan* an attempt to show what happiness really is, the power to fly, the power to race over the church steeples, the power to soar over the ocean. I do not agree with those critics who only see in *Peter Pan* the embodiment of happiness. If one reads the character of Peter Pan at all carefully, it can be seen that he has a certain wistfulness about him, which is akin to melancholy.

For the whole essence of Peter Pan is melancholy, it is the symbol of a striving against the inevitable, a striving not to grow up that we all really wish, though we pretend that we would on no account be children again. Peter's wish not to grow up is that he shall not reach that stage that he can no longer fly. For grown ups cannot fly, they have not faith that they can, that is reserved for little children. (pp. 120-21)

In a sense Peter Pan wants to be something else to what he is, he very much wants a mother, yet he wants to remain at the same time as he is. To a limited extent then Peter Pan is symbolic of humanity's strivings.

I do not think that most children really understand the true significance of *Peter Pan*, they look upon it as a delightful fairy story, about a boy who refuses to grow up and has delightful adventures and hairbreadth escapes. It is for the older folk to see the symbolism and philosophy that lies behind, the pathos of Peter, the utter sadness of the Never, Never Land. . . . One of the most poignant incidents in Peter Pan is that one where Tinker Bell to save Peter has drunk poison. The only thing that can save Tinker Bell is if the children say they believe in fairies, and if they do they must clap.

And so every Christmas in the heart of London, the children in the audience of a West End theatre clap to proclaim that they believe in fairies. And perhaps, almost unconsciously some of their parents clap also. It is the secret of the charm of *Peter Pan,* the beautiful child's world of the fairy, so far removed from the cold, commercial and bitter world that has long lost fairyland because it has long lost its childlike innocence. (p. 122)

Patrick Braybrooke, in his J. M. Barrie: A Study in Fairies and Mortals, *J. B. Lippincott Company, 1925, 162 p.*

THOMAS MOULT

The *Peter Pan* mood is fixed in us by the time the curtain goes up on Act One—"the night nursery of the Darling family . . . whose top window, the important one, looks out upon a leafy square from which Peter used to fly up to it, to the delight of three children and no doubt the irritation of passers by." It is an indefinable mood, this of the greatest children's play of modern times. Nay, more than a children's play, or how else shall we explain the poignant touches that are everywhere, as when the dramatist speaks in his stage-directions about the cards over the doors of Bloomsbury lodging houses "inviting homeless ones to come and stay with the hospitable inhabitants"; or when he announces that "Wendy and John came in,

Barrie at the age of eight.

looking their smallest size, as children tend to do to a mother suddenly in fear for them"?

Peter Pan is unquestionably a play for grown-ups as well as young people. Doubtless this explains in some measure its vitality. . . . Readers of all ages can laugh at the quaint notion about the bed in which all the children of the Never-land sleep. "Though large, it is a tight fit for so many boys, and Wendy has made a rule that there is to be no turning round until one gives the signal, when all turn at once." And do not even the babies in an audience at the theatre lean forward as though to cry out the truth to Mrs. Darling in that lovely last scene when she goes into the apparently empty bedroom of the nursery and although she "sees the bumps as soon as she comes in, she does not believe she sees them"? (pp. 160-61)

[There] is no doubt that the publication at last of the "book of words" of Sir James Barrie's fairy-play is a literary event of magnitude. It is one, moreover, that those who don't care a brass farthing for literary events will wish to celebrate in the best possible manner—by acquiring a copy. Much as they have loved the stories of Peter already published, part of their appreciation was due to the fact that a snack is the next best thing to a feast. And now the feast has arrived. It will surely be partaken of by many enchanted generations. . . . (p. 161)

Thomas Moult, "'Peter Pan': The Book of Words," in The Bookman, *London, Vol. LXXV, No. 447, December, 1928, pp. 160-61.*

J. B. PRIESTLEY

Barrie wrote his fantasy of childhood, added another figure to our enduring literature, and thereby undoubtedly made one of the boldest bids for immortality of any writer of his generation. This is not to say that even in *Peter Pan* he contrived to avoid all dangers, for there are those of us who have never felt quite comfortable in the presence of Mr. and Mrs. Darling, Nana, Wendy, and Tinker Bell. Nevertheless, it remains a masterpiece, and it is a masterpiece just because the more ambitious of the novels were failures, patchwork. . . . Wendy, though not altogether successful, is simply the essential Babbie, Grizel, and the rest, all rolled into one solid little girl. Peter Pan is the real Sentimental Tommy who has slipped out of Scotland, has given up pretending to write books and make love, said farewell to all those grown-up tricks, shed his black coat and trousers, and now exists in his own natural element. As for Captain Hook (with his concern for "good form"), Smee and his sewing-machine, the crocodile, and the rest, there is nothing like them, and they are worth a host of little ministers and quaint weavers who are not successful in being either reasonable adults or elves. Here then, in *Peter Pan,* Barrie is supremely himself. (p. 117)

[*Peter Pan*] remains the masterpiece, and if its author wins immortality it will be through the suffrages of Peter and his innumerable friends. Sir James Barrie has received some of the highest honors within the reach of a man of letters and has been praised without stint for some three decades; but it is safe to prophesy that his name will endure chiefly because he once wrote a pantomime: his name will come round with the Christmas trees and the crackers. It will be a quaint but not unenviable kind of immortality. (p. 119)

J. B. Priestley, "Sir James Barrie," in English Journal, *Vol. XVIII, No. 2, February, 1929, pp. 106-19.*

J. A. HAMMERTON

[*The following excerpt is taken from* Barrie: The Story of a Genius *which, along with Denis Mackail's* Barrie: The Story of J.M.B. *(1941), is considered a benchmark of Barrie scholarship. In his Author's Note, Mackail calls Hammerton's book "a monument of industrious research."*]

[*The Little White Bird*], wherein the immortal Peter makes his earliest appearance, ranks among the author's finest adventures in that realm of fantasy and faëry which he was soon to enter as conqueror by way of the stage. But it did not appreciably advance his standing in the world of letters. *Peter and Wendy*, with all its moonbeam beauty, is still a 'book of the play,' a restatement in story form of a thing that had already come to wondrous life upon the stage: a thing upon which, in the long run, its author's reputation may chiefly rest: his surest grip on fame. (p. 3)

In *The Little White Bird*, there is probably as much of the innermost Barrie as in any book he has ever written. His humour is here at its finest, his sentiment at its purest. It matters not a fig that in its general outline it conforms to no literary convention with which one is familiar. (p. 233)

The outstanding thing about *Peter Pan* is that its author did not make a resolve that he would write a fairy play and sit down in cold blood to fill the bill. It was a thing of slow growth. It was mainly to please his dreamy self. . . . [This] eerie, fairy thing . . . was really the play of his heart. . . . (p. 247)

The secret of *Peter Pan*, what is it? (p. 252)

I would incline to attribute the hold the play has taken upon old and young alike to the amazing skill with which a group of the most universal of human experiences is assembled and presented to the material eye with a naturalness that implies both faith and knowledge. Consider for a moment some of these. All children, doubtless little Zulus as well as little Scotsmen, want to 'fly.' It is a natural impulse which has often led to broken noses; it is the commonest of dreams, and possibly in another million years human beings may have developed the necessary physical equipment for flying and such a scene as that of the opening act of *Peter Pan* may be as common as walking downstairs to-day. Then, when Peter remarks to the children that there are pirates in the Neverland, John, grabbing his tall Sunday hat, exclaims: 'Pirates! Let us go at once!' What more natural? Lives there a boy since the days of Mayne Reid or W.H.G. Kingston who would not have responded with equal alacrity? Redskins, too, make their appearance very soon, wolves also, and Peter had shown the Lost Boys how to frighten the wolves away by looking at them through his legs, a bit of wood lore every boy inherits with that which enables him to catch birds by putting salt on their tails. Then Mermaids are there. Wendy was 'awfully anxious to see a mermaid,' like every other child that has been born for many generations back. The building of Wendy's house by the Lost Boys, what is it but the most natural of all the make-believe games of childhood? The lagoon, the kite, and the walking of the plank and a dozen other elemental memories of our childhood's days; the stories told to us, the stories we read ourselves; these are the things that make the whole entrancing entertainment the loveliest experience for grown-ups and by a perfect wizardry of presentation make it equally alive for the children whose memories have not yet begun to lay by the precious things which in years to come they will delight to take out and fondle again. What Barrie really does in *Peter Pan* is to 'flipe' the mind of his own boyhood, as a Scotsman might say: to turn it inside

out, as he used to do with his jacket in some of his games at Kirriemuir. The result is an imaginative epitome of all boyhood, with which is interwoven just the right amount of 'feminine interest,' but no sex consciousness. In the ordinary way nothing would more readily repel a healthy boy than any suggestion of the feminine, but he is caught in the motherly coils of Wendy before he knows where he is, or it may be that his own masculine interests are so predominant throughout the play, that he is never conscious of this feminine element which has done its work by capturing at the outset both mothers and fathers and the whole range of girlhood. (pp. 254-55)

[*Peter Pan*] the most celebrated, and most certain of immortality, among all Barrie's creations. . . . (p. 267)

J. A. Hammerton, in his Barrie: The Story of a Genius, *Sampson, Low, Marston & Co., Ltd., 1929, 344 p.*

F. J. HARVEY DARTON

The play of *Peter Pan* came a year later than *The Admirable Crichton*. But its substance had been in the novel, *The Little White Bird*, and had been hinted at in *Tommy and Grizel* (1900), where Tommy, as T. Sandys, meditates a work which should deal with a boy who hated the idea of growing up. The chapters from *The Little White Bird* (beginning with chapter thirteen) which were more or less part of the play were separately issued in 1906 as *Peter Pan in Kensington Gardens*. . . . In that form . . . the tale suggests both George Macdonald and a fusion of Hans Andersen's tales with the more ethereal passages in Grimm; a little of Charles Lamb might be added for the London flavour of the writing. Later—in 1911—Barrie made the play into a story, under the title of *Peter Pan and Wendy*. (pp. 70-1)

Consider first the novel. . . . It would be fair to say that some parts of it came near to frightening its eager readers. The fancy of the Kensington Gardens portion is exquisite. Some of its prettiest whimsies are not used in the play; for instance, the absurdly pathetic transformation of the parish boundary stones into little tombstones—just the sort of invention a wise humorist would make on the spot (as maybe Barrie did) for young friends. Kensington Gardens themselves, of course, are in no way vital to the play, and their rather too pretty-pretty statue of Peter Pan (given to the Gardens by Barrie himself . . .) has little to do with the play: it is inspired, if by anything, by a passage in *The Little White Bird*. Indeed it ignores altogether a very important half of Peter of the play. Peter in stone is a delicate figure piping to rabbits, wood nymphs, and various other creatures. There is no trace of his valour, and no vestige of the play's ever-present humour. Now killing pirates was Peter's skilled trade, if ever he had one. (pp. 71-2)

It would be superfluous to describe the play. But it is curiously interesting in some of the details we now take for granted. They show the omniscience of the eternal boy in Barrie—the ideas which have occurred to other people and been forgotten. (p. 75)

The wonders of the Never Never Land—a place, like the Swiss Family Robinson's island, "almost too satisfactory"—have many analogues. Underground homes are common knowledge. Examples occur, as scientists say, in *Aladdin*, *Big Klaus and Little Klaus*, the epic of the Nibelungs, and *Alice in Wonderland*, to name only a few classics of Subterranea. The name of the Never Never Land is found in the early records of Australian travel. As for the pirates, and the swelling speech of Jas. Hook and Pan, the Flying Stationers of Thrums surely provided them. Crocodiles are recurrent beasts in most works of real and fictitious adventure. . . . But the memory of man runneth not to the swallowing of clocks, nor to such fastidiousness of greed that the creature must needs follow Jas. Hook over land and (apparently) sea for another taste of him. (pp. 76-7)

But it was not details like these which lifted the play above the plane of inspired exuberance, high though that level is. It was other qualities, new to the stage, which hitherto Barrie alone has shown. One is the capacity for sheer simplicity. Barrie tells you more by what he leaves out than by what he says, as in the reticent wistfulness, the sad almost silent grace, of Mrs Darling's mother-love and Peter's ineffectual flutterings against the shut window. Another is the translation of happy visions into a spiritual truth which is almost fact. Peter could never grow up. He did not wish it? I wonder would he have grown up if by doing so he could have found a Mrs Darling? But he must flicker off into the Land of Lost Children, where imaginary heroisms come true. "Fetch me that doodle-do!" bellows Hook: and when panic fear falls upon that black soul, "What are you?" he asks. "I am youth, I am joy, I am life. . . ." That triumphant shout is the war-cry of Fairyland, with which he must lead the Lost Children. He, poor happy exile, does not know that it is needed also on the earth to which he guides them back. He hardly knows, perhaps, how tremendous a thing it is for him, an immortal, to contemplate death, though he is ready to do it. Even to mortals "to die would be an awfully big adventure."

Again, there is the almost impudent use of the audience as an accomplice—a conspirator, not in realities, but in things of the imagination, as in the snatching of Tinker Bell from death. "Do you believe? If you believe, clap your hands. A fairy can never die if you believe in him.". . . [When] the appeal first came, there was a second's pause, and then the young in all sincerity, the old both because they too were rapt and because they perceived a superb stage trick, broke into thunder genuine and entirely spontaneous. They *did* believe. Afterwards, when they thought it over, the older persons realized that they had been cheering a plain truth to which they had seldom given conscious attention.

That—the perception, the communication, of some magic that lies beyond the dust of existence, something east of the sun and west of the moon—was the "lesson" or "message" of *Peter Pan*. (pp. 78-80)

Mankind has known many Pans—for the name, being interpreted, means Everything. The Greek Pan, the goat-footed god, died to the sound of a great moaning heard by ships at sea, when Christ was crucified. . . . [Some], like Shelley, make him a teeming god of fullness, growth, ecstasy, or send him piping down the vale of Mænalus. Yet others again, as Mr Kenneth Grahame in *The Wind in the Willows*, would have him "the Friend and Helper" of all good beasts. Peter, if you *must* "moralize the fable," may have some of the best qualities in these several modes of god, with the addition of vivid attributes known to us from the Barrie revelation. It is immaterial. The main thing is to know laughter and tears through him and with him, and be thankful for both. (pp. 81-2)

F. J. Harvey Darton, in his J. M. Barrie, *1929. Reprint by Scholarly Press, 1970, 127 p.*

F. J. HARVEY DARTON

[*Children's Books in England was originally published in 1932.*]

[*Peter Pan*] has influenced the spirit of children's books, and the grown-up view of them, more powerfully than any other work except the *Alices* and Andersen's *Fairy Tales*. (p. 317)

The play was received with unbounded gladness. It was in no way like anything known before. Naturally to-day, after the lapse of a quarter of a century, the rapture which first greeted the new phenomenon has been slightly soiled. In 1904-6 Barrie was at the height of popularity, and some of the enthusiasm for anything he wrote was a little uncritical. Reaction, so far as there has been any, has not in the least diminished his claim to originality, but repetition has made some of even his freshest fancies appear sentimental or trivial, or both. It is necessary for those who are old enough to recall the performances—and the audiences—of 1904-5 to reassure themselves that they had truly seen a revolution (almost a revelation) in the presentation of imaginative ideas to children. So much of *Peter Pan* seems obvious now: so little of it was then.

When the play is considered in detail it becomes clear that one thing Barrie did was to remember a hundred small whimsies and scraps of dream and beloved traditional illusions which most of us have forgotten, though to us also they were once life itself. There is a precedent for almost everything in the romance: a precedent in the warm embers of memory rather than in fact. The dialogue and the stage-business both made the old fires glow again, with an unearthly vividness which they had never quite possessed when they were first lit. Probably the Never Never Land, for instance, . . . had come to Barrie, and to boys of many lustres before him, from some arid Parleyish book, or even from a talkative geography of about 1820 or so, when Australia was becoming exciting. The idea of dispersing wolves by looking through your legs at them is an old traveller's tale. Pirates we knew all about ever since Morgan sacked Panama or Drake took the *Cacafuego*. Lagoons were in books like Ballantyne's *Coral Island*, for which, in 1913, Barrie wrote an Introduction with the glorious beginning: "To be born is to be wrecked on an island". Peter crying cockadoodle-doo is Jim Hawkins in *Treasure Island* or, more artificially, Capt. Boldheart in Dickens's *Holiday Romance*. Flying is eminent in *Peter Wilkins*. Peter's elusive shadow is to be found in *Peter Schlemihl* . . . , as well as in *A Child's Garden of Verses:* indeed, Stevenson's poems contain almost in themselves alone enough raw material for the play. The crocodile might be a recollection of Waterton's travels. Red Indians are Fenimore Cooper. And so on. Barrie's preface to the printed play shows the humorous windings of his mind at work.

Then, again, some of the English sentiment was common form; perhaps too common in places. The ritual of going to bed, the anxiety about a dress tie, the mother-love . . . , the song of birds at sunset—these had been in books, in poetry and in plays often enough before. There was little throughout that a well-read person could feel sure he had never read, seen, or heard before—by itself. The change—a transformation scene, in the theatre sense—wrought by Barrie was in uniting all the particular gleams of memory into one universal radiance. He made the old young as they watched his puppets: he made the young live the stage-play visibly, as they lived it in the secrecy of their minds by themselves. It was not acting that was taking place for an audience: it was the all-conquering reality of fairyland, with not an atom of afterthought or seriousness prepense.

It does not matter if to-day the whole crowd of spectators does not clap its hands at Peter's impassioned plea for faith in fairies. What matters historically is that Barrie made all but shrivelled pedagogues see the value, even the necessity, of that nonsensical creed. And the influence of his concrete presentation has travelled far beyond the stage. He was no entire innovator as, in a sense, Lewis Carroll was. But he had the almost sudden effect of one in the way in which *Peter Pan* surprised, stirred and enlightened that slow-moving, thorough-going organism, the English mind. We had thought of his ideas for ourselves, now and then, here and there. We knew children really had these fancies, and that they were beneficial, not harmful. But an inhibition, a social fog, a Baconian Idol, had prevented us from being clear-headed and kept us silent. (pp. 318-19)

F. J. Harvey Darton, "The 'Eighties and To-Day: Freedom," in his Children's Books in England: Five Centuries of Social Life, *second edition, 1958. Reprint by Cambridge at the University Press, 1970, pp. 299- 326.*

FRANK SWINNERTON

Peter Pan, the children's entertainment which is less a play than a portmanteau of games and insights, has given the utmost pleasure to many children and many adults for twenty years. Lines from it, remembered from the past, are as familiar to grown-up children as are lines from the Gilbert and Sullivan operas. And yet as one recalls *Peter Pan,* and its admitted charms for many, one does, I think, hesitate. Although there has been no entertainment for children which approaches it in popularity in the whole of modern theatrical history, and although it has contributed greatly, I surmise, to the decline and fall of the English Christmas pantomime, there is in *Peter Pan* something approaching an exploitation of the child mind. As it entertains, so it deceives. When Peter says that "to die will be an awfully big adventure," he makes me shudder. When he demands to know whether the audience believes in fairies, and poor over-excited tots thunder out their applause, I wonder whether Barrie is a human being or a demon. For I do not think that Barrie himself believes in fairies.

This you will say is a moral criticism. So it is. But surely it also suggests why I believe *Peter Pan* to have its fair share of mawkishness. It is to entertain the children; that is agreed. So was *Alice in Wonderland.* And yet *Alice in Wonderland* contains not the smallest hint of sentimentality. It is genuine gold throughout. There is not the smallest hint of sentimentality in any one of the Gilbert and Sullivan operas, which are genuine gold throughout. *Peter Pan* is sentimental. For this reason Barrie's work is at the present time seriously undervalued by many who, if they knew the major plays and the early books of Kirriemuir sketches, would recognize in it a positive contribution to modern letters. (pp. 117-18)

Frank Swinnerton, "Fancy Fair: Barrie, Milne, James Stephens," in his The Georgian Scene: A Literary Panorama, *Farrar & Rinehart, 1934, pp. 105-29.*

THE JUNIOR BOOKSHELF

When, on June 24th, the body of Sir J. M. Barrie was laid to rest in the cemetery "up the hill" in Kirriemuir, there passed from among us one whose fame will last for many generations. That fame will rest on *Peter Pan,* for it is through that play that children in their thousands will keep his name alive. The Archbishop of Canterbury . . . said, "It is a commonplace to say that in him there abode the essential spirit of a child. With children he was all his life a fellow citizen of the happy land of make-believe." . . . [*Peter Pan*] is universal: it, and the story written from it, has been translated into almost every civilised language.

Barrie was ultimately a writer for children and for those adults who have retained, as he had to so remarkable a degree, the elements of child mentality. And that is the secret of his uni-

versality, for the most sceptical among us and the most cynical retain some of that early youth, and no matter how jealously we may try to hide our "weakness" from our fellow-grown-ups, we have to admit to ourselves an enjoyment of fine children's books when they are sufficiently make-believe to be frankly removed from normal everyday adult life. Barrie wrote what he did, perhaps, as an escape from the heart-breaking discouragement of a world that makes one sceptical of man's progress. He created a realm of fantasy of his own and we and our children have been admitted into that enchanted land. We shall therefore remember him with affectionate gratitude because he leads the children into their own country of make-believe and gives to us periods of the rejuvenating experience of an occasional peep into a world which we have half forgotten.

"Sir J. M. Barrie," in The Junior Bookshelf, *Vol. 1, No. 4, July, 1937, p. 26.*

JAMES A. ROY

Perhaps Mr. Alfred Noyes got nearest the secret of [*Peter Pan*'s] lasting appeal when he called the play "an exquisite illustration of a very ancient and beautiful phrase about the width and height and wonder of the kingdom of little children" [see excerpt dated December, 1905]. Barrie put it in a slightly different way in the beginning of *Peter Pan:* "All the characters, whether grown-ups or babes, must wear a child's outlook as their only important adornment." That is absolutely essential. If you believe in fairies, in the incredibly real intangible things in life, and in a Never-Never Land where things that seem most inconsequent fall into their places like the pieces of coloured glass in the old-fashioned kaleidoscope, then *Peter Pan* will appeal to you. If you are what is called a realist, the play will not. (p. 180)

Peter Pan is not only a fairy tale that can be appreciated by both old and young; it embodies a profound philosophy of life, which is found in the symbolic significance of Peter himself. Peter is both mortal and fairy. The mortal part of him is the eternal boy that is in all of us, the sensitive and imaginative child who lives in a world of make-believe, where he has the most wonderful adventures with the most amazing people, with pirates and fairies and crocodiles. The fairies are, if you will, moods by which we can escape, for the time being, from the prison of the flesh and the trammels of material things. Very few of us realize that we are all Peter Pans, that humanity itself is Peter Pan, eternally childish and foolish, making the same mistakes, and remaining unchanged because it has not the will to change. Peter is terribly lonely; but he possesses that greatest of all assets—courage, and knows the happiness which courage brings. (pp. 181-82)

[The] modern writer to whom Barrie is most closely akin in spirit, is Hans Andersen. Andersen's life was a tragedy—a defeat which issued in victory. His tragedy was that he was never able to grow up, to adapt himself to the privileges and responsibilities of the grown-up world. . . . So he was thrown back on his own thoughts and took refuge in a world of dreams. His tales and legends, like those of Barrie, developed into a blend of the fantastic and the autobiographical. Things that Andersen tells us about sound utterly impossible, because they have never happened to us. But as he continues with his story he plays the trick on us that Barrie is so fond of playing, which he no doubt picked up from the Ancient Mariner. He makes us listen to him, and the moment we begin to do that, we are lost. (p. 182)

Some people who do not understand Barrie would have it that he is teaching cowardly evasion, and that Peter Pan, instead of being the most attractive of all the fairies, is the very personification of selfishness. To be sure, Peter is selfish, just as any child is selfish, without being aware of it. But Peter is also a symbol of that youth which we would all gladly recapture. (p. 189)

> *James A. Roy, in his* James Matthew Barrie: An
> Appreciation, *Charles Scribner's Sons, 1938, 256 p.*

DENIS MACKAIL

[*The following excerpt is taken from* Barrie: The Story of J.M.B.,
which is considered a classic of Barrie scholarship.]

Volumes could be written on all that [*Peter Pan*] has meant to generation after generation of playgoers of all ages; on what it has added to English and American imagery, and literature, and language; and on the ten thousand and one details of its inner history, as the ripples began leaving St. Martin's Lane [where the Duke of York's Theatre, the venue in which the play premiered, was located in London] and then spread all over the earth. . . . [The man who wrote it] assured us afterwards that he couldn't remember writing it . . . and was telling the truth to this extent—that though he had put his heart and soul and all his thoughts into it, something deeper and still more individual had actually guided his pen. An alchemy, as mysterious and often as disturbing to him as to anyone else, which had taken his own sadness and nostalgia for childhood, his games with the little Davieses, and thirty years of constant if not always conscious preoccupation with the stage, and had turned them into dialogue and direction, and three hours of magic, utterly different from anything yet known.

But welcomed and recognised [in 1904], and almost unanimously, by the Press and the public alike. Queues at the box-office, and addicts already beginning to join them even as they emerged from a matinée. Only a play, of course; a sentimental play; a play, as they would say nowadays, of escape; and a play, if one stops to think, with cruelty in it as well as charm and beauty. It didn't alter anything. It righted no wrongs, and solved no problems. It didn't pretend to face a single objective or material fact. It was whimsical, if you like, for the word can't be avoided for ever. But there it was, . . . at the right hour, with the right manager, the right producer, the right players, the right scene-painters, dress-designers, and musical composer. Success. . . . Mr. J. M. Barrie not only in the top class now, but slipping quietly, and with an only slightly deceptive air of having done the whole thing purely to please himself, into a class that was entirely his own. (p. 367)

> *Denis Mackail, in his* Barrie: The Story of J.M.B.,
> *Charles Scribner's Sons, 1941, 736 p.*

GEORGE JEAN NATHAN

Something has happened either to me or to *Peter Pan*. When I first saw it on its initial production long years ago, it delighted me, lambkin that I then was. And when I saw it revived later on, young and tender as I still was, it continued to do so; and I recall that I wrote of it as if it were something pretty special in the way of fantasy. But now, seeing it again at this time in my life, I find it altogether too cute and flimsy for my taste and not anything like the picnic I once thought it was. (p. 270)

The play that captivated me in the far yesterdays failed me, and despite the training to work myself into form seemed to my resistant adult eyes a feebly manufactured flight of fancy,

*Peter, George, and Jack Llewelyn Davies in a photograph
taken by Barrie.*

and one that, though deliberately calculated for children, whether in fact or in mind, was itself childish. (p. 271)

What is the reason? . . . The answer, I think, is that what originally impressed us as Barrie's remarkable imagination and warming gentleness has come to be seen, in the first case, as simply a mouthful of sugar blown at the out-of-reach stars and, in the second, as the kind of gentleness born of self-conscious weakness rather than of sympathetic strength.

I don't wish to imply that a certain mild measure of appeal doesn't still inhere in the play. It is, however, of a left-handed sort, like the mushy but irresistible appeal of the juvenile lyric of ''Home, Sweet Home'' or the sound of a little dog licking its paws. But for the most part it is only the occasional stage tricks like the piano-wire aviation and the Tinker Bell lights that interest the persisting share of innocence that ever stubbornly remains in the adult composition, since the fantasy otherwise in its determined sweetness too much resembles a valentine addressed to someone else and opened by mistake. (pp. 271-72)

Peter Pan is the same play it was in the early Nineteen Hundreds; in other words, a ruthlessly sentimental fabrication that has the taste of pastry and that, like pastry, is appetizing if you confine yourself to only a few nibbles but rather hard on the digestion if you wolf it whole. (p. 272)

> *George Jean Nathan, in a review of ''Peter Pan,''*
> *in his* The Theatre Book of the Year, 1949-1950: A
> Record and an Interpretation, *Alfred A. Knopf, 1950,*
> *pp. 270-73.*

MARIETTA KARPE

[What makes] sophisticated, mature adults take [*Peter Pan*] so seriously? How is it possible that all audiences . . . , not only at children's matinees but also in the evenings always answered with a rousing ''Yes!'' to the question: ''Do you believe in fairies?'' What special magic does this play have that would cause adults to revert willingly and cheerfully back to childhood? The theme of this play must touch on a basic and universal need, shared by everybody, which has made audiences react that way for the period of half a century. . . .

[*Peter Pan*'s success] is especially astonishing if we consider the childlike simplicity and unsophistication of its plot. However, if we examine the story more closely, we find that it deals with the basic problems of life: with the problem of aging and death versus eternal youth and immortality. The author of *Peter Pan,* Sir James Matthew Barrie, is concerned with these problems from his earliest works on and seems to struggle with them all his life.

One fact becomes immediately obvious: children who fly through the air at night in their nightgowns are obviously dead children. The only way that a child can accomplish the feat of never growing up is by dying at an early age. (p. 104)

[In] some of the other writings of Barrie's, before and after *Peter Pan,* the idea of children and also mothers coming back from the grave occurs quite frequently. In fact, one might call it the leading idea which goes through his whole work. (p. 105)

Barrie's preoccupation with this eerie theme warrants closer attention. Who is this person in Barrie's mind who comes back from the dead? A first quick answer to this question is given in Barrie's autobiographical book *Margaret Ogilvy.* . . . In this book he writes in the most glowing and loving terms about his mother and his early intensive relationship to her. The book was written in 1896, one year after his mother's death. In describing what kind of a person his mother was he says in the beginning: "God sent her into the world . . . to open the minds of all who looked to beautiful thoughts." This is a significant expression because years later, when he tells how Peter Pan teaches Wendy and her brothers how to fly, he lets Peter say: "You just think lovely wonderful thoughts and they lift you up in the air." Here it is his mother's spirit that gives people the magic ability to fly. Another even more direct and almost conscious hint as to Peter Pan's connection with the author's mother is given in the fact that this part was written for and is always played by a grown-up woman actress—a strange concept of a little boy who never grew up!

But the person or persons incorporated in the symbol of Peter Pan become more obscure and complicated as we continue reading Barrie's autobiographical book, *Margaret Ogilvy.* In writing about his mother he very soon relates that she had another son, David, six-and-a-half years the author's senior, who died suddenly at the age of 13, when James was almost seven years old. Barrie does not say how it happened, but his devoted biographer Hammerton tells the story how David and his friend, while away at boarding school, went ice skating and David was fatally injured in a fall. He died a few hours after the accident, so suddenly that his mother was unable to get to his bedside before his passing. . . . It seems that after this tragedy the mother went into a deep depression. For many weeks she stayed in bed, her face turned to the wall, without speaking to anyone, crying for her dead boy. Little James must have been terrified at the spectacle and tried to keep away from her until one day his older sister encouraged him to go into the mother's bedroom and speak to her, ". . . and say to her that she still has another boy." In moving terms he describes in *Margaret Ogilvy* what happened on that memorable afternoon which was to be decisive for the whole pattern of his later life.

He entered the darkened room and was scared and quiet. Finally his mother said: "Is that you?" He writes: I thought it was the dead boy she was speaking to, and I said in a little lonely voice, "No, it's not him, its just me." At that, his mother held out her arms, and he flung himself into them. After that he spent a lot of time sitting on her bed, trying to make her forget David, and trying to make her laugh. He even kept a record on paper of how often she laughed at his tricks and antics such as standing on his head, etc. He tried to become

like the dead brother who knew so well how to whistle and who "stood with his legs apart, and his hands in the pockets of his knickerbockers," a familiar pose adopted by Peter Pan. (pp. 105-06)

So we find James Barrie, at the age of not quite seven and from then on all through his life, faced with the problem of an invincible rival for his mother's love. A little boy of that age might feel strong enough to fight a living father against whom he can feel aggression and with whom he can finally successfully identify, but to have as rival a dead brother, older and superior to him in every way, this truly is an unequal fight! How could he possibly have a chance! But he bravely attempts it, putting his whole life into the effort, and achieves in the creation of Peter Pan his ultimate victory by combining the figures of David, the dead boy who never grew up, his mother, since the part of Peter is written for a woman, and the image of himself into one charming "careless boy" who wins the hearts of an audience of millions. (p. 107)

In 1895, his mother died. We might assume that his mother's death changed the character of Barrie's oedipal struggle. While his mother was living, he tried, for 29 years, to substitute David in her feelings, but when she died, she joined as it were her dead son in Barrie's conception of death since he was a deeply religious man. Now it almost looked as if his lifelong rival finally won out, and Barrie might have come to a morbid solution of his conflict, that is, joining his dead mother and brother by suicide. Instead, he turns into the direction already mapped out by his early literary success, the direction into which his mother's interest in literature and writing had lead him. He carried on the fight in his imagination and wins his ultimate victory as the creator of the boy who teaches millions how to fly into the Never-neverland of our dreams. . . .

While James Barrie shows an almost idolizing affection for his mother, he rarely speaks of his father whom he describes as "a most loving and always well-loved husband, a man I am proud to call my father." In the character of Captain Hook, however, the father is portrayed as a murderous monster, castrated, full of hate and sly subterfuge. This dual personality is expressed in the theater by the author's stipulating that Mr. Darling and Captain Hook be played by the same actor, thus identifying the two characters. (p. 109)

When James was small, his mother vividly described her own childhood as her father's little companion and helper, and these stories impressed themselves deeply on the boy's sensitive mind. As James spun stories around the image of his mother as a little girl, the child-housekeeper-mother for her own father, we see the origins of the character of Wendy who becomes the mother-sister-housekeeper of Peter Pan. Thus the characters of two children became the imaginary companions of little James: The little girl who grew up to become a mother and who in a sense was already a mother when still a child; and the little boy who died and therefore never grew up.

As he was keeping company with his grieving mother and developing the roots of the ideas which later were to blossom forth in his literary work, a most intimate relationship sprung up between mother and son. While he undertook the futile attempt to replace David in his mother's love, he became his mother's therapist. By letting her talk to him for days on end about herself, her childhood, and her feelings, he relieved her sorrowing mind. And *vice versa,* in "counter-transference" as it were, his own mind was shaped and deeply influenced by her stories. Later, in sublimation of his oedipal needs, he becomes with his *Peter Pan* the therapist for the whole world, helping his audiences to deny aging and death. The tremendous success on stage and screen of this character of Peter Pan, the impersonization of eternal youth and immortality, shows that the audience responds instinctively to the reassurance that somewhere in Never-neverland a little boy lives on forever. James Matthew Barrie finally succeeded in his great childhood desire to bring his mother's darling boy, David, back to life. (p. 110)

> Marietta Karpe, "The Origins of Peter Pan," in The Psychoanalytic Review, *Vol. 43, No. 1, January, 1956, pp. 104-10.*

JOHN SKINNER

[In her] biography, *Portrait of Barrie,* Cynthia Asquith, Barrie's secretary for twenty years, denies the evidence which proves Barrie was "The Boy Who Wouldn't Grow Up", the sub-title of *Peter Pan.* There is undeniable confirmation in Barrie's journals that he unconsciously identified himself with Peter Pan, but Cynthia Asquith argues that he is the opposite, "more than old". She doubts he "ever *was* a boy". Here lies the riddle and perhaps the answer for Barrie was contradictory in personality: old and young; gay and depressed; sadistic and tender; ambitious and modest; humble and a snob. Barrie's contradictions are explained partially by comparing his life with his letters, journals, plays, and novels, for, like everybody else his phantasies were unconsciously rooted in his life experiences. (p. 112)

[James M. Barrie] solved the dilemma of growing up by remaining an emotional child. His unconscious motive seems to have been to join his mother in her childhood, which would enable him to displace his brothers and sister, as well as his father, and to remain in childhood with his young mother, the major theme of *Peter Pan,* for Wendy is the mother of lost boys. Boys usually long to become the hero; to defeat their fathers by becoming strong and powerful, but Barrie reversed this wish and attempted to remain "the happy boy". Barrie postponed his maturation by this mechanism but also denied that Margaret Ogilvy had aged and become his mother. Passive, regressive defiance of the reality of growing up made it unnecessary to live in open defiance of the father. Barrie escaped the requirement of overt rebellion by running back toward the illusory happiness of childhood.

This psychological device enabled him to deny that his mother, whom he prefers to remember as "Margaret Ogilvy" rather than as Mrs. David Barrie, was the mother of other children and in *Peter and Wendy* he realized that after two he would have to grow up, the age at which his mother conceived the sister who was to replace him. His description of this period in a child's life is sad and wistful:

> All children, except one, grow up. They soon know that they will grow up, and the way Wendy knew was this. One day when she was two years old, she was playing in a garden. . . . Mrs. Darling put her hand to her heart and cried: "Oh, why can't you remain like this forever! . . . ." henceforth Wendy knew that she must grow up. You always know after you are two. Two is the beginning of the end.

Wendy also realized that it would displease her mother if she grew up; her mother loved her as a baby, which provided an additional incentive for the young child to postpone maturation, and to enjoy a lifetime of immaturity.

In *Portrait of Barrie,* Cynthia Asquith feels that Barrie's estimations of himself are unreliable and with chilly disapproval she dismisses the assumption that he may be the boy he wrote about. Her description of his photograph, taken when he was seven, emphasizes that his face was adult and sober.

> In that tiny Kirriemuir cottage where Barrie was born, it had been, by a strange inversion of the laws of nature, not the mother, but the infant son, who had ceaselessly strained, plotted, contrived to make and keep, the other happy; . . . . from earliest infancy he had been constrained to play on his emotions, . . . to distract, console and amuse the mother, who never for one moment allowed him to forget her grief for her adored elder son.

James Barrie may not have realized the awful requirements of his mother's love in infancy but he tells us that he learned it at seven and in *Margaret Ogilvy* he realized that the role of mother and child had been reversed. He described himself in *Margaret Ogilvy* as "Her Maid of All Work" and his schoolboy response to girls was maternal; "you wanted all at once to take care of them."

Sir James M. Barrie, Bart., realized the truth at sixty when he entered his personal diagnosis in a notebook, observing wistfully and sadly: "The Man Who Couldn't Grow Up or The Old Age of Peter." He was even more explicit two years later, by which time it was much too late to escape, for Peter Pan could no longer be denied: "It is as if long after writing *P. Pan* its true meaning came to me. Desperate attempts to grow up but can't." He had known it since he was two.

The inconsistencies of James M. Barrie's character are psychologically consistent although apparently contradictory. He seems to have become preoccupied with death, sorrow, unhappiness and pain quite early in life. Many of his personality traits were apparent prior to the death of his brother and his earlier sorrows were probably felt before his brother died, for he realized that "Two is the beginning of the end." He was displaced by a sister at three, and he says in *Peter and Wendy* that "All children, except one, grow up." James M. Barrie, masquerading as the great exception, Peter Pan, hoped to displace his young sister through boyhood and eternal dependency. He could defeat the baby by becoming more dependent than she; more of a baby than the baby.

In the first version of *Peter Pan,* Mrs. Darling remonstrates: "But Peter, won't you ever do anything useful?" Peter answers:

> Don't want to be useful. But I'll be good to the dead babies. I shall come and sing gaily to them when the bell tolls; and they won't be frightened. I shall dance by their little graves and they will clap their hands to me and cry, "Do it again, Peter do it again", for they know I'm funny and it's the funny things they like.

Later, when Wendy is willing to go with Peter to Never-Never Land, he asks her, "But what as, Wendy, what as?" She replies: "As your mother. Oh, Peter, how I wish I could take you up and squdge you." They discover that a baby has been born, "a fairy and a girl", to which Peter protests: "You won't bother much with me now." Wendy consoles him with the promise that even the baby will grow up and become a mother to him: "Yes, darling, it's for you I want her. You see, you will always by young, but I shall grow old and die, and then she will be here to be a mother to you." In this primitive, childish, inverted logic, women bear daughters to provide mothers for their young sons; sisters do not exist; and "all children, except one, grow up''; the son has again changed places with someone else through a denial of time, age, and logic; his infant sister will some day become his mother; death and age are cheated by ''the boy who wouldn't grow up.'' (pp. 118-20)

[Peter Pan and James M. Barrie] did not proceed from an essentially infantile, passive, orally incorporative happiness toward the active combativeness of the genital Oedipus. Each remained with his mother, oblivious to life, ''The Happy Boy'', ''The Boy Who Couldn't Grow Up''. (p. 140)

> *John Skinner, ''James M. Barrie; or, The Boy Who Wouldn't Grow Up,'' in* American Imago, *Vol. 14, No. 2, Summer, 1957, pp. 111-41.*

NAOMI LEWIS

A curious piece of Kirriemuir-Kensington—a hitherto unpublished scene from *Peter Pan*—has turned up in . . . [*When Wendy Grew Up: An Afterthought*]. Briefly, the tale is this. Frohman, who had backed the original play in 1904, could not come over from America to see the London production until the third season (1907-8). On the last night, as a tribute to his visitor (and without the Lord Chamberlain's permission) Barrie added an Epilogue, an answer to the question: What happened to Wendy when she grew up? It was to be played once and never again. 'All those privileged to witness this never-to-be-forgotten and only performance of this striking act', wrote a stray critic in the audience, 'will acknowledge it to be the finest thing that Mr Barrie has ever done.'. . .

We are not the Lord Chamberlain, of course—but what can we possibly observe about this indecent and macabre little play? Only that here is a compelling instance of the fact that it isn't what you say that counts but the look on your face while you are saying it. Barrie's literary obsession with his own devouring mother is always taken as a sentimental tribute. This *Afterthought* should crystallise anyone's suspicions that it is, throughout his plays, a deep and abiding revenge, unrealised now only because *Peter Pan* is still accepted, by and large, on the terms of 1904. It was just possible to write these things at that point in time, between the late soft end of the Yellow Book period and the early edge of the middle domestic Georgian. . . . But at no other moment could the monstrous birth of Peter and Wendy ever have taken place. (p. 880)

[The] whole thing is absurd. Nobody could make a play out of this, in the Nineteen Fifties. (p. 881)

> *Naomi Lewis, ''Spirits of the Age,'' in* New Statesman, *Vol. LIV, No. 1398, December 28, 1957, pp. 880-81.*

ROGER LANCELYN GREEN

[The following excerpt was originally published in 1960.]

Peter Pan holds a peculiar position: his is the only story of recent centuries to escape from literature into folklore. For every one person who has seen the play or read the story there are hundreds who know perfectly well who and what Peter Pan is. Besides being a fairy-tale character, he is also a symbol— of what, precisely, even Barrie could not find words to describe: 'I'm youth, I'm joy! I'm a little bird that has broken out of the egg!' cries Peter—and Hook cannot understand, but says blankly, 'Oh . . . Well, to it again,' as he raises his cutlass. (p. 160)

Barrie insisted that what he used [in *Peter Pan*] was only a fraction of what was there, but he alone could draw out the very essence of childhood and the imaginative world into which

most children can retire. Perhaps it was because he himself could still slip away—escape, if you like—for brief moments into that world. (p. 164)

[Barrie used] all the old dreams of children and story-tellers since the world began: to fly, to run away from the responsibilities of growing up and yet to assume all the prerogatives of the grown-up, to fight without being hurt, to kill without shedding blood or causing pain, to flirt with death the unrealised—. . . and, drawing nearer to the particular, to build a hut, to live in a cave, to foil pirates and redskins, mermaids and wolves, to sail a ship, to be marooned. . . We have all been to our own Never, Never Land and known its possibilities. This 'map of a child's mind,' wrote Barrie, 'is always more or less an island, with astonishing splashes of colour here and there, and coral reefs and rakish-looking craft in the offing, and savages and lonely lairs, and gnomes who are mostly tailors, and caves through which a river runs, and princes with six elder brothers, and a hut fast going to decay. . .' The island has always room for more details: a corner of Tarzan's jungle or a back entrance to Kôr, a scrap of lunar landscape or a province of Narnia. But in its essentials it is still the same and ever present, though Barrie alone of mortals caught it for a magic moment and brought away a reflection of it that nearly all of us can recognise. (pp. 164-65)

The play was not published until 1928, when Barrie revised it considerably, and wrote many delightful stage directions, besides an amusing Introduction, the 'Dedication' to the Davies boys [see Author's Commentary]. However, in 1911 he had made the play into a book, *Peter and Wendy* (*Peter Pan and Wendy* in later editions); so good a book that it is surprising to find the short versions still being reissued. It is even stranger to find how comparatively little known the real book seems to be.

The style is not always easy for the child reader, and a few of the conceits are definitely of the adult Barrie variety; but these are only stray motes in the sunbeam. All the play is digested into the story, and much more besides, with a finality and a conviction that only Barrie could achieve. All the questions are answered, too, including what happened 'When Wendy Grew Up', which Barrie wrote first as an additional scene to the play, *An Afterthought,* which was acted for a single per-

Leinster Corner, Lancaster Gate, London, where Barrie wrote Peter Pan.

formance (February 22, 1908) and published for the first time in its original form in 1957. Altogether *Peter Pan and Wendy* is a perfect book for children, and children who find it at the right age are engrossed by it and remember it vividly. It should be better known, and would gain by appearing in some popular edition, and certainly with worthy illustrations: in this respect it has never been well served.

Barrie wrote another version of *Peter Pan* which is the least known of any: a scenario for a silent film that was never made. This waif of Never, Never Land, which was first published in 1954 in the present author's *Fifty Years of 'Peter Pan'*, can stand comparison unflinchingly with Peter Pan's other two media, and contains many delightful touches and intriguing suggestions not to be found in either but every bit as genuine and authentic. (p. 170)

[*Peter Pan* is] the best play for children ever written. (p. 171)

> *Roger Lancelyn Green, "J. M. Barrie," in* Three Bodley Head Monographs, *edited by Kathleen M. Lines, The Bodley Head, 1968, pp. 137-88.*

MARCUS CROUCH

[*Peter Pan*] has become embedded deep in the national consciousness. No other play has such a continuous tradition of performance; no other character in a children's book, not even Alice, is such a household name. It is difficult to approach *Peter Pan* in a proper mood of critical detachment to discover if it is a major work of creative imagination or a masterpiece of sentimental whimsy. Several generations of children, who are not concerned with the psychological interpretation of symbols, have had no doubt at all; for them this is a story of high adventure and high spirits. (p. 17)

> *Marcus Crouch, "The Edwardian Age," in his* Treasure Seekers and Borrowers: Children's Books in Britain 1900-1960, *The Library Association, 1962, pp. 12-31.*

BRIGID BROPHY, MICHAEL LEVEY, AND CHARLES OSBORNE

It's not a fault—it may even lend him the virtue of a poetic elasticity—for an author not fully to comprehend his own theme. The *Oedipus Rex* is a great poetic tragedy even though Sophocles most probably never articulated the facts of the Oedipus complex to himself in so many words. Neither is any theme impermissible in itself. Incest, castration and homosexuality are proper subjects for drama—even drama designed for children, whose own unconscious minds nightly design them fantasies on those subjects anyway. The only thing that is aesthetic murder is for an author to half-know and yet wantonly not-know—and then to tease and flirt with what he can't help, but won't admit to, knowing. Because its author plays peep-bo with his own knowledge of his theme (his theme being incest, castration and homosexuality), *Peter Pan* is an aesthetic massacre of the innocents—though it is also perhaps the most copybook example of stagecraft, of engineering an audience's emotions, in the repertory of the theatre.

The incest theme is announced at once. The children are introduced during a let's-pretend game in which John and Wendy, who are brother and sister, play-act being husband and wife and claim their brother Michael as their son. This prefigures the relation between Wendy and Peter Pan, an erotic relation, in which they flirt over a kiss and provoke Tinker Bell to sexual jealousy, but also a relation in which Wendy mothers Peter. In the Never Land, Peter introduces her to the boys as 'a mother

for us all'; she is even addressed as 'mummy'; yet presently Peter is playing father.

What small boys in the throes of the Oedipus situation feel about fathers is epitomized in the casting of the same actor as Mr Darling and as the villain and danger of the piece. What small boys in that situation would like to do to fathers, the play's castration theme, is introduced with the crocodile, who has already actually snapped off one of Captain Hook's members. The animal might have been created to illustrate what Freud called 'the infantile recurrence of totemism'—and from a literary point of view there is certainly more life in the totem sea beast which pursues Barrie's sea captain than in what must surely be its model, the sea beast pursued by Melville's.

The homosexual theme Barrie does not introduce explicitly until the last act. But it has of course been present all along in the transvestite casting of Peter Pan him/herself and has been flirted at us in the play Barrie makes with that transvestism in the dialogue and action. It is an actress who, playing Peter, hurts Wendy's feelings by a display of unequivocally virile pride ('He crows like a cock') and assuages them ('the artful one', comment Barrie's stage directions) by 'popping on to the end of the bed' and assuring her 'Wendy, one girl is worth more than twenty boys'.

Girls in drag flirting with girls straight have, of course, a hundred theatrical precedents. (Barrie was denied the extra kink Shakespeare enjoyed whereby his girls were really boys, anyway.) But the history of the play's genesis in Barrie's mind contains a sex-change unique to Barrie's mind. The germ of *Peter Pan,* according to its author, was a let's-pretend game which he, already in his forties, regularly played with a family of small boys. Some tableaux from the game were made into a photograph album. A dog—or, to be exact, two successive dogs—took part in the game and appeared in the photographs. Both these real-life dogs were male. When, however, Barrie transposed the real-life dog into the dog character in the play, he changed its sex. Nana is, of course (as a nanny), female. But the rôle of the dog in the play is, of course, taken by a human. And Barrie specified that the human who played the part of the dog should be a boy.

No one who has taken in the sex-alternations of Nana can feel much surprise when, towards the end of the play, Wendy at last comes explicitly out with the homosexual theme, which she does during her account of the sex differentiation of fairies: 'the mauve fairies are boys and the white ones are girls, and there are some colours who don't know what they are'.

Barrie was almost contemporary with Freud. Both were men of genius. Both were gifted observers of children—though Barrie perhaps limited his observation to boy children. It seems unlikely he knew much about girls' fantasies, since he keeps Wendy back from an active part in the battle against the pirates; and, while he was about the free invention of a world ideal for children, he really might have seen to it that his invention freed Wendy from sewing and washing. On the other hand, it may be only by undertaking the chores that Wendy was admitted to the ideal world at all. Barrie writes of one of the earlier stages of the story as being before 'we let women in'. At her very first encounter with Peter, Wendy does a spot of mending for him. That may have been her immigration permit.

Barrie's observations, one-sided though they may be, coincided with many of Freud's. Barrie knew that the two great preoccupying questions of childhood are 'Where do babies come from?' (hence Wendy's and Peter's speculative dissertations on where fairies come from) and 'How do you tell boy babies from girl babies?' During the game where John and Wendy play-act their parental fantasy, the important question 'Boy or girl?' is rapped out four times in a minute's dialogue. *Peter Pan* is by way of being Barrie's *Interpretation of Dreams*. (Freud, four years the elder, published his four years earlier.) *Peter Pan,* subtitled 'the boy who would not grow up', is full of insights into the unconscious, that core in everyone which *cannot* grow up. Indeed, the play itself *is* a dream, as the final stage direction implies: Peter Pan 'produces his pipes' and 'plays on and on till we' (the audience) 'wake up'. Barrie's play states almost as plainly as *The Interpretation of Dreams* itself the significance of dreams of flying. (As it were: Wendy and John express their wish for a child, then fall asleep and dream of flying.) For once Barrie makes concession enough to girls' wishes to let Wendy fly, too. But of course she's shot down.

Freud, however, was an honest non-fiction thinker. Barrie was a dishonest artist. Freud saw that children have the utmost right—who more?—to know where children come from, and that to laugh at them for their quaint ignorance of sex is a dishonourable act on the part of adults who have deliberately kept them ignorant. For taking this honourable view Freud was at first ignored and then abused as a besmircher of children's innocence. Barrie, on the other hand, became a bestseller and, presently, a baronet, largely on the strength of a play whose dialogue is one long tease of children's sexual curiosity (the last thing Barrie is prepared to do is *answer* their questions; he assures them it's much nicer for them to believe in mauve, white and indeterminately coloured fairies) and whose often very witty stage directions are one long snigger behind his adult hand at the children's quaint innocence. His most dastardly stage direction is probably the one where he actually hints that the way you get a baby is to buy it: Mr Darling, he tells us, earlier in his married life, 'did all the totting up for' Mrs Darling, 'while he calculated whether they could have Wendy or not'.

It's not enough, however, for Barrie to betray children. He betrays art. He does it brilliantly. That superb piece of engineering (the engineering, however, of an instrument of torture), the scene where Peter Pan appeals to the children in the audience to keep Tinker Bell alive by clapping to signal their belief in fairies, is a metaphor of artistic creation itself. All characters in all plays are kept alive by the audience's belief in them. But the belief properly exacted from audiences is belief of the kind Coleridge distinguished as 'poetic faith', a 'willing suspension of disbelief for the moment'. Peter Pan blackmails the children, cancels the willingness of the suspension of disbelief, and disrupts the convention on which all art depends when he threatens to hold the children morally responsible for Tinker Bell's death unless by a real act—an act done in the auditorium, not on the stage—they assert their literal belief in what they know to be an artistic fiction. It is his culminating, cleverest and most diabolical flirtation with children's innocence. By perpetrating it he destroyed his own innocence as an artist. (pp. 109-12)

Brigid Brophy, Michael Levey, and Charles Osborne, "'Peter Pan'," in their *Fifty Works of English and American Literature We Could Do Without, 1967. Reprint by Stein and Day Publishers, 1968, pp. 109-12.*

HARRY M. GEDULD

To the majority of readers *Peter Pan* is the essential Barrie. Everyone has encountered it in one form or another. Yet beyond the nursery it is frequently as unfamiliar as *Gulliver's Travels*. To reacquaint ourselves with Barrie's "legendary creation," it is first necessary to forget the pantomime and Walt Disney perversions of the original stories. We must then follow Peter through several of Barrie's works; for, although Peter was never to grow up, he nevertheless developed as a character from book to book and through more than one genre.

Peter Pan's story passed through three distinct stages: (1) a children's story in six chapters carved out of an "adult" novel, (2) a children's play similar in only a few respects to the children's story, and (3) a children's story in seventeen chapters based closely upon the play and its separately published sequel. Barrie first brought Peter Pan to life in a long digression, occupying chapters XIII-XVIII of an "adult" novel entitled *The Little White Bird, or Adventures in Kensington Gardens*. The title of the book was evidently taken from the Grimm brothers' familiar folk tale "Hansel and Gretel," in which the lost children are guided first to the gingerbread house and then out of the forest by a little white bird. Two years later, using substantially different story material, Barrie completed a three-act play entitled *Peter Pan, Or The Boy Who Would Not Grow Up*. A final published version of this play, revised and extended to five acts, was not to appear for many years. But in the interim, he turned back in 1906, to *The Little White Bird* and excerpted the six "Peter Pan" chapters, which he published in a slightly adapted form as the children's story, *Peter Pan in Kensington Gardens,* illustrated by Arthur Rackham.

In 1911 another children's story, *Peter and Wendy,* appeared. This was a narrative based on the unpublished play, using practically all the dialogue, and adding a final chapter about what happened "When Wendy Grew Up." The book was later reissued as *Peter Pan and Wendy,* or simply as *Peter Pan.* Barrie's five-act play, *Peter Pan, Or The Boy Who Would Not Grow Up,* was not given its definitive form until 1928, nearly a quarter of a century after the original production. By this time the text had undergone numerous changes and had been provided with a long dedication in which the author gave a tongue-in-cheek account of the genesis of his play. *When Wendy Grew Up: An Afterthought,* published posthumously in 1957, completed the dramatic version of the Peter Pan story. Barrie wrote this sequel to his play in 1908. It was performed only once, in honor of the American producer, Charles Frohman, and was excluded from published editions of the play. Nevertheless, it patently belongs with the story, as Barrie indicated when he turned it into narrative form for the final chapter of *Peter and Wendy.*

In *Peter and Wendy* Barrie compares Mrs. Darling's romantic mind to a Chinese box, a comparison equally appropriate to the structure of *The Little White Bird,* in which several plots are enclosed, one within the other, among them the children's story which was to be separately published as *Peter Pan in Kensington Gardens.* (pp. 53-4)

[The] main narrative is not so much a love story as a conflict of shadow and substance, a rivalry between the Creator-Artist (the narrator) and the Creator-Mother (Mary), in which a writer's literary fantasies are unfavorably contrasted with reality, represented by a living child [David, Mary's first-born son, for whom the narrator becomes virtually a second father]. (p. 55)

Throughout the book, Barrie emphasizes David's possession by, dependence on, and "creation" by the narrator who furnishes his clothes, invents his fantasies, takes him to a pantomime in which he witnesses a clown making and unmaking fantasies, ''kidnaps'' him, and later borrows him from his mother so that he may undress and sleep with the child. The narrator in effect seeks to usurp the function of the mother as well as the father, and the episode that culminates in David's climbing into bed to sleep with his mother's benefactor is plainly a wishful adaptation of the prototypic situation in which Margaret Ogilvy slept with the christening robe that symbolized her favorite son.

Contained within the David story are two fantasy-tales: one, the Peter Pan narrative in its earliest published form; the other, the story of the dog Porthos who was eventually to become Nana of the *Peter Pan* play and *Peter and Wendy*. While the first appears as the substance of the narrator's entertainment of David, the Porthos tale is the narrator's own fantasy experience. It concerns the brief transformation of a dog who is almost human into William Paterson, a simple, honest, doglike man. Porthos as William Paterson is a tragic failure: he attempts to identify himself with the narrator and to adapt himself to the world's harsh realities, but he soon reverts to the old canine form in which he can remain oblivious to the shortcomings of man and continue to perform his duties as guardian of David. When Porthos reappears in *Peter Pan* and *Peter and Wendy*, he has undergone a change of sex and a change of name; but his function as guardian is retained. (pp. 56-7)

[In] the later developments of the Peter Pan story, Barrie definitely points to an identification of Porthos-Nana with the prototypic father. Mr. Darling uses the dog as a substitute for himself by feeding it his own medicine. Ultimately, he expresses his understanding of his relationship with the dog by climbing into its kennel to take its place. Mr. Darling's faults are evidently those Barrie ascribed to his own father: he is ''dog-like'' and an unsatisfactory guardian for allowing his offspring to fly away. As dog or as man, the character is an ineffectual one. The world flows on indifferently past William Paterson as it had done past Barrie's father. The dog-man loses all faith in human nature and then recoils from the world, accepting a life of mindless servility.... Nana is unable to save the Darling children from flying away with Peter Pan any more than the senior David Barrie was able to save his son from a fatal fall on the ice. The dog's attempts to alarm the household and drive away the intruder are suppressed by Mr. Darling when he leaves Nana chained in the yard. In departing with Mrs. Darling for a pleasant evening with the neighbors, he has unwittingly shackled his own guardian instincts, as did the senior David Barrie in allowing his son and namesake out of his care to stay with Barrie's elder brother, Alexander. (pp. 57-8)

As a synthesis of fairy, adventure, and pirate story, *Peter Pan* is a perennial children's favorite. In writing it, Barrie imposed a collage of childhood enthusiasms and a wide range of elements from popular children's literature upon the prototypic material. Children who enjoy the story are not, of course, consciously aware of its psychological substructure, but its enduring popularity among young people must be attributed in part to the story's correspondence to their own ineffable Oedipal fantasies. Like speaks to like, and *Peter Pan*, blending autobiographical, fantasy-psychological, and literary material makes its wide appeal on many levels. (p. 58)

In using as publishable material the stories he had told the Davies children, Barrie first concentrated on his hero as he had emerged in the Kensington Gardens setting. Chapters XIII-XVIII of *The Little White Bird* present a Peter Pan who is different in many respects from the hero of *Peter and Wendy* and the play on which it is based. (p. 59)

When Barrie came to write the later work, he rejected most of the material concerning the baby Peter as too infantile for older children. The eternal boyhood of the hero, his encounter with the heroine, and the building of the heroine's house are among the few elements that are unaltered from *The Little White Bird*.

Associations between Barrie's hero and the goatlike Pan of Greek mythology are definite in *The Little White Bird* but more obscure in the later books. The baby Peter, in *Peter Pan in Kensington Gardens*, rides a goat and plays an instrument that corresponds to the syrinx, Pan's musical pipe of seven reeds. When the narrator of *The Little White Bird* takes off David's socks, the child puts his toes to its mouth as if to play them like the reeds of a pipe. The mythological Pan lived in an Arcadian grove where he fell in love with certain nymphs who did not requite his affection, but Barrie places his baby Pan in an island on the Serpentine in Kensington Gardens and sometimes in a wooded area in the same park where the eternal child comes upon the little girl Maimie, who returns his affection but eventually leaves the garden to go back to Mommy. (pp. 59-60)

[Barrie] points clearly to the identification of David with Peter Pan. Maimie whom Peter-David marries according to fairy ritual is the ''Mommy'' of the prototypic story, but her name also suggests Jaimie (*i.e.,* James Barrie).... (p. 60)

Younger than her braggart brother Tony..., Maimie is subjected to his bullying...; but she admires him and tries to imitate his magnificent swagger. At night, however, Tony reveals another side to his character: the braggart is a coward in the dark. Maimie terrifies him with fantasies of a monster who is coming to bore into him with its horns. This ''monster'' is presumably Peter's goat.

Maimie decides one day to remain in Kensington Gardens after lockout time when the fairies hold their court and Peter Pan comes out to play. Tony also agrees to stay behind, but, when the hour arrives, he deserts Maimie. When the fairies find her alone sleeping in the snow, they hit upon the idea of building a house around her. When Maimie wakes up to find herself inside a fairy house built exactly to her size, she knocks her head against the roof in a manner that recalls an early episode of *Alice in Wonderland*. But, where Alice outgrows her house, Maimie's shrinks slowly away; she stands aside to watch it disappear and bursts into tears as it vanishes into nothingness. At this precise moment a naked little Peter Pan appears to comfort her. Barrie's description of his appearance before Maimie is a fantasy account of an immaculate childbirth: the house (womb) shrivels as the naked newborn infant arrives.

This episode recurs with some elaboration of sexual imagery in *Peter and Wendy*. There the house is built not by fairies but by lost boys who acquire a mother in Wendy (Maimie), when one of their number shoots her down (impregnates her) with an arrow. Peter Pan pulls the arrow from Wendy's breast and is relieved to discover that she is still alive. While the girl remains unconscious, the house is built round her and a chimney is provided by placing Mr. Darling's (*i.e.,* father's) top hat on the roof. Peter Pan, who shows more understanding of the significance of the house than most of Barrie's commentators, wants to order babies to come out of the house before

Wendy wakens, but the other lost boys prevent him from doing so:

> We've made the roses peeping out,
> The babes are at the door,
> We cannot make ourselves, you know,
> 'Cos we've been made before.

Peter knocks on the door; and, as Wendy emerges, the children appeal to her to become their mother. At night, the lost boys sleep underground, in a womb-tomb of earth, like the dead David Barrie. Wendy retires into her little house, and Peter Pan stands guard outside with a drawn sword.

The image of the womb as house or nest is recurrent in *The Little White Bird* and in *Peter Pan in Kensington Gardens*. Near the beginning of *The Little White Bird*, before David is born, the narrator sends Mary her doll's house. Mother Mary is directly associated with the fairy house-builders, for we are told that she too speaks in the affected "fairy way," pronouncing all her *r*'s as *w*'s. When Mary's baby is born, the narrator bemoans his loneliness, regretting that alone one cannot build a nest. Later, the narrator's "baby," Peter Pan, escapes from his island in the Serpentine to the little wood where he meets Maimie by sailing across the lake in a thrush's nest. While talking to Maimie, Peter, stroking the fur on her pelisse, tells her that he loves her because she is like a beautiful nest. Peter's own nest, in which he sleeps in a foetal position, evidently symbolizes the "womb" of artistic creation—the poet's "nest"; for the narrator informs us that it was made by the thrushes out of a five-pound note discarded by the poet Shelley. Patently, Barrie's emphasis is repeatedly on birth: the birth of babies, of a book, of a house. (pp. 60-2)

[After *The Little White Bird*], Barrie shifts his focus of interest away from problems of birth or rival creativity to revert, in *Peter Pan* and in *Peter and Wendy*, to the old theme of usurpation of identity. The new emphasis—indebted to the conclusion of *The Little White Bird* that artistic creation is the sterile equivalent of maternal creation—represents Barrie as a pirate bent on stealing a mother, a monstrous thief whose missing hand, replaced by an iron hook, was devoured by a crocodile. Peter Pan here confronts an adversary who, in his passion to destroy his rival, will reach into the Neverland, down even into the womb of earth where the dead David sleeps in the guise of Peter Pan. (p. 62)

The play, *Peter Pan*, written prior to *Peter and Wendy*, though not published until many years after, provided Barrie with the basis of the prose narrative that augments the Peter Pan story in *The Little White Bird*. All that will be said about *Peter and Wendy* later in this chapter applies to the play. The dramatic dialogue and, in one form or another, most of the stage directions were incorporated into the story, so that the play exists embedded within *Peter and Wendy* as well as in its separate published form. How the original three-act play became transformed through numerous reworkings and productions into the five-act play incorporated into the definitive edition of Barrie's dramatic works is a complex subject beyond the scope of this book. . . . Our concern is with the relationship of the play in its final, five-act form to *Peter and Wendy*.

With the exception of chapter IV, "The Flight," every episode in the story is fully represented in the play. All the characters are also retained, though it is notable that in actual productions the same actor usually doubles the roles of Mr. Darling and Captain Hook. And, for obvious technical reasons, productions of *Peter Pan* limit the flight to a brief spectacular performance by actors suspended from wires. The prose narrative is not subject to such technical restrictions, and so Barrie was able to recount dialogue and incidents occurring in mid-flight en route to the Neverland. The episodic and chronological parallels between play and story are remarkably close. Chapters I, II, and III of *Peter and Wendy* correspond to Act 1 of the play; Chapters V and VI relate to Act 2; Chapter VIII relates to Act 3; Chapter X (with its material slightly transposed) and Chapters XI through XIII are the narrative equivalent of Act 4; Chapters XIV and XV represent Act 5, Scene 1, and Chapter XVI represents Act 5, Scene 2. The final chapter is a narrative version of the dramatic sequel, *When Wendy Grew Up*, which Barrie excluded from the definitive text of the five-act play.

Barrie's skill at transforming fiction into drama was as considerable as his talent at adapting drama from fiction. (pp. 62-3)

The measure of his achievement becomes impressive when we compare *Peter Pan* with *Peter and Wendy* and discover that the story is scarcely richer in detail than the play. The whole of the Neverland is gradually revealed over the last four acts, each of which is located on a different part of the island or on Hook's ship, the *Jolly Roger*. The setting of Act 4 provides for a simultaneous view of the Home under the Ground and the wood above it in which redskins battle with the pirates. Act 5, Scene 2, is a little structural masterpiece, developing what becomes a crowded chapter of narrative through three brief inner scenes arranged with a fluency that anticipates screen-writing at its best. Excluding the sequel, Barrie requires only eight scene changes for the dramatic version of a story he later tells in sixteen chapters.

In three respects *Peter Pan* is more enlightening to a student of Barrie's work than *Peter and Wendy*. It is only in the dramatic version that we find the long dedication "To the Five" Davies children, with its whimsical account of the genesis of the Peter Pan legend. The dedication also alludes briefly to *Mary Rose*, and in the play of *Peter Pan* and nowhere else do we learn from Mr. Darling that his wife's first name is Mary A—— the name of Barrie's wife and the heroine's in *The Little White Bird*. Finally, in the first scene of Act 5, where there are a number of minor differences from the story, Captain Hook communes with his ego in a long soliloquy that was not to be worked into *Peter and Wendy*. At the heart of this soliloquy the significance of the prototypic situation to the adult Barrie comes plainly to the fore. Hook complains that no little children love him: "they play at Peter Pan. . .the strongest always chooses to be Peter. . .they force the baby to be Hook."

Countless revivals of *Peter Pan* have ensured that Barrie's most enduring theatrical success is also the world's most popular children's play. . . . The play's perennial success confounded even [George Bernard] Shaw who tried without success to drive it from the boards with *Androcles and the Lion*. Shaw told his biographer, Hesketh Pearson,

> When *Peter Pan* was in its first great vogue Max Beerbohm caricatured Barrie reading it to a circle of elderly people and children. The elderlies were beaming with enjoyment: the children were all asleep. I agreed, and wrote *Androcles* to show what a play for children should be like. It should never be childish; nothing offends children more than to play down to them. . . . Like all other [great children's] plays and tales it should go over the heads of the audience occasionally because this makes them feel that they are superior people with highbrow tastes.

Unfortunately for Shaw, most children are not Shavians. They prefer *Peter Pan* to Shaw's *Androcles,* and will presumably go on doing so as long as there are Christmases and theaters for pantomimes.

Compared to *The Little White Bird, Peter and Wendy* has a basically simple structure. There are no Chinese boxes here, no fairy-tale digressions within an adult novel. The chapters located within the Darling household and framing the Neverland episodes—the narrative equivalent of *Peter Pan in Kensington Gardens*—are integral to the story they enclose. Instead of a series of loosely linked episodes, we now have a coherent children's novel whose three structural divisions—Peter's arrival at the Darling household, the adventures in Neverland, and the return of the Darling children—embody the prototypic story stripped of the artist-mother theme previously imposed upon it.

Few elements of *Peter Pan in Kensington Gardens* are salvaged for *Peter and Wendy.* In the later book, Peter is more evidently based on the prototypic David than on the Kingsley "water-baby" called Peter Pan in *The Little White Bird.* The new Peter is courageous and clever, but also conceited; and his "cockiness". . .infuriates Captain Hook more than the injury Peter inflicts on him. Scarcely a hint remains of earlier assocations with the mythological Pan. Peter still has his pipes, but there is no mention of the goat. The earlier Peter had flown away from his mother when he was seven days old, and he was still a naked newborn babe when Maimie encountered him in Kensington Gardens. The new Peter had fled from home when he was a day old, but he appears fully clothed and about Wendy's age when he arrives at the Darling household.

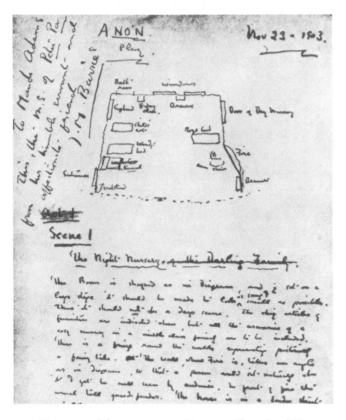

First page of the manuscript of Anon: A Play, *dated November 23, 1903, which was shortly to become* Peter Pan.

The locale of Peter's greatest adventures is now an elaborate fantasy-island, a child's dream world reached by taking the second turning to the right and keeping straight on until morning. (The direction seems to anticipate the route to the fantastic world of James Branch Cabell.) Rejected with the original locale are the fairies who have been replaced by the "predatory" island population of crocodile, beasts, redskins, and pirates. Wendy is substituted for the lost girl Maimie Mannering; and, like Maimie, she supplies Peter with thimble-kisses and is provided in turn (though under somewhat different circumstances from Maimie) with a wonderful makeshift house-in-the-woods. . . . *Peter and Wendy* is a children's story; but, unlike its predecessor, it is directed at an audience that is beginning to outgrow the nursery—and at the incipient maternal instincts of little girls and at the adventurous and belligerent spirits of little boys.

A detailed plot summary of Barrie's most famous story should be unnecessary, but readers who left the nursery behind more years ago than they care to remember may need to be reminded that the plot of *Peter and Wendy* turns mainly on the rivalry of Peter and Captain Hook for the possession of the substitute mother, Wendy. The scene of this conflict is the Neverland where lost boys sleep in a subterranean home. Manifestly, the island represents more than unactualized possibilities. . .: it is also Barrie's Hades, a land of the dead. The lost boys who "live" there have left the maternal womb for that of the earth.

Attracted by stories told to the Darling children by their mother, Peter, on one of his flights from Neverland, hovers about the window of the nursery. In effect, fiction keeps him from returning immediately to his tomb-home—just as Barrie kept David alive in his books. Peter had first left the Neverland in order to return to his own mother whom he had deserted years before. But his return home was long overdue; another baby had taken his place, and the window was barred against him. (The cold glass of the window recalls the ice on which David Barrie fell to his death.) While visiting the Darling household, Peter conceives the idea of taking both the stories and Wendy back with him to Neverland where they can be anything he desires them to be.

While Peter is eavesdropping at the Darling household, he suddenly has his shadow cut off when Nana the dog slams down the window. Nana, whom we have already identified with Porthos and William Paterson as a father-figure, is appropriately the boy's "killer": the one who severs shadow from substance. The dog, being a brute, does actively what the prototypic father was supposed to have done passively through neglect. . . . The dull nature of David Barrie senior and his imputed guilt are subsequently depicted in Mr. Darling's humiliating retreat to the dog's kennel. In *The Little White Bird,* Kensington Gardens magic had transformed dog into man, but in *Peter and Wendy* the "guilt" of the father who remains permanently outside the Neverland turns man into brute.

The severed shadow of Peter, recalling the memory of Peter-David, is retained by mother Darling. Before stuffing the shadow into a drawer. . ., Mrs. Darling hangs it out of the window. She soon withdraws it because she fears that its exposure to the public gaze would lower the tone of her household or, in other words, that it would create a public spectacle of the Darling home as Barrie and Margaret Ogilvy had done through their preoccupation with David's memory. Later, Wendy, a virgin mother like Grizel, sews Peter's shadow back on his feet, thereby effecting a fusion of memory and reality, of shadow and substance, that makes Peter complete and enables him to return to the Neverland. Wendy's act of attaching the shadow to Peter expresses Barrie's own desire for his mother to give up the memory of the dead son and become free for the attentions of the younger brother.

Apart from Hook, Peter's relations are mainly with female characters. In one way or another, all the male figures other than Peter and Hook are minimized. Michael and John, inconsequential characters named for the two older Davies children, are relegated to subordinate positions in Neverland; Mr. Darling is reduced to the level of a dumb animal; and in the sequel, *When Wendy Grew Up,* the heroine's husband is never characterized.

The female figures who surround Peter are based on the inevitable prototypes: the girl-mother (Wendy), the inveterate spinster (the fairy-light Tinker Bell), and the desirable "blood sister" (Tiger Lily). Barrie specifies that Tinker and Tiger are both Bell(e)s, Tinker by name and Tiger as "the belle of the Piccaninnies." The former is the bell(e) of light, the latter the belle of darkness. Like Barrie's sister Maggie, Tiger Lily is pursued by young "braves" who desire to marry her; but she is "coquettish, cold and amorous by turns" and staves off her admirers with a hatchet. Like Barrie's sister Jane, Tinker Bell is the "useful" spinster (a fairy who mends pots and pans) who dies young and is buried beside Peter in her subterranean boudoir situated beside Peter's bed.

At the climax of the book Peter kicks his rival into the crocodile's maw and then proceeds to assume Hook's identity by donning the pirate's clothes and by imitating his stance and his hook. Peter fights Hook in order to "become" Hook; he adopts the personality of his dead rival as Barrie had assumed the identity of David in the prototypic story. The "substitutions" that pervade the book signify that the two male figures of the prototypic situation are now interchangeable.

Peter, the boy who "becomes" Hook, is also the lad who will never grow up and the rival who returns repeatedly from the Neverland to claim the girl-mother as his own. . . . Numerous related images reinforce the themes of identity assimilation and "eternal return" or rebirth. In the assimilation of identity, dog becomes nurse; man, dog; girl, mother; hand, hook; "tomb," home and womb; thimbles, acorns; buttons, kisses; hollow trees, tunnels or "suits of clothes"; and a top hat and a mushroom, chimneys. In exemplifying the theme of rebirth, the lost boys lose their mothers and find mother-substitutes (Wendy, and later Mrs. Darling); and, as we have previously noticed, they are symbolically reborn at the conclusion of the housebuilding episode: Peter loses Wendy and finds a new "Wendy" (the heroine's daughter Jane, who subsequently provides him with yet another new "Wendy" in the person of her daughter Margaret); Mr. Darling, who was previously William Paterson who was Porthos, "becomes" Nana, thus transforming repeatedly from dog to man, and back again. Finally, the inhabitants of Neverland are described as living in endless pursuit of one another: the lost boys who are pursued by pirates (the stealers of mothers); redskins (the conscience) scalp or unmask the pirates; beasts (uncontrolled passions) seek to devour the redskins; and a crocodile consumes James (Hook's first name). Birth, uninhibited passions, conscience, and illicit desire for the mother pursue the lost boys. The pattern of pursuit on the island manifestly conforms to the psychological development of a child.

In *Peter and Wendy* Barrie had endeavored to entice his mother from the memory of David. *Tommy and Grizel* had suggested

the consequences of such an attempt. Tommy Sandys suffocated in the coat that symbolized the identity he had tried to assume. But Peter-David assumes the identity of another and survives. Since the identity he assumes is that of the pirate-thief Hook (Barrie), it appears that Barrie had come to regard his attempted assimilation of David's identity as a gradual destruction of his own. Once Barrie had thought to contain David; but now David threatened to overwhelm or to absorb Barrie. (pp. 64-9)

> *Harry M. Geduld, in his* Sir James Barrie, *Twayne Publishers, Inc., 1971, 187 p.*

PENELOPE SCAMBLY SCHOTT

Peter Pan has flown a long and changeable journey through the Neverlands of the critics. First admired, and then downgraded, Peter is now being psychoanalyzed. This latest approach was hinted at as early as 1923 by Louis Wilkinson, buttressed in a flip manner in 1968 where Peter was included in *Fifty Works of English Literature We Could Do Without* [see excerpt above], and presented in full dress in the 1971 critical study by Harry Geduld [see excerpt above]. Wilkinson notes Barrie's general parlour retreat from love and sex, Brophy, Levey, and Osborne assert the theme of *Peter Pan* to be "incest, castration and homosexuality," and Geduld elaborates every detail as dark and portentous psychological symbol within the context of the rest of Barrie's literary production.

Geduld sees Barrie as a writer of recurrent sentimental fantasies, reflecting autobiographical and psychological experiences, and resulting in repeated distortions of a prototypic family situation. While that situation—Barrie's attempt to replace his dead older brother, and his peculiar relationship to his mother—does indeed exist and seems to intrude on the writing, Geduld misuses it. Relapsing into an ultraorthodox Freudianism which is an equivalent distortion, he is so preoccupied with symbols and dream transformations that he overlooks the available surface.

Therefore, it seems useful to reexamine *Peter Pan* from the point of view of common sense rather than depth psychology. There are elements of biography and sex-role expectation which seem important accompaniments to any probings of the author's unconscious.

Peter Pan, as both play and novel—and here I shall deal with the novel—has attained the status of a classic everyone misremembers. We recall, from our separate childhoods, the flying, the adventures with Indians and pirates. We even remember, I suppose, that finally the children went home. But who remembers what happens after they get home? We remember the adventures, but not the attitudes—if, indeed, we ever noticed them; the middle, but not the frame. Yet, what happens in the Darlings' house anticipates and reflects, I would almost say "determines," what happens in the Neverland. Those fabulous doings of boys, Indians, mermaids, fairies, and pirates are in some sense less important than the London frame of the story set in the Darlings' house.

Not only does the real story take place in London, but there is another misunderstanding prevalent: *Peter Pan* is in no way a "boy's book." Although the fantasy began as a series of tales invented for and dramatized by a family of five little boys—the Davies—and although before they "let women in" the story was called *The Boy Castaways,* Wendy's arrival was totally necessary. Unlike many stories meant for boys, *Peter Pan* offers few of the expected lessons in courage, ingenuity, perseverance, or other stereotypes of "manliness." After all the excitement subsides, the story has little to say to boys. Young or old, they do not really count. If the story is to be labeled for didactic content, it is a chronicle of assumptions about sexual roles, and, ultimately, a training manual for mothers.

Barrie's views regarding the natures and roles of men and women have a very clear double origin: lingering Victorianism and his own peculiar experiences. The best and most revealing introduction to his personal attitudes is his memorial or love testament to his mother, *Margaret Ogilvy*. . . . This odd little work maintains one point of view while giving the modern reader enough data to see quite an opposite view. Even as Barrie idolizes his mother, she shows through the details he lovingly presents as an overly possessive, selfish, and destructive woman. He reports, for example,

> Biography and exploration were her favorite reading, for choice the biography of men who had been good to their mothers. . . .

At the age of six, when his older brother died and his mother became an invalid, Barrie began his long career of being good to his mother. "I sat a great deal in her bed trying to make her forget him, which was my crafty way of playing physician." Particularly, he tried to cheer her and "kept a record of her laughs on a piece of paper." One sees the desire to amuse his mother as shaping the sometimes cloying whimsey of the later writing.

Mother and son continued to spend long hours together, during which she talked of her childhood. They had read that a novelist "is better equipped than most of his trade if he knows himself and one woman," and his mother insisted that she was the only woman Barrie knew. "'Then I must make you my heroine,' I said lightly." Though said lightly, it cost dear; the women in Barrie's writing are all either versions of Margaret Ogilvy or, as becomes apparent, other idealized mothers. Even the prototype for Wendy is clearly spelled out in Barrie's account of his mother's childhood:

> She was eight when her mother's death made her mistress of the house and mother to her little brother, and from that time she scrubbed and mended and baked, and sewed. . .and gossiped like a matron with the other women, and humored the men with a tolerant smile. . . .

The girl-as-mother and the patronizing attitude toward men both show up in *Peter Pan*. One is never told Wendy's precise age, but certainly eight is safely prepubescent.

Then there is that other aspect: From Barrie's account of his childhood in *Margaret Ogilvy*, one would never surmise that he had a father who lived to healthy old age. Mr. Barrie, senior, is in fact mentioned only once in a rather perfunctory way. Much more revealing are Margaret's comments about men in general. "Gentle or simple, stupid or clever, the men are all alike in the hands of a woman that flatters them." The degree to which she wrote off men was sufficiently extreme that Barrie could indicate it in a parenthesis:

> Indeed she could never be brought to look upon politics as of serious concern for grown folk (a class in which she scarcely included men). . . .
>
> (pp. 1-3)

After his mother's death and her commemoration in *Margaret Ogilvy*, Barrie's greatest emotional attachment was to Sylvia Davies whom he met the following year. Much of her attraction seems to have been in her prodigious motherhood, and it was for her boys that Peter was originally invented. (p. 3)

When Barrie transforms his Davieses into his Darlings, certain things are highlighted. The changes are revealing. Mrs. Darling is idolized, Mr. Darling—poor George—is made into a pompous fool, the boys become part of a rather motley assortment, and—from no obvious prototype in the Davies family—there emerges a Wendy. Once Mrs. Darling has been identified, the question becomes that of how she operates in *Peter Pan* and what, really, is going on in the whole fantasy story.

The novel opens with a report of Mrs. Darling and Wendy discovering the inevitability of growing up, after which Barrie asserts, "until Wendy came her mother was the chief one." Here the chronology seems to go backwards, for as Mrs. Darling is Sylvia Davies, Wendy contains aspects of Margaret Ogilvy. To some extent, however, the two will turn out to be one.

> Just as Mrs. Darling has a romantic mind, like the tiny boxes, one within the other, that come from the puzzling East, however many you discover, there is always one more,

so, too, the generations of mothers are self-contained and perpetual. Reinforcing this notion, Barrie added the last section **"When Wendy Grew Up,"** which reports the endless chain and succession of mothers.

These are the important women—along with Nana, who is something of a double transvestite, originating with the male dog Porthos and usually played by a man. Their function is always mothering. Wendy verges briefly on sexuality as, using Peter's ignorantly reversed terminology, she would prefer "thimbles" to "kisses," but things remain sufficiently unclear to insure that she is never satisfactorily thimbled. As she and Peter play house in the Neverlands and she asks his true feelings toward her, Peter answers, "those of a devoted son." Wendy's dissatisfaction with this answer unsettles Peter.

> "You are so queer," he said, frankly puzzled, "and Tiger Lily is just the same. There is something she wants to be to me, but she says it is not my mother."

Nor do Tinkerbell or the mermaids want to mother, and all of these young ladies show brief flashes of nonmaternal jealousy. But the intrusion of sexuality is suppressed, and Wendy must settle for feeding, darning, and spring-cleaning—as must all the generations of Wendys. (pp. 4-5)

[In] the world of *Peter Pan*, London or Neverlands, men never understand. They are petty, vain, and self-deceiving. They do not, one might say, grow up. Both Mr. Darling and Captain Hook are preoccupied with the appearance of good form. It is for more than convenience or economy or oedipal conflicts that they are generally played by the same actor. Yes, Mr. Geduld, Peter gets to kill the father figure and wins the kiss from Mr. Darling's wife, but ultimately neither Captain Hook nor Mr. Darling is of any consequence. Both are incurably ridiculous; even the ticking crocodile has more dignity. The only likeable male character is the pathetic pirate Smee at his sewing machine, "ever industrious and obliging," whom Wendy would take as her "pet pirate." But he, too, has sexual designs on Wendy: "See here, honey," he whispered, "I'll save you if you promise to be my mother." So we discover that even the most appealing of the men is mother-hunting.

Men seem to want mothers because they need reassurance. In the all-important London frame, Mr. Darling goes to great pains to be impressive and respected, quickly forgetting little episodes like his temper tantrum over a recalcitrant necktie, tamed only by Mrs. Darling. He worries that his colleagues will not respect him because he has a dog for a nurse, but that is not the worst of it.

> Nana also troubled him in another way. He had sometimes a feeling that she did not admire him. "I know she admires you tremendously, George," Mrs. Darling would assure him, and then she would sign to the children to be specially nice to father.

But poor George never feels sure of himself. When, finally, the children have returned home and asked Mrs. Darling's permission for the lost boys to stay, Mr. Darling "thought they should have asked his consent as well as hers, instead of treating him as a cypher in his own house." At this point the children interview each other as to whether each thinks him a cypher. "It turned out that not one of them thought him a cypher; and he was absurdly gratified." But Mr. Darling's problem is that he is indeed a cypher, very much like Mr. Barrie, senior, in *Margaret Ogilvy*. While women nurture, console, and cajole, men bluster ineffectually or disappear.

Peter himself, in the world of his story, is very much a "little man." His outrageous cockiness is intended to be charming, as are his selfishness, his short memory, and his whole appearance. He charms Mrs. Darling because he still has his baby teeth and "his first laugh." Apparently that pervasive male childishness is most winning in a child, but never, one hastens to add, never in a real child.

Always observant, Cynthia Asquith understood this aspect of Peter—and Barrie—very well, as she writes to her husband:

> Peter Pan isn't a boy, is he? He is a wish-fulfillment projection in fable form of the kind of mother—Barrie's an expert at her—who doesn't want her son to grow up.

If the men are cyphers and Peter is a mere wishful projection, the book is then left to the women. They dominate it at beginning and end. Here one discovers Barrie's most loving portraits of Sylvia Davies and Margaret Ogilvy. One sees why he prefers Mrs. Darling to Wendy, Sylvia to Margaret, but taken all in all there is little to choose between them, and the roles they play are scarcely to be recommended.

Just as Mrs. Darling covers for her childish husband, so too Wendy insists that the lost boys show respect to Peter. "Father knows best," she always said, whatever her private opinion must be. And all that domestic busywork is portrayed as a kind of badge of honor. At first encounter, Wendy is rather patronizing about resewing Peter's shadow.

But she was exulting in his ignorance. "I shall sew it on for you, my little man," she said, though he was as tall as herself. Wendy enjoys her self-assumed martyrdom of stockings and stove. Darning her way through a basketful,

> . . .she would fling up her arms and exclaim, "Oh dear, I am sure I sometimes think spinsters are to be envied."

Her face beamed when she exclaimed this. The approving narrator assures us,

> Really there were whole weeks when, except perhaps with a stocking in the evening, she was never above ground. The cooking, I can tell you, kept her nose to the pot.

All this while the boys are busy having adventures.

But, presumably, Wendy enjoys all her domesticity. It was, in fact, the original bribe Peter cunningly offered to get her to

the Neverland. Children and housework: "How could she resist. 'Of course it's awfully fascinating.'" When she first reaches the Neverland, the lure is repeated as the lost boys implore, "O Wendy lady, be our mother."

> "Ought I?" Wendy said, all shining. "Of course it's frightfully fascinating, but you see I am only a little girl. I have no real experience."

It appears, however, that Mrs. Darling and Nana have been commendable models, as Wendy fills her role very well—even to protecting her children from the pirates's fiendish cake.

But there is another side to what Barrie portrays as Wendy's innate femininity. Just as she cannot resist the appeal to her maternal talents, she is susceptible to other forms of flattery. Oh, daughters of Eve as chronicled by the sons of Adam. When Peter is trying to lure her from under her covers back in the night nursery, he assures her,

> in a voice that no woman has ever yet been able to resist, "Wendy, one girl is more use than twenty boys."

So Wendy gets up and subsequently proves and proves again her usefulness. But even the nefarious Hook, despite his own doubts about good form, can charm the unworldly Wendy. Leadng her away captive,

> He did it with such an air, he was so frightfully *distingué*, that she was too fascinated to cry out. She was only a little girl.

Yes, Wendy was only a little girl (though old enough to want thimbles), but she was not entirely unlike her mother. As mothers and daughters become that stack of Chinese boxes, they become extremely similar to each other. And the beloved Mrs. Darling doesn't seem very much more grownup than Wendy. Living in a world of party dresses and sentiment, she copes with little more challenging than uncooperative neckties.

Perhaps it is the lost boys who have the real truth about mothers, even as Barrie may have known the truth about Margaret Ogilvy. Nibs reports that all he remembers about his mother, "is that she often said to father, 'Oh, how I wish I had a cheque-book of my own.'" Even more significant, Tootles uses his long-lost mother's supposed objections to get out of being cabin boy to the pirates.

> He knew that mothers alone are always willing to be the buffer. All children know this about mothers, and despite them for it, but make constant use of it.

When, at last, the Darling children decide to go home, the lost boys are bewildered.

> They knew in what they called their hearts that one can get on quite well without a mother, and that it is only the mothers who think you can't.

If one assumes, for the moment, that children know the truth about mothers, the final verdict is devastating. Mothers are greedy, easily duped, and ultimately expendable.

The effect here is very much like that in *Margaret Ogilvy*. Even as Barrie idolizes, he undercuts the beloved idol—always proclaiming his devotion. As the bereaved parents sit alone in the night nursery, Mr. Darling in ostentatious penitence in the kennel and Mrs. Darling with a pain about her heart, the narrator looks at her and confesses, "Some like Peter best and some like Wendy best, but I like her best." Here is no great revelation.

But, in the end, Barrie's preference does no good. Peter takes Mrs. Darling's kiss and flies away with it, all the children grow up, and finally, in that added last episode, "Mrs. Darling was now dead and forgotten." Now Wendy is the mother and the daughter is Jane, and when Peter comes back, still with his first teeth, to take his "mother" for spring cleaning in the Neverland, it is Jane who goes with him. And then Jane grows up, and it is her daughter Margaret who goes.

It is not surprising that the last of the series given a name should be Margaret, after Barrie's mother. She is the enduring image of the girl-mother, a guise in which the author would like to see himself.

As he writes at the end of *Margaret Ogilvy,* should his mind wander in old age,

> . . .it will not, I believe, be my youth I shall see but hers. . .a little girl in a magenta frock and a white pinafore, who comes toward me through the long parks, singing to herself, and carrying her father's dinner in a flaggon.

And the child-mother, perhaps Barrie's deepest self, will go on forever.

> When Margaret grows up she will have a daughter, who is to be Peter's mother in turn; and thus it will go on so long as children are gay and innocent and heartless.

But real children are not gay, innocent, or heartless. Nor, fortunately, are they psychologically sophisticated when it comes to what they read, but, indifferent to the gusts of literary criticism, they fly happily on to any sort of magic island. Adult readers have forgotten *Peter Pan*—or reread it psychoanalytically—while boys and girls alike enjoy it. Boys continue to enjoy the irresponsible warfare, and generations of girls have envied Wendy her little house,

> With roses peeping in, you know,
> And babies peeping out.

Until our daughters prefer pirates to pots, daring to darning, I suppose they will continue to do so.

But one small girl I know thinks it very unfair that Wendy can't fly as well as her brothers. I, for one, will forgive Margaret Ogilvy only when my own Wendy is allowed to fly. Let us hope, for all our children, that they do not need to wait for Neverneverland. And, while we wait, let us remember what is really going on in *Peter Pan.* (pp. 5-9)

> Penelope Scambly Schott, "The Many Mothers of Peter Pan: An Explanation and Lamentation," in Research Studies, *Vol. 42, No. 1, March, 1974, pp. 1-10.*

ALISON LURIE

The current idea of *Peter Pan* as a shallow, cloyingly cute fantasy is probably based on memories of the Disney film, or some similarly oversimplified and sugared version of the story in print. The original play is more interesting and complicated, just as its author, James Barrie, was a more original and complex man than he is now generally reputed to be.

Current opinion is not absolutely wrong: Barrie *was* a whimsical romantic with an emotional, occasionally a maudlin, devotion to mothers and children. But he was also a shrewd, cynical, and highly successful journalist and dramatist who had made his way from a weaver's cottage in a remote Scottish village to a town house in South Kensington. As the seventh

of eight surviving children, and the adopted uncle of five more, he knew very well that juvenile charm and innocence are often accompanied by profound egotism and an unconscious capacity for cruelty. Moreover Barrie knew, for the most bitter and private reasons, what a boy who didn't grow up would really be like. He was that boy. (p. 11)

The play *Peter Pan* is on its simplest level a combination of the stories [Barrie] told the Davies children in Kensington Gardens and the games he invented for them in Surrey. . . . But the play is much more than this. To start with, it is a classic English Christmas pantomime. . . .

Like *Mother Goose, Dick Whittington,* or *Aladdin,* **Peter Pan** presents a medley of incongruous fantasy settings—the mermaids' lagoon, the forest full of wolves and Indians, the pirate ship. There are music, songs, dancing, and a transformation scene; a chorus of children (the Lost Boys) appears. The original production of *Peter Pan* even ended with the then traditional harlequinade. . . .

The conventional pantomime characters are all included. Peter Pan of course is the Principal Boy (like Peter, always played by a young woman in tights)—youthful, imaginative, courageous, somewhat boastful. Wendy is the Principal Girl, full of gentle innocent feminine charm. Captain Hook plays the Demon King and Tinker Bell the Good Fairy; Nana, the dog-nurse, is the Dame (like her, traditionally a male comic part). *Peter Pan* even observes the pantomime tradition, inherited from the old mystery and morality plays, that the villains enter from stage left and the good characters from stage right. . . .

In **Peter Pan** every wish comes true, from early fantasies of flying to the resurrection of the dead: the Lost Boys, missing children who live underground in the Never Land in a sort of cozy tomb, finally return to London where they are adopted by the Darlings. The whole play is an elaborate dream-fulfillment of intense but contradictory childhood wishes: to be grown-up at once and never to be grown-up; to have exciting adventures and be perfectly safe; to escape from your mother and have her always at hand.

No wonder that **Peter Pan** was received with overwhelming enthusiasm, and that it has become the most famous children's play ever written, as well as the greatest success in recent British stage history. . . .

But there is a private, darker side to the play. The crocodile who follows Captain Hook, relentlessly ticking . . . , stands for the threat of death and time that hangs over all the characters except Peter. And there is a hidden identification of James Barrie not only with the Darling children's innocent playfellow Peter Pan but with their kidnapper, Captain James Hook, who shares the author's name and his fondness for cigars. The plot of acts 3 through 5 turns on the rivalry between Peter and Hook for possession of Wendy. Not possession in the physical sense, of course: in spite of our associations (or the Edwardians') to his name, Peter Pan is completely asexual. "You mustn't touch me," he cries in the final published version of the script. "No one must ever touch me." Hook, too, only wants Wendy so that the pirates may have a mother.

In fact Peter Pan and Captain Hook are not so much opposites as two sides of the same coin. After Peter has defeated Hook in their final duel there is a tableau; Barrie writes in the stage directions:

> The curtain rises to show Peter a very Napoleon on his ship. It must not rise again lest we see him on

the poop in Hook's hat and cigars, and with a small iron claw.

According to Peter Davies, whenever Barrie "was strongly attracted by people, he wanted at once to own them . . . whichever their sex." Assuming that what Barrie wanted in 1904 was to own Sylvia Davies and her sons, it is possible to see Peter Pan as the innocent embodiment of this desire, and Captain Hook as the guilty one. In the play, of course, neither of them succeeds, and we are not sorry. (p. 12)

*Alison Lurie, "The Boy Who Couldn't Grow Up,"
in* The New York Review of Books, *Vol. XXII, No.
1, February 6, 1975, pp. 11-12, 14-15.*

MARGERY FISHER

The strange, brief fantasy, *The Little White Bird* (which afterwards became *Peter Pan in Kensington Gardens*) has echoes of myth in it, for the god Pan is present in more than Peter's name and Maimie's present to him of an imaginary goat; it has echoes of *Cinderella* and *The Snow Queen* in the sub-plot of the Duke of Christmas-Daisies and his inconvenient heart; it presents in an almost throw-away manner the central point of Peter's inadequate personality. To this fantasy many congenial additions were made when Barrie wrote the play of *Peter Pan*. . . . The struggle in Peter between his moments of affection and his inhuman self-sufficiency, the reason for his eternal youth—these ideas are made less painful by a dramatic presentation. The crowded cast of characters allows Barrie's audiences to recall the most enjoyable figures of childhood—pirates, Redskins, mermaids, fairies, 'mothers and fathers'.

Peter Pan has many forms as a written story but ideally it should be seen first and then read. It contains ideas that are

Program from the first production of Peter Pan *in 1904 at the Duke of York's Theatre in London.*

primitive, natural and essential and the humour and energy of the spoken word carries these ideas easily. Peter's remark 'To die will be an awfully big adventure' is easy to ridicule unless it is spoken and unless we see the boy marooned on a rock with the sea rising. Hook's 'Fetch me out that doodle-doo' and his last despairing 'Floreat Etona' as he is swallowed by the crocodile; Peter's malapropism, 'Dark and conister man, have at thee!'; the extraordinary mixture of emotion, terror and comedy needs to be heard, for, once heard, its complexity will remain in the mind of the reader. Similarly the characters, so simple and so subtle, live in action. Children will understand the full nastiness of Mr Darling's character if they have actually seen him pouring his medicine into the dog's dish, and a good actor can convey a great deal more of Peter's personality than psychological analysis can discover. (p. 275)

*Margery Fisher, "Who's Who in Children's Books:
Peter Pan," in her* Who's Who in Children's Books:
A Treasury of the Familiar Characters of Childhood,
Holt, Rinehart and Winston, 1975, pp. 273-75.

KATHLEEN BLAKE

Treasure Island is the fulfillment of the "sea-dreams" of its boy hero, Jim Hawkins. . . . But whereas *Treasure Island* is the dream, *Peter Pan* is about dreaming, and waking. (p. 165)

Treasure Island is a good book. So is *Peter Pan*—but of a different sort utterly, for Barrie is concerned with showing how the palpable absolute conjured by such as Stevenson is both forever and never, and in particular, never again. "On these magic shores children at play are forever beaching their coracles. We too, have been there; we can still hear the sound of the surf, though we shall land no more." (p. 168)

The surf and the coracles define Neverland. It isn't that what happens in Neverland never happened before, never would, and never could. Just about everything that happens there has happened before—in books.

In Neverland life falls into ideal shapes, "like in a book." Who is James Hook? He is the pirate captain, part history and part literary creation. . . . [Stevenson] uses Defoe's Blackbeard to define his own Flint: "Blackbeard was a child to Flint." Barrie extends the system of piratical relations. James Hook was Blackbeard's bo'sun, and if Long John Silver (alias Barbeque, the Sea-Cook) is the only man who did not fear Flint or even the ghost of Flint, Hook is the only man "of whom Barbeque was afraid" and whom "the Sea-Cook feared."

Captain Hook is also the Byronic hero in his boys' book manifestation. Like Byron's Corsair he is a "man of loneliness and mystery." . . . Hook's eyes express their balefulness in two glowing red spots. He suffers the "blighted bosom" of a Corsair, a self-torment as ineffable as Manfred's. Hardened by his thousand crimes, he yet harbors in his soul an unlooked-for reservoir of exquisite sensibility: "No little children love me!" But no such inklings of humanity soften his relations with the general rout. Like the Corsair among his band on the pirate isle, "With these he mingles not but to command." Hook is a "grand seigneur." (pp. 168-69)

The pirate chief always exacts a shuddering respect, for his is a "not wholly unheroic figure." Above all he has class. Often born an aristocrat, he possesses, even more importantly, the inner stuff of the gentleman. . . . Silver is always as spruce as possible in his fine broadcloth suit, in contrast to his slovenly cohorts, while Hook cringes to observe Wendy's eyes upon his soiled ruff. Silver despises his unruly, rum-sodden crew as unworthy of the sea, a pack of low tailors, while Captain Hook is "frightfully *distingué*," so superior to the rest that he "never felt more alone than when surrounded by his dogs. They were socially so inferior to him." To be genteel is to inspire fear, according to the code of Long John Silver. Hook too has the breeding to be most sinister when he is most polite. The line of literary inheritance connects Hook to the attractively wicked Silver; to Ballantyne's pirate, whose straightforward ferocity of expression "rendered him less repulsive than his low-browed associates"; to the Byronic hero, whose "name could sadden and his acts surprise, / But they that feared him dared not to despise." Captain James Hook draws his crew from Flint's *Walrus* (drawn by Stevenson from the pages of Defoe), and his life's blood from printer's ink.

While life on any desert island goes by formulas, Neverland *is* formulas, and on it form is a way of life. The island is the land of dreams (it is the landscape of a child's mind) and its presiding spirit, Peter, is good form, a kind of embodiment of the play spirit, playing at islands.

There are moments when Jim Hawkins strides the thin line between living his adventures and playing them. . . . (pp. 169-70)

But if there is a hint of the game player in Jim, it is outright in Peter. Make-believe and real are the same thing to him. He does nothing to simply get something done. He never just lives; he has adventures. And he organizes his life in order to have them. Even *not* having adventures, doing the sorts of things John and Michael have done all their lives, is something he plays at, "a new game that fascinated him enormously." After saving Tiger Lily, Peter engages the forbidding Hook when he doesn't have to because he "could never resist a game." The sport of the combat is the point, and the lines of opposition are arbitrary. For example, having once led his boys nearly to victory in battle with the redskins, he suddenly switches the sides; the encounter continues with boys as redskins, redskins as boys. (p. 171)

The formula adventures that make up *Peter Pan* are presented in a style insistently "like in a book." It is as if the narrator (I call him Barrie for convenience) were saying: I tell it this way because this is what is needed for the sort of story I am telling. In Stevenson's words: "The right kind of thing should fall out in the right kind of place; the right kind of thing should follow." But it is a kind of cheating to reveal this principle of order within the story itself. Barrie's content is the content of romance, but his style subverts romantic illusion. He wants to establish the character of the terrible pirate captain; he proceeds as follows: "Let us now kill a pirate, to show Hook's method. Skylights will do." He wants us to know that the pirate chief is not beyond all admiration; he stills the ticking of the crocodile as it waits below to receive Hook: "We purposely stopped the clock that this knowledge might be spared him: a little mark of respect from us at the end." Things happen because the story requires them: "Will they [the children] reach the nursery in time? If so, how delightful for them, and we shall all breathe a sigh of relief, but there will be no story. On the other hand, if they are not on time. . . ."

Barrie assumes certain conventional narrative stances that appear particularly artificial because they are contradictory. He elaborately insists that he is bound, if reluctantly, to stick only to the truth. He wishes he could report that Peter talked to the Never bird, "but truth is best, and I want to tell only what really happened." At the same time, Barrie is constantly intervening. He controls what happens much more than it controls him. For instance, he says that he might interfere with the denouement by breaking the news of the children's return to Mrs. Darling in advance so that she could give them the cold shoulder they deserve.

He has the power to lead his readers astray, as for example when he slips and writes the wrong ending. Two things are suggested here. One is that the narrator doesn't know everything and that something new has happened to change the plot since he heard the children's plans upon leaving Neverland; this implies the primacy of the story over its teller. Yet a second effect is just the reverse, for we have just read an ending as straightforwardly reported as any in the rest of the book, which then turns out to be a pure fiction, something that never "happened" at all. We are reminded of the narrative presence and power—not to mention caprice.

He asks us to time the events of the great battle between boys and pirates by our watches. Again the suggestion is double. Barrie invites us to the illusion—you are there, your time is the characters' time. Yet he strains the illusion by addressing us as readers. How can readers time the events themselves? We can only time the telling (or the reading) of those events.

Barrie hovers in the background in the form of addresses to the reader, rhetorical questions, asides on mothers. He speaks to his characters and they talk back.

The narrative presence suggested by a line like "We now return to the nursery" is conventional and unobtrusive in itself, but Barrie makes a point of obtruding conventions: "In the meantime, what of the boys? We have seen them at the first clang of weapons, turned as it were into stone figures, open-mouthed, all appealing with outstretched hands to Peter; and we return to them as their mouths close, and their arms fall to their sides." The forward action of the characters and the plot comes to a dead stop when the narrator is not there to supervise it.

Such action is not the most important thing. Some passages have nothing to do with forwarding it. Barrie writes a conversation between himself and Mrs. Darling. He says he could spare her ten days of pain by announcing the children's return in advance. She replies that the cost would be too great in the children's loss of ten minutes of the happiness of surprising her. This interchange is curious because it takes place on some secondary (or is it primary?) plane, outside of "the story" and without effect on it. Mrs. Darling *is* surprised on the night of the children's return. Her foreknowledge is entirely hypothetical. In fact, the hypothetical is the presiding narrative attitude, which the reader is obliged to share: "Let us pretend to lie here among the sugar-cane and watch them [the boys] as they steal by in single file."

Peter Pan never allows us to enter for long into the sea-dream because the story repeatedly reminds us that it is pure dream, or game—arbitrary, conventional, made-up, literary. "Let us pretend." Art so overtakes nature in these woods that the coyotes come out second best at coyote calls. The Indians traverse every inch of ground between the lines of the boys and the pirates wearing their moccasins backwards because that is what they are supposed to do.

These "confiding savages" confide in the rules. Hook breaks them by failing to wait for the traditional dawn attack. The daring originality of this breach stands testimony to his "subtle mind," his "gigantic brain." But in a realm where the game properly played is what counts, he suffers the bad conscience of the ulterior-minded cheat. Hook knows that the highest value is good form, but he violates it here as elsewhere—in an unfair fight with Peter on the rock, and in fretting about good form itself: "was it not bad form to think about good form?" The true game player plays it straight, like the Indians, like Peter, like Stevenson. He may know that it is a game and enjoy its formal dimension, but he stays inside the frame so that its artificial limits do not impinge. In Barrie's work they impinge. He constantly reminds us of the frame. One might say that the narrator of *Peter Pan* is a dramatization of bad form. To rough out an equation: Hook is to Peter as Barrie is to Stevenson as adult is to child.

Peter remains a perpetual child because he does not remember things. In particular, he does not remember when he has been treated unfairly. He is fighting fair on the rock in the lagoon, and Hook bites him. This would undermine the faith of any other confiding boy by revealing the instability of the whole idea of fair fight, precisely because it is just an idea. "No one gets over the first unfairness; no one except Peter. . . . I suppose that was the real difference between him and all the rest." When Mr. Darling slips the medicine behind his back instead of taking it on the count of three as Michael does, Michael presumably begins to grow up. Adults cheat. They do not cut clean of the game. Mr. Darling wants to be admired by his children just as if he had taken the medicine, except that he happened to miss his mouth. And Hook has a passion for good form. The cheat upsets the system because he is both in it and out of it. One doesn't know where one is with him, and the game is demoralized.

Peter Pan, that "terrible masterpiece" as Peter Davies calls it, is a *tour de force* of literary demoralization. Barrie presents himself as an adult forever banished from Neverland, a disgruntled onlooker cut off from his characters and doing maximum damage to their romantic world. His subversion is occasionally deliberate: "Nobody really wants us. So let us watch and say jaggy things,in the hope that some of them will hurt." More often it comes of trying too hard to do the right thing. He goes through all the forms of the island narrative—in fact he hates to let any of them go and has to toss a coin to choose between them—but he is a fallen man because he perpetually shows that he knows they are forms. A narrator who writes, "Hook did not blanch, even at the gills," is a fallen narrator. Good form is not to know one has it, like the childish Smee. Consciousness of form is bad form—a truth which is torture to Hook and, for Barrie, theme, style, and a last great desert-island book. (Let me not claim too much; it is just that to read *Peter Pan* is to feel that it *should* have been the last, as *Don Quixote* should have been the last knights-in-armor romance.) (pp. 172-75)

Peter Pan is a more serious book than *Treasure Island.* Whereas, essentially, as Richard Aldington says, "an adult can get nothing more from *Treasure Island* than a boy does," *Peter Pan* is a boys' book not only for boys. Though Stevenson's book is "serious like a game properly and strenuously played," it is not a serious statement about "existence." Neverland adventures are only pretend; yet Barrie's book is very much about matters of life and death because it is about the loss of the island and the loss of childhood. To grow up is to hear the clock ticking for you, like Hook; to be "dead and forgotten," like Mrs. Darling; to be replaced by your daughter in Peter's affection, like Wendy, and she by her daughter after her. Good form means absorption in the shape of the moment, taking it absolutely for granted as when playing or dreaming. Peter lives eternally because for him each moment is all there is. But

Barrie calls him "heartless," and he calls him "tragic" for the same reason. . . . Peter sneers at the "laws of nature" as figured by mothers, who represent the cycle of life that transforms a child into someone who has children into someone finished off altogether. . . . One cannot quite get away with being an eternal boy, it seems, for even Peter has mysterious bad dreams and cries in his sleep. . . . (p. 176)

In *Sir James Barrie* Harry M. Geduld sums up the prevailing modern reaction to Barrie's works: "serious critical interest in his novels and plays has recently been hostile, when it has not been negligible or non-existent." Since the waning of the tremendous popularity that he enjoyed in his lifetime, Barrie has been of interest, if at all, mainly biographically, for his pathology. His personal oddities were made for Freudian critics: his love for his mother; his short stature; his take-over of somebody else's children and the extravagance of his immersion in the games he created for them; his idealization of women, which kept him at safe arm's length from them; his probable impotence; his divorce. Because he himself was preoccupied with childhood (in some ways doubtless even arrested in childhood), a misleading simplification has been practiced on his most famous work: *Peter Pan* is taken as representing the charming fulfillment of the desire for perpetual childhood, being as such sentimental and even neurotic. Only very recently, with Alison Lurie's essay in *The New York Review of Books* [see excerpt dated February 6, 1975], has a voice been raised contrary to the general chorus. Lurie attributes to Barrie a more self-conscious and even self-critical treatment of the theme of childhood than he has been given credit for before. She bases her analysis on *Tommy and Grizel* and *Mary Rose.* Her reading of *Peter Pan* is more conventional however since it stresses the attraction of eternal youth, whereas I think that here too the attraction (and surely it is attractive—we shouldn't be so bent on psychological well adjustment as to deny that) is explored in large part as a *dilemma.* It is worth dipping into the play version to illustrate Barrie's undercutting of a position like Peter's. Peter has no weight, he doesn't eat, and he can't be touched. There is pathos, even tragedy, in his isolation from the life force. When she leaves him, Wendy says she would like to give him a hug. He half understands, as the author tells us between the lines of dialogue: "If he could get the hang of the thing, his cry might become 'To live would be an awfully big adventure!' but he can never quite get the hang of it." There has been considerable distaste of Peter's line in both play and novel: "To die will be an awfully big adventure." It should be realized that no matter what his life—or maybe because of his life—Barrie was aware of and more than hints at the sterility, and even morbidity, of the ideal of perpetual youth.

An index of the ambivalence, far from naive, of his attitude toward childishness as a way of life is the sophisticated self-reflexiveness—more possible in the novel than the play and thus giving the novel the fuller resonance—in his handling of boys'-book formulas as a way of literature. *Treasure Island* is the sea-dream pure and fine, its apotheosis. *Peter Pan* is the dream's deathblow, elegy, and obsessive half-life, artfully rendered in the medium of bad form. Just about everything that happens in Neverland has happened before in books. But these things can never happen again in the same way for the grown-up narrator and the grown-up reader. Barrie makes it all the harder for us to play the dream straight, to beach our coracles one more time. (pp. 177-78)

Kathleen Blake, "The Sea-Dream: 'Peter Pan' and 'Treasure Island'," in Children's Literature: Annual of the Modern Language Association Group on Children's Literature and The Children's Literature Association, *Vol. 6, 1977, pp. 165-81.*

JOHN GRIFFITH

Peter Davies, the boy whose name suggested "Peter" for James Barrie's hero, knew first-hand what went into the making of *Peter Pan.* He had watched the shy, moody and oddly aggressive Barrie befriend him and his brothers more out of a need for playmates than for sons, and he had seen the story of Peter Pan emerge from Barrie's obsession with youth, play, and brittle, airy fantasy. Thus aware of both the charm and the emotional sources of Barrie's work, Davies called it a "terrible masterpiece."

The work quickly came to be regarded as a classic, and this has meant, among other things, that most people have lost sight of what is terrible about it. Assisted by Walt Disney's moviemakers and uncounted editors, abridgers and illustrators, the story of Peter Pan has been enshrined as a cheerful, whimsical celebration of childhood, a story about flying and swordflights and other adventures, with a little puppy-love interest thrown in on the side. But in the form Barrie himself gave to the story, it is more than that; it is a work of classic fantasy which insists on its very unreality and reveals the psychological sources from which such a deliberately insubstantial fantasy springs.

Barrie's fantasy world, "the Neverland," is first presented as part of "the map of a person's mind," created from the welter of conscious and unconscious material stored there. It is an ambiguous place: one part of the psyche desires and therefore creates it; another part denies and retreats from it, insisting it is only make-believe, when it threatens to become too real. The conflict of desire and fear which Barrie's characters feel may appear to be the classic dilemma of children's literature: the conflict between staying home and running away. And the adventures of the Darling family may seem similar to those of Jim Hawkins in *Treasure Island* or the children in the Narnia Chronicles. But the Neverland is, in a subtle way, much more dangerous. The worlds of Treasure Island and Narnia do not threaten or lure the characters in quite the same way. The Neverland is more disturbing in a sense because it is too desirable. And therefore Barrie must deny it all the more emphatically.

For, in Barrie's mind, the issue of whether to fly away or stay at home was really settled before the story ever began. Any biography of him shows that the idea of ever really detaching himself from his home and mother would have been unbearable. His imagination had committed itself absolutely to the image of the faithful child who would remain a child. Therefore the departures had to remain sheerest game and make-believe. Moreover, Barrie undercut the fantasy because he apparently could not bear its implications. For in the Neverland there exists for him a mother-wife figure whom he can't, even there, embrace and a villain of a father he can slay. Such visions were very likely too frightening for him to stand by, so that as soon as he hinted at them he had to repudiate them. And since he could neither fulfill them nor get rid of them, he was immobilized.

That is why the fantasy of flying to the Neverland takes the form it does in *Peter Pan.* (pp. 28-9)

The Pirate Ship, *a scene from the first production of* Peter Pan. *Nina Boucicault as Peter, Gerald du Maurier as Hook, and Hilda Trevelyan as Wendy are usually considered definitive in their respective roles.*

Barrie's excessive attachment to his mother comes as no surprise to anyone who has read *Peter Pan,* with its rhapsodic effusions on the glory of mother love. The same exaggerated concern for his mother which generated those passages generated the fantasy of the Neverland—and generated, too, the need to insist that the Neverland is not real. For, on the one hand, the Neverland is the product of a half-hearted wish for a world away from the tempting, guilt-producing influence of a mother about whom one cares too much. In a fundamental way, it is conceived as a world without mothers; its basic business goes on without them: exploring, fighting, running risks—things which boys do away from home. Peter has come there to escape his own mother; the Darling children come as an elaborate way of teasing their mother by their absence. But, on the other hand, the fantasy of a motherless world is ultimately impossible for Barrie. Appealing as it might be to project an island free from the tensions of his relationship with mother, his attachment for her is still the greatest principle of his thinking and wishing. A world without the mother on whom his deepest desires are fixed is miserably incomplete; it is no fun at all. In short, a mother must be imported; and Peter immediately fetches one. Thus the primary intention of the Neverland—to be a world free from the anxieties of the mother-fixation—is immediately compromised, since Barrie's imagination is so thoroughly infused by that fixation.

Peter's own attitude toward mothers is a clear expression of this simultaneous wish to be free of their bothersome presence, and to have their unlimited devotion. "Now, if Peter had ever quite had a mother, he no longer missed her," says Barrie. "He could do very well without one. He had thought them out, and remembered only their bad points." When he meets Mrs. Darling at the beginning of the story, he gnashes his teeth at her; when he finds Wendy grown up and a mother at the end of the story, he gives, "a cry of pain" and "[draws] back sharply." Yet at the same time he inarticulately craves a mother. He brings Wendy back with him in the first place to mother him and the lost boys; when he returns in the last chapter, he announces, "I came back for my mother, to take her back to the Neverland." "He does so need a mother," the new little girl Jane says. "'Yes, I know,' Wendy admitted rather forlornly; 'no one knows it so well as I'."

The little girls Peter takes back to the Neverland are, of course, always to be his make-believe mothers, not his real one; that is important to Peter and Barrie. Why this should be so is easy to understand. It is not simply that a real mother can boss you around and force you to grow up, as Peter says; in his very running off to the Neverland Peter has shown that real mothers don't have that kind of authority over him. There are differences more important than this between real and make-believe mothers; and Barrie makes it clear that they have something to do with sexual desire.

Sex is bound to be a worrisome subject for a person emotionally overburdened by the love of his mother. He faces the terrifying possibility that his passionate feeling for her will shade toward erotic desire—and that is absolutely taboo. He knows he must not feel what he is afraid he does feel. Barrie's fantasy handles this precarious wish/fear with great ingenuity. He has Peter choose for his mothers a series of girls, not quite women themselves but on the verge of becoming so. He brings them back to the Neverland to be his mother—but, once there, they play house, with Peter taking the part of the husband. All along, Barrie reminds us that this is all in play; the girl is not really Peter's mother, nor is she really his wife. Hence the incest-

taboo is not really being broken. Barrie's fantasy does include a degree of eroticism, but it is assigned only to the girl/woman, never to the boy. *His* innocence is preserved, immaculate. (pp. 30-2)

Peter and Wendy's dual relationship as son-and-mother and husband-and-wife is not the only one that needs to be safely insulated in make-believe. Peter's relationship with Captain Hook is another. The climactic event of the Neverland adventure, of course, is that Peter brings their ancient conflict to an end by killing Hook. On the face of it, there isn't anything especially taboo about a hero's killing a storybook villain like Hook. But if one observes how Barrie has imagined him, one sees that Hook's death at Peter's hands is indeed an event which must be kept make-believe.

For Barrie establishes a clear connection between Hook, that wicked, unfamilied man who "has no little children to love him," and Mr. Darling, Wendy's father, the only other man with any prominence in the story. Barrie stipulated that the same actor should play both Hook and Darling on the stage, and the two characters are crucially alike. In the first place, neither of them is really grown up. Darling "might have passed for a boy again if he had been able to take his baldness off"; and when Hook goes to his death in the duel with Peter, he is mentally a schoolboy still; in his mind he is "slouching in the playing fields of long ago." And not only are they boys, but they are bad boys—cheaters and sulks who lack good form and who try, by unfair means, to steal attention and respect. Darling is obsessed with having the good opinion of his neighbors, his children, and his wife, but he does nothing to deserve it. He throws a tantrum when he cannot tie his tie, he cheats in the medicine-taking treaty with Michael, he uses his remorse over the children's absence to get attention for himself by moving into the kennel. Hook, too, cheats and sulks (he calls it brooding) and behaves like a petulant child. In one espisode, just after Peter has made the noble gesture of giving Hook a hand up so they can fight on the same level, Hook bites him. In another, he violates the "unwritten laws" of romantic warfare by attacking the redskins rather than waiting for them to attack him. Like Darling, he struts and fumes in an effort to make people look up to him, he postures, dresses splendidly, and he lords it over his crew. But all his concern for good form is vain—for "was it not bad form to think about good form?"

Whimsically but insistently, Barrie emphasizes that these men compete with the boys for the mothers' favor. Darling rivals the children bumblingly and indirectly, pretending not to, revealing his jealousy only in sporadic outbursts; he wheedles and whines for the motherly attention that Mrs. Darling gives spontaneously to her children. Hook, who hates the boys openly and nakedly, tries to kill them, attempting to steal Wendy to be his own mother. And it is a great satisfaction in Barrie's fantasy to see Peter put the men's ridiculous aspirations to rout. Hook, of course, he kills, rescuing Wendy from his clutches and then spurning him with his foot. He registers his victory over Mr. Darling when he casually takes "the sweet, mocking kiss" from Mrs. Darling's lips, a kiss which Mr. Darling had tried and tried in vain to get.

Obviously Barrie is not as nervous about the fantasy of a boy killing the father-like rival as he is about the boy's becoming the mother's husband; he feels no need to render Hook's death doubly make-believe as he has done with the marriage of Peter and Wendy. It is sufficient that Hook dies in the Neverland. (Barrie does emphasize the unreality of his death by mentioning that, within a year of its happening, Peter has forgotten all about it.) The saving power of make-believe does its work. The boy may freely perform the deeds in the Neverland which would destroy him in the real world—because in the real world he would have to face the forbidden nature of his desires, and feel guilty about them. That is the great magic of the Neverland: it is a place for people who are "gay and innocent and heartless"—that is, free of guilt.

What Barrie's Neverland demonstrates, then, is one of the primary values of make-believe. Make-believe is the power of the mind to create its own psychologically insulated place—"for the Neverland is always more or less an island"—in which one can act out, symbolically and therefore recklessly, the desires which the real world denies him. There is no penalty to pay, because make-believe actions don't count.

To call this an escape from the real world is accurate enough, in one sense; but in another it is exactly wrong, since ultimately those very concerns from which the mind most eagerly desires to free itself become the preoccupations of the fantasy-world itself. In his eagerness to create a pleasing fiction, this kind of fantasist creates a mirror-image of the real world—the real world, that is, as it appears in his own mind.

Not all fantasy is of this sort, of course; the fantasy I am discussing is the kind produced by writers—like Barrie, Carroll and Andersen—who create out of a discernible need to arrogate the fantasy-rights of children as a way of expressing, in sportive modes, their own troubled thoughts. For this purpose, the sportiveness is of special importance, since it is the means by which disturbing feelings can be made pleasurable. Such fantasy asks at every point *not* to be taken seriously, *not* to be believed in. It emphasizes the absurdity or the arbitrariness or the insubstantiality of its surface details—and thereby muffles its deeper meanings. In introducing a chapter on the mermaids' lagoon in the Neverland, for instance, Barrie writes:

> If you shut your eyes and are a lucky one, you may see at times a shapeless pool of lovely pale colours suspended in the darkness; then if you squeeze your eyes tighter, the pool begins to take shape, and the colours become so vivid that with another squeeze they must go on fire. But just before they go on fire you see the lagoon. This is the nearest you ever get to it on the mainland, just one heavenly moment; if there could be two moments you might see the surf and hear the mermaids singing.

Literally, this means that the lagoon is an optical illusion, but what Barrie is doing here is describing the quality of evanescence. All through his story, incidental details have the same qualities, which serve to make things diminutive and insubstantial. The mermaids play rugby with "bubbles made in rainbow water"; the lost boys wear animal skins "in which they are so round and furry that when they fall they roll"; the chimney of Wendy's house is made by knocking the bottom of John's hat out and clapping the hat on the roof; even Hook smokes two cigars at once "in a holder of his own contrivance." These and a hundred other minutiae emphasize how unserious, and therefore inconsequential, and therefore innocent, the events of the story are.

It is ironic that this kind of whimsy should be considered especially appropriate to children's literature, when children generally show less appreciation for it than adults. It is the rhetoric of lovers, stage magicians and jolly uncles. Children don't indulge in it themselves very much, and they don't particularly seek it out in books. The most popular kids' fiction—like the Nancy Drew and Hardy Boys series, the Tarzan books

and so on—are notable for their rather ponderous seriousness, their avoidance of Barrie's arch "Let us now kill a pirate, to show Hook's method" kind of narrative. All the canny modernizers, abridgers and popularizers of *Peter Pan* recognize this. They leave out the whimsical trimmings—the addresses to the reader, the entirely ornamental details—and keep the plot. . . . It seems that ordinary readers share enough of Barrie's interest in the fantasy of a child who defeats the father and plays house with the mother to be attracted by his story; but they don't need the camouflage Barrie provides. Barrie sensed the "wickedness" of his fantasy much more strongly than most of his readers do, and instinctively took steps to render the story exaggeratedy innocent. In *Peter Pan,* whimsy, wit and fantasy are put to one of their most important psychological uses—rendering the unthinkable harmless. (pp. 32-6)

> *John Griffith, "Making Wishes Innocent: 'Peter Pan'," in* The Lion and the Unicorn, *Vol. 3, No. 1, Spring, 1979, pp. 28-37.*

NICHOLAS TUCKER

[*Peter Pan*] is a play that gets so close to children's own fantasy life that it even includes various common violent, morbid or sadistic feelings normally omitted in child-centered writing. Another major attraction for children, though, is the enigmatic figure of Peter himself: someone that many girls like Wendy will want to mother, and almost all children will wish to imitate, especially when it comes to flying. Yet this is also a hero who arouses pity, at the moment when he refuses to join the Darling family, defiantly if sadly insisting on returning to the unconvincing pleasures of games with Tinker Bell and other microscopic fairies. But if Peter had joined the other children and accepted the shaky family discipline of Mr and Mrs Darling, he would—in the eyes of his young admirers—certainly have been happier but ultimately much less exciting in the memory. He is, therefore, an intriguing, even slightly alarming hero, who represents to children the height of their fantasy ambitions along with a splendid, if pitiable refusal to compromise with adult authority. In this sense, Peter is almost a sacrificial figure, willing to forgo all the domestic comforts and mothering that mean so much to children in order to preserve his eternal, unflawed heroic status. And when, oppressed by fear of loneliness, he tries to keep the Darling children with him by flying back quickly and closing the bedroom window against their return, even he is sometimes greeted with resounding boos from his audience. For although children may be happy for someone else to act the uncompromising child hero, they do not really want this role for themselves or for the more ordinary Darling children, whose wish to return and stay at home they fully understand. An otherwise attractive hero who can also be pitied, however, has everything to offer: sympathetic admiration unchecked by accompanying envy, which could be why Peter has always been so especially loved by so many children over the course of the century. (pp. 48-9)

> *Nicholas Tucker, "Fly Away, Peter?," in* Signal, *No. 37, January, 1982, pp. 43-9.*

WILLIAM BLACKBURN

Readers of the contemporary adolescent novel may be expected to laugh at the notion that J. M. Barrie's *Peter Pan* has anything in common with such novels. The most obvious virtue of the adolescent novel is the determined realism with which it addresses the problems of growing up today; critics have yet to weary of praising its modernity . . . and sympathy. . . . Even the most hidebound of conservative critics, i.e., anyone who refuses to believe that modernity and vulgarity are necessarily the paramount literary virtues, might find it difficult to argue that Barrie's novel also addresses the problem of growing up, and that it does so in a fashion superior to that of much contemporary fiction. After all, Barrie somehow contrives to bring his novel to a close without once mentioning adultery, abortion, drug addiction, homosexuality, prostitution, divorce, lesbian rape, or even birth control; *ergo,* he cannot possibly have anything to say to modern adolescents. Also everyone knows that *Peter Pan* is a sentimental celebration of the freedom and innocence of childhood; everyone, that is, except a few critics who mutter darkly about psychological infantilism and tend to sneer at the novel as a monument to Barrie's own failure to grow up.

Barrie's partisans and detractors both should reread *Peter Pan;* both are likely to find the experience a surprising one. Those who teach the adolescent novel can also profit from Barrie's story because it too deals with the price of maturity and because, despite its lack of ferocious and doctrinaire realism, it deals with it in a way that reveals the chief limitation of much contemporary fiction.

For purposes of illustration, it is useful to compare *Peter Pan* with one of the most highly-acclaimed of recent adolescent novels, Richard Peck's *Are You in the House Alone?* Peck's novel tells the story of Gail Osburne, a teen-age girl whose parents have fled the evils of Manhattan for the bucolic security of Oldfield Village, where Gail is promptly terrorized and raped by Phil Lawver, scion of one of Oldfield's most powerful and respected families. There is a good deal in Peck's novel to justify its critical acclaim. Peck deals sympathetically with adolescent alienation and does not criticize Gail for "beginning to feel pretty cut off from everybody." His novel recognizes that not all adults are *ipso facto* villainous—though even his most candid adults are misfits . . . and that not all adolescents are trustworthy. . . . Peck hints at Gail's limitations ("I was just beginning to see my parents as people once in a while, and not just as parents"), while insisting on the shortcomings of her parents ("We were a great little family for secrets") and the community ("I felt strangled by the place. Everything so neat and perfectly organized. On the surface.") It is Gail's discovery of what lies beneath the surface that gives the novel its thematic richness. In its own way, Gail's story is a kind of mid-seventies *Paradise Lost,* an account of the loss of innocence; her story is prefaced with an idyllic memory of a moonlight swim with her first love . . . , and ends with Gail confronting a world in which human compromise and human weakness are the real facts of life. . . . (pp. 47-8)

Peck's account of the fall of Gail Osburne, however, has its weaknesses too—weaknesses which are typical of so much modern fiction for adolescents. At times Peck cannot resist the temptation to fall into the kind of cliché likely to appeal to teen-age readers: a contemporary of Gail's "sounds real normal. Kind of like a teacher"; Gail wonders "if there's such a thing as a bright spot in a school day" (guess what the answer is); a typical attempt to talk with her mother "sounded weirdly like my mother practicing ventriloquism with me as the dummy." One might benignly ignore such cheap shots as a way of establishing *rapport* with the reader, but for the fact that they indicate a general shallowness, a glibness which oversimplifies the problems Peck apparently addresses so fearlessly. . . . There can be no doubt that Gail is the victim of a bitter injustice, but Peck should be able to show this without glibly denouncing the entire legal system and blithely ignoring the problems in-

volved in seeing that justice is done. In short, the strength of Peck's novel lies in the sympathetic frankness with which it presents the adolescent protagonist and acknowledges her point of view; its weakness lies in its readiness to achieve that sympathy by the sacrifice of complexity and in its failure to provide an adequate context for its adolescent readers.

What, we may well ask, does Barrie's *Peter Pan* have in common with *Are You in the House Alone?,* and how can Barrie's novel help us understand the shortcomings of contemporary adolescent fiction? We can only answer these questions by recognizing the novel for what it is, neither a shallow celebration of childhood nor a sentimental monument to the author's inability to come to terms with his own maturity. There are, it is true, elements of both a celebration of childhood and of compensation for its loss in the novel. Most of Barrie's critics go awry in failing to give adequate consideration to the tension between these elements, a tension which lies at the heart of *Peter Pan.* On the first page of the novel, Mrs. Darling asks a rhetorical question of her two-year-old daughter, Wendy: "Why can't you remain like this forever?" The entire novel may usefully be regarded as Barrie's attempt to answer this question.

Barrie's novel resembles *Are You in the House Alone?* because it deals, however obliquely, with the problems of maturation and with the loss of innocence which growing up demands. Maturation is acknowledged as a process of loss; of the Neverland, Barrie tells us: "On these magic shores, children at play are forever beaching their coracles. We too have been there; we can still hear the sound of the surf, though we shall land no more." Adults cannot hope to return to Peter's island, which is not a place but a state of mind,

> though if you shut your eyes and are a lucky one you may see at times a shapeless pool of lovely pale colors suspended in the darkness; then if you squeeze your eyes tighter, the pool begins to take shape and the colors become so vivid that with another squeeze they must go on fire. But just before they go on fire you see the lagoon. This is the nearest you ever get to it on the mainland, just one heavenly moment.

We all recognize the lost heavenly land behind the wall of fire; Barrie's subtle invocation of the Garden of Eden guarded by the angel with the sword of fire (Genesis 3:24) tells us that childhood is indeed a type of the lost paradise.

The unreflecting and spontaneous freedom of childhood is concentrated in Peter Pan, the boy who refuses to grow up. Peter has fled the perils and responsibilities which lie in wait for all children. He tells Wendy: "'I ran away the day I was born. . . . It was because I heard father and mother . . . talking about what I was to be when I became a man.' 'I don't want ever to be a man,' he said with passion. 'I want always to be a little boy and to have fun. So I ran away. . . .'"

Peter's flight is apparently a success. "Innocent and gay and heartless," Peter "had his first laugh still." He is entirely free of the adult's need to calculate: Peter "just said anything that came into his head." Unlike Captain Hook or Mr. Darling, Peter need not fret about his social position, for Peter "did not know in the least who or what he was." The boy enjoys a freedom from the tyranny of facts known only to very young children, madmen, and, to a lesser degree, artists; to him "make-believe and true were exactly the same thing," and he frequently disconcerts the boys who follow him when "in the middle of a fight he would suddenly change sides." Peter also enjoys the blessing of forgetfulness: "Peter had seen many tragedies, but he had forgotten them all,'' and so, does not share the vulnerability of other children. When Hook bites him at a critical moment, Peter is at first "quite helpless. He could only stare horrified. Every child is affected thus the first time he is treated unfairly. . . . No one ever gets over the first unfairness; no one except Peter. He often met it, but he always forgot it." Pan is, as his name implies, the god of all in Neverland. There he lives in splendid anarchy, exempt from time and memory and remorse, waging a jolly and unending war against the adult world, represented by Hook and the Piccaninny Indians, his every whim gratified.

The sweetness of Peter's life is underscored by the fate which befalls the children who decide to return to the mainland with Wendy: "Before they had attended school a week, they saw what goats they had been not to remain on the island. . . . It is sad to have to say that the power to fly gradually left them," and sadder yet to see that they also lose the power of belief: "the bearded man who doesn't know any stories to tell his children was once John." Even Wendy, who "grew up of her own free will a day quicker than other girls," cannot hold back her tears when she sees Peter for the last time and must tell him that she has grown up.

So, in all these ways, Barrie reminds us of the cost of maturity. His book is in large measure a romance insofar as romance is, as Northrop Frye says in *The Anatomy of Criticism,* "the nearest of all literary kinds to the wish-fulfillment dream," with its "perennially childlike quality . . . marked by its extraordinarily persistent nostalgia, its search for some kind of imaginative golden age in time or space." The innocent childhood of the hero is "in later phases . . . often recalled as a lost happy time or Golden Age"—just as Barrie's partisans insist he recalls it in *Peter Pan.* Yet this romantic view of childhood, influential though it certainly is throughout the novel, does not do full justice to the complexity of Barrie's thought.

Despite the persistent romantic misreading of the novel, Peter does not enjoy Barrie's full approval. Peter has bad dreams, a reflection of his isolation ("for hours he could not be separated from these dreams, though he wailed piteously in them"). There is something more than a little sinister in the means Peter must use to maintain his position on the island: "his band were not allowed to know anything he did not know," and when his followers "seem to be growing up, which is against the rules, Peter thins them out." Peter saves Tiger Lily from the pirates by giving "a marvellous imitation" of Hook's voice, and, once the pirate chief has been dispatched to the crocodile, Peter is only too eager to add Hook to his repertoire of roles ("he sat long in the cabin with Hook's cigar-holder in his mouth, and one hand clenched, all but the forefinger, which he bent and held threateningly aloft like a hook."). Peter's emotional growth is also arrested by his decision to remain on the island. . . . At the novel's opening, Peter needs Wendy to tell him what a kiss is, and he fails utterly to understand Wendy's maturing interest in him. When Tinker Bell saves Peter's life by drinking the poison left by Hook, the baffled boy can only ask, "But why, Tink?" Peter maintains his freedom and security by forfeiting the possibility of love.

Barrie's awareness of the limitations of perpetual boyhood is also conveyed in his treatment of an adult character who bears an interesting relationship to Peter, Mr. Darling. Mr. Darling is, like Peter, vain and pompous, given to authoritarianism and the grand gesture—as when, after the children have gone to Neverland, he insists on punishing himself by living in Nana's doghouse. Like Peter, "whatever he did he had to do in ex-

cess," and we recognize the echo of Peter in Mr. Darling's words to the lost boys when he tells them they can sleep in the drawing room: "I am not sure that we have a drawing room, but we pretend we have and it's all the same." The man's resemblance to Peter is continually brought home to the reader—Mr. Darling "might have passed for a boy again if he had been able to take his baldness off"—and it is through this resemblance that Barrie emphasizes the limitations of Peter. What might be considered charming in the boy is beyond a doubt foolish in the man.

Barrie's most profound criticism of the paradisal "innocence of childhood is implicit in his summation of children as 'innocent and gay and heartless," "the most heartless things in the world." We have seen that Peter's life in Neverland is based on his rejection of the adult world, the world of time. He is "the only boy on the island who could neither write nor spell, not the smallest word. He was above all that sort of thing." Peter is a prehistoric creature. Since he is exempt from history and time, death is meaningless to him. He must lose everyone and everything he knows, but he need never remember the loss. To Peter death seems only "an awfully big adventure"; therefore, he remembers nothing, not even Wendy.

To remember is, in this novel, to be an adult. The memories of the other children are somewhat fluid: Peter's alone is totally unreliable, and, though this saves him much pain, this is also the source of his heartlessness. When Wendy is astonished that Peter does not remember Captain Hook, Peter can say grandly, "I forget them after I kill them." He also asks, "Who is Tinker Bell?" and such insouciance, likewise, grates when we meet it in other contexts, as in the Spartan epitaph "Mrs. Darling was now dead and forgotten." Exempt from time, and its burden of an irrevocable past, Peter is likewise exempt from remorse; as his final meeting with Wendy demonstrates, to be without memory is to be without a heart.

Peter's heartlessness is a consequence of his rejection of the adult world, a world devoured by time. We sympathize with the adults in Barrie's novel because time takes everything from them, as it does from us, and so makes them like ourselves. Hook is, for this reason, something of a tragic antagonist in the novel. If Peter is the archetypal child, Hook is certainly the archetypal adult, for he is obsessed with time, as grotesquely symbolized by the alarm clock in the crocodile which pursues him to his death. "Terribly alone," cursed with acute self-consciousness and the knowledge of his failure to live up to his ideals, Hook is also obsessed with good form, the lost grace and innocence of childhood which Peter cannot help possessing. "A dark and solitary enigma," Hook is in fact fallen man, the maimed and insecure captive of that world of time which Peter shuns. He, no less than Milton's Satan, carries hell within him, for he is never able to reconcile himself to the loss of bliss that maturity brings. Hook's insight does not make him good—Barrie is not writing *that* kind of fantasy— but it does make him a candidate for our sympathy in a way that Peter can never be so long as he remains heartless. Barrie, who once remarked that "to be born is to be wrecked on an island," insists that the heart has a price, a price Peter is unwilling to pay. One can find a heart only by leaving Neverland, and this is the consolation Barrie offers us for the loss of Paradise, for our exile from those magic shores whence "we can still hear the sound of the surf, though we shall land no more." Hook and Mr. Darling, because they cannot leave childhood behind, cannot find hearts. Barrie contends that it is only in the acceptance of time, and of loss, and of the risks of love, that a heart is to be found. In the "Intimations" ode, Wordsworth admits that "Shades of the prison-house begin to close / Upon the growing boy." Was Barrie thinking of those lines when he shows Peter staring in through the barred window as the Darling children are re-united with their parents: "He had ecstasies innumerable that other children can never know; but he was looking through the window at the one joy from which he must be forever barred." Peter shall be forever free and forever heartless.

So Barrie's novel is perfectly frank about the fact that childhood is a lost paradise, but he also tells us that it may be a paradise well lost. In this he resembles Milton and the great romantic poets. . . It is this sense of the *felix culpa,* this awareness that one must lose Paradise in order to find love, that balances the nostalgia for childhood in *Peter Pan* and make the novel so much richer than its partisans and detractors alike are apt to realize.

An author is, of course, at liberty to present the loss of childhood innocence without any accompanying consolation. This is how Rousseau presents it in his account of his first meeting with injustice in the *Confessions*: . . . . (pp. 48-52)

[We] may note that the difference between the English romantics and Rousseau is very like the difference between Barrie and many writers of adolescent novels today. Both parties stress the loss of childhood innocence, but not all seek to offer the reader such honest consolation as may be found for the loss. In a work which does not provide consolation, the impulse to criticism and recrimination is dominant, as it is in Rousseau. Peck's *Are You in the House Alone?*, like its numerous and inferior imitations, is more inclined to recrimination than consolation. It lacks the balance of Barrie's novel. Of course, a writer ought to tell the truth, but to offer young people little more than a confirmation of their suspicion that adults have messed everything up, and that the world is invariably a nasty place, is to cheat those readers. Such fiction encourages, not mature strength, but only snide cynicism. The problem is one of balance and emphasis and of providing a context in which the reader can make some sense of human evil and human shortcomings. Only when writers are willing to refrain from a trendy sensationalism and to attempt to grapple honestly with the moral complexities of life, as Barrie, for all his difficulties,

Michael Llewelyn Davies, dressed as Peter Pan, tussles with Barrie's Captain Hook.

grapples in *Peter Pan,* can they hope to produce the kind of literature that our young people so desperately need. (pp. 52-3)

William Blackburn, " 'Peter Pan' and the Contemporary Adolescent Novel," in Proceedings of the Ninth Annual Conference of the Children's Literature Association, *1982, pp. 47-53.*

JOHN ROWE TOWNSEND

[*Peter Pan*] with its brilliantly stagey incidents and characters, has delighted many thousands of children and adults. The book [*Peter and Wendy*], considered on its own, is less satisfactory.

There is no doubt that Barrie created two or three vivid and memorable characters: Captain Hook, with the hook in place of his lost hand, and the ticking crocodile, and possibly Peter Pan himself, though it is doubtful whether the idea of a boy who never grows up is as appealing to children as it is to parents. The profound effect that *Peter Pan* has had on parents is illustrated by the fact that the name Wendy, now quite common, was invented by Barrie.

But much of the time the author is winking over the children's heads to the adults, and putting in jokes that to children are meaningless—as for instance in Captain Hook's preoccupation with good form (in a *real* children's story what would a pirate chieftain care for good form?) or in the parody of a military commentator analysing Hook's battle with the Indians—'To what extent Hook is to blame for his tactics on this occasion is for the historian to decide', and so on. There is a taste of saccharine about some parts of the book; notably Wendy's mothering of the lost boys. I believe also that the kind of fantasy in which the children's nurse is a dog and in which Father banishes himself to the dog-kennel is a different sort of fantasy from that of the Never Never Land, and the two do not mix. All in all, *Peter and Wendy* is not a very good book; I am sure it benefits unduly from the fame of the play. (pp. 106-07)

John Rowe Townsend, "The Never-Lands," in his Written for Children: An Outline of English-Language Children's Literature, *second revised edition, J. B. Lippincott, 1983, pp. 101-10.*

JACQUELINE ROSE

Peter Pan offers us the child—for ever. It gives us the child, but it does not speak *to* the child. . . .

Peter Pan stands in our culture as a monument to the impossibility of its own claims—that it represents the child, speaks to and for children, addresses them as a group which is knowable and exists for the book, much as the book (so the claim runs) exists for them. . . . *Peter Pan* has never, in any easy way, been a book for children at all. . . . (p. 1)

Behind *Peter Pan* lies the desire of a man for a little boy (or boys). . . . (p. 3)

Suppose, therefore, that Peter Pan is a little boy who does not grow up, not because he doesn't want to, but because someone else prefers that he shouldn't. Suppose, therefore, that what is at stake in *Peter Pan* is the adult's desire for the child. I am not using 'desire' here in the sense of an act which is sought after or which must actually take place. It is not relevant, therefore, to insist that nothing ever happened, or that Barrie was innocent of any interest in sex (a point which is often made). I am using desire to refer to a form of investment by the adult in the child, and to the demand made by the adult on the child as the effect of that investment, a demand which fixes the child and then holds it in place. A turning to the child, or a circulating around the child—what is at stake here is not so much something which could be enacted as something which cannot be spoken.

The sexual act which underpins *Peter Pan* is neither act nor fantasy in the sense in which these are normally understood and wrongly opposed to each other. It is an act in which the child is used (and abused) to represent the whole problem of what sexuality is, or can be, and to hold that problem at bay. This is something which . . . surfaces constantly throughout the history of *Peter Pan*—it is part of the fabric of the work. But the fact is either not known, or else it is displaced (as with Carroll) onto Barrie himself, and then disavowed (Barrie as the innocent of all innocents).

To call *Peter Pan* a fantasy does not, therefore, absolve us of the sexual question. It focuses it more sharply. At the moment when Barrie was writing *Peter Pan,* Freud was making his most crucial (and in this context least known) discovery that sexuality works above all at the level of fantasy, and that what we take to be our sexual identity is aways precarious and can never be assumed. Sexuality persists, for all of us, at the level of the unconscious precisely because it is a question which is never quite settled, a story which can never be brought to a close. Freud is known to have undermined the concept of childhood innocence, but his real challenge is easily lost if we see in the child merely a miniature version of what our sexuality eventually comes to be. The child is sexual, but its sexuality (bisexual, polymorphous, perverse) threatens our own at its very roots. Setting up the child as innocent is not, therefore, repressing its sexuality—it is above all holding off any possible challenge to our own.

The problem is not, therefore, J. M. Barrie's—it is ours. Ours to the extent that we are undoubtedly implicated in the status which *Peter Pan* has acquired as the ultimate fetish of childhood. All Barrie ever did was to write *Peter Pan*. . . . But it is we who have recognised *Peter Pan* ('recognised' in both senses of the term), and given it its status. *Peter Pan* has been almost unreservedly acclaimed as a children's classic for the greater part of this century. Its presence in our culture is in fact so diffused that most of the time we do not even notice it. We take it for granted as something which belongs to us and to children, without there being any need for us to ask the question of the relation between the two. Like all children's classics, *Peter Pan* is considered to speak for everyone—adult and child. . . . The child and the adult are one at that point of pure identity which the best of children's books somehow manage to retrieve. Time and again in its history, *Peter Pan* has been set up as the very emblem of that purity and identity. But this, I would say, has only been possible (and desirable) because it reveals so crudely the travesty on which any such notion rests. (pp. 3-5)

Peter Pan is a myth, but its status as such rests on the very difficulty which most commentaries refuse to recognise, or else recognise in order to diagnose and remove. *Peter Pan* is a classic in which the problem of the relationship between adult and child is unmistakably at the heart of the matter.

Peter Pan was not originally intended for children. It first appeared inside a novel for adults, J. M. Barrie's *The Little White Bird,* as a story told by the narrator to a little boy whom the narrator was trying to steal. In order for it to become a work for children, it was extracted from its source, transformed into a play, and sent out on its own. *Peter Pan* emerges, therefore, out of an unmistakable act of censorship. The book which

it leaves behind is one of the most explicit accounts to date of what it might mean to write fiction for the child. *The Little White Bird* is the story of the difficulty of that process—the difficulty of the relation between adult and child, and a question about the sexuality of each. What is the sexuality of the narrator? What is the origin of the child? What is *going on* between them? Questions which are never quite answered in the book, but which provide the basis for the telling of *Peter Pan.* The rest of *Peter Pan's* history can then be read as one long attempt to wipe out the residual signs of the disturbance out of which it was produced. *The Little White Bird* is an origin of sorts, but only in the sense that no origin is ever left behind, since it necessarily *persists*. *The Little White Bird* shows what cannot, or must not, be allowed to get into fiction for children, but the problems to which it so eloquently bears witness do not go away. They remain in such a way as to undermine, finally, any simple notion of children's fiction itself.

Thus the result of that first act of censorship was that *Peter Pan* was both never written and, paradoxically, has never ceased to be written. Barrie himself certainly couldn't manage it. He did not write the play until twenty-four years after its first production. The publication had nothing to do with children, since it was the only children's text in a volume of collected plays (this was the main publication although in the same year it was printed on its own). The story from *The Little White Bird* was eventually published separately, but it cannot be described as a book for children. It was released onto the fine art collector's market, at a time when a whole new market for children's books was developing, a market which it completely by-passed and to which it never belonged. Barrie persistently refused to write a narrative version of the play, and, when he did, it was a failure, almost incomprehensible, and later had to be completely rewritten along the lines of a new state educational policy on language in [1915]. During this time Barrie authorised *Peter Pan* to a number of different writers, which means that its status as a classic for children depends at least as much on them as it does on Barrie himself. Barrie may well be the source of the play, but this constant dispersion of *Peter Pan* challenges any straightforward idea of origin or source. Above all it should caution us against the idea that things can simply be traced back to their beginning, since, in the case of *Peter Pan,* what followed is at least as important as what came before.

What has followed has been a total mystification of all these forms of difficulty and confusion. Barrie *is Peter Pan,* despite the fact that he could not write it. *Peter Pan* is a classic for children, despite the fact that they could not read it—either because it was too expensive, or because it was virtually impossible to read. Nowhere has it been recognised that there might be a problem of writing, of address, and of language, in the history of *Peter Pan. Peter Pan's* dispersion—the fact that it is everywhere and nowhere at one and the same time— has been taken as the sign of its cultural value. Its own ethereal nature merely sanctions the eternal youth and innocence of the child it portrays, and for which it is most renowned.

The sexual disavowal is, therefore, a political disavowal. A disavowal of the material differences which are concealed behind the category of *all* children to which *Peter Pan* is meant to make its appeal. (pp. 5-7)

The material and sexual aspects of *Peter Pan* have been the vanishing-points of its history. They are there, however, and they can be exposed. But what we have been given instead is a glorification of the child. This suggests not only a refusal to acknowledge difficulties and contradictions in relation to childhood; it impies that we *use* the image of the child to deny those same difficulties in relating to ourselves. (p. 8)

Children's fiction emerges . . . out of a conception of both the child and the world as knowable in a direct and unmediated way, a conception which places the innocence of the child and a primary state of language and/or culture in a close and mutually dependent relation. It is a conception which has affected children's writing and the way that we think about it to this day. We can see it, in differing forms, in such apparently diverse types of writing as the fairy tale and the adventure story for boys. . . . Both types of writing are present in *Peter Pan* which condenses a whole history of children's fiction into its form. They can also be seen in the works of Alan Garner who is considered by many to be one of the most innovatory writers today. But what I want to stress in both cases is the idea which they share of a primitive or lost state to which the child has special access. The child is, if you like, something of a pioneer who restores these worlds to us, and gives them back to us with a facility or directness which ensures that our own relationship to them is, finally, safe. (p. 9)

Peter Pan is sometimes scoffed at today for the excessive and cloying nature of its innocence. It is in fact one of the most fragmented and troubled works in the history of children's fiction to date. *Peter Pan* is peculiar, and yet not peculiar, in so far as it recapitulates a whole history of children's fiction which has not yet come to an end. (pp. 10-11)

> *Jacqueline Rose, in her* The Case of Peter Pan; or, The Impossibility of Children's Fiction, *The Macmillan Press Ltd., 1984, 181 p.*

HUMPHREY CARPENTER

[The play *Peter Pan*] has generally been recognized since its first appearance as, in its strange way, a work of genius. Yet it also inspires, even from its warmest admirers, expressions of distaste: at its whimsicality, its sentimentality, and perhaps other qualities not so immediately apparent. Nowhere has the reaction to it been better expressed than by . . . [Peter Llewelyn Davies]. Looking back at it many years later and contemplating the effect it had had on him and his brothers, and perhaps on a whole generation, he called it 'that terrible masterpiece'. (p. 170)

Peter Pan is the only piece of Barrie's writing that gets the whole Barrie into it. (p. 176)

The principal model for Peter Pan is, of course, Barrie himself. Peter is everything that Barrie had been and had become. He is neither child nor adult, and he is entirely sexless. (p. 177)

Peter is also an adventure-story addict, just as Barrie had been in childhood (when he soaked himself in Penny Dreadfuls and in *Treasure Island*) and had remained. In student days Barrie wrote in his notebook: 'Want to stop everybody in street & ask if they've read *The Coral Island*. Feel sorry if not.' Peter's adventures in the Never Never Land, and those of the Lost Boys, are largely inspired by Ballantyne's *The Coral Island,* together with touches of Robert Louis Stevenson; and on this level the play is a joyful celebration of children's literature itself, and of the rich imagination which is childhood's greatest asset. Yet, typically, Barrie does not let Peter simply indulge in this; Peter is always standing back from the action, and regarding it and himself in a quizzical light. He loves to hear *stories;* indeed it is this which brings him to the Darling nursery in the first place. . . . Nor are all the adventures themselves

'real' ones. We are told that the Lost Boys wear coats of 'the skins of animals they think they have shot', and in the Home Under the Ground non-existent meals are sometimes served. . . . Barrie seems to be saying that the childish imagination, splendid as it is, has the most terrible limitations, and can never (without growing up) come to terms with the real world. *Peter Pan* thus manages—and it is a triumph of ingenuity—both to celebrate imagination and to give a rather chilling warning of its limitations. And is Barrie also suggesting that even the most brilliant and effective writer—such as himself—does not know whether to believe in his own creations? The theme of belief, so important . . . to *Peter Pan* at its deepest level, is touched on here.

Peter 'is' Barrie in so many other respects. He is the manipulator of other people's emotions, who carries them off from the real world that they inhabit to a country of his own invention, where they can act parts that he chooses for them in dramas of his own devising. He is also the outsider, the observer, who flirts with both mother and child (just as Barrie did), but who in the end is cut off from real relationships. . . . From this isolation, this knowledge that he is not a 'real' person, comes Peter's otherwise inexplicable sadness, which pervades the play and provides a superbly judged counterpoint to what would otherwise be an overabundance of 'adventures'. Again Barrie is reminding his audience of the limitations as well as the marvels of childhood, and of the price that has to be paid by those who choose to remain as children. Though the play is in a sense a celebration of immaturity, it is an awful warning to those who choose to remain immature. (pp. 178-79)

Barrie, though he appears to be extolling the joys of not growing up, of remaining within the dream, is in fact saying just the opposite, for the events of *Peter Pan* are framed by a 'real' world in which money has to be earned and family relationships can be extremely difficult. Mr Darling, with his bad temper and his money worries, has been put into the play to make just this point. Moreover, the Never Never Land is a deliberately unreal Arcadia: it is visibly stuck together out of bits of well-known stories, and to visit it requires an act of belief which the children cannot sustain as they grow up. *Peter Pan* is arguably more 'true to life' in this respect than is any other major work of children's literature which preceded it. To use J.R.R. Tolkien's terms for the two layers of narrative found in many works of fantasy, it not only presents us with a 'secondary' (make-believe) world, but reminds us that the 'primary' (real) world is there all the time, and must be returned to if maturity is to be achieved.

But Peter rejects the possibility of returning to it:

> PETER *(passionately):* I don't want to go to school and learn solemn things. No one is going to catch me, lady, and make me a man. I want always to be a little boy and to have fun.

For him, in consequence, there can be no maturity, no increase in wisdom, no procreation, not even death. There is only forgetting and starting out all over again. Peter is condemned to live out the same events every time a new generation of children follows him to the Never Never Land; this much is made clear by the continuation of the story in *Peter and Wendy,* and is indicated by Barrie's difficulty in finding a satisfactory ending for the play. There can be no ending, only a return to the beginning.

On the negative side then, Peter is a victim of his own worship of immaturity. On the positive side, he expresses almost everything that children's literature up to 1904 had been trying to say and do. He is at the same time a child himself and a child's dream-figure, the archetypal hero both of magical fairy tale and adventure story. Indeed he is so archetypal that one almost begins to believe Barrie's assertion about the play that, 'I have no recollection of having written it.' He seems not just the invention of one writer, but a character from mythology. He is god-like. Indeed in a sense he is God-like.

Gillian Avery has observed that the fairy-fashion which over-whelmed English nurseries and their books after the success of *Peter Pan* invoked something akin to religious feeling.

> There was during these years a yearning in those who wrote for children to present them with some sort of faith to replace the Christian teaching which had been implicit in Victorian books (even with writers who had no particularly fervent religious feelings) and which had become unfashionable. Children's writers generally deprecated the 'progressive' attitude . . . which sought to remove all mystery and to base everything on scientific fact. They also recognized that it is difficult to preach an ethic convincingly in the absence of a faith, and so fairies became the new guardian angels.

This in a way was what Barrie himself was doing in *Peter Pan*. But he was attempting more than his imitators tried to do. He was following in the steps of Charles Kingsley, George MacDonald, and Kenneth Grahame: working from a largely religious impulse, he was attempting to replace conventional religion with something of his own devising which would summon up religious feelings in his child and adult readers. And unlike them he made a complete success of it. *Peter Pan* is an alternative religion.

Kenneth Grahame's vision of Pan in 'The Piper at the Gates of Dawn' fails to invoke real religious awe because it takes over a stock symbol and uses it without any depth of feeling. But Barrie, unlike Grahame, was able to write with deep feeling about a character whom he named Pan.

Barrie's choice of 'Pan' as Peter's second name was, to say the least, ingenious. It implies that Peter is a figure of classical mythology. . . . (pp. 180-81)

Peter Pan has almost nothing about him of the classical Pan except his pipes and (in *The Little White Bird*) the brief appearance of the goat. But Barrie was influenced less by ancient tradition than by recent fashion, for Pan was a recurrent figure in the work of those 'nineties writers who turned their backs on Christian doctrine but wished to evoke religious awe. (p. 182)

Peter Pan is in many respects remarkably like the central figure of the Christian religion. At one moment he goes willingly towards death so as to save another, proclaiming: 'To die will be an awfully big adventure.' He can bring the dead back to life: when Wendy is shot to the ground by Tootles' arrow he revives her by building the Wendy-house around her. He can perform other miracles too. . . . Peter is surely Christ-like when he takes the children on a journey through the skies to his own heavenly land. The Lost Boys who dwell there seem to be the souls of the dead; Peter says of them: 'They are the children who fall out of their prams when the nurse is looking the other way.' Like Christ on earth, he is half human, half immortal. Like Christ, his only close relationship is that of son to mother.

Hook is the Satan to Peter's Christ, a Satan in the manner of *Paradise Lost*. Despite his supposedly nightmare qualities he is not really a figure of terror (as is, say, Blind Pew in *Treasure Island*) but a morally ambiguous and, as Peter says, 'not un-heroic' character. He has the injured and more than slightly comic pride of a fallen angel nursing his dignity. (pp. 182-83)

To encounter Peter Pan and Hook—the Christ and Satan of Barrie's religion—is something that can only be achieved by belief. The play is largely about faith. The Darling children can only fly if they 'think lovely wonderful thoughts and they lift you up in the air'; the fairy dust sprinkled on them by Peter is not in itself enough (faith is necessary as well as the sacraments). At the end of the story, as it is told in *Peter and Wendy*, the children gradually lose their belief in Peter, and so cannot see him any longer. . . . And, at the greatest crisis in the play, not only the characters in it but the audience itself is called on to make a demonstration of faith:

> PETER: . . . Tink, dear Tink, are you dying?. . . She says —she says she thinks she could get well again if children believed in fairies! *(He rises and throws out his arms he knows not to whom, perhaps to the boys and girls of whom he is not one.)* Do you believe in fairies? Say quick that you believe! If you believe, clap your hands!
>
> (pp. 183-84)

The public affirmed its faith in Barrie's newly minted religion.

Of course, it was not really new. Barrie was dealing with symbols which children's writers had been using for almost a half century before him. Most of all he had taken up that familiar figure the Beautiful Child and had turned it to brilliant use. In fact he had split it into two. One half he made into a child-god, Peter Pan himself, who is an expression of all that the child-worshippers of Mrs Molesworth's generation had tried to say. Peter is a kind of heavenly equivalent of Little Lord Fauntleroy. The other half, the mortal child (in the characters of Wendy and her brothers), is like Wordsworth's infant who comes into this world at birth with a memory of the heavenly life he used to lead. But Barrie's children have not come from the Christian heaven, but from fairyland. (p. 184)

Yet Barrie was a man of boxes-within-boxes, and he could not create anything without mocking and standing back from it. *Peter Pan* established a quasi-religion, the early twentieth-century fairy cult; but the play itself is, on its deepest level, a satire of religion and a mockery of belief.

'To die will be an awfully big adventure,' says Peter at his grandest moment; but it is a piece of empty self-observing rhetoric. The stage directions to this scene remark that his self-sacrifice in the Mermaids' Lagoon is quite unnecessary—he could perfectly well swim or fly to safety, but he wants to be a hero. . . . Moreover, Peter's words derive not from any faith in the Christian after-life, or in any other external religion, but from stories about Peter himself. . . . By putting these words into the play Barrie is making Peter in effect a worshipper at his own altar. The apparent religious awe invoked by the speech is therefore utterly deceptive. Peter knows nothing at all about real death, which he could not experience anyway, given the utterly cyclical and sterile nature of his existence. Yet Barrie throws the words in simply for the effect they produce at that moment, and also one suspects for mockery too. (pp. 184-85)

If Peter is Christ-like, then he is a Christ of an extraordinarily self-regarding kind. As Wendy remarks to him, 'It is so queer that the stories you like best should be the ones about yourself.' Is Barrie here remarking on, say, the overwhelming preoccupation of the Christ of St John's Gospel with his own nature?

Is he saying that in the end all religions are utterly introverted, are concerned only with themselves?

Barrie's audience is meant to realise that the Never Never Land is entirely untrue. The 'secondary world' in *Peter Pan* does not exist except in the children's imaginations. The play is constantly hinting at this. The introductory remarks to Act II state that the Land can only be seen in dreams ('In the daytime you think the Never Land is only make-believe . . .') and in *Peter and Wendy* Barrie describes it as simply 'a map of a child's mind', the ideal adventure-land, 'not large and sprawly, you know, with tedious distances between one adventure and another, but nicely crammed'. There is no question about it being real. Unlike his predecessors who created Arcadias, Barrie is constantly stating that his dream-land *is* a dream. The play is a detailed map of the earthly paradise, the secret garden, more detailed than that made by any other writer. But at the same time it is a statement that such a territory is only to be found in the imagination. Barrie invokes religious belief in this creation only to dismiss it as childish nonsense.

And it is this, surely, which accounts for the terrible whimsy which overlays *Peter Pan* and almost everything else that Barrie wrote. He does not believe in his own creations. How could he do so, given his extraordinary detachment of mind from himself, from other people, and from everything they say and do? His whole self is not engaged in the creation of his stories:

there is always a part which stands back and mocks them. And so comes the whimsy: it is partly satirical, a deliberate exaggeration and mockery of such things as parental affection and a delight in fairy stories; and it seems also to be a kind of mockery of his audience, a deliberate giving-them-what-they-want, a tongue-in-cheek pandering to the popular taste which demanded pretty stories for the nursery, and liked to hear about loving mothers and beautiful children. It is in this spirit, surely, rather than with any sincerity, that we are told that 'when the first baby laughed for the first time, the laugh broke into a thousand pieces and they all went skipping about, and that was the beginning of fairies'. Barrie wants to show us the appalling depths to which our sentimentality towards children can lead us. One part of him is being horribly sentimental; the other part is standing back and mocking it. Anthony Hope, author of *The Prisoner of Zenda,* was one of the few dissenting voices at the premiere of *Peter Pan,* and is said to have remarked amid the rapturous reception of the play, 'Oh for an hour of Herod.' But Barrie himself is playing Herod to his own creation. At the heart of the sentimental dream is a cynical, mocking voice. (pp. 185-86)

Humphrey Carpenter, "J. M. Barrie and 'Peter Pan':
'That Terrible Masterpiece'," in his Secret Gardens:
A Study of the Golden Age of Children's Literature,
Houghton Mifflin Company, 1985, pp. 170-87.

Betsy (Cromer) Byars

1928-

American author of fiction and picture books and illustrator.

Byars is recognized as one of the most popular and prolific authors of contemporary realistic fiction for middle grade and junior high school readers. Called "one of the best writers for children in the world" by critic Nancy Chambers, Byars is lauded for creating adventurous works which blend humor and sympathy to address the universal emotions of childhood. Concentrating on themes of maturation and relationships with family, peers, and animals, she frequently portrays the growth of respect and understanding between child and adult characters. A distinctive mixture of unsentimental pathos, humor, and fundamental optimism coupled with an attraction to life's oddities allows her to examine successfully subjects usually considered too disturbing to young readers. Her noncondescending, sensitive presentations of such difficult topics as parental abandonment and wife abuse, as well as her focus on fragmented families, point to Byars's timeliness and belief in the maturity of children. Her works often feature troubled but likeable male protagonists who are misfits or loners, and she generally includes unconventional adults who are sometimes distinguished by their eccentricity. To lighten the heaviness of her subject matter and to advance her plots, Byars uses comical situations and witty dialogue. These techniques, combined with her insight into children's fantasies, fears, and experiences, help make her works consistently well liked. For a younger audience, Byars has written several picture books, mainly centering on anthropomorphic animals, two of which she has illustrated in pen-and-ink and watercolor drawings.

Byars is commended as a thoughtful and original writer who creates fresh, convincing characterizations, skillful portrayals of human interaction, vibrant images, and deceptively simple prose. While occasional critics find her plot endings contrived, Byars is well regarded as a compassionate explorer of the social and moral issues confronting her audience.

Byars has received numerous adult- and child-selected awards for her works. *The Midnight Fox* won the Lewis Carroll Shelf Award in 1970 and *The Summer of the Swans* was awarded the Newbery Medal in 1971. In addition, *The House of Wings* was a National Book Award finalist in 1973 and *The Night Swimmers* was a *Boston Globe-Horn Book* Honor Book in 1980 and won the American Book Award in 1981. Byars received the Regina Medal in 1987 for her body of work.

(See also *CLR*, Vol. 1; *Contemporary Literary Criticism*, Vol. 35; *Something about the Author Autobiography Series*, Vol. 1; *Something about the Author*, Vols. 4, 46; *Contemporary Authors New Revision Series*, Vol. 18; *Contemporary Authors*, Vols. 33-36 rev. ed.; and *Dictionary of Literary Biography*, Vol. 52: *American Writers for Children since 1960; Fiction*.)

AUTHOR'S COMMENTARY

[The following excerpt is taken from an address given in Canterbury, England in September, 1985.]

Photograph by Edward Byars. Courtesy of Betsy Byars.

[It] has now been twenty-five years and twenty-five books [since I began writing], and every time I sit down to write a book, I feel like that character in the old fairy tale who, in order to survive, has to spin straw into gold. What I know about spinning straw is nil and I have learned from hard reality that no little man in a funny suit is going to pop out of the woodwork to strike a deal.

I went to a school once in Virginia, and I had ages five to fourteen in the gym, and I told the kids that after I talked, they could ask questions. One little boy in the front row put up his hand and held it up all during my speech and so I called him first. His question was, 'All my life,'—he was seven—'All my life I have wanted to write a book, but I've never been able to get enough paper.' Well, I explained that writers never wait for the perfect sheet of paper, that sometimes I write on old envelopes, and he shook his head. Then I explained that one of the things publishers do really well is provide the paper for the printing of the book. He's still shaking his head, and I'm relieved to see a teacher's hand up. The teacher's question was, 'Some of the children are beginning to write stories of their own and they would like some tips on plot construction.'

Now, up until this moment, I had never even thought of plot construction. I had started out instinctively writing books that had very simple, from point A to point B plots, in which you take your characters from point A to point B and you let things happen to them along the way. That was all I was capable of at the time because just getting the book down on paper was enough of a challenge. I couldn't clutter up my mind with a plot. I did two of these point A to point B books, and I was getting easier with my dialogue and description, and so on my next book I constructed what I considered my first real plot. If I had wasted one moment thinking about what I was doing, I'm sure I couldn't have done it. So at this point, looking back on my career, I can see something about plot construction, but standing in the gymnasium in front of hundreds of kids, and after already blowing the paper question, I blurted out that I never let myself think about plot construction, and added, foolishly, that I also never let myself think of theme or characterisation.

My one goal in writing, then and now, is to get my story down on paper, because until the story is on paper, I don't have anything to work with. And I rely totally on instinct. If my instinct tells me the story is not moving fast enough, I speed it up. If my instinct tells me I've told this too quickly, I divide the chapter and add some bull. And the difference between someone who has been writing for twenty-five years and someone who is just starting, is the quality of this instinct. When I first started, I agonised over everything—should I take this out? Should I change this? Is this funny? Is this stupid? And every time I changed something I had the feeling I was ruining a potential masterpiece. After twenty-five years I have learned to follow my instinct without question. (pp. 6-7)

[For example, *Cracker Jackson*] had been written in the first person and submitted to the publisher that way. It had been accepted and rewritten four or five times. I was ready to send it in for the last time. I sat down for one quick read, and I had not read but two or three chapters before I realised that I had made a terrible mistake in letting Jackson tell the story. I should have told it. I sat there for about three seconds while the thoughts flashed through my mind that I had a contract for this book and the editors liked it as it was and I had already spent the money I had got for it, and then I went to my typewriter and started over.

The opening sequence I worked over more than anything I have ever written.

> 'There's a letter for you.'
>
> 'For me?' Jackson was pleased. He didn't get that much mail. 'Where?'
>
> 'On the coffee table.'
>
> The envelope was pink. There were yellow roses on the flap. His name and address were in pencil. There was nothing to indicate danger.
>
> 'Who's it from?' his mother asked.
>
> 'Well, let me open it.'
>
> He lifted the flap, took out the sheet of paper, and unfolded it.
>
> There was only one sentence. He read it and stopped breathing.
>
> 'Keep away, Cracker, or he'll hurt you.'

I'm sure you're thinking that the passage seems incredibly simple, that I couldn't have worked on it at all. That, to me, is the whole goal of writing. You write until it seems you have not worked on it at all, and then you stop. As long as the

passage reads as if you've worked on it, you aren't finished. You have to work on it some more.

But there has to be more to this spinning process than just instinct, and of course there is. Now when I first started writing, I was strictly on my own. I didn't know any editors, any other writers, and I was not getting very far very fast. I finally decided to get a degree in Library Science so I would have something to fall back on. One of my library courses was in children's literature, and my teacher said during class one day—this seemed at the time, the first concrete 'put the straw in slot A' instruction I had received—she said—and I'm sure she said it better than I'm going to now—that in a good children's novel, the main character was different at the end of the book than he or she was in the beginning. That made instant sense to me. If what happened to your character was important enough, then the person would be changed, and if it was a weak story and nothing really happened, then you couldn't write all those wonderful paragraphs that start out, 'Now she saw that . . .' or 'All of a sudden she knew . . .' I took this straight to heart. I started looking for the kind of stuff, raw material, straw, that had good strong fibres, and actually that has become part of my formula, if you want to call it that. I take characters, ordinary people, and throw them into a crisis, and I think that is one reason I haven't done a sequel—I feel one crisis is enough for anybody.

Then I came to realise that in order to make the story more dramatic, I had to somehow put the main character on his or her own. I had to get rid of the parents. I am certainly not the first author to come to this realisation, but I don't know of any author who has taken to ridding herself of parents with the fervour that I have. Parents went to Hunter City to give birth, to Europe on holiday, to Ohio to work, to Detroit seeking work. I favoured occupations involving travel like truck driving and country western singing. I fell back on pneumonia, plane crashes, car accidents and coal mine disasters. In *The pinballs* I managed to get rid of six parents in two and a half pages, which I consider something of a record, something for other writers to shoot at.

I noticed that a story had more immediacy, more impact if it happened in a short length of time. This was a gradual realisation, just a sort of lassitude that came over me when I had to start a chapter with, 'Two months later, Tom still had not . . .' I didn't like gaps like that. Of my novels, ten take place in no more than two or three days, four are a matter of weeks, two take place in one summer, and the rest prove my point.

Then it came to me that the real secret of spinning straw into gold was the idea itself. When an author gets an idea that suits her abilities and interests perfectly—no matter if the parents are on the scene, no matter if the story takes ten years to unfold, then the author will write better than she actually can, she will write above her abilities, and the end result will be a golden story. This is true. I've had the experience a time or two myself. But what are you going to do while waiting for this idea that will unlock your hidden talents? Because sometimes—many times actually—I had no idea whatsoever and had to face the unfortunate truth that in order to spin straw into gold, you at least have to have the straw. So I used whatever came my way. *The night swimmers* is a good example. I was visiting a friend in West Virginia and she had a small swimming pool. As we were leaving to go out one night, she commented that she was very worried because whenever they went out, some neighbourhood kids came over and swam in the pool. She was terribly worried one of them would drown. As soon as she said that, I thought THE NIGHT SWIMMERS, and as soon as I got home, I put a sheet of paper in my typewriter and typed 'THE NIGHT SWIMMERS by Betsy Byars'. All I needed now were 150 pages and I would have a book.

I started writing instantly. The kids—incidentally if I can pick how many characters I'm going to have I pick three and mix up the sexes, and in my own mind my books are divided into one-character books and three-character books. This was a three-character book, and the kids were sneaking out of the bushes in their underwear to swim in the pool. My intention at this point was to do a mystery. I love mysteries and here was my chance to write one. The kids would see something going on in the house, but they wouldn't be able to tell what they had seen, and I was very excited over this idea. The trouble with the plan soon became apparent. I couldn't think of anything for the kids to see—nothing. The time was dragging on, the kids were getting waterlogged, and I had nothing.

At this point in my life we were getting ready to move from West Virginia to South Carolina. We had lived in this house for twenty years, and I was going through closets and chests daily. One morning I came across a diary my daughter had kept when she was ten. I would not have read it if I had come across it when she was keeping it, but my daughter was now grown-up and I needed a laugh so I opened it. The whole diary was how much she hated her sister. I had realised there was a bit of 'sibling rivalry', but this was hatred. And as I read, I remembered that when I was growing up my mother would sometimes come in the bedroom I shared with my sister and draw a chalk line down the centre of the room to prevent us from crossing over and killing each other. At this point I decided to change *The night swimmers* from a mystery to a book about a brother and sister who get to the place where they hate each other. I'm sure that if I hadn't changed, I would still be sitting ther waiting for the mysterious event the children would see in the house.

I'm a very practical writer. With every book I come to halts; some are so severe that I literally have no idea how this story is going to end. I have learned to live with these halts, and if I just go on about my life as if nothing is wrong, sometimes my brain will throw me a bone. If that doesn't happen, I do one of two things. First, I read the manuscript as if I am the reader. In a children's book, for example, if you write a two-hundred word paragraph on a tree, somebody better fall out of that tree. Kids don't want to waste time reading about something that is not going to matter in this story, so that's what I'm looking for. In *The two-thousand-pound goldfish* I came to one of these halts, and on reading and rereading the manuscript I discovered that I had been sending the reader signals about the poor health of the grandmother. Now I did not want the grandmother to die. And the main reason was that in the US people are continually getting up lists—lists of books on divorce, books on various diseases, and I realised that if the grandmother dies, somebody will put this book on a list entitled 'Death and Dying', and I didn't think I could stand that. Finally I realised that grandmother had to die, and not only that, I was going to have to have a funeral. The book would probably end up on a 'Funeral' list.

The other thing I do when I come to a halt is go to the library. I take down book after book and read opening sentences in each chapter. And I will think, 'Of course, the phone is ringing and it's . . .' and I will hurry home to start writing.

Some things that I had never thought were important turned out to be vital to the writing of books. Research has made an enormous difference. Although I never got my Library Science degree, my library training has proved invaluable. If it's in the library, I can find it. If it isn't, I know how to get it. *The house of wings* came about through research. We had had a local story in the newspaper about a sandhill crane that had got lost and injured in migration, and I thought, well, I'll read about cranes and see if there's anything in it for me. (pp. 6-11)

I got a lot of tips from other weavers. Some I listed to, some I didn't. An English teacher wrote me shortly after *Trouble river* was published to deplore my use of the double negative. In that book, grandma uses the double negative almost exclusively, and the English teacher wrote that she was trying to break her students of using the double negative, and I had reinforced it. I wrote back that I would try, but occasionally there is no substitute for the double negative. (p. 11)

Other things people told me I had accepted. A librarian told me I had made a mistake in not having chapter headings in one book, that one of the ways children select books is by reading the chapter titles, and ever since she told me that I have worked as hard on my chapter titles as I do on my book titles. I try to make them almost a book synopsis, and at the same time intriguing enough to make them have to read the book.

Another librarian told me that the two things kids always find funny are wise-cracking kids and bathroom humour. Since that time, I have had at least one wise-cracking kid and, if possible, bathroom humour in every book I have written. . . .

I finally learned the value of that old, old advice, 'Write about what you know.' I first heard that chestnut when I was in second grade and I thought it was the worst advice I had ever heard. Oh, it's fine to write about what you know if you are a wild game hunter in Africa, but if you are a seven-year-old girl living in a small rural cotton mill town, then you'd better make stuff up. I did this for a long time, even into my professional writing career, but the first real success that I had was in writing about what I knew—kids, family life, and so on. The reason I ignored that bit of advice was because nobody ever told me the reason for it. I finally figured it out for myself. The most important asset an author has is a feeling of authority. I don't know which word came first, author or authority, but they're closely linked in my mind. When I'm writing about something that I know happened because I was there, I write with an authority. I put a lot of my life in my books. Of course, I have to update it somewhat because a fifty-year-old childhood would not exactly fit into my today stories. (p. 12)

I learned the importance of having something read well, and that the only way you can be sure is to read it aloud. If it doesn't read aloud well, then there's something wrong and you need to work on it some more. I have a friend who reads her whole book into a tape recorder and listens to it. I couldn't do that because I can't stand the sound of my voice, but I do mutter a lot over my typewriter. I now have a word processor, which I love, and that's what it's particularly good at—getting something to read right, allowing me to change, change, and change again until it reads right, and then it is.

But this spinning process turns out to be even more complicated than all these things. It's an individual thing. An author has to take her personal strengths, whatever they are—humour, pathos, simplicity, a way of creating new worlds, or a way of bringing back old ones, craziness, sanity, whatever she has, and she has to somehow work that in with the strands of straw. And as if that wasn't enough, she has to, at the same time, not get so involved that the story can't grow on its own. Whew! If this were one of my books, how easily I would wrap it up. 'Suddenly I saw that . . .' 'Now I understand that . . .' And maybe the truth is that simple. We authors write the best we can, with what skills we have, what tricks we've learned, and then if we are lucky, very lucky, the straw actually will be turned into gold, for a fleeting moment by the miraculous mind of a child. (p. 13)

> *Betsy Byars, "Spinning Straw into Gold," in The School Librarian, Vol. 34, No. 1, March, 1986, pp. 6-13.*

GENERAL COMMENTARY

INA ROBERTSON

Reviewers have not always been . . . kind to Betsy Byars. Her early books received little praise from critics, but fortunately for all who have been captivated by her later works, she did continue to write and has created outstanding modern, realistic stories enjoyed by children and adults.

When her first book, *Clementine,* was published in 1962, one reviewer wrote, "The concept is a nice enough projection of imaginative play, but the writing verges on the precious." . . . Her second book, *The Dancing Camel* (1965) fared somewhat better when another writer declared, "It offers a tidy little moral without much meat" [see *CLR*, Vol. 1]. *Rama the Gypsy Cat* (1966) was treated more kindly and affirmed to be "true both to the accidents of life and to cat psychology" [see excerpt below dated January 15, 1967], but *The Groober* (1967) was classified as a marginal book to be given careful consideration before purchasing. . . . (pp. 328-29)

But beginning with *The Midnight Fox* in 1968, . . . books by Byars have been placed on recommended reading lists while reviewers and readers acclaim her distinctive style of writing books that young people of today can understand and accept. Byars is now viewed as an artist who can create vivid characters, use deft dialogue, inject just enough humor into situations, fashion plots that are convincing and tightly structured as well as entertaining, and make a comment on today's world. She is a thoughtful, sensitive writer with extraordinary ability to help her readers view those portions of society captured in her books.

Many of Byars' books do not have the more traditionally-accepted happy endings. Aiden Chambers, British writer and critic, believes that Byars challenges children as readers and challenges the commonplace assumptions about children and childhood. For many years it was assumed that children needed happy endings to their stories, but Chambers acknowledges that Betsy Byars does not feel children need or want clear-cut, optimistic endings. Chambers writes:

> Plainly, Byars believes that children of seven or eight and older are not only able, but willing to take on and make their own, without psychological damage . . . harsh truths about life which we all, children and adults, often wish were otherwise. And quite properly in my view, she accepts the responsibility as an author for offering children such truths communicated in a form they can connect with.
>
> On the surface, Mrs. Byars offers children an appealing text, seemingly easy to lift from the page and make their own. A text full of fun and interest. Her subjects are all child-attractive—bullies, animals, physical danger, fears universally known. But she

composes her stories so that once absorbed by the surface attractions, her readers are led to contemplate the deeper issues of her tale without their feeling any strain in doing so. Indeed, they wish to do so. The challenge is hidden, but the responsiveness of her readers shows that it is eagerly accepted.

Byars states that she must present challenges in her books. She wrote, "Living with my own teenagers taught me that I must not write down to my readers; I must write up to them. Boys and girls are very sharp today. When I visit classrooms and talk with students, I am always impressed to find out how many of them are writing stories of their own and how knowledgeable they are about writing." (p. 329)

And this may be the secret of Betsy Byars' success as an author of books for young people. For in addition to her compassion, humor and insight, she has a true respect for her audience which is unmistakably clear in all her books.

Many of Byars' books are contemporary realistic fiction, but no discussion of her works would be complete without giving special attention to the picture book she wrote and illustrated in 1975, *The Lace Snail.* Described as a quiet simple story by her publishers, the book tells of the Snail, who, on her way to the pond, started to leave a trail of lace behind her. Everyone wanted to know why.

> "How do you do that, Snail?" they asked.
>
> The Snail didn't know.
>
> "It's just the way life is, I think," she said.

Snail philosophically accepts the fact that she can create fine lacy patterns "which she generously shares with all of the animals in her environment. She subtly points out that all are deserving of lace, from the lowest bug to the huge hippo". . . . The book is illustrated in two colors, black and green, with large uncluttered pages showing the animals and the lace created by the Snail. The lace has a pointillistic quality, looking as if it were made by quickly touching the tip of the paint brush to the paper, making intricate lace patterns overlaid on the dark green animals. With her soft green and black colors adding to the story, the author tells her readers that the most generous gifts are those given naturally.

If success is measured by awards, Byars is extremely successful, for in addition to the Newbery Medal for the *Summer of the Swans* in 1971, her books have received recognition from many sources. . . . Byars' books have been translated into Danish, Dutch, Finnish, German, Japanese and Norwegian. *Trouble River, The 18th Emergency, Summer of the Swans, The Winged Colt of Casa Mia* and *Pinballs* have been dramatized and presented on national television. Byars' books are available in a variety of formats: cloth, paper, filmstrips with cassettes or records, and selections from her writings have been included in graded-reading series.

The Pinballs was the recipient of a recent noteworthy award, when it was placed on the "Special IBBY (International Board of Books for the Young) International Year of the Child Honor List" in the category of "Promoting Concern for the Disadvantaged and Handicapped." (pp. 329, 331)

The Pinballs is a modern story of child abuse, a topic much in the news today. Three lonely foster children, a girl and two boys, each bearing scars of parental neglect or abuse, come together in a foster home. This new setting provides a supportive environment and they begin to understand and to care for one another. (p. 331)

Ina Robertson, "Betsy Byars—Writer for Today's Child," in Language Arts, *Vol. 57, No. 3, March, 1980, pp. 328-34.*

LOIS R. KUZNETS

I am looking forward to hearing and seeing Betsy Byars at the Eighth Annual ChLA Conference in Minneapolis. Not only am I, naturally, interested in whatever she has to say about children's literature, but I am, frankly, curious to find out whether Byars, in person, presents some of the same contrast between book and cover that I sense when I read her biographical blurbs or look at her picture on the dust covers of her novels.

Why, I wonder, does she choose usually to write about mobile, fragmented American families when she, herself, seems clearly to have led a stable and settle existence, married with four children, in a West Virginia community not far from the North Carolina region where she was born and brought up? More whimsically, I wonder, too, how someone who seems never to have changed her conservative page-boy hair style is so willing to be experimental in both form and substance of her books.

In preparation for writing this review, I read as many of the some eighteen Byars' children's books as I could get my hands on (several for the first time, I must admit). I am not given to such grand accolades as British *Signal* editor, Nancy Chambers, tosses off, "... Betsy Byars goes on being one of the ten best writers for children in the world." ... Still, I was impressed by both the quantity and quality of Byars' books since her first, *Clementine,* a humorous and delicately controlled depiction of a young boy's projection of self on a dragon-shaped stuffed sock (of all things!)

Whatever its variety, the corpus of Byars' work seems generally to exhibit several characteristically American traits: 1) she often depicts "the call of the wild," the fascination that rural field, forest, stream, animal and bird exert on most Americans, even those from modern urban areas; 2) she expresses the fascination with mass-produced objects and entertainment that is similarly a part of our "culture," with a lower-case "c"; 3) she is concerned with bringing to the attention of her readers the consciousness of creatures (both animal and human) that are inarticulate, naturally or unnaturally, and often maimed and vulnerable; 4) she is interested in the role that a combination of imaginative playfulness and self-depreciating, "Woody Allen" type humor has in the growth and development of her typical young protagonists. These traits, combined with the contemporary American sensitivity to the breakdown of the nuclear family, seem to me to be exhibited to a greater or lesser extent in most of Byars' novels.

Her Newbery Medal winner, *The Summer of the Swans,* is perhaps the best known of these, but is not, I think, typical of her best work. *The Summer of the Swans* is distinguished from the usual tale of "ugly duckling into swan," by the perceptive portrayal of a retarded child, Charlie, younger brother of Sara, the developing adolescent protagonist. But some of Byars' strengths are muted in this book. Novels like *The Midnight Fox, The House of Wings,* and *The Winged Colt of Casa Mia* displayed Byars' talents to better advantage. Male, rather than female protagonists, seem to be Byars' forte in characterization through thought and speech patterns. Byars' success in the depiction of animals non-anthropomorphically which has been clear since her early *Rama the Gypsy Cat,* is fully evident in the latter three books where all three protagonists have relationships with vulnerable wild creatures. These creatures are not merely symbolic, as the swans are in *The Summer of the Swans.* They are real to begin with, have relationships with the protagonists, and gradually acquire symbolic meaning in the characters' lives. Their presence gives a richness and depth to the depiction of the character's development; Sara's relationship to Charlie is perhaps meant to do the same, but does not work quite so well because it is overshadowed by teen-age romance.

Byars' fictional children rarely appear in the habitat of conventional nuclear families; they have been deserted, or temporarily abandoned by one parent or both; the parents are sometimes victims of circumstances beyond their control, but are often themselves infantile and occasionally vicious. Some of the most satisfactory relationships that develop are between children and other relatives: grandmother and grandson in *Trouble River,* grandfather and grandson in *The House of Wings,* uncle and nephew in *The Winged Colt of Casa Mia,* and, to a less satisfactory extent, aunt and nieces and nephew in *The Summer of the Swan.* The adults in these cases are by no means stereotypical and any one interested in nonconventional portraits of the elderly might look closely at the first two of these works. Foster parents in *The Pinballs* and a friendly policeman in *The TV Kid* also serve as parent substitutes; peers often try to do the same, as in *After The Goat Man* and *The Pinballs,* with some success. Her recent *The Night Swimmers* depicts mothering as an unfair and distorting burden on an older sister.

Byars at the age of one. She comments, "This is the only time I was a cute kid. It was downhill from here on." Courtesy of Betsy Byars.

In some of these books, the seriousness in the children's situations and the shallowness of the help provided do not seem to warrant the optimistic note on which the books end. Several reviewers of Byars' *Good-bye, Chicken Little* have commented on a dichotomy between seriousness of situation and comic tone in that book as well. In contrast to the optimism that, perhaps inappropriately, characterizes books like *After the Goat Man* and *The Pinballs*, there seems to be a swing toward pessimism in *The Cartoonist*. The young cartoonist is completely alienated from a TV-freak mother, an irresponsible older brother, and a powerless grandfather. He comes down from the attic into which he has locked himself, but back into a world in which he also cannot expect the kind of understanding he craves from his older sister, his best friend, or his teacher, all of whom seem also to have failed him; he is a wonderfully imaginative cartoonist (his ideas for cartoons display Byars' wry humor at its best), but nobody else but the reader has discovered this by the end of the book; it seems doubtful that his cartoons can control the chaos, or make up for the emptiness of his real life.

There is a bias in my taste towards classic children's literature that makes me like best those Byars' novels that express her own love of nature as part of the development of her characters and like less those Byars' novels that move clearly in the direction of the modern "problem" novel. Of the latter, I find *The TV Kid* by far the most satisfactory. The protagonist is, first of all, not permanently maimed or seriously deprived in spite of the fact that he is living with a single parent struggling to make her own living. He has simply slipped part of the way into the world of TV, which, in itself, has provided him with some creative opportunities in fashioning fantasies. His preference for these fantasies yields to the pain and reality of a rattlesnake bite acquired in the dubious situation of breaking and entering summer houses in order to play out these fantasies.

Not only do I find the problems and solutions in *The TV Kid* to be fitted to each other in seriousness, but it is the one Byars book in which I am fully comfortable with her depiction of an adult female of parental age as both unconventional and yet a successful parent. Depictions of such females in other books seem to be either stereotypical or condemning, or both. Yet Byars is capable of depicting a spirited grandmother in *Trouble River* and unconventionally competent or aggressive young girls in *After the Goat Man, The Pinballs,* and *The Night Swimmers.*

The body of Byars' work has been made up of realistic novels for the middle-age child, but she has written a few books for a much younger audience. The most distinguished of these is a picture book *The Lace Snail*. . . . Combined with the tough but vulnerable little boy dialogue of which Byars is a master, is the whimsy of a snail who, for a brief period, finds herself making a trail of lace rather than slime and who gives the lace to anyone who asks for it, big or small, bug or hippo, polite or rude, saying "You deserve lace as much as anyone."

The element in Byars' style that I find most attractive and memorable is her capturing of imaginative, quirky observations and putting them into colloquial speech patterns. I hope that Byars is as funny in person as she can be in print. (pp. 31-3)

Whether she is funny or not, I'm looking forward to running across not only Betsy Byars in Minneapolis, but also many more of Byars' young boys, in their American settings. (p. 33)

Lois R. Kuznets, "Betsy Byars' Slice of 'American Pie'," in Children's Literature Association Quarterly, *Vol. 5, No. 4, Winter, 1981, pp. 31-3.*

STUART HANNABUSS

One of the writers to move on through the obviousness of everyday reality to what young people feel deep down is Betsy Byars. She often uses a kind of fantasy to do this, developing it as a way of expressing the central characters' preoccupations, and then allowing them to mature through these preoccupations to some kind of compromise with other people. In doing this she encourages readers to give themselves a pretty close look too. *The Eighteenth Emergency* moves through the fantasy of Benjie's having seventeen solutions to disasters that might happen to his coping with the eighteenth which is all too real: the bullying of Marv Hammerman at school. It is a funny and scary book at the same time, full of twists and turns and eccentric turns of phrase. . . . Her more recent *The Cartoonist* takes a young man who locks himself in the attic room of the house because he does not want to give up his personal space to his feckless and over-rated elder brother. Simple enough as a storyline, but shown from within most sensitively: the attic is the only place where Alfie feels happy, where he can express himself fully in his cartoons, through which he works out lots of his thoughts. His gesture to stay put takes on increasing power when the reader knows what is involved and the final solution, helped by a convenient twist of fate, is no weak escape clause. By the end we have all worked pretty hard and our emotions are deeper for the experience. Throughout Betsy Byars brings in touches of droll fantasy, which amuse *and* tell us much about the way the hero's mind works, that is the closeness between real life and his mixed up view of it:

> . . . He could never come down the ladder into the harsh light of the living room, no matter what happened. It was impossible . . . Maybe when he was very old, he thought, eighty or ninety, when there was nothing left of the boy he had been, maybe then he would come down. He would be an old man, straggly beard, long grey hair, as thin as a skeleton, bent with arthritis and malnutrition. He would lift the trapdoor at last, trembling with effort, shaking in every limb, and slowly climb down the ladder. There in the faded living room he would discover that his family—Mom, Alma, and Pap—had moved away years ago. A new family lived in the house now, a family who hadn't even known he was up there. He would stand bewildered and lost, blinking in the light, as frightened and confused at seeing the strangers as they were at seeing him. . . .

Betsy Byars' skill at getting inside the mind in this way allows her astonishing scope to explore ways in which young people cope with things that start by being too big for them and then finally fall into perspective. (pp. 173-74)

Stuart Hannabuss, "Beyond the Formula: Part II," in The Junior Bookshelf, *Vol. 46, No. 5, October, 1982, pp. 173-77.*

I. V. HANSEN

Within the space of 10 years, Betsy Byars has brought her vivid portraits of small boys full circle. This is not to suggest that her female protagonists lack vitality: Sara, in *The Summer of the Swans,* is a character rich in teenage humour and genuine compassion; Carlie, in *The Pinballs,* has a steely determination to set against the harsh reality of her situation; Retta, in *The Night Swimmers,* takes on her elder sister responsibilities with a kind of nobility. But Byars' boys are the characters that ring so true.

The gallery of portraits is uneven, understandable in a writer whose output is extensive: one cannot get it right every time. The balance and sense of proportion are sometimes skewed, as in the period that produced Alfie in *The Cartoonist* and Jimmie in *Good-bye, Chicken Little*: here, the light framework of the novels cannot quite bear the load it is expected to carry, and the boys themselves are comparative shadows, in my view, Alfie almost indiscernible and Jimmie almost peripheral. Nevertheless, Byars has given us five or six other small boys who are totally genuine, whose very gestures and facial expressions show them sliding into a life independent of the pages of a book. Their appeal as characters is wide: the 10 or 11 year old reader giggles in recognition, the 22 year old education student is delighted to discover them, and parents laugh in relief that the world may be, after all, as they know it. I am aware of one theologian who quotes from Byars in lectures.

It would appear at first that American cultural imperialism has made the Byars novels readily accessible to English speakers. Outside the United States, readers are familiar with New World youth through television family situation series, as they are familiar with popsicle sticks, apartment buildings, and those wide suburban streets, with school classrooms and Hallowe'en and baseball. It may be claimed, however, that Byars' young characters have a universality to be seen matched by English, Dutch, Yugoslav, and Australian television characters, for example, and in children's novels the world over. Byars' ambience is secondary: it is the people of her novels who behave so familiarly. (pp. 3-4)

Parents who cannot understand what their children are saying, the gravity of playing games, the importance of television to children, these are some of the elements of which Byars' protagonists are made. Two of the novels in particular encapsulate the world of the author's young boy, novels separated in publication date by almost a decade. They are *The Eighteenth Emergency*, first published in 1973, and *The Cybil War*, first published in 1981. In the former novel, Benjamin Fawley, called Mouse, and his friend Ezzie fantasise about life's great emergencies, such as how best to deal with Emergency Five—being choked by a boa constrictor, and Emergency Nine—approach of mad elephants. Now Mouse faces the Eighteenth Emergency, how to escape from Marv Hammerman, the school bully, and his associates, Tony Lionni and the boy in the black sweat shirt. Impelled by a series of English lessons on the concept of honour, Mouse finally confronts Hammerman, and although sorely beaten for his pains, limps tall back to Ezzie. In *The Cybil War*, Simon Newton and his friend, Tony, are both enamoured of Cybil Ackerman, Simon ever since third grade, and between the two boys there develops a veritable civil war. After numberless vicissitudes, Simon finally has the unalloyed delight of cycling the streets with his Cybil, and the war is over.

Structurally, the novels are closely related. Byars' boys never have accessible fathers: Mouse's father has been driving a truck for the past two years and Mouse hardly ever sees him; Simon's father has left home to embrace an alternative life-style, living on boats and in forests, and has written letters only seldom. Mrs. Fawley deals at home with cosmetic orders and tells Mouse he imagines things; Mrs. Newton attends Parents Without Partners meetings and everlastingly asks Simon, "What's wrong?" Neither boy has domestic support when he needs it most.

Both novels have peripheral male figures—old, large men. Mr. Casino distresses Mouse: a one-time furniture mover, whose strength was legendary, Mr. Casino has been reduced to a shambling hulk by a stroke. One of Mrs. Fawley's neighbourly gestures is to have Mouse take Mr. Casino for walks. Mouse senses the power of sinew and muscle that he craves slumbering useless in this vast man. Simon's friend, Tony, has a grandfather he calls Pap-pap. But Pap-pap is hugely sentimental and prone to floods of tears, brought on by the memory of the smell of his mother's apron or by hearing that Simon's father has left home: he can offer to Simon no firmness of purpose.

There are dogs. In *The Eighteenth Emergency* is Garbage-Dog, "good old G.D.," a nondescript stray who lives near Mouse's apartment building, and who provides Mouse and Ezzie with both solace and amazement, like the time when the boys found a live turtle in his mouth. Simon, in *The Cybil War,* has his own dog, T-Bone, whom he dresses as a pirate for a pet show and who offers him at least some private comfort: T-Bone, in the living room, opens his eyes but does not lift his head and thumps his tail once on the hearth. (pp. 5-6)

Ezzie is a warm friend, ineffectual, but warm. When Hammerman stalks Mouse, Ezzie is on the look-out. (p. 6)

The relationship between Simon and Tony, however, has never been certain. Tony makes up stories about Simon for cheap laughs. Whether by chance or design on the part of the author, Tony's surname is Angotti. One of the minor characters in *The Eighteenth Emergency* is the statuesque Viola Angotti, a girl at Mouse's school who refuses to allow the diminutive hero to put her in a garbage-can and hits him in the stomach harder than he has ever been hit before. With, therefore, a possible older cousin by fiction like Viola, small wonder Tony Angotti tells lies all the time. Behind his friend's back, Tony invites the desirable Cybil to the movies, pairing off Simon with the undesirable Harriet Haywood in their foursome. At times Tony could be relied upon, like the time when the boys attempted to drill a spy-hole between their adjoining classrooms and Mrs. Albertson discovered them, but not now.

Elementary school teachers figure in both novels. Mr. Stein copes well with boys: if they arrive late, like Mouse, claiming to be ill, Mr. Stein shows he has no reliance on thermometers, for "over the years he had developed an eye for the faker." And he knows his class and will not be distracted. . . .

On the other hand, *The Cybil War*'s Miss McFawn numbers boys among her nonfavourites. (p. 7)

Byar's individual icon or stamp in her novels is the way in which, true to type, her small boys reflect, privately or in company, upon prior experiences, how they recall singular incidents from their past, the "like the time when" motif. Mouse remembers measuring Garbage-Dog's legs as part of an arithmetic assignment on using the ruler and how the class could not believe in such short legs—two and seven-eighths inches; and he remembers how Ezzie used to keep a tooth in his pocket, able to produce it for a teacher as an excuse for leaving the classroom for a drink of water. Simon's memories are sorrowful ones, on the other hand; he remembers writing in third grade an Arbour Day "tribute to trees," and it comes out violently antiarboreal, because he has with finality just realised his father *is* gone; another time he remembers with alarm how, suffering temporary blindness from poison ivy at camp, he is led to the toilets by a boy named Marvin Rollins who refuses to tell him if there are any Daddy-long-legs on the toilet seat. (p. 8)

What often saves the boys from going down under the pressure of their circumstances is a quirky articulateness in thought and speech, wherein lies much of the novels' humour. Mouse's mother is always asking him why he is called Mouse: she explains how nicknames stick and how in later life he will regret the name:

> "I don't think you have to worry. I'm not planning to be president of anything." But the idea had stuck with him. "I, Mouse Fawley, do hereby swear that as president of this great company . . ." It did sound bad. "And now we take great pride in presenting the distinguished and honourable president of our university—Mouse Fawley!" Very bad.
>
> (p. 9)

The Eighteenth Emergency and *The Cybil War* swing in a wide arc and appear to meet. They have much in common, passages of totally natural dialogue, shrewd observations of the world of the child, set comic pieces (Garbage Dog and the turtle, Cybil's and her friends' pet show), young heroes coping with themselves, the technique of memories "like the time when." On the surface, there would appear to be a formula here. The evidence of the Byars' *oeuvre* does not suggest this completely. Between these two titles she has produced stories more sharp-edged, like *The Pinballs, The Cartoonist,* and *Good-bye, Chicken Little.* She had perhaps fallen prey to the realist style in American children's books, but the amused warmth of her worldview has not quite allowed her to pursue social issues. Hers is a fine capacity for delineating the ordinary and the personal. Therefore, in *The Cybil War* (despite an earlier mild flirtation with fantasy in *The Winged Colt of Casa Mia*), Byars returns to problems of simply having to be with others. Perhaps her incidents are in themselves trifling and she elevates them to tragic dimensions, but her ending of the novel is not contrived: Simon must pay for his happiness.

What *The Cybil War* finally demonstrates is the superiority of *The Eighteenth Emergency,* that the two novels do not quite meet in their arc. For the earlier novel has a delicate seriousness lacking in the later one. It is true that the treachery Simon uncovers in his erstwhile friend is a powerful discovery, but Simon glides without great cost into his later contentment. The price Mouse pays is much higher, and the ultimate reward is greater. After the confrontation with Hammerman, Mouse, with aching breastbone and bleeding nose,

> . . . made his way down the sidewalk with his eyes closed. He thought suddenly that if he could see where he was going it would probably not be down Fourth Street at all. He was probably walking across some foreign field. If he could look up, he would not see the tops of buildings, the flat blue sky with a jet trail drawn across it. He would see gold and scarlet tournament flags snapping in the wind. There would be plumes and trumpets and horses in bright trappings. Honour would be a simple thing again and so vital that people would talk of it wherever they went.

The Eighteenth Emergency is a wry, sometimes uproariously humorous story, and yet the medieval vision Mouse has slips easily into its fabric. Byars has not been able to repeat the novel's quality. It is, if not a great children's book, at least a very fine one. The pity of it is that *The Cybil War,* for all its promise, cannot match *The Eighteenth Emergency.* Yet with both titles we should be grateful to Byars for her portraits of small boys in a sometimes bewildering and unfair world: her light touch is the secret of her accessibility. (pp. 9-10)

I. V. Hansen, "A Decade of Betsy Byars' Boys," in Children's literature in education, *Vol. 15, No. 1, Spring, 1984, pp. 3-11.*

DAVID REES

Betsy Byars is a prolific writer; almost every year since the late sixties she has produced a novel for children. With such a large output, one might expect to find a body of work with a considerable diversity in quality, a wide assortment of interests, differing structures, implied readers of varying ages. The surprise is that this is not so. Betsy Byars's novels are all much the same length (shorter, in fact, than many children's books), have similar structures, differ little in quality, and the implied reader is usually a child of between nine and twelve years old. Nor does the material of her books show much variety. She usually writes about children who are loners, or who have acute difficulties in their families or with their peer groups, who are forced to operate in trying situations that make them grow up a little. The narrowness of range is quite remarkable. Such comments could also apply to Judy Blume, but Betsy Byars's work shows what children who only read Judy Blume are in danger of missing—originality and inventiveness, lack of repetition, wit and good sense, a succinct prose style with terse, vivid perceptions and ironical observations of life. If any children's writer can be said, as Jane Austen commented about the themes and people in her own novels, to work on a "little bit (two inches wide) of ivory," it is Betsy Byars.

As in the novels of M. E. Kerr, adults are major figures in those of Betsy Byars, but they are not . . . at the center of the action, the characters around whom the narrative revolves. They certainly influence events and people, but Betsy Byars's stories are the stories of the child protagonist. That child either has only one parent, as in *The Night Swimmers, The TV Kid, The Cybil War, The Cartoonist,* and *Good-bye, Chicken Little,* or has been abandoned temporarily by both parents—*The Midnight Fox, The House of Wings, Trouble River*—or is without parents at all—*The Pinballs* and *After the Goat Man.* Grandparents, therefore, assume an importance that is unusual in children's books, and often it is the grandparent who is one of the most memorable characters in the story, because he or she is strong, cross-grained, highly individual—*Trouble River, After the Goat Man, The House of Wings*—or weak, selfish and ineffectual—*The Cartoonist, The Cybil War,* Great-uncle C. C. in *Good-bye, Chicken Little.* It is not surprising, given these circumstances, that the central child character is often a misfit, unhappy, ill-at-ease, depressed. Yet not too much of a misfit; there is no one who is really neurotic in these books. One of their strengths is that it is always possible for the reader to become involved and concerned about what happens to the child. However deprived the background, the reader can usually see something of himself or herself in the characters Betsy Byars creates.

There are certain differences of theme, tone of voice, and structure in the fourteen books between *The Midnight Fox* and *The Animal, The Vegetable, and John D Jones,* but they are small. One of her novels, *Trouble River,* has a historical background, and two of them—only two!—employ a first person narrator (*The Midnight Fox* and *The Winged Colt of Casa Mia*), a device Betsy Byars does not handle well. *The Winged Colt of Casa Mia* also happens to be her sole work of fantasy, a medium in which she is not really skillful. It is the realistic, everyday, humdrum details of ordinary existence that show her at her best; some of her finest writing concerns children doing simple, indeed silly little things just to pass the time—Sara dyeing her sneakers in *The Summer of the Swans,* the Monopoly game that lasted a day and a half in *After the Goat Man,* and, in *The Midnight Fox:*

> Petie was transferring the ant from one sneaker to the other, crossing his legs all kinds of different ways, so that no matter which way the ant ran he was always on the sneaker. This ant must have thought, Wow! There are one thousand boys lined up here and I will never get to the end of them.

However, despite her success as a writer of realistic fiction, some of her stories are marred by improbability. *The Eighteenth Emergency* is one of her most popular and most widely read books, but it is one of the least convincing, a short story spun out to novella length, with characterization that is really caricature: Mouse Fawley's fear of almost everything doesn't sound genuinely felt—the language and concepts of the seventeen emergencies are too unreal, too amusing—and his acceptance of being beaten up as a matter of honor does not ring true. He does not, in fact, owe a debt of honor—Marv, a junior version of The Incredible Hulk, may well be annoyed that Mouse has written "Marv Hammerman" under a picture of Neanderthal Man, but hitting Mouse until the blood flows is not, by any standards except those of revenge justice, a way of retaliation the reader should be asked to approve. Lennie, the main character of *The TV Kid,* seems to be cured of his mindless addiction to television by being bitten by a rattlesnake; the book appears to be saying that some violent external shock, such as a snakebite, can jolt a withdrawn unhappy child into the world of reality. Temporarily, of course, it could do so—Betsy Byars's portrayal of the pain that absorbs Lennie's whole attention is well done, and moving; but it does not prove that the sudden conversion is permanent, though that is implied. Betsy Byars clearly dislikes television. In several of her books, attention is drawn to the cheap escapism and the lack of intelligent content of many children's programs, and to the vulgar banality of most commercials. In particular, she seems—rightly—to be bothered by the negative effect of a great deal of television watching on the development of children's minds and imaginations. One applauds this, and though other authors . . . have made similar statements, Betsy Byars is perhaps alone in making television addiction the main theme of a story. Yet in *The TV Kid* her moral concern is too obtrusive; the book is spoiled by the narrative being manipulated to illustrate a point. *The Cartoonist* should have been her masterpiece: only in *The Night Swimmers* is her humor so amusing, her observation so sharp, her ability to make the reader sympathize with one character and despise another so effective. But it is marred by the way the narrative develops. Alfie has locked himself in his room, an attic, and he refuses to come out; his brother and sister-in-law have been told they can move in there and he is very resentful. His mother threatens to call the fire department, but her daughter, Alma, says he has got to come down by himself; there are things she has had to accept and work out by herself, and that is what Alfie must do. This seemingly intractable problem, however, is solved not by Alfie, but by the expedient of the brother and sister-in-law deciding *not* to move into the attic. It is all too easy, therefore, for Alfie to come out. The conclusion of this otherwise exceptionally fine novel—a witty, humane, absorbing story—is a rather lame anticlimax.

Betsy Byars is particularly good at opening sentences, first paragraphs, first chapters. *The Night Swimmers* begins with this sentence:

> When the swimming pool lights were turned out and Colonel and Mrs. Roberts had gone to bed, the Anderson kids came out of the bushes in their underwear.

Not only is this a marvelously rich invitation to read on, but it is a powerful image that seems to dominate the book. A strong, central, visual image often leaves a vivid impression on Betsy Byars's readers—Grandma, in *Trouble River,* shooting the rapids, sitting in a rocking chair perched on the middle of a raft, is one example, despite the resonances it has with more than one rapid-shooting movie; Grandfather in *After the Goat Man,* alone in his cabin, defying the builders of the new freeway is another; Sammy and his grandfather in *The House of Wings* staring at each other from opposite ends of a pipe that runs beneath a main road is a third:

> It was a strange sensation. It was as if they were the only two people in the world, staring at each other through the center of the earth.

"The game of Monopoly had been going on for a day and a half" is the opening sentence of *After the Goat Man,* and the first words of *The Animal, The Vegetable, and John D Jones* tell us a great deal about Clara's position in the family—

> Clara sat in the back seat of the Mercedes, staring out the window. In the front seat her father and sister had been having a discussion about television for twenty miles.

The first two pages of *The Pinballs* plunge us immediately into an absorbing, dramatic situation. The day Harvey was to be awarded third prize for writing an essay on "Why I am Proud to be an American," his father, half drunk, "accidentally threw the car into drive instead of reverse. In that wrong gear, he stepped on the gas, ran over Harvey and broke his legs." As a result, Harvey is taken away from his father and put into a foster home. All this before page three! But it is the opening chapter of *The Cartoonist* that is best of all. It is a model first chapter that any would-be writer of the short novel should study; for it establishes, briefly, the outlines of all the main characters, hints at the tensions, the way the plot will develop, suggests where our sympathies are to be withheld, gives a sense of place, social class, and a feeling that this narrative will totally engross the reader. It is all done with great economy—brief, telling phrases and an ironic sense of humor. One would like to quote all eight pages, but . . . [one example] will have to suffice. These are the opening words—

> "Alfie?"
>
> "What?"
>
> "You studying?"
>
> "Yes," he lied.
>
> "Well, why don't you come down and study in front of the television? It'll take your mind off what you're doing," his mother called.

Of all the adults in Betsy Byars's novels, none is more striking than Alfie's mother—a silly, domineering, empty-headed, selfish woman who leaves a trail of breakage and unhappiness wherever she goes, a character one would not be surprised to find in a story by M. E. Kerr. (pp. 33-8)

One of the prerequisites of the short novel, if it is to make a strongly effective impression, is the author's ability to be epigrammatic, to be the master of the short phrase or paragraph that says a lot and which will stay in the mind. Betsy Byars is as good in this as M. E. Kerr. When Carlie, in *The Pinballs,* hears that Harvey's father is coming to visit him, she says,

"Whoo, next thing you know they'll be letting germs and viruses in." Roy, in *The Night Swimmers,* is a sensitive, anguished child—

> Once in kindergarten he'd accidentally colored his George Washington face mask green and had not been allowed to march in the Parade of Presidents with the other kids. He had waited in the classroom with Miss Penny, weeping with the pain of exile, vowing never to be left out of anything again.

John D, in *The Animal, The Vegetable, and John D Jones*

> thought of himself as an antidote to the world's new niceness. He saw the world as a great big bland glass of niceness, and he was an acid tablet, dropped in to start things fizzing.

The story of *Good-bye, Chicken Little* is the reaction of Jimmie Little to his Uncle Pete's death. Uncle Pete is an immature, overgrown schoolboy, and he dies, after a drinking bout, walking on a frozen river in answer to a challenge that he dare not cross from one side to the other because the ice might not be safe. The ice cracks; he falls in and is drowned. Jimmie

> felt strange. As soon as his mother had called Uncle Pete a boy, he had found that he himself no longer felt like a boy. He was not a man yet, he knew that, but something vital, something important about boyhood, had been taken away from him with his mother's words. He wasn't sure he would get it back. . . .

In *The House of Wings* Sammy asks

> "Where's my mom and dad?" His grandfather rocked slowly back and forth like a buoy in the water.
>
> Then his grandfather said one word. "Gone." It was like the sound of an old sad church bell in the hot empty yard. "Gone." . . .

Indeed, the word does sound like "an old sad church bell." Sammy's grandfather tries to explain the importance of all life, human, animal, bird, fish, and wants to convey the reverence he feels but which his grandson lacks. He says—

> They're going to find one dead planet after another, that's what I think. You'll be picking up the newspaper and reading one sorry headline after another. No life on Jupiter. No life on Mars. No life on this planet. No life on that planet. And not until you've seen every one of those headlines, not until you know there's not any life anywhere, *then*, boy, is when you'll know how precious life is.

Animals play an important role in Betsy Byars' work, for there are more than the usual cats and dogs one is likely to find in most children's books, though even these she observes as distinctive creatures. Garbage Dog, in *The Eighteenth Emergency,* is a neglected stray, as timid as the central character. His fears parallel those of Mouse Fawley. . . . It is, however, wild animals that interest Betsy Byars more than domestic pets. The swans in *The Summer of the Swans* and the goats in *After the Goat Man* act as powerful symbols; the best writing in *The TV Kid* concerns the rattlesnake and the effects of its bite. Horses dominate *The Winged Colt of Casa Mia,* and if they are not as well realized as the menagerie of creatures Grandfather looks after in *The House of Wings,* that is because of the poor quality of the first-person narration. (It is an unusual and interesting device in a children's book to make the first-person narrator an adult, but Betsy Byars does not succeed in portraying Uncle Coot, the sardonic, reclusive ex-Hollywood stunt man, to sound totally credible.) The horse, Alado, has wings and can fly like

Pegasus; fantastic though that is, it comes over as more plausible than the voice of the main character. Maybe the nephew should have been the narrator—the element of wonder at the fantastic would have sprung naturally from him, particularly as he saw his uncle as a "wonder," not unlike the flying horse in his feats of daring as a stunt man. The portrayal of the fox in *The Midnight Fox* is excellent—as physically real as the fox in *The Iron Giant* by Ted Hughes—

> Her steps as she crossed the field were lighter and quicker than a cat's. As she came closer I could see that her black fur was tipped with white. It was as if it were midnight and the moon were shining on her fur, frosting it. The wind parted her fur as it changed directions. Suddenly she stopped. She was ten feet away now, and with the changing of the wind she had got my scent. She looked right at me.

The description is accurate, detailed, vivid, and the words "as if it were midnight and the moon were shining on her fur" is illuminating, the one needed touch of poetry. *The House of Wings* has several good passages describing birds. Grandfather and the wounded blind crane, observed together by Sammy, make a strange duo—

> Then gently he lifted the bird against his side. The tips of his white elbows were as sharp as knives, and the crane's stick legs ran, scissors-like, in the air for a moment. It was a picture of sharp and impossible angles.

The repeated "i" sounds of "lifted," "tips," "stick," "scissors," "picture" well emphasize the "sharp and impossible angles." In the same story, the raccoon asleep in the middle of the bed after eating five jars of jelly, and the owl who fell down a chimney and was discovered next morning in the stove's ashes, are anecdotes related with simplicity and a sense of wonder. The owl is beautifully observed:

> The owl made a faint hissing sound, like steam escaping. Then he swooped down into the tub and pounced on the grasshopper with both feet. His talons curled around the grasshopper, and he put it in his mouth . . . Then suddenly Sammy noticed how intently the owl was staring at him. He took a step backward. He said quickly, "That was the only one I could find." He backed out into the hall and went quietly down the stairs.

This time it is the verbs that make this effective—"swooped," "pounced," and "curled" contrasting with "put" and "intently . . . staring;" then Sammy's movements—"took a step backward," "backed out," "went quietly." Betsy Byars's writing at its best is as fine as that of the great stylists of contemporary children's authors—Philippa Pearce, Paula Fox, Lucy Boston. The material from which she makes a children's novel is often similar to the material M. E. Kerr uses in a young adult novel, but she is the better *writer* of the two.

She is, as I said, a good observer of the trivia children concern themselves with; she is also effective in portraying the fantasies that go through their heads, and their memories of extraordinary situations. Harold, in *After the Goat Man,* cannot forget that when he was six the kids in his class put on a Noah's Ark play; the pairs had all been chosen, so he had to be an extra hippopotamus. (He is a very fat boy.)

> In his dreams all the other animals had clomped happily into the ark. The heavy wooden door had slammed shut. The extra hippopotamus had been left alone.

Tommy, in *The Midnight Fox,* feels adults always seem to worry about the wrong things—

> One time Petie Burkis's sitter came out and Petie was stuck up in this tree, about to fall, and she said, "Petie, come down out of that wind—you're going to get earache!" Petie made up a headline about it— BOY BREAKS TWENTY-SEVEN BONES— AVOIDS EARACHE.

Mouse Fawley's seventeen ludicrous emergencies are another example of a child's fantasies; so are Harvey's lists, in *The Pinballs,* of the awful things that have happened to him; and, in *The TV Kid,* Lennie imagining himself to be a winning contestant in a television quiz show. John D in *The Animal, The Vegetable, and John D Jones* is writing a series of books with titles like *You Are Smarter Than Your Teachers.* Alfie, in *The Cartoonist,* has his comic strips, and Harold, in *After the Goat Man,* his self-important visions of himself as a TV or radio announcer. All these situations are seen as amusing, and hopefully temporary—necessary stages a child may have to go through before he can cope with the real world.

The material of *The Pinballs* is uncannily similar to that of *The Great Gilly Hopkins* by Katherine Paterson, though, as both books were published within a year of each other, it is unlikely that either writer knew what the other was doing. (*The Pinballs,* in fact, preceded *The Great Gilly Hopkins.*) Harvey, Thomas J., and Carlie live in a foster home—Thomas J. because he has no parents; Harvey and Carlie because their home situations are so intolerable that they have been removed by order of the courts. Mrs. Mason, their foster mother, is not the larger-than-life figure of Mame Trotter in *The Great Gilly Hopkins*; she is somewhat colorless—but nevertheless almost as saintly. The chief parallel between the two books is in the characters of Carlie and Gilly—both of them mixtures of toughness and insecurity, never at a loss for an answer, and both commanding a wide vocabulary of wit and repartee. However, Carlie is no more of a successful creation than Gilly Hopkins. She is, we are told,

> hard as a coconut. She never said anything polite. When anyone asked her how she was, she answered, "What's it to you?" or "Bug off."

But, in fact, like Gilly Hopkins, she is generous, compassionate, not a desperate problem.

Neither character comes over to the reader as the author wants us to see her. The trouble is that the authors fight shy of portraying the real nature of many kids who find themselves in foster homes, perhaps because some adults would object to such material. Writers of teenage novels avoid the depiction of adolescent sexuality for similar reasons. In answer to the question, how real do you want your realism? Mr. and Mrs. Average Parent, Librarian, and Teacher would say, of children's books and young adult books, not too absolutely real. Alas!—for the kids frequently have a different answer.

The Summer of the Swans and *The Night Swimmers* are probably Betsy Byars's finest books. *The Summer of the Swans* has an exciting well-paced narrative, as good as that of *The Cartoonist,* but it does not depend on a *convenient* chance for its outcome; chance, yes—but one that is more likely than that of Bubba and Maureen simply changing their minds about living in Alfie's attic. It is the story of the summer Sara Godfrey finds all the certainties of childhood no longer certainties; in particular, the story of the day her mentally retarded brother disappears. Much of the plot is concerned with the search for him. Sara

finds him, by chance—but it is plausible, for it is very likely that Charlie has not strayed far. For Sara, finding Charlie restores at least one of the certainties she thought she had lost. Looking after Charlie had become a nuisance; it stopped her fully enjoying herself with her friends, but when she faces the awful possibility that her brother might be dead, or at least badly injured, she realizes how much she loves him, how necessary he is to her existence. And if the other certainty she would like to restore to her family—the return of her father—does not happen, she advances a step towards maturity in finding her first boy friend, Joe Melby—someone she thought she had always despised. Characterization in this novel is excellent—not only Sara herself, but her elder sister Wanda (this relationship is exceptionally well done; tense and quarrelsome, but also affectionate and important), eccentric Aunt Willie, Sara's best friend Mary, Charlie, ineffectual Dad. The dialogue, too, never falters. *The Summer of the Swans* thoroughly deserved the Newbery Medal it was awarded in 1971.

"So much happens here, so simply, in the taut space of a few summer days, that every word and gesture has to count," said *The School Library Journal* review of *The Night Swimmers*: an accurate assessment, for though this novel is as brief as most others written by Betsy Byars, it is perhaps the most complex. The Anderson children have no mother; their father is a second-rate Country and Western singer—he once made the number thirty-seven position on the charts—and he is usually away from home at night. Retta, the eldest child, has to cook, keep house, and act as surrogate mother to her two brothers. . . . The story concludes with [the] father realizing that he has more responsibilities to his children than he had thought, but it is no conventional happy ending. The insights in this book are memorable; the words have a forceful bluntness that is as striking as the language in *The Cartoonist.* Retta "felt as bewildered as a child whose dolls have come to life and are demanding real care and attention;" "the unswallowed, unspoken pain of her mother's death stayed in her throat so long that sometimes she thought she would die of it," and—

> She had suddenly felt as if she were seeing her father so clearly that her image of him might be damaged forever, the way one's eyes are damaged by looking directly at the sun.

The Night Swimmers is a somber and powerful achievement.

In the realistic novel for children and young adults that delineates the everyday events of school and home, the pleasures and pains of parent-child relationships—and those with brothers, sisters, friends—contemporary American writers have produced a much more impressive body of work than the British. Between them, Betsy Byars and M. E. Kerr leave their rivals, both British *and* American, far behind. Their main strengths are in focusing on the importance of adults to teenagers and children, in portraying relationships with wit, subtlety and complexity, and—particularly Betsy Byars—in achieving the goal of high literary excellence. (pp. 38-46)

> *David Rees, "Little Bit of Ivory: Betsy Byars," in his Painted Desert, Green Shade: Essays on Contemporary Writers of Fiction for Children and Young Adults, The Horn Book Inc., 1984, pp. 33-46.*

DENISE M. WILMS

Becoming jaded is an occupational hazard for reviewers, especially now that mass-market fiction and nonfiction books abound. Yet as each new publishing season arrives, there are certain authors whose latest offerings do spark a sense of anticipation. Betsy Byars is one of them. Over the years she has published about 24 books; recently there has been usually one book a year. On that basis, she might be called a prolific author; she can also be called an enduring one. Of the 24 books I found record of, 20 are still in print. . . .

[She] is principally known as a novelist. Her success in this form brought her a Newbery award for *The Summer of the Swans* in 1971. Most of her novels can be characterized as contemporary realistic fiction. She is quick to incorporate current trends. *Cracker Jackson* deals with wife abuse. *The Computer Nut* deals with computers. *The Pinballs* portrays the effects of child abuse. *The TV Kid* is about a boy who is mesmerized by television.

This topical nature of Byars' subject matter implies a writer who appears to make calculated decisions regarding her books' marketability. But where many trendy novels wind up short on substance and on praise, the majority of this author's books have met with critical approval as well as strong popular appeal. Somehow, she has managed to translate her ideas into well-wrought stories that almost never succumb to clichés or easy stereotypes.

As a long-time reader of children's books, I am always amazed at the feat of telling a good story—to tell a string of good stories is truly remarkable.

I have to confess that part of the reason I find Betsy Byars an enjoyable author is my own preference for contemporary stories. . . . I never had difficulty with "problem novels" per se; my disdain was reserved for stories that didn't make the grade in authenticity. I refused to say good things about books that somehow tipped you off that the author was on the outside, looking in.

I have never had that feeling about Betsy Byars. Her realistic fiction, whether it falls into the "problem novel" category or not, has always had a reality about it that has been completely alluring. Her characters and the world they move in are so credible that it is impossible to think that anything could be otherwise. (p. 267)

Her stories imply she knows children; she has an unerring instinct for appealing to their sensibilities. Her books, with their careful attention to character development and their authentic voice, have a resonance that's unmistakable. Because their substance grows so surely out of craft, their impact is strong. Whether she's writing about a character who could be the reader, or someone who is clearly different, her humane views and clear lessons stand firm, all in the guise of good, solid, middle-grade entertainment. (p. 269)

> Denise M. Wilms, "Cracker Jackson," in Booklist, *Vol. 82, No. 3, October 1, 1985, pp. 267-69.*

ZENA SUTHERLAND AND MAY HILL ARBUTHNOT

Although few of her books are humorous, there is in most of Betsy Byars' writing a quiet, understated sense of humor that children quickly recognize and enjoy. More evident, and just as much appreciated, are her compassion and her understanding of the deepest emotions of children. And, as in *The Midnight Fox* there is an empathy with children's love of animals. Tom, an urban child visiting relatives, has had no interest in animals, but he is so caught by the beauty of a black fox that he becomes absorbed in watching her and her cub; when his uncle pens the cub as bait to trap the mother, Tom releases it, and is delighted when his aunt and uncle prove to be understanding about his deed.

Byars with her husband and daughters at the University of Illinois, Urbana, in 1956. The barracks in the background is where Byars began her writing career. Courtesy of Betsy Byars.

The compassion depicted in Tom appears again in Byars' Newbery Medal book, *The Summer of the Swans,* one of the early books about a retarded child. Charlie's sister Sara is loving and protective, terrified when Charlie is lost, and glad of the help of a friend, Joe, in finding him. Sara, fourteen and shy, accepts a party invitation from Joe, and comes to a turning point. Like the swans she and Charlie have watched, she knows for the first time that she will move from a first, awkward flight to the confidence of being in her own element. The book has a tender quality and has enough action to balance the quiet unfolding of a situation.

In *The Night Swimmers* Byars again explores a situation and a turning point in a child's life with insight, again writes with tenderness and grace, again creates a memorable character. Retta is the oldest of three children; motherless, she is a mother to her younger brothers, since their father, a country-western singer, is away at night and asleep for most of the day. Secretly they swim, at night, in a neighbor's pool; it's one of the many ways that Retta tries to keep her brothers busy and happy. She is bereft when they develop other interests, confused by her own reactions of jealousy and resentment. The situation is resolved when a friend of their father's takes over; she's a tough, cheerful woman who's determined to marry Retta's father. Only when she realizes that she can be a child, that somebody else will assume the role of protector, does Retta accept the change in her role, in a story that is touching but never saccharine.

Byars has written some fantasy and some lightly humorous stories like *The Cybil War,* but her strong forte is in depicting troubled children. In both *After the Goat Man* and *The House of Wings* she deals perceptively with boys and their relationships with grandfathers who have lived solitary lives; in *The Pinballs* she depicts the camaraderie of those who are joined in misfortune, in a vivid story about three foster children who gain security from each other and their affectionate foster parents; in *The TV Kid,* a hospitalized child gets over his addiction to television shows; in *Cracker Jackson* a child reacts to the abuse of someone he loves. In *Good-bye, Chicken Little* a child, appalled by his uncle's death, learns that people have different ways of handling grief. In all her books, Byars affirms a respect for children's resiliency and strength. (pp. 352-53)

> *Zena Sutherland and May Hill Arbuthnot, "Modern Fiction: Books for the Middle Group," in their* Children and Books, *seventh edition, Scott, Foresman and Company, 1986, pp. 340-57.*

RAMA, THE GYPSY CAT   (1966)

Cats are less likely to be centered on in juvenile fiction than dogs, horses, or other loyal, animals—the errant Black Beauty way of life is too well suited to their personality. Tears may not flow very rapidly for Rama, but she is characteristically independent. You can sympathize with her even at the times when she finds new humans to replace the old—the chain goes from a gypsy woman (who might have taken Rama from a little boy), to a poor, backwoods little boy who saves the cat's life, to a westward heading peddler who come closest to fitting her footloose spirit. Even when she wanders off on her own to have, say, a murderous scrap with a rival, Rama is fittingly feline. The story is episodic and moody, and the frank approach may rub some readers' fur the wrong way, but objective cat lovers will appreciate this.

> *A review of "Rama the Gypsy Cat," in* Virginia Kirkus' Service, *Vol. XXXIV, No. 21, October 15, 1966, p. 1103.*

Rama's adventures are true both to the accidents of life and to cat psychology. . . . Never is there a trace of anthropomorphism. The Peggy Bacon pictures catch the look of a real cat as completely as the text catches his character. This has an open-ended plot like life itself. More will happen to Rama.

> *Anne Izard, in a review of "Rama the Gypsy Cat," in* School Library Journal, an appendix to Library Journal, *Vol. 13, No. 5, January, 1967, p. 64.*

TROUBLE RIVER   (1969)

For 12-year-old Dewey, homesteading on the prairie was all work and no pleasure, except when he stood on his raft and dreamed of Huck Finn adventures on the Mississippi. For the old, like Dewey's Grandma, the prairie was a frightening place of "strange sounds and long stillnesses." It is this feeling of frontier life that Betsy Byars captures, with effortless effectiveness.

One night, while Dewey and his Grandma are alone in their cabin, an Indian attacks. The two slip away on Dewey's raft—into Trouble River's current, toward possible safety, away from certain death. Grandma rides in style in her rocking chair, "like a lady on a steamboat." But it's not melodrama that the author plays on—even when wolves attack, and when Dewey discovers a smoldering neighbor's cabin where his family may have perished. There's only one false note: would Grandma's rocker have stayed right side up while the raft went through the rapids?

Miss Byars has a talent for plot and dialogue that makes her low-keyed story a skillful portrayal of the growing respect between a young boy and an old woman.

> *Margaret F. O'Connell, in a review of "Trouble River," in* The New York Times Book Review, *September 14, 1969, p. 30.*

Average adventure fare. . . . Both Dewey and Grandma are unreal characters, though Grandma provides a certain—reader concern-negating—comic relief, with her tales and fondness for her gold spectacles and cobbler-made shoes. On the whole, a routine achievement, with another youthful hero triumphant.

> *Ann M. Montgomery, in a review of "Trouble River," in* School Library Journal, *an appendix to* Library Journal, *Vol. 16, No. 2, October, 1969, p. 138.*

[Betsy Byars] never disappoints a reader. . . . [*Trouble River* is a] strong vivid story by a writer who understands boys and old people too and the fears they had on the frontier a century ago. Perfect collateral reading for social studies units on the West.

> *Judith Higgins, in a review of "Trouble River," in* Teacher, *Vol. 90, No. 3, November, 1972, p. 74.*

AFTER THE GOAT MAN   (1974)

José Ortega y Gasset described a novelist as one who "moves with cumbrous baggage like circuses or nomadic tribes, carrying the furnishings of the world on his back." In this novel Betsy Byars has chosen to travel light—she has sorted through her cumbrous baggage, exercising great discipline in selecting only essential furnishings and ruthlessly discarding superfluous gewgaws that might distract the reader from her characters.

Byars has accomplished this difficult feat in a story which spans 24 hours but becomes a paradigm of life—full of pain and irony, but studded with frequent bursts of fun and laughter. The dialogue sounds so familiar, we become part of the story as quickly as Figgy gets hooked on Monopoly.

Before we're aware of what's happening, we know three people: tomboy-tough Ada, whose restless energy seems to flow from the same life force as Carson McCullers's Frankie; Harold, a fat boy whose rueful observations and crackling wit form the core of the novel; and defenseless Figgy, one of life's Victims, clinging to a rabbit's foot to ward off an unfathomable world.

Figgy has an immediate problem. His thorny grandfather, the town's oddball nicknamed the Goat Man, has barricaded himself with his shotgun in their old cabin in a last ditch attempt to halt the wrecking crew from flattening their home for a superhighway.

In a crisis which develops when they set out to talk the old man away from the cabin, Ada, Figgy, Harold and the Goat Man become linked by their mutual caring, generosity and gentleness. It is Byars's most affirmative statement: in a world which deals out sudden and often harsh hurts, we can comfort each other. An intuitive sense of the bond between himself and the Goat Man ("I know how you feel because I, too, was the extra hippopotamus") brings a guarded optimism to Harold, whose self-image may be the only part of him that has not been overinflated in his fat-plagued life.

Never losing control of her material (and God knows a fat kid, an uprooted old man and a puny boy scared silly could be prime candidates for a pile of damp Kleenex in the hands of a lesser writer), Byars remains a dispassionate craftsman, weaving a sturdy homespun tale with the simple words of plain people.

She raises thundering questions, but, lacking the egotist's compulsion to provide pat answers, she challenges us to respond to her characters, to react to their situation—to reach toward our own conclusions rather than to swallow the novel passively.

And of course she succeeds. One spends many hours rereading the perceptions of Harold and wondering what's going to happen after *After the Goat Man.*

> *Alice Bach, "Plain Talk, Moon Talk and a Toothless Toothache," in* The New York Times Book Review, *December 15, 1974, p. 8.*

The restrained plot, developed through spare, unsentimental prose, effectively and clearly delineates the need to recognize individual dignity and the pangs of adolescence. A compassionate and artistic treatment of human problems. (p. 51)

> *Mary M. Burns, in a review of "After the Goat Man," in* The Horn Book Magazine, *Vol. LI, No. 1, February, 1975, pp. 50-1.*

A fairly slender story-line holds together a trio of characters whose personalities are individual enough to compensate for any lack of action. The Goat Man of the title is shadowy and undeveloped: a pity—the aged rebel who defies the bulldozers offers an opportunity for strong characterisation which is sidestepped in favour of the three children. . . .

[A] discerning study of relationships.

> *G. Bott, in a review of "After the Goat Man," in* The Junior Bookshelf, *Vol. 40, No. 1, February, 1976, p. 38.*

THE LACE SNAIL (1975)

The Newbery Medalist displays her dual gifts as author-illustrator here in a beautiful picture book for younger readers. But many older people, including adults, will find themselves caught up in the enchantment of the delicate drawings and the unusual story. A snail, making her way toward a pond, begins to leave a trail of gossamer-fine lace in various intricate patterns. All the animals she meets—from lady bugs to a hippopotamus—beg her to fashion them something from the magic lace. When she has pleased them all with parachutes (the holes in the fabric don't matter because the bugs who use them can fly anyway), hats and even a lacy hammock for a crocodile, her capacity for producing the lace fails and she arrives at the pond for a needed rest. The quiet tale treats interesting creatures, including turtles and an ominous snake, in a sympathetic and appealing manner.

> *A review of "The Lace Snail," in* Publishers Weekly, *Vol. 208, No. 11, September 15, 1975, p. 59.*

The slight story has nothing to capture children's interest, and it is further weakened by the animals' slang conversation—e.g., in "we got lace, man, LACE!" or "Look at me, you guys."—which is not in keeping with the overall mood. Byars' green-and-white illustrations are attractive but unexciting, adding one more reason to pass this by.

> *Jane E. Gardner, in a review of "The Lace Snail," in* School Library Journal, *Vol. 22, No. 3, November, 1975, p. 42.*

In a surprisingly successful blend of quiet tenderness and contemporary, often slangy, dialogue, Betsy Byars has written a witty picture book, appealing despite the slight story line. The illustrations are spacious, with animals in strong, dark green and a contrasting note of delicate, lacy black on white.

> *Zena Sutherland, in a review of "The Lace Snail," in* Bulletin of the Center for Children's Books, *Vol. 29, No. 7, March, 1976, p. 106.*

THE TV KID (1976)

[Betsy Byars] has done an impressive job of researching this story. Like a police chase in "The Rookies," her plot careens forward; sentences, short and clean, are bursts of exchanged gunfire. But the ending is a copout. His hospital ordeal, we are told, has shown Lennie the dichotomy between trying to live in the plastic (Mrs. Byars's thematic catchword) domain of network TV and making it in the real world. So what else, Lennie's amply lectured contemporaries may wonder, is new? Lennie's teacher hasn't the answer. Instead of sending her born-again charge back to his science book to learn the difference between a petiole and a stipule, she lets him recoup that humiliating 59 with an "extra-credit" report on his crawl-space misadventure. A benign adult evasion of the hard choices that may help to explain the nation's sagging SAT scores.

> *Cathleen Burns Elmer, in a review of "The TV Kid," in* The New York Times Book Review, *May 2, 1976, p. 40.*

Betsy Byars has made a special corner for herself in the sensitive handling of growing rapport between adults and children; she also has the storyteller's gift of being able to create a gripping sequence of events to effect the changes in relationship that inform her plots. In *The TV Kid,* however, the story is too thin and the formula too near the surface. . . . The television fantasy sequences which open the story and feature Lennie starring in quiz shows of mind bending fatuousness are vigorous and hilarious. But with the main events of the narrative, a slice of real adventure during which Lennie nearly dies of a rattlesnake bite and learns to love life itself, instead of at one remove, the book becomes predictable and banal.

> *Sarah Hayes, "The Wings of Summer," in* The Times Literary Supplement, *No. 3879, July 16, 1976, p. 879.*

This is a most sympathetic study of a child whose flight from reality ends in a convincing way. That it is a narrative with suspense and color is the more remarkable because there is only one dramatic incident, there are few characters to give variety, and the major part of the book is given over to Lennie's internal monologues. (pp. 4-5)

> *Zena Sutherland, in a review of "The TV Kid," in* Bulletin of the Center for Children's Books, *Vol. 30, No. 1, September, 1976, pp. 4-5.*

THE PINBALLS (1977)

When Sid Fleischman observed, "Comedy is tragedy; but it is tragedy in motley" and "Comedy . . . is alchemy; the base metal is always tragedy"—he might well have been talking about Betsy Byars' latest book. The stark facts about three ill-matched, abused children living in a foster home could have made an almost unbearably bitter novel; but the economically told story, liberally spiced with humor, is something of a tour de force. Ideal but never idealized, the foster parents Mr. and Mrs. Mason are modest, patient, and quietly loving; one summer two boys and a girl come to live with them. Thirteen-year-old Harvey arrives in a wheel chair, his legs having been broken when his father, driving in a drunken rage, accidentally ran over him. Three years before, his mother had vanished, gone away to live in a commune and "find herself by getting back to nature." Sharing Harvey's room was Thomas J, a younger boy. As a two-year-old toddler, he had been found abandoned near the home of elderly twin sisters; six years later he was discovered by the authorities when the eighty-eight-year-old ladies, looking "like matching salt-and-pepper shakers," simultaneously broke their hips and ended up in the hospital. The girl Carlie, repeatedly beaten up by her stepfather, was a cynical, rude teenager, "hard . . . as a coconut," who concealed beneath her brittle exterior a keen mind and a courageous spirit. "'Harvey and me and Thomas J are just like pinballs. Somebody put in a dime and punched a button and out we came, ready or not, and settled in the same groove.'" Goaded into furious action by Harvey's deteriorating condition and impenetrable depression, Carlie finally took matters into her own hands, injecting life into the listless Thomas J as she swept him along in her grim determination. A deceptively simple, eloquent story, its pain and acrimony constantly mitigated by the author's light, offhand style and by Carlie's wryly comic view of life.

Ethel L. Heins, in a review of "The Pinballs," in The Horn Book Magazine, *Vol. LIII, No. 4, August, 1977, p. 437.*

The plight of children battered or abandoned by their parents is not, one might have thought, the most appealing subject for a book for the young. Even in our present enlightened age when no topic seems too sacred or too daring to be aired in a children's novel, authors still shy away from themes and characters that may disturb rather than shock the young reader. . . .

In her new book, *The Pinballs*, Betsy Byars helps to fill the gap a little. The "pinballs" of the title are three children. . . . The three children, each damaged and deformed in different ways by adult indifference, are taken into care and become the foster-children of kindly Mr and Mrs Mason. In this new, stable environment, rebellious Carlie, withdrawn Harvey and timorous Thomas J. help each other to adjust to their desperate situations and learn from each other and from the Masons that they are not "pinballs" after all.

Given such a theme and such characters, it is only to be expected that *The Pinballs* should be a moving book. And, coming from such a writer as Betsy Byars, it is only to be expected that it should be extremely funny into the bargain. Yet, despite the incidental comedy in this story and the deceptive simplicity of its telling, Betsy Byars has written a serious book about a disturbing subject, investing it with the insight, sympathy and sense of comedy that have distinguished her more recent work. *The Pinballs* is a book to remember.

Lance Salway, "Against the Odds," in The Times Literary Supplement, *No. 3943, October 21, 1977, p. 1247.*

Although the circumstantial problems of the three children remain unsolved at the end, Carlie sees that, unlike pinballs, people are able to influence their destinies and change the quality of their lives, in particular, by attempting to improve things for others. The extensive, often witty, contemporary dialogue carries the burden of the slight, rather obvious plot and reveals character. The child characters seem deliberately assembled and are overdrawn for effect, and the adults are flat and functionary. Conversation and behavior tend to provoke amusement rather than empathy. The conclusion is heavily

foreshadowed, and the whole thing trivializes what is a serious, contemporary social problem. (p. 516)

Alethea K. Helbig and Agnes Regan Perkins, in a review of "The Pinballs," in their Dictionary of American Children's Fiction, 1960-1984: Recent Books of Recognized Merit, *Greenwood Press, 1986, pp. 515-16.*

THE CARTOONIST (1978)

The Cartoonist is not for every pre-teen. Some may be turned off by the slow-paced character development, and many will not appreciate its West Virginia humor. But youngsters with stoutly guarded realms of their own surely will identify with Alfie and his attic hideaway, where he draws "super caterpillar" cartoons and dreams of breaking out of the shadow of an older, domineering brother.

It's a one-dimensional little book, yet curiously appealing. Alfie's battle for privacy, while childish, is poignant—almost praiseworthy. The memory of his "victory" lingers long after the last page.

Diane Casselberry, "Spy Thriller for Would-Be Heroines," in The Christian Science Monitor, *May 3, 1978, p. B9.*

Alfie Mason, the hero of Betsy Byars' novel, *The Cartoonist* transforms events—often painful—and his life—nearly always difficult—into art. He is a true artist. He even works on his cartoons in an attic, the only room he likes in his crooked house and the one place where his family can't get at him. (p. 1)

How Alfie struggles, at first foolishly and mulishly, then bravely, to keep his attic, and how he finally does save it for himself is the heart of Byars' story. She tells it splendidly, with clarity, verve and grace. There is a real dilemma, not a worked-up one: there is real comedy, not condescending gags. Alfie's Mom and Pap are original comic inventions. They are awful, yet vaguely endearing. And the subsidiary characters—Tree Parker, Alfie's friend; the Finley twins, local Typhoid Marys who want to be gossip columnists when they grow up; and Mrs. Steinhart, the math teacher—are as substantial and living as the Mason family.

But it is Alfie himself who has that rare quality in fiction—any fiction—charm. (p. 4)

Paula Fox, "A Room of His Own," in Book World— The Washington Post, *May 14, 1978, pp. 1, 4.*

I kept waiting for [*The Cartoonist*] to get underway—which it does when we're halfway through. . . .

A quiet tragedy of forgotten hopes and tawdry expectations, it is a much better book than at first appears, with deft lines of black comedy and occasional insights into the secret world of childhood. But it never fully grips the imagination. Too much conversation and the usual diet of transatlantic verbiage only manage to reveal the iceberg tip of what this story might have been.

Peter Fanning, "Hot and Horny Youth," in The Times Educational Supplement, *No. 3308, November 24, 1978, p. 45.*

Manuscript page from The Glory Girl *(1983). Courtesy of Betsy Byars.*

GOOD-BYE, CHICKEN LITTLE (1979)

Jimmie Little became filled with anxiety the year his father was killed in the coal mine, and he began to call himself Chicken Little. As time went on, he began "to notice that his . . . family drew attention to themselves in the wrong way. They did silly, senseless things that made them look foolish even when they succeeded." But his mother's brother Pete did not succeed when he tried to walk across a frozen river four days before Christmas. He was drowned. After her initial shock Jimmie's mother, who had a strong sense of family solidarity, decided to hold a Christmas party, assembling assorted relatives and going so far as to fetch ninety-two-year-old Uncle C.C. from the nursing home. Jimmie continued to be morosely unappreciative of his mother's activities until it occurred to him that his family was really remembering and honoring Pete, and the boy learned to see each of his relatives as a "unique, one-of-a-kind individual." As in the author's other works, the extended terse dialogue gives the narrative a characteristic quality of understated, often wry humor; but after the realism and the seriousness of the opening incident, the sudden change of mood seems disconcertingly incongruous. Although the author is obviously attempting to account for the transformation of the boy's emotional attitudes, she fails to make a successful transition between the tragic and the comic portions of the story. (pp. 189-90)

> *Paul Heins, in a review of "Good-bye, Chicken Little," in* The Horn Book Magazine, *Vol. LV, No. 2, April, 1979, pp. 189-90.*

[Betsy Byars] has tackled the tough subject of guilt—that particular kind of guilt we feel after the death of someone close. Could we have prevented it? Why did we say what we did?. . .

It's not a simple story. The working out of such complex emotions never is, and the subtleties of redemption may be lost on some of Byars' younger readers. But for children who've had a taste of being made to grow up quickly, Byars offers some solace as well as an absorbing narrative.

> *Alice Digilio, in a review of "Good-bye, Chicken Little," in* Book World—The Washington Post, *May 13, 1979, p. K2.*

A theme like [death and guilt] could result in an intolerably depressing children's book, but Betsy Byars is sensitive to the dangers, and never lets things get too heavy. In a way this is the trouble, the rest of the book works too hard to amuse the reader. Jimmie's mother is a scatty comedienne and an appalling driver. His ancient Uncle C.C. . . . is comically forgetful and testy, and a transparent liar. When the whole family gets together for a Christmas party in memory of Pete the whole thing is too whacky for words.

The main anxiety that his uncle's death touches off in Jimmie is a fear of being afraid. His father's death, some years earlier, had reduced him to such a state of unconfidence that he had taken to referring to himself as "Chicken Little." But the book shows him to be less vulnerable than he fears, able to come to terms with loss and draw comfort from his family relationships.

For the first time I found Betsy Byars' touch uncertain in this book. So much of what gives meaning to Jimmie's experience precedes the action of the book that it is hard to share it; a formula for avoiding the portrayal of too much pain has resulted in a book where it is hard to take the pain really seriously.

> *Myra Barrs, "Dicing with Death," in* The Times Educational Supplement, *No. 3311, November 23, 1979, p. 35.*

THE NIGHT SWIMMERS (1980)

Whenever I finish a book by Betsy Byars, I have an overwhelming urge to put a star beside the title along with code letters, P.I.—Parents Invited. Indeed, it would be a shame for parents to miss out on Mrs. Byars's books, for no matter how off-beat her characters are, readers (adults and children alike) are bound to identify with them. For Mrs. Byars has uncanny ability to know the secret lives, the outward postures and the exact words her characters would surely use.

In *The Night Swimmers,* Betsy Byars features a motherless family that consists of Shorty, the father (a small-time country music singer) and his three children: Retta, the oldest who is in charge; Johnny, who is ready to strike out on his own; and chubby little Roy, who doesn't want to miss anything. At the beginning of the summer Retta looks forward to a vacation of companionable, fun-filled days. "We're going to do all the things rich people do," she says. "Only we have to do them at night."

Since their father works at night, they have no trouble getting out. And since Colonel Roberts's private swimming pool is within walking distance, they have no trouble finding an agreeable, if dangerous, pastime. The trouble comes when Johnny makes friends with Arthur, a boy with ideas of his own. Retta, of course, resents being excluded, but what is worse, she is no longer in control. She likes feeling strong, and in the past there have been moments when she has felt strong enough "to be put on a Mother's Day Card," but no longer. And certainly not after the night when Roy almost drowns. "I can see how you can be a good mother," she says, "if you're there all the time. . . . But when they get away from you, well, I just don't see how mothers do it."

In this case, there is a solution, but the memorable parts happen on the way. With her customary skill, Betsy Byars drives every nail home and wastes not a one.

> *Jean Fritz, in a review of "The Night Swimmers,"* in The New York Times Book Review, *May 4, 1980, p. 26.*

It is only in mediocre children's novels or stories that parental absence is viewed as an undisguised blessing, a licence for "adventure." Betsy Byars's work is of an altogether higher order. It is just as accessible and entertaining to children, while twice as nourishing, because, however dire the straits of her young characters, humour is never long absent from the scene. In *The Night Swimmers* she has written a short novel that makes the reader hold his breath, cry and laugh; not for one moment are the emotions disengaged. . . .

Betsy Byars's skill at showing Retta, half child, half the kind of nagging mother that television programmes invariably depict, is consummate. The child in Retta longs for fun and excitement—which is how the nocturnal expeditions to a private swimming pool in a rich family's garden begin. But there is also in Retta the instinctive recognition that she must keep her brothers occupied and half-afraid of her, or she may lose control. . . .

The denouement to this story with Roy rescued by the owner of the pool and with the children's father called back from the Hoedown to take on the responsibilities he had not realized were his, is handled by the author with her accustomed dexterity. For Retta, adult intervention could be a blow to pride or a blessed relief. There is a moment when, inevitably, her feelings waver between the two. Then,

> She saw Roy lying on the sofa. Suddenly she realised how young, how vulnerable he was. She looked at Johnny. . . . She felt as bewildered as a child whose dolls have come to life and are demanding real care and attention.

There are many ways in which the author can distance the agonies children endure; humour is Betsy Byars's chosen path. . . .

> *Elaine Moss, "Dreams of a Surrogate Mother," in* The Times Literary Supplement, *No. 4034, July 18, 1980, p. 806.*

Not a long story, in biggish print, and with three juniors, on page one, creeping out of the bushes to swim in the Colonel's pool at night, when the upstairs light has just gone out. This is a good start. It is a likely book to coax a reader. The sympathy in it and the humour have to carry it along because not a great deal happens. There is a lot of feeling for Retta. . . . The children are most sympathetic, especially the youngest, with his subtle way of waking people up by standing quietly beside them and breathing on them. Retta's wish not only to cope, but to provide sports, to make a family, and to be loved and respected is readily understood. There is enough excitement at the close to heighten the story and there is a happy and quite unforced ending. (pp. 27-8)

> *D. Atkinson, in a review of "The Night Swimmers,"* in The School Librarian, *Vol. 29, No. 1, March, 1981, pp. 27-8.*

Although the conclusion is simplistic, events happen rapidly, scenes come alive, dialogue is extensive and natural, and humor abounds. The author describes the ways, feelings, and attitudes of the children with warmth and sympathy. Except for Arthur, a stock figure who functions as the author's voice, the children are dynamic characters, but the adults are types and somewhat eccentric. Retta's compulsive behavior is handled sensitively. (pp. 473-74)

> *Alethea K. Helbig and Agnes Regan Perkins, in a review of "The Night Swimmers," in their* Dictionary of American Children's Fiction, 1960-1984: Recent Books of Recognized Merit, *Greenwood Press, 1986, pp. 473-74.*

THE CYBIL WAR (1981)

Betsy Byars to a large extent dispenses with particular details of place, relying on an extremely precise choice of words through which her characters give us the illusion of action. Her acute sense of conversational forms stands her in good stead in *The Cybil War*, which is hardly a tale of action (a few blocks on bicycles and a move from one room to another more or less sums it up) but, rather a compact study of two relationships—the doomed alliance of Simon Newton and Tony Angotti, doomed because of Tony's compulsive and disloyal lying, and the growing friendship between Simon and the girl he ardently admires, Cybil Ackerman, a girl who to his amazement seems able to ignore public opinion and back her own judgements in the most testing situations. Betsy Byars's skill in extending the role of dialogue beyond mere communication has perhaps never been more evident than in the scene at Harriet Haywood's party when for embarrassing reasons Tony has to remove his aunt's poodle, though he had been confident that her costume of nappy and bonnet, and her special tricks, would win him the prize. A touch of narrative added to dialogue can be astonishingly effective when it is used rarely. Here are the final stages of Tony's downfall:

> Tony glanced behind him to see that the trouble was with Miss Vicki. 'You are *not* praying.' He jerked the leash as she again tried to put her head between her paws. 'No praying!'
>
> The crowd around Harriet's porch watched in pleased silence as Tony Angotti, head down, walked out of sight, dragging the prayerful Miss Vicki behind him.

Sparing with words, Betsy Byars always elicits both picture and mood with them; there is no-one like her for creating small, significant neighbourhood dramas. (pp. 3911-912)

> *Margery Fisher, in a review of "The Cybil War,"* in Growing Point, *Vol. 20, No. 2, July, 1981, pp. 3911-12.*

There is absolutely nothing wrong with *The Cybil War* . . . except that it is by Betsy Byars. And that makes all the difference in our expectations.

In book after book Mrs. Byars has, through her use of metaphor, created unforgettable characters. Her crane in *The House of Wings* symbolizes an elusive bond between grandfather and boy. The swans in Newbery winner *The Summer of the Swans* provide a poignant counterpoint to the gentle, retarded, curious

Charlie. A river and an old lady in a rocking chair on a raft set the tone for *Trouble River.*

In *The Cybil War* there are no cranes, swans or rafts. There are just three rather ordinary youngsters who encounter very ordinary situations: the dilemma of who will play Mr. Indigestion in a nutrition play, a dog show in which a pooch named T-Bone is dressed as a pirate, and a mock Miss America pageant. If this sounds mundane, you've found the problem.

Mrs. Byars can be funny, her dialogue can be enchanting, and she has created an appealing character in Pap-Pap, Tony's grandfather, who cries a lot, sometimes just because "the moon is full . . . and it's so beautiful." But neither the humor, nor the dialogue, nor Pap-Pap makes this more than a dated, easily read and easily forgotten book.

Mrs. Byars writes of Cybil's house: It "was like a commercial for living . . . an advertisement to show how zestful ordinary day-to-day life can be." Perhaps this was what Mrs. Byars was trying to impart in this book. Frequently, however, the portrayal of an ordinary situation with ordinary characters turns out to be ordinary. We want more from Betsy Byars.

> *Patricia Lee Gauch, in a review of "The Cybil War,"* in The New York Times Book Review, *July 19, 1981, p. 21.*

A joy. . . . The writing seems deceptively simple, but it has a polished fluency and spontaneity. The children, separately and together, are vividly characterized; the relationship between Simon and his mother has a particular warmth, and the story is permeated by an affectionate humor, especially in the dialogue.

> *Zena Sutherland, in a review of "The Cybil War," in* Bulletin of the Center for Children's Books, *Vol. 34, No. 11, July-August, 1981, p. 209.*

THE ANIMAL, THE VEGETABLE, AND JOHN D JONES   (1982)

Although the whole story is told by the author, alternate chapters are from the viewpoint of John D or from the viewpoint of Deanie and Clara, the daughters of a divorced man who has his children with him for a fortnight's beach vacation. To their horror, Dad has arranged for John D's mother to share the beach house. Deanie and Clara bicker a great deal, but they are united in their contempt for John D, an emotion he cordially returns. Only when Clara comes close to drowning do her sister and John D see beyond the pettiness of their hostility; Deanie even softens toward John D's mother, toward whom she had felt resentment. This doesn't have as strong a story line as some of Byars' stories, but it has the same perceptive exposition of the intricacy of ambivalent relationships. The use of shifting viewpoints works well, partly because of the smoothness of the writing style, partly because the characters and relationships are so quickly and definitely established. (pp. 183-84)

> *Zena Sutherland, in a review of "The Animal, the Vegetable, and John D Jones," in* Bulletin of the Center for Children's Books, *Vol. 35, No. 10, June, 1982, pp. 183-84.*

The Animal, The Vegetable and John D. Jones by Betsy Byars explores with . . . subtlety the conflict that can arise between siblings, between children and their parents, and between families when brought together in confined surroundings. Betsy Byars is an American writer with a successful string of children's books to her credit. Although this one is set firmly in

the United States (with some expressions unfamiliar to British readers), the characters and situations will be universally recognized. . . .

[The] development of plot, which results in self discovery for both Clara and John D., and a realization that the world is a more tolerable place than they had supposed, is achieved with considerable effect and economy of effort.

The characters of the children are well drawn and many a child (and adult) will readily understand why John D. chooses to put himself into such an uncomfortable position, and why Clara feels constrained to test her own physical endurance to the point of danger. A thoughtful, entertaining book for nine-year olds.

> *Brian Baumfield, "Misdeeds and Misunderstandings," in* The Times Literary Supplement, *No. 4138, July 23, 1982, p. 794.*

The first chapters of this thought-provoking novel about real, rather unstable, typically American teenagers seem exaggerated and trivial. Delores is the only one who appears rational and balanced. But the climax of the last chapters builds up powerfully and convincingly. Background detail is well defined, but the references to current "Pop" personalities could give this book a short relevant life. The characterisation could help some mixed-up teenagers to understand themselves and their motives.

> *A. Thatcher, in a review of "The Animal, the Vegetable, and John D. Jones," in* The Junior Bookshelf, *Vol. 46, No. 5, October, 1982, p. 195.*

THE TWO-THOUSAND-POUND GOLDFISH   (1982)

Betsy Byars is at her best taking an uncommon situation and treating it to a simple, forthright exploration. *The Two-Thousand-Pound Goldfish* is a provocative and compelling example.

Warren Otis, 8, has cinematic daydreams, magnificent spectacles in which bizarre creatures terrorize helpless victims, including his grandmother and older sister, Weezie.

Warren hasn't seen his mother for three years, ever since she went "underground" as a fugitive wanted by the F.B.I. for violent protest activities. He misses her terribly; or, at least, he thinks he does, since he can barely remember her. What he really misses is the *idea* of a mother; someone to hug him, tuck him into bed, bake cupcakes for him—a juvenile ideal of maternal love.

Warren focuses his emotional energies on cows that squirt radioactive milk, and Bubbles, a giant goldfish who lives in a sewer. Imagined disasters distract Warren from his personal ongoing sense of disaster. There is a remarkably skillful blend of imaginative fantasy and reality here.

Eventually, Warren gets a chance to speak with his mother on the telephone but what he hears is not the voice of the mother of his dreams, but an echo of someone blurry and remote who is never going to play a significant, nurturing role in his life.

Mrs. Byars' straightforward narration lets pure gut feelings come through. The rationale for the mother's behavior and her actual motives are never really explored, but that's not important. The impact of Warren's having to cope with the fact that he's not the No. 1 priority in his mother's life *is* important. It's not an easy concept to grasp, but he will eventually accept it, and survive. In the end, he imagines a movie in which his

2,000-pound goldfish is released from the sewer and sent out to sea. With this, his first nondestructive cinematic finale, he takes the first step toward banishing his own demons.

Marilyn Kaye, in a review of "The Two-Thousand-Pound Goldfish," in The New York Times Book Review, *November 28, 1982, p. 24.*

Abandoned by his mother, slighted by his older sister and cared for by a grandmother who has all the compassion of an irritable cab driver, young Warren Otis teaches us about the power and awe of a child's imagination and inventiveness.

This is a wonderfully crafted story. And if it doesn't leave your hands sore from applause for Warren's bottomless faith in love and in himself, then you have much to learn from this 10- or 11-year-old kid. . . .

It is Warren's older sister who keeps in touch with their mother, by waiting, one day each month, beside a phone booth for the mother to call. When Warren finally gets in on one of the calls, his imagined and loving portrait of his mother is shattered. All his sister can do to assuage his grief is, in her commonplace way, to explain that life is dull and painful and populated by wicked people. Warren totters on an edge between adopting his sister's surrender or plowing ahead with his own, rare strength of character.

If there is tragedy in the loss of childhood dreams, there is also reason to celebrate the rare child who grows into maturity with his inventiveness and wonder intact. Warren is a young man for adults to admire and children to emulate.

The story's infrequently yet clear references to the sexual behavior of the mother and the illegitimacy of Warren and his sister are pointed out here so that parents can judge for themselves the propriety of the book in their homes.

Tim Murray, in a review of "The Two-Thousand-Pound Goldfish," in Best Sellers, *Vol. 42, No. 9, December, 1982, p. 364.*

The problem of writing about emotional isolation is that it may be difficult to communicate the sense of characters who are not communicating, so this latest of Betsy Byars' accounts of the painful process of growing up, while bringing off as brilliantly as ever her combination of bleakness and hilarity, is yet a little disappointing: several of the main characters are reminiscent of others in earlier books but seem less strongly drawn. Thus Warren, the central character is, like the hero of *The Cartoonist,* escaping from an unsatisfactory home life into the world of his imagination, but the family he cannot get close to are less vital and convincing.

The fantasy is glorious: Warren's escape is into the construction of imaginary horror films, and the reader is entranced by such concepts as the cow which squirts radio-active milk, the giant skunk which turns men into wer-skunks, and, Warren's latest creation, Bubbles, the goldfish flushed down the toilet that has grown to enormous size through absorbing chemical waste and become a man-eater. The film is worked out in such loving detail one almost begins to remember having seen it.

Moreover, this exuberant fantasy has real point; the misery of Warren's life is that he has been without his mother since he was five because she has, in a sense, absorbed chemical waste and become a monster: that is, she has become an urban terrorist on the run from the police. This situation, which must have been a reality for a number of American children since the sixties, is handled without melodrama; the life lived by Warren

and his older half-sister Weezie with their irritable and slatternly grandmother is simply grey and depressing. It is hardly surprising that Warren retreats from it into the visionary sewer where Bubbles lurks, though Weezie, one of those strong-minded girls on whose aching shoulders the Byars world often rests, is determined that he shall grow out of his dependence on his dreams.

What actually breaks the dependence is the nature of reality; when grandmother dies, Warren is forced to realize that real fear is quite different from fun fear, that though he hadn't liked grandmother much, he had loved and will miss her, that even her mother's funeral will not bring his mother home, and that talking to her on the telephone, a privilege for which he and Weezie fight like maniacs, will not ease his pain. This is an admirable frame; if it is not filled in as richly as in some of the earlier works, it still provides a liberal education for the emotions.

Audrey Laski, "Fun Fear," in The Times Educational Supplement, *No. 3466, December 12, 1982, p. 25.*

THE GLORY GIRL (1983)

Betsy Byars has a gift for exposing the soul of the lost child—the damaged, the alienated, the unloved. Her stories may not always live up to expectations, but her characters have credibility. They tend to rise above situations and plots.

Anna Glory, 12, is the only person in her family who can't carry a tune, a miserable state of affairs when one's family is a gospel singing group. Onstage, her parents and siblings bask in the glow of spotlights and spiritual fervor. Meanwhile, untalented Anna sits in the back of the auditorium and waits to perform the only function for which she's suited—selling Glory family records and tapes.

Suddenly, the family hears that Uncle Newt, Mr. Glory's brother and a onetime bank robber, has been paroled. The parents respond to this news with hostility and fear, but Anna harbors a peculiar sense of connection with this unknown and obviously unloved person. Newt makes no contact with the family, but Anna senses his presence during a performance and in a restaurant where some obnoxious boys hassle her sister. Later, when the family's bus is wrecked, Newt appears. In the rescue effort and its aftermath, Anna confirms her affinity with this other alienated soul and moves toward a recognition of her own worth.

The rest of the Glorys are vaguely defined. There's the harsh, quick-tempered father and an insipid mother who plays favorites among her offspring. The beautiful sister spends her time setting her hair, while the frenetic twin brothers count the stitches they accumulate through various scrapes. While Mrs. Byars makes no explicit judgments about the family's piety, they do come off as a pretty sleazy bunch. She avoids the religious angle and concentrates instead on a situation in which a young person is made to feel inadequate.

The story is thin, but the tension builds neatly and the writing is polished. The plot, particularly the climax, may carry a hint of contrivance, but *The Glory Girl* is rescued by its striking and appealing protagonist. In the end, it's Anna who becomes its salvation.

> *Marilyn Kaye, in a review of "The Glory Girl," in* The New York Times Book Review, *November 27, 1983, p. 34.*

Betsy Byars proves once again that she can treat difficult situations with humor, empathy, and piercing insight. . . . By the end of the book Anna may not have changed from an ugly duckling to a beautiful swan, but she discovers that her unique personality—more sensible and compassionate than the other members of her family—can be appreciated by others as much as the ability to sing would have been. This is an important lesson for every adolescent who feels alienated from his family, left out of the crowd.

All the main characters are multi-dimensional. Even Anna, who is a well-behaved young lady, is shown reading her father's mail on the sly. Her father and mother, brothers and sister are presented as complex, evolving humans. . . . The skillful characterizations make this book ring as true as an old gospel song.

> *Ruth Livingston, in a review of "The Glory Girl," in* Best Sellers, *Vol. 43, No. 9, December, 1983, p. 344.*

Since Betsy Byars' theme is always the same—the difficulties of beginning to grow up into a real human being—her great gift is for finding, each time, a new situation to frame it. This time, her protagonist is a girl, Anna Glory, who like many other Byars youngsters, feels herself to be an outsider in her own family. . . .

Betsy Byars has written about the fringes of show business before, but this is a special kind; the Glory family are Gospel singers, travelling about in a beat-up bus to give religious concerts, and one of the subsidiary themes of the book is the contrast between the Christian professions which are their stock-in-trade and the uncharitable feelings which animate most of the family most of the time. . . .

The means Betsy Byars takes to reveal to the family the true qualities of Newt and Anna are perhaps a little melodramatic—the Gospel bus is forced off the road by some wild boys, and uncle and niece drag the others out of it before it can be carried away by the river—but the clean, matter-of-fact tone in which

she relates the episode makes it work. As ever, she is very good on the way that one may love one's family without much liking them, and the modest improvement in everybody at the end of the book is both plausible and satisfying to the feelings.

> *Audrey Laski, in a review of "The Glory Girl," in* The Times Educational Supplement, *No. 3526, January 27, 1984, p. 29.*

THE COMPUTER NUT (1984)

While doing a self-portrait on her father's office computer for an art project, Kate is contacted by the mysterious BB-9. Continued communication via the computer reveals BB-9 as a (supposedly) extra-terrestrial yearning for a taste of earthly humor. Plot and characterization fall short of Byars' usual perceptive fare. Shallow Linda is abruptly dropped as a friend mid-way through the story, and Kate turns to solid Willie who never comes alive as more than a willing accomplice. The adults all sigh tiredly, and even BB-9 is a one-dimensional disappointment. Readers never see BB-9 land or take off, and Byars is not entirely successful in portraying him as a credible alien. This is not convincing as either an alien-from-another-world story or as an addition to the plethora of computer fiction.

> *Caroline Ward, in a review of "The Computer Nut," in* School Library Journal, *Vol. 31, No. 2, October, 1984, p. 155.*

Byars' unerring talent for shaping true characterizations is especially apparent in her dialogue, though a few typical speech patterns read even worse than they sound ("'See, it's like . . .'"). The emerging relationship between Kate and Willie is deftly handled, and while BB-9's one-liners are truly dreadful, his anxious desire to crack a successful joke is affecting and funny at the same time. One the whole this has a lighter tone than the novelist's more substantive works, but the breezy quality won't bother young readers, who will be easily hooked on the fascinating sci-fi premise that underlies the story.

> *Karen Stang Hanley, in a review of "The Computer Nut," in* Booklist, *Vol. 81, No. 4, October 15, 1984, p. 303.*

Betsy Byars's forte is the contemporary (American) scene, and within that, the things real kids say and do, and the painful comedy attendant upon the brink of adolescence. She has a sharp ear for language and a sharp eye for behaviour, so that her books are consistently readable and, just as consistently, a little too slick. It is characteristic of her to have identified the current computer fad as a good subject, and to have made the computer nut of her title not a boy, as one might have expected, but a girl. . . .

Curiously, many of [the alien's] jokes depend on puns ("You remind me of a roll of film—underdeveloped"), a way of thinking that seems peculiarly human in its delight in confusion. Machines prefer clear distinctions and the gratuitousness of laughter seems rather outside their range. Behind this lies the book's more general failure to exploit the intriguing if unpoetic possibilities of computer language. If, as it seems, *The Computer Nut* is primarily addressed to young buffs, why does it not take advantage of the many verbal oddities, limitations and short cuts characteristic of this mode of discourse? The alien's computerized messages are typographically isolated and indentified by capitals, but their semiotic distinctiveness begins and ends here. They employ implausible complex subjunctive forms, and there is a notable absence of that BASIC terminology only too familiar to the programmer—ENTER, RUN, GOTO, GOSUB, REM, INKEY$, PRINT, PLOT, PEEK, POKE and HEX. All this suggests that, while Betsy Byars can recognize a trendy topic when she sees one, she has not acquired even the most rudimentary knowledge of the subject, available from any beginner's manual; the result is, as a computer might clumsily point out, a TYPE MISMATCH or an IMPROPER ARGUMENT.

> *Julia Briggs, "Young Buffs," in* The Times Literary Supplement, *No. 4270, February 1, 1985, p. 130.*

CRACKER JACKSON (1985)

To combine the wretched story of an abused wife and a baby with the lighthearted pranks of two eleven-year-old boys would be an audacious undertaking in the hands of a less skilled storyteller. Young Jackson discovers that his ex-baby sitter has been beaten by her husband; and, spurred by affection for her, the boy enlists his friend Goat to help drive her to a home for battered women. The pathetic story of Alma, with her adored baby, tidy home, and treasured collection of Barbie dolls, is relieved by flashbacks to the two boys' antics at school and by their hilarious, if potentially lethal, attempt to drive her to safety. Interwoven within the brief story are the multiple threads of Jackson's parents' divorce; his changing relationship to Alma, wherein the once-protected becomes the protector; and amusing sketches of Goat and his long-suffering circle of family, teachers, and classmates. That Jackson's mother ultimately rescues Alma in no way diminishes Jackson's heroic devotion; the story is one of loyalty in many forms—of parent to child, of child to adult, and of friend to friend. The author's gift for depicting misguided adults for whom one still feels sympathy—even Alma's brutish husband is no exception—and for transforming unlikely young people into heroes is again splendidly in evidence. The book belongs in the same distinguished category as *The Summer of the Swans* and *The Pinballs* in its expert blend of humor and compassion.

> *Ethel R. Twichell, in a review of "Cracker Jackson,"* in The Horn Book Magazine, *Vol. LXI, No. 3, May-June, 1985, p. 310.*

The problems in *Cracker Jackson* are solved convincingly, without prettifying. Betsy Byars . . . reveals her characteristic economy of organization and expression. This story has no bright fireworks and, in spite of the intense subject and Alma's palpable anguish, no hysterics.

Mrs. Byars can write low-key humor deftly. Jackson's eternal problems include his shame at a nose that runs "most of the time." He is compiling a list of acts his nose will make impossible: kissing girls, singing opera, being a brain surgeon.

Goat McMillan, his best friend, is a good enough foil for serious Jackson. But, with Goat, Mrs. Byars's signature fades a little. Goat regularly acts so much like a standard free spirit that a reader could tire of or disbelieve him. Goat even shares his full name with a character in the author's earlier book *The Cartoonist.*

There are some small cracks in the plot that suggest quick writing from habit. "Car wreck," says Alma, referring to some bruises, and that startling remark passes by her hearer far too easily. Goat is performing a tale about Percy—who becomes "Morrie" in the telling. Jackson's mother's reaction to Alma's

baby, Nicole (named for a character on "All My Children"), is so detached it is almost mean.

These are cavils, because the plotting and characterization do work and the details remain vivid. For example, Mrs. Byars shapes the story so that Alma's pristine collection of "unplayed-with" Barbie dolls, of all things in this story told from a boy's point of view, will come to represent the horrors that accompany battering when Jackson encounters them smashed and mauled.

> *Mary Louise Cuneo, in a review of "Cracker Jackson," in* The New York Times Book Review, *August 4, 1985, p. 21.*

Cracker Jackson is in many ways a typical Byars novel. It's relatively brief, but tightly focused, and, in the end, dramatic and moving. It's aimed at middle-graders, with characters and settings that are well within the range of such youngsters' experiences. (p. 267)

In developing a story for children about wife abuse, Byars has made some interesting creative choices. The very idea of a book on that subject may seem odd. Unlike child abuse, where the victim is young—and therefore of immediate interest to the reader—wife abuse involves an adult as the principal victim. Byars neatly circumvents that apparent barrier by incorporating Alma's victimization into the experiences of Jackson Hunter. Alma is a beloved person to Jackson; he has dear memories of her as his childhood baby-sitter, so anything that might hurt her is of grave concern to him. Alma's problem is therefore Jackson's problem.

Jackson's worries about Alma automatically snag the reader, who is now made to sympathize not only with Alma as victim, but also with Jackson, as a concerned but essentially powerless child who wants to set something right. Making Alma the victim also allows Byars to keep the story's psychological and emotional impact in control. What if it were Jackson's mother who was abused? If that were the case, the problems of shaping a story that was credible but yet not overpowering would be much more difficult. Since Alma is outside of Jackson's family, both he and the reader are able to view the problem with much more rational concern.

Byars draws the reader completely into the story by way of Jackson's and Alma's characterizations. In fact, memorable characterizations are central to almost all of Byars' work. They're central to her success too. Her finest novels, including *The Summer of the Swans*, might best be labeled character studies. Think back to Tom, in *The Midnight Fox*, who is a boy loathe to accept change, or Sara in *The Summer of the Swans*, who finds adolescence thoroughly upsetting the summer she is 14.

Cracker Jackson is a character most notable for his ordinariness. Like Ezzie in *The Eighteenth Emergency* or Lennie in *The TV Kid*, Jackson seems like an average child in every way. He lives with his divorced mother but talks regularly with his father, rides a neon-painted bike, and has a best friend who stands by him the way best friends are supposed to. Yet Jackson, as real and ordinary as he seems, soon displays a heroic quality; the fact that he fails in his attempt to help Alma in no way diminishes his stature.

Alma, the baby-sitter and the story's main victim, is a beautifully drawn character, and the latest in a line of what I call Byars' eccentrics. These are characters who deviate from the norm whether mildly or otherwise; they may be central to the story, as is Tom in *The Midnight Fox*, or more peripheral; they

Byars with her grandchildren. Courtesy of Betsy Byars.

are intriguing figures that challenge our perceptions of people and nudge us to rethink our acceptance or rejection of those who are in some way different. Regardless, Alma is warm, loving, generous, and a not very bright woman-child who is similar to Jackson in her powerlessness. She's unable to muster the nerve to leave her husband, Billy Ray, until he strikes out not only at her but at her baby too. Alma is the sort of person you might look down on in real life. Her world is narrow and defined by the shallower elements of popular culture. She named her baby Nicole after a character on "All My Children." She has a collection of Barbie dolls she wants her daughter to have one day; she thinks Jackson's mother's flight attendant uniforms are the height of fashion. Yet for all of these naive preferences, Alma is never portrayed derisively. She is a person of worth in Jackson's eyes because of the unconditional love and understanding she extended to him as a young child. His esteem makes her a worthy person to the reader too.

Byars' exposition of character is very skillful. Personalities are built up layer by layer through dialogues and monologues that spotlight critical moments in the present or the past. These are often offbeat and their novelty increases their effectiveness at making highly individualized characters. Flashbacks occur again and again in Byars' work, and they serve her well. You can see them at work in *Cracker Jackson*. They begin in the first chapter, when Jackson receives the letter that gets the story off like a shot. The letter says, "Keep away, Cracker, or he'll hurt you." Though its unsigned, Jackson knows it's from Alma.

Still, the gut-wrenching message sends him back to an earlier time when another anonymous letter jolted him just as severely. . . . This recollection sets up Jackson as a vulnerable, impressionable boy who has spirit enough to fight back. It also hints at the pattern for the rest of the book; that is, Jackson is sensitive to a problem—Alma's safety—and then tries to do something about it.

This flashback of Jackson's also has a good dose of humor in it, which, I think, is the second critical element in Byars' appeal. It's a strong suit for her and very important to the sharp characterizations that anchor her work. It runs from quietly wry, to brash, to outright slapstick, and it shows her keen eye for the foibles of adults and the mischief of children. . . . In fact, in *Cracker Jackson,* almost all of the characters are, at one point or another, the target for Byars' sharp sense of the absurd. (pp. 267-68)

The book's comic high point is the desperate drive Jackson takes with Alma and his friend Goat. . . . Of course he has no license; his only driving experience has been steering the car from his grandfather's lap. He calls Goat, and together they set out on a very serious but very funny trip.

In *Cracker Jackson,* Byars' humor works to several advantages. First of all, it warms up the reader. A funny book is an easy book to read, and youngsters starting *Cracker Jackson* will be hit not only with the jolt of an anonymous warning but also with a taste of fun. Later the humor accents the characters in a way that makes them especially real and believable. Humor also advances the plot—as in Jackson's car drive, but most importantly, it provides a necessary counterpoint to the book's serious subject while never making light of it. Even as they laugh, young readers will not for a moment forget that Jackson must save Alma.

Plotting is another essential aspect in a novel's development; its soundness is reflected in how credibly the story moves forward and how closely the reader stays involved. . . . In problem novels, plots are often weak points. The story is too expository; endings are too happy—or conversely, too hopeless.

Plotting in Byars' work seems to grow inevitably out of character. It is a measure of her skill that plot can't be easily considered apart from character. The things Jackson sees and does as the story moves forward seem inevitable, not because of subject matter but because of who Jackson is. Therefore, the plot is never predictable; you never know just which way it's going to turn. Yet it isn't quirky or devious; it *seems* like it's simply an outgrowth of Jackson's thoughts and emotions: he gets the letter. He's worried. He tries to find out without getting close to Alma if she's in trouble. When he finds out she is, he tries to help her. By having the reader view everything through Jackson's eyes, Byars avoids being disappointingly obvious. Yet the plot never drags. Readers worry about Alma; they wonder what Jackson will do. When he does take action, it can be funny (the car ride); when Jackson sees the awfulness of Alma's situation, the reader may well be moved to tears. There is always a state of tension about what is going to happen to the characters in *Cracker Jackson.*

There are some other things worth noting about this plot. One is that the violence is never viewed directly. In a book about wife abuse, you might expect at some point that Jackson will witness Billy Ray beating Alma. But there never is such a scene. You only see the aftereffects of violence: Alma's bruises, Alma's fear. Perhaps the most chilling episode in the book is Jackson seeing the aftermath of Alma's most serious beating. . . . Opting for this indirect view of the story's violence accomplishes a couple of things. On the most basic level, it's simply true to Jackson's circumstances. He doesn't live that close to Alma, he probably would have no occasion to see her abused. From an aesthetic viewpoint, the tactic works because there is something even more disturbing and more threatening in *implied* violence. Seeing the disquieting signs is scarier for Jackson—and for the reader—than would be the actual spectacle of a fight.

Byars is also subtle about describing a common pattern of abuse and of victim behavior. Alma at first denies Billy Ray's violence toward her; then she tries to excuse it; she also backs out of her first attempt to leave Billy Ray. The elements of case history are here, but they never appear as such within the story's development.

Byars' skill as a storyteller is well honed. In *Cracker Jackson* she has pulled off a successful depiction of a problem that children hear about and perhaps even see—all in terms they can understand and perhaps learn from. (pp. 268-69)

> *Denise M. Wilms, "Cracker Jackson," in* Booklist, *Vol. 82, No. 3, October 1, 1985, pp. 267-69.*

THE GOLLY SISTERS GO WEST (1985)

Traveling by horse-drawn covered wagon, May-May and Rose Golly joke and bicker their way along the American frontier, entertaining the locals with their singing and dancing as they go.

Pictured as vigorously middle aged, the two sisters have six cheerful minor adventures, such as singing inside their moving wagon to console themselves for being lost, then discovering that their first audience has meanwhile assembled outdoors, and inventing "The Dance of the Squashed Hat" in honor of the hat demolished during one of their squabbles. Byars makes masterful use of the controlled vocabulary of this genre, ingeniously incorporating repetitions and contriving, apparently effortlessly, the cadences and word choices of natural speech. . . .

This is Byars' first easy reader; more would be welcome.

> *A review of "The Golly Sisters Go West," in* Kirkus Reviews, *Vol. LIV, No. 14, July 15, 1986, p. 1122.*

Byars applies her distinctive brand of quirky humor to two adventuresome women determined to dare the frontier with minimum experience. . . . The dialogue and antics are convincingly like those of rivalrous young siblings anywhere on the block. The story lines are cleverer than much easy-to-read fare, and the old-West setting adds flair.

> *Betsy Hearne, in a review of "The Golly Sisters Go West," in* Bulletin of the Center for Children's Books, *Vol. 40, No. 3, November, 1986, p. 44.*

Byars catches some nice nuances in the relationship between the rival sisters, and there are some funny sequences, but most of the incidents precipitated by the sisters are only mildly amusing. . . . Byars is a winner in her books for older children, but here the lack of plot punch, dead-on dialogue, and characterization makes this a disappointment.

> *Nancy Palmer, in a review of "The Golly Sisters Go West," in* School Library Journal, *Vol. 33, No. 4, December, 1986, p. 122.*

THE NOT-JUST-ANYBODY FAMILY (1986)

About two-thirds of the way through Betsy Byars's new novel for children, *The Not-Just-Anybody Family,* a kindly bus driver says to 12-year-old Maggie Blossom, "You take care of yourself. You the only member of your family doing all right. Everybody else in jail, in the hospital."

Everybody else includes 11-year-old Vern, who has busted into jail to be with his grandfather Pap, who was arrested for firing his shotgun on Spring Street after two teen-agers in a Toyota purposely ran over his collection of 2,147 beer and pop cans, scattering them all over the road, and 7-year-old Junior, who has broken both legs trying to fly off the top of the Blossoms' barn (he was wearing wings; they just didn't work). Then there is the family dog, whose name is Mud, lost in the shuffle when Pap is taken away to jail, the subject of a humanitarian all-points bulletin as he tries to make his way back home across the busy city. The Blossom children's mother, Vicki, a rodeo trick rider, is away on the circuit while all this is going on; the children's father was killed a few years ago by a runaway steer in a rodeo accident in Nebraska.

In successive chapters we follow the adventures of Junior in the hopsital, Pap in jail, Mud on the loose, Vern and Maggie trying desperately to get the family back together and home again. Though their mother leaves them phone numbers where she can be called in an emergency, there is a mix-up this time, and Vern is unable to reach her. Eventually she learns what's going on by reading it in the newspaper and to everyone's relief (particularly the reader's), rushes home.

The jacket copy calls this book a "delightful comedy of errors." I wonder. A grandfather who goes after teen-agers with a shotgun? Children left alone to fend for themselves, so terrified of the police (Pap has a still in the cellar) that they run three miles without stopping or jump off the barn trying to fly away when they see them coming? A mother so careless she doesn't realize that if she is not registered at a motel in her own name her children can't find her? *The Not-Just-Anybody Family* may not be just anybody's laugh riot; few scenes in the book are without pathos, and the one where Vern tries to call his mother because he misses her and discovers she isn't where she is supposed to be and can't be located brought tears to my eyes. Vern especially misses the good old days when his father was alive and they were all happy together. Tragicomedy would be a truer description of what goes on here.

Still, Betsy Byars's light touch and her skillful interweaving of the various plots give *The Not-Just-Anybody Family* a reassuringly farcelike quality. There is enough comic exaggeration to give even the most faint-hearted readers hope that all will not be lost, that everything will turn out fine. The society depicted here—police, judges, newspaper reporters, bus drivers, motel owners, fast-food restaurant patrons (they drop food next to Mud and anxiously report his presence to proper authorities)—is caring and sympathetic. The Blossoms are well-rounded and believable characters, however peculiar. Mud is particularly well drawn, a resourceful toilet-water drinking, leg-lifting, zoysia-grass-scratching dog after my own heart....

Funny-ha-ha maybe not; well worth reading, certainly yes.

Susan Kenney, in a review of "The Not-Just-Anybody Family," in The New York Times Book Review, *June 15, 1986, p. 38.*

A fluent tongue is needed to pronounce the title of this book, and a strong stomach for reading it; though no doubt Betsy Byars . . . was wise not to call it *The Blossoms. The Not-Just-Anybody Family* is a tough, entertaining American urban romance, in the best tradition of stories about children carrying more than adult responsibilities and almost magically winning the day. But the overpoweringly demotic language, full of trade names and abbreviations, can be puzzling, and I felt at times that a glossary or subtitles should have been added for United Kingdom readers.

The adventures of the Blossom family are a far cry from the Famous Five. Layers of American life are evoked of which English children can have little conception....

Through Mud, we get a brilliantly vivid ditch-level view of American urban life, as he lies "under the carryout window of a Dairy Queen", and is fed substantial morsels of hamburger and bacon cheeseburger, ending his meal with chocolate milkshake. Other people's waste is meat and drink to the Blossoms. Mud doesn't like the rich end of town, finding chlorinated swimming-pool water less to his taste than water from the family lavatory. His agonized negotiation of the congested and polluted Interstate is thrillingly told, and the dog's heroic odyssey rounds off a comforting happy ending. But this is not a story for the squeamish. Having endured Ralphie's anatomical fantasies and Mud's meals of leftovers, serious queasiness may set in when reading of the food actually chosen by members of the Blossom family. Like Dickens's Maggie in *Little Dorrit*, who had "Chicking", Mrs Byars's Maggie enjoys hospital

food—"She had bought a pimento cheese sandwich from a vending machine, heated it miraculously in a small oven, and washed it down with an ice-cold Mello-Yellow." The Blossom family's favourite breakfast is squashed, fried shredded wheat with lots of syrup. But for the stout-hearted, this is an excellent read.

Katherine Duncan-Jones, "Down at Ditch Level," in The Times Literary Supplement, *No. 4342, June 20, 1986, p. 691.*

The author has a sure hand with the telling details and desperate problems of people living at the poverty level—what they eat and wear, why they avoid authority—and a gift for short, pithy, authentic characterizations. The story of the pathetically self-reliant, eccentric, but deeply loving family makes a book that is funny and sad, warm and wonderful.

Ann A. Flowers, in a review of "The Not-Just-Anybody Family," in The Horn Book Magazine, *Vol. LXII, No. 5, September-October, 1986, p. 588.*

THE BLOSSOMS MEET THE VULTURE LADY (1986)

Mad Mary, who lives in a cave and collects her meat from the highway, rescues Junior Blossom from a cage and takes him home to keep him safe when she thinks that he has been abused. Actually, Junior had made that cage himself, hoping to trap a coyote and win a reward. His disappearance brings out his entire family (introduced in *The Not-Just-Anybody Family*), and each one's personality, fears, and needs is highlighted during the search. This is a lively, likable family, handled lightly but surely by an author known for her ability to write believable dialogue and present the desires of her characters with humor and understanding. Mad Mary's history, sketched throughout the story, brings readers more and more into contact with an independent, determined woman who has created a workable life for herself. If some would argue that mental illness rather than independence drove her to the cage, then at least her illness is that of a genuinely caring person bewildered by the world of man. This is a short book, moving from one character to another and back again in a way that may confuse less sophisticated readers. The situation isn't as dramatic as in *The Not-Just-Anybody Family,* and the action is more diffused through the characters' internal lives. Yet thoughtful readers will find the story to be satisfying, and Mary and Junior's friendship heartwarming.

Sara Miller, in a review of "The Blossoms Meet the Vulture Lady," in School Library Journal, *Vol. 33, No. 3, November, 1986, p. 86.*

Betsy Byars, who has looked straight in the eye of the scariest things a child can imagine—a parent's death or betrayal—here introduces readers of around ten or eleven to an outsider, one of those frightening beings who wander on the edges of society, sleep rough and talk only to themselves....

As anyone who has read Byars's *The Not-Just-Anybody Family* already knows, the Blossoms are not exactly an uptight American clan, ruled by convention.... But even these open-minded youngsters think Mad Mary might be a witch, and they instinctively fear her, as does their mother—and the family dog, too, for that matter. Only Pap, who went to school with Mary, believes that she is gentle, if unsociable.

Mad Mary has lived in the wild for fifteen years and shucked off human traits like smiling and taking off one's boots at night and caring about other people. Then she comes across Junior Blossom, a dreamy, emotional eight-year-old. . . .

Byars, having arranged this meeting fraught with strangeness and possibilities, makes Mary comprehensible and responsive too quickly, and allows Junior to slip without a struggle into a happy, mindless crush on her, there in the cosy cave with all the pretty vultures floating overhead. The dialogue gets a bit saccharine; children may begin to wish that Mad Mary would rip open a rabbit with her bare hands and that Junior would ask her some embarrassing questions. The manhunt also loses its drive around this time (although charmingly sidetracked by a love scene between Junior's sister and her young admirer, who has an artificial leg).

Similar sentimentality crops up towards the end of other Byars books, including the otherwise tough-minded and savvy *The Pinballs* and even the inspired *The Night Swimmers,* but it hurts more here. It touches with its deadly sogginess the vivid details, the snappy colloquial dialogue, the slightly outlandish flourishes and the rambunctious Americanness. But children, after all, love a happy ending, and the sentimental last chapters cannot sink this story, or defeat these characters. Nor do they totally subvert the serious issues of safety and conformity that Byars has raised for chilren just beginning to face the world outside.

> *Alice H. G. Phillips, "Happily Ever After," in* The Times Literary Supplement, *No. 4365, November 28, 1986, p. 1344.*

The whole Blossom family—including Vicki, the mother, who returned near the end of the first book, *The Not-Just-Anybody Family*—is back for another romp that includes laughter, tears, understanding, and compassion. Betsy Byars has again created a genuine, original character in the person of Mad Mary, a.k.a. the vulture lady. . . . Byars's talents shine in this title as she produces natural dialogue and wildly funny yet plausible situations. . . . Middle readers will once again find that Byars has written a winner.

> *Elizabeth S. Watson, in a review of "The Blossoms Meet the Vulture Lady," in* The Horn Book Magazine, *Vol. LXII, No. 1, January-February, 1987, p. 55.*

THE BLOSSOMS AND THE GREEN PHANTOM (1987)

Junior is certainly the center of attention in Byars' third comic novel about *The Not-Just-Anybody Family.* The boy is laboring to launch his greatest invention yet—a rickety homemade hot-air balloon he dubs the Green Phantom and hopes will be mistaken for a flying saucer. While Junior is busy with his balloon, Pap is stuck in a dumpster, having fallen in when he tried to rescue an unfortunate puppy someone had tossed in. Meanwhile, Junior's mother, Vicki, is teaching her daughter Maggie acrobatic riding so the two can become the first mother-daughter trick riding team in the history of rodeo. When Junior's Green Phantom threatens to flop, he suffers a crisis of confidence that draws the Blossoms and their friends together (except for Pap, hopelessly caught in the dumpster) in a determined effort to make sure that Junior's beloved project succeeds. Their unity gives the novel heart and celebrates the importance of family love, but humor is what makes the story enjoyable. Byars' comic touch softens the harshness of the Blossoms' relative poverty and highlights the endearing eccentricities that make each personality anything but a stock

character. With Junior's success and Pap's safe return comes a sense of pleasure and satisfaction that will make readers look forward to a promised fourth installment.

> *Denise M. Wilms, in a review of "The Blossoms and the Green Phantom," in* Booklist, *Vol. 83, No. 14, March 15, 1987, p. 1125.*

With her uncanny ability to make the absurd touching and the ludicrous a matter of aching uncertainty, the author plays off one set of events, Junior's helium-filled UFO collapsing on Farmer Benson's chicken house, against another, Pap's humiliating tumble into a garbage dumpster. . . . The family life, spiced by a mother who isn't afraid to hand her children a good tongue-lashing, is warmly and convincingly pictured while the authenticity of Mud's hurt feelings over a new puppy are equally authentic. The genuine amusement of the story is tinged by hints of mortality and human limitation, yet soars on the triumphs of Pap's and Junior's notable if incongruous achievements. (pp. 207-08)

> *Ethel R. Twichell, in a review of "The Blossoms and the Green Phantom," in* The Horn Book Magazine, *Vol. LXIII, No. 2, March-April, 1987, pp. 207-08.*

Byars develops her story subtly, using shifting points of view to delineate her characters. Each chapter leads logically and simply into the next; yet by the end of the story readers understand several different viewpoints and have followed a subplot involving Pap, Mud, and an abandoned puppy. This is no small accomplishment for independent readers in fourth or fifth grade and is excellent preparation for more complex reading. The Blossoms are totally real and believable, yet quirky enough to be fun. Maggie yearns for her mother's approval and companionship, but values friend Ralphie for his flamboyance as well as his faithfulness. Vern is anxious to win a friend of his own, to separate himself from his "different" family and be like other people; like Junior, he misses his dead father. Junior is a free spirit, inventive and adventurous but in need of support. And in Pap, imprisoned in and rescued from a garbage dumpster, Byars conveys the poignance of aging and the value of deep and lasting affection. This is a story about love in its many forms. Like Byars' best, it is rock-solid and full of chuckles, and it lingers in the mind.

> *Dudley B. Carlson, in a review of "The Blossoms and the Green Phantom," in* School Library Journal, *Vol. 33, No. 8, May, 1987, p. 96.*

A BLOSSOM PROMISE (1987)

It had been the worst flood in the history of the state, the newspaper said, but for Vern Blossom and his friend Michael it was the chance to build a raft and have an adventure. Maggie was participating in her first rodeo along with Mom, and Junior, the youngest Blossom, was getting ready to visit his adult friend Mary. Byars moves easily from one pattern to another, building suspense for each child and for their grandfather, who has a heart attack (not fatal) when he rescues Vern and Michael, capsized and in danger of drowning. The smoothly-knit plot is pulled together by the crisis, and the strength of family love is made manifest. Style, dialogue, structure, and characterization are all deft, and the story is given depth by its percipience, and appeal by its humor.

> *Zena Sutherland, in a review of "A Blossom Promise," in* Bulletin of the Center for Children's Books, *Vol. 41, No. 3, November, 1987, p. 44.*

As life would have it, events are once again tumultuous in the Blossom fold. . . .

Byars' fourth (and she says final) work on the Blossom family, *A Blossom Promise,* will not disappoint fans of her previous works. . . . Once again the simple dignity and zest for life exhibited by the Blossoms are showcased. While Pap's obvious frailty gives each Blossom pause, their uninhibited response to even this rather serious situation is pure Blossom: brimming with love, unaffected, and unique. As with the other works of the quartet, *A Blossom Promise* should be accessible to those with even marginal reading skills and is a perfect candidate for a booktalking session.

> *Kevin Kenny, in a review of "A Blossom Promise,"* in Voice of Youth Advocates, *Vol. 10, No. 5, December, 1987, p. 232.*

The final volume of the Blossom Family Quartet rounds out the adventures that began with *The Not-Just-Anybody Family.* All the familiar characters are included, the various members of the Blossom family and their friends—Mad Mary, Ralphie, Michael—but the story stands firmly on its own. . . . The characters are as engaging as ever, and the author uses her sharp-eyed powers of observation to humorous advantage. . . . Although readers will be relieved that Pap's attack is not a fatal one and sympathize with Maggie's determination to see that the family settles down, some of the vitality of the earlier books is missing from the last volume. The pacing is haphazard, with most of the action occurring at the beginning of the book. The last chapter when Junior goes off to spend the night, finally, with Mad Mary is a trifle too transparent an attempt to tie things up neatly. Still, the book will be read with pleasure by readers who have enjoyed the other Blossom books. (pp. 61-2)

> *Nancy Vasilakis, in a review of "A Blossom Promise,"* in The Horn Book Magazine, *Vol. LXIV, No. 1, January-February, 1988, pp. 61-2.*

THE BURNING QUESTIONS OF BINGO BROWN   (1988)

Once again, Byars gives us a memorable character in her portrait of Bingo, poised for his first steps into adulthood—if only he can find out what he's supposed to do.

Bingo—like his school-assigned diary—is full of questions. What can he do when he falls in love with three girls within minutes, when he's not yet up to "mixed-sex" conversation? What should he do when he discovers that Billy Wentworth, who calls him "Worm Brain," is moving in next door? And how can he respond when his teacher, Mr. Markham, hands out strange assignments: writing laudatory letters about Markham to Markham's girlfriend, and, later, writing another letter to convince someone not to commit suicide? Bingo puzzles over these ever more serious questions as he confronts a world of suddenly vulnerable adults.

In less capable hands, Bingo's explorations and the events he faces, which take a more serious turn when Mr. Markham attempts suicide in the second half of the book, could be melodramatic and uneven in tone. But Byars never loses touch with the realities beneath the wryly humorous surface. She communicates her compassion for all her characters to the reader who—like Bingo—will be wiser by the book's end.

> *A review of "The Burning Questions of Bingo Brown,"* in Kirkus Reviews, *Vol. LVI, No. 6, March 15, 1988, p. 451.*

Bingo Brown is one of Byars's most ingenuous and likable male characters since Junior Blossom. He is a fairly ordinary sixth grader, with a number of extraordinary questions. . . . Without resorting to the knee-slapping antics of her last few books, Byars relays Bingo's questions and his answers, in a way that is so believable that readers may wonder if there isn't a Bingo in their classrooms.

> *A review of "The Burning Questions of Bingo Brown,"* in Publishers Weekly, *Vol. 233, No. 14, April 8, 1988, p. 95.*

What an irresistible beginning: "Bingo Brown fell in love three times during English class." . . . Byars does a superb job of presenting a boy just on the edge of maturity. Bingo . . . is peeking through a keyhole into the adult world, while at the same time is actively participating in sixth-grade life. Witty, offbeat, yet beautifully real, Bingo's story scores.

> *Ilene Cooper, in a review of "The Burning Questions of Bingo Brown,"* in Booklist, *Vol. 84, No. 16, April 15, 1988, p. 1426.*

Ann Nolan Clark

1898-

American author of fiction, nonfiction, and picture books; biographer; and reteller.

Clark is recognized as an eminent interpreter of the American Indian experience for middle-grade and younger children. Throughout her distinguished literary career, which spans nearly four decades, she has exhibited unfailing respect for native traditions, beliefs, and ideals; shown sensitivity to ethnic minorities in their struggle to integrate their own values with those of the dominant society; and stressed themes of universal brotherhood and appreciation of nature. A versatile writer, Clark has created picture books, verse, realistic fiction, historical fiction, and biographies that attest to her understanding and love of children from such diverse backgrounds as the deserts of the southwestern United States, the jungles of Costa Rica, and the villages of South Vietnam. She brings her vast experience as a teacher and teacher trainer for the U.S. Bureau of Indian Affairs and the Institute of Inter-American Affairs in Central and South America to her many works. Finding that the children of the various Indian tribes she taught had no textbooks or readers reflecting their rich cultures, Clark immersed herself in their language and customs and produced bilingual books for and with them. *In My Mother's House* (1941), which authentically details the everyday life of the Pueblo Indians, was written for five pupils in simple verse whose cadence patterns their native speech. Best known for *Secret of the Andes* (1952), in which a Peruvian shepherd boy discovers his royal lineage and ultimately accepts a sacred trust from his Inca ancestors, Clark combines a search for identity and vivid descriptions of the Andes mountains with a pervading element of mysticism. She has also written realistic fiction centering on non-Indian peoples such as the Vietnamese, Finnish, and Irish and has retold a Vietnamese version of *Cinderella*.

Critics praise Clark for her poetic prose, the dignity with which she treats her subjects, and her ability to capture the beauty and distinctions of disparate cultures. Although reviewers point out that some of her tales are slow-moving and may not appeal to all children, they agree that her stories read aloud well because of their lyrical quality and that their geographic and historic backgrounds are well researched. Clark has not only created books that give Indian and immigrant children pride in their heritage, she has also allowed other young readers to encounter a diversity of cultural experiences that underscore our universal human kinship.

In My Mother's House was designated a Caldecott Honor Book in 1942 and *Secret of the Andes* won the Newbery Medal in 1953. Clark received the Regina Medal in 1963 for her body of work.

(See also *Something about the Author*, Vol. 4; *Contemporary Authors New Revision Series*, Vol. 2; and *Contemporary Authors*, Vols. 5-8, rev. ed.)

AUTHOR'S COMMENTARY

[The following excerpt is taken from Clark's Regina Medal acceptance speech given on April 16, 1963.]

Photograph by Jack W. Sheaffer

When I received the letter saying that the Regina Medal was being given to me, I could not believe it. The Regina Medal is such a tremendous honor and it came so quietly. (p. 14)

Inner questionings began clamoring for answers. Did I deserve this honor? Why had it happened to me? What had enabled me to reach a place where this medal could be mine?

There were certain facts I knew. I knew them with clarity and honesty. My receiving this award could not be for what I am. I fall far short of any measure of greatness. It could not be for knowledge, I have little knowledge and smaller wisdom. It could not be for writing gift. There are those with greater story sense. There are those with greater force and power in writing skills.

What then did I have that had brought me to this day, this hour that I stand here before you?

Time passed. Answers came to mind and were discarded for newer ones. There was one that kept returning. Like a small persistent voice it kept worrying at the edges of my thoughts. It kept on and on repeating, "If it is not for what you are or know or can do, it must be for something that you believe. Something that you believe."

What I believe? What do I believe? The teachings of my faith, of course. But I was born into my faith. My faith is my heritage.

I have not suffered in its growth within me nor—yet—in the defense.

I asked myself, "What is this belief that has not been given to me, nor laid down before me, but I, myself, have developed? Was it born because of something I have seen or people I have met in my journeying along life's trail?"

Gradually the answer came. It must be because of my belief that people need people, that an acceptance of people by people is important and necessary and vital.

I believe that this acceptance need not be built upon complete understanding. Complete understanding is probably impossible to achieve among groups of people. It may be impossible between individuals. I think it is not absolutely necessary that we must understand in order to accept.

I believe that acceptance of people by people is not built with words nor treaties nor resolutions for co-existence.

It is built upon tolerance—tolerance for other people's values. It is built upon respect—respect for the traditions and customs of other nationalities, races and culture. It is built with sharing—sharing of experiences of tangibles and intangibles of everyday living among the peoples of the world. (pp. 14-15)

I could go on and on far past my allotted talking time in telling you of people of our country and of other countries, people of town and settlement, pueblo and encampment, in the cool, dark rain forest, on the wind-swept Alto Planos, in the muggy coastal swamps, on the wide sand stretches, people of the Americas who accept strangers, who tolerate strange values, who respect strange customs and who share with others all that they have. They are everywhere. They need only to be found and to be told about. I think especially do they need to be written about in our books for children. Children need to know that tolerance and respect, sharing and giving is a natural life-way for many, many people. (p. 17)

Ann Nolan Clark, "Fragments of a Journey," in Catholic Library World, *Vol. 35, No. 1, September, 1963, pp. 14-17.*

GENERAL COMMENTARY

MAY MASSEE

[*May Massee was Clark's friend and first editor.*]

[Ann Nolan Clark] began teaching in earnest in a school in Gallup where Mabel Parsons was the principal. . . . She taught Ann how to teach and made her love the teaching. Once started on the right path, Ann's vivid imagination made her enter so completely into the lives of her Indian pupils that she knew what was wrong with the textbooks provided for them. So she wrote new ones that were exactly right. The children loved their new geographies and readers and so did their mothers and fathers and their uncles and their aunts. The whole village got a new idea of reading and the use of books.

When she taught in a high school they had a Kelsey hand press, and the older children for their English lessons made books for the little ones. They printed and bound the books and it all became really a community project. That is great teaching.

It was natural that the Bureau of Indian Affairs should discover this amazing teacher and find that she had a gift for writing. Willard Beatty, Director of Indian Education, persuaded her to give up her classroom teaching, spend a year each with

various tribes and write books to be used as readers, printed in Navajo and English or Sioux and English, Zuni and English, etc. First drafts of a geography made for and by the Tewa Indians in the Tesuque Pueblo in Santa Fe were the basis of *In My Mother's House,* about which Mr. Beatty wrote me that Indian children loved the book so much, he thought white children would too. We agreed and they do. . . . It was followed by *Little Navajo Bluebird,* the appealing story of a little Navajo girl and her difficulties in adapting herself to the differences between the traditional Indian customs that she loved and the white people's world which had absorbed her brother and now was beckoning to her adored elder sister and even to Doli herself.

The Inter-American Educational Foundation commandeered Mrs. Clark's services for five years to travel and live in Mexico, Guatemala, Costa Rica, Ecuador, Peru and Brazil. She was training native teachers for work with underprivileged children. There is the background for *Magic Money, Looking-for-Something,* and *Secret of the Andes.* And for her fidelity to the background of her stories, her understanding and her skill, I would like to quote from a letter from Mabel Parsons, who probably knows Ann better than anyone else does.

Ann had the good fortune to be part of a very strict family with the highest sense of honesty and responsibility. Everything she has written is honest reporting based on her own experiences. She never "makes up" anything in her life or in her writing. I think this explains why her stories ring true—they are true.

How can Ann write about Navajos so that one old medicine man, who had one of her stories read to him by a Navajo interpreter, said, "It is as good as a Navajo could write"? He meant, of course, that Ann wrote as an Indian felt. She did not imagine this, she knew it, and not only because she had known many Indians, but because she understands the oneness of mankind—skins, habits, ways different, but at heart the same. Ann's understanding of Indians, Latins and the many kinds of people that crowd and cluster up her life is the basis for her writing, but only that—because then come hours and days of patient, careful thinking and planning, selecting and discarding sentence by sentence and word by word. She does not just sit down and write, she sits and works and works. The rhythm and flow of words that so pleases a reader is not just turned on and off at will. It would be nice if it were. It is shaped and manipulated with a great skill inborn in a keen, well-disciplined mind and developed by an honest, painstaking workman.

(pp. 259-61)

May Massee, "Ann Nolan Clark," in The Horn Book Magazine, *Vol. XXIX, No. 4, August, 1953, pp. 258-62.*

EVELYN WENZEL

Ann Nolan Clark's books for children fall into two classifications: the bilingual ones written for Indian children primarily as text-books and published by the U.S. Office of Indian Affairs; and those regularly published for all children. The textbooks came first, the others later, but there is surprisingly little difference in quality between the two types.

The Indian Reader Series definitely presages the later books and constitutes far better literary fare than many readers regularly used in public schools across the country. These are truly delightful stories telling of familiar details of the everyday living of the Navajo, Sioux, and Pueblo children; revealing humor and sensitive understanding of these people as individual personalities as well as a minority culture with its problems; and written in simple, often poetic language which has an Indian ''flavor'' even in English. The readers conform in some degree to the conventional reader format—manuscript printing, short sentences, repetitive words and phrases, many illustrations, and a somewhat controlled vocabulary—but they have a literary quality superior to many of their counterparts in English.

These books contain much that is simple informative material. In the chapter called ''Branding,'' in *Singing Sioux Cowboy,* children are told

> Cowboys cut the calves from their mothers
> They drive the calves into my uncle's corral
> Mother calves bawl
> Baby calves bawl
> Cowboys work fast
> Cowboys yell ''Yi-peee''

The ''Little Herder'' series describes the work of a Navajo girl in each of the four seasons. In autumn she is busy sorting the wool:

> I am helping my mother sort the wool
> This pile we will keep
>   to spin into yarn for weaving
>   because its strands
>   are long and unbroken

Much of this material was later incorporated into the longer story of *Little Navajo Bluebird. Young Hunter of Picuris* tells a story of life in a Pueblo town:

> Up, up, up
>   to Picuris
>   a red-brown town
>   a mud walled town
>   that hides in a pocket
>   of the purple mountains
>   above the read brown hills.

But many of the readers have a stronger thread of story and open with a ''come-hither'' note no reader could resist. *Who Wants to Be a Prairie Dog?* is ''for little Navajos who have not learned to hurry'' and begins by addressing the reader

> This little boy is Mr. Many-Goat's son.
> If you do not believe his story it is because
> You are not short,
> Nor fat
> Nor slow
> And never, never have
>   you been down a
>   prairie dog hole.

A series of four stories are introduced in this intriguing fashion:

> These are stories
>   told just for fun.
> They are not true.
> They never were.
> They could never be.
> But what does it matter
> in just-for-fun stories?

Could there be a beginning better calculated to relax the young reader and make him eager to read about the Pine Ridge Porcupine who lived at the Agency, or about Mister Raccoon in the watermelon patch?

Then there are stories with more serious overtones, meant to present some of the problems of the people of whom they are written. Here Ann Nolan Clark's artistry is at its best, for only a teacher who knows and loves children and a person who has lived and felt with these people could deal with such problems so simply and effectively. *Little Boy with Three Names* tells about a Pueblo boy's summer at home after his first year at Boarding School and shows him confronted with the puzzle of his school name (Little-Joe), his home name (Tso'u), and his church name (Jose la Cruz). Here is a truly artistic handling on a child's level of the problems of conflicting cultures. (pp. 328-330)

Ann Nolan Clark's name appears on two textbooks written for all children: *A Child's Story of New Mexico,* written with a co-author, and *Buffalo Caller,* one of the Row, Peterson Basic Social Education Series. The first is rather a traditionally organized geography text; the second, primarily an information book containing the thread of a story.

Much better known than these textbooks are Ann Nolan Clark's commercially published books for children. With the exception of *In My Mother's House* these books were published somewhat later than the textbooks. *In My Mother's House,* originally written for Indian schools in and around Santa Fe, was published as a trade book and immediately became popular and loved by teachers and children alike. It is a book difficult to classify, for, like any piece of art, it becomes for the reader what he wants at the moment. Is it geography, history, poetry, philosophy, or religion? It is none of these, yet it is all of them, and scaled so perfectly ''to size'' for young children that it almost seems to have been written by them under the guidance of an artist teacher. And perhaps, indeed, it was. . . .

After *In My Mother's House,* Ann Nolan Clark becomes the story-teller again, now on a reading level for older children. The addition of the story, however, in no way lessens their value as information books or detracts from their appeal as poetry. The story does enable her to do something for which she feels a strong responsibility: to help Indian children understand their own problems of growing-up and to interpret to children of other cultures these people she knows and loves so well. (p. 330)

And so she proceeds to tell the stories of the children she has known: of Doli, in *Little Navajo Bluebird,* who must decide whether she will leave her beloved home in the hogan and go away to School; of Tony in *Magic Money,* who has a ''secret want,'' and of his sister Rosita who wants shoes before she goes into the city to work; and, last of all, of Cusi, who finds for himself the ''secret of the Andes'' and faces and solves his own problem. *Magic Money* and *Little Navajo Bluebird* are beautiful family stories. Tony and Doli, though faced with problems, enjoy the security of love and understanding that all children need. Cusi must discover for himself how this need is being filled for him, for he thinks he wants above all else a family of parents and brothers and sisters. *Looking-for-Something* is the story of Gray Burro, who has the typical human problem of being bored with things as they are and who ''follows his ears'' into new and strange places until he finds what he is looking for.

It is appropriate that *Secret of the Andes* should have received the Newbery Award, for it seems above all the other books to have a message in it. Mrs. Clark, herself, says that ''It had been a gradual piling up of all that I had learned, and of all that I believed.'' Cusi is not, at first glance, an ordinary boy, but he shares in common with many boys a need for a "family" of his own and he faces a serious vocational choice—whether to remain in the valley and carry on Chuto's work or to go out into the world. The real message of this book is in the way he makes this choice. The Indian belief in an inner directing force which must be respected and fostered with great patience and understanding is one which our culture could well ponder upon and study. For Cusi, coming into manhood meant learning "to read his own heart." He had been restless and full of questions about the mystery of his past but Chuto would not answer, for "the time is not now to know." When the time for knowing did come, Cusi realized that in his heart he must have known all along. Chuto in his wisdom had known, but had been willing to wait: "Of course you knew, but you had to find out that you knew." This is indeed a message for teachers who, with all of their specialized training and access to scientific knowledge, have scarcely begun to know how to wait for youth to "read its own heart."

Few teachers have given themselves so single-mindedly to understanding a people as Ann Nolan Clark in her long years of work among the Indians; and few writers have been able to effect communication between cultures so sensitively and artistically. (pp. 330-32)

> *Evelyn Wenzel, "Ann Nolan Clark: 1953 Newbery Award Winner," in* Elementary English, *Vol. XXX, No. 6, October, 1953, pp. 327-32.*

CLAIRE HUCHET BISHOP

Ann Nolan Clark has specialized in the American Indian, North and South of the equator. This was no decision of the mind on her part; she is not a sociologist. Neither was it an initial determination to work for better interracial appreciation. Ann Clark's specialization was not intentional at the start. It grew naturally out of the meeting of life's circumstances and a warm imaginative heart. (p. 281)

The deceptive simplicity of the story [*In My Mother's House*] conceals ten years of utter dedication to the discovery of the way Indians feel. It reveals a quiet and steady groping at an understanding from the heart. Ann Nolan Clark lived with the tribes, learned not only their different languages but also their ways of life and their philosophy. She put herself in the gentle, unhurried, receptive mood which alone can open the path to inner interracial communication; an obscure, modest labor of love which in no way precluded the development of an outstanding career.

The book is about My Mother's House, inside and around it, as seen and experienced by an Indian child. It is expressed in rhythmical form which is natural to the Indians. The sentences are very short because Mrs. Clark knows that the Indian child who is learning to read English has to translate back into Indian each sentence and then again into English in order to fully understand it.

The wonder is that with so many technical handicaps at the start, the book comes out, not as a feat of skill, or proficiency at using a vocabulary list, but as the literary accomplishment of a poet. Using but everyday well known recurrent happenings told in simple words, Mrs. Clark has recreated a unique atmosphere. The familiar, humdrum routine of the days and seasons at the pueblo glows with a sort of ritual sacredness. There is nothing there that a young child whatever his color, cannot understand and yet, somehow, he is introduced to a certain life's dimension infinite in space and time. To the Indian children the very familiarity of the pattern is enchanting, to

the White children this is a surprise and a revelation. The quality of this book is such that all through the years it has been loved not only by Indian and White children, but also by adults. Personally, each time I have opened it, I have been caught over and over again by the serene magic of its earthy song, and, more than once, I have been pacified—

> My heart is the holding-place,
> My heart is the keeping place. . . .
>
> Always will I keep
> In my heart
> The things that belong there,
> As lakes
> Keep water
> For the people.

Already are present here the simplicity, the directness, the lyricism, the loftiness and nobility which characterize Ann Nolan Clark's writing. (pp. 282-83)

In My Mother's House, a direct product of teaching the Tesuque children, was followed by *Little Navajo Bluebird* which deals with Indian-White relationship. Doli, the little Indian girl, has to solve this huge problem for herself in a very personal way. There is no preaching, no fiery declaration. This is a simple, honest, rhythmically slow moving Indian story written by someone who has learned to look at life the way Indians do. The White contribution inserts itself in its proper place while the lasting values of the People remain respected. Ann Nolan Clark herself feels that respect deeply. In *Little Navajo Bluebird* she shows this reverence plainly when she deliberately foregoes a sensational, picturesque description of "the Gods." The reader is left without any mental picture whatsoever, and that is as it should be, for sheer curiosity or scholarly anthropological concern should have no place here—this is sacred ground. (p. 283)

This "Third World" of North, Central and South America, scandalous evidence of Christians' inhumanity, these Indian peoples holding fast, mutely, for centuries, to their own traditions, beliefs and sense of values, come to life in Ann Nolan Clark's books. One wonders how a woman, born to the United States average standard of comfort and hygiene as well as to current regards for material values, could have bypassed the filth, the primitive conditions, the ignorance, and, seeing it all, yet perceived the uniqueness of the Indian spiritual contribution. Should it be said, in religious terms, that Mrs. Clark has a charism?

If so, it does not lie in flaming denouncing of blatant exploitation, criminal indifference, shameful abuses or corrupt economic systems. Her dedication is to reveal the Indian children first to themselves then to the Whites in such a way that both sides will acquire, on each other, a new perspective born of mutual respect and appreciation. Mrs. Clark does not minimize the difficulties on the path to understanding as she shows so well in *World Song.* There, the White boy is eager to feel that nothing separates him from his Indian friend. He declares, "You and I are alike." But the Indian boy does not agree. He knows that sheer will power and good intentions cannot bridge the gap. The latter is eventually spanned through sharing in common a mutual love, that for birds. In this new unsentimental, authentic relationship, many different people come to be included—the Indian, a Spanish, a Chinese and the United States boy. Wisdom knows no curtain.

There are times however when Indian tradition is all powerful, all inclusive, starkly uncompromising, a calculated, deliberate rejection of the white conqueror's entire world. And that too,

Ann Clark understands. *Secret of the Andes* is the story of an Inca boy in present day Peru who becomes heir to the four-hundred-year-old-kept secret about the hidden gold which never reached the Spaniards after they murdered Atahualpa. It is hard to say what is the most outstanding in this book, the plot itself or the style, the author's grasp of Indian lyricism or her knowledge of Incas' traditions, her ability to vibrate to the grandiose landscape of the Andes or that of rising to Indian philosophic heights. The latter lead her to a 'non-White' happy ending of the story—Cusi turns away, not only from the White world from which he cuts himself off completely, but also from the legitimate warmth of human family relationship. Irrevocably he sets his gaze toward the mountains from whence comes no material reward but the austere blessing of a consecration to a four century old lost cause. To my mind, *Secret of the Andes* is one of the summits of American literature for the young. . . . That such a book received the Newbery Medal is more than justified.

Had Ann Nolan Clark written but *Secret of the Andes* she would have acquired the right to be remembered lastingly. But many more moving stories has she set down with talent and art, stories of Indians and mixed Indians and of poor children of Spanish descent in the Latin Americas. With such a colorful, rich background of customs as those people have, it would have been easy to create interest through sheer picturesqueness and local mores. But though her children are true to their particular surroundings, condition and culture—and thereby introduce the reader to the externals of the Americas' 'Third World'—yet their feelings are apprehended not as curiosities but as deep, fundamental human reactions. Children the world over can understand poor little Costa Rica Tony of *Magic Money* who wants to earn enough money to buy two oxen for his Grandpa. Or the boy of *The Desert People* who sings of the animals and the way of life in the wide open country throughout the annual cycle of the changing moons when each morning his father calls,

> Morning stands up, my sons,
> Stand up to meet it.
> Go forth into the dawn,
> running.

Or the child in *Tia Maria's Garden*. . . . who sings of the desert—his auntie's fenceless garden—its plants, its animals, the magic of endless walks and discoveries. . . . (pp. 283-84)

Ann Clark's books cover a wide age range, from four to 14, at least they do so officially. It seems to me truer to say that they have no age limit. Also, several of her books have been translated into foreign languages.

The life of all those underprivileged children bereft of material possessions is rich in feelings. The simple happenings which would hardly make a ripple in the life of an average young White United States citizen are of tremendous significance to the Indian or to the Latin American youngster. The drama is twofold—the conditions of the experience and the impact of the experience on the child. The latter is the more important. It is the intensity and depth of feeling the child brings to the experience, his capacity to live his small human drama to the limit, even up to the wrenching of his own heart, this is what makes the stories unforgettable. The stream of consciousness in those children runs deep as in the little Mexican orphan Pascqualita who, in *A Santo for Pasqualita,* wishes for her own saint's likeness.

That this deep stream of consciousness should not be tampered with in any way is convincingly set forth in Ann Clark's books.

In this fluid world of ours where millions of people are awakening there is also the problem of the underprivileged child befriended by some well-intentioned people belonging to another prosperous or victorious race. Such a 'lucky' child is in fact, without his knowing it, a human being inwardly divided, who will, all his life, play at being what he is not and who, unaware of the inner clamoring of his own roots, will remain incapable of authentic knowledge of himself. Thus *Santiago,* the Indian orphan boy who, until he is 12 years old, knows nothing of his own people and lives happy and carefree in the house of a lovely, proud descendant of a Spanish family. But an Indian clansman snatches him out of this comfortable world of make-believe and rudely sets him back on the arduous bitter path of his Indian heritage. Stark, harrowing adventures, one after the other, harden the boy and force him into a true knowledge of himself, until at last he can accept himself as he is and not as he would have appeared—even to himself—to be had he remained in the Spanish house. However, the merciless experience has gone deep enough to reveal to him that his own true way is not the hard but uncomplexed going back to the ancestral pattern of life. To do this would be the denying of a part of himself just as would his acceptance to enter the Whites' world. Santiago chooses the narrow path of his own authenticity, ''I have found my place in the Divine One's pattern—it is to help Indian children to be good Indians in the modern world . . . , I want to teach.''

Santiago's tragedy points to a worldwide problem—the danger for the peoples of underdeveloped countries to turn into artificial human beings following their introduction to the Western and to the technical worlds. The outcome of Santiago's tragedy points to a harmonious way out, one of many undoubtedly. What is important is to maintain full authenticity. This is the problem of Gandhi returning from London University, that of Mouloud Feraoun of Algeria, that of Leopold Senghor, President of the Republic of Senegal. Because these are great names we happen to know about their dilemma. But the Santiagos are already legion and tomorrow they will be many more. Ann Nolan Clark's books leap over borders thousands and thousands miles long.

And this she does without ever leaving the world a child can understand. Though Mrs. Clark was the only woman to a UNESCO conference on the education of underprivileged children, yet there is nothing in her of the stereotyped social worker. None of her stories are 'cases,' and that is why they touch us so much, children and adult alike. The artist in her eclipses the teacher and the spiritual experience transcends the ethical. Even her gay animal stories retain something of this double characteristic. In *Looking-For-Something* the little burro cries with joy when the boy takes him in,

> Oh! This is what I wanted.
> To be somebody's burro.
> To belong to somebody.
> This is the SOMETHING
>   that I have been looking for.

And in the simple story of *Blue Canyon Horse* there is a touch of philosophy which gives it a bigger dimension,

> The little horse stumbles climbing forward.

and

> The price of too much freedom is pain.

Her writing has the unhurried quality of the Indian song and its compelling rhythm. She has a sweeping sense for the grandeur of this hemisphere's landscape, of its untamed, harsh magnificence. With a few words and short sentences she knows how to paint some of these breath-taking American horizons or to make you feel the fury of the elements. . . . (pp. 284-85)

But the song of this hemisphere which Ann Clark perceives is not detached from man. On the contrary it is intimately linked with him. Often I have wondered whether our White avid restlessness on this continent was not a manifestation of our own rootlessness in its soil. It is as if we were standing on the crust of the land as so many objects set there, not as growing trees nursed deep in the ground. There was a time in my life when that feeling choked me so that I looked desperately for a link which would enable me to grasp somewhat the inner meaning of this particular part of our planet's land and to relate myself to it. I turned to the seventeenth-century French Jesuits' *Relations* and, through them, came my first authentic contact with this hemisphere. Later, much later, came Ann Nolan Clark's books. Here was solace—a White, North American woman had become at-one with the land, and, as the Jesuits did, she had done so through the Indians who themselves live an im-memorial, deep rooted friendship with this hemisphere's na-ture. This feeling permeates all Mrs. Clark's books. . . . This feeling of intimate relatedness between this hemisphere's na-ture and man, Ann Nolan Clark carries . . . through many beautiful Indian songs that she has recreated for us and which are to be enjoyed almost in every one of her books. Every one of these songs should be quoted and many of them could be learned by heart by the children so that later in life these verses may come up naturally to their lips in the midst of the American landscape.

No wonder that Ann Nolan Clark's books are a joy to the Indians, both young and old, who recognize themselves, their traditions, their sense of values, their suffering and their hopes. Also, her books introduce the Indians to what is relevant for them in the White man's culture and which they can assimilate without betraying their own ways. . . . (p. 286)

To us Whites, children and adults, Ann Clark opens the door to Indian culture, not through easy picturesqueness, but through inner contact which brings respect. Gone is the short sighted effort of making the Indians over into Whites. There is appre-ciation for what they are, racially and culturally.

Reading Mrs. Clark's books makes one feel sometimes that we have much more to learn from the Indians than they from us. Much that we can offer can be had, directly or indirectly, through money, whether hygiene, technique or even schooling. But no amount of money can buy serenity, reverence for nature, at-oneness with the universe, family devotion, sense of the sacred in everyday life.

Social reformers may miss in Ann Nolan Clark's books a ring of indignation. It may seem insufficient to them to make state-ments such as,

> Indians must keep their land.
> They must keep the land they have;
> They must not sell it;
> They must not let other people
> Take it.
>
> Indians must keep
> What land they have.
>
>   (*In My Mother's House*)

Some people may point out that Indians have mighty little land left and that it would be better to denounce the cause of this iniquity. But this is not Mrs. Clark's vocation. She has been called to work slowly at the redress of the wrongs, through

thoughtful teaching and talented writing. Her dedication is to point to the Indians that, without betrayal, some of the White man's ways are acceptable and good. To us Whites, she shows the Indian path of ever present and everlasting Beauty. Children of both races reading her books have begun to tread the road where they may eventually meet in true friendship.

Mrs. Clark pursues her work in behalf of the Indians and she also keeps up with her writing. One can but hope that many more books will come out of the distinguished pen of the poet-philosopher-teacher and mother Ann Nolan Clark. All those who already know her work, so typically feminine in its service to earth children's mutual understanding, will applaud at the well deserved recognition bestowed upon her as the recipient of the Regina Medal for 1963. (pp. 286, 333)

> *Claire Huchet Bishop, "Ann Nolan Clark," in Cath-olic Library World, Vol. 34, No. 6, February, 1963, pp. 280-86, 333.*

MAY HILL ARBUTHNOT

In My Mother's House and *Secret of the Andes* represent some-thing of Mrs. Clark's range of experience with primitive peoples. Furthermore, she is able to interpret their ways of life so that modern children respect them. . . . Her writing reflects her love for these peoples. *Secret of the Andes,* a Newbery Medal win-ner, is the story of a dedicated Peruvian Indian boy, the last of a royal line. *Santiago* is about a Guatemalan youth, raised in a Spanish home but determined to find his place in the world as an Indian. Both of these perceptive stories are for children eleven to fourteen.

For younger children Mrs. Clark has written three books that give authentic pictures of the life and ideals of our desert Indians. *In My Mother's House* is written as if a Tewa child were speaking simply and beautifully of the small world he knows and holds dear. The cadenced prose of the text is matched by the rhythmic beauty of the illustrations [by Velino Herrera]. (pp. 452-53)

Little Navajo Bluebird tells the dramatic story of a Navaho child who loves her home, her family, and the old ways of life. . . . Children nine to eleven to enjoy little Doli, and through her story acquire a better understanding of the Indian's problems of adjustment. . . .

Blue Canyon Horse is about the Havasu Indians, who, with neither roads nor wagons, must depend on horses in their can-yon home. The book begins with the flight of a young mare to the high mesa above the canyon, where the wild horses live. All winter the hero grieves for his lost horse but never loses hope that she will return. And sure enough, in the spring she comes back with her colt to the friendship of her master. No outline can give a fair picture of the beauty and simplicity of this story, with its account of the little mare running wild and free and the interludes of the boy's hurt and longing, his dream "misted, unreal, unfinished, but in it flickers a spark of hope." For the oldest or the youngest children, Mrs. Clark writes with a sense of the inner life and ideals of a people. Her cadenced prose is beautiful and unique. (p. 453)

> *May Hill Arbuthnot, "Here and Now: Ann Nolan Clark," in her Children and Books, third edition, Scott, Foresman and Company, 1964, pp. 452-53.*

ARNOLD A. GRIESE

Ann Nolan Clark's answer to the question, "What factors con-tributed significantly to your success as a writer?" could be paraphrased in the simple statement "other people." Such an answer points to one of her basic character traits—humility. A genuine humility that makes it possible for her to accept what others have to offer. To accept especially the richness found in minority cultures. This richness which so often lies hidden from those of us belonging to the dominant culture who are apt to judge the other culture in terms of our own. In the early 1960's when rigorous attention was given to the education of minorities, the term ''culturally disadvantaged'' was first used and then, as minority cultures were better understood, the term was changed to ''culturally different.'' Twenty years earlier Ann Nolan Clark had already arrived at her own clear distinction between these two terms. (p. 649)

It seems appropriate at this time to study examples of her writing in more detail to determine the specific elements that contribute to their excellence as literature. (p. 652)

[Two] outstanding characteristics of Ann Nolan Clark's writing are: theme, in which she sensitively depicts the Indian traditions and world view while at the same time relating them to the broader arena of universal human concerns, and literary style, in which she uses words to produce prose that has many of the essential elements of poetry.

Theme is defined here as the author's unconscious attempt to portray—through the interactions of story characters with each other and with the physical elements of their surroundings—universal human traits, beliefs, aspirations, and values. Ann Nolan Clark's stories abound with strong, suitable themes for children. Thus in *Blue Canyon Horse* she expresses, through the feelings and actions of an Indian boy and a wild horse, the bond of friendship that can exist between man and animal—a bond so strong that it even overcomes the animal's natural instinct to be free.

Similarly, in *Summer Is for the Growing* she deals with the universal need of children for something permanent as they face the change that is an integral part of growing up and which is, in a broader sense, an integral part of every culture regardless of how unchanging it may appear. This theme is subtly conveyed through passages such as the following which reflect the thoughts of the main character, Lala, a young girl of Spanish descent:

> Lala sat up in the high carved bed. How good it was, she thought, that each special sound belonged to the special person making it. It was good too, to know that each sound came from its special place and in its special time. Each morning was the same.

This experience takes place in 1851, in a hacienda, to a girl who is born into a place of privilege. But it is also a universal experience. An Indian child of an earlier period awakening in his wigwam, a child in the ghetto of today awakening to the sounds of a mother moving about as she prepares for the day, or a child awakening in his own room in suburbia—all of these children probably would have experienced such a moment, would have cherished it, and would have unconsciously been strengthened by the feeling of permanence it implied. (pp. 652-54)

[Because] of her extensive knowledge of, and appreciation for, Indian tradition, Ann Nolan Clark is able to focus on specific facets of that tradition while at the same time incorporating this distinctively Indian view into the broader framework of theme as previously defined. Thus in the following excerpt taken from *In My Mother's House* she conveys the importance

of nature—physical surroundings, seasons, growing things, etc.—in the Indian world view:

> Trees are good to us;
> They give us things,
> Many things.
>
> Trees give us
> Shade
> From sun;
> They give us
> Shelter
> From storm.
>
> Trees give us
> Fruits and nuts,
> Apricots,
> Little and yellow,
> And plums and apples

In this instance we can assume the child of today in the dominant white culture has not experienced a similar closeness with nature. But the style of writing allows such a child to identify with the Indian child's point of view and, perhaps, even find value in applying it to his own life. (p. 654)

Style has also been mentioned as an outstanding attribute of her writing. Style is, of course, an all-pervading characteristic of literature and it is all but impossible to identify all the elements that account for distinctive style. It is possible, however, to identify specific elements that contribute significantly to a particular author's style.

One of the elements that contribute significantly to Ann Nolan Clark's style is her natural awareness of detail aimed at promoting imagery and a facility to communicate such images to the reader's mind through the use of appropriate concrete words. In the following passage from *Blue Canyon Horse* she uses specific detail to communicate—through imagery—the Indian's awareness of his natural surroundings:

> The night is still
> The stars above are far away.
> The night winds hush the noisy waters,
> The canyon is shadow-filled and stilled.

In the following passage taken from the opening sentences of *Santiago* she uses specific detail to subtly develop characterization:

> Today was his birthday. Today he was twelve years old. . . .But only his dark eyes showed his happiness. His face was still. His hands were quiet. His thin body was poised as he gravely greeted his guests.

Another important element in her style is effective use of simile, metaphor, and personification—especially the latter. Effective use of personification is demonstrated in these lines from *Tia Maria's Garden:*

> Sun likes the sand,
> I think, because
> even in the morning
> he touches it
> to make it warm.

(p. 655)

A final significant element in her style is the creation of a sense of rhythm through carefully selected repetition of words and phrases. This is demonstrated in the following passage taken from her Newbery Award winner *Secret to the Andes:*

> There was no sound, there was no movement. No wind blew through the twisted, tangled branches of

a tree. No bird chirped its morning prayer. No twig broke beneath the fleet foot of a running fox. . . .

(pp. 655-56)

In making this closer examination of Ann Nolan Clark's writing, some consideration should be given to her treatment of plot. If we define plot as the generation of a problem or conflict taken from within the everyday happenings in a child's life, and if the attempted solutions stem from the child's attitudes, actions, and inner resources, then her stories can be said to contain rigorous plots. This is especially apparent in stories such *Navajo Bluebird, Santiago* and *Medicine Man's Daughter* where the main characters are caught up in the larger conflict between the Indian culture and the dominant white culture. However, if plot is interpreted as involving rigorous action and adventure (as exemplified in the ''Hardy boys'' series) then her plots will not fulfil the criteria. She has a definite view as to what plot should be and expresses it in the following statement from *Journey to the People:*

> On the other side of the mountain there can be, but there need not be, bandits in hiding, lost treasures waiting to be found, villains filled with gleeful malice, or damsels in distress. But there need not be these things. Instead, there can be—just the other side of the mountain, the adventure of having reached there and the prospect of return. These things are real. They happen to us every day. . . .I make a plea for recognizing and enjoying the small, simple realities of life.

A close examination of her writing would not be complete without trying to answer the criticism expressed by some, that children are not naturally drawn to reading her stories. (pp. 656-57)

As the preceding examples from her stories—those used to demonstrate outstanding elements of style—show, her writing is closely akin to poetry. Thus it may well be that children do not spontaneously choose her stories for their own silent reading; no more than they would spontaneously choose poetry for this same purpose. This suggests that teachers, and parents, take time to share this type of writing through oral reading during story hour or any other similar convenient period. Considering the strong themes contained in her writing, her effectiveness in building bridges of understanding between cultures, and the poetic quality of her style, it would seem important that every effort be made to properly introduce children to her stories.

The problem, and its solution, are summed up in the following review of *The Desert People* by M. S. Libby in the May 13, 1962, issue of the New York Herald Tribune Books:

> Ann Nolan Clark writes a simple prose poem to express her feelings about a group of people. . . .This kind of book often puzzles the young when they pick it off the library shelves and glance at it. They will receive it cordially and share imaginatively in another way of life if a wise teacher introduces it. . . .

Apparently many wise teachers, and parents, are introducing Ann Nolan Clark's books to children for all her books, whether old or more recently published, continue to be sold out and new printings made. . . . This places them in the category of the classics which are usually defined as books that continue to be read with the passage of time. Considering that books she has written over thirty years ago continue to be read by a substantial number of children today suggests that Ann Nolan Clark is not only a builder of bridges of cultural understanding

but also a literary artist whose status as a writer for children will not be diminished by the passing years. (p. 657)

Arnold A. Griese, ''Ann Nolan Clark—Building Bridges of Cultural Understanding,'' in Elementary English, *Vol. XLIX, No. 5, May, 1972, pp. 648-58.*

BARBARA BADER

> The land
>   around my mother's hogan
>   is big.
> It is still.
> It has walls of red rocks.
> And way, far off
>   the sky comes down
>   to touch the sands.

So begins *Little Herder in Autumn,* the start of Little Herder's story. It is incantatory, an Indian chant; it is direct, a child's talk; it speaks precisely and allusively, poet-fashion. (p. 162)

[The] Little Herder series is outstanding in any company. They continue to be issued by the Bureau of Indian Affairs . . . and to be used in Indian schools. (p. 163)

Mrs. Clark learned from the Indians, adults and children,. . . not only a mode of expression but a way of feeling. Little Herder looking upon the land around her mother's hogan, her Pueblo counterpart saying of ''Home,'' ''This is my Mother's house . . . I live in it,'' is saying this is mine and I am me, it is part of me and I am part of it: for a child, any child, a wonderful thing. To bolster them, teachers of Indian children encouraged them to express what was theirs, and Mrs. Clark put what was theirs into words that were, in effect, their own; but beyond the value of her work in teaching Indian children or, in the case of *In My Mother's House,* in teaching white children about Indians, was its value as an example of children speaking in their own voice, naturally, about what was closest to them. (p. 166)

Barbara Bader, ''Of the American Indian,'' in her American Picturebooks from Noah's Ark to the Beast Within, *Macmillan Publishing Company, 1976, pp. 158-66.*

MYRA POLLACK SADKER AND DAVID MILLER SADKER

No author represents [the] movement of presenting an accurate portrayal of Indian life more than Ann Nolan Clark. . . . *In My Mother's House* is representative of the kind of story Clark writes, relating the everyday events in Indian society rather than focusing on the unusual and the more adventurous stories. Clark's literary style demonstrates a sensitivity to detail, a strong sense of rhythm, and an emphasis on the use of simile and metaphor. . . . (p. 180)

The ceremonies and daily activities of the Navaho are presented in Clark's *Little Navajo Bluebird.* The close relationship between Navaho and nature is stressed, and white civilization is seen as a competitive force that offers definite advantages to the Navaho. *Secret of the Andes,*. . . although not about an Indian in the United States, is an effective story of a Peruvian Indian boy who grows to understand his heritage and his responsibilities as the last in a royal line. The activities and ceremonies of the Papago Indians are recounted in *The Desert People,* another realistic book for elementary children.

Ann Nolan Clark, noted for her many fine books for younger children, has also written several insightful books appropriate for older children. *Journey to the People* consists of ten essays that reflect the author's experiences of over fifty years of working among the Zuni, Navaho, Pueblo, Sioux, and Guatemala Indians. Clark refutes some common misconceptions about Indian beliefs by discussing Indian concepts of land, work, time, and spiritual life. In *Circle of Seasons* Clark provides a description of the rites and practices of the Pueblo year and a sense of reverence for and appreciation of the closeness of the Pueblo to nature.... (p. 181)

> *Myra Pollack Sadker and David Miller Sadker, "Native Americans in Children's Books," in their* Now Upon a Time: A Contemporary View of Children's Literature, *Harper & Row, Publishers, 1977, pp. 163-90.*

ALETHEA K. HELBIG AND AGNES REGAN PERKINS

Although artlessly plotted, [Ann Nolan Clark's] novels show that she understands the Indians and has great sympathy for them. The books are shallowly characterized and tend toward message but are high in atmosphere and mood and employ a simple, poetic style. Her more recent novels have moved in a different direction, relating the experiences of immigrants to this country, among them, *All This Wild Land* about Finns, and *To Stand Against the Wind* about Vietnamese. (p. 104)

[*Little Navajo Bluebird* is a] realistic novel of Navajo family life set in Arizona in the mid-1900s. The loosely plotted story follows one year in the life of little Doli, the Bluebird.... Sentences are short and language easy. The loose, contrived plot moves without surprises to its expected conclusion. It serves as a device by which the author can present details of daily life among the Navajos as the seasons change. The sense of family comes through strongly, Doli changes believably, and Uncle and Trader are genial and likeable, but Uncle's Wife is too obviously a role model. The book's claim to memorability lies in its graphic picture of Navajo life, customs, and beliefs intended for the young. Verses from chants, stories about and many allusions to the gods, and descriptions of such activities as peach picking in Canyon de Chelly, the Sing for Hobah, the Night Chant for Doli, gathering pinon nuts in the mountains, weaving, silverworking, sheepherding, and games come together for a vivid depiction of Navajo life. (p. 302)

[*Magic Money* is a] realistic novel of family life set in Costa Rica near San José at an unspecified time but probably in the mid-1900s.... The two main characters [Tony and Grandpapa] seem real, even if Tony is a trifle too babyish, but the rest of the family seems assembled for effect. There are good scenes of daily work (doing the washing, picking coffee berries, making sugar, going to market) and of pleasure (the peasants' picnic and the family party), but the way of life seems idealized, and the peasants are depicted as almost perpetually laughing in text and in [Leo Politi's] illustrations, supporting the popular stereotype of Central Americans. Although contrived, the story is diverting, holds the interest, and moves to a satisfactory conclusion. The book seems intended to instruct young readers about peasant life in Costa Rica. Read today, it holds ironies, for example, that Costa Rica compares to the United States in opportunity for peasants to rise and that the Patron is considered a good man because he provides so well for his workers. (pp. 321-22)

[*Santiago* is a] realistic novel of the problems of the modern Maya in finding their role in Guatemala society as seen through the experiences of an educated Maya youth.... Although sentences are short and vocabulary easy enough for younger readers, the earnest, even urgent, tone and the underlying concepts require a more mature audience. Descriptive passages are alive

with imagery, but characterization is minimal. AFter a gripping start filled with human interest, the novel degenerates into a fictionalized social science text about the Guatemala of the mid-twentieth century. Santiago's experiences seem intended to show the life choices open to modern youth there and move predictably to an instructive conclusion. (pp. 449-50)

[*Secret of the Andes* is a] novel set in the mid-1900s among the Indians of the Peruvian mountains, which combines realism, legend, and here and there a touch of fantasy.... The pace is slow, the plot seems contrived, Cusi changes predictably, the atmosphere is overly mystical, and the mystery of Cusi's background, while it adds some suspense, seems an unnecessary complication. The best part of this novel lies in its rhythmical prose, in its descriptions of the hill Indians' way of life, in the sense it conveys of their respect for nature and pride in their ancient culture so drastically altered by the coming of the Spaniards. (pp. 459-60)

> *Alethea K. Helbig and Agnes Regan Perkins, in a review of "All This Wild Land" and others, in their* Dictionary of American Children's Fiction, 1859-1959: Books of Recognized Merit, *Greenwood Press, 1985, pp. 104, 302, 321-22, 449-50, 459-60.*

IN MY MOTHER'S HOUSE (1941)

AUTHOR'S COMMENTARY

In My Mother's House was written for five little Tesuque children, four boys and one girl about nine years old. It was first called *Home Geography* because that is what it is.

I had been teaching in the pueblo for four years. These children had begun school the first year I taught them. At first I had to teach them English. Later I taught them to read but I was dissatisfied with what they had to read. We had attractive books but not one story that was "Tesuque."

Even the Indian stories were from the white viewpoint and instead of taking an Indian fact for granted, the story explained it, which is interesting and necessary for white children but bores the little Indian.

For example, one part of the book is about spring fields. The Pueblo Indians do not like to "bruise mother earth" in the spring before she has become fruitful, therefore at that time the horses go unshod and all the older Indians and the conservative younger ones wear moccasins and not hard leather shoes—but to explain that to Indian children would be unnecessary and something which the older ones would resent as they have become very secretive in their folkways, but to ignore it would not be Indian so I took it for granted. The book has many such places.

Indian Pueblos are matriarchal and the life of the village centers around the fireplace in the mother's house. The house, the children, and the house furnishings belong to the mother. Crops in the field and game on the mountain are the property of the men, but they must be brought home and placed before the mother's door and then they become her property.

I believe that Indians have a far greater rhythmic sense than we do. I think design and pattern is more important to them than to us and so the book is written in a style that fits in with that thinking. Also I think that Indians have to translate English back into Indian and retranslate it again to English, therefore I made short lines with natural breaks in the sentences. We have found that this helps greatly in remedial reading. (pp. 475-76)

May Massee, "Newbery to Ann Clark," in Library Journal, *Vol. 78, No. 6, March 15, 1953, pp. 475-77.*

This book about the Tewa Indian children of the Tesuque pueblo, near Santa Fé, tells of everyday things with the unstudied poetry, the simplicity and directness of childhood. Here is a realistic book for little children transfigured by imagination; a rare achievement and one very welcome in the field of children's books about the Indians. An interest in the American Indian past and present comes early and the books on this subject prepared for boys and girls from 7 on are legion. They are simple enough, many of them, for beginners in reading, they are usually accurate, but for the most part they look on from the outside and are remote from the inner spirit of Indian life.

Ann Nolan Clark has worked for ten years with Indian children of all ages. She has lived for a year at a time, or longer, with a tribe, to try to catch their ways of thinking. *In My Mother's House* first took form in the children's notebooks. Finding there was a need in the Indian schools for books written from the Indian point of view, she began, with the permission of the government, to write some of these books. As used in the villages the books are done in English and Spanish, or English and Navajo, or English and Sioux. They are illustrated by Indians and published by Indian printers.

And so Miss Clark's book, with its lovely pictures [by Velino Herrera], its sensitive rhythmical descriptions of the house that

> does not stand alone.
> Its sister houses are round it;
> Its sister houses are close to it.
>
> Like holding hands,
> The houses stand close together
> Around the plaza,

of the "brown fields that will turn to green."

> Little green corn ears
> Dancing,
> For the rain,
> For the sun,

of the

> Yucca
> Growing
> So tall
> Like candles,

and the rest, is more than a beautiful picture book. It gives to little children as no other book has a sense of knowing Indian boys and girls and the feeling of experiences shared.

With its short sentences and clear type the text is well suited to the needs of beginners in reading; when read aloud a little at a time it will hold children as poetry does, by its rhythm and the beauty of its language. . . . A distinguished American book.

Anne T. Eaton in a review of "In My Mother's House," in The New York Times Book Review, *May 4, 1941, p. 11.*

[It] would be hard to find use of words—call it poetry or prose as you prefer—carrying a beautiful meaning more clearly to a

young mind: what life means to a primitive community, close to earth and sky. At the heart of all is the family in "my mother's house" that my father made with adobe bricks and that my mother plastered with brown clay, smoothing walls and floor "for me to live there."

> My mother's house,
> It does not stand alone—
> Its sister houses are around it:
> Its sister houses are close to it.
> Like holding hands,
> The houses stand close together
> Around the plaza.

Telling sometimes what a Tewa Indian child knows, sometimes what he believes, whether of life-giving water, of sheep and cows and many horses lithe and parti-colored, of juniper, chamiso, guaca and yucca, blankets and earthenware, and of the spirit that holds all these together, the quiet, rhythmic record goes on. . . . This book met the judgment of all the people of Tesuque pueblo before it was offered to ours. Even a very small English-speaking child could understand every word of it; sometimes the smaller a child is, the more apt he is to get the overtones of words. Read it aloud to someone, old or young; read it gently, letting it take its own time. It has something the rest of America has forgotten, and that civilization must remember when it begins to build again.

May Lamberton Becker, "Three Prize Winning Books, Spring 1941," in New York Herald Tribune Books, *May 11, 1941, p. 8.*

The simple, direct text, containing repetition in word and beat, reinforces the style of traditional Native American literature and seems adaptable to singing or chanting, reflecting its evolution from the oral tradition. The more authentically and realistically presented style of this early work does capture the essence and style of the Pueblo world-view more closely than later works dealing with the same concepts—it is not an attempt to "Americanize" the style, but it does reflect a common attempt to "civilize" the Native American in some portions of the text and illustrations. . . .

Each segment the text deals with, be it Home, Council, Pasture, pueblo, Pipeline, people, fire, wild plants, Birds, Mountains or others, contributes to the whole picture of the young boy's life as a Pueblo Indian. "I string them together / Like beads. / They make a chain, / A strong chain, / To hold me close / To home, / Where I live / In my Mother's house." (p. 249)

Linda Kauffman Peterson, in a review of "In My Mother's House," in Newbery and Caldecott Medal and Honor Books: An Annotated Bibliography, *by Linda Kauffman Peterson and Marilyn Leathers Solt, G. K. Hall & Co., 1982, pp. 235-378.*

LITTLE NAVAJO BLUEBIRD (1943)

Winner of one of the Herald Tribune's Spring Festival prizes, for her luminously beautiful presentation of Navajo life, *In My Mother's House."* Mrs. Clark shows in her new book the same qualities that gave distinction to her earlier work. These are first of all the capacity to identify herself spiritually with the Navajo scheme of things, while retaining the power of looking at it from the outside. This is a gift rare enough to call for special tools by which to carry it out: these are provided by her other distinguishing quality—ability, whether natural or acquired and probably both, to speak and write in the Navajo rhythm and with these turns of phrase. Applied, as here, to a story turning on a situation familiar to children's literature—the difficulty of applying "Americanization" to these Americans—the result is a story with special meaning to those interested in this process.

For Doli, approaching her sixth summer and making ready to learn all kinds of women's work, has an elder brother who has been so thoroughly Americanized at the government's school that he scorns home ways and has indeed left home forever. Her adored big sister, Hobah, is just old enough to be taken off, willing or otherwise, to the school. How will little Doli, child of her people, with their music in her bones and their prayers part of her life, reconcile her love for the brother and for a sister who seems ready to take his path, with her love of her mother's house? Through the year the life of the village goes on around the child through whose eyes the child reader sees it. They thus witness even the ceremonies at which the Gods appear, and take part in the great Sing, with its sand paintings and consecrations, that take place when sister Hobah goes off to school. Songs of home, of family affection, of nature, sound throughout the story. When big brother returns, Doli has brought him, and in doing so has shown our children how rugs are woven, what part peaches play in Navajo life, and other arts, trades and tasks of Doli's people. But the charm of the book is in its evocation of Doli's love of life and in her definition—which is that of her people—of what life means to man.

May Lamberton Becker, in a review of "Little Navajo Bluebird," in New York Herald Tribune Weekly Book Review, *April 4, 1943, p. 8.*

Ann Nolan Clark, whose distinguished picture-story book *In My Mother's House* appeared two years ago, has caught in this story for 7 to 10 year olds the same reality and quiet beauty. *Little Navajo Bluebird* does not seem so much a story about the Indians of the Southwest as it seems an actual bit of Indian life which Miss Clark, because of her long intimate acquaintance with the Navajos, her knowledge of their ways and her imaginative understanding of what they think and believe, is able to put before the reader. . . .

There is a quiet rhythm in the writing which suits the author's sensitive feeling for places and seasons and growing things, and we find in this book the calm that comes from living in stillness and in close association with the forces of nature, a calm good for the modern child whose life is often over-full and over-stimulated. The drawings [by Paul Lantz] deepen the book's peaceful quality. *Little Navajo Bluebird* is a book about the Indians which is not only a good story but which will start young readers on the road to intelligent sympathy with their fellow-Americans in the Southwest.

Anne T. Eaton, in a review of "Little Navajo Bluebird," in The New York Times Book Review, *May 16, 1943, p. 16.*

Ann Nolan Clark develops, with sympathy, the patient growth of Little Bluebird, loving her home with its individual sense of beauty and art,. . . seeing as she grows wiser, how the Red Man's Trail and the White Man's Trail can come together to enrich the Indian's life. While this is a happy personal story for little girls, it presents truly one of the problems an Indian child faces today.

Alice M. Jordan, in a review of "Little Navajo Bluebird," in The Horn Book Magazine, *Vol. XIX, No. 3, May-June, 1943, p. 169.*

MAGIC MONEY **(1950)**

A rambling, little idyll of Costa Rica too tremulously in the genre for most American children to take. Tony had a secret, and he needed money for his secret. So Grandfather helped him to work, even though he was very little. But somehow Tony seemed to go to sleep when he should be working and even though there was a grand party at the Patron's, and handsome Roberto was happy and beautiful, and Rosita had a lovely pair of shoes, Tony was not happy, for he wanted something for his grandfather. Finally Grandfather helps him to make a wooden ox and cart—like Grandfather's before he lost his oxen. When the wooden ox and cart are sold Tony is jubilant for now Grandfather may buy his oxen, which was Tony's secret all along. A pleasant story, but the gay, lilting measure of the speech, so charming to an adult, may puzzle and annoy a child acclimated to the flat intonations of American speech.

A review of "Magic Money," in Virginia Kirkus' Bookshop Service, *Vol. XVIII, No. 16, August 15, 1950, p. 464.*

[*Magic Money*] is a realistic story of the everyday life of a country boy who lives in Costa Rica. With an intimate first-hand knowledge of the country and its people Miss Clark has given a warm human touch to the life of the whole family to which nine-year-old Tony belongs. . . . Of special interest to children who are learning that Central America is something more than just a country on the map, *Magic Money* deals with common problems of childhood with rare understanding and regard for children's emotions and secret desires.

Anne Carroll Moore, in a review of "Magic Money," in The Horn Book Magazine, *Vol. XXVI, No. 5, September-October, 1950, p. 356.*

In this beautifully written story of Costa Rica, the lovable nine-year-old hero wants more than anything in the world to earn money for a Secret. . . . The ending is much better than the usual stereotyped one for a story with this theme. Pictures [by Leo Politi], characterization and plot all help to make this a "must." (pp. 379, 381)

Jennie D. Lindquist and Siri M. Andrews, in a review of "Magic Money," in The Horn Book Magazine *Vol. XXVI, No. 5, September-October, 1950, pp. 379, 381.*

SECRET OF THE ANDES **(1952)**

[*The following excerpt is taken from Clark's Newbery Award acceptance speech given on June 23, 1953.*]

Everyone asks me, "How did you happen to write *Secret of the Andes?*" For months that question has met me at every turn. One night in May I sat me down to think it out—how had I come to the writing of that book? Had it been an inspiration of a moment? No. Had it been a long-cherished dream at last fulfilled? No. It had been a very uneventful, natural writing. It had been an easy book to write. It had been a gradual piling up of all that I had learned, and of all that I believed.

My thoughts kept marching back and back and back until I was a child again in the town of my birth in New Mexico. . . .

Did this small town have anything to do with an Indian herdboy of Peru who came to life in the pages of a book a half century later?

I think it did. It think it had much to do with my writing *Secret of the Andes*. (pp. 249-50)

It was the days of early Las Vegas that set the pattern for my thinking. It set the pattern for my acceptance of people and folkways and traditions. It set the pattern which the years have deepened.

New Mexico gave to its early children four culture patterns. It gave us the culture pattern of the Indians who lived in our houses and who slept by our fires. When Juana [an Apache Indian] sang to me and washed my face and fed me, she gave me more than acts or words. She gave me an at-homeness with things Indian and primitive.

New Mexico gave us the culture pattern of the Colonial Spanish who lived on their vast land grants. As children we saw the strip of carpet stretched on the ground from the surrey to the church steps for the Doña to walk upon. We knew that the golden beads and bracelets and bangles that she wore had been mined at the family gold mine and designed for her by the family craftsman. We knew that she had servants to do her will. We also saw her feed those servants, tend them in their illnesses, and care for their well-being. We grew up knowing the responsibility of service to the person who serves you. We accepted this belief. (p. 251)

New Mexico gave us the culture of the French trapper, his ways of dress, his manner of speech, his tradition. Mora and Taos were the trapper towns. I went there often with my father. I remember them as exciting and gay and vivid and alive. I do not know why they were, but this is the way I remember them. As children we knew about the Hudson's Bay Company. It might not have been in operation then, but its people were there in Mora and in Taos.

New Mexico gave us the culture pattern of the people "from the States." It was a culture pattern made up of many nationalities, each clinging stubbornly to the European customs and traditions of its forebears. I know our household clung to ours. Our grandfather saw to it. I know that as well as being a little Indian, a little Spanish, a little French in our ways and our thinking, and "back East" because of mother and father, we were above and beyond and completely Irish because grandfather said so.

But all of this gave us understanding, a tolerance and acceptance and appreciation and ease with different peoples who have other ways of thinking and other ways of living.

New Mexico gave that to all her early children, and for me it has made my life-way rich and warm and wide.

When I grew up and left Las Vegas for greener pastures, it was natural that I chose my classrooms among the kinds of people whom I knew. I have worked with Spanish children from New Mexico to Central and South America, with Indian children from Canada to Peru. I have worked with them because I like them. I write about them because their stories need to be told. All children need understanding, but children of segregated racial groups need even more. All children need someone to make a bridge from their world to the world of the adults who surround them. Indian children need this; they have the child problems of growing up, but also they have racial problems, the problems of conflicting interracial patterns between

groups, and the conflicts of changing racial patterns within the group. Anyway you look at it, it's rugged to be a child. Often I think more of us did not survive the experiences than meets the eye. (pp. 252-53)

Indians have wonderful balance. Generations ago they learned that what cannot be cured, must be endured. I do not like morals in stories—at least, if they show. But often I think that groups of children have messages for other groups of children and for grown-ups, too. I have taught North American Indian children for twenty years. I have known these children in all sorts of situations, in Give-Away get-togethers of the Dakota Sioux, in tight little complex villages of the Pueblos, in lonely Navajo hogans, and in the cottonfields of the Papago. Each group and each child has had some message, some story to tell. (p. 254)

Where customs are different, they assume importance. Those of us who dress alike can afford to be casual in our awareness of clothes. Clothes customs to an Indian child can be an agony.

Manuel came from a southern pueblo. He told me this when he was grown. It had almost stopped hurting then. Manuel's grandfather adored him. When it was time for Manuel to begin school, the old man decided that his grandson should have everything. He left the pueblo and went to the nearby white town and stayed there for several days. Each morning the old man sat himself down in the road by the public school. He watched the children. He would not visit with anyone. He would not answer questions. He watched the school. He watched the children. At last he knew what he had wanted to know. He trotted the fifteen miles back to the pueblo and the next morning he took Manuel to the trading post. He bought him Levi's with button rivets, a plaid shirt with a handkerchief pocket, a red neckerchief to wear cowboy fashion, and a pint-size ten-gallon hat.

When the first day of school came, grandfather took Manuel to school and sat in the schoolroom to make certain that the grandson was inducted properly. All went well until mid-morning when the grandfather gave a gasp of dismay and took Manuel home. When they were out of the school, the old man pointed to Manuel's feet. He had forgotten to buy the proper shoes. The little boy was wearing deerskin moccasins made for him by this same old man. Manuel did not return to school that year. (p. 255)

I could keep on telling you stories—about the boys who stole the teacher's watch, but not because they wanted a watch. The teacher had a habit of taking his watch out, looking at it, snapping it shut and putting it back in his pocket again every time he was asked a question. The children got the idea that the watch was magic, and looking at it would give the answers to all questions. So they took the watch to "borrow" the magic. About another boy in Guatemala who walked with his father twenty-five kilometers in a tropic downpour to bring me the live, family rooster so I could take it with me and have the man on the plane cook it for me when I was hungry. About my own small boy on his first communal Indian rabbit drive, who, when I asked him why he said he had killed half a rabbit, said, "It lay down and was dead for a little while and then it got up and ran off." About Pat, the small grandson, who said to me, "Look, Grandmother, even the flowers are glad to see us. Look how they are bowing to us."

These are the reasons I write about children. If the children like what I write, that's a gift to me from my grandfather's fairies in Ireland.

The boys I write about are part of all the boys I have known. They are part of their laughter and their dreams, their hurts and their brave, big hopes. They are the boys who have walked with me and talked with me and have been my friends.

I knew Cusi in *Secret of the Andes* under many other names and in many other places. I also knew him in the market place in Cuzco. (pp. 255-57)

I knew [Cusi] in Ecuador. I knew him in Peru. All my life I had been getting ready to understand him. *Secret of the Andes* is part fact, part imagination, part history, part legend—all so mixed up together that for me it happened. (p. 257)

> *Ann Nolan Clark, "Newbery Award Acceptance," in* The Horn Book Magazine, *Vol. XXIX, No. 4, August, 1953, pp. 249-57.*

The Inca boy, Cusi, and his search for a family are portrayed in a story that is crystal clear as the cold mountain-like waters, as ethereally expressed as the morning air that softens the tips of the Andes. One day convinced by an errant minstrel that his lonely llama herd's life in Hidden Valley—with only old Chuto, the llama Misti, and the dog Suncco, for company— was far from complete, Cusi starts a journey to brilliant Cuzco, but with these words in his ears: "Grieve not if your searching circles". Miss Clark's skill as a story teller, as interpreter of Indian feelings, mountain feelings, dramatic contrasts between the age of Inca civilization and the newness of the modern world, are put to much better use at this age level than at the younger, though her marked immersion in the genre, the interpolation of Incan songs and myths, the whole idyllic quality, may still be a bit hard to take.

> *A review of "Secret of the Andes," in* Virginia Kirkus' Bookshop Service, *Vol. XX, No. 3, February 1, 1952, p. 70.*

A story distinguished by lyrical writing which conveys the atmosphere of the Peruvian mountain lands and the dignity of an ancient Indian people with a heartbreaking impact. Not an action story, the plot hinges on abstract concepts and has a mystical quality. As a result, the exceptional fifth- and sixth-grader will enjoy it most.

> *Anne B. McCreary, in a review of "Secret of the Andes," in* Library Journal, *Vol. 77, No. 9, May 1, 1952, p. 799.*

In another of her thoughtful, deeply felt books, giving children a sympathetic sense of far-away Indian life, Miss Clark takes us to Peru. Her tone here is one of beauty and mystery, of the elation of living alone in very high places, of the passing along through the centuries of the two ancient Inca treasures, their llamas and their hidden gold.

A small boy and an old man guard the llama flock, high in the Andes. The great day comes when the boy is to see the outer world and be tested by it. Before meeting humans, he meets mysterious dream Incas. At last he accepts his fated task with joy—to be one of those who always guard the great secret. Perhaps the story will seem confused to children who find here no clues to place it in time, knowing not yet the Inca background. To an adult, the atmosphere, the songs and prayers quoted, the glimpses of ancient monuments, are most touching and illuminating. Some children under twelve, and many over

that age, will be moved by the spell and gather a rare feeling given in no other book about South America.

> *"Some of the New Honor Books," in* New York Herald Tribune Book Review, *May 11, 1952, p. 7.*

[Mrs. Clark has] made a rare contribution to literature for older boys and girls in *Secret of the Andes*. . . . I regard it as one of the most beautiful and original books for children and young people of our time. Ann Nolan Clark has lived close to all she has written about. She has been able to translate personal knowledge and experience into memorable words with a universal appeal.

Secret of the Andes touches me deeply in my search for beauty to share with boys and girls who are far more responsive to the call of poetry and prose than is commonly admitted. The Inca shepherd boy Cusi and the wise old guardian of the herd of llamas are living characters. (pp. 160-61)

Legend springs to life in a new form and because the book is at once true and full of mystery it casts a spell on a reader. . . . (p. 161)

> *Anne Carroll Moore, in a review of "Secret of the Andes," in* The Horn Book Magazine, *Vol. XXVIII, No. 3, June, 1952, pp. 160-61.*

From a hidden mountain valley of Peru is drawn this rarely beautiful and subtle story of Cusi. . . . Perceptive young readers will respond to the beauty of the telling, with mysticism in Incan songs and vivid description of wild and unvisited grandeur in the high Andes.

> *Virginia Haviland, in a review of "Secret of the Andes," in* The Horn Book Magazine, *Vol. XXVIII, No. 3, June, 1952, p. 174.*

LOOKING-FOR-SOMETHING: THE STORY OF A STRAY BURRO OF ECUADOR (1952)

This is one of those exquisite poetic stories . . . that librarians and teachers—and most parents—will welcome, but that children rarely accept spontaneously as their own. In this case, the slender thread of story deals with the adventures of an inquisitive little gray burro who wanders from spot to spot in Ecuador seeking the thing that he will feel is his for him alone. He doesn't find it in the banana grove or the mines or the village— but he does find it in the farming country where a small boy claimed him as his own.

> *A review of "Looking-for-Something," in* Virginia Kirkus' Bookshop Service, *Vol. XX, No. 4, February 15, 1952, p. 123.*

This engaging little burro will appeal to younger children entirely aside from the fact that he introduces us to the strange land of Ecuador. . . .

Here, as in her book about American Indians, ***In My Mother's House***, Miss Clark writes in a simple, primer style. The type lines are arranged for primer-age eyes to cope with, and there is much repetition. . . . It means that many second or third graders will be able to enjoy it who otherwise might not tackle Ecuador.

> *Louise S. Bechtel, "Three 1952 Prize Books," in* New York Herald Tribune Book Review, *May 11, 1952, p. 6.*

BLUE CANYON HORSE (1954)

There's a stark simplicity of theme and free verse form that lends to the story of a mare and her colt and the Indian boy who loved them the beauty and feel of the canyon pasture and the mesa heights. The little mare deserts her owner and the quiet of the valley when she hears the call of freedom. She joins a band of wild horses for a summer and a winter. And then—with her colt—she comes back to human friendship and the boy who loves her. When the boy kills a cougar that has landed on her back, she knows that through him she has found safety. . . . Not a book for an action-loving child, but for one to whom the rhythmic oneness of thought and text add meaning.

> *A review of "Blue Canyon Horse," in* Virginia Kirkus' Bookshop Service, *Vol. XXII, No. 14, July 15, 1954, p. 436.*

The poetic quality of Mrs. Clark's *In My Mother's House* distinguishes also this book. . . . [*Blue Canyon Horse* is] a moving story of great beauty. It should be read aloud—and children will want it more than once. Obviously both the author and the Indian artist [Allan Houser] love the country of the canyon and the mesa; together they have made this one of the outstanding books of the fall.

> *Jennie D. Lindquist, in a review of "Blue Canyon Horse," in* The Horn Book Magazine, *Vol. XXX, No. 5, October, 1954, p. 330.*

[*Blue Canyon Horse*] is a simple story but a moving one, dealing with elemental needs and mirroring clearly the wild setting. Told in the lyric style which distinguished *In My Mother's House*, this has beauty and literary value, as well as appeal for young horse lovers.

> *Elizabeth Hodges, "The Runaway," in* The New York Times Book Review, *October 10, 1954, p. 38.*

SANTIAGO (1955)

Santiago takes a leading place among [Mrs. Clark's] Indian heroes, another in whose character and purpose she epitomizes her ideal Indian—one who is a true Indian and a good Indian in the world of today, which, she says, it is not easy to be. Her admiration of the Indian's heritage and her belief that he must be loyal to it emerge naturally as a theme out of her intimate acquaintance with such people and scenes as she draws in her story. The book's distinction derives from her power to express her ideas, to create a varied array of characters and re-create actual scenes in prose that is rich and beautiful.

Santiago's wanderings during the five groping years in which he seeks to find his true purpose give him a strong taste of life: among the pagan-Christian highlanders, in a warm family circle of "lifters" of coffee on a sub-tropical finca, with the chewing-gum gatherers or "chicleros" in their mosquito-y rain forest, and with a mixture of peoples on the modernized banana plantation of his North American friends. He hears the beautiful prayers of the highlanders and the songs of the coffee workers, feels the terrors of the chicle jungle, sees Communists demonstrating in the big capital. He is strong and intelligent, but perplexed and human in his errings and tragic involvements; honest and loyal, though afraid; and, finally, aware and firm, has become a man, knowing that he will return to his own village "to help Indian children be good Indians in the modern world."

> *Virginia Haviland, "Some of the New Honor Books," in* New York Herald Tribune Book Review, *May 15, 1955, p. 6.*

[This is] a book whose range and scope reflect not only Mrs. Clark's closely observed experience of life in Guatemala but her long first-hand knowledge and understanding of Indian people. . . .

[The] book is an absorbing one and vitally related to questioning youth of today. . . .

It is a triumphant story of a living, growing boy in today's world and adds another cubit to Mrs. Clark's stature as a writer. (p. 178)

> *Anne Carroll Moore, in a review of "Santiago," in* The Horn Book Magazine, *Vol. XXXI, No. 3, June, 1955, pp. 177-78.*

Once you accept the compulsion of the boy Santiago to leave his gentle foster home to lead the primitive life of the Indian, you find yourself saying, "the greatest Clark yet." Not even in *Secret of the Andes* is the boy's reaction to life so poignant, the feeling of race so strong, the conception of beauty and mysticism so clarified. And all this in a book for young people in a thoroughly normal and fascinating story.

> *Siddie Joe Johnson, in a review of "Santiago," in* Library Journal, *Vol. 80, No. 12, June 15, 1955, p. 1510.*

THE LITTLE INDIAN BASKET MAKER (1957)

[*The Little Indian Basket Maker*] concerns a small Papago Indian girl of Arizona, and takes her through the process of learning to weave the mats and baskets for which this tribe is famous. The rhythmic text is well suited to reading aloud to primary children, and beginning third grade readers can handle it alone.

> *A review of "The Little Indian Basket Maker," in* Bulletin of the Children's Book Center, *Vol. X, No. 8, April, 1957, p. 99.*

This very easy story of a Papago Indian girl is written in a distinguished style. Especially good for the beginning reader, it has . . . repetition of words and phrases, and the occasional unfamiliar regional words add flavor and color. Has the careful selection of words, as in readers, without being dull.

> *Allie Beth Martin, in a review of "The Little Indian Basket Maker," in* Library Journal, *Vol. 82, No. 12, June 15, 1957, p. 1684.*

A SANTO FOR PASQUALITA (1959)

[Pasqualita] is a 10-year-old orphan adopted by an aged Santero and his wife. A Santero is a local craftsman who makes statues of their patron saints for the devout people of the countryside. The girl loves her new home, and makes herself happily useful in the kitchen after her new grandmother has taught her the skills with which "a cook in her kitchen holds the home in her hands." The only sorrow of Pasqualita's life is that she does not have a santo—a patron-saint statue—because her grandfather cannot find a model for her San Pasqual.

The text of *A Santo for Pasqualita* is highly stylized: printed in verse-like lines, and relying on poetry's terseness for effect after effect. The book is one for children far above average. Others will probably jig with the jag of the physical lines, and miss many carefully wrought meanings full of verbal loveliness, while trying to follow the slight, special story.

> *Mary Louise Hector, in a review of "A Santo for Pasqualita," in* The New York Times, *April 19, 1959, p. 30.*

A delightful book. . . . Pasqualita tells her own story, and the trust and love that she expresses are completely natural and convincing. The literary style has a fragility and a lyric quality that will appeal to a limited group of readers; and the book may, like other books by this author, perhaps be best introduced by being read aloud. (p. 147)

> *Zena Sutherland, in a review of "A Santo for Pasqualita," in* Bulletin of the Children's Book Center, *Vol. XII, No. 9, May, 1959, pp. 146-47.*

WORLD SONG   (1960)

A rather slight story which covers visits made by a boy from the suburbs of Chicago to the Navajo country of the South West and to Costa Rica. Mrs. Clark's approach to her characters and situations is more adult than childlike. She is very adept at local color. The reader can almost see and hear the sights and sounds of the areas she describes, and she makes the local customs very clear and understandable.

> *A review of "World Song," in* Publishers Weekly, *Vol. 177, No. 14, April 4, 1960, p. 57.*

Red looked at the thousands of songbirds. They know no lands, he thought. They know no boundaries. They sing their songs for the world to hear. And that is the burden of this story—a story which, I am afraid, is only for the unusual child.

Should Red go with his parents to a Costa Rican coffee plantation for two years or stay at his grandfather's trading post on the Navajo reservation? His grandfather made the decision. "Way the world is today, you'd best get to know all kinds of people and how to get along with them." But in Costa Rica Red was very lonely, unable to break down barriers of language and custom. Not until the flocks of yellow warblers came was the jinx broken. Here was something he loved and which was also loved by the Costa Ricans. They took him to the ancient Indian Bird Woman where they sat in the dawn waiting for the birds. Juanito broke the silence: "Look at us," he said in wonder. "We represent our races, the races of mankind. We understand one another. We are friends."

Ann Nolan Clark . . . has a wonderful idea here and she has expressed it in beautiful words—sometimes a bit over-whelmingly. The children seem precocious in what they say and the amount of information about everything slows the slight story. As a 10-year old once said about an equally nice idea, "Too much talk for what happened."

> *Phyllis Fenner, "The Warblers Came," in* The New York Times Book Review, *July 10, 1960, p. 24.*

The message of the book is brotherhood and understanding, and it is expressed in a style that is spiritual—even mystical at times. The device that cements the understanding—a love of birds—is not one that has wide appeal for the audience; the literary style and the concepts of the book further indicate that this story will probably be most appreciated by the more sen-

sitive or perceptive child. For the average audience, it is a little slow and esoteric. (p. 176)

> *A review of "World Song," in* Bulletin of the Center for Children's Books, *Vol. XIII, No. 11, July-August, 1960, pp. 175-76.*

THE DESERT PEOPLE   (1962)

The author's poetic prose and Allan Houser's illustrations combine to produce a beautiful description of the life of the Papago Indians through the year's seasonal changes. To be read to preschool and primary children and by third grade and up. This is wonderful intercultural material for any age. A really beautiful book. (pp. 2615-16)

> *Elsa Berner, in a review of "The Desert People," in* Library Journal, *Vol. 87, No. 3, July, 1962, pp. 2615-16.*

[*The Desert People* is a] beautifully written book. . . . The writing has dignity and a quiet strength; it has, above all, a distinguished lyric quality. . . . A good book to read aloud to younger children.

> *Zena Sutherland, in a review of "The Desert People," in* Bulletin of the Center for Children's Books, *Vol. XV, No. 11, July-August, 1962, p. 173.*

PACO'S MIRACLE   (1962)

One beautiful, affectionate story after another has come from the pen of Ann Nolan Clark, picturing in a quiet, poetic fashion the lives of the Indian and Spanish children she knows so well. Again and again she returns to the theme of the wise old man who teaches a child to appreciate the beauties of nature and kinship with all living things. In this story Paco first lived happily up in the New Mexican mountains with the Old One, a one-time trapper who has renounced his work and is determined "to live the rest of his days in friendship with all wild creatures" and to teach this gospel to the boy. Then he lived with a young man, Tómas, and Pita, his bride, in a valley village, happy yet yearning for his mountain animals. When Tómas' house was chosen as the one where the Posada would be welcomed on Christmas Eve, Paco's animals called to him and made it possible for him to help Pita greet the Posada with dignity and pride even though an avalanche kept Tómas away.

This is a deeply religious story, mingling the pantheism of Saint Francis with the spirit of Christmas. It will be read aloud with pleasure in many schools at Christmas (especially Catholic schools) and used by teachers to give children descriptions of Spanish customs in the villages of our Southwest.

> *Margaret Sherwood Libby, in a review of "Paco's Miracle," in* Books, *September 2, 1962, p. 10.*

[*Paco's Miracle* is] a gentle story that verges on the mystical at its close. . . . A bit sentimental at the close, but acceptably so as an ending to a warm and sympathetic portrayal of a kindly community of people and of the newlywed couple who have accepted with love an orphaned child.

> *Zena Sutherland, in a review of "Paco's Miracle," in* Bulletin of the Center for Children's Books, *Vol. XVI, No. 3, November, 1962, p. 39.*

[*Paco's Miracle*] beautifully describes Spanish formal customs, marriage ceremonies, Christmas celebrations, shawls, and mantillas. . . . Although the story repeatedly discusses tortillas and donkeys . . . and undervalues the French and Spanish languages . . . , it does illustrate in an attractive writing style the theme of kindness to all things.

> *Isabel Schon, in a review of "Paco's Miracle," in her* A Bicultural Heritage: Themes for the Exploration of Mexican and Mexican-American Culture in Books for Children and Adolescents, *The Scarecrow Press, Inc., 1978, p. 59.*

MEDICINE MAN'S DAUGHTER (1963)

Deep in the Navajo country lived Chanter, most famous and powerful of medicine men. His daughter, Tall Girl, lived with him, and lived only to carry on the work of her father. Others had roamed beyond the stark wilderness to attend a Catholic school. After receiving an awaited sign, Tall Girl realized that she must follow those who had gone in order to learn more about medicine. The uncomplicated story is shrouded in an impenetrable silence—an Indian silence which is sustained too long. For, although the author skillfully writes in a poetic style, there is not enough of a story to reenforce the clear writing. Tall Girl's dedication has obviously inspired the author, but the result of inspiration does not captivate the reader. More plot, less poetry, in this case, would have been advantageous. This story is not comparable to *World Song*. . . .

> *A review of "Medicine Man's Daughter," in* Virginia Kirkus' Service, *Vol. XXXI, No. 5, March 1, 1963, p. 240.*

The information about Navajo life is fascinating, the descriptions of the country are lovely, and the author has created an intense mood—a sort of absorbed rapture; the story is, however, very slow-moving.

> *Zena Sutherland, in a review of "Medicine Man's Daughter," in* Bulletin of the Center for Children's Books, *Vol. XVI, No. 11, July-August, 1963, p. 171.*

Although [Tall-Girl's] precipitous acceptance of the mission school strains credibility, and the picture of the conflicting cultures tearing at the Navahos dissolves in sentimentality, this is nonetheless an affecting though slow-moving story of a gifted Navaho girl with a passion for helping her people.

> *Helen E. Kinsey, in a review of "Medicine Man's Daughter," in* The Booklist and Subscription Books Bulletin, *Vol. 60, No. 3, October 1, 1963, p. 150.*

TÍA MARÍA'S GARDEN (1963)

> Tia Maria's garden has no fences. It goes on and on from our door to where the sky bends down to touch the land.

Thus a small boy takes the reader with him and his aunt on a walk through the New Mexican desert to see the many things that live and grow there. He also captures its mood throughout the day. In gentle rhythmic prose, Ann Nolan Clark has developed another quiet, introspective picture-story of the country she loves so well. Its only fault is that occasionally it loses impact because the author is a little bit preachy. . . . The book begs to be read aloud to be its most effective.

> *Harriet Quimby, in a review of "Tia Maria's Garden," in* The New York Times Book Review, *Part II, May 12, 1963, p.29.*

A slow and gentle text in which a boy describes the desert scene through which he loves to walk. . . . The illustrations [by Ezra Jack Keats] appropriately and handsomely echo the evocation of mood. The writing has a lyric quality, but the lack of pace or plot will probably limit the book's appeal to those readers who can appreciate the quiet, tender quality of the writing.

> *Zena Sutherland, in a review of "Tia Maria's Garden," in* Bulletin of the Center for Children's Books, *Vol. XVII, No. 2, October, 1963, p. 24.*

BEAR CUB (1965)

The relentless, unsentimental rules of animal life are described in the rather somber sequences of a text which follows the birth and training of a grizzly cub to the time nature dictates that his mother leave him on his own. Together, they had survived a forest fire by hiding in a pool. In the passages dealing with the course and effect of the fire, the 1953 Newbery Medal winner achieves a vitality that is not in evidence at either the start or the conclusion of a book which will probably need a strong adult push before it moves with juvenile readers.

> *A review of "Bear Cub," in* Virginia Kirkus' Service, *Vol. XXXIII, No. 14, July 15, 1965, p. 674.*

In poetic language, Miss Clark has told the story of the . . . grizzly bear cub. . . . While scientifically accurate, one suspects that a child would prefer a simple descriptive narrative, and that the poetic language will appeal most to adult admirers of good children's books.

> *A review of "Bear Cub," in* Science Books: A Quarterly Review, *Vol. 1, No. 3, December, 1965, p. 162.*

BROTHER ANDRÉ OF MONTREAL (1967)

Mrs. Clark, familiar to us for books set in New Mexico, has written the story of Brother André, founder of the Oratory of St. Joseph in Montreal. In preparation for the book she visited the parts of Quebec connected with his life and was very impressed with the beauty of the country and the fall colouring. The unfortunate result of this is a number of purple passages. The book suffers from a plethora of words. Perhaps Mrs. Clark found her material too slim for the length required by the series and padded the narrative with pairs and series of verbs and adjectives. This can be effective when used occasionally but becomes tiresome here. In spite of its defects of style it is a sincere effort and Mrs. Clark's admiration for her subject is evident, perhaps a little too much so.

> *M. I. Robertson, in a review of "Brother André of Montreal," in* In Review: Canadian Books for Children, *Vol. 1, No. 4, Autumn, 1967, p. 13.*

SUMMER IS FOR GROWING (1968)

Characters and scenes are sharply drawn in a slow-paced, descriptive story about New Mexican hacienda life following the acquisition of the territory by the U.S. in the mid-nineteenth century. Lala is being reared and trained for her future duties as mistress of a hacienda according to traditional Spanish customs but when a wily, old Indian chief forces her to bargain her prized Appaloosa foal for the freedom of a wagon-train child orphaned by an Indian raid, her decision is influenced by the ideas and ideals introduced by the Americans.

> *A review of "Summer Is for Growing," in* The Booklist and Subscription Books Bulletin, *Vol. 64, No. 20, June 15, 1968, p. 1184.*

This slight plot and the stereotyped characters fail to convey any real feeling for the hacienda and its people or for the changes coming with United States possession of New Mexico. The attempt to convey information is too apparent in incident, conversation, and description.

> *Jean Pretorius, in a review of "Summer Is for Growing," in* Library Journal, *Vol. 93, No. 12, June 15, 1968, p. 2536.*

In her award-winning style, Mrs. Clark weaves a story of indescribable warmth and color. Contrasting the customs of hacienda life in New Mexico with the developing spirit of the United States, she reveals the values in both. Young Lala symbolizes the best of the two worlds as she meets the challenge of growth.

> *Sister M. Claudia, in a review of "Summer Is for Growing," in* Catholic Library World, *Vol. 40, No. 2, October, 1968, p. 148.*

ALONG SANDY TRAILS (1969)

Along Sandy Trails is a photographic counterpart and complement to *In My Mother's House*—which is where the Papago Indian girl and her grandmother end up after spending a day in the desert. "There are so many things in this quiet land"— and the color photos [by Alfred A. Cohn] accompanying the typically parapoetic Ann Nolan Clark text, display them to advantage. The little girl's favorite—the quail—and the grandmother's—the giant cactus—are dwelt on at some length without, however, depicting their stated activities/attributes precisely or fully (e.g. we don't see the cactus making walls and fences or supplying water). It's appreciative natural history, then, with some reflection of the Indians' relation to it but only limited evidence of tangible involvement. And just this aspect—that it's fundamentally a catalog of desert flora and fauna— is likely to deter the younger child who responds to something more active and personal.

> *A review of "Along Sandy Trails," in* Kirkus Reviews, *Vol. XXXII, No. 17, September 15, 1969, p. 995.*

Ann Nolan Clark has enriched with poetry a well-selected set of sensitive photographs of the Arizona desert. . . . Grade school children will see the variety and beauty of life in the desert from the viewpoint of a small Papago Indian girl as she takes a walk with her grandmother. Together they see small friendly animals and birds (squirrels, a roadrunner, quail), the gleaming colors of desert plants and blooms (ocotillo bush, paloverde tree, cactus) and the glowing beauty of the desert sky. All suggest a pleasant, romantic quietness, with hardly a hint of the Papago poverty and the harsh conditions of desert life. Nevertheless, it's a beautiful book that libraries in the southwest will want.

> *Evelyn R. Downum, in a review of "Along Sandy Trails," in* Library Journal, *Vol. 95, No. 4, February 15, 1970, p. 766.*

CIRCLE OF SEASONS (1970)

A few quotations representative of the author's different voices reveal the strengths and the weaknesses of her account of the hallowed Pueblo cycle of ceremonies—a cycle in which every day has its sacred specialness, be it secular or religious, and if the latter, pagan or Christian. The preponderant stage-setting passages weigh most heavily in their unvarying hymn to Earth Mother: "A brilliant sun shines down a world so glistening white it sparkles with myriad iridescent splintered stars." The adoption of what is apparently an Indian cadence is stiff . . . and more than occasional: "The people wait for solstice, but not yet are the counted days enough for this to happen." Sometimes, however, a deft nuance tells a whole urgent story: ". . . dark-blanketed men move silently, doing the tasks they have been given the privilege of doing". . . . Majesty, timelessness, spirituality, are conveyed as Mrs. Clark, teacher, friend, and neighbor to the Pueblo people, speaks from her personal peephole. But facts to grasp, scenes to really envision, are rarely extricable from the rhapsodic timbres; only a strong Bleeker background or its equivalent would begin to make this readable—and then there is of course the question of appeal.

> *A review of "Circle of Seasons," in* Kirkus Reviews, *Vol. XXXVIII, No. 10, May 15, 1970, p. 561.*

A book with both literary and anthropological interest. The author's poetic style perfectly suits her subject—the yearly ceremonies, rituals, and fiestas of the Pueblo Indians. With an understanding fostered by years of teaching Indian children, writing about them and for them, she evokes significance and beauty. . . . The book is a striking evocation of a way of life rich with mysticism and symbolism. (p. 401)

> *Virginia Haviland, in a review of "Circle of Seasons," in* The Horn Book Magazine, *Vol. XLVI, No. 4, August, 1970, pp. 401-02.*

[This book] features a beautiful layout and poetic writing. A well-written, concise description of Pueblo past and present is given in the foreword. The book notes that not all Pueblo Indians live in their ancestral pueblos and mentions the importance of maternal descent. Ceremonies are described as part of a way of life; age is seen as important. Indian ambivalence about school celebrations of white Thanksgiving is described: "White ways may be good but they are difficult to comprehend and to accept." Watch for occasional stereotyping: "Pueblo Indians are gentle, kindly, laughter-loving people." The book concentrates on "man-work", and only deals in a perfunctory way with women. Good.

> *Mary Jo Lass-Woodfin, in a review of "Circle of Seasons," in* Books on American Indians and Eskimos: A Selection Guide for Children and Young Adults, *edited by Mary Jo Lass-Woodfin, American Library Association, 1978, p. 54.*

HOOFPRINT ON THE WIND (1972)

Ten year-old Patcheen, whose father and older brother have been killed in one of the sudden storms that take so many of these Irish islandmen, insists that "'tis himself be seeing" a Connemara pony on the cliff, but his father's old cronies deny it (do they protest too much?) and others tease him for imagining things. Then on a visit to the Galway fair Patch meets a gentleman who expresses interest in the pony and even visits the island to pursue the matter. Patch is tempted by the man's offer to train him to show the horse all over Ireland and even America, but he gradually comes to realize that his father had bought and imported the horse to upbreed the island stock. Though the need for all the secrecy is never quite clear, Patch, confident now that "his hands are big enough to hold his Da's dream," answers the stranger: "Myself be not minding, mister, if the Islanders be saying 'tis myself that be seeing a horse that's not here." Mrs. Clark's superior recreation of the textures of the harsh island life—where the boys "make land" for growing potatoes by spreading sand and dried seaweed on limestone beds—is marred by her obtrusively overdone dialect, which never flows like (say) the lines of Synge but gets awkwardly bogged down in the *ings* (several per sentence), and uses the ubiquitous *'tis, myself* and *after* in ways no proper Irishman would dream of.

> *A review of "Hoofprint on the Wind," in* Kirkus Reviews, *Vol. XL, No. 22, November 15, 1972, p. 1304.*

The characters are well drawn except for their sometimes excessive dialect; action is lively; and the setting . . . is vividly realistic. The strongest impact of the book, however, comes from the feeling of love and closeness in Patcheen's family and among the loyal islanders.

> *Barbara Joyce Duree, in a review of "Hoofprint on the Wind," in* The Booklist, *Vol. 69, No. 15, April 1, 1973, p. 763.*

YEAR WALK (1975)

Ann Nolan Clark, who took us to visit the Irish Islands in *Hoofprint on the Wind,* now introduces the Spanish Basques and their sons who became large-scale sheepherders in Idaho along about 1910. Once again the scenery is inviting as 16-year-old Kepa, along with his dog and his mule Patto-Kak, guide some 2,000 sheep through rolling hills and brushlands—surviving misadventure from flood, coyote, snow and unfriendly cattlemen and conquering loneliness with the help of a wise old prospector, a guitar and a whittling knife. Yet when Kepa encounters another human being the dialogue is wooden ("I can't tell you what this means to me, son") and his eventual decision to stay in America and court Chris, the daughter of his employer and godfather, is so managed and predictable that Kepa's individuality fades from sight. Nor will many readers care for the supposedly Americanized Chris who pines away when her affections are not immediately reciprocated and who later weepily promises that "you . . . will walk the trails and I, like my mother did, will cry because you walk them." Much of this stiffness stems from Clark's self-conscious efforts to evoke the laconic, sturdy Basque character, but Kepa mostly seems to be going nowhere slowly. Ironically, it's the sheep who provide some sense of direction and excitement here and for readers content to share the clear air and open spaces with them, it might just be enough.

> *A review of "Year Walk," in* Kirkus Reviews, *Vol. XLII, No. 2, January 15, 1975, p. 71.*

The novel's structural and plotting patterns are too familiar and underscore the studied, worn air that clings to the telling,

but the appealing characters and rich detail are enough to hold readers to this comfortable historical fiction.

> *A review of "Year Walk," in* The Booklist, *Vol. 71, No. 12, February 15, 1975, p. 617.*

Ann Nolan Clark's books are always a delight to read, and this one is well up to her high standard. Mrs. Clark doesn't just sit down and write a story—she does her homework thoroughly before she writes. Her books are in refreshing contrast to some of the shallow, carelessly researched stuff that manages to get in print. . . . [The] beauty of this story is in the way Mrs. Clark has provided an ample amount of excitement and action without resorting to violence or unrealistically dangerous situations which call for miraculous solutions by the hero. Instead, the story moves smoothly but engrossingly through the year's walk, full of authentic detail about herding sheep in the true Basque tradition, and sprinkled with subtle but profound inspiration for emerging adults in the form of homespun Basque sayings. There is even a touch of romance—poignant, natural, and in perfect taste and harmony with the story as a whole.

Kepa, of course, triumphs and enters his eighteenth year sure of his future, and leaving the reader thoroughly appreciative of his remarkable experience.

> *Marvin S. Sharpe, "Basque Boy Tends Flock in Idaho Wilds," in* The Christian Science Monitor, *May 7, 1975, p. B2.*

ALL THIS WILD LAND (1976)

[In *All This Wild Land*] the Finnish mother, Hilma, frets so vocally—and eleven-year-old Maiju steels herself so often by muttering *sisu* (courage)—that one's sympathies are numbed by the time Isa (Father) dies in a snowstorm and the two women decide to carry on alone. Clark delineates Finnish customs and community feeling, and the hardships of Minnesota homesteading, with evident fondness and accuracy. Against this background, Maiju's silent friendship with a homeless half-Sioux girl seems somehow naive and her resentment of Hilma's new suitor unduly babyish; however, a less venturesome audience may find the reactions appropriate and be content to savor vicariously the blended flavors of sour-rye bread and wild venison.

> *A review of "All This Wild Land," in* Kirkus Reviews, *Vol. XLIV, No. 16, August 15, 1976, p. 906.*

A sympathetic portrayal of yet another culture that is part of our melting pot, this is a keenly felt tale of Finnish immigrants who are ill-equipped for the rugged pioneer life in America in 1876. . . . Though it's a bit heavy on Finnish customs, the good characterizations and winsome story line spell another good read from the author of . . . *Secret of the Andes.* (pp. 55-6)

> *Nancy M. Abruzzo, in a review of "All This Wild Land," in* School Library Journal, *Vol. 23, No. 3, November, 1976, pp. 55-6.*

Like close friends, the characters Ann Nolan Clark gives us in *All This Wild Land* are people we quickly get to know and care about. Several hours after finishing the book, I was still thinking about them as real people. . . .

Sympathetic toward both the immigrants and the Indians on whose land they settle, Mrs. Clark writes sensitively of the conflict between two peoples who need land of their own. The author also stresses the role of women in settling the land in this very satisfying book that should appeal to boys as well as girls.

Wendy Moorhead, "From Appalachia to Chinatown—Adventures in Americana," in The Christian Science Monitor, *May 4, 1977, p. B2.*

TO STAND AGAINST THE WIND (1978)

Clark uses her main character to remember events that befell him and his family before and during the Vietnam War up to their coming to the United States as refugees. Em recalls methods of rice planting, cultivation, and harvesting, the preparations for his sister's wedding, and the celebration of the Tet holidays, showing how strong a role tradition plays in making family life stable and harmonious. Attitudes toward ancestral worship, astrology, and war are worked in unobtrusively. Em's relatives are engaging as characters, and his friendship with the disillusioned, kind, foresighted American reporter Sam is interesting. But dialogue is sparse and stiff in this studied, slow-paced, pastoral novel of the culture of a Vietnamese Mekong River delta village prior to its destruction through aerial bombardment. (pp. 142-43)

Larry Chamberlain, in a review of "To Stand against the Wind," in School Library Journal, *Vol. 25, No. 2, October, 1978, pp. 142-43.*

The trouble with this novel is that consciousness of its crafting belies its intended impact. The story . . . is replete with details of custom and culture, carefully assembled to validate the unfolding events. But these small facts form a barrier, the scenes unfold as if from a distance, and emotional involvement is never complete. And yet the slow drama is not without impelling force. . . . The record speaks for itself; its fullness of effect will depend on whether or not one accepts Clark's stylistic approach.

Denise M. Wilms, in a review of "To Stand against the Wind," in Booklist, *Vol. 75, No. 8, December 15, 1978, p. 684.*

Most of the story is concerned with the tragedy of [the Vietnam War], and Clark evokes it sympathetically and poignantly. Unfortunately, the several shifts between past and present halt the flow of the narrative and are not always clearly defined. The writing style and dialogue are excellent, however, and the book gives a touching picture of the disruption and disaster that came to a rural community in South Vietnam. . . .

Zena Sutherland, in a review of "To Stand against the Wind," in Bulletin of the Center for Children's Books, *Vol. 32, No. 8, April, 1979, p. 132.*

IN THE LAND OF SMALL DRAGON (with Dang Manh Kha; 1979)

This Vietnamese Cinderella story is told in the stylized, metric form we are told is traditional and interspersed with little proverbs or other italicized comments. "A man's worth is what he does, / not what he says he can do," is one such passage; "In truth, beauty seeks goodness; / What is beautiful is good" better represents the theme. This version of the rivalry between the virtuous heroine and her treacherous half-sister plays some effective changes on a theme that can always draw response. However, for those accustomed to Western storytelling the distancing manner of this telling requires some adjustments, and the compensating rewards of this particular sample are limited. The authors do well enough with concrete description and straight narration, but the italicized statements often verge on the platitudinous and the pretty phrases aren't as sharp as they should be. . . .

A review of "In the Land of Small Dragon," in Kirkus Reviews, *Vol. XLVII, No. 10, May 15, 1979, p. 572.*

[*In the Land of Small Dragon*] couples [illustrator Tony] Chen's well-conceived and strongly composed work with an equally strong text by Ann Nolan Clark, and the result approaches perfection in the art of making picture books. (p. 50)

The poetic text, retold in the traditional Vietnamese metric form, is sprinkled with Oriental terms, while proverbs, an apt introduction to Vietnamese thought, appear here and there throughout the understated text. These and many small details of setting make the story Eastern and individualize it, setting it off from its more familiar European cousin. . . . *Small Dragon* is an especially lovely book which should provide pleasure for many readings.

One cannot think of *In the Land of Small Dragon* without recalling some of Clark's carefully drafted phrases. . . . (pp. 50-1)

Alethea K. Helbig, "The Wheat and the Chaff: Separating Some Retellings," in The World of Children's Books, *Vol. VI, 1981, pp. 46-52.*

Paul Galdone

1914-1986

Hungarian-born American illustrator of picture books, poetry, fiction, and nonfiction; reteller; and picture book author.

A prolific illustrator for over four decades, Galdone is best known for creating bright, humorous picture books which present traditional nursery rhymes and folk tales to preschoolers and primary graders. Recognized for interpreting a wide variety of sources while retaining their original spirit, he helped to establish the trend of devoting a whole edition to a single Mother Goose rhyme, Aesopian fable, folk tale, or Bible story. He is also acknowledged for the success of his dashing yet controlled artistic style, for his strong compositions, and for his consistent professionalism. Galdone addressed such favorite tales as those by Jacob and Wilhelm Grimm, Charles Perrault, and reteller Joseph Jacobs as well as less familiar accounts from India, Sweden, the Philippines, and his native Hungary. Reducing the texts to their simplest elements by judicious editing and streamlining, Galdone effectively used such techniques as repetition and word patterning, characteristics which make his lively renditions appealing to very young children. Although his retellings generally adhere closely to their sources, the occasional tempered ending—for example, Cinderella forgiving her stepsisters at the end of the story—reflect Galdone's basic optimism and humanity.

Galdone began his career with the acclaimed illustrations for Eve Titus's *Anatole* (1956) and *Anatole and the Cat* (1957), both featuring a Parisian cheese-testing mouse, followed by a separate series written by Titus and starring Anatole's British counterpart, the mouse master sleuth Basil of Baker Street. With the publication of *Old Mother Hubbard and Her Dog* (1960), Galdone began the succession of cheerful, multicolored versions of classic early childhood literature, distinguished by double-page spreads, oversize figures, and brief, repeatable texts, all of which make his books popular for storytelling and reading aloud. An established sculptor and landscape artist, he combined a practiced sense of balance and design with realistic details from nature, a flair for facial expression and movement, and a distinctive talent for comedy. He is especially praised for his knowledge and portrayal of animals, giving them personalities without sacrificing accuracy for caricature. As an artist, Galdone favored pen and watercolor, interspersing vigorous black and white sketches among his gaily imaginative paintings. Meticulous in his research, Galdone designed appropriate settings which ranged from Antarctica to medieval Europe, but most commonly placed his characters in rural America. He is also noted for illustrating single narrative poems such as Henry Wadsworth Longfellow's *Paul Revere's Ride* (1963), the nonfiction of such science writers as Paul Showers and Franklyn M. Branley, and the fiction of authors such as William O. Steele and Ellen MacGregor. In addition, Galdone provided the art for the verse of his daughter Johanna and was the author of *Paddy the Penguin* (1959), the story of a penguin who yearns to fly.

Critics applaud Galdone for his fresh recastings of old tales, humane views, and outstanding craftsmanship. Although several reviewers point out that his later works lack his earlier zest and that his pictures often outshine his texts, most ob-

Courtesy of Joanna Galdone

servers agree that he has made an essential and enduring contribution to children's literature by keeping the well-loved nursery rhymes and traditional stories of an earlier time accessible, entertaining, and relevant to young audiences.

Galdone has won several awards for his illustrations. Two of his works were designated as Caldecott Honor Books: *Anatole* in 1957 and *Anatole and the Cat* in 1958, both written by Eve Titus.

(See also *Something about the Author*, Vols. 17, 49 [obituary]; *Contemporary Authors New Revision Series*, Vol. 13; and *Contemporary Authors*, Vols. 73-76, 121 [obituary].)

GENERAL COMMENTARY

BETTINA HÜRLIMANN

[*The following excerpt was originally published in German in 1965.*]

Paul Galdone is notable for his completely successful interpretation of the humour of nursery tales and rhymes (as well as his bold re-illustrations of Edward Lear). His colour drawings match the atmosphere of his subjects and contrast with the much more consciously modern graphic work of Margot Zemach in her illustrations to traditional folk-tales. (p. 21)

Bettina Hürlimann, ''Picture-Books in America,'' in her Picture-Book World, translated and edited by Brian W. Alderson, Oxford University Press, London, 1968, pp. 18-21.

CHARLOTTE S. HUCK AND DORIS YOUNG KUHN

A recent trend has been the publication of picture books portraying only one Mother Goose rhyme. Paul Galdone has illustrated five of these books, including *The Old Woman and Her Pig, The House That Jack Built, Old Mother Hubbard and Her Dog, Tom, Tom, the Piper's Son,* and *The History of Simple Simon.* These narrative verses have action and humor and lend themselves well to individual presentations. Galdone's pictures have much sly humor and his animal ''personalities'' are delightful. (p. 103)

The First Seven Days is a picture book by Paul Galdone telling the story of creation in rich color. Several of the double-page spreads appear to be overcrowded. The text is slow and dignified, in keeping with the story. . . .

Another handsome book is Galdone's *Shadrach, Meshach and Abednego.* Nebuchadnezzar's golden image is pictured as a huge creature, and the figures of the characters are powerful. Although the story is simplified, the author retains the rhythm of the chant and uses repetition effectively. The three loyal, courageous boys are portrayed as quietly determined in their faith. (p. 201)

Paul Galdone has led the way in illustrating many books of a single narrative poem. Beginning with Lear's amusing tale of *Two Old Bachelors,* Galdone then illustrated three patriotic poems: *Paul Revere's Ride* by Longfellow, *Barbara Frietchie* by Whittier, and *The Battle of the Kegs* by Hopkinson. The stirring tale of how the colonists were warned by Paul Revere's midnight message is appropriately illustrated by Galdone's vigorous drawings in moonlit blues and blacks. During the preparations for the illustrations of this book, Galdone made a special trip to New England in the spring, the time of the ride, and traced Paul Revere's route through the villages. In *The Battle of the Kegs,* he has captured the rollicking good humor of the old Revolutionary ballad that told of the colonists' plan to float kegs of gunpowder down the Delaware River in order to damage the English ships. His illustrations for *Barbara Frietchie* portray the courage of that intrepid old lady who waved the Union flag in defiance of Stonewall Jackson's orders. Oliver Wendell Holmes wrote *The Deacon's Masterpiece or The Wonderful One-Hoss Shay* over a hundred years ago; but unlike the remarkable shay that was built to last a hundred years to a day and then went to pieces all at once, the original humor of this poem endures. The amusing illustrations add to the fun of this poem that defies obsolescence. By way of contrast, Galdone's illustrations for *Three Poems of Edgar Allen Poe* seem quite melodramatic. Perhaps the haunting love ballad of ''**Annabel Lee,**'' terrifying rhythms of ''**The Raven,**'' and singing repetition of ''**The Bells**'' demand such interpretation. Emotion is more difficult to portray than action, however. With these books, Galdone has established a trend for illustrating books of a single poem. These editions are popular with both teachers and children who find that the illustrations increase their enjoyment of the poems. (pp. 432-33)

Charlotte S. Huck and Doris Young Kuhn, in a review of ''The Old Woman and Her Pig'' and others, in their Children's Literature in the Elementary School, second edition, Holt, Rinehart and Winston, Inc., 1968, pp. 103, 201, 432-33.

BERNARD J. LONSDALE AND HELEN K. MACKINSTOSH

[Paul Galdone's] illustrations of *The Three Wishes,* a tale that dates back to Greek mythology and has appeared in many languages, give the story vitality, newness, and a decidedly humorous twist. Tom is treated in an hysterically funny way in Mr. Galdone's illustrations for *Tom, Tom the Piper's Son.*

Mr. Galdone followed the style of the chap books for his version of *History of Simple Simon.* Each blunder that Simon makes is illustrated with a delightful picture against the background of the times.

The expressive faces on the characters in the illustrations of *The Horse, the Fox, and the Lion* give color and life to Galdone's adaptation of one of the popular tales by the Brothers Grimm. The text and illustrations carry the reader rapidly through the story. . . . The brightly colored illustrations complement the text from its sad beginning to its happy ending.

Mr. Galdone has done a masterful job of retelling and illustrating the popular tale of the monkey who outwits the crocodile in *The Monkey and the Crocodile,* a Jataka tale from India. Mr. Galdone is skilled in combining humor with touches of excitement in animal stories. (pp. 242-43)

Bernard J. Lonsdale and Helen K. Mackintosh, ''Picture-Story Books: 'The Three Wishes' and others,'' in their Children Experience Literature, Random House, 1973, pp. 242-43.

MARCUS CROUCH

[Paul Galdone] was essentially an artist of the 'Sixties. Indeed, with his older contemporary Roger Duvoisin, for many admirers he came to represent the children's picture-book of that decade. Like Duvoisin too, although an American citizen by naturalization, he was a product of the European tradition so that, however much he assimilated the imagery of his adopted country, the basic ingredients of his work clearly identified him with his Eastern European origins. (p. 153)

His first major success came in 1956 with *Anatole,* the first fruit of his long and rewarding association with the New York writer Eve Titus. In the following year this book introduced him to a British audience.

There were, I believe, nine 'Anatole' books in all. They are all now, sadly, out of print in this country, so that it may not be inappropriate to remind readers that Anatole is a mouse, a mouse *magnifique* in fact. He lives in a mouse village outside Paris with his wife Doucette and their six children, Paul and Paulette, Claude and Claudette, and Georges and Georgette. Anatole dresses in traditional Parisian-artist style in smock and black beret set off with a smart red neckerchief; he rides a bicycle. His future is assured—although many subsequent adventures put it in peril—when he begins a long and mutually beneficial association with M. Duval who owns a cheese factory. Anatole's analytical mind and delicate palate make him ideal for cheese-tasting. He makes nightly inspections, leaving critical comments stuck into each cheese. In subsequent books the joke is varied and extended, and incorporated into exciting and amusing adventures, but the essence is all there in the original book. It is above all the Frenchness of the stories, conveyed equally in Eve Titus' finely and economically written texts and in Galdone's exquisite and gravely restrained drawings, which gives them their individual quality and their powerful appeal.

In 1958 the same partnership produced the first of another series of mouse stories, this time with an English mouse, Basil of Baker Street. Basil lives in the cellar of 221 Baker Street and models his detective methods on those of the occupant of Apartment B upstairs, to whom he bears an uncanny resemblance. The five 'Basil' stories have a charm which does not depend entirely on a knowledge of the originals which they parody, but they are, I think, just a little less successful than the 'Anatole' books. One remains in print in an English edition.

Even before *Anatole,* Galdone had tried his hand at a picturebook to a traditional text (*Did You Feed My Cow?* 1956; no English edition.) During the next decade this was followed by a series of books on which, with *Anatole,* his reputation is based.

The first of these was *Old Mother Hubbard and Her Dog* (1960; English edition 1961), and in the same year what is perhaps the finest of these books—it is certainly my personal favourite—*The Old Woman and Her Pig* appeared. A steady stream of these books was published into the early Seventies. Most of these were sponsored in this country by The Bodley Head. After 1971 the Bodley Head association came to an end, and although Galdone continued to make his traditional picturebooks until 1980—the last, I believe, was *Cinderella* in that year—these later books, although drawn with the familiar professionalism and technical excellence, lacked something of the old sparkle. A number of these later books survive in print but not one from his heyday.

What we remember most of the Galdone magic is his humour. It is not just that his pictures contain many excellent jokes, although this they certainly do, but that his was essentially a comic view of the world. The drawings do not often excite laughter but they give a deep and rich sense of satisfaction. Galdone took particular joy in drawing animals, exploring their potential for humour without ever being false to their real physical natures. (In this respect his work stands comparison with that of Leslie Brooke, than which there could be no higher praise.) We may recall most readily his pigs, all bulge and complacent obstinacy, or the vast bulk of an ox dominating the page, but his humans repay study too, each an individual portrait. Galdone was the complete artist, with a technique perfected and obedient to his will. Although also a painter of landscapes and portraits, he was particularly happy in his submission to the stern disciplines of book-art. In the 'landscape' format which he favoured he made masterly use of the very wide and narrow double-spreads, producing pictures which were richly pleasing in themselves and which encouraged the turning of the page to reveal further delights. His settings and costumes belonged to rural America, but the drawing invites comparison with Continental work of the same period, especially that of Janacek in Czechoslovakia and Stokowski in Poland. I fancy, however, that Galdone was always restrained by the limitations imposed by the commercial realities of American publishing.

Like many another artist and writer Galdone seems to have outlived his fame. All of his best work is out of print, at least in this country, and he is in danger of oblivion. May we perhaps hope for a posthumous revival? Surely there is room, in our darker world, for the innocence, the sharp observation, and the comic version which his work so joyously conveys. (pp. 153-55)

Marcus Crouch, "Paul Galdone," in The Junior Bookshelf, *Vol. 51, No. 4, August, 1987, pp. 153-55.*

ANATOLE (1956)

[Anatole *was written by Eve Titus.*]

Anatole is certainly "a mouse of action, a mouse of honor, a mouse *magnifique*." . . . An expert on cheeses he looks very dashing in his maillot as he bicycles forth to prove he is a self-respecting animal. Paul Galdone has done some fine, spirited pictures, among his best, showing Anatole, his family and his friend, Gaston. He uses broad tricolor bands of white, clear blue and rosy red for the end papers, and these same colors very effectively again in some scenes, while others are sketched in grey or deeper blues and reds. Altogether a gay and Gallic offering for the young.

Margaret Sherwood Libby, in a review of "Anatole," in New York Herald Tribune Book Review, *September 23, 1956, p. 7.*

Usually such unified blending of story and illustration is successful when one person is responsible for both. Mrs. Titus and Mr. Galdone together, however, have expertly captured the piquant and the quaint in the French setting.

Mary Lee Krupka, "Enterprising Mice," in The New York Times Book Review, *November 18, 1956, p. 49.*

Lively red and blue illustrations give this light tale the Parisian atmosphere it deserves, but the black and white pictures are as effective in their own right. The same expressive lines appear in all the illustrations and possess a mouselike quickness about them. At the hands of Paul Galdone, Anatole, complete with beret, scarf, and smock, has dignity, pride, and ingenuity. The gray washes and active lines of the black and white pages give the book a free-flowing looseness and informality that reflect the spirit of the book. Much akin to the spirit of Maurice Sendak's *A Very Special House* or *Madeline* of Ludwig Bemelmans, *Anatole* is a refreshing addition to the Caldecott Honor Books.

> *Linda Kauffman Peterson, "Anatole," in* Newbery and Caldecott Medal and Honor Books: An Annotated Bibliography, *by Linda Kauffman Peterson and Marilyn Leathers Solt, G. K. Hall & Co., 1982, p. 309.*

ANATOLE AND THE CAT (1957)

[*Anatole and the Cat was written by Eve Titus.*]

As light and artistic as a Parisian chef's souffle, the story of a little mouse, Anatole, who works as a cheese taster evenings in a French cheese factory and succeeds in trapping the owner's cat, is a blend of impish wit and Gallic gaiety. Paul Galdone's illustrations in red, white and blue personify a smock-clad and beret-capped mouse sprinting on his bicycle between the tall houses of narrow French streets. We say, *Vive Anatole.*

> *A review of "Anatole and the Cat," in* Virginia Kirkus' Service, *Vol. XXV, No. 15, August 1, 1957, p. 523.*

[Anatole] proudly carries on his duties at the Fromagerie Duval until M'sieu Duval's cat appears—disobediently, at night. Anatole's cleverness in handling this situation builds up satisfying nonsense, pictured with amusing drawings of factory and family activity. The cat—a "You-Know-What" in mouse-parent language—is sketched with as real a personality as Anatole's. (pp. 392-93)

> *Virginia Haviland, in a review of "Anatole and the Cat," in* The Horn Book Magazine, *Vol. XXXIII, No. 5, October, 1957, pp. 392-93.*

Truth may be stranger but fiction's more fun, especially in Paris with resourceful Anatole. Gracefully formal dialogue and amusing illustrations, many done in the red, white and blue of the tricolor, are just right for a young reader's version of how a French mouse might speak and look.

> *Mary Lee Krupka, "A Job to His Taste," in* The New York Times Book Review, *November 10, 1957, p. 38.*

Anatole is a mouse *magnifique*. He makes the world safe for cheese tasters. He promptly and most ingeniously bells the "YOU KNOW WHAT." *Vive* Anatole! No wonder Paul Galdone has made the end papers vast French flags. Anatole is reasonable, intelligent and extremely French. He has inspired the artist to make some of his most amusing pictures. Especially attractive is the clear blue title page with Anatole bicycling madly down a dusky street. Young children, already fond of this independent Gallic character, will cheer the double achievements recorded here.

> *"Beguiling Animals in Handsome Pictures," in* New York Herald Tribune Book Review, *November 17, 1957, p. 4.*

BASIL OF BAKER STREET (1958)

[*Basil of Baker Street was written by Eve Titus.*]

Into Basil's (the noted mouse detective) apartment on No. 221-b. Baker Street, Mrs. Judson, the "mousekeeper", ushers the frantic Proudfoots, whose twins, Angela and Agatha, have been kidnapped. Basil, who is well equipped to find the girls, having very literally followed in the footsteps of Sherlock Holmes, and his companion, Dr. Dawson, set out in pursuit, and after much cogitation and derring-do, reunite the little girls with their parents. This miniature detective story follows many of the conventions of the A. Conan Doyle classics, though its simple structure and elementary clues are geared to the logic of the young reader. The text, itself, does not fully exploit the humorous possibilities of the situation although Paul Galdone's elegant Victorian illustrations will delight both children and adults with their graceful wit. Eve Titus and Paul Galdone, who have previously collaborated on the very successful *Anatole* books, once again happily join forces in this charming mousery.

> *A review of "Basil of Baker Street," in* Virginia Kirkus' Service, *Vol. XXVI, No. 9, May 1, 1958, p. 335.*

Mr. Galdone's Basil is as British and as Holmesian (look at him in his British ulster and deerstalker hat!) as the character of Anatole, in the book of that name also written by Miss Titus, is Gallic. The expressive and amusing gray wash drawings in this book have been arranged in a less crowded and more effective manner than the pictures in the Anatole books. Great fun!

> *"Ghostly Adventure and Mystery from Jungle to Mousehole," in* New York Herald Tribune Book Review, *May 11, 1958, p. 5.*

PADDY THE PENGUIN (1959)

A very wistful penguin looks longingly at the Arctic sky, wishing that—since he has wings, he could fly like a proper bird. Penguin games are all very well, on ice and in water, swimming, follow-the-leader, high-jumping, sliding and skidding—but to fly, that was what Paddy really wanted. A helicopter is the instrument of fulfillment to Paddy and his young companions as the whole community of baby penguins go for a joy ride high above the ice. Paul Galdone whose animal stories and drawings have won him a considerable reputation catches the humor of the penguin without sacrificing accuracy in his treatment of the aquatic bird.

> *Varda Pinckard, in a review of "Paddy the Penguin," in* Virginia Kirkus' Service, *Vol. XXVII, No. 13, July 1, 1959, p. 438.*

The drawings are delightful, but the book seems to waver between factual and fictional; all of the action is quite within the realm of possibility until the episode of the mass parachuting—yet there is no real story, the major part of the book describing true penguin behavior, yet the accuracy of the observation being confused by the fictional aspect. (p. 147)

> *A review of "Paddy the Penguin," in* Bulletin of the Center for Children's Books, *Vol. XIII, No. 9, May, 1960, pp. 146-47.*

THE OLD WOMAN AND HER PIG (1960)

The classic story of the old woman and her pig is told here with the pictures by Paul Galdone. A time-tested story, Paul Galdone's expressive drawings reach into the essence of each object involved—the sassy pig, the grumpy bull dog, the rigid stick, the playful water, the stubborn ox, the pompous butcher, the limp rope, the capricious rat, and the greedy cat. With humor and logic, the somewhat sadistic element of the story becomes less forbidding.

> *Varda Pinckard, in a review of "The Old Woman and Her Pig," in* Virginia Kirkus' Service, *Vol. XXVIII, No. 2, January 15, 1960, p. 47.*

Paul Galdone has done an outstanding piece of work in providing the delightful illustrations and artistic book design for this dearly loved folk tale. The whole is dramatic in appearance, appropriately quaint, and full of warm-hearted humor. Young children will enjoy it and many will memorize the text. Highly recommended.

> *Elizabeth Mitchell, in a review of "The Old Woman and Her Pig," in* Junior Libraries, *an appendix to* Library Journal, *Vol. 6, No. 7, March, 1960, p. 135.*

Has no one ever made a picture book of this before? It is perfect material for an artist as skilled and resourceful as Paul Galdone. . . . The difficulty here is to achieve variety in a repetitive story, but it seems no difficulty to Mr. Galdone who brings to his task humor, pace and a fine feeling for design.

> *A review of "The Old Woman and Her Pig," in* The Junior Bookshelf, *Vol. 24, No. 5, November, 1960, p. 288.*

OLD MOTHER HUBBARD AND HER DOG (1960)

A delightful edition of a favorite nursery rhyme. The text is the original, the illustrations have humor and jaunty style; it is notable that the illustration of **"The poor dog was dead"** shows an animal enjoying to the fullest his own trick of "playing dead." Each page has one line of text, so that each of the amazing dog's activities is separately pictured.

> *Zena Sutherland, in a review of "Old Mother Hubbard and Her Dog," in* Bulletin of the Center for Children's Books, *Vol. XIV, No. 7, March, 1961, p. 109.*

Galdone is even better in his pictures for *Old Mother Hubbard* [than in the *Anatole* books]. The naive doggerel sets his imagination roving in a way both fanciful and realistic, and the matter-of-fact resourcefulness of his charming dog is admirable and endearing. This is a most pleasing book.

> *A review of "Old Mother Hubbard and Her Dog," in* The Junior Bookshelf, *Vol. 25, No. 5, November, 1961, p. 268.*

Charming pictures, one colour on grey, set M. H.'s activities in the Regency period, making the most of street scenes and rustic interiors. The artist has obviously studied the early cuts closely, and his own dog, who posed for him, has the right attitudes and shaggy looks for the old rhyme.

> *Margery Fisher, in a review of "Old Mother Hubbard and Her Dog," in* Growing Point, *Vol. 2, No. 2, July, 1963, p. 192.*

THE HOUSE THAT JACK BUILT (1961)

A picture book that gives a joyful interpretation of the familiar nursery rhyme. The rhyme has been left intact, and the illustrations are delightful: the first picture of the cow with a crumpled horn shows the dog being tossed, not hurt but completely surprised, into the grass; a second picture, when the lines recur, shows the cow benignly licking the dog, with only one startled eye visible in the dog's rather apprehensive face.

> *Zena Sutherland, in a review of "The House That Jack Built," in* Bulletin of the Center for Children's Books, *Vol. XIV, No. 10, June, 1961, p. 158.*

Mr. Galdone's double-page pictures for the familiar nursery rhyme are alive with color, humor, and action. But the book presents a dilemma. One would not want a child to miss Caldecott's version, with its subplots and sub-subplots within the incomparable drawings. Also not to be missed is the amusing French-English version with Frasconi's clever and beautiful illustrations. How many Jack's houses does a child need?

> *Margaret Warren Brown, in a review of "The House That Jack Built," in* The Horn Book Magazine, *Vol. XXXVII, No. 3, June, 1961, p. 258.*

This ancient cumulative rhyme is a natural for illustration. It seems strange that Leslie Brooke never used it; one can just imagine his man all tattered and torn. Paul Galdone has found plenty to interest him here, and has made probably the best to date of his traditional picture-books. His cat is superb, his cow with the crumpled horn clearly related to the ox who played a disobliging part in *The Old Woman and Her Pig*, his dog, playing truant from Old Mother Hubbard's establishment, really too nice to worry cats. As ever, Mr. Galdone finds comfort in the limits of the printed page, and each double-spread makes a pleasing design. The end-papers, in white and black on salmon, are exceedingly delightful.

> *A review of "The House That Jack Built," in* The Junior Bookshelf, *Vol. 26, No. 3, July, 1962, p. 118.*

THE THREE WISHES (1961)

Another tried and true folk tale illustrated in the comic manner of Galdone. This time the artist chooses the rich reds and browns of the moods to match the mood of a hunter's haven. Facial expressions are his forte and he uses them to the hilt in this simple retelling.

> *A review of "The Three Wishes," in* Virginia Kirkus' Service, *Vol. XXIX, No. 19, October 1, 1961, p. 915.*

A read-aloud version of the familiar folk tale about the kind woodsman who spared a tree and was granted three wishes. The story is told with simplicity of structure, but in folk style: "Hasn't thou naught for supper, dame?" or "He was dazed, as you may fancy, with wonderment and affright . . ." The illustrations are attractive in their simplicity and humor, but the text seems to strain a bit for effect in the use of language. (pp. 76-7)

> *Zena Sutherland, in a review of "The Three Wishes," in* Bulletin of the Center for Children's Books, *Vol. XV, No. 5, January, 1962, pp. 76-7.*

As she was coming home
she came to a stile,
and she said:
"Pig, pig, get over the stile,
Or I shan't get home tonight."

"I won't," said the pig.

From The Old Woman and Her Pig, *pictures by Paul Galdone. McGraw-Hill Book Company, 1960. Copyright © 1960 by Paul Galdone. Reproduced with permission.*

[*The Three Wishes*] is not outstanding though sprightly enough. The chief charm of the drawings is in the forceful portrayal of the man and his wife as they chat with each other at supper time, he wishing for black pudding, she wishing to have it on his nose, and he, finally using up the third precious wish given him by a fairy in the forest, wishing it off again. The fairy is certainly unimaginatively conceived, part Pinocchio, part gauzy-winged fairy, part leprechaun, and we wonder if the small children will not be bothered that, while the three wishes were given to the *man,* the *wife* was able to use up one of them. Magic doesn't usually work this way.

> *Margaret Sherwood Libby, in a review of "The Three Wishes," in* Books, *January 14, 1962, p. 12.*

THE FIRST SEVEN DAYS: THE STORY OF THE CREATION FROM GENESIS (1962)

The complete first chapter of Genesis in the beautiful King James Version is made into a child's picture book by an artist who has enlivened innumerable gay children's books with his drawings. While his interpretations will appeal to children they have dignity, avoid being saccharine, and one feels they are Paul Galdone's own visualization of the scenes described, not pictures made merely to please children. The cover in a hand-

some deep blue woven cloth is imprinted with a sun, moon and earth in yellow, the end papers show blue skies with heraldic angels blowing golden trumpets, and the various scenes are done in a fine pen and ink line with a blue wash or a combination of bright blue with touches of red, yellow and green. We wish more of our outstanding illustrators would follow Mr. Galdone's example and interpret short passages and stories, keeping them always in the exact words of the text and letting their briefness be the sole concession to a young audience.

We have had the D'Aulaires' pictures for the Lord's Prayer and the longer beautiful books of Dorothy Lathrop, *Animals of the Bible,* and Helen Sewell, *A First Bible,* but what of individual stories or parables? A rich variety of picture books of this sort would allow parents to choose either the fairly conventional like Mr. Galdone's or the deeply mystical, inspired perhaps by Blake or Rouault.

> *Margaret Sherwood Libby, in a review of "The First Seven Days: The Story of the Creation from Genesis," in* Books, *April 22, 1962, p. 9.*

[This] book is handsomely illustrated, some of the pages being softly lovely, some stark, and all in good taste. An excellent book for reading aloud to younger children also; useful in religious education collections as well as in home, school, or public libraries.

Zena Sutherland, in a review of "The First Seven Days: The Story of the Creation from Genesis," in Bulletin of the Center for Children's Books, *Vol. XV, No. 11, July-August, 1962, p. 171.*

THE HARE AND THE TORTOISE (1962)

An ingratiating picture-book treatment of Aesop's fable. The drawings mingle lively forest animals with flowers and grasses done in green, brown, and yellow. Although a little undisciplined in composition, the double-page spreads provide plenty of visual entertainment.

Patricia H. Allen, in a review of "The Hare and the Tortoise," in School Library Journal, *an appendix to* Library Journal, *Vol. 8, No. 9, May, 1962, p. 82.*

Paul Galdone's folk-tale books are free of adult interpolations. Although he fills in the background his interpretations are those of a consistent and recognisable world, even if the zoology is that of America. **The Hare and the Tortoise,** beautifully drawn as ever, is limited in colour to a background of soft greens and yellows, and after the richness of earlier books in this series this comes as a disappointment.

A review of "The Hare and the Tortoise," in The Junior Bookshelf, *Vol. 27, No. 3, July, 1963, p. 125.*

TOM, TOM, THE PIPER'S SON (1964)

To his now-impressive set of nursery-rhyme picture books the artist adds a fresh, lively, and humorous piece in a fully illustrated, little-known version of a traditional rhyme found in *A Treasure of Pleasure Books for Young Children* (published in London in 1850). End papers give the words of the more familiar rhyme, and each pair of pages adds a pictured quatrain about Tom's piping bewitchment of animals and humans. Whether black-and-white or three-color, the drawings are absorbing with their jolly details and continuity of action.

Virginia Haviland, in a review of "Tom, Tom, the Piper's Son," in The Horn Book Magazine, *Vol. XL, No. 2, April, 1964, p. 170.*

Paul Galdone has ideal material for his art in a set of ridiculous rhymes about Tom who, on this occasion, is not stealing pigs but making the most unlikely people dance to his piping. This is a slight but most enjoyable book, full of good observation and unforced gaiety, and with drawing as impeccable as ever.

A review of "Tom, Tom, the Piper's Son," in The Junior Bookshelf, *Vol. 29, No. 4, August, 1965, p. 209.*

SHADRACH, MESHACH AND ABEDNEGO: FROM THE BOOK OF DANIEL (1965)

Mr. Galdone has used the words of the King James version of the Bible for the stirring story of the heroes whose love for God enabled them to survive being cast into the fiery furnace. This chapter from the Book of Daniel has rhythmic passages, with the mouth-filling names of King Nebuchadnezzar and the three Babylonians who defied his command to worship the new golden image, and such sequences as ". . . the sound of the cornet, flute, harp, sackbut, psaltery, dulcimer, and all kinds of musick. . . ." Added to the splendid undiluted text is a pictorial interpretation in red, gold, and black, which creates

dramatic images: the great sphinxlike statue, impressive soldiers, blazing furnace, and contrastingly serene captives.

Virginia Haviland, in a review of "Shadrach, Meshach and Abednego: From the Book of Daniel," in The Horn Book Magazine, *Vol. XLI, No. 2, April, 1965, p. 162.*

Whatever is the artist of Mother Hubbard and the mouse *magnifique* doing wandering loose in the Old Testament? Paul Galdone's pictures of the fiery furnace are far from the exquisite meticulousness of his more familiar work. They are dramatic enough and make realistic sense of a somewhat mystifying story, but it is difficult to like them. The harsh colours, appropriate to the subject and the setting, are most unlovely.

A review of "Shadrach, Meshach and Abednego: From the Book of Daniel," in The Junior Bookshelf, *Vol. 29, No. 5, October, 1965, p. 275.*

The text is based on the book of Daniel, the story tidied up and made simple and continuous. The pictures suggest the East with their friezes and architectural backgrounds, and there is a clever switching from close-up to broad crowd scenes. Vivacious colour alternates with grey and black in a pleasing whole.

Margery Fisher, in a review of "Shadrach, Meshach and Abednego: From the Book of Daniel," in Growing Point, *Vol. 4, No. 6, December, 1965, p, 630.*

THE HISTORY OF SIMPLE SIMON (1966)

[Paul Galdone] is perfectly at home with **Simple Simon,** which he chooses to do in period style, with nicely mannered printer's ornaments round the pictures. In adopting nineteenth-century limitations he foregoes some of his virtuosity, but he gains in directness and good design. A charming book, indeed. . . .

A review of "The History of Simple Simon," in The Junior Bookshelf, *Vol. 31, No. 1, February, 1967, p. 31.*

Mr. Galdone is skilful at finding exactly the right idiom for his nursery rhymes brought up to date: this will give pleasure to grandmothers and grandchildren, and many of the verses will be new to both.

A review of "The History of Simple Simon," in The Times Literary Supplement, *No. 3404, May 25, 1967, p. 453.*

THE HORSE, THE FOX, AND THE LION (1968)

A little-known, decidedly lesser Grimm story (*The Fox and the Horse*) is the basis for an amusing set of pictures as the old horse, turned out by the ungrateful farmer, is assisted by the fox in capturing the lion, thereby assuring himself of the farmer's protection for the rest of his life. The disconsolate old horse, even his hair drooping, the smirking fox and the wide-eyed lion so exactly express their states of mind that you hardly need the text. You don't, of course, need the book otherwise.

A review of "The Horse, the Fox, and the Lion," in Kirkus Service, *Vol. XXXVI, No. 2, January 15, 1968, p. 47.*

From Shadrach, Meshach and Abednego: From the Book of Daniel, *illustrated by Paul Galdone. Whittlesey House/McGraw-Hill Book Company, 1965. Copyright © 1965 by Paul Galdone. All rights reserved. Reproduced with permission.*

Mr. Galdone's tale, adapted from a lesser-known work of the Brothers Grimm, is Indian merely by virtue of the author-artist's choice of costume for his one human protagonist. With illustrations on the grandest of scales, this simple tale should particularly please youngest listeners. (A spiritedly drawn lion, the fall guy of the story, steals the show.)

Selma G. Lanes, "Picture Book Passport," in The New York Times Book Review, March 17, 1968, p. 30.

THE WISE FOOL (1968)

[*The Wise Fool*] is Paul Galdone's rendition of a tale borrowed from Rabelais. . . . Galdone drops the reader right in the middle of Paris in the Middle Ages, with drawings broad enough to appeal to the youngest listener and a tale subtle enough to delight the most sophisticated reader. (p. 55)

Selma G. Lanes, "Picture Books," in The New York Times Book Review, May 5, 1968, pp. 54-5.

It is doubtful whether this small snippet from the third book of Rabelais' *Gargantua and Pantagruel* merits the full picture book treatment. Paul Galdone has kept faithfully to the original story. . . . The adapter has converted the original 'Seyn John the Fool' into 'Lord John the Looney' and as this is the only point where he diverges from the original and without any advantage there would seem to be little point. Paul Galdone's bright, humorous illustrations are up to his usual standard, but,

apart from the first two illustrations showing a general view of Paris and a street, they do not live up to the claim on the jacket of 'bringing to life the atmosphere of the market place in sixteenth-century Paris'—for thereafter he concentrates on the main characters and spectators, who are well portrayed in wash and line, and there is no background illustration. Much of the wit of Rabelais is of a subtle nature and one wonders whether the point of the Fool's Wisdom will be taken by the six to nines. I rather doubt it. (pp. 27-8)

Edward Hudson, in a review of "The Wise Fool," in Children's Book Review, Vol. IV, No. 1, Spring, 1974, pp. 27-8.

HENNY PENNY (1968)

How nice of Paul Galdone to bring back **Henny Penny**! And to bring back that famous Cassandra in the most ebullient Galdone fashion! Now *there's* a man who knows gusto when he sees it. And his happy readers will know it, too, when they see his jolly pictures.

A review of "Henny Penny," in Publishers Weekly, Vol. 194, No. 11, September 16, 1968, p. 71.

The prolific artist is at top best in a sprightly and bright four-color rendition of this favorite, cumulative nursery tale. His Cocky Locky, Ducky Lucky, Goosey Loosey, and Turkey Lurkey form a speeding, lengthening animated procession—until they accept Foxy Loxy's shortcut to the King's palace. The text differs from the original Jacobs and also from the Flora Annie Steel version, substituting pleasanter names than Ducky-daddles, Goosey-poosey, and Foxy-woxy, and shortening and tidying the sad ending. (pp. 161-62)

> *Virginia Haviland, in a review of "Henny Penny," in* The Horn Book Magazine, *Vol. XLV, No. 2, April, 1969, pp. 161-62.*

A rather puzzling allusion on the dust-jacket to a 'final surprise for the reader that reveals a more sympathetic side to Foxy Loxy' appears to refer to the fact that he never passes on the hen's warning to the somnolent king; certainly the fox eats the poultry—no right-minded child would have it otherwise. Paul Galdone has chosen to depict the animal characters in the story in an almost naturalistic style, merely pointing up an eye here and a beak there to suggest excitement. His colours are bright and a little obvious and the interpretation as a whole seems to me a little dull.

> *Margery Fisher, in a review of "Henny Penny," in* Growing Point, *Vol. 9, No. 4, October, 1970, p. 1605.*

THE MONKEY AND THE CROCODILE: A JATAKA TALE FROM INDIA (1969)

The old Indian tale of the monkey who outwits the crocodile lends itself particularly well to the form of the picture book, especially one by an artist who has already proved his ability to give humor and great liveliness to animal stories. The large pages give excellent scope for the many monkeys swinging in the branches of a mango tree, for shore and river with the long toothy crocodile, and for the monkey's wide leap. It has the humor, plot, and movement to make it a good book for any young child, even one unused to stories; the brilliant colors, clear pictures, and brief text should make it very successful for sharing with groups of children.

> *Ruth Hill Viguers, in a review of "The Monkey and the Crocodile: A Jataka Tale from India," in* The Horn Book Magazine, *Vol. XLV, No. 6, December, 1969, p. 668.*

This attractively illustrated version of one of the better known Jataka tales is a welcome addition to the picture-book collection. The crocodile wants a meal of monkey, but the intended prey is far wilier than his antagonist. When the monkey eludes the crocodile one more time, by telling him to open his mouth (which means that he must close his eyes), the monkey leaps on to his head, and from there to the river bank, his tree, and safety. The crocodile, impressed by his adversary's ingeniousness, promises to leave him alone in the future. Children's pleasure in the story will be increased by the clear, cheerful, and lively pictures in pen-and-ink and water color. Particularly certain to elicit an enthusiastic response is the double-page spread showing the crocodile jaws stretched open to snatch the monkey, who has already nimbly jumped onto the crocodile's head. This offers delightful viewing, and is an excellent choice for storytelling purposes.

> *Mary B. Mason, in a review of "The Monkey and the Crocodile: A Jataka Tale from India," in* School Library Journal, *an appendix to* Library Journal, *Vol. 16, No. 6, February, 1970, p. 71.*

The Monkey and the Crocodile is based on a Jataka, one of the animal fables of India which describe the exploits of the Buddha in his animal incarnations. There is fun and sound observation both in the writing and the illustration, but this is a lesser Galdone book. The pictures, big, lively and colourful as they are, lack the exquisite composition of his best work. (pp. 278-79)

> *A review of "The Monkey and the Crocodile: A Jataka Tale from India," in* The Junior Bookshelf, *Vol. 34, No. 5, October, 1970, pp. 278-79.*

THE LIFE OF JACK SPRAT, HIS WIFE AND HIS CAT (1969)

Paul Galdone, who has enlivened many a folktale with his droll interpretations here offers a colorful depiction of the lives and love of Jack Sprat and his wife, Joan, utilizing text from an 1820 chapbook. Children hear and see how a smart-looking, skinny Jack courts a fat Joan; learn the comical details of the couple's eventful ride home from the church; make the acquaintance of Jack's one-eared cat; view the twosome's daily activities; and finally, rest satisfied with the knowledge that Jack and Joan are eventually wealthy as well as loving. Children will delight in the contrast between the buxom Joan and the puny Jack, and will probably ask to have repeated the rhymes about the one-eared cat. A more detailed version of the story than those found in editions of Mother Goose rhymes, this is for funfilled listening and viewing.

> *Pat Byars, in a review of "The Life of Jack Sprat, His Wife and His Cat," in* School Library Journal, *an appendix to* Library Journal, *Vol. 16, No. 5, January, 1970, p. 48.*

[Paul Galdone] is right back on form after some poorish work recently. The naive chapbook rhymes of **Jack Sprat** prompt him to some of his most charming inventions. . . . Mr. Galdone is a kindly artist. Even the rat and mouse escape, to play pat-a-cake while Jack and Joan doze by the fire and the cat plays with a ball of wool. These gay and apt pictures, all in excellent colour, are in the high tradition of the picture-book; one sees the shade of Caldecott nodding approval.

> *A review of "The Life of Jack Sprat, His Wife and His Cat," in* The Junior Bookshelf, *Vol. 34, No. 6, December, 1970, p. 347.*

The full version of the nursery rhyme about Jack Sprat and his wife runs to twenty-three four-line stanzas, and Paul Galdone has made a delightfully rustic picture-book of it. It is all in full colour, in double-page spreads across the landscape format, bled to the page edges. Set in an Oxfordshire village, in carefully observed period detail, these pictures illuminate all the rumbustious humour of the verses, and will be enjoyed by children from about four to seven. This is Galdone at his best, producing something fresh and full of humour and movement, which yet has an earthily traditional flavour.

> *John A. Cunliffe, in a review of "The Life of Jack Sprat, His Wife and His Cat," in* Children's Book Review, *Vol. 1, No. 1, February, 1971, p. 14.*

ANDROCLES AND THE LION (1970)

Androcles and the Lion [is] a 1st-century A.D. legend of which we now have a Christian version with pictures by Grabianski and a pagan version adapted and illustrated by Paul Galdone. Grabianski's text has Androcles meeting and befriending the lion in Africa before coming up against him during a persecution of Christians in the Roman arena. The treatment is somber and serious, and the pictures rather go out of their way to emphasize the cruel and gory. Galdone's version, in which Androcles is just a runaway slave, has a lighter touch. If there's nothing especially memorable about the writing or the pictures, neither is there anything objectionable, and some would say that a story of simple virtue rewarded still has a place in the world. Well, doesn't it?

> *Harve and Margot Zemach, "Old Tales in New Picture Books," in* The New York Times Book Review, *June 21, 1970, p. 22.*

A picture-book version of the story of the Roman slave whose kindness to a lion was repaid by the saving of his own life is told very simply. Some of the humor of the Shavian version is reflected in the illustrations, but the book has less humor than does Daugherty's *Andy and the Lion*; it is, however, adequately written and should be useful for storytelling and reading aloud as a straight version of the original legend.

> *Zena Sutherland, in a review of "Androcles and the Lion," in* Bulletin of the Center for Children's Books, *Vol. 24, No. 1, September, 1970, p. 8.*

THE THREE LITTLE PIGS   (1970)

Three little pigs to savor, and a wolf to lord it over: from the clover-sprigged jacket (*three*-leaf of course) to the third little pig covering the steaming pot from which the wolf's tail protrudes, this is a blithe, unbloody business with a leer on the face of the wolf that you can only laugh at. The text is Jacobs tightened, the drawings are jaunty rustic (with houses inventively framed in straw, sticks, bricks), the whole is more adroit and much more tasteful than Palazzo, more childlikely than the verse version of du Bois. No one will want to abandon Leslie Brooke but like Galdone's **Henny Penny,** this animates the tale for the widest possible audience.

> *A review of "The Three Little Pigs," in* Kirkus Reviews, *Vol. XXXVIII, No. 15, August 1, 1970, p. 794.*

Since the text of this book follows the Joseph Jacobs version very closely, it is the illustrations which are important, and Paul Galdone gives new life to the childhood classic with his colorful and realistic pictures. In each one, he manages to capture the mood of the moment, and, through subtle touches, adds much to the story. Pathos is evidenced in the parting scene of the Mother Sow and her piglets, as they wave goodbye to each other, with tears streaming down their faces. The precarious placing of the ladders during the house-building efforts of the first two pigs gives some indication of the instability of their respective homes. In the case of the third pig, his plumb line is a sign of the care with which he did his construction. The pictures of the fox are also excellent, for the facial expressions show his many emotions. In the one of him sitting

But the crocodile was still determined to catch him. He searched and searched and finally he found the monkey, living in another tree.

Here a large rock rose out of the water, halfway between the monkey's new home and the island. The crocodile watched the monkey jumping from the river bank to the rock, and then to the island where the fruit trees were.

"Monkey will stay on the island all day," the crocodile thought to himself. "And I'll catch him on his way home tonight."

From The Monkey and the Crocodile: A Jataka Tale from India, *written and illustrated by Paul Galdone. The Seabury Press, 1969. Copyright © 1969 by Paul Galdone. Reprinted by permission of Clarion Books/Ticknor & Fields, a Houghton Mifflin Company.*

outside the brick house, readers can almost hear him say, "I can't wait." All in all, a very appealing edition of a beloved story.

> *Florence E. Sellers, in a review of "The Three Little Pigs," in* School Library Journal, *an appendix to* Library Journal, *Vol. 17, No. 2, October, 1970, p. 122.*

Paul Galdone is never less than amusing and perhaps he would not expect any more extravagant claims to be made for his visualisation of *The Three Little Pigs*. He has chosen to illustrate the traditional form of the story, much as it is relayed by Halliwell, and his pictures have a like anonymity. Only in a few places—the medieval yokels selling straw, sticks and bricks, the playful designs around the house-building scenes—does Galdone's individual style show up, the rest might be any-body's talent.

In the choice of text and the sequence of pictures his book has an almost exact similarity to William Stobbs's treatment of the story. With its greater emphasis on design and its insistently two-dimensional illustrations the Stobbs version is perhaps more serious, more dramatic, but a librarian would probably argue a good case for buying both editions. For reading aloud, the Stobbs text is undoubtedly better, but Galdone should be easier for children to read for themselves. (pp. 164-65)

> *Brian W. Alderson, in a review of "The Three Little Pigs," in* Children's Book Review, *Vol. I, No. 5, October, 1971, pp. 164-65.*

THE HISTORY OF LITTLE TOM TUCKER   (1970)

The familiar rhyme of Little Tom Tucker who sings for his supper is vividly enhanced here by Paul Galdone's humorous and colorful illustrations. This version, first published in England around 1820, expands the story of Tom who doesn't much like school and won't learn to read. The lesson that "All boys that can read are my betters" is finally learned, however, and ". . . Tom learned to read / Quite pretty indeed, / And very soon after to write." He goes on to perform other notable deeds, among them courting a lovely lady. The tale ends on a happy note:

> Now Tom's got a wife,
> And Tom's got a knife,
> And Tom can sit down to his supper
> As blest as a king,
> And each night can sing,
> After eating his white bread and butter.

This is bound to be popular with those who enjoyed *The House That Jack Built, The Life of Jack Sprat His Wife and His Cat, Old Mother Hubbard and Her Dog* and *The Old Woman and Her Pig*. Again, Mr. Galdone does much to renew interest in an old favorite. (pp. 41-2)

> *Barbara Gibson, in a review of "The History of Little Tom Tucker," in* School Library Journal, *an appendix to* Library Journal, *Vol. 17, No. 5, January, 1971, pp. 41-2.*

The verses of *Little Tom Tucker* are typical doggerel of the chapbook kind; they come from Kendrew of York. The only possible excuse for reprinting them is Paul Galdone's pictures, and a very good excuse they provide, too. Mr. Galdone needs only a few hints to set him off on excursions of his own, and he makes out of the trivial rhymes a whole world of Tom and

his family and friends. There are a few excellent jokes, but it is the completeness of the picture and the consistency of its detail which matter most.

> *M. Crouch, in a review of "The History of Little Tom Tucker," in* The Junior Bookshelf, *Vol. 35, No. 4, August, 1971, p. 216.*

THREE AESOP FOX FABLES   (1971)

The Fox and the Grapes, The Fox and the Stork, and *The Fox and the Crow,* the first and third seemingly adapted from Joseph Jacobs' retelling, are literately and simply retold here for the picture-book audience. The winsome trickster's success and defeats are expressively captured in large line drawings washed in reds, greens and browns, and the appealingly guileful fox on the jacket makes you want to grin back. Small children will delight in these favorite tales, which will be useful in story hours and which can be read independently by second and third graders.

> *Ruth M. McConnell, in a review of "Three Aesop Fox Fables," in* School Library Journal, *an appendix to* Library Journal, *Vol. 96, No. 12, June 15, 1971, p. 2125.*

THE TOWN MOUSE AND THE COUNTRY MOUSE   (1971)

This artist, who often seems to me niggardly of his talents, has really let himself go in an emphatic statement in colour of the difference (in terms of costume and environment) between a flamboyant mouse at Court and his monkish counterpart. The stately point—'What good is elegance without ease, or plenty with an aching heart'—rounds off a simple text, good for reading to quite small children and wittily interpreted by the artist.

> *Margery Fisher, in a review of "The Town Mouse and the Country Mouse," in* Growing Point, *Vol. 10, No. 5, November, 1971, p. 1830.*

The fable of the town mouse and the country mouse is understandably popular with writers for the very young. For children it has all the characteristics of a nursery classic—archetypal characters, a simple dramatic plot with thrilling climax and reassuring ending.

As one would expect from [British publisher] The Bodley Head, the text is based on an eighteenth century version of Aesop whose well turned phrases are a delight to read aloud. Unfortunately the illustrations hardly match their elegance.

Paul Galdone's spirited picture book versions of *The House that Jack Built, Old Mother Hubbard* and other nursery classics established him in the early nineteen sixties as a lively and sympathetic illustrator of nursery rhymes, with a nice (if somewhat unvarying) line in humorous dogs, cows, rustic milkmaids and the like. His strength lies in his expressive use of line but recently he has burgeoned into full colour and in the process his illustrations have lost a great deal of their individuality. Mr. Galdone has nothing to *say* in colour—he merely lays it on top of his original composition and in doing so effectively obscures the essential wit and vitality of his basic line.

This will undoubtedly find a ready response in children but we should recognise how much more they *might* have gained if the text had been illustrated with a greater sensitivity to its essential qualities.

Eleanor von Schweinitz, in a review of "The Town Mouse and the Country Mouse," in Children's Book Review, *Vol. 1, No. 6, December, 1971, p. 199.*

This is another fine example of Paul Galdone's skill as an illustrator and interpreter of folktales and fables. . . . Through his superb full-color paintings, Galdone portrays the contrast between quiet country life and gay but precarious city life. Double-spreads of the green-eyed cat with fangs exposed, the yapping, snapping dog, and the appealing characterizations of the mice will delight young readers and listeners. Although there are many other versions of this well-known fable, Galdone's is worth looking at.

Mary B. Mason, in a review of "The Town Mouse and the Country Mouse," in School Library Journal, *an appendix to* Library Journal, *Vol. 18, No. 8, April, 1972, p. 126.*

OBEDIENT JACK: AN OLD TALE   (1971)

This is the third—and best—version of the Lazy Jack story to appear in the past year or so (following Jacobs' *Lazy Jack* illustrated by Barry Wilkinson, and the livelier *Lazy Jack,* retold and illustrated by Kurt Werth. Galdone's big, striking watercolors have a humorous folk quality, and in the retelling Jack is pictured as a very well meaning and appealing, if rather stupid, boy. The basic story remains the same—though Jack is always obedient in following his mother's instructions on how to carry home his day's pay, he always manages to lose it and arouse her ire until the end of the story, when his literal interpretation of her instructions wins him the hand of the wealthy merchant's daughter. This retelling of Jack, especially good for reading aloud, also obviates the need in the near future for any more versions of this amusing but currently overdone tale.

Gail Abbott Furnas, in a review of "Obedient Jack: An Old Tale," in School Library Journal, *an appendix to* Library Journal, *Vol. 18, No. 4, December, 1971, p. 53.*

Paul Galdone has the favourite old tale of the stupid boy—his name varies according to the country from which the version comes—who always followed his mother's instructions—after the event. Galdone has been below his best for some time now, and this is nothing special. The drawing is adequate, but Galdone can do this in his sleep. There is little of his best humour and warmth.

M. Crouch, in a review of "Obedient Jack: An Old Tale," in The Junior Bookshelf, *Vol. 36, No. 1, February 1, 1972, p. 24.*

THE THREE BEARS   (1972)

A fresh retelling of the familiar three bears nursery tale. Galdone presents a mischievous, impulsive Goldilocks minus a front tooth and the usual prettiness that has conventionally characterized her. The humorous, representational illustrations help children picture the desirable home and family life of the three bears. The initial double-page spread, which shows the father bear pushing the youngest family member in a swing while mother proudly watches at the door of their log cabin home, is especially pleasing. Another realistic touch, the teddy bear of the Little Wee Bear which experiences the same mishandling as a real child's toy, will also enable children to better

relate to the story. Four- to six-year-olds are sure to enjoy Paul Galdone's interpretation, and they should gain good visual concepts of size and of right to left from the delightful pictures and the use of various type sizes.

Evelyn R. Downum, in a review of "The Three Bears," in School Library Journal, *an appendix to* Library Journal, *Vol. 18, No. 1, September, 1972, p. 63.*

The story of the three bears must exist in more picture-book versions than almost any other fairy tale. The reviewer would be foolhardy who hailed any one edition as the definitive treatment, but Paul Galdone's *The Three Bears* is certainly hard to fault. Most important, he achieves an approach that is distinctively his own: his three bears are beautifully groomed, civilized creatures, living a life of rustic contentment in an astonishingly verdant forest, while his Goldilocks is a horrid, beringleted, over-dressed child who rampages wantonly through the bears' tidy home looking and behaving like Just William's despised sidekick, Violet Elizabeth. The brief, simple text manages to avoid tedium without omitting any of the traditional elements, and Mr Galdone must be congratulated on bringing freshness and vitality to a story that almost every English speaker over the age of four must know by heart.

"Old Friends, New Faces," in The Times Literary Supplement, *No. 3709, April 6, 1973, p. 385.*

The trouble with *The Three Bears* in its most familiar version is Goldilocks. How could the sweet young thing implied by the name behave so badly. Paul Galdone solves the problem admirably; his Goldilocks is a horrible little girl to whom stealing food and breaking furniture comes naturally. From her first appearance—missing front teeth and all—to the traumatic moment when she opens one blue eye and sees the bears at her bedside she is consistent. The bears are less human-like in habit and costume than usual; indeed the Great Big Bear is the only one to wear anything and he only spectacles. This is an unfussy version with none of the customary interior jokes, and not the worse for that. Not in Galdone's very finest manner but thoroughly welcome nevertheless.

M. Crouch, in a review of "The Three Bears," in The Junior Bookshelf, *Vol. 37, No. 3, June, 1973, p. 173.*

THE THREE BILLY GOATS GRUFF   (1973)

The brothers Gruff are most goatish and sly in this retelling of the classic and the troll is a genuine terror. All the elements of the story are realistically portrayed and culminate in dazzling action. Children should be wide-eyed when the goats flummox the wicked troll and send him over the rickety bridge to a watery grave.

A review of "The Three Billy Goats Gruff," in Publishers Weekly, *Vol. 203, No. 21, May 21, 1973, p. 50.*

Though the source of this version of a traditional tale is not acknowledged, Galdone's illustrations are in his usual bold, clear style. The three Billy Goats Gruff are expressively drawn, and the troll looks appropriately ferocious and ugly. The large, lively, double-page spreads are sure to win a responsive audience at story hour; however, storytellers may prefer the version illustrated by Marcia Brown as the text is written in more colorful language.

Then the Little Wee Bear looked at his bed.

"SOMEBODY HAS BEEN LYING IN MY BED—AND HERE SHE IS!"
cried the Little Wee Bear in his little wee voice.

This woke Goldilocks up at once. There were the Three Bears all staring at her.

From The Three Bears, *written and illustrated by Paul Galdone. The Seabury Press, 1972. Copyright © 1972 by Paul Galdone. Reprinted by permission of Clarion Books/Ticknor & Fields, a Houghton Mifflin Company.*

Mary B. Mason, in a review of "The Three Billy Goats Gruff," in School Library Journal, *an appendix to* Library Journal, *Vol. 20, No. 1, September, 1973, p. 57.*

Every generation, of artists as well as children, has to rediscover these immortal stories. Every country too, for Paul Galdone's American vision is quite different from the English interpretation of William Stobbs. The Billy Goats have one of the most perfect of all folk-tale texts, with not a word too many and each one in the right place. Mr. Galdone keeps faithfully to the familiar words and matches them with pictures which prance joyously across the pages. The goats are nicely differentiated. The troll is a fearsome creature, but not so terrible as to make his defeat at the hands—or the horns—of the Big Billy Goat Gruff improbable. The economics of production have taken from Mr. Galdone's pictures some of their former richness of colour, but his line is as strong as ever. (pp. 148-49)

M. Crouch, in a review of "The Three Billy Goats Gruff," in The Junior Bookshelf, *Vol. 38, No. 3, June, 1974, pp. 148-49.*

THE MOVING ADVENTURES OF OLD DAME TROT AND HER COMICAL CAT (1973)

Reminiscent of Old Mother Hubbard, Old Dame Trot bounces through a similar series of rollicking adventures with her cat. Paul Galdone's delightful pictures enlarge the text with sly humor. For example, Old Dame Trot is shown weeping sadly as Puss supposedly lies dead at her feet—but winking one green eye. The type is large enough to be easily read, but some of the words ("butcher," "leather," "chamber") will challenge beginners. In any case, primary graders will enjoy hearing about Old Dame Trot and her comical cat at story hour.

Alice Ehlert, in a review of "The Moving Adventures of Old Dame Trot and Her Comical Cat," in Library Journal, *Vol. 98, No. 12, June 15, 1973, p. 1993.*

Some minor differences apart, the story of Old Dame Trot and her cat runs strikingly parallel to that of Old Mother Hubbard and her dog, a rhyme which Paul Galdone has already successfully illustrated. According to the Opies, Dame Trot is of greater antiquity than Old Mother Hubbard, so it is just her misfortune, now re-emerging from comparative obscurity, to read like a weak imitation of the later work. Paul Galdone's pictures for this edition are full of life and fun, with numbers of mice on every page goggling unharmed at the strange activities of the devoted Dame and her crazy, accomplished pet.

"More Picture Books Received," in The Times Literary Supplement, *No. 3719, June 15, 1973, p. 686.*

HEREAFTERTHIS (1973)

Paul Galdone injects rollicking fun into this traditional English folk tale with his slyly humorous pen-and-ink and watercolor illustrations. The double-page spreads are filled with action—the wife in pursuit of a stray dog, oblivious to the inundation of ale behind her; the robbers' feast; and the happy denouement as Jan and his wife make their way home, each holding one end of their door which is weighted down with the robber's loot. This is sure to delight children at story hour.

Margaret Maxwell, in a review of "Hereafterthis," in School Library Journal, *an appendix to* Library Journal, *Vol. 20, No. 3, November, 1973, p. 39.*

The Galdone-Jacobs heroine in *Hereafterthis* scatters her wheat to the wind and her wisdom to the world, in bold, full-color pictures that spill off the pages in a wash of deep reds, browns and purples. One wishes the retelling had been extended a bit, but there's more than enough to please the young reader in Paul Galdone's robust illustrations: Eyes glint at the sight of silver. Peasants and robbers rush onstage and off in a flash of red leggings, bristling chins, trailing cloaks and waggling bustles. It's all great fun—especially if you read the Joseph Jacobs text aloud.

> *Ann Sperber, in a review of "Hereafterthis," in* The New York Times Book Review, *January 6, 1974, p. 8.*

THE LITTLE RED HEN (1973)

The familiar story of the busy little hen and her three lazy friends is delightfully illustrated with pictures that have color and vitality, the humor of the story extracted in full and most evident in the faces of the dog, cat, and mouse. The setting is a dilapidated farmhouse, and the text and pictures are nicely correlated: Galdone at his best. (pp. 63-4)

> *Zena Sutherland, in a review of "The Little Red Hen," in* Bulletin of the Center for Children's Books, *Vol. 27, No. 4, December, 1973, pp. 63-4.*

Paul Galdone's **The Little Red Hen** is more satisfying [than Janina Domanska's version.] His breezy, seemingly effortless full-color drawings establish a homey background and give the characters distinct, appealing personalities. He makes clear, as Domanska does not, that these animals all live with the hen, so she has a right to expect them to share in the work. And, happily, it leaves in every "And she did."

> *Doris Orgel, in a review of "The Little Red Hen," in* The New York Times Book Review, *January 6, 1974, p. 8.*

In **The Little Red Hen** Paul Galdone returns to the manner, but not the format, of his most successful work. . . . A repetitive text is a challenge to the artist to achieve sufficient variety while sustaining the mood of the story. This Galdone does perfectly. Here is an artist whose humour comes from a fundamentally humorous view of life; he does not need to make jokes to be profoundly funny. A small masterpiece. (pp. 15-16)

> *M. Crouch, in a review of "The Little Red Hen," in* The Junior Bookshelf, *Vol. 39, No. 1, February, 1975, pp. 15-16.*

THE HISTORY OF MOTHER TWADDLE AND THE MARVELOUS ACHIEVEMENTS OF HER SON JACK (1974)

Here is a verse version, first published in England in 1807, of the well-known "Jack and the Bean Stalk." The jolly pictures by Galdone can stand up to his other fine creations and hold their own. Old Mother Twaddle finds a sixpence and sends son Jack to the fair to buy a fat, tasty goose.

> When Old Mother Twaddle
> Had sent Jack to the fair,
> She hastened with onions
> And sage to prepare
> A savory stuffing
> For the delicate treat,
> And thought with what glee
> Of the tidbits she'd eat. . . .

But as we all know, Jack trades his coin for the famous bean instead of the goose. He climbs the beanstalk, slays the giant,

marries a fair damsel he meets in the monster's castle, grabs the treasure and they all live happily ever after, which is, after all is said and done, exactly the ending one wishes to find.

> *A review of "The History of Mother Twaddle and the Marvelous Achievements of Her Son Jack," in* Publishers Weekly, *Vol. 205, No. 11, March 18, 1974, p. 54.*

In this form, the tale is simpler and shorter than the Joseph Jacobs retelling. The lively pictures provide just the right accompaniment; the story begins and ends with scenes of folksy domesticity while the suitably loutish monster, roaring and tippling, overspreads several pages in between.

> *Ethel L. Heins, in a review of "The History of Mother Twaddle and the Marvelous Achievements of Her Son Jack," in* The Horn Book Magazine, *Vol. L, No. 3, June, 1974, p. 273.*

A verse rendition of "Jack and the Beanstalk" with a new twist—here, a young maiden greets Jack at the top of the beanstalk and agrees to marry him after the lad chops off the sleeping giant's head. Jack invites his mother up for the wedding at which Mom cries "and they lived very happy / to the end of their lives." Cheerful, cosy pictures of the cottage and the fair at which Jack buys the magic bean effectively expand in scale to play up the giant's menacing proportions. Although this is not a replacement for the prose version of the story widely available in collections, e.g., Haviland's *Fairy Tale Treasury, Arthur Rackham Fairy Book*, etc., this spirited and broadly comic version will be a welcome addition to fairy tale collections and to the picture book hour.

> *Barbara Thiele, in a review of "The History of Mother Twaddle and the Marvelous Achievements of Her Son Jack," in* School Library Journal, *an appendix to* Library Journal, *Vol. 21, No. 1, September, 1974, p. 59.*

LITTLE RED RIDING HOOD (1974)

"Do I find you here, you old sinner!. . . Long enough have I sought you!" exclaims the huntsman before cutting Little Red Riding Hood and her grandmother out of the greedy wolf's belly. This, then, is a thoroughly conventional Red Riding Hood, both for better (the unbowdlerized Grimm ending) and for worse (the half-modern, half-archaic adaptation). And as usual, Galdone's pictures pose no surprises—the blond, angel-faced Red Riding Hood and the wolf with his lolling pink tongue, pink nightgown, and ruffled cap are bloodless, storybook cutouts, but this illustrator's ability to establish eye contact with the reader is really effective here. None of the impish subtlety of deRegniers and Gorey, but then, "all the better to catch hold of you with, my dear."

> *A review of "Little Red Riding Hood," in* Kirkus Reviews, *Vol. XLII, No. 22, November 15, 1974, p. 1199.*

For families which lack a copy of the old classic, here's just the ticket—a softer version of the original, graced by the pictures of a master. Paul Galdone stresses the comic here, rather than the moralizing or the macabre tone. It's clear that he finds the villainous wolf a dashing fellow, and the vapid blond girl looks just the kind of a dullard who would mistake her grandmother for a wolf. We get a happy ending, after enjoying striking woodland scenes and charming interiors (the quilt on grandma's bed could make parents positively covetous).

> *A review of "Little Red Riding Hood," in* Publishers Weekly, *Vol. 206, No. 22, November 25, 1974, p. 45.*

In a retelling that adheres to the Grimm version with both Grandmother and Red Riding Hood eaten up and later rescued by a passing huntsman, Galdone's customary dazzle of washed line work shows a vacuous Red who seems devoid of artistic character when placed beside the splendidly villainous wolf. But the story's drama is still well maintained in sweeping close-up scenes that can easily be viewed by story-hour listeners.

> *A review of "Little Red Riding Hood," in* The Booklist, *Vol. 71, No. 9, January 1, 1975, p. 460.*

THE FROG PRINCE   (1974)

Galdone's frog leaps his determined way through this well-known folk tale in pursuit of the princess, who, having promised him a place at her table and in her bed in return for retrieving her ball, is reluctant to fill her end of the bargain. Galdone's princess comes across as what she is—a petulant, self-willed child, who gets more than she deserves when the frog becomes a properly handsome prince in the best fairy tale tradition. A humorous version, with full-color wash-and-ink illustrations that perfectly capture the spirit of the tale.

> *Margaret Maxwell, in a review of "The Frog Prince," in* School Library Journal, *Vol. 22, No. 1, September, 1975, p. 82.*

With the colorfully washed line work that has become his trademark, Galdone pictures a pond, a princess, and a castle à la fairy-tale convention. Focal to the illustrations is a bug-eyed, insolent frog realistically drawn from live models captured for short-term use on the artist's Vermont farm. Similar in flavor and format to **Little Red Riding Hood. . . .**

> *Barbara Elleman, in a review of "The Frog Prince," in* The Booklist, *Vol. 72, No. 3, October 1, 1975, p. 233.*

Paul Galdone is in a sense the American William Stobbs. Both artists know how to pour new life into an old story. In his latest offering Mr. Galdone takes one of the most familiar stories in the world. Admittedly his free rendering of the Grimm text is not very well done, missing both the timelessness and the colloquial ease of the oral folktale. (And while he was about it, would it not have been wise to omit the curious episode of Iron Henry which hangs uncomfortably on to the tail of the main theme?) However, it is the pictures that matter, and these are wholly admirable. Unlike the words they relate the fantasy to a recognisable, if exotic, world. As always, Mr. Galdone is superbly professional in his handling of the long oblong page, into which he drops his designs with due regard to their dramatic and decorative quality.

> *M. Crouch, in a review of "The Frog Prince," in* The Junior Bookshelf, *Vol. 41, No. 5, October, 1977, p. 276.*

THE GINGERBREAD BOY   (1975)

Galdone has already proven many times over that he is perfectly at home with those traditional nursery tales that are still pre-schoolers' favorites, and his expressive, unassuming style just right for their very young audience. Here he takes us, with his runaway gingerbread hero, from the benign old couple's cottage through a country landscape that streaks by like the backdrop in a Western chase film. We must admit that his ogling threshers and mowers have less individual appeal than the typically Galdone-y loping cow, stuffed looking horse and ever-so-self-satisfied fox, but children will follow along breathlessly with every one of them right up to that last *snip snap snip* when the Gingerbread Boy goes "the way of every single gingerbread boy that ever came out of an oven."

> *A review of "The Gingerbread Boy," in* Kirkus Reviews, *Vol. XLIII, No. 3, February 1, 1975, p. 119.*

From The Frog Prince: Adapted from the Retelling by the Brothers Grimm, *by Paul Galdone. McGraw-Hill Book Company, 1975. Illustrations copyright © 1975 by Paul Galdone. All rights reserved. Reproduced with permission.*

The Gingerbread Boy is a variant of the English tale of Johnny-Cake which lacks the conciseness of the text in Joseph Jacobs. The story, with its repetition-with-variation formula, lends itself well to picture book treatment, but Mr. Galdone never really catches fire, being content with stereotype characters and settings. All done with immaculate professionalism, but we expect more of so distinguished an artist.

> *A review of "The Gingerbread Man," in* The Junior Bookshelf, *Vol. 40, No. 5, October, 1976, p. 262.*

Paul Galdone has approached *The Gingerbread Boy* in a . . . respectful spirit. His jovial, mob-capped old couple and the other human pursuers of the traditionally-shaped cookie are rustic in the usual picture-book style, with smock-frocks and square-cut hair and farm implements at the ready, and it is not unexpected that the animals express surprise or eagerness in a near-human way, with the fox's mask manipulated to suggest a Victorian villain. The water-colours are accomplished and pleasing and the artist has made good use of a long page to suggest the forward rush of the chase.

> *Margery Fisher, in a review of "The Gingerbread Man," in* Growing Point, *Vol. 15, No. 5, November, 1976, p. 2993.*

GERTRUDE THE GOOSE WHO FORGOT (1975)

[Gertrude the Goose Who Forgot *was written by Joanna Galdone.*]

[A] neat cumulative text in relaxed verses describing how the absent-minded goose, while looking for her lost key, gathers up various articles of clothing so that in the end she is suitably dressed for the party to which she is escorted by her mate. The tour round the farmyard introduces numerous animals, each presented in bland colour with slightly humanised expressions. Like Petunia, Gertrude has visible personality and is clearly a family pet. . . . [A] pleasant little tale.

> *Margery Fisher, in a review of "Gertrude the Goose Who Forgot," in* Growing Point, *Vol. 15, No. 4, October, 1976, p. 2974.*

Gertrude is vintage Galdone. At his best, this artist is unmatched as a master of the landscape picture book, and Gertrude waddles beautifully across the wide double-spreads in search of her lost key. . . . The neat verses, by Mr. Galdone's daughter, move the action forward briskly.

> *M. Crouch, in a review of "Gertrude the Goose Who Forgot," in* The Junior Bookshelf, *Vol. 40, No. 5, October, 1976, p. 261.*

PUSS IN BOOTS (1976)

Like Stobbs last year, Galdone trims Puss's tale for younger listeners and sacrifices also the dash and splendor of Marcia Brown's illustrations. However, if Galdone's obvious, unsophisticated style is not what you'd associate with Perrault, he has it all over Stobbs for movement, expression and light-hearted humor. And if Brown made the peasant and his cat convincing courtiers, there is something to be said for Galdone's depiction of the king and his entourage as beefy louts in finery. A *Puss* for the people.

> *A review of "Puss in Boots," in* Kirkus Reviews, *Vol. XLIV, No. 7, April 1, 1976, p. 384.*

Galdone follows Perrault's story line faithfully, as Puss works mischief to obtain a fortune for his master. The writing, fluid and readable, makes even this familiar tale sound fresh—no mean feat. Galdone's large, humorous caricatures—easily seen for story hour—have great gusto, and Puss is the embodiment of cleverness and knavery (the elephant, however, has a disproportionate trunk and looks bluish in the review copy). This lacks the sophisticated detail in Marcia Brown's version, yet it is pure Perrault, pure Galdone, and children will love it.

> *Michael John Lafian, in a review of "Puss in Boots," in* School Library Journal, *Vol. 23, No. 1, September, 1976, p. 100.*

The appeal of Puss in Boots is perennial, and so is its challenge to the illustrator. Paul Galdone responds splendidly to the comic element in the story, rather less to its courtliness and elegance. This means that it appears what in fact it is, the account of a highly successful "con". However, if Mr. Galdone misses some of the subtleties of the original, he catches and embellishes every joke. He is at his happiest with the big double-spread page, over which his designs flow with immense vitality. Here is much joy, all of it well within the child's range.

> *M. Crouch, in a review of "Puss in Boots," in* The Junior Bookshelf, *Vol. 42, No. 5, October, 1978, p. 250.*

THE MAGIC PORRIDGE POT (1976)

The story of the magic porridge pot gone out of control is an old favorite (and one of ours) and Galdone gives it an amusing twist by having the mother forget the magic words (frantically shouting "halt!" and "cease!" instead of "stop!" as the porridge flows down the village streets) and the little girl come to the rescue. There's no twist to the pictures though—they're workaday Galdone, with some child-level comic-book touches, such as a cat hanging from a tree branch to escape the rising river of porridge, but certainly without the overall eye appeal of De Paola's 1975 Italian version, *Strega Nona.* Ah well, some like it obvious.

> *A review of "The Magic Porridge Pot," in* Kirkus Reviews, *Vol. XLIV, No. 20, October 15, 1976, p. 1132.*

Galdone portrays this simple folk tale in his usual style—*not* that of Breughel as the jacket obliquely implies—but with minimal spark. A poor peasant woman and her daughter are helped by a witch who presents them with a porridge pot capable of replenishing its contents. It is the mother who activates it, out of appetite rather than mischief. The legitimacy of her desire to kindle the pot robs the story of tension: the mother simply isn't very bright and needs to be rescued by the daughter. Some readers may revel in the chagrin felt by the mother, but the grain of truth hopefully to be found in folk tales is garbled here and most collections will prefer to stick with Tomie de Paola's rendition of the sorcerer's apprentice theme in *Strega Nona.*

> *Dana Whitney Pinizzotto, in a review of "The Magic Porridge Pot," in* School Library Journal, *Vol. 23, No. 4, December, 1976, p. 49.*

Two recent versions of this familiar tale, De Paola's *Strega Nona* and Towle's *The Magic Cooking Pot*, spring to mind as being richer and more novel. But Galdone has a way of getting back to basics; his text is fast moving and economical, and the familiar lines and washes conjure up a medieval backdrop with peasantry ever ready to catch a child's wandering eye.

Denise M. Wilms, in a review of "The Magic Porridge Pot," in Booklist, Vol. 73, No. 8, December 15, 1976, p. 606.

THE TABLE, THE DONKEY AND THE STICK: ADAPTED FROM A RETELLING BY THE BROTHERS GRIMM (1976)

Paul Galdone has wisely chosen a story which is less familiar than most of the others he has retold and illustrated. Entitled "The Wishing-Table, the Gold-Ass, and the Cudgel in the Sack" in the Pantheon complete edition of Grimm, the robust tale of magic and trickery concerns a stupid tailor who unjustly punished his three sons and drove them from home. A minor episode and the irrelevant coda in the original version have been judiciously omitted by the artist whose typically entertaining illustrations—full of verve, exaggerated characterizations, and earthy humor—make a well-balanced picture book.

Ethel L. Heins, in a review of "The Table, the Donkey and the Stick," in The Horn Book Magazine, Vol. LIII, No. 2, April, 1977, p. 149.

The story is a humorous one and the humor is enhanced by Galdone's drawings which capture the silliness of the situations and the gullibility of the characters. There is, however, one problem with this folk tale. Over one third of the story is concerned with how the tailor, who was deceived by the lying family goat, drove his sons into the world. Yet, after the old man has discovered his mistake and driven off the goat, this business is completely dropped. The result is a rather unbalanced plot. One would have hoped that with the reteller's right of editing, Galdone might have shortened this opening section considerably. (pp. 17-18)

Jon C. Stott, in a review of "The Table, the Donkey and the Stick," in The World of Children's Books, Vol. II, No. 2, 1977, pp. 17-18.

CINDERELLA (1978)

The enduring fairy tale seems likely to go on forever, tempting every writer and artist to create personal versions of Cinderella's trials and triumphs. Galdone's telling is kinder to the wicked stepmother and stepsisters than [Anne] Rogers's. When the scullery maid gets her prince, she forgives her selfish relatives, after they abase themselves and plead for pardon; ". . . as she hugged them she said she loved them with all her heart and asked them always to love her." Galdone infuses his paintings with glowing colors, elegance and wit—his individual touches, in short.

A review of "Cinderella," in Publishers Weekly, Vol. 214, No. 21, November 20, 1978, p. 60.

This is an eminently robust version of the story, in contrast to the quieter, more romantic tone of, say, Marcia Brown's classic work. Even the few completely serious scenes, such as Cinderella sitting sadly alone in front of the hearth or confronting her fairy godmother, sing with energy. Moreover, the ambitious spreads reflect Galdone's essential lightheartedness of style; comedy seeps through in the pompous, snobby faces of the stepmother and sisters. Dialogue gives the text an informal feeling but does adhere to folktale conventions: says the godmother to Cinderella, "Now . . . go again to the garden, child,

From The Amazing Pig: An Old Hungarian Tale, *retold and illustrated by Paul Galdone. Houghton Mifflin/Clarion Books, 1981. Copyright © 1981 by Paul Galdone. All rights reserved. Reprinted by permission of Clarion Books/Ticknor & Fields, a Houghton Mifflin Company.*

and you will find six lizards behind the watering pot. Bring them to me." Visually, this has surefire child appeal; it's a good working interpretation.

Denise M. Wilms, in a review of "Cinderella," in Booklist, Vol. 75, No. 9, January 1, 1979, p. 750.

[Mr. Paul Galdone] is certainly the most confident performer of all [those whose books are reviewed here]—choosing for his text an honest-to-goodness abridgment of Perrault's original and building his double-page pictures round it with typical zest (wherein of course lies the weakness, because Mr. Galdone is now so proficient a maker of picture books that everything flows forth with mechanical ease and all the character of his early books has gone).

Brian Alderson, "Prettification," in The Times Educational Supplement, No. 3340, June 20, 1980, p. 42.

ANATOLE AND THE PIED PIPER (1979)

[*Anatole and the Pied Piper* was written by Eve Titus.]

Cheers for Titus, bringing another buoyant story of dear Anatole, the most gifted mouse in all of France. Galdone, who did the honors in the nine previous tales of Anatole, matches the swift telling and fraught events with his brightly hued paintings. A day that promises pleasure begins when Anatole's wife, Doucette, takes 24 smiling schoolmice to a picnic in the woods. But there a frustrated human composer, Grissac, kidnaps the mice and imprisons them in his Paris studio. The heartless man needs inspiration for his "Mouse Minuet," which he cannot succeed with as he has with "Waltz of the Whales" and "Hippo's Hop." His captives' reactions now tell him which notes to sound and he is elated by his progress. But in the mouse community, Anatole and his friends, the pigeons of Paris, are hatching the plot that ends in the rescue of the mice children and a delightful surprise.

> *A review of "Anatole and the Pied Piper," in* Publishers Weekly, *Vol. 215, No. 26, June 25, 1979, p. 123.*

It would be hard to imagine an Anatole who wasn't parented by Galdone as well as Titus, for the artist captures all the brio and humor of the author's writing. In this newest tale, the mouse-hero's wife takes an active part, for it is she, Doucette, who thinks of the way to rescue two dozen schoolmice who have been captured by Grissac. . . . Nice nonsense. . . .

> *Zena Sutherland, in a review of "Anatole and the Pied Piper," in* Bulletin of the Center for Children's Books, *Vol. 33, No. 3, November, 1979, p. 60.*

KING OF THE CATS: A GHOST STORY (1980)

In this retelling of a century-old English tale, a woman and her cat wait long into the evening for the return of the grave-digger husband. Finally he bursts into the cottage wild-eyed and demands, "Who is Tom Tildrum?" As he goes on to recount a funeral procession of black cats that he witnessed, his own cat, Old Tom, is much affected by the description. When the gravedigger reports that the head of the procession spoke to him, charging him to "Tell Tom Tildrum that Tim Toldrum's dead," Old Tom shrieks "What—old Tim dead! Then I, Tom Tildrum, am King of the Cats!" and he rushes up the chimney and is never seen again. Illogical. Fun. Great for reading aloud to a circle of wriggly children. The wonderful weather-beaten full-spread illustrations are of a scale for group showing. Because it is short, strange, beautifully illustrated, dramatic but not really frightening, it will do well in most libraries. (pp. 55-6)

> *Mary B. Nickerson, in a review of "King of the Cats: A Ghost Story," in* School Library Journal, *Vol. 26, No. 9, May, 1980, pp. 55-6.*

Unlike the artist's recent **Hans in Luck,** which had some shallowness in its illustration, this shows Galdone at his best. Scenes are dramatic and clear, with characters' faces individualized to memorable effect. The mildly spooky story (retold from Joseph Jacobs) is first-rate and perfect for telling aloud, especially at Halloween. . . . A soundly executed venture with suspense and energy to spare. (pp. 1363-64)

> *Denise M. Wilms, in a review of "King of the Cats: A Ghost Story," in* Booklist, *Vol. 76, No. 18, May 15, 1980, pp. 1363-64.*

Galdone follows closely, in his adaptation, the version by Joseph Jacobs on which this tale is based (from *More English Fairy Tales*) but has simplified the exposition and removed the dialect from the dialogue. A smooth retelling, the story is handsomely illustrated by large-scale pictures that fill, but do not crowd, the pages; Galdone's draughtsmanship is at its best here, with effective composition and use of color to create the eerie graveyard scenes and the staring, frightened eyes of the old gravedigger and his wife as he tells the tale of the burial service for the King of Cats. The style isn't quite as flavorful as that of Jacobs, but the simplified language makes this version a good choice for telling to young children or for reading aloud.

> *Zena Sutherland, in a review of "The King of Cats: A Ghost Story," in* Bulletin of the Center for Children's Books, *Vol. 34, No. 1, September, 1980, p. 13.*

THE AMAZING PIG: AN OLD HUNGARIAN TALE (1981)

Once more a king announces a contest for his daughter's hand; once more a poor peasant sets out to win it; and once more Galdone disarms with his down-to-earth egalitarian humor. . . . Never mind that Galdone's pictures have become predictable—they still give his stories more life and simple fun than many more ambitious illustrators can summon.

> *A review of "The Amazing Pig: An Old Hungarian Tale," in* Kirkus Reviews, *Vol. XLIX, No. 6, March 15, 1981, p. 352.*

A king promises his daughter to any man who tells him something he *can't* believe. The son of a poor peasant sets out to win her hand by spinning a tale of his family's fabulous pig. After elaborating on its accomplishments, the son allows that the pig is going blind and must be led—"And that is why my father hired your own grandfather as a swineherd to look after him." The king roars, and you can guess the finish. Galdone's quick lines and full-color washes do their work well. The facial expressions he provides are sharply apt, particularly for the pig, and page composition shows the artist's sure touch for luring young eyes through the story.

> *Denise M. Wilms, in a review of "The Amazing Pig: An Old Hungarian Tale," in* Booklist, *Vol. 77, No. 16, April 15, 1981, p. 1152.*

THE THREE SILLIES (1981)

Galdone's flashy and infectiously nonsensical color paintings captivate one as much as his swift version of Jacobs's circular tale of stupidity. A swain courting a farmer's daughter finds her with her mother and father weeping in their cellar. The reason is an axe, stuck in the ceiling. What if the young woman and her fiancé marry and have a son who would be killed if the axe should fall on him? The suitor laughs at their foolishness, removes the tool from its perilous niche and departs. He swears he will come back to wed his betrothed only when he finds three people sillier than they are. Little readers will have a high old time, going on the quest and discovering epic ineptness that persuades the bridegroom to return and exchange vows with his intended.

> *A review of "The Three Sillies," in* Publishers Weekly, *Vol. 220, No. 17, October 23, 1981, p. 63.*

A genial rendering of the classic Joseph Jacobs' tale—with less suggestion of witlessness and less pictorial ingenuity, perhaps, than the Margot Zemach version (now o.p.), but probably more popular appeal. Galdone makes the foolishly despairing daughter ("Suppose my young man and I were to be married, and we were to have a son, and he was to grow up . . .") a pretty, beribboned, bubble-headed blonde; he depicts her horror-struck parents as Dickensian ninnies; and he gives her fiancé (who goes off in search of "three bigger sillies") the aspect of an amiable, indulgent young blade. In this mock-Victorian interpretation, the conclusion comes off particularly well—"So the young man went home and married his own dear silly"—and the two hearts set below, one grinning, one demure, reinforce the feeling that what we have is not so much a dimwit tale as a valentine. (pp. 1404-05)

A review of "The Three Sillies," in Kirkus Reviews Vol. XLIX, No. 22, November 15, 1981, pp. 1404-05.

Slapstick is central to this tale of stupidity, and Galdone capitalizes on all opportunities. Children will relish spectacles like the old woman pushing her cow up a ladder or a rotund traveler trying to jump into his pants. As usual, the artist's scenes maximize the story's drama; here's more practiced fun from a prolific visual storyteller. (pp. 498-99)

Denise M. Wilms, in a review of "The Three Sillies," in Booklist, Vol. 78, No. 7, December 1, 1981, pp. 498-99.

WHAT'S IN FOX'S SACK? (1982)

A fox' sly conniving to get something for practically nothing goes awry when a woman substitutes a watchdog for the boy he's managed to acquire in his manipulative ploys. The tale does nicely with Galdone's broad cartoon illustrations, which make the most of simple dramatic close-ups and adeptly pace the story. Vintage Galdone, and as such a good pick for story hours or for readers on their own.

Denise M. Wilms, in a review of "What's in Fox's Sack?" in Booklist, Vol. 78, No. 17, May 1, 1982, p. 1158.

The repetitious text, built on a series of refrains makes the final interruption of the expected sequence fun. But, although the pictures are bright and busy, they do not always convey the excitement or humor necessary to lift the pedestrian text. A typical Galdone offering, from the slapdash watercolors to the unleavened text; good for story hour, but only if the animation of the storyteller adds the zest that the overall production lacks.

Kristi L. Thomas, in a review of "What's in Fox's Sack?" in School Library Journal, Vol. 28, No. 10, August, 1982, p. 97.

It's partly the marvelously expressive faces (animal and human) that Galdone gives his characters, partly the vitality of his drawing, and partly the exuberant humor of the illustrative details that make this version of an English folktale so engaging. . . . There's a restrained use of repetition and a pattern within the story, nicely told and as appropriate for storytelling as for reading aloud.

Zena Sutherland, in a review of "What's in Fox's Sack?" in Bulletin of the Center for Children's Books, Vol. 36, No. 2, October, 1982, p. 25.

THE MONSTER AND THE TAILOR: A GHOST STORY (1982)

In intent, another "Scary Story"—following *The Tailypo* and *King of the Cats;* in actuality, a lame excuse for a story framing a central scare sequence. A poor tailor is sent to the graveyard to stitch up the Grand Duke's new trousers ("Only then will I have good luck when I wear them—that is what my soothsayer told me"). There, a ghostly monster begins to emerge behind him, intoning: "Do you see this great head of mine?" "Do you see this great neck of mine?" Etc., etc. As the monster materializes bit-by-bit in the background, the tailor bravely stitches away . . . until, finishing in the nick of time, he makes

the Grand Duke's castle just inches ahead of the pursuing creature. . . . The tailor-monster dialogue is in the best oral ghost story tradition, and Galdone's pictures of the confrontation have a properly threatening aspect when seen at a distance. But for the single child, listening or looking, it's a crudely executed artifice.

A review of "The Monster and the Tailor: A Ghost Story," in Kirkus Reviews, Vol. L, No. 16, August 15, 1982, p. 935.

Galdone masterfully engineers his tale through line-and-wash illustrations that milk the giant's fright potential for all it's worth. There's a severe letdown, then, when the giant simply disappears at the finish; children are sure to wonder where he went. Nevertheless, the preceding excitement is not to be missed; it's sure to hold youngsters spellbound.

Denise M. Wilms, in a review of "The Monster and the Tailor: A Ghost Story," in Booklist, Vol. 79, No. 5, November 1, 1982, p. 370.

Galdone's vigorous drawings, full of movement, humor, and color, are the stellar feature of an adapted story for which no source is cited. . . . This has some suspense, but there's really little action, and the story, albeit adequately told, ends abruptly. (pp. 65-6)

Zena Sutherland, in a review of "The Monster and the Tailor: A Ghost Story," in Bulletin of the Center for Children's Books, Vol. 36, No. 4, December, 1982, pp. 65-6.

HANSEL AND GRETEL (1982)

There have been several handsome editions of *Hansel and Gretel* in recent years. Zwerger's and Jeffers' to name two. Now here is another choice, Galdone's, illustrated in his own unmistakable style. He has used the late-nineteenth-century version of the story by E. V. Lucas upon which to base his bold ink-and-watercolor drawings. Except for the witch, who still has some comic nuances to her character, everyone is portrayed in a realistic, even poignant manner. Some drawings, especially faces, are better executed than others, and the gingerbread house seems almost unappetizing. But as in the past, Galdone's large, eye-catching illustrations should be popular. Though the text is long, this would work in group session.

Ilene Cooper, in a review of "Hansel and Gretel," in Booklist, Vol. 79, No. 10, January 15, 1983, p. 676.

Hansel and Gretel continues to challenge today's illustrators (18 versions in print), inviting two more here to try their luck on the forest waifs. Svend Otto S. has made a totally unconvincing interpretation. . . . Paul Galdone also misses the mark but not as completely. His children, parents and witch are convincing enough but the color wash separations are not. The density of the washes frequently overpowers the soft penciled features of the characters' faces. Both artists have done much better work.

Jim Trelease, "Once Again upon a Time," in Book World—The Washington Post, May 8, 1983, pp. 13, 21.

THE TURTLE AND THE MONKEY: A PHILIPPINE TALE (1983)

Described as "a Philippine tale," this story of a turtle who finds a banana tree in the river and a monkey who cheats her out of its fruit begins with a catchy folklore situation but ultimately trails off in bits and pieces. As Turtle can't carry the tree to her garden by herself, she asks Monkey for help and agrees to give him his share in return. Monkey then insists on splitting the tree now, not the bananas later, and chooses the showier top half for himself. Though it is Turtle's half that survives and bears fruit, once more she must turn to Monkey, offering him some of the bananas if he will climb the tree and throw some down. Instead, he merely climbs up and eats his fill. Snappy enough so far, the story needs only a fitting come-uppance, but Turtle's strewing thorns and prickers around the tree and Monkey's painful hopping about on his descent doesn't quite answer. Grafted onto this is a briar-bush routine, with Monkey threatening reprisal and Turtle begging *not* to be thrown into the river . . . and then, when she is, paddling happily downstream, the bananas forgotten. Even Galdone's drawings lack spirit, with repetitive, minimally varied shots of Monkey and Turtle facing off against a slapdash tropical background.

> *A review of "The Turtle and the Monkey: A Philippine Tale," in* Kirkus Reviews, *Vol. LI, No. 6, March 15, 1983, p. 304.*

The brains-over-brawn moral is easy to see, and Galdone's proficient spreads are easy to take. This is not inspired in either telling or illustration, but it is workmanlike. The visual pacing is practiced and effective, bringing the story to life very well. It's a practical pick for the picture-book shelf.

> *Denise M. Wilms, in a review of "The Turtle and the Monkey: A Philippine Tale," in* Booklist, *Vol. 79, No. 20, June 15, 1983, p. 1338.*

This Philippine tale is told in a direct style which effectively allows Galdone's illustrations to convey the emotional strife between the two characters. The ink and watercolor illustrations, although not as intense as those in **The Monkey and the Crocodile,** succeed in portraying the turtle as being slowmoving yet patient, resourceful, crafty, and having great eye contact!

> *Ronald A. Jobe, in a review of "The Turtle and the Monkey: A Philippine Tale," in* Language Arts, *Vol. 60, No. 6, September, 1983, p. 772.*

THE ELVES AND THE SHOEMAKER (1984)

Librarians who have purchased the recent Birrer version of this traditional Grimm story will have to balance the latter's innovative, folk-art appeal against Galdone's familiar, energetic style. His telling, like the Birrers', is efficient; his pictures are, as usual, literal and dramatic—young audiences will have no trouble holding on to the story as it unfolds. Although the draftsmanship is true and dynamic, color is used sparingly; the predominant grays, blacks, and tans make for a muddy look that can't hold a candle to the Birrers' glowing scenes. On the other hand, Galdone's spreads have a compelling dramatic quality that the Birrers' more static compositions don't convey. This is very serviceable; add it where budgets and demand warrant.

> *Denise M. Wilms, in a review of "The Elves and the Shoemaker," in* Booklist, *Vol. 80, No. 20, June 15, 1984, p. 1483.*

Galdone's version resembles the Grimms' original fairy tale in that he preserves an air of formality and sticks to the sequence of events penned by the folklore brothers. . . . The pictures in flashing hues emphasize the secret helpers' impishness; they seem to be performing the service more for a lark than in the name of sweet charity. It's a dandy adaptation, more fun than most of the many versions available. (pp. 104-05)

> *A review of "The Elves and the Shoemaker," in* Publishers Weekly, *Vol. 225, No. 26, June 29, 1984, pp. 104-05.*

Lucy Crane's pleasantly phrased retelling of the folk-tale provides opportunities for the artist's typically robust treatment of human faces and figures and for his favourite dramatic combinations of geranium red and bright yellow paint; the elves, with skinny bodies and huge bulging eyes, move lightly when naked and strut comically when they have put on the clothes made for them by the shoemaker's wife. The feeling of goodwill and domestic felicity is very evident in this interpretation. (pp. 4584-85)

> *Margery Fisher, in a review of "The Elves and the Shoemaker," in* Growing Point, *Vol. 24, No. 6, March, 1986, pp. 4584-85.*

THE TEENY-TINY WOMAN: A GHOST STORY (1984)

Galdone's version of this old English ghost story is much like Seuling's in its retelling, but his art contrasts sharply. Where Seuling's pictures are contained miniatures featuring a doll-like protagonist, Galdone opts for his characteristic brisk spreads and a teeny-tiny woman who looks larger than her role in the story implies. His deft cartoon lines and color washes are proficient though not inspired; however, youngsters might make a game of seeing how many faces they can find in the story's inanimate objects. The cupboard holding the bone is the prime example, but there are lots more to be found, all in keeping with the story's sense of ghostly silliness.

> *Denise M. Wilms, in a review of "The Teeny-Tiny Woman: A Ghost Story," in* Booklist, *Vol. 81, No. 7, December 1, 1984, p. 522.*

Galdone's version of the rhythmic, repetitive old ghost story can't miss as an amusement for the younger set. The teeny-tiny woman who lives in a teeny-tiny house in a teeny-tiny village goes for a teeny-tiny walk, etc. Opening the gates to a churchyard, she finds a bone that will add flavor to the soup she plans for supper. Back home, she goes to bed but is alarmed by a voice, not at all teeny-tiny and progressively louder, demanding, "Give me back my bone!" The rollicking effects are heightened by Galdone's full-color pictures. He cleverly details the appointments of the woman's Victorian-era cottage and, best of all, the setting outside. Objects scudder and soar in the increasing gale preceding the rain that pushes the TT woman, huddled in her bonnet and shawl, back from the graveyard along the road to her TT home.

> *A review of "The Teeny-Tiny Woman: A Ghost Story," in* Publishers Weekly, *Vol. 227, No. 2, January 11, 1985, p. 72.*

Galdone has directed his considerable talent and style to [this] traditional British ghost story. . . . [The] comfortable, cozy country and cottage scenes defuse whatever scariness young readers might conjure up. Fences, trees, balustrades and cupboards in murky, inky tones are designed to suggest watchful faces and add to the atmospheric tension of the narrative, a definite contrast to the sunny, sweet version illustrated by Barbara Seuling. While Galdone's illustrated story is an adequate addition to folk tale, ghost story, Halloween collections and beginning reader shelves, it still doesn't replace hearing the original story told aloud in the dark around a campfire.

> *Dana Whitney Pinizzoto, in a review of "The Teeny-Tiny Woman: A Ghost Story," in* School Library Journal, *Vol. 31, No. 6, February, 1985, p. 63.*

RUMPLESTILTSKIN (1985)

A Galdone-illustrated folktale can be counted on for visual thrust and expression, but in recent years those Galdone trademarks have become perfunctory. Here, slapdash diagonals of heaped straw do for dynamic vitality, and the miller's daughter with her oversized sad eyes is unattractively and one-dimensionally formless. Without seeming to try, Galdone can point up his story with a subtle detail (the ring of keys in the king's hand) or a sideways glance (a gloating one from the dandily dressed dwarf on the title page; a sinister one from the jewelery-laden king). But this is a garish, overbearing sort of expressiveness. Certainly these pictures will project to storyhour crowds, but they are all blare and no echo.

> *A review of "Rumplestiltskin," in* Kirkus Reviews, *Vol. LIII, No. 11, May 15, 1985, p. J25.*

It's always interesting to see the different styles in which artists interpret the classics. In Galdone's lavish application of royal red and other glittering colors, this fairy tale's settings in woodland and palace assume lively realism. The story moves briskly, introducing conniving Rumpelstilskin as a kindly old man, eager to help the miller's daughter spin straw into gold. Failure means death so the maiden agrees to her benefactor's terms. She promises to give him her firstborn in return for producing the gold. Even toddlers have probably heard the end, where Rumpelstiltskin is outfoxed and pounds himself into the ground

in his rage. But it's like hearing a brand-new story in the master's words and vivid scenes.

> *A review of "Rumplestiltskin," in* Publishers Weekly, *Vol. 227, No. 20, May 17, 1985, p. 117.*

Visually and stylistically similar to Galdone's other fairy-tale renderings, this is a straightforward version of the Grimms' story about the little man who helps a girl spin straw into gold. Although the passionless text is somewhat bland, Galdone plays against this by offering expressive, boldly colored drawings that are highlighted with bright blues, golds, and oranges. Donna Diamond's recent black-and white interpretation of the story makes a more unusual choice for libraries, but as a garden-variety staple useful for story hours (the large size is a plus), this Rumpelstiltskin succeeds on its own merits.

> *Ilene Cooper, in a review of "Rumplestiltskin," in* Booklist, *Vol. 81, No. 19, June 1, 1985, p. 1399.*

CAT GOES FIDDLE-I-FEE (1985)

Galdone presents his picture-book version of a cumulative folk song that will be familiar to fans of folksinger Sam Hinton. While the addition of a boy and his grandmother to the usual cast of barnyard animals changes the tone a bit, it neither adds to nor detracts much from the familiar version. The jacket flyleaf copy indicates that this is a song, but unfortunately no music is appended. Galdone's line-and-watercolor illustrations have all the verve and accessible good humor associated with his work, and the varied and irresistible rhythm of the verses carries the nonsense along at a good pace, enhancing its appeal to the very young. Whether told or sung, this is a diverting selection for preschool story times. (pp. 258-59)

> *Carolyn Phelan, in a review of "Cat Goes Fiddle-I-Fee," in* Booklist, *Vol. 82, No. 3, October 1, 1985, pp. 258-59.*

This traditional barnyard song is readily available in collections (with music and/or accompanying motions) and also in at least one other picture book version, illustrated by Diane Stanley. Nevertheless, Galdone does a workmanlike job both in the

From Three Little Kittens, *illustrated by Paul Galdone. Clarion Books, 1986. Copyright © 1986 by Paul Galdone. All rights reserved. Reprinted by permission of Clarion Books/Ticknor & Fields, a Houghton Mifflin Company.*

retelling and the illustrations. His cast of characters—unlike Stanley's tarted-up pigs with ties and cats in silk and plumes—appear in their natural fur and feathers, crunching apples, pecking for bugs and eating hay. The line-up is the traditional one—with the addition of a grandmother for the final stanza, presumably to lend a sense of conclusion to the text. The cartoon illustrations are bright and cheerful, with each new animal being individually introduced on a double-page spread, then joining the other animals under "yonder tree" in the succeeding double-page layout—a design device that reinforces the rhythm and balance of the song itself. This edition will prove useful to librarians and parents who feel more comfortable holding and showing a book while they sing. (pp. 72-3)

> *Kristi Thomas Beavin, in a review of "Cat Goes Fiddle-I-Fee," in* School Library Journal, *Vol. 32, No. 4, December, 1985, pp. 72-3.*

A cat that sees and hears everything is featured in this familiar cumulative rhyme-song about the feeding of a group of barnyard animals. The refrain and the emphasis on sound words ("Duck goes quack, quack, / Hen goes chimmy-chuck, chimmy-chuck") make this attractive to young children playing with language, and the repetitive structure invites new readers to be successfully independent with minimum practice.

Other artists have interpreted this verse differently, but Galdone is true to his well-developed style of comic realism. His animals are so clearly represented that very young children will identify them with ease. The wide-eyed cat bursts with acrobatic energy, much too busy to be sly or proud, and smiles his way through all those "fiddle-i-fees."

> *Janet Hickman, in a review of "Cat Goes Fiddle-I-Fee," in* Language Arts, *Vol. 63, No. 2, February, 1986, p. 192.*

THREE LITTLE KITTENS (1986)

Galdone's brisk pen-and-wash drawings have a way of making characters seem slightly larger than life. His three little kittens with their wide yellow eyes and otherwise expressive postures create a visual focus that will carry readers securely through this energetic depiction of the familiar nursery rhyme. All eight verses are here in large print, several lines to a page. A skilled, effective version to use with preschoolers.

> *Denise M. Wilms, in a review of "Three Little Kittens," in* Booklist, *Vol. 83, No. 3, October 1, 1986, p. 271.*

[A] cartoonist who interprets the mystique of cats is Paul Galdone.... His work is not "flashy" in the conventional sense, but his style is consistent, self-assured, and very positive. His 1986 rendition of the classic rhyme "Three little kittens, they lost their mittens" is by far the best version we have seen. He gives us vigorous, animated cats that are loosely structured with spidery lines and comically characterized. He places huge foreground images of these cats in environments that are subdued and radically scaled down. Yet the interiors in *Three Little Kittens* are a pleasure in themselves, an encounter with nineteenth-century styles of American ornamentation.

> *Donnarae MacCann and Olga Richard, in a review of "Three Little Kittens," in* Wilson Library Bulletin, *Vol. 62, No. 3, November, 1987, p. 63.*

OVER IN THE MEADOW: AN OLD NURSERY COUNTING RHYME (1986)

Adapting and illustrating the old nursery rhyme in a full-color picture book, Galdone chooses ten animal families to show hiding, jumping, gnawing, squealing, buzzing, cawing, quacking, oinking, swimming, and sleeping in their homes in the meadow. The familiar thump of the rhythm and satisfying clip of the rhyme keep the pages turning at a good pace, while the sunny watercolor illustrations provide a rewarding series of detailed, happy tableaux. Although the format is not oversize, the pictures are most effective seen from a little distance. Not to deny the pleasure it will give as a lap book, this interpretation seems particularly well suited for reading aloud in library and classroom story times. Fine versions by Theodore Rojankovsky and Ezra Jack Keats are still in print, but children will enjoy the gaiety of Galdone's interpretation.

> *Carolyn Phelan, in a review of "Over in the Meadow: An Old Nursery Counting Rhyme," in* Booklist, *Vol. 83, No. 8, December 15, 1986, p. 646.*

The familiar counting rhyme is given new text and illustrations in this cheerful book.... Using rhyme and repetition, the deceptively simple verse provides a vehicle for counting and for identification and recognition of numbers, colors, animals, wildflowers, noises, and actions. The artwork is vibrant and beautifully composed. Unfortunately the colors are not always as described: "pink" pigs are a light pumpkin shade; a "pond so blue" is a weak green; a "red barn door" isn't red. Those familiar with earlier versions may question the need for a rewrite, and they may also wonder what happened to a credit to Olive Wadsworth, who wrote the original *Over in the Meadow*.

> *Leda Schubert, in a review of "Over in the Meadow: An Old Nursery Rhyme," in* School Library Journal, *Vol. 33, No. 6, February, 1987, p. 68.*

THE COMPLETE STORY OF THE THREE BLIND MICE (1987)

[*The Complete Story of the Three Blind Mice was written by John W. Ivimey.*]

The jolly, lilting and expanded poetical version of *The Three Blind Mice*, by John W. Ivimey, a turn-of-the-century British writer, was found in an antique children's book and exuberantly illustrated by Paul Galdone just before his death earlier this year. The three impecunious mice sleep in the field of a farmer and gorge on his cheese crumbs next morning. The farmer's wife, however, doesn't like their high jinks. In a hair-raising chase through bramble briars that blind the pitiable creatures, she does the notorious foul deed with the knife. The blind and stub-tailed little rodents are truly dreadful to behold—too horrible an end to an illustrated children's book. Mercifully, they acquire a salve to make their tails grow anew, and at the end they build a Cotswold thatch cottage, and each learns a trade. It's preachy; still—the mice are real. Their blind misery will wrench the heart of anyone who has ever had a hamster *in extremis*. The upbeat end is in scale, conclusive, proper. *Vale*, Paul Galdone. (pp. 28-9)

> *Peter F. Neumeyer, in a review of "The Complete Story of the Three Blind Mice," in* The New York Times Book Review, *November 29, 1987, pp. 28-9.*

What brings this amusing cautionary tale to vivid and entertaining life is Galdone's masterful artwork. He infuses such vigor and humor into his illustrations that the text becomes fresh and exciting. The bold, action-filled double-page spreads in warm colors view the scenes in fields and farmhouse from various perspectives and include all kinds of intriguing background details. The goggle-eyed mice in neck scarves, the leather-faced farmer, and his stout wife in mobcap and shawl are delightful.

> *Patricia Pearl, in a review of "The Complete Story of the Three Blind Mice," in* School Library Journal, *Vol. 34, No. 7, March, 1988, p. 168.*

Patricia (Grace) Lauber (Frost)

1924-

American author of nonfiction and fiction and editor.

Lauber is recognized as a versatile writer best known for creating lively, authoritative informational books for all ages in both the natural and social sciences. Her more than sixty works on subjects as diverse as animals, rivers, planets, robots, and cattle ranching reflect her contagious curiosity, observance of the interdependence of all living things, and regard for the work of scientists and historians. Acclaimed for her up-to-date research, thoroughness, and imaginative presentations of scientific facts and historical overviews, Lauber provides simple introductions to such complex fields as astronomy, botany, and geothermal energy. Her books, several of which are considered to be outstanding examples of their kind, are praised for their skillful condensation of vast amounts of information; accurate, intriguing details; readability; and appealing use of analogies children can understand. For the last three decades, Lauber has interspersed light, humorous fiction for younger children with solid, entertaining nonfiction in science and the social studies for readers up through senior high. For example, between her first book *Clarence the TV Dog* (1955)—based on the antics of her own pet—and the first of several sequels, she wrote nonfiction books on the Netherlands, France, and Scotland. Lauber broke from her usual straightforward scientific writing with a speculative examination of early Nordic, Indian, and Oriental travelers in *Who Discovered America? Settlers and Explorers of the New World Before the Time of Columbus* (1970). Documenting her facts with cultural comparisons and archaeological investigations, she pioneered the first such ambitious undertaking for children. The celebrated *Volcano: The Eruption and Healing of Mount St. Helens* (1986) demonstrates how volcanoes can both destroy and encourage life while revealing Lauber's commitment to ecological recovery. In the late 1960s, she began selecting the drawings and photographs for her books, which are often commended for their beauty and suitability. A former editor-in-chief of *Science World*, chief science editor of *The New Book of Knowledge*, and consulting editor of *Scientific American Illustrated Library*, Lauber has also contributed to several series, such as the *Look-It-Up* books and the *Challenge* books.

Critics praise Lauber for her ability to clarify sophisticated concepts and dramatize factual material with neither condescension nor sensationalism. They admire her scholarship, literary excellence, and the way she attracts, involves, and stimulates young readers to further inquiry. Although a few reviewers complain that the plots or characters of her fiction seem slightly contrived, the majority of critics agree that Lauber exemplifies the best qualities of nonfiction writing for children with her timeliness, accuracy, perceptiveness, and joyous enthusiasm.

Lauber won the Washington Post/Children's Book Guild Nonfiction Award in 1983 for her body of work in informational books for young readers. She received the Eva L. Gordon Children's Science Author Award in 1987; her *Volcano: The Eruption and Healing of Mount St. Helens* was selected as a Newbery Honor Book in the same year.

Photograph by Roy A. Gallant. Courtesy of Patricia Lauber.

(See also *Something About the Author*, Vols. 1, 33; *Contemporary Authors New Revision Series*, Vol. 6; and *Contemporary Authors*, Vols. 9-12, rev. ed.)

AUTHOR'S COMMENTARY

To many people an "appealing" science book is a contradiction in terms, for science tends to have a spinachlike reputation. Apart from books about young animals there is little subject matter that one might describe as cuddly or heartwarming. Readers of science books are unlikely to feel the hair rise on the backs of their necks or to laugh or cry, except perhaps for highly personal reasons. They may well have to work hard to understand the content. And so science is often viewed as being somewhat unpalatable—but good for you; few would deny the importance of scientific literacy, particularly in others.

Yet, that is an adult view. Children are not born turned off by science, and if they grow up that way, it is because they have "caught" that attitude, along with the common cold and other scourges. Children are born curious, wanting and needing to understand the world around them, wanting to know why, how, and what: the very questions that scientists ask. Science has a natural appeal to children, to their powers of reasoning and questioning, their intuition and imagination. The business of writers and publishers of children's science books is to make that appeal apparent. There is more to it than producing a book that will engage and hold a child's interest, because most children's books are selected and paid for by adults. To reach the child one must first get by the adult—and then compete for time and attention, most notably against the pablum of television.

Strangely enough, however, it is television that has probably provided the biggest push toward making science books more appealing, at least to the eye. It has created a picture-oriented society, and the children of today have never known any other kind. In days gone by, most editors lavished their resources on picture books for the very young, while a typical science book was illustrated with simple line drawings that could most kindly be characterized as "clear." Today we are seeing a number of handsome science books that take advantage of advances in printing technology and are prompted by an editorial awareness of the picture-oriented reader and of the fact (a whole generation to the contrary notwithstanding) that appearances do count. Books today can and should be generously and well illustrated, with photographs and art that embody content and extend the text. Layout, use of white space, and readable type should also serve to draw the reader in, to make the book inviting. All books deserve good graphics, but science books perhaps have the greatest need to make a good first impression, to say, "Pick me up and look inside" or "Turn the page." Good illustrations can also be effectively used to draw readers (or the selectors of books) toward subjects that are important, but less popular than such all-time favorites as dinosaurs, whales, snakes, young animals, and volcanoes. The hand that might not otherwise reach for a book bearing on microbiology probably cannot resist turning pages that show what an electron microscope sees.

Still, illustrations can do only so much. Books are for reading, and once someone has been enticed into picking up a science book, the text begins to count heavily. A problem confronting both writer and reader in the 1980s is that science, even in the areas suitable for children, has advanced by quantum jumps in the last twenty years or so, and, advancing, has become appreciably harder than it used to be. More is known. New concepts abound. New complexities arise.

Within memory, natural scientists have moved from finding and classifying plants, animals, and protists, to anatomy and physiology, and to understanding the relationships that exist among living things and their environment. Today it does not suffice to produce, even for very young readers, a book that simply shows, names, and describes turtles. Every young reader is capable of grasping a bigger picture—how turtles make a living, how some can survive in cold water, who and what their enemies are, and what role turtles play in the natural world. Young children are perfectly capable of understanding how a big cactus survives in a desert and how, in surviving, it provides food and shelter for desert animals. The total picture is more complex and also more interesting. It is significant and important because it permits chidren to grow up knowing about the interdependence of living things. (pp. 5-6)

Most writers of children's science books are not themselves scientists, but people who understand science and know how to write for children. The rapid advances in many scientific disciplines mean that these writers must work harder than they used to. Gone are the days when "facts" stayed reliably the same for years on end. Gone, too, are the days when research could be done in the comfortable convenience of a good home library. To be up-to-date, writers must go to primary sources: scientific papers and journals and the scientists who know in what direction research is moving. Once the information has been collected, it must be digested, a process that may take considerable time and effort. It is only when this assimilation is complete that the writer is ready to consider how best to tell the story.

I use the word "story" because I believe that the best science books have a story line: that one thing leads to another, that it is possible to build tension so that the reader really wants to find out what happens next. Science is not simply a collection of known facts to be learned. It is open-ended (with plenty of room for future scientists). It is a continuing process and a *human* activity. In the practice of it, paths lead to dead ends: What to do next? Key pieces of evidence, earlier overlooked, are discovered. Puzzles are solved as all the pieces suddenly fall into place. There is excitement aplenty to stimulate the mind. As the story unfolds, the reader should become aware that because science is a human activity, it contains errors. The point is important partly because the reader should realize that science is, sooner or later, self-correcting, that questioning minds are always probing, testing, doubting. It is also important because the writer must take cognizance of the errors that are incorporated into textbooks and encyclopedias, which even adults tend to view as gospel, but which by their very nature are years in the making, always partly out-of-date, and constantly being revised. It is confusing for a child to find "facts" that are categorically stated in a textbook being flatly contradicted in another book. The considerate writer will indicate what is a new discovery, or even go so far as to tell what it was that other scientists "used to think."

Good science books also give the reader an overview, a framework into which the specifics fit. Young readers need an idea of the whole before they can see how the pieces come together to form that whole. My own favorite cookbooks are very good in this respect. The authors, in addition to telling me what to do, tell me why and how, and what the final result should be—and what to do if mine doesn't come out quite the way it was supposed to. I am at ease with such a cookbook because I understand what I'm doing and where I'm supposed to come out. The young reader of a science book deserves no less.

At a more specific level, it is obvious that science books ought to be accurate; but taking dead aim at some of the concepts and theories of modern science is seldom possible. They are too hard and unfamiliar. Some do lend themselves to step-by-step explanation; others do not. The best a writer can do is to put across the general idea. In either case, it is essential to develop relevance, to find familiar expressions of the unfamiliar. (pp. 7-8)

The writers of children's science books have always used analogies and have always looked for familiar counterparts to the unfamiliar. Obliged, when writing about volcanoes, to define magma as molten rock with gases dissolved in it, we all turn to soda pop as an example of the familiar. Soda is a liquid with a gas (carbon dioxide) dissolved in it. The gas makes the bubbles when the container is opened. This is not an explanation, but children do not need to understand precisely what is meant by a gas dissolved in a liquid. What they do need to understand is that the phenomenon is not esoteric, but everyday and familiar. They will then have a good idea of what happens when a volcano erupts violently, when gases burst out carrying molten rock along with them. The explosion is, on a large scale, exactly what happens if a bottle of soda is shaken before being opened. Today the need for finding ways of putting across the unfamiliar is greater than ever before. Success in doing so depends on the writer's assimilation and understanding of the material.

The writing of good science books for children is not easy. Many mind-bending hours go into the writing of a book that is appealing to a child's mind and sense of wonder. The end result should be so seamless and natural that a reader of any age might think, "Of course that's the way it is." The book should read as if it had, in fact, been easy to write. Our reward for achieving this is sometimes to be treated by other adults as if we were slightly simpleminded. (If we aren't, why are we writing easy books for children instead of hard books for grown-ups?) And so, just as virtue is said to be its own reward, the intellectual satisfaction of having mastered difficult subject matter and making it clear to others is the one reward the writer of a good book can be sure of. On occasion there is also the reward of having made something so clear and interesting that an adult (perhaps the book's editor or a reviewer) who was long ago taught not to like science, suddenly begins to see what it's all about and becomes enthusiastic. But the greatest reward of all comes from children who have found in a trade book something they were not finding in their texts, who are full of enthusiasm, and who write letters asking for "more." (p. 9)

> *Patricia Lauber, "What Makes an Appealing and Readable Science Book?" in* The Lion and the Unicorn, *Vol. 6, 1982, pp. 5-9.*

GENERAL COMMENTARY

ROSE FRIEDMAN

In these days of widening communications, children are becoming better acquainted with peoples of distant lands. This new series of books [the "Challenge Book" series, which includes Lauber's *Battle Against the Sea: How the Dutch Made Holland* and *Highway to Adventure: The River Rhone of France;* Jean Bothwell's *Cobras, Cows, and Courage: Farm Life in North India;* and Wanda Tolboom's *People of the Snow: Eskimos of Arctic Canada*], describing how several peoples have met the challenge of their different environments, furthers that acquaintanceship.

The most dramatic of these four volumes pictures the courage and perseverance of the Dutch in winning their land from the sea. After giving a capsule picture of the natural forces that shaped early Holland, the author concentrates on the coastal region. The crude dikes built by Frisian settlers, improvements by the Romans, and the treacherous inroads of the sea are described briefly. The rest of the book is a panorama of the flood of 1953 and the struggle of the people to regain their land. The account of the tremendous dike-building project, the reconstruction of the country and the development of plans for a permanent hold-back of the sea is gripping and informative.

In *Highway to Adventure,* the same author profiles the Rhone, tracing it from its glacial source and describing its influence on the development of France. The reader is taken on an oil-barge tour down the river through glacier-cut gorges and a man-made canal to Arles and the colorful Camargue—where cowboys and gypsies mingle with ranchers, farmers and fishermen. At this point the narrative becomes overburdened with historical facts, but it picks up liveliness again in the portrayal of how modern inventions helped France harness the rebellious river for electricity, flood control and irrigation. . . .

These authoritative, well-integrated and splendidly illustrated books fill a definite need among 10-to-14-year olds. Recommended, however, is a pronouncing dictionary of geographical terms.

> *Rose Friedman, "Challenged by Nature," in* The New York Times Book Review, *December 30, 1956, p. 12.*

CLARENCE, THE TV DOG (1955)

Clarence, a very remarkable dog who enjoys television, catches a burglar by untying his shoelaces, and makes friends wherever he runs, is the hero of one of the funniest dog stories I have ever read. Pure nonsense that children of all ages, but especially 8-12 will love. Good for reading aloud to groups. Every school and public library will be the happier for owning a copy of this book.

> *Phyllis Fenner, in a review of "Clarence, the TV Dog," in* Junior Libraries, *an appendix to* Library Journal, *Vol. 2, No. 1, September 15, 1955, p. 42.*

Everyone in the book is believable and funny, simpler than life and twice as natural. Clarence does display a degree of paternal feeling for his own puppies which is rare in the species, but most engaging. This story has wit and economy in the telling, with room for the reader to laugh.

> *Marjorie Fischer, "Gifted Pooch," in* The New York Times Book Review, *November 13, 1955, p. 36.*

The activities of a small, but unusual dog whose greatest pleasure in life is watching TV. The episodes, told in the first person by the dog's owner, are obviously based on real happenings, but they are told with a forced and labored humor that takes from them much of their potential appeal and any semblance of reality.

> *A review of "Clarence, the TV Dog," in* Bulletin of the Children's Book Center, *Vol. X, No. 2, October, 1956, p. 23.*

BATTLE AGAINST THE SEA: HOW THE DUTCH MADE HOLLAND (1956)

This is the first in a new series of books designed to show how people of different countries have dealt with the problems peculiar to their regions—in this case, the Dutch and their dikes. . . . [*Battle Against the Sea*] outlines the history of Holland, briefly and with sole reference to its relations with the ocean. The broad outlines of Earth's climatic trends are traced and we see how the dunes were created and how the Frisians came to live on them. Roman dikes follow and then with the balance, the greater part of the book, the accent is on the present and the terrific fights the Dutch have had to put up against such disastrous storms as the one in 1953. Human and mechanical angles are explored and much is made of the heroism and effort involved in the struggle against the awful floods as well as the actual paperwork and planning for the elaborate pumping and dike systems which have also taught much to the rest of the world. Emotionalized but informative. (pp. 166-67)

> *A review of "Battle Against the Sea," in* Virginia Kirkus' Service, *Vol. XXIV, No. 5, March 1, 1956, pp. 166-67.*

An absorbing, factual account of "How the Dutch Made Holland"—virtually wresting it from the sea time and time again. Vivid descriptions of the various floods, including the last, most disastrous one of 1953 are given with details of past, present, and contemplated schemes for combatting them. Although students in grades 6-9 are the ones best able to read it themselves, it will be very welcome to the teachers of the fourth grade where the Lowlands are frequently studied.

> *Miriam S. Mathes, in a review of "Battle against the Sea," in* Junior Libraries, *an appendix to* Library Journal, *Vol. 2, No. 8, April 15, 1956, p. 116.*

Battle against the Sea is the over-dramatized story of the 1953 floods and the rebuilding of the dykes of the Netherlands which followed. The American spelling of 'dike' is preferred and the correct name of the country is never used. The information is interesting and the dramatic style will command the young reader's attention.

> *J. A. Morris, in a review of "Battle against the Sea," in* The School Librarian and the School Library Review, *Vol. 12, No. 1, March, 1964, p. 91.*

HIGHWAY TO ADVENTURE: THE RIVER RHONE OF FRANCE (1956)

Through well-written text and excellent photographs, the reader is taken on a voyage down the Rhone River in France from its start in the high Alps to the Camargue delta country where the River divides and flows into the Mediterranean. Through the semi-narrative style of describing family life on a barge, the author shows what the river means to France as a source of water power and the problems that are created by its tremendous force. The surrounding countryside is described in terms of its physical geography and products. In a final section the plans that are being made for harnessing the river's power are discussed. An interesting presentation, somewhat weakened by the unnecessary fictionalization.

> *A review of "Highway to Adventure," in* Bulletin of the Children's Book Center, *Vol. X, No. 4, December, 1956, p. 52.*

Interesting, much-needed material done in a warm, lively manner. Author has skillfully woven into her account of present-day life on the river barges and along the shores of this mighty river the historic background of the French people and their hopes for the future. Fine for supplementary material in grades 5-8 and also good adventure reading. (pp. 23-4)

> *Margaret McFate, in a review of "Highway to Adventure: The River Rhone of France," in* Junior Libraries, *an appendix to* Library Journal, *Vol. 3, No. 5, January 15, 1957, pp. 23-4.*

VALIANT SCOTS: PEOPLE OF THE HIGHLANDS TODAY (1957)

Another zestful description of a geographic area, its people and their problems is added to the *Challenge* series by Patricia Lauber, general editor, in this first hand account of the beauty and hardship of life in the Scottish Highlands. Succinctly it tells of the strikes against the Highlands in the past two centuries—of timber wealth stripped away, uncontrolled emigrations, and the radical drop in acreage under cultivation. The

story of Scotland's current fight to recoup its economic losses is clearly and simply told. . . .

> *A review of "Valiant Scots," in* Virginia Kirkus' Service, *Vol. XXIV, No. 10, May 15, 1957, p. 351.*

CLARENCE GOES TO TOWN (1957)

Clarence, the dog whose liking for TV was recorded in an earlier book, goes to New York in this one with Brian and Sis and their mother, who is to mind a dress shop for Aunt Min. The city seems unfriendly until Clarence goes to work on the neighbors. He helps rid the apartment house of mice. Then he wins a wealthy customer for the shop by knowing the difference between synthetic, as Brian says, and real Persian lamb. Scarcely pausing to shake himself, he wins a trip to Europe for a neighbor, catches two dog thieves at a dog show, works up a clientele for a neglected French restaurant, gets lost on a ship, and finally attacks a wild-smelling beast which turns out to be made of old Davy Crockett hats. This is a funny book, a fine mixture of the probable and improbable—sensible nonsense.

> *Marjorie Fischer, "A Dog Has His Day," in* The New York Times Book Review, *November 17, 1957, p. 38.*

This sequel to **Clarence the TV Dog,** is not quite so funny as the earlier book, but it will be happy reading for boys and girls of 8-12, whether or not they have read the first title. . . . Recommended for all libraries.

> *Mildred C. Skinner, in a review of "Clarence Goes to Town," in* Junior Libraries, *an appendix to* Library Journal, *Vol. 4, No. 4, December, 1957, p.28.*

PENGUINS ON PARADE (1958)

A fascinating account of the life cycle and behavior of the penguins that inhabit the Antarctic regions, for young people in the upper elementary grades. Detailed description of the leading varieties is given with a discussion of the birds' evolutionary development and their remarkable adaptation to their environment. . . . Subject matter is similar to that found in *Penguins* by Darling, but presentation is for slightly more advanced readers.

> *Elizabeth F. Grave, in a review of "Penguins on Parade," in* Junior Libraries, *an appendix to* Library Journal, *Vol. 4, No. 8, April 15, 1958, p. 46.*

[**Penguins on Parade**] is a rollicking book. . . . Anything about penguins is funny, and this attractive volume . . . takes full advantage of the humor of these quaint creatures. The information is amazingly complete. Here are answers to just the sorts of questions the 10-to-14's inevitably ask—how they live, what they eat, how they raise their young, how many kinds there are. This book is good fun for any age.

> *Millicent J. Taylor?, in a review of "Penguins on Parade," in* The Christian Science Monitor, *May 8, 1958, p. 15.*

DUST BOWL: THE STORY OF MAN ON THE GREAT PLAINS (1958)

This dramatic and beautifully clear account of how lush grasslands became, through man's carelessness, the Dust Bowl, is highly recommended for junior high school reading. Photographs, mostly from the Soil Conservation Service, and maps, done by Wes McKeown, supplement the excellent text. Will be useful in all school libraries. May even be used from fifth grade (good readers) up to high school.

> *Mildred C. Skinner, in a review of "Dust Bowl: The Story of Man on the Great Plains," in* Junior Libraries, *an appendix to* Library Journal, *Vol. 4, No. 9, May 15, 1958, p. 44.*

RUFUS, THE RED-NECKED HORNBILL   (1958)

When an exotic bird from Thailand escaped several years ago from a New York pet shop, the whole city followed Rufus on his lively escapade amid the city sky-scrapers. Now, the story of this impetuous hornbill is retold in a humorous though factual treatment.... Apart from the interpretation of human thoughts attributed to the bird and the device of constant repetition of detail, this book might well captivate the parent reader as well as the child, who inevitably will be fascinated by Rufus' unconventional antics.

> *A review of "Rufus, the Red-Necked Hornbill," in* Virginia Kirkus' Service, *Vol. XXVI, No. 19, October 1, 1958, p. 752.*

"Rufus wanted to see the town. And the town wanted to see Rufus." This is the essence of a wonderfully comic tale.... Nice Mr. Schlesinger tries to capture Rufus but spends most of his time going up and down in elevators. Both pictures [by Polly Cameron] and text take advantage of the repetition, as should anyone reading the story aloud. Children in the early grades will no doubt want to read it for themselves....

> *Rod Nordell, in a review of "Rufus the Red-Necked Hornbill," in* The Christian Science Monitor, *November 6, 1958, p. 14.*

A read-aloud picture book based on an actual happening.... Text and illustrations draw the incident out in a rather repetitious fashion; since the fictional story reflects, for the most part, real events, it seems unnecessary to attribute to the bird emotions and purpose of a human variety, and to present at the same time, the type of newspaper-reporting details that would not appeal to small children.

> *A review of "Rufus the Red-Necked Hornbill," in* Bulletin of the Center for Children's Books," *Vol. XIII, No. 3, November, 1959, p. 48.*

CHANGING THE FACE OF NORTH AMERICA: THE CHALLENGE OF THE ST. LAWRENCE SEAWAY   (1959)

In *Changing the Face of North America,* Patricia Lauber deftly weaves the history of the St. Lawrence-Great Lakes area into the story of the waterway's construction. Clearly and concisely she spells out the economic factors that impelled the United States and Canada to combine in the undertaking. In brisk, journalistic style, she highlights the construction program of recent years, and perceptively evaluates the meaning of the Seaway for the future of North America.

> *Howard Boston, "New Big Ditch," in* The New York Times Book Review, *April 26, 1959, p. 38.*

This book on the St. Lawrence Seaway treats some of the same aspects covered in the more detailed [*St. Lawrence Seaway* by

Clara Ingram Judson]; by comparison it is a bareboned but equally valuable account written with great clarity.

> *A review of "Changing the Face of North America: The Challenge of the St. Lawrence Seaway," in* The Booklist and Subscription Books Bulletin, *Vol. 55, No. 18, May 15, 1959, p. 514.*

THE QUEST OF GALILEO   (1959)

The refusal of Galileo to accept on faith the authority of Aristotle and other classical scholars created severe problems for him. For the modern world, it provided new avenues along which science could pass. This text . . . charts the contributions of Galileo—his experiments with motion, gravity, and astronomy. The text further traces his influence on succeeding scientists, showing the far reaching effect his investigation of the heavens with a spy glass has had in the field of science and the exploration of space. A compact and informative book . . . A convenient supplement to elementary and junior highschool science courses.

> *A review of "The Quest of Galileo," in* Virginia Kirkus' Service, *Vol. XXVII, No. 12, June 15, 1959, p. 403.*

The story of the man who destroyed the Aristotelian view of the universe is told clearly and forthrightly in this large and attractive book.... Extraordinarily good is the description of the experiments Galileo conducted and the conclusions he drew therefrom. There is a coolness about Miss Lauber's style (which might so easily have become florid) that makes her refreshing to read. I am particularly glad that she gave adequate mention . . . to Galileo's discovery of numerous stars too feeble to be seen without a telescope. His starry discoveries have usually been obscured by his planetary findings, particularly by the four moons of Jupiter. My only regret is that the author did not tell the story of Galileo and the Inquisition in greater detail. In these days of threats to intellectual freedom, his story is particularly timely.

> *Isaac Asimov, in a review of "The Quest of Galileo," in* The Horn Book Magazine, *Vol. XXXV, No. 5, October, 1959, p. 396.*

ADVENTURE AT BLACK ROCK CAVE   (1959)

Many longer and more pretentious mystery stories pale beside this short story by Patricia Lauber.... Chris takes his landlubber friend Addie out to Black Rock Island in his precious but leaky old rowboat, the Doughnut, the very first day of her visit. He has noticed a mysterious light there at night and suspects someone is searching for buried treasure. They find a strange cave and two uncouth men who chase them off the island with threats. Reporting this at home they are warned to keep away but luck is against them. Partly due to Addie's way of following directions to the letter, like throwing out an anchor, for instance, and partly due to a bad storm, they find themselves again on Black Rock. This time it is more terrifying, but the mystery is solved with some of the credit going to Addie for doing the right thing even if for the wrong reason. Funny as well as exciting, and quick reading for the over nines.

> *A review of "Adventure at Black Rock Cave," in* New York Herald Tribune Book Review, *November 1, 1959, p. 8.*

A pleasant "easy-to-read" book, not unusual in plot or characterization; the plot is credible, however, and the characters are believable, albeit just slightly burlesqued. Addie, for example, is a bit too naive; the villains are just a bit too crusty.

A review of "Adventure at Black Rock Cave," in Bulletin of the Center for Children's Books, Vol. XIII, No. 5, January, 1960, p. 84.

THE STORY OF NUMBERS (1961)

The author attempts to trace the various methods of counting, from antiquity to our present system. The contributions of the ancient civilizations are briefly sketched. Approach is superficial and offers little stimulation to the intelligent child. Less story and more concrete examples would make book more valuable. Slow 3rd-graders, if interested, will find Waller's *Numbers* more appropriate and astute 3rd-graders will prefer Bendick's *Take a Number* or Adler's *Numbers Old and New*. Science has been sacrificed for readability.

Thomas Goonan, in a review of "The Story of Numbers," in School Library Journal, an appendix to Library Journal, Vol. 8, No. 2, October 15, 1961, p. 164.

The Story of Numbers offers an excellent opportunity for third, fourth, and fifth graders to enrich their understanding. It not only presents authentic factual material, but also gives odd and exotic information especially fascinating to the young. Thus they can learn that a tribe of South American Indians who counted on figures and toes expressed twenty as "the fingers of both hands and both feet" (which came out *lanàmriheyem cat yracherhaka anamichirihegem* in their language) and that some English shepherds had numbers that followed a rhyming scheme. The author also includes a table of numbers from million to vigintillion that should settle that eternal question once and for all.

Fritz Kain, "Math Trio," in The New York Times Book Review, November 5, 1961, p. 50.

YOUR BODY AND HOW IT WORKS (1962)

An excellent book on human physiology and morphology for the middle-grades reader. The explanations are lucid, accurate, and simply stated. . . . The writing is straightforward, but rather informal, and the author gives each topic enough coverage without being technical or fulsome. An index is appended.

Zena Sutherland, in a review of "Your Body and How It Works," in Bulletin of the Center for Children's Books, Vol. XVI, No. 2, October, 1962, p. 30.

BIG DREAMS AND SMALL ROCKETS: A SHORT HISTORY OF SPACE TRAVEL (1965)

Sometimes when a title seems chosen primarily to pique curiosity and inspire interest, there is the danger that the casual browser may not realize the actual nature of the book's contents. In that case, noting the subtitle is necessary. For instance, the dramatically titled **Big Dreams and Small Rockets** . . . has the prosaic subtitle **"A Short History of Space Travel."** The history of rocketry and space exploration has, of course, been told a number of times in recent years; but Miss Lauber brings

a charming style to the task, and aims it well at the upper elementary-school children. (p. 414)

Isaac Asimov, "Views on Science Books," in The Horn Book Magazine, Vol. XLI, No. 4, August, 1965, pp. 413-14.

A concise, well-written history of rockets beginning with the ancient Chinese war rockets and ending with the V2, the first practical large-scale space rocket. . . . Materials are well chosen and the author has been fair in evaluating the contributions of her subjects.

Ovide V. Fortier, in a review of "Big Dreams and Small Rockets: A Short History of Space Travel," in School Library Journal, an appendix to Library Journal, Vol. 12, No. 1, September, 1965, p. 2886.

THE STORY OF DOGS (1966)

I think that this whole story is very nice indeed. It is truly scientific and yet told in a way that should awaken the interest of all intelligent young readers. I like particularly the legend at the beginning. I always used to say that the division of humans on one side and animals on the other was wrong, and that there really were three categories: humans, dogs, and animals. I also think that the short presentation of the social behavior of wolves gives an understanding of how these animals have fitted so well into human society. This is an excellent book. (p. iii)

Konrad Lorenz, in a foreword to The Story of Dogs, by Patricia Lauber, Random House, 1966, p. iii.

Here is an excellent and concise history of the probable evolution of the domestic dog written for younger children. The overall perspective is good and the relationship to man and domestication of the early "dogs" lucid. The physiological and environmental conditions resulting in and making possible this domestication are intelligently explained. The illustrations and archaeological documentation further broaden the scope of this book.

Fred Geis, in a review of "The Story of Dogs," in Appraisal: Children's Science Books," Vol. 1, No. 1, Winter, 1967, p. 9.

"This is an excellent book," Konrad Lorenz wrote in a short foreword [see excerpt above]. "It is truly scientific and yet told in a way that should awaken the interest of all intelligent young readers." He is correct. It tells a clear and simple story of the dog's evolution and domestication, carefully but unobtrusively, noting where scientific speculation fills gaps in knowledge. There is also a full measure of the warmth in man/dog relations. A minor flaw is that the author says too little about what a dog-owner must do to make the relationship flourish: choose a sound puppy and invest patience and skill in its training.

A review of "The Story of Dogs," in Science Books: A Quarterly Review, Vol. 2, No. 4, March, 1967, p. 312.

THE LOOK-IT-UP BOOK OF MAMMALS (1967)

An alphabetical handbook of mammals, elsewhere designated an encyclopedia. In sentences of few words, in words of few syllables, is fundamental information—location, habitat, physical characteristics, breeding and feeding habits—for more than a hundred variously related animals, domestic and wild. A brief introduction characterizes mammals generally, a brief conclusion classifies them, but this is less science than respectable supermarket reference, the kind of thing you get when you break up a pictorial encyclopedia into its component subjects for secondary sales. Because text and [Guy Coheleach's] color illustrations are accurate as far as they go and style is simpler than content, this might come in handy for retarded readers; for others, there's . . . a host of better books.

> *A review of "The Look-It-Up Book of Mammals,"* in Kirkus Service, *Vol. XXXV, No. 17, September 1, 1967, p. 1051.*

What begins with aardvark and ends with zebra and in between has a picture and description of almost every mammal one can think of? It's *The Look-It-Up-Book of Mammals,* by Patricia Lauber. It is concise and attractive, full of pertinent information easy to find and understand. School libraries should find it useful as well as any individual child with a special interest in animals.

> *Marian Sorenson, "Name an Animal, We'll Name a Book,"* in The Christian Science Monitor, *November 2, 1967, p. B11.*

The format of, and idea behind, this book are to be commended. It presents brief descriptions and illustrations of most mammals, in alphabetical order, with some cross referencing by different names. The descriptions, however, combine fact with childish commentary which might be appropriate for very young children, but not for those in the age bracket for which this book is intended. One does not need to describe chipmunks as ". . . a bright-eyed little animal that scurries about . . ." to be interesting or readable. Nonetheless, the obvious advantages of the format make it a useful book. . . .

> *Fred Geis, Jr., in a review of "The Look-It-Up Book of Mammals,"* in Appraisal: Children's Science Books," *Vol. 1, No. 3, Fall, 1968, p. 17.*

THE LOOK-IT-UP BOOK OF STARS AND PLANETS   (1967)

Simply and honestly written, here are a hundred pages of alphabetized entries, *asteroids* and *atoms* to *Venus* and *zodiac,* that a child can understand and enjoy. The brief text displays unfailing good taste about where to start and how far to go.

> *Philip Morrison and Phylis Morrison, in a review of "The Look-It-Up Book of Stars and Planets,"* in Scientific American, *Vol. 217, No. 6, December, 1967, p. 140.*

A reference book in dictionary form covering astronomy, astrophysics and space travel, which is remarkably thorough considering its length. It is very good and clear on such obscure points as the difference between mass and weight. One naturally wishes that more had been included, but for the most part the author made a wise selection. I could wish that a pronunciation guide had been included with the Greek alphabet given on page 12. The one point on which I caught the book as out-of-date was the appearance of the other side of the moon. As a result of low resolution Russian pictures, it did seem smoother than the front side, but subsequent Lunar Orbiter high resolution photographs have shown the reverse to be true: the back side is rougher than the front side, and contains virtually no seas or level areas. This is probably more in the librarian's

domain when judging the book as suitable for children of given ages: I found the very short sentences jarring and rough reading; the sentence length seems to indicate a lower intended reader age than the content does.

> *Edmund R. Muskys, in a review of "The Look-It-Up Book of Stars and Planets,"* in Appraisal: Children's Science Books, *Vol. 2, No. 1, Winter, 1969, p. 17.*

BATS: WINGS IN THE NIGHT   (1968)

Bats enough to drive you . . . in a book that packs a lot of information into a brief, simple text that describes anatomy and habits (especially echolation) but features the varieties of bats around the world (between 800 and 900 kinds, and everywhere but Antarctica). From the flying fox of the Old World (also various) to the vampires of Central and South America to the cannibals of Asia and Australia, they are slowly being understood, and even now much remains in question—which is one of the attractions of this treatment, that it explains (and sometimes illustrates) who has found out what and how. Another is the photographs showing every kind close up and/or in action. Much better than Kohn (*The Bat Book*) in this respect, more extensive than Ripper, it complements Brauner's involving *Silent Visitor,* and, on its own, both piques and satisfies curiosity.

> *A review of "Bats: Wings in the Night,"* in Kirkus Service, *Vol. XXXVI, No. 19, October 1, 1968, p. 1119.*

A well-organized and carefully researched study, much superior to *The Bat Book* by Bernice Kohn. Inaccuracies of generalization, which marred the latter book, have been avoided here by scrupulous adherence to sources and by special chapters on such sub-topics as flying foxes, vampire bats, and cannibal bats. Credits are provided for the many excellent black-and-white photographs and for the findings of scientists reported in the text. (From the viewpoint of the specialist, it would appear that better balance might have been achieved in acknowledging contributions of individuals to bat research; Bloedel is recognized for one experiment on fishing bats, for example, while no mention is made of Greenhall's ten years of work on vampires.) However, the presentation of the material itself is sound, clear and eminently readable, serving as an excellent example of good scientific writing for children. (pp. 87-8)

> *Della Thomas, in a review of "Bats: Wings in the Night,"* in School Library Journal, *an appendix to* Library Journal, *Vol. 15, No. 3, November, 1968, p. 87-8.*

WHO DISCOVERED AMERICA? SETTLERS AND EXPLORERS OF THE NEW WORLD BEFORE THE TIME OF COLUMBUS (1970)

The title's a challenge, the book a search—as conducted by archaeologists, ethnologists, plant geographers, philologists, art historians—for the Siberians who crossed the ice-free land bridge to Alaska and spread through the interior; for their descendants the Paleo-Indians—Sandia man, Clovis man and Folsom man (found in reverse order, finds detailed), their shelters and their (surprisingly few) bones; for the Archaic people, bereft of big game and forced to settle down, who developed distinct cultures based on agriculture (in the Middle West, the

Mound Builders, in the Southwest, Pueblo Bonito, further south the Mayas, Aztecs, Incas). Whereupon the question arises—were these wholly indigenous or were there "Visitors from Distant Lands?" What of the stone with a Phoenician inscription found at Parahyba in Brazil? What of less tangible, more plausible traces of cultural transference like pottery from Ecuador akin to contemporary work in Japan, the complex Ecuadorian raft with an Asiatic counterpart, the common Hindu-Buddhist and Mayan art motifs? What of the game of parcheesi? One of several maps that (literally) show the world from a new angle supports the thesis that Asian ships sailing *straight* along the coastline could have reached the New World repeatedly. Harder to account for are the Indian legends and myths of bearded, fair-skinned gods (and the singular appearance of the Inca ruling family). Which brings us to "Vinland the Good," the two sagas that tell differently of its discovery and attempted settlement, and the problem of determining where it was—partly solved by the recent find at L'Anse au Meadow in Newfoundland. But the Norsemen probably penetrated further, into New England, and some disappeared, as had Irish monks earlier; were these the fabled white gods? The stage is set—by miscalculation—for Columbus' illusory 'discovery' and the misconceptions of his contemporaries until, lost knowledge reacquired, the existence of the New World was firmly established. This is the first such synthesis for children, intrinsically enlightening and excellently accomplished.

> *A review of "Who Discovered America? Settlers and Explorers of the New World Before the Time of Columbus," in* Kirkus Reviews, *Vol. XXXVIII, No. 10, May 15, 1970, p. 566.*

Who *did* discover America? Almost everyone might have, according to this convincing author, who assumes that human beings did not spring indigenously from the soil of these Western continents, but came from somewhere else. (p. 28)

In **Who Discovered America?** the reader is the discoverer, following a concise account of the known and speculative evidence in the New World's beginnings and re-beginnings, discoveries and rediscoveries.... A long-view examination of human and animal migrations and development during and after the Ice Age flows easily into a discussion of pre-Columbian outside influences and their possible origins. In all, Patricia Lauber's presentation is up-to-date and her writing dust-free.... The bibliography looks as if it would be most helpful in further clearing the mists from earliest America. (pp. 28, 30)

> *Robert J. Anthony, in a review of "Who Discovered America?" in* The New York Times Book Review, *May 24, 1970, pp. 28, 30.*

After reading this book, it is impossible to say definitively who discovered America—a circumstance testifying to the careful and extensive research that went into this thoroughly interesting and absorbing book. Patricia Lauber destroys the myth of Columbus discovering America in 1492 by describing the ancient travellers—Indian, Oriental, and Nordic—who explored and settled on our continent. She documents her facts with archeological investigations and cultural comparisons; the many graphic reproductions, photographs and maps are extremely informative visual supports. Discussing the work of archeologists, sociologists, and linguists, as well as exploration, this unique title is a worthwhile addition to any children's collection.

> *Nancy Barnwell, in a review of "Who Discovered America?" in* School Library Journal, *an appendix to* Library Journal, *Vol. 17, No. 1, September, 1970, p. 162.*

THIS RESTLESS EARTH (1970)

A lucid introductory examination of earth dynamics which covers earthquakes, volcanoes, mountain building, and includes a well-developed section on continental drift. The author's thoughtful development of the subject and choice of vocabulary make this book well-suited to junior libraries, while the completeness and timeliness of the coverage also make it appropriate for senior high school earth science students. Because of the focus on continental drift and the formation of the solar system, this book is an excellent introduction to Bullard's adult book, *Volcanoes: in History, in Theory, and in Eruption.* The illustrations and black-and-white photographs are adequate; the index is useful. Unfortunately, there is neither a bibliography nor a glossary.

> *Richard H. Maki, in a review of "This Restless Earth," in* School Library Journal, *an appendix to* Library Journal, *Vol. 17, No. 3, November 15, 1970, p. 120.*

The text provides unusually lucid and readable explanations of some rather sophisticated concepts. It is, perhaps, especially noteworthy for its correlation of observations and interpretations that are all too often presented in a disconnected and unrelated fashion.

> *Ronald J. Kley, in a review of "The Restless Earth," in* Appraisal: Children's Science Books, *Vol. 4, No. 1, Winter, 1971, p. 19.*

OF MAN AND MOUSE: HOW HOUSE MICE BECAME LABORATORY MICE (1971)

This is a comprehensive, well-researched account of the *mus musculus* or house mouse as a laboratory animal. After an informative account of the position of mice in history (e.g., worshipped by the Greeks, cursed by Bishop Hildebert, etc.), Lauber gives a rundown of the genealogy of the laboratory mouse. Reasons for selection of mice as laboratory animals for research in areas as diverse as cosmetology and muscular dystrophy are clearly stated. Of particular interest is the explanation of genetics from the work of Mendel to present research in the field and the discussion of mutant strains.... [There] is a detailed index; and, a selective bibliography is included in which works appropriate for young readers are indicated with an asterisk. Unique in its coverage for the age group, this is a must where more material on laboratory animals is needed.

> *Everett C. Sanborn, in a review of "Of Man and Mouse: How Mouse Mice Became Laboratory Mice," in* School Library Journal, *an appendix to* Library Journal, *Vol. 18, No. 7, March, 1972, p. 1179.*

Three topics are discussed in **Of Man and Mouse.** These are mice, genetics, and the research conducted by the Jackson Laboratory of Bar Harbor, Maine. Although it is written simply, there are so few books written about mice and the research at Jackson Laboratory that it may have some value even for adults.... The current research at Jackson is well-covered. Unfortunately, the romance is left out.

A review of "Of Man and Mouse: How House Mice Became Laboratory Mice," in Science Books: A Quarterly Review, *Vol. 8, No. 1, May, 1972, p. 62.*

EARTHQUAKES: NEW SCIENTIFIC IDEAS ABOUT HOW AND WHY THE EARTH SHAKES (1972)

With the dramatic but not unduly dramatized opening example of the 1964 disaster in Alaska, Lauber sets the stage for a brisk, uncomplicated discussion of earthquakes and tsu-nami, (commonly, tidal waves). A 1923 quake in Tokyo Bay introduces the Pacific "Ring of Fire," a mystery whose gradual solution readers will follow with unwavering interest; and specific California quakes, especially the famous one in San Francisco in 1906, are worked into an uncommonly clarifying explanation of what's going on along the San Andreas fault. New findings from the developing field of plate tectonics are utilized throughout, and the author's consistently felicitous analogies make it all strikingly clear to even the least science-minded of intermediate grade students.

A review of "Earthquakes: New Scientific Ideas About How and Why the Earth Shakes," in Kirkus Reviews, *Vol. XL, No. 19, October 1, 1972, p. 1148.*

Earthquakes: New Scientific Ideas about How and Why the Earth Shakes provides remarkably current coverage of recent developments in one of the fastest moving fields of the earth sciences. Errors are few and insignificant; the arrangement and balance of the presentation is commendable. Moreover, the nine interesting chapters are written with the needs of young people in mind. Young people (and their inquiring elders) who want to know what new earth science terms like "continental drift" and "plate tectonics" are all about, will come away from this . . . easily read volume with a much improved appreciation of this ever-changing planet and an understanding of why these earthquake-caused changes will always be with us. Indeed, as the author points out, without these earthquake-caused changes we would have no dry land to live on.

A review of "Earthquakes: New Scientific Ideas About How and Why the Earth Shakes," in Science Books: A Quarterly Review, *Vol. 8, No. 4, March, 1973, p. 322.*

EVERGLADES COUNTRY: A QUESTION OF LIFE OR DEATH (1973)

A carefully researched, well organized, readable account of the Everglades. The interdependence of life in this area is clearly drawn and will be understood by most young students of ecology. There is an especially informative chapter about man's manipulation of the water supply to the Everglades National Park. Good black-and-white photographs [by Patricia Canfield], maps, a selected bibliography, and an index augment this up-to-date presentation, which is much better than the Grahams' *The Mystery of the Everglades* and more current than Floethe's *Sea of Grass* and Helm's *Everglades: Florida Wonderland*.

Linda Lawson Clark, in a review of "Everglades Country: A Question of Life or Death," in School Library Journal, *an appendix to* Library Journal, *Vol. 20, No. 1, September, 1973, p. 146.*

In 1968, bulldozers began carving up Florida's Big Cypress Swamp for a proposed jetport. In 1970, environmentalist pres-

sure brought the project to a halt and preserved for a time the Everglades of southern Florida. At this point, Patricia Lauber begins her detailed and carefully researched study of this precariously balanced ecosystem. . . . In chapter increments she develops the concept of this balance. . . . The flora's role in the development and maintenance of the ecosystem is examined, first separately and then as part of the complex food chains which bind the Everglades into a tight web of interdependence. Ms. Lauber lays her groundwork so carefully that the final chapters on the threats to this web's deterioration seem almost unnecessary, but do serve to underscore the tenuous relationship between man and his environment. The section on food chains could stand alone for its clarity. The single difficulty arises in finding an audience for the book, a task hampered by the specificity of the title and some of the subject matter. Aided by a fine index, maps and bibliography, and beautifully illustrated with Patricia Caulfield's photographs, nature lovers and ecology students will find this book a rewarding one. (pp. 23-4)

Judith Botsford, in a review of "Everglades Country: A Question of Life or Death," in Appraisal: Children's Science Books, *Vol. 7, No. 1, Winter, 1974, pp. 23-4.*

COWBOYS AND CATTLE RANCHING: YESTERDAY AND TODAY (1973)

After Glen Rounds' garrulous reminiscences of *The Cowboy Trade* and any number of literary field trips to ranches past and present, the need for another cowboy book is doubtful. But Patricia Lauber has assimiliated the lore and science of cattle ranching with her usual facility—interweaving details on the organization of 19th century cattle drives, modern breeding and roundup procedures, and the businesslike orgainzation of today's large ranching operations with a careful historical rundown and visits to the typical Flying V and Big Cypress spreads. Despite their overall poor quality, the 124 photographs include a large sampling from 19th century archives which convey the authentic look of the old west; these, combined with the emphasis on the practical, unromantic side of the cowboy's job, will add to this documentary's appeal for the more mature western fan. (pp. 975-76)

A review of "Cowboys and Cattle Ranching: Yesterday and Today," in Kirkus Reviews, *Vol. XLI, No. 17, September 1, 1973, pp. 975-76.*

The historical portion of Lauber's survey predictably lacks the depth and analytics of Seidman's *Once in the saddle*, but her description of modern-day cattle ranching is more specific. . . . With its plentiful photographs and journalistic text this comprises a useful introduction to today's cattle business. (pp. 340-41)

A review of "Cowboys and Cattle Ranching: Yesterday and Today," in The Booklist, *Vol. 70, No. 6, November 15, 1973, pp. 340-41.*

A generally good historical treatment of cowboying and cattle ranching. The history of cattle and the cowboy in America, from 1493 to the end of long cattle drives and introduction of barbed wire, is excellent. However, the cowboy's changed life since then is scantily treated in two biographic sketches of cattle ranchers—one in Florida, the other in Wyoming. There is much detail about care, keeping, and breeding of modern cattle, some of which may not be understandable to city-born children. The text is copiously illustrated with photographs and prints (most of which are labeled), but the brand marks flanking chapter headings are not explained. Lauber's coverage is fuller than that of Glen Round's *The Cowboy Trade* but it is not as readable nor humane.

> George Gleason, in a review of "Cowboys and Cattle Ranching: Yesterday and Today," in School Library Journal, an appendix to Library Journal, Vol. 20, No. 3, November, 1973, p. 65.

TOO MUCH GARBAGE (1974)

A plea for reduction in the amount of garbage and suggestions for disposing and recycling what is produced are presented in simple terms. The opening chapter, which introduces this subject via a "typical" family in "Fairtown," uses dated-looking drawings, but black-and-white and full-color photographs illustrate the remainder of the text. This covers basically the same information as Hahn's *Recycling: Re-Using Our World's Solid Wastes* but is for slightly younger readers.

> Carole Ridolfino, in a review of "Too Much Garbage," in School Library Journal, Vol. 21, No. 7, March, 1975, p. 88.

More than a ton of garbage a year for each person in the United States! Where does it come from? What is in it? Where does it go? How might it be a valuable resource? By showing the problems from the viewpoints of members of a typical family in what might be a neighboring town, the young reader is led to develop a personal concern over many aspects of solid waste disposal. The loss of resources, the waste of energy in collecting and disposing of trash in dumps and landfills, the threats to health and to aesthetics of eye and nose are all vividly discussed in terms easily understood by children. . . . Although written for third grade level, this book should appeal to children from the second to the sixth grade, and it ought to be available to all of them—and to their parents.

> Edmund C. Bray, in a review of "Too Much Garbage," in Science Books & Films, Vol. XI, No. 1, May, 1975, p. 32.

SEA OTTERS AND SEAWEED (1976)

This survey for beginners stresses the sea otter's key role (through its feeding habits) in keeping a balance of life in the kelp beds where it lives. The text clarifies the distinction between northern and southern sea otters and includes information on the animal's mating and parenting behavior. The easiest to read of all the introductions on this endangered species, this also contains some information . . . not found in other titles.

> Juliet Kellogg Markowsky, in a review of "Sea Otters and Seaweed," in School Library Journal, Vol. 23, No. 6, February, 1977, p. 66.

The introduction of biological topics in general and the scientific method on the elementary school level can be extremely tedious, and if an author uses a bland, dry, antiseptic approach, he or she runs the risk of turning off a future biologist to scientific study. To avoid this, one must choose a fascinating topic and present it as interestingly as possible. Lauber has chosen wisely with sea otters—utterly charming creatures with irresistable appeal to youngsters. Keeping technical terms to a minimum, Lauber deals with many different facets of biology; animal behavior, mammalian physiology, marine biology,

ecology and even botany on the most elementary levels. The aspects of ecology—the otter's need for protection, threats of extinction and the relationship of all living things in the webs of life—are well presented. . . . Particularly pleasing is the introduction of scientific method through scientist Jud Vandevere, whose observations on field study show youngsters how very exciting and fascinating a career in biology can be. I highly recommend this book as an introduction to the life of sea otters.

> Robert R. J. Grispino, in a review of "Sea Otters and Seaweed," in Science Books & Films, Vol. XIII, No. 1, May, 1977, p. 43.

MYSTERY MONSTERS OF LOCH NESS (1978)

An apparently well-researched essay dealing with the perennial question of the existence and nature of the Loch Ness monster. After a brief historical rundown of citings, complete with captioned photographs and two-color illustrations, the author settles into a detailed discussion of the possible biological origins of the creature. In this context Lauber analyzes each possibility from the standpoint of environment, anatomical structure, and other scientific points, leaving readers with the question to puzzle out for themselves. This will make interesting, unsensationalized reading and spur children on to discussion.

> Judith Goldberger, in a review of "Mystery Monsters of Loch Ness," in Booklist, Vol. 74, No. 20, June 15, 1978, p. 1621.

Under the guise of answering the catchy rhetorical question "What might the Loch Ness monster be?" Patricia Lauber discusses the salient characteristics of mammals, amphibians, reptiles, fish, and mollusks, providing a thorough foundation for later acquaintance with biology. This book is easily accessible to bright six or seven year olds and holds material of interest right through the sixth grade.

> Sue Bottigheimer, in a review of "Mystery Monsters of Loch Ness," in School Library Journal, Vol. 25, No. 3, November, 1978, p. 47.

In the light of the ambiguous nature of the evidence, a question mark would seem to be appropriate at the end of the title. In the absence of hard evidence, the author nevertheless assumes the presence of one or more monsters. Even worse, the author devotes two-thirds of the book to the origin, the nature of the home, and the possible categories of animals that may satisfy the skimpy, illusive evidence. Nor does it satisfy reasonable standards of evidence to write: "Pictures and sonar findings have caused some scientists to take a fresh look at Loch Ness. They now think that the monster is not a joke after all." Who are these scientists? And who are the people who think it may be a joke? What is the nature of the reasoning that each group marshalls in support of its point of view? What induces some people to see an animal and others to see only bubbles when looking at the same photograph? If sonar can locate and identify submarines, why can't it do the same for a monster? When scientific evidence has been clearly established, there is usually widespread agreement in the scientific community. Is there such agreement about a Loch Ness monster? If not, why not? It is disingenuous to devote half of the book to speculating about which animals are likely candidates for monster status in the absence of evidence about the presence of any monster at all. It appears suspiciously like fill to round out a book that lacks sufficient substance to stand on its own. (p. 24)

Lazar Goldberg, in a review of "Mystery Monsters of Loch Ness," in Appraisal: Children's Science Books, *Vol. 12, No. 2, Spring, 1979, pp. 23-4.*

TAPPING EARTH'S HEAT   (1978)

This small volume introduces younger students to geothermal energy and its uses. Beginning with an intriguing description of the formation of a volcanic island, the author carefully explains the structure of the earth's interior—the source of geothermal energy. She illustrates various earth science concepts with simple experiments that younger children can do on their own at home or in school. Thus, children on a concrete operational level can actually see how a geyser erupts, how water pressure in the earth increases with depth, and how water makes a turbine in an electric generator spin. The author relates each new concept to something in the child's experience. For example, in explaining how water flashes into steam in a fumarole, she writes:

> How do you test a pan to see if it is hot enough for pancakes? You don't touch it. You let a few drops of water fall on it. Remember what happens? . . .
> The same thing happens underground.

This quote also illustrates her use of questions to get the young reader to do some inferring and predicting on her own. In its simplicity the text does not lose scientific accuracy. The author even lists some of the problems involved in harnessing geothermal energy. However, a larger number of examples of present and future uses for geothermal energy would be desirable. In general, the text is an adequate and well-organized introduction for upper elementary students. (pp. 34-5)

Martha T. Kane, in a review of "Tapping Earth's Heat," in Appraisal: Children's Science Books, *Vol. 12, No. 2, Spring, 1979, pp. 34-5.*

This little book on geothermal energy will capture the interest and imagination of many young minds. Well illustrated [by Edward Malsberg], and with many topical experiments, it remains lively from the attractive cover through its discussions on geology, atomic energy, and ecology—all simply explained and all relative to the main theme. In this age of alternate energies, a children's book on geothermal energy is very appropriate, for it makes young people aware of energy problems they will soon face.

Kent C. Freeland, in a review of "Tapping Earth's Heat," in Science Books & Films, *Vol. XV, No. 2, September, 1979, p. 101.*

WHAT'S HATCHING OUT OF THAT EGG?   (1979)

What's Hatching Out of That Egg? is a simple and captivating book. It opens with the photograph of an egg in its natural setting, and the reader is invited to guess its identity. Sequential pictures show the hatchlings and the animals at progressively older stages until the adult appears. Meanwhile the text offers clues: It describes the egg or nest, then gives several general facts which help substantiate an early hunch, and by the time most readers have guessed, they see the answer. The process is repeated for ten more animals—including an ostrich, an alligator, a frog, a snake, and a platypus. I suspect that a child could learn more from this guessing game than from a straight narrative. In any case the book is fun; it has excellent photographs drawn from a variety of sources and builds up to a well-

made point at the end—that eggs are formed when sperm cells join egg cells and that the new animal in an egg is like its parents. With an index. (p. 555)

Sarah Gagné, in a review of "What's Hatching Out of That Egg?" in The Horn Book Magazine, *Vol. LV, No. 5, October, 1979, p. 555.*

Lauber's introduction to the basic concepts of embryology is both clever and confusing. A guessing game featuring species of birds, reptiles, mammals, insects, and spiders is set into a glossy photo format. In several instances the text or pictures reveal too much, spoiling the suspense necessary to keep up the game. The textual transition from one animal to the next is not always clear—sections flow together in spite of a thin black line framing the first page for each animal. The photographs are generally well chosen, but a few are repetitive or poorly composed or reproduced. . . . A final section gives very short shrift to the chicken and attempts to compare and contrast the development of egg into fetus in mammals with the process of egg laying by other species. The information on how sperm joins egg is vague and unclear. Ernest Prescott's *What Comes Out of an Egg?* is at least as informative, but since the subject is very popular for curriculum use, this will also be wanted in many libraries. (pp. 75-6)

Margaret Bush, in a review of "What's Hatching Out of That Egg?" in School Library Journal, *Vol. 26, No. 4, December, 1979, pp. 75-6.*

HOME AT LAST! A YOUNG CAT'S TALE   (1980)

Small, the narrator, lives with his brother Biggers in the library, which, with its two attentive librarians, is fine with both of them. Biggers reads a lot of stories, however, and insists they must go out in the world, face hardship, climb the ladder of success, and find a real home. All this the two kittens do, but their youthful innocence creates obstacles and confusions: they are hired by two dogs to "take care of mice," for instance, but decide this means baby-sitting. While a passing tomcat does the real job, the two cats hightail it for their true home—the library—which may not have beds and an icebox but certainly has love and a place for them. A homey story, just right for older primary-graders and free of unnecessary overlays of sophistication.

Judith Goldberger, in a review of "Home at Last: A Young Cat's Tale," in Booklist, *Vol. 77, No. 5, November 1, 1980, p. 406.*

A petite (6¼ x 7¼), dainty volume with a simple situation and an overcomplicated plot—that doesn't, finally, get anywhere. . . . The book has its incidental charms (the cats' names, for one) but it's not only intricately structured, some of its assumptions are plain dumb and its ending is soppy. The content, the form, and the format never quite get together—for any age level.

A review of "Home at Last: A Young Cat's Tale," in Kirkus Reviews, *Vol. XLIX, No. 1, January 1, 1981, p. 7.*

SEEDS: POP, STICK, GLIDE   (1981)

The years have seen many books published for children about seeds, their varying methods of dissemination and their basic diversity. In this [, Lauber's collaboration with photographer

Jerome Wexler], we have the Mercedes of the introductory seed books. The information is organized by means of dispersal; thus the travelers are grouped by how they move (by water, by animals and people, by wind and by their own means). The text is vivid and assumes very little on the part of readers except a willingness to perceive the natural world. . . . This book, in its enthusiasm for the plant kingdom, is an irresistable beacon for young explorers to make their own discoveries. *Seeds* not only informs, it fosters an appreciation of the plant world and makes wondrous what is too often seen as commonplace. This is more striking and less demanding than Winifred Hammond's *The Riddle of Seeds*.

> *Steve Matthews, in a review of "Seeds: Pop, Stick, Glide," in* School Library Journal, *Vol. 27, No. 8, April, 1981, p. 114.*

The subject of seeds reminds me of a kindergarten classroom with a jar of disintegrating plant stalks in it or of an outline for biology giving four methods of seed dispersal. But Lauber's book brings to life the subject of adaptations for seed dispersal with fresh and fascinating examples in [Wexler's] magnificent black-and-white photographs. . . . The text deals with plants as novel as witch hazel and as common as maple and sticktights. Not once does Lauber use the word *adaptation* in her text, and I am glad. It lets the novelty of nature's inventions speak for itself. Index.

> *Sarah Gagné, "Views on Science Books: Plants," in* The Horn Book Magazine, *Vol. LVII, No. 3, June, 1981, p. 331.*

This is a super book. (p. 24)

The text is remarkable. It manages to go into sufficient depth to surprise and fascinate an adult reader, yet uses sentence structure and vocabulary that will allow comfortable reading by intermediate readers. The only technical word in the entire book is clearly defined, illustrated, and reused several times in context.

There are no separate captions for the pictures. The text is usually so closely related to the photographs and the photographs at different magnifications so obviously related to one another that only twice in 119 illustrations might there be a question as to what the reader is seeing. In the text itself, I was aware of only one ambiguous sentence and one editorial slip that produced an apparent internal inconsistency. This is a high quality book in every respect. (pp. 24-5)

> *Marion P. Harris, in a review of "Seeds: Pop, Stick, Glide," in* Appraisal: Children's Science Books, *Vol. 14, No. 3, Fall, 1981, pp. 24-5.*

JOURNEY TO THE PLANETS (1982)

A far more imaginative and exciting presentation than Seymour Simon's shorter but similarly structured . . . *Long View Into Space*. At the start of Lauber's journey, and it's a compelling start, beautiful photos of earth as seen from space, then closer and closer details of particular areas, involve readers in a search for signs of intelligent life as it might be conducted by observers from space. This leads to an examination of the conditions for life on earth and then to a basic geological briefing—all accompanied by spectacular photos. . . . Then there's a review of how "astronomers think" the solar system began, which prepares us for a review of its parts. Reading Lauber's description of conditions on the harsh, airless moon, and viewing

the reinforcing photos, you imagine how it feels to be there. She inspires a spirit of inquiry among readers as she reviews different theories of the moon's formation (incorporating how scientists arrived at the conclusions); what Mariner 10 discovered about Mercury; how false assumptions about Venus were cleared up—and how conditions on Venus limit the extent of our probes; etc. Mars is approached in terms of whether there is life there, then examined according to the questions, answers, and speculation resulting from progressive explorations. Jupiter and its moons and rings are vividly described ("Europa looks like a billiard ball with cracks"; "When the first pictures of Io were received, watching scientists were astounded. 'It looks like a pizza!' one of them said"), as is the puzzle of Saturn's rings: "Scientists think that just as sheep dogs keep a flock together, these two moons may keep material within the F ring." And so a sense of discovery accompanies us all the way to Neptune and Pluto (the last of which may not be a planet at all), which were discovered when "astronomers were trying to find out why Uranus sometimes speeded up and sometimes slowed down." A stimulating experience for the eyes, mind, and imagination. (pp. 606-07)

> *A review of "Journey to the Planets," in* Kirkus Reviews, *Vol. L, No. 10, May 15, 1982, pp. 606-07.*

Popular account of the Earth, Moon and planets as seen from space. And popular it will be! Popular with kids because of its handsome collection of black-and-white photos . . . and because of the clearly written text with such apt comparisons as the "surface of Venus is hotter than a self-cleaning oven, which at 800 degrees turns the remains of food to fine dust." Popular with teachers and librarians because Lauber has the rare ability to explain things simply without compromising scientific accuracy. This careful and competent author is among the first to use the full range of photos now available to us; with the space program at its current funding, we'll have to make these photos last a long time.

> *Margaret L. Chatham, in a review of "Journey to the Planets," in* School Library Journal, *Vol. 28, No. 10, August, 1982, p. 118.*

This is an adequate summary of planetary information, about as up-to-date as is practical for a hard-cover book. Ms. Lauber follows the traditional outward-from-the-sun format only after the sensible preliminary of describing the earth, which we know most about, and giving a very terse but, as far as we now can tell, reasonably adequate outline of the formation of the sun and solar system.

There are a few discrepancies which suggest that she may have depended on secondary sources for some of her information. The polar caps of Mars are, according to current belief, mostly carbon dioxide, not mostly or entirely water. The number of active volcanoes seen on Jupiter's satellite Io seems to be varying as more and more books are written. The version I heard at JPL during the Voyager 2 Jupiter flyby was: eight seen by Voyager I; six of these still active and one inactive at the time of the Voyager 2 flyby, though the latter had emitted enough material to change its "Devil's Footprint" appearance considerably before quieting down; and one which simply was not visible from Voyager 2's trajectory, so nothing could be said about it.

This was a verbal report, given at one of the press briefings; I could be wrong, too!

These descrepancies are the sort which good students should spot and cross-check with other publications; they don't bother me much. (pp. 39-40)

> *Harry C. Stubbs, in a review of "Journey to the Planets," in Appraisal: Children's Science Book, Vol. 16, No. 1, Winter, 1983, pp. 39-40.*

[Journey to the Planets *was revised in 1987.*]

The outstanding work of Patricia Lauber includes *Seed: Pop, Stick, Glide; Volcano: The Eruption and Healing of Mount St. Helens* and *Dinosaurs Walked Here.* These and other of her books set a standard of excellence in all aspects of their design and execution. The revised edition of *Journey to the Planets* more than meets this high standard and will be welcomed by readers of age ten and up.

This book introduces readers first to Earth and then to each satellite and planet in our solar system. New information from American and Soviet explorations as well as earthbound instruments and new theories bring this completely up-to-date. Black-and-white photographs and drawings illustrate the detailed, masterfully written text. Both metaphors and concrete examples draw the reader in and make these remote and awesome places real. The importance of understanding our neighboring planets so that we may better understand and cherish our own is emphasized. A first purchase for any library, even those owning the 1982 edition. (pp. 39-40)

> *Diane F. Holzheimer, in a review of "Journey to the Planets," in Appraisal: Children's Science Books, Vol. 21, No. 1, Winter, 1988, pp. 39-40.*

TALES MUMMIES TELL (1985)

Mummies, says Lauber, tell much about the diseases, diets, and life spans of ancient peoples. Before getting down to their messages, however, she looks at the mummies themselves. Taking off from particular mummies, "natural and manmade," that have been found in several parts of the world, she explains how the corpses are preserved (usually by quick drying) and how carbon 14 dating helps determine their age, then describes the different elaborate methods used by the ancient Scythians, the Jivaro head-hunters of South America, and the Egyptian embalmers.

As for scientists' readings of mummies, X-rays reveal that the ancient Egyptians were plagued by parasites from the Nile and sand in their daily bread. Examination of Peru's mummies confirms that Indian diets and general health were far worse after the Spanish came. Finally, there is speculation about the "bog people" of Denmark and why they were all put to death before being deposited in the bogs.

This approach to mummies-as-text gives Lauber's book a distinguishing slant (and a good title), though the cultural and environmental information her readers glean from all these specimens is secondary to the perennial appeal of the mummies themselves. Whatever its target, though, her wide-ranging text informs without sensationalism. . . .

> *A review of "Tales Mummies Tell," in Kirkus Reviews, Juvenile Issue, Vol. LIII, Nos. 5-10, May 15, 1985, p. J39.*

This book is intended to be an informative introduction for young readers, and it will undoubtedly be successful as a first source for them beyond narrower encyclopedia listings. The author presents reasonably detailed descriptions of mummies, mummification processes, and the information to be obtained from the study of these phenomena. The geographic scope of the topic is worldwide, extending well beyond the usual treatment of the more famous Egyptian examples. Both human and animal mummies are treated with a refreshing and innovative approach that emphasizes what scientists can learn about ancient societies and life styles. Well written and profusely illustrated, the book also contains suggestions for current additional readings that will challenge readers who wish to go further. Aside from a few general statements, particularly those that perpetuate the "Black Legend" against the Spanish in Latin America, the numerous facts are pertinent and accurate. A useful addition to elementary and junior-high libraries, this book will certainly provide the impetus for young readers to go beyond an initial fascination with mummies to the tales that mummies tell.

> *William O. Autry, Jr., in a review of "Tales Mummies Tell," in Science Books & Films, Vol. 21, No. 2, November-December, 1985, p. 79.*

When most people hear the word "mummy" they think of Egyptian mummies, but Patricia Lauber's marvelous new book is about all well preserved bodies, animal as well as human, from many corners of the world. Readers will pick up a great deal about the ways scientists, historians and archeologists work from reading this superb account.

I had a difficult time reading this book from start to finish because family members kept appropriating it! Not until I secreted it away beneath tamer titles could I hold on to it long enough to read it through.

This is the sort of book I love. A fine blend of science and history of an exotic topic with plenty of mystery to keep me turning the pages. Some of the mysteries are solved in these pages but others actually open up more provocative questions and leave the reader with much to wonder about. Photographs from museums all over the world add dimension to a well organized text, informed by the author's obvious enthusiasm for her subject.

X-rays of mummies' bones and teeth reveal information about disease, health and diet which give us clues to life in the distant past. The processes by which these relics first came to be preserved, were then later discovered and studied are fascinating in themselves, even before we get to the remarkable "tales mummies tell."

The tales themselves are of short, squalid lives snuffed out early by disease or violence. Many people were mistreated in some horrible way. These facts, along with several eerie photographs, may make this disturbing reading for some children under ten. Regardless of that, this is a distinctive book which supplements other titles on this subject well and as such deserves a place in every library.

> *Diane Holzheimer, in a review of "Tales Mummies Tell," in Appraisal: Children's Science Books, Vol. 19, No. 2, Spring, 1986, p. 33.*

VOLCANO: THE ERUPTION AND HEALING OF MOUNT ST. HELENS (1986)

Mount St. Helens's powerful explosions in 1980 shook the country for hundreds of miles. . . . With Lauber's taut prose and well-edited photographs, the reader relives the eruption and healing. The author begins with scientists' predictions, 123 years before the volcano blew; documents the actual blast; then traces the surviving plant, animal and insect life which continue to develop to this day. Lauber also explains how these survivors created a base on which other life forms could take hold. . . . The book—and Mount St. Helens—stand as testimony to the tenacity of life. This is a magnificent, awe-inspiring work.

A review of "Volcano," in Publishers Weekly, *Vol. 229, No. 26, June 27, 1986, p. 96.*

As dynamic as it is informative, this recounts the sequence of developments in Mount St. Helens' eruption with a smoothly energetic style that makes the facts flow cohesively. Even more important to the intelligent conception of the book is Lauber's devotion of half the space to the ecological recovery of plant and animal life in an area that appeared totally decimated. Color photographs of the highest quality, along with key diagrams and maps, are a major part of the book's impact. The balance of informational details and larger scientific concepts marks this as an exceptional sample of natural history narrative.

Betsy Hearne, in a review of "Volcano: The Eruption and Healing of Mount St. Helens," in Bulletin of the Center for Children's Books, *Vol. 40, No. 1, September, 1986, p. 12.*

The dramatic story of Mount St. Helens is told in a gripping style and with extraordinary color photographs. Evident throughout the book are Patricia Lauber's careful scholarship and talent for distilling material to present it in an extremely smooth narrative. Her choice of photographs—primarily from the United States Forest Service files—is excellent. The sets of before and after photos are especially effective. The second half of the book deals with the volcano's gradual return to life as a mountain with the renewal of animals and plants. The fascinating descriptions and photographs of new greenery growing through cracks in the ash crust and of the emergence of underground survivors, such as ground squirrels, are striking in contrast to the desolate background of charred terrain. The material is well organized and presented in a beautifully designed book. Index.

Elizabeth S. Watson, in a review of "Volcano: The Eruption and Healing of Mount St. Helens," in The Horn Book Magazine, *Vol. LXII, No. 5, September-October, 1986, p. 609.*

It is not clear who said: "A child is not a vase to be filled, but a fire to be lit." The author, unfortunately, has remained elusive. But the statement is nonetheless true and applies to children as they read, especially to children reading nonfiction. You can almost divide the nonfiction they read into two categories: nonfiction that stuffs in facts, as if children were vases to be filled, and nonfiction that ignites the imagination, as if children were indeed fires to be lit. (p. 710)

As we agonize over evaluating nonfiction, we are lucky to have an occasional book that can serve as a stellar example of the genre, such as Patricia Lauber's **Volcano: The Eruption and Healing of Mount St. Helens.** The 1987 Newbery Committee showed great wisdom in choosing this perfect book for a Newbery Honor Book. Patricia Lauber has fulfilled all the demands for strong nonfiction writing. The organization is masterful. She starts with the eruption itself, grabbing the reader on the very first page. She places most of the vital geological information toward the end, never slowing down the action. She

includes simple diagrams that clarify at a glance. She begins on a high note, and she ends on a high note: All plants and animals, she says on the last page, will rejuvenate themselves—just as the mountain itself will be rejuvenated. This idea reaffirms all that has come before. The writing itself generates excitement. Sometimes the details are so vividly described that we can actually feel the heat from the molten lava and see clearly the touches of green appearing through the gray ash. The vocabulary is enriched by strong verbs that move the action forward: "[The mud flow] churned down the river valley, tearing out steel bridges, ripping houses apart, picking up boulders and trucks and carrying them along. Miles away it choked the Cowlitz River and blocked shipping channels in the Columbia River." Sometimes vivid figures of speech make the mountain seem almost human. But never does Patricia Lauber lapse into "isn't-nature-wonderful?" hyperbole. (pp. 712-13)

From Patricia Lauber's masterly book we learn that solid information can be captivating in the hands of a gifted writer. Too many nonfiction authors have produced worthy-but-dull books that will reach only skilled readers, only young people who are already interested in the subject, only the intellectual elite. What about ordinary children, especially those who have yet to discover the pleasure of reading? We should not forget them.

We can—and certainly will—buy solid informational books when we need them. But we should save the stars in reviews for vivid, exciting books—for the kind being written by Patricia Lauber, Rhoda Blumberg, and all the other authors who have a real flair for language. We should save our highest accolades for those rare books we know will "light a fire." (p. 713)

Jo Carr, "Filling Vases, Lighting Fires," in The Horn Book Magazine, *Vol. LXIII, No. 6, November-December, 1987, pp. 710-13.*

FROM FLOWER TO FLOWER: ANIMALS AND POLLINATION (1986)

Although the text mentions other means of pollination (the wind, self-pollination), the focus here is on how animals seeking pollen or nectar effect the fertilizing that insures the reproduction of plants. The excellent photographs [by Jerome Wexler], many magnified, are so carefully integrated with the text that only rarely does the lack of labels seem unfortunate. The text is adequately organized, gives a great deal of information about the process of pollination (including many facts about bees) and is accurate; however, it's a bit heavier in style than most of Lauber's books and is in a dull format. A relative index gives access to the contents of the book.

Zena Sutherland, in a review of "From Flower to Flower: Animals and Pollination," in Bulletin of the Center for Children's Books, *Vol. 40, No. 8, April, 1987, p. 150.*

A first class book which entirely lives up to its name. Text and photographic illustrations work closely together to provide the reader with a technically accurate, and an aesthetically pleasing learning experience. . . .

Children are immediately attracted by the clear, detailed photographs. From there, they move to the text, which is well-written and to the point. The reader is invited to become actively involved by working with a pin and the flower of a butterfly weed. In addition, many young readers are encouraged to take the temperatures of certain plants, after they see it done on page 44. It is an interesting surprise to learn that the skunk cabbage can maintain an internal temperature of 72°F, even when surrounded by freezing air.

Add this to your library if you possibly can.

> *Clarence C. Truesdell, in a review of "From Flower to Flower: Animals and Pollination," in* Appraisal: Children's Science Books, *Vol. 20, No. 4, Fall, 1987, p. 36.*

The process of pollination and adaptation of plants to attract specific pollinators are well described. Scientific concepts are presented clearly and in a logical sequence. . . . My only criticism is that in a few instances, the author refers to the bright colors of the flowers but this cannot be shown through the illustrations as they are all in black-and-white. . . . However, in general, this book is quite good.

> *Leonard H. Friedman, in a review of "From Flower to Flower: Animals and Pollination," in* Science Books & Films, *Vol. 23, No. 3, January-February, 1988, p. 175.*

GET READY FOR ROBOTS! (1987)

Although this is not information-packed, it's "user friendly," with little of the futuristic glamorization that often accompanies books on robots. The text opens with a dream sequence of that common misconception of robots as household companions and then sets out to show their actual current capabilities. There's a bit of background on computer signals, sensors, dependence on robots for dangerous or intricate manufacturing jobs, and of course employment of robots in satellites and space probes. The illustrations [by True Kelly] are not as clear as the text in delineating what robots can or can't do. . . . In spite of these quibbles, the book offers fairly straightforward treatment of a popular topic for a young audience that needs the material.

> *Betsy Hearne, in a review of "Get Ready for Robots!," in* Bulletin of the Center for Children's Books, *Vol. 40, No. 7, March, 1987, p. 129.*

Lauber tells clearly and accurately what robots can and can not do now, and then moves on to what we hope they will be able to do in the future. . . . This should answer many students' questions, and at the same time draw a clear line between what is factually true and what is speculatively possible.

> *Sylvia S. Marantz, in a review of "Get Ready for Robots!," in* School Library Journal, *Vol. 33, No. 10, June-July, 1987, p. 85.*

A light breezy picture book about robots. Not terribly comprehensive or exact, but not intended to be. Illustrations are often more decorative than informative, but the book still offers a wide range of information about robots.

Robot arms are included, and industrial robots are shown working on an assembly line. There is even a device which goes up trees and cuts off limbs with a chain saw. Maybe the concept of robot is stretched a little too far, but this is preferable to restricting the concept to devices which look like humans, as is often done in books for children. (pp. 36-7)

> *Clarence C. Truesdell, in a review of "Get Ready for Robots!," in* Appraisal: Children's Science Books, *Vol. 20, No. 4, Fall, 1987, pp. 36-7.*

DINOSAURS WALKED HERE, AND OTHER STORIES FOSSILS TELL (1987)

Within each fossil lies a story of what that fossil once was, and how that fossil was made. Lauber's book is a key to those stories, explaining in a clear, readable style the processes of fossil information and new scientific theories derived from the fossil record. Like Lauber's **Tales Mummies Tell,** the book focuses on recent discoveries rather than reiterating outdated information. . . . The clarity of Lauber's style is matched by the exquisite color photographs and drawings that illustrate the book. It is aimed at a slightly older audience than Aliki's *Fossils Tell of Long Ago,* but younger children will certainly enjoy listening to the text and looking at the pictures. This stunning book is science at its finest—it is captivating, beautifully designed, and it both answers and evokes questions.

> *Cathryn A. Camper, in a review of "Dinosaurs Walked Here and Other Stories Fossils Tell," in* School Library Journal, *Vol. 34, No. 1, September, 1987, p. 189.*

In a crisp, well-honed text Lauber distills and relates a great deal of information about fossils, making clear their origins and what we can learn from them. The first few sentences set up the book brilliantly:

> Once there were dinosaurs. They roamed the earth for 140 million years but died out long before there were people to see them, tell of them, or draw their pictures. Even so, we know about them because we have found their bones, teeth, skin imprints, and footprints preserved in rock. These remains and traces of dinosaurs are called fossils.

The description of the continental drift theory is equally inspired. One frieze of simple drawings with brief captions and two short paragraphs explains the theory and points out how the discovery of the same fossils in different parts of the world helps to support it. The photographs and prints are extraordinary; both compositon and clarity are far above average. They come from various sources, and great care was obviously taken with their selection. Children who have read Aliki's *Digging Up Dinosaurs* will find this book a natural next choice. Index.

> *Elizabeth S. Watson, in a review of "Dinosaurs Walked Here and Other Stories Fossils Tell," in* The Horn Book Magazine, *Vol. LXIV, No. 1, January-February, 1988, p. 86.*

Fossils tell fascinating tales, and so does Lauber. Here she relates the prehistoric stories revealed by paleontologists around the world. . . . She also creates vivid scenarios to demonstrate plausible scientific interpretation of fossil finds; for example, a saber-tooth tiger's attack on a giant ground sloth is retold through fossils found at La Brea. . . . Throughout, the writing is clear, concise, and accurate. Best of all are the exceptional and abundant illustrations. Looking at these pictures is like examining the most outstanding fossil collections of the world or stepping back in time to the days of the dinosaurs. Finding a fossil and imagining an ancient life is exciting. A child or young student who finds the superb book will be excited, for on its pages animals and plants dead for millions of years come alive.

> *Peter Roop, in a review of "Dinosaurs Walked Here and Other Stories Fossils Tell," in* Science Books & Films, *Vol. 23, No. 3, January-February, 1988, p. 174.*

SNAKES ARE HUNTERS   (1987)

Snakes are the focus of this Let's-Read-and-Find-Out Science Book, a short, informative and well-paced introduction to the natural history and habits of these reptiles. The basic facts about snakes are clearly presented: they have no legs, they have scales and ''spectacles'' instead of eyelids. And snakes are hunters; in the wild, all snakes stalk, capture and eat other animals. Lauber, an award-winning science writer for children, also explores aspects of cold-bloodedness, hibernation, reproduction and growth.

> *A review of ''Snakes Are Hunters,'' in* Publishers Weekly, *Vol. 233, No. 4, January 29, 1988, p. 429.*

The selection and organization of material are excellent, and the style is clear except in one case: the statement that ''Snakes die if temperatures are below freezing'' is not true unless readers deduce that she means outside of the ''safe shelters for winter'' that are described. . . . The book is nonetheless valuable for the information it provides and for the friendly presentation of a subject that frightens many children.

> *Betsy Hearne, in a review of ''Snakes Are Hunters,'' in* Bulletin of the Center for Children's Books, *Vol. 41, No. 6, February, 1988, p. 120.*

Harry Mazer

1925-

American author of fiction.

Mazer is recognized as a moralistic yet nondidactic writer who has created a variety of thoughtful realistic novels for young adults which focus on survival and the discovery of inner strength. Often acknowledged for his insight and perceptiveness, he is well known as the author of well-paced tales with strong plots and significant themes, lightened by humor, that deal frankly with such topics as war, the homeless, divorce, drugs, unwed motherhood, and airplane disasters. His stories, which feature teenagers coping with traumatic situations ranging from domestic crises with brutal, preoccupied, or absent adults to life-threatening battles against the natural elements, are set not only in contemporary times but also in Depression-era New York and Europe during the Second World War. A firm believer in the resilience of youth, Mazer characteristically portrays his protagonists getting into trouble, running away, and coming back changed and ready to confront the same problems with new vigor. Considered a controversial figure by those parents, teachers, and librarians who object to his use of strong language and occasional treatment of pre-marital sex, Mazer is praised by other observers for his presentation of alternative solutions and frequently open-ended conclusions which lend themselves well to classroom discussions.

Mazer is best known for his autobiographical *The Last Mission* (1979), in which an idealistic Jewish fifteen-year-old lies about his age to join the Air Force, gets shot down over Germany, and, alone among his crew, survives to tell a school audience at home the truth about war. Popularized by the television production in 1978, *Snow Bound* (1973) is the adventure of two runaway teenagers who get lost in a snowstorm, overcome their differences in order to survive, and return home chastened and wiser. *The Island Keeper* (1981) is a contemporary Robinsonnade featuring Mazer's only female protagonist, who contends successfully not only against the hostile Canadian wilderness but also with her feelings of grief and rebellion. Praised for well-developed characters who win the devotion of his readers, he has written two books each about two of his heroes: illegitimate Marcus, who first appears as a lonely fourteen-year-old obsessed with the need to find his father in *Dollar Man* (1974), grows into the infatuated seventeen-year-old senior who craves more than friendship with his childhood friend in *I Love You, Stupid* (1981); thirteen-year-old Willis, son of an alcoholic, triumphs over his background by becoming a champion runner in *The War on Villa Street* (1978) and transcends his situation as a nineteen-year-old factory hand in the love story *Girl of His Dreams* (1986). Mazer collaborated with his wife, young adult novelist Norma Fox Mazer, on *The Solid Gold Kid* (1977), a thriller concerning the kidnapped son of a millionaire.

Critics laud Mazer for his sensitivity to the problems and feelings of young people, his emphasis on moral victories of integrity and compassion, and the absence of romantic, predictable endings in his books. Several of his works are also considered outstanding examples of literature for young adults. Although some critics discredit his use of raw language, most

Photograph by Ruth Putter

reviewers agree that Mazer's stories successfully convey the anguish, joy, and hope of growing up.

Mazer has won several adult-selected awards for his books.

(See also *Something about the Author*, Vol. 31 and *Contemporary Authors*, Vols. 97-100.)

AUTHOR'S COMMENTARY

Realistic fiction for the young reader is under attack and so are its authors. For a decade there has been an exciting expansion of children's literature. "Forbidden" subjects were dealt with—sex, broken homes, violence, death. Like Pandora's box, once the lid was off more and more of what was hidden came to light. It was an exhilarating time for writers and I think for readers as well.

Now the lid is being pushed down by those who want pretty fictions, a return to a make-believe world. The call is out for safe books, light fiction, romances, pure entertainment. And in the background, conglomerates, those crocodiles of business, with their narrow concerns for profit, are gobbling up publishing companies. We are seeing more nonbook books produced and marketed as products. It's not a good time for books, authors or readers.

I feel that I'm riding a dark wave. Sense tells me that things are not likely to improve soon, yet I think the need for realistic fiction is greater than ever. The world is not getting saner, calmer or more peaceful. Young readers need real books to make sense of the world, to validate their experience. So while there is little to crow about I remain hopefully committed to the realistic direction of adolescent fiction.

> *Harry Mazer, in an excerpt from* Literature for To-day's Young Adults, *edited by Aleen Pace Nilsen and Kenneth L. Donelson, second edition, Scott, Foresman and Company, 1985, p. 484.*

GENERAL COMMENTARY

KEN DONELSON

Harry Mazer writes about young people caught in the midst of moral crises, often of their own making. Searching for a way out, they discover themselves, or rather they learn that the first step in extricating themselves from their physical or moral dilemmas is self-discovery. Intensely moral as Mazer's books are, they present young people thinking and talking and acting believably, and for that reason, some parents and teachers may object, particularly to the language in *The Last Mission.* The necessity of making one's own moral judgments appeals to young people who recognize that moral decisions that matter are never possible outside situations which reflect and approximate real life.

Snow Bound may well be Mazer's best known book, and it is certainly one of the best will-they-or-won't-they-be-rescued thrillers of the last several years. Tony LaPorte, spoiled rotten by his doting and doltish parents, sets out to punish them when he is not allowed to keep a stray dog by stealing his mother's old Plymouth and taking off for parts unknown. Enroute to nowhere, he spots hitchhiker Cindy Reichert, and they ride off into the sunset. They don't get there as Tony proves his prowess at the wheel by wrecking the car in a desolate area during a blinding snowstorm. While each despises the other for the situation they're in and their early plans for escape are vague and inevitably fail, they do ultimately save themselves from the cold and a pack of feral dogs.

As Tony, no longer the selfish person he had been, lies in the hospital bed reflecting on the past few days, on all he and Cindy faced, on all the havoc he has wreaked trying to prove whatever it was he set out to prove, he recognizes that he has faced himself and a moral crisis, and he won. . . .

Snow Bound is a story of people facing somewhat melodramatic problems in reasonably believable ways. As a story of sheer adventure, it is one of the best books of its kind, second only, for me, to Robb White's *Deathwatch.* But Mazer's novel goes little beyond the adventure, and most youngsters reading it are likely to miss the moral engagement. If they catch sight of it, they surely will think the morality simpleminded, and they will be right. Still, it is a grand tale of adventure.

The Dollar Man carries Mazer's concept of the moral dilemma arising from the crisis one step further. Marcus Rosenbloom, fat and fatherless and frightened, refuses to let his loving and delightful mother, Sally, and her boyfriend, Bill, help him. He *knows* that his father, wherever and whoever he is, is a great person. He cannot and will not understand why no one at home will talk about his father. (p. 19)

Marcus decides to ignore his family since they refuse to help, and he sets out to find his beloved and misunderstood father. After getting in trouble at school, Marcus finds a lead that takes him to his wealthy father. Unhappily for Marcus but believably for the novel, the father hadn't realized Sally had decided against an abortion and instead had Marcus. He tries to buy Marcus off with a twenty dollar bill and a new wrist-watch, but Marcus isn't having that, and he leaves his father behind along with the money and the watch.

The Dollar Man may lack the thrills of *Snow Bound,* but it represents a great advancement in writing. Marcus' dilemma is real and, judging from newspapers and court records, not uncommon. His search, foolish as it may appear to some of his family and futile as it turns out, is necessary for Marcus, and the hitherto ineffectual young man carries the search to its logical conclusion. But more important than the search itself is Marcus' grudging but inevitable willingness to accept reality. Marcus is truly a person with a moral quest, and he can take pride in his personal proof that he is a "searcher and a doer."

The Solid Gold Kid, written with his wife Norma Fox Mazer, represents no advancement in Mazer's work. It tries, with limited success, to combine the thrills of *Snow Bound* with the moral dilemma of *The Dollar Man.* The result is a pleasant enough thriller, a diversion, not a bad book and often quite a nice book, but nothing more.

The plot is simply told. Derek Chapman, sixteen, and a millionaire's son may not be as spoiled as Tony of *Snow Bound,* but Derek has a sense of self-importance born of his money. One day, he is kidnapped along with four other young people standing and waiting at the same bus stop. Terror and suspense follow as the evil kidnappers make their plans, and the five young people plan this and then that escape. The end of the book is intriguing, for Derek escapes first and he waits anxiously wondering what has happened to the other four. His relationship with Pam, clearly not of his social class, develops from hot pursuit and passion to an honest and growing affection as they seek to escape. When Pam the last to be found, is wounded and then bitterly tells Derek to leave her hospital room, the reader may wonder if this too will not work out neatly and romantically, but it does not, and the ending is realistically ambiguous. But all in all, a disappointing book.

The Last Mission represents an amazing leap in writing, far surpassing anything he had written before. Whether young people will find the book easily—given the language some parents and teachers and librarians may not encourage young adults to read it—is unclear, but there is no doubt but that *The Last Mission* is a brilliant addition to adolescent literature. It is apparently largely autobiographical, and it is unquestionably the bloodiest and the most moral book Mazer has written.

Jewish Jack Rabe so desperately *must* get into action during World War II to destroy Hitler that he uses his older brother's identification and lies his way into the Air Corps when he is only fifteen. He trains as a waist gunner on a B-17, makes Staff Sergeant, goes through combat duty out of England, survives twenty-four missions before being shot down the next time out, watches his best friend die, is captured by Germans, makes his way back safely, and is discharged from the service.

That brief and hackneyed plot sounds like so many other war stories (and war films), but Mazer's novel is not trite or commonplace. Jack dreams about the glory of being a hero, and he pictures the general heroism of war, but his dreams do not approximate the dullness and boredom of much of his service life just as they do not suggest the blood and bitterness of losing his best friend in battle. Jack learns, slowly, how very stupid and hellish war is, even that war, the last of the Holy Wars when goodness fought evil.

The book has authentic sounds of men at war, the pointlessness and boredom.

> He pushed the breakfast tray away. Chipped beef in a cream sauce on toast. 'Shit on a shingle'. It turned Jack's stomach.
>
> 'Eat it,' Chuckie said. 'It's good for you.'
>
> 'You want it? You can have it.' He reached into his pocket for a cigarette.
>
> Chuckie glanced at him. 'Cut out the cigarettes before breakfast, Jack. No wonder you're so fucking jumpy.'
>
> 'Fuck off,' Jack answered automatically. The swearing in the Army was like nothing he'd ever heard before. When he was home he'd known all the swear words and used them sometimes, but never where his mother or any grown-up could hear. But in the Army, everyone swore, all the time, everywhere, about everything.

And *The Last Mission* conveys better than any other young adult novel, and better than most adult novels, the feeling of war and the desolation it leaves behind. After Germany surrenders, Jack's war is over, and he requests a discharge. Back home after the family welcomes him back (he's never written them, a fact that will disturb some readers but is believable given Jack's circumstances and his deep-felt belief in the holiness of his cause), he drifts. War was not what he thought it would be, but then neither is peace, for he finds no peace within himself. Chuckie's death and Jack's living leave him still at war, and he does not find his peace, though he does find solace of a sort, when he is asked by the high school principal to speak on Veterans Day as the school's youngest veteran. (pp. 19-20)

Paxton Davis called *The Last Mission* a "rare" experience, and so it is [see excerpt dated December 2, 1979 for *The Last Mission*]. Perhaps this is Mazer's way of writing out something from his past that has haunted him, but whatever the motivation, this book is a remarkable achievement, both for its theme and its portrait of a young man who searches and acts and finds the search futile and the actions incoherent. But that dark trip into war and into himself was something far more necessary and far more moral than anything he had done before. He may not have liked everything he found on that trip, but he began to find himself and what and who he was and even what he might become.

The Island Keeper fuses some elements from *Snow Bound* and *The Last Mission*. Fat, rich, lonely, and unattractive sixteen-year-old Cleo Murphy still grieves for her mother, killed in a car crash, and her younger sister, Jam, recently dead in a boating accident. Her grandmother has no sympathy and little time for Cleo, and Cleo's father is equally cold and distant. So flying from Chicago to New York and another summer camp she knows she'll hate, Cleo decides to head for the last place she and her sister had had a wonderful time, Duck Island in Big Clear Lake. She buys camping gear, avoids the caretaker on her father's property, steals a canoe, and paddles out. So far, the book has all the promise of a good adventure tale, but then reality steps in when Cleo discovers that the cabin she had planned on using has burned, and she must make do with few creature comforts. And make do she does.

> She knew nothing about real life, what real people did. Whatever she knew she had learned from reading.

And she learns. Having run off without plan, she learns to plan. Having run off as a lark, a momentary gesture, she learns the danger of caprices and carelessness. She finds a small hole in a hill, makes a home of sorts, and vows to stay one day longer, and she renews that vow for several days until she realizes she will stay there until she knows why she has come in the first place. From a young girl without strength or will, she learns how to handle problems by herself and for herself and her needs. When the caretaker canoes in to find her—her father is searching, we later learn, everywhere for Cleo—she hides, not quite sure why except that she has yet to get from the island all there is to learn. When the raccoon steals all her freeze-dried food, Cleo is depressed, but again she makes do, she survives. (pp. 20-1)

The Island Keeper is no romanticized version, wouldn't-it-be-wonderful-to-be-alone-on-a-desert-island book. She tries to befriend and tame a chipmunk and a small owl, but while both will take food from her, neither trusts her. . . .

And August comes and goes and September and it's cooler, and a cold mist hangs over the lake, but still Cleo hangs on. And then it is time to leave, a storm hits, and her canoe is crushed by a falling tree, and the game, whatever it was that she had been playing, is no longer a game but survival. October brings colder weather, and death is near. She builds a raft and it too fails. . . .

And she knows she is truly alone and she cries out of despair. . . .

And then she grows up, not as a Job with burdens and punishments heaped upon her without cause. She had caused her own burdens, her own punishments. She had pretended that out of this mystic retreat to the island paradise something, she knew not what, would come, and nothing had happened. But this she knew; she had to work out her destiny and survival on her own. No more fun and games and minor, temporary disappointments. (p. 21)

She came to the island fat and lonely and incapable of handling problems and desolate. She left the island on foot across the ice seven months later slim, independent, capable, in almost every sense her own master. She had not found easy answers, indeed she may have found no answers, but she had rid herself of searching for easy answers and she had, like Jack Raab in *The Last Mission,* found herself.

Whether *The Island Keeper* represents a great advance in Harry Mazer's writing is doubtful because *The Last Mission* is such a superb book, but *The Island Keeper* is no inferior work, no let down after a great work. It has the danger of *Snow Bound* but heightened and much more believable. It has the self-imposed quest of *The Last Mission,* and it clearly fits into Mazer's persistent theme of the seeker and the doer, in this case in the metaphor Mazer uses for his dedication in *The Island Keeper.*

> To the young who stand at the threshold of an uncertain world. Courage.
>
> (p. 25)

Ken Donelson, "Searchers and Doers: Heroes in Five Harry Mazer Novels," in Voice of Youth Advocates, *Vol. 5, No. 6, February, 1983, pp. 19-21, 25.*

GUY LENNY (1971)

Twelve-year-old Guy Lenny is suddenly beset with all the complications of the adult world he has just begun to enter. His divorced father has a girl friend, Emily, who is pleasant enough but who threatens the secure man's world Guy has known since early childhood when his mother left her family to marry an Army officer. When his mother reappears after seven years, Guy's father, who wishes to remarry and knows his son's opposition, suggests that the boy live with his mother and her husband. Guy feels manipulated by both parents and reacts by briefly running away. But he returns, with a "sense of his own strength and separateness," knowing "that he wouldn't cry again. There were no more lies they could tell him." Although there is little overt action in the story, the transformation of a reasonably content boy into an alienated young man is well handled. Guy Lenny is a likeable hero and the supporting characters—both adult and juvenile—are believable.

> *Sharon Karmazin, in a review of "Guy Lenny," in* School Library Journal, *an appendix to* Library Journal, *Vol. 18, No. 2, October, 1971, p. 122.*

Two new paperbacks [**Guy Lenny** and Lois Duncan's *A Gift of Magic*] really make children think—about themselves, about their parents, about how they treat people. Both concern children whose parents want to marry for a second time, although there's plenty of other action in each story. . . .

[**Guy Lenny** is an] open-ended story, with the grownups sure "everything will work out perfectly." Guy's not so sure. The language is right in this book—and so is Guy, young and tough, but not quite tough enough.

> *Judith Higgins, in a review of "Guy Lenny," in* Teacher, *Vol. 90, No. 6, February, 1973, p. 125.*

The story ends abruptly, leaving the reader uncertain about Guy's future. This open-endedness and the tracing of the main character's change from a reasonably happy and contented boy to a youth alienated from his world are excellent stimuli for discussion. (p. 471)

> *Sharon Spredemann Dreyer, "Annotations: 'Guy Lenny'," in her* The Bookfinder: A Guide to Children's Literature about the Needs and Problems of Youth Aged 2-15, *Vol. I, American Guidance Service, Inc., 1977, No. 627.*

SNOWBOUND (1973)

A more mismatched twosome would be hard to imagine. Tony, 15, is the spoiled, handsome son (there are three sisters) of working-class Americans caught in the mindless upward-mobility spiral. Following an argument Tony "borrows" his mother's car and, on impulse, heads north in a blizzard to visit a relative. Cindy, slightly older, is the motherless only child of a physician father, too busy and detached to take note of her emergent womanhood. Bookish, sharp in her way, Cindy has trouble relating to others. When the bus she is taking home from her grandmother's is delayed by the storm, Cindy (also on impulse) hitches a ride with Tony.

It is hate at first sight, scarcely sweetened by subsequent events. Tony gets lost in the storm and wrecks the car on the desolate Tug Hill plateau of upper New York State. In their struggle to get out, to survive, these chance companions come to terms

with themselves and each other, discovering in two weeks' compacted anguish what many fail to learn in a lifetime—that we are all accountable for one another. Cindy says it best in the loving, intensely alive and outgoing letter to Tony that ends their adventure: "You are my brother now, and though you hardly need . . . more sisters, you're stuck with me for life."

Occasionally a plot turn seems contrived: The car trunk and Cindy's tote bag turn out to be survival kits. Both youngsters, though wilderness nitwits, sometimes behave like group leaders from "Outward Bound." Yet the final measure of the book's capacity to enthrall lies in the *mature* reader's willingness to suspend disbelief. **Snow Bound** is a crackling tale; Mazer tells it with vigor and authority.

> *Cathleen Burns Elmer, in a review of "Snow Bound," in* The New York Times Book Review, *August 12, 1973, p. 8.*

The authors of **Snow Bound** and *A Figure of Speech* are husband and wife. Their craft must benefit from their relationship, because both of them tell extremely engrossing tales for early adolescents.

Snow Bound, as its subtitle indicates, is a story of raw survival. The two teenagers who are stranded in a blizzard in the most desolate part of New York State contend with the familiar perils from cold, near-starvation, inability to signal rescuers, and despair. These are expertly described, but the real merit of the book is in the representation of the psychology of the two young people. Both are independent and, in different ways and to different degrees, defiant. The boy is bold and impulsive, the girl is intelligent and vexed by what she sees as her stiffness in relating to others. She is the more mature of the two and her eventual responsibility for their rescue alters the thinking of both of them. The relationship that develops between the two of them is sensitively handled, never foolishly romanticized, and will probably be an easy thing for young readers to identify with.

> *Tom Heffernan, in a review of "Snowbound: A Story of Raw Survival," in* Children's Literature: Annual of the Modern Language Association Seminar on Children's Literature and The Children's Literature Association, *Vol. 4, 1975, p. 206.*

THE DOLLAR MAN (1974)

Overweight, awkward and shy, Marcus Rosenbloom cuts a cool, heroic figure in his fantasies where he is given courage by the example of the father he has never known but variously imagines as a spy, a military hero and a benevolent "dollar man." Meanwhile Marcus' efforts to change his image by dieting become futile, self-inflicted torture and a plan to make himself more dashing by wearing a plumed black hat falls flat. But when he is framed on a charge of smoking pot in school and reluctantly, but with dignity, takes the rap for his guilty "friends" the incident turns out—as Vivian, an older teenager who has a crush on this 5'11" fourteen year-old, predicts—to be "the best thing that ever happened to you." Indeed it gives Marcus the courage to seek out the father who doesn't know he exists and—when Dad proves to be a self-centered, money preoccupied businessman who tries to buy off this inconveniently appearing son with a watch and a twenty dollar bill—his shattered hopes leave him able for the first time to appreciate his mother's cheerful independence and his own character—less than dashing perhaps, but more than a laughing stock or pawn. Not incidentally, this is an outstandingly empathetic and realistic study of the psychology of a food addict and, moreover, a sensitive interior view—undistorted by the self-discounting sarcasm that has become a narrative cliche—of the kind of kid who is usually shoved into the background . . . but who in this case deserves the front and center attention Mazer accords him. A rare combination—uncompromising yet ever so easy to connect with.

> *A review of "The Dollar Man," in* Kirkus Reviews, *Vol. XLII, No. 16, August 15, 1974, p. 882.*

Marcus Rosenbloom is fat and he daydreams. He has a large fantasy life and a large rubber tire of fat around his gut. Both seem to be the result of an understandable, greedy emotional hunger—the acute longing of adolescence—for love, identity, communication, roots. Fourteen-year-old Marcus's search for self-identity takes the form of a search for his father, whom he has never known. . . .

Marcus is supported by a solidly-realized cast of characters: his blunt, best friend, Bernie; Bernie's older sister, Vivian, whose friendship is easy, open, warm and direct and with whom Marcus falls in love while they're hand wrestling; Wendy, a self-styled adolescent witch, who encourages Marcus into pseudo-psychic self-confrontation under a bed piled with party-goers' coats; and a grandmother as humanly peculiar and real as your own.

Marcus is successful. He doggedly seeks out and finds his father—an anonymously-named George Renfrew, with whom none of the good guys in this book would have much in common. And once he has confronted him and learned what kind of person his father is, Marcus can begin to be himself. The idea is not novel, or even presented with extraordinary subtlety or style, but there is such charged energy in Mazer's work and Marcus is such an authentic person that you care, very much, what happens.

> *Tobi Tobias, in a review of "The Dollar Man," in* The New York Times Book Review, *November 17, 1974, p. 8.*

Positives and negatives of a one-parent family are convincingly explored in this novel. . . . (p. 111)

This is an important book because of its realistic exploration of the pressures on a child by his peers and society when he has only one parent. The positives of the mother-son relationship are explicit enough not to be obliterated by Marcus's obsession over finding his father. (p. 112)

> *Binnie Tate Wilkin, in a review of "The Dollar Man," in her* Survival Themes in Fiction for Children and Young People, *The Scarecrow Press, Inc., 1978, pp. 111-12.*

THE SOLID GOLD KID (with Norma Fox Mazer, 1977)

Separately, both members of this husband and wife team have produced books of uncommon interest. . . . Together, alas, the Mazers seem to cancel out each other's virtues. The best that can be said about **The Solid Gold Kid** is that the authors have hit on a plot with 14-carat potential. The mass kidnapping of five teenagers, previously strangers, is a premise that's virtually guaranteed to keep youngsters turning pages.

The solid gold kid himself is Derek Chapman, the lonely, insecure son of a self-made millionaire. While waiting for a bus outside the gates of his private school, Derek unsuspectingly hitches a ride with Pearl and Bogie, a self-styled Bonnie and Clyde who have been planning to kidnap him for a cool half-million in ransom. Just as innocently, Derek invites five townies who happen to be standing at the bus stop to share the back of the van with him. Thus Pearl and Bogie, luckless as they are desperate, are stuck with four accidental hostages.

Our introduction to the five victims is the first hint of heavy going ahead. This supposedly random bunch is as calculatedly balanced as the cast of a singing Pepsi commercial. In addition to Derek, there is Jeff, a nattily dressed black whose drive to be realistic about their predicament verges on cynicism, and Eddie, a working-class ethnic type who passes remarks about "boogies" and tends to identify with his captors. And there are two girls: Pam is blonde, idealistic and outspoken; and Wendy is Jewish, asthmatic and apparently the weakest member of the group.

Pearl and Bogie's plans go wrong from the outset, and the kids are carted around, bound and half-starved, from one hideaway to the next. Their attempts to escape provide some solid suspense. And, surprisingly, the most exciting scene centers on Wendy, who turns out to be a gymnast and an absolutely fearless one. When the group is locked in the cabin of an abandoned fire tower, Wendy calmly rigs a rope trapeze, swings her way down to the stairs below, and frees her companions. This getaway, like several others, is foiled by the surprise return of the kidnappers. By the time Derek is rescued six days later, he is under the impression that all his fellow victims are dead.

Unfortunately, the Mazers aren't content to spin a straight action adventure. They gum up the works trying to make serious statements. Often, these teenagers sound less like crime victims than self-conscious participants in a weekend encounter group. Especially annoying is the attempt to deal with Derek's guilt over being disgustingly rich. First, the other young people berate him for being the cause of the plight. Then, after they've been rescued and Derek's father has arranged to pay for their hospital bills, they seem to forgive him. "Being rich is just one of those miserable facts of life you have to live with— like my limp, maybe," says Pam. This is the kind of dialogue that passes for profundity here.

On another occasion, Derek muses lugubriously, "It was fate, I told myself, and I thought of fate like a giant hand scooping up the five of us, squeezing us together in this unbearable, hateful intimacy." Actually, young readers know as well as the Mazers do the difference between fate and contrivance. They may well be satisfied with the latter, and as a thriller this is passable fair. Too bad it tries so hard to be more.

> *Joyce Milton, "A Kid's Ransom," in* Book World— The Washington Post, *July 10, 1977, p. H10.*

The Mazers create a believable situation and explore actions and reactions with percipience; the characters are sharply defined, and their relationships develop logically. But this is more than a perceptive analysis of people under stress, it is also an adventure story with a strong plot, good pace, and well-maintained suspense.

> *Zena Sutherland, in a review of "The Solid Gold Kid," in* Bulletin of the Center for Children's Books, *Vol. 30, No. 11, July-August, 1977, p. 178.*

Two writers have combined their distinct talents to produce a skillfully written and credibly plotted suspense story with fascinating psychological overtones. . . . The teenagers, from diverse racial and social backgrounds, are incisively individualized characters; closely confined and under the pressure of constant terror, their attitudes toward one another alternate between genuine solicitude and snarling hostility. The appalling events reach a climax with a breathtaking police chase; but more significantly, the reader feels that the story is essentially concerned with the human capacity for survival and with the futility of violence and hatred. (pp. 451-52)

> *Ethel L. Heins, in a review of "The Solid Gold Kid,"*
> *in* The Horn Book Magazine, *Vol. LIII, No. 4, August, 1977, pp. 451-52.*

THE WAR ON VILLA STREET (1978)

Eighth-grader Willis Pierce runs off his frustrations every day, mile after mile, in secret—just as if his father were after him, drunk, or Rabbit Slavin's gang, vengeful. When retarded Richard Hayfoot attaches himself to Willis, his troubles seem complete; but Willis is a tough survivor and one by one (just as he has run the miles) faces each torment as it comes, including a beating by the gang, the tedious coaching of Richard for an upcoming athletic event in exchange for much-needed money, and the reality of his father's alcoholism. At the story's end, a loner with his back against the wall has gained self-respect that ironically draws others and will take him through the world against all odds. The plot elements are familiar, but Mazer has an inveterate sense of using them to build tension. Moreover, he has smoothed out his style, developing characters in relationship to each other with skill and feeling. Careful work, good reading. (pp. 547-48)

> *Betsy Hearne, in a review of "The War on Villa Street: A Novel," in* Booklist, *Vol. 75, No. 6, November 15, 1978, pp. 547-48.*

This is a moving, fast-paced story that once more proves Mazer's understanding of adolescence. The treatment of the retarded boy and Willis' difficulty in adjusting to him is sympathetic and honest. The few expletives in the story should not be a bar to purchase of this novel which belongs on library shelves along with Mazer's former successes, **Snowbound** and **The Dollar Man**. . . .

> *Robert Unsworth, in a review of "The War on Villa Street," in* School Library Journal, *Vol. 25, No. 4, December, 1978, p. 62.*

The story is adequately written, the characterization and dialogue capably handled, but the ending—the fight, the thinking period, the realization that Willis can't let his father's problem dominate his own life—seems so tied to the familial situation that all of the material about the girls Willis likes, the gang he detests, the retarded boy he's been helping seems more padding than preparation for the dénouement.

> *Zena Sutherland, in a review of "The War on Villa Street," in* Bulletin of the Center for Children's Books, *Vol. 32, No. 5, January, 1979, p. 84.*

THE LAST MISSION (1979)

Mazer has attempted a kind of *All Quiet on the Western Front* for World War II, which turns out to be a deeply felt, but oddly sketchy tale based upon his own experiences. Jack Raab, a 15-year-old from Brooklyn, runs away from home in 1943

with his older brother's ID and fools the army into inducting him. He trains as a gunner on fighter planes and, after a slow start, soon develops a close comraderie with his crew, and in particular with fellow New Yorker Charlie O'Brien. They successfully complete bombing mission after mission, but as the war winds to a close in Europe, they are shot down over Germany. After a short imprisonment, the Germans let Raab go when the allies are close to victory. He then learns to his horror that he alone of his crew has survived. In a moving finale, Raab meets the parents of Charlie O'Brien and is welcomed back at his high school. Instead of glorifying his feats, however, Raab tells the student body that war is death and destruction. Mazer seems to keep his distance in telling this autobiographical story—the characters take second place to the action. Raab's growing distaste of the fighting is believable but the rest—his relationship to family, his Jewishness, even his first romantic friendship—is not developed. Still, it's a welcome relief from the two kinds of war stories usually written for teens—romantic heroics and actionless character studies.

> *Jack Forman, in a review of "The Last Mission," in* School Library Journal, *Vol. 26, No. 3, November, 1979, p. 91.*

War is by nature an almost incommunicable experience, yet it provides one of mankind's most fundamental narrative sources; most everyone who has fought and survived wants to tell what fighting and surviving were like. Harry Mazer fought in World War II, and in this novel tells the story brilliantly.

It is surely his own experience, and a rare one it is. . . .

What gives Mr. Mazer's novel its force . . . lies less with details of Air Force training and service, though he does them well, than with the emotional substance upon which the experience builds. For Jack Raab is no mere author's pawn. The reader feels his shock and grief at losing his friends, suffers with him the doubts and apprehensions that being a Jewish prisoner inevitably raise, and, especially, experiences with him the bewildering mixture of relief and repugnance that comes with returning to civilian life. . . .

Ultimately **The Last Mission** gains its force from its authority: it is an authority that has been won at high cost and never deceives itself. Harry Mazer is a prize-winning writer for young people. No wonder.

> *Paxton Davis, in a review of "The Last Mission," in* The New York Times Book Review, *December 2, 1979, p. 41.*

Told in a rapid journalistic style, occasionally peppered with barrack-room vulgarities, the story is a vivid and moving account of a boy's experiences during World War II as well as a skillful, convincing portrayal of his misgivings as a Jew on enemy soil and of his ability to size up—in mature, human fashion—the misery around him.

> *Paul Heins, in a review of "The Last Mission," in* The Horn Book Magazine, *Vol. LVI, No. 1, February, 1980, p. 63.*

THE ISLAND KEEPER (1981)

Cleo Murphy is an overweight 16 year old whose mother and younger sister have died in accidents. She decides to run away from her unhappy home with her wealthy but uncaring father and nagging grandmother to her father's isolated island in On-

Bubbles, and when the two finally "do it.

tario. When she arrives she discovers that their cabin has burned, and animals soon destroy her food supply. She manages to forage for food, hunt, fish and make a shelter in a cave. In the fall her plans to return to Chicago are upset when her canoe is wrecked in a storm. Winter sets in, and she finally escapes by walking back to the mainland over the frozen lake. Her experiences have given her a new confidence, and she comes to terms with her bereavement. The story of Cleo's past is told in imaginary scenes and conversations with her family, the effect of which seems stilted and artificial and adds no real conflict. The sentence structure is repetitive, and the runaway/survival plot was more successfully handled in Mazer's *Snow Bound*. The character of the Canadian wilderness is far more vividly realized in other adventure novels such as Farley Mowat's *Lost in the Barrens* or its sequel, *The Curse of the Viking Grave*.

> *Lorraine Douglas, in a review of "The Island Keeper,"*
> *in* School Library Journal, *Vol. 27, No. 8, April,*
> *1981, p. 142.*

[The] story is a Robinson Crusoe saga, and very well done, a record both believable and suspense-filled, and—when Cleo finds her canoe smashed and faces being on the island for the winter—exciting. She gets away by crossing the frozen lake, and she finds that her father and grandmother are no more understanding than they were before the long period in which they didn't even know if Cleo was alive. It may be realistic, but it's a rather sad ending: Cleo simply decides to go back to boarding school. She has the thought of the island to sustain her, but otherwise her life hasn't changed. The author maintains interest with skill; like O'Dell's Karana, Cleo has to learn wilderness living, and the details of her coping are all believable and nicely paced.

> *Zena Sutherland, in a review of "The Island Keeper,"*
> *in* Bulletin of the Center for Children's Books, *Vol.*
> *34, No. 9, May, 1981, p. 176.*

Written in a snappy, vernacular style *The Island Keeper* would make an entertaining read for a city child who fancies that life in the wilderness offers an enviable way to escape human complexity, even though there is much in the book that strains belief. The story is perhaps more interesting because the author has chosen a female character to enact what traditionally would have been a boy's adventure story.

> *Feenie Ziner, in a review of "The Island Keeper,"*
> *in* The New York Times Book Review, *September*
> *13, 1981, p. 50.*

I LOVE YOU, STUPID! (1981)

Marcus Aurelius Rosenbloom is an aspiring writer and a sex-obsessed senior. He figures the only impediment to maturity is sexual initiation—when is he going to get laid? The plot is artful: Marcus' erotic dreams play over every young female he meets—except for Wendy, a girl he used to know in grade school. Wendy's back in town and falls for a friend of Marc's; Marcus is babysitting for the child of Karen, a cool young divorcée whom he hopes will admire him as a writer and lover. It takes most of the book to get them together, but it's better that way; Marcus and Wendy are friends who become lovers. They're honest and humorous; their conversations and adventures are fresh and funny. Once they make love, Marcus looks for a pretext to do it every day, and Wendy begins to feel bugged. "'Sex is not a good enough reason for sex,'" she

says, and they break up. A family graduation party brings them back together and nicely underscores the affective ties that make love and sex dynamic. A worthy, lighthearted but thoughtful treatment of a perennial preoccupation.

> *Kay Webb O'Connell, in a review of "I Love You,*
> *Stupid!" in* School Library Journal, *Vol. 28, No. 2,*
> *October, 1981, p. 152.*

I Love You, Stupid!, which reinforces the old theme that women exist for men's sexual pleasure and satisfaction, underscores the need for feminist novels about adolescent sexuality.

Marcus Rosenbloom, an aspiring high school writer, is obsessed with sex. He sees every young woman as a sexual object ("She was like a ripe juicy Florida orange, like whipped cream and chocolate flakes") or a seducer ("She'd always been something of a witch, a spider luring him into her web"). Marcus reduces women to "the three B's: bones, boobs, and butts." He takes a baby-sitting job because he's infatuated with Karen, the child's mother, not out of a desire to earn money or care for small children. When he finally makes a sexual overture towards Karen, he is rebuffed and decides to develop a sexual relationship with his friend Wendy. They make a pact to cross the wall of virginity that separates childhood from adulthood together. It's interesting to note that although they talk about birth control methods and Marcus even buys some prophylactics, there is no mention of using any birth control devices when the two finally "do it."

Marcus and Wendy's relationship is characterized by one sexual encounter after another until Wendy comes to the realization that Marcus is interested only in sex. (Most young women would probably have deduced this sooner.) The conflict is simplistically resolved when Marcus tells Wendy, "I love you, stupid" and Wendy appears satisfied that things will be different.

There is a parallel plot about Marcus' development as a writer (he submits a story to *Playboy*, of course). When a story of his is accepted by a local newspaper, it seems that he is on his way to a successful writing career. In contrast, Wendy's desire to go to Forestry School is not taken seriously; friends refer to her as "Ranger Wendy." The adult females have fairly traditional occupations—a preschool teacher, an office worker and the curator of a small art museum.

As Wendy says, "Sex is not a good enough reason for sex." And writing a sexist book about sex is not a good enough reason for writing a book. *I Love You, Stupid!* depicts the excitement and confusion of the awakening of male sexuality, but there is little effort to place them in the context of a respectful, equal relationship. Young men may need stories to help them understand their sexual feelings, but not at the expense of the humanity of young women.

> *Lauri Johnson, in review of "I Love You, Stupid!"*
> *in* Interracial Books for Children Bulletin, *Vol. 13,*
> *Nos. 4 & 5, 1982, p. 27.*

American writers were first in the field of believable novels about the traumas of growing up, and this one is in the best traditions of the genre, disconcertingly authentic, funny, touching, with crisp dialogue. Its theme is the over-riding fascination sex holds for adolescents, and the sometimes ludicrous discrepancy between fantasy and reality. Marcus hopes to become irresistible to the opposite sex by various poses ("He was jacketless. *Rugged individualism*. The wind found holes in his his trousers. *Modest poverty*. He set a fast pace. *Olympic style*") The opposite sex is unimpressed. Then he meets by chance

Wendy, an old childhood friend. To his surprise, he finds they can talk about anything and everything, including sex, and gradually he realises the importance of friendship in their relationship; a relationship which convincingly ripens into love.

> *Barbara Sherrard-Smith, in a review of "I Love You, Stupid," in her* Children's Book of the Year: 1982, *Julia MacRae Books, 1983, p. 59.*

HEY, KID! DOES SHE LOVE ME?   (1984)

Even in high school, Jeff Orloff dreamed of Mary Silver, plastering his walls with photos of her. Her family moved away when she graduated, but now, two years later, Mary is back with a baby, renting a room from Jeff's best friend Danny's mother. So Jeff, just out of high school, hangs around Danny's house, helping Mary with baby Hannah, driving them to the doctor and the dentist, and gradually winning her friendship and the pet name Sir Walter Teddybear—but not the love and sex he wants from her.

Jeff projects all this with self-mocking humor and frequent lapses into Mitty-like scenarios cast as film scripts—for Jeff, though resisting family pressure to start college or a career, dreams of being a film director when he is not dreaming of Mary. His campaign builds up to a frazzled but (for readers) flat four-day stint caring for Hannah, while Mary attends the acting workshop he has urged on her. Then, instead of the loving reunion he's envisioned, Mary returns with bubbling plans to join a commune of actors doing street and community theater. For Jeff, her departure is followed by gloom, despair, a car accident, a bout with reality, and at last a move to Los Angeles and a job on the movie lots—"need I add, not as a director,"—as a dishwasher moving up to security guard.

This outcome makes sense, and the story is free of the maudlin banality of similar YA novels. Jeff is likable, decent without any moralistic self-consciousness; his sense of humor gives a refreshing edge of awareness to his normal self absorption.

> *A review of "Hey, Kid! Does She Love Me?" in* Kirkus Reviews, *Juvenile Issue, Vol. LIII, Nos. 5-10, May 15, 1985, p. J-42.*

With all of the Wildfire books and others like them on the market, a love story has to be great to make it just on the basis of author or title alone. The problem with this book is that its love angle just does not get off the ground. . . . The story develops as the relationship between Mary and Jeff does not— and the relationship between Jeff and Hannah—the "Kid!" of the book's title—does. And therein lies the book's problem. Most young readers want some action, some sort of contact in their love stories, and this has very little—especially early in the book where most readers' attentions are caught. This book just does not have what it takes to make it today.

> *John Lord, in a review of "Hey, Kid! Does She Love Me?" in* Voice of Youth Advocates, *Vol. 8, No. 3, August, 1985, p. 187.*

Jeff Orloff is always framing shots, directing actions, zooming in for close-ups and spouting terse, clipped dialogue. He sees himself as a future film director and throughout the book Mr. Mazer skillfully uses Jeff's "directing" to reveal his character.

Jeff loves Mary but Mary does not return his love. Exit Mary. Exit Jeff. With these bare facts Mr. Mazer has written a wise, warm, funny and touching book. . . . Jeff wants more than

friendship but Mary wisely keeps him at arm's length. She never succumbs to his sexual advances. Once she accidentally gives Jeff a bloody nose while fending him off. Mary steadfastly refuses to use Jeff and sex as a comfort or escape. Mazer handles the sexual encounters realistically with humor and sensitivity. . . .

There is no pat, predictable ending—just two young people in a loving relationship, still searching, still struggling, still growing.

Through Mr. Mazer's skillful storytelling young people are presented alternatives. [Jeff's best friend] Danny decides to marry after his girl gets pregnant. This choice contrasts sharply with the decisions Jeff and Mary make. (It is chiefly through Mary's strength that both are freed to pursue their dreams.) Abortion is mentioned but neither girl chooses it. The realities and difficulties of caring for a child, though presented with humor, are never minimized. Without preaching this book says to young people: there are alternatives, try out your ideas, have a dream and dare to follow it; don't be afraid to care. (p. 280)

> *Corrine Falope, in a review of "Hey, Kid! Does She Love Me?," in* Best Sellers, *Vol. 45, No. 7, October, 1985, pp. 279-80.*

WHEN THE PHONE RANG   (1985)

In what is, these days, a not-so-outlandish turn of events, 16-year-old Billy Keller learns in a phone call that his parents have been killed in a plane crash, leaving him, his brother and his sister orphaned. Mazer, a critically acclaimed YA author, then examines the effects (emotional and practical) on the Keller children.

While the death of parents and the struggle of children without parents are not uncommon themes in novels for teens, Mazer's solution to the Keller's situation is unusual. Faced with the dissolution of the remaining family unit—oldest son Kevin to return to college, Billy and 12-year-old Lori to go to various relatives—the children decide to stay together. Kevin drops out of college to live with Billy and Lori; and as the three grope their way through the next months, they grieve, make mistakes, and get into minor trouble, but by the time summer arrives, they know they can make it. They are the survivors.

Mazer, competently handling a devastating subject, has written a story that combines believable pathos with humor, touching detail, and enough kid appeal (despite his grief, Billy discovers an inexplicable interest in girls) to create a page-turner that is not a tear-jerker. In fact, perhaps the book's one flaw is that too little attention is paid to the emotional readjustment of Billy and his siblings. But Billy is an appealing character whom the reader is behind all the way—and nobody is more relieved than the reader when the Keller kids emerge intact and optimistic.

> *A review of "When the Phone Rang," in* Kirkus Reviews, *Vol. LIII, No. 18, September 15, 1985, p. 991.*

Through dialogue and the thoughts and actions of Billy, the narrator, Mazer skillfully conveys the five stages of grieving. He creates credible characters, balances a meaningful theme with a rapidly evolving plot and incorporates splashes of humor while maintaining the established mood and tone. The author's sensitive penetration into adolescent emotions in stressful circumstances makes this a novel with many enduring qualities.

Cynthia K. Leibold, in a review of "When the Phone Rang," in School Library Journal, *Vol. 32, No. 3, November, 1985, p. 100.*

This is a solid novel by an author whose works are almost invariably critical and popular successes. It's also, however, very sad, perhaps too disheartening for wide appeal. . . . It's hard to view the book objectively, to believe that the Kellers accomplish the many, intricate feats that Mazer describes. One would also question that an airline official would telephone news of the parents' fate to a young boy.

A review of "When the Phone Rang," in Publishers Weekly, *Vol. 228, No. 18, November 1, 1985, p. 65.*

CAVE UNDER THE CITY (1986)

The author of many celebrated YA novels returns to his Bronx roots to tell a moving survival story of two brothers [during the depression] who suddenly find that they have no one to rely on but themselves. . . .

A tale of runaways and hardships that has resonance today (Tolley: "I don't want to hear people making stupid remarks like the only hungry people are too dumb or too lazy to work''), with scenes and characters that are hard-edged and vivid. Tolley and Bubber will be hard to forget.

A review of "Cave Under the City," in Kirkus Reviews, *Vol. LIV, No. 19, October 1, 1986, p. 1510.*

In this gripping story set in the Bronx during the Depression, Tolly (about 12) and his brother, Bubber (about 6), are thrust into an odyssey of survival when their father has to leave town to seek work and their mother and grandmother are both too ill to care for them. Rather than be separated or sent to a children's shelter, the two flee to the streets where they are forced to take care of themselves through wit, endurance, and often painful compromise of their values. When Tolly becomes ill, Bubber leads him home, where they find that their father has returned and the brothers can resume their old lives. But they are not the same boys: each has had his character honed by the experience. Bubber has become a quiet realist, accepting loss while retaining hope. Tolley has become angry at the grownup world, and at his father in particular. Although filled with sharply detailed incident, the book is more character and atmosphere than plot, and hence, concentrating as it does on the changes in Tolley and Bubber, seems to stop rather than end. While occasionally relentless in its portrayals of the boys' struggle, this is compelling and well told in Tolley's believably adolescent voice, resulting in a harsh but credible story with some resonances of the plight of today's homeless. (pp. 105-06)

Christine Behrmann, in a review of "Cave Under the City," in School Library Journal, *Vol. 33, No. 4, December, 1986, pp. 105-06.*

What might have been a stark survival story is lightened by Mazer's deft handling of the bantering exchanges between the boys. The story is significant for its pictures of a time and the opportunities for open-ended inquiry about the choices and actions of the characters, but it will linger in the mind for the portrayal of the relationship between these two brothers. (p. 212)

Hanna B. Zeiger, in a review of "Cave Under the City," in The Horn Book Magazine, *Vol. LXIII, No. 2, March-April, 1987, p. 211-12.*

THE GIRL OF HIS DREAMS (1987)

This is a love story that's sweet without being sugary, original without being outlandish, sophisticated without being outré. It's the story of a nice young man, Willis, who was the main character in **The War on Villa Street,** who is a factory laborer, a dedicated runner, a shy loner who knows exactly what the girl of his dreams is like. She isn't the least bit like Sophie, who's a loner, too, having left the farm where her brother treated her like a servant and come to the city to be independent. They are both simple, good people who learn that reality can be better than a dream as they stumble toward a permanent relationship. The characterization has depth and compassion, the story is taut in structure and smoothly written, and the subplot (Willis crashes a college track meet and almost wins) is exciting and credible.

Zena Sutherland, in a review of "The Girl of His Dreams," in Bulletin of the Center for Children's Books, *Vol. 41, No. 5, January, 1988, p. 95.*

No run-of-the-mill boy meets girl story here. **The Girl of His Dreams** is romantic without being either mushy or explicitly sexual. Willis and Sophie are attractive characters who will interest and involve readers. Friends and lovers, they grow in trust and maturity page by page. They embrace and pull back. The many minor characters in the story are also realistically drawn and motivated. The action is well-paced, deliberate, and will hold readers' attention. Mazer has yet another winner in this satisfying, skillfully-realized title. This book may be enjoyed in its own right; with the previous book, the two together add up to a special treat. (p. 87)

Libby K. White, in a review of "The Girl of His Dreams," in School Library Journal, *Vol. 34, No. 5, January, 1988, pp. 86-7.*

Mazer's characters are down to earth, very ordinary people who are flawed, inept, and good. Their eccentricities, loneliness, and dreams are lightly touched with humor. Sophie, of course, is nothing like Willis's dream girl, but she certainly turns out to be more interesting. Their relationship develops awkwardly; "being close with someone isn't easy," as Willis comes to realize after losing Sophie and winning her back. Their story is moved along by Sophie's belief in him and his dreams. She begins to coach him in his running and to encourage his competing against the champion. Though Willis wavers, he does ultimately enter the championship race in a totally improbable and comic way. The outcome of the race, which gives Willis greatly improved future prospects, seems a bit unrealistic but conveys a rather nice message to the reader: you can be more than you are. This well-paced story is a fine illumination of everyday life. (p. 210)

Margaret A. Bush, in a review of "The Girl of His Dreams," in The Horn Book Magazine, *Vol. LXIV, No. 2, March-April, 1988, pp. 209-10.*

Walter Dean Myers

1937-

Black American author of fiction, picture books, and nonfiction.

Myers is recognized as a versatile author whose works, often set in Harlem, stress the positive attributes of the experiences and environment of his characters without shunning the negative elements. Considered an important black writer, he is often praised for his appealing characterizations, natural dialogue, exciting plots, successful integration of topics, and superior use of detail. Although he has written a variety of books for several age ranges, Myers is best known for his realistic fiction for young adults, in which his protagonists confront problems typical of adolescence—developing trust, making choices, becoming self-aware, and dealing with family relationships—as well as issues of particular concern to black readers, such as breaking out of the ghetto, avoiding drugs, and realizing individual potential despite the barriers of background. Underlying these works is the message that, despite the odds they face, young people can survive and succeed through inner strength and the support of family, friends, and community.

Myers's goal of offering accurate, hopeful, pertinent literature to children is reflected throughout his career. He began by writing picture books for the primary grades which stress togetherness and other values, and later created a controversial fairy tale, *The Dragon Takes a Wife* (1972), which combines black characters and language with more traditional elements. With *Fast Sam, Cool Clyde, and Stuff* (1975), Myers created his first novel for young adults. Perhaps his most popular work, *Fast Sam* blends humor and poignancy to present a nostalgic view of friendship in Harlem, the neighborhood of Myers's youth; *Mojo and the Russians* (1977) and *The Young Landlords* (1979), which also center on the urban adventures of black teenagers, further demonstrate Myers's sensitivity to the joys and sorrows of adolescence. Although Myers is noted for the lighthearted approach and often outrageous premises with which he invests his humorous books, he has also written serious fiction for young people which addresses such topics as adoption and foster parenting, the plight of neglected senior citizens, and suicide. He is perhaps most appreciated for *It Ain't All for Nothin'* (1978), in which a twelve-year-old boy decides whether or not to turn his father over to the police after a robbery; *Hoops* (1981) and its sequel *Outside Shot* (1984), which follow the emotional development of a gifted basketball player as he struggles through high school in Harlem and college in Indiana; and *Motown and Didi*, a love story about two teenagers who learn to trust each other. Myers has also created works in several other genres: a science fiction novel, a fantasy set in Africa, nonfiction on social welfare, mystery stories often set in exotic locales, and a novel/workbook which presents a harsh, personalized look at unplanned pregnancy.

Myers is applauded for creating affirmative and entertaining stories which are both realistic and optimistic. Critics also acclaim him for his writing style, which uses both fast pace and restraint, as well as for the believability of his characters and situations, the suspense of his plots, and the emotional involvement which characterizes several of his books. While reviewers periodically find his characterizations thin or under-

Courtesy of Walter Dean Myers

developed and note that his books vary in the success of their concepts and execution, most state that Myers verifies his artistic strength through his accurate reflection of emotion in works which demonstrate his belief in the young.

Myers received the Coretta Scott King Award in 1980 for *The Young Landlords*, the Edgar Allan Poe Award runner-up 1982 for *Hoops*, and the Coretta Scott King Award in 1985 for *Motown and Didi*.

(See also *CLR*, Vol. 4; *Contemporary Literary Criticism*, Vol. 35; *Something about the Author Autobiography Series*, Vol. 2; *Something about the Author*, Vols. 27, 41; *Contemporary Authors New Revision Series*, Vol. 20; *Contemporary Authors*, Vols. 33-36, rev. ed.; and *Dictionary of Literary Biography*, Vol. 33: *Afro-American Fiction Writers after 1955*.)

AUTHOR'S COMMENTARY

I write books for children, filled with the images I've accumulated over the years, with stories I've heard from my father and my grandfather. Many take place in the Harlem of my youth. The names of boyhood friends, Binky, Light Billy, Clyde, creep into the stories, and memories of them and of summer days playing endless games of stoopball next to the Church of the Master on Morningside Avenue keep the stories ever alive for me. I'm drawn to the eternal promise of childhood, and the flair of the young for capturing the essence of life.

When I began writing for young people I was only vaguely aware of the problems with children's books as far as blacks were concerned. My own encounters with black symbols and black characters were no less painful than those of the generations that followed me. There was the first mention of blacks in history. There were "slaves" being led from ships. Not captives, slaves. In truth, I don't remember Little Black Sambo, the large red lips pouting from the page, the wide eyes, the kinky hair going off in all directions, as being particularly bothersome. I'm not sure if it was the awe in which I held the tiger, or if I had just separated myself from this image. But later I do remember suffering through the Tom Swift books, and the demeaning portrait of Eradicate, the major black character in the series.

The pain was not so much that the images of my people were poor, but that the poor images were being made public. There they were in books for all of my white classmates to see. I had already internalized the negative images, had taken them for truth. No matter that my mother said that I was as good as anyone. She had also told me, in words and in her obvious pride in my reading, that books were important, and yet it was in books that I found Eradicate Sampson and the other blacks who were lazy, dirty and, above all, comical.

When the images of Dinah, the black maid in the Bobbsey Twins, Friday in "Robinson Crusoe," Eradicate in Tom Swift and the overwhelming *absence* of blacks in most books were telling the children of my generation that being black was not to be taken seriously, they were delivering the same message to white children. I knew that no homage to racial equality delivered by my teachers could, for me, offset even one snicker when Friday was depicted as a "savage," or when Dinah or Eradicate Sampson said something stupid.

I once worked in a personnel office in lower Manhattan where we hired both administrative and technical workers. I soon discovered that the hiring process was not so much a careful analysis of the applicant's abilities as it was a matching of appearance and behavior with the image of the successful candidate. When my otherwise liberal co-worker chose white males over women and black applicants, he was simply responding to what had been his cultural experience, that blacks and women were not the kinds of people who filled certain positions. I wonder how many books he had read—how many images of blacks—had led him to believe that a black man would not be a successful chemist or sales manager. Had he ever seen a black person in a book who was not an athlete or a service worker?

The 1960's promised a new way of seeing black people. First, and by far most important, we were in the public consciousness. Angry black faces stared out from our television sets, commanded the front pages of our tabloids. We were news, and what is news is marketable. To underscore the market the Federal Government was pumping money into schools and libraries under various poverty titles. By the end of the 60's the publishing industry was talking seriously about the need for books for blacks.

Publishers quickly signed up books on Africa, city living and black heroes. Most were written by white writers. In 1966 a group of concerned writers, teachers, editors, illustrators and parents formed what was to be called the Council on Interracial Books for Children. The council demanded that the publishing industry publish more material by black authors. The industry claimed that there were simply no black authors interested in writing for children. To counter this claim the council sponsored a contest, offering a prize of $500, for black writers. The response was overwhelming. It was the first time I had actually been solicited to write something about my own experience. That first year Kristin Hunter, a fine writer from Philadelphia, won the prize in the older children's category and I won in the picture book category for my book *Where Does the Day Go?* Subsequently, the winners of the contest, authors such as Sharon Bell Mathis, Ray Sheppard and Mildred Taylor, have gone on to produce books that not only have won national recognition but, not incidentally, have made nice profits for their publishers. The industry proudly announced that it had seen the error of its ways and fully intended to correct the situation.

I felt proud to be part of this new beginning. Langston Hughes, the brilliant black poet and novelist, had lived a scant half mile from me in Harlem. He had written for young people and I fancied myself following in his footsteps. I had learned from Hughes that being a black writer meant more than simply having one's characters brown-skinned, or having them live in what publishers insist on describing on book jackets as a "ghetto." It meant understanding the nuances of value, of religion, of dreams. It meant capturing the subtle rhythms of language and movement and weaving it all, the sound and the gesture, the sweat and the prayers, into the recognizable fabric of black life. . . .

I understood, and I know the others did too, that it was not only for black children that we wrote. We were writing for the white child and the Asian child too. My books did well, and so did the books of other black writers. . . . Things were looking up. I believed that my children and their counterparts would not only escape the demeaning images I had experienced but would have strong, positive images as well. And, though I was not happy with all the titles being published, the quality of the books written by blacks in the 70's was so outstanding that I actually thought we would revolutionize the industry, bringing to it a quality and dimension that would raise the standard for all children's books. Wrong. Wrong. Wrong.

No sooner had all the pieces conducive to the publishing of more books on the black experience come together than they started falling apart. The programs financed by the Johnson Administration and his Great Society were being dismantled under President Nixon. By the time President Ford left office the "Days of Rage" had ended and the temper of the time was lukewarm. Blacks were no longer a hot political issue. The libraries were the major markets for black children's books, and when they began to suffer cutbacks it was books on the black experience that were affected most.

In 1974 there were more than 900 children's books in print on the black experience. This is a small number of books considering that more than 2,000 children's books are published annually. But by 1984 this number was cut in half. For every 100 books published this year there will be one published on the black experience. Walking through the aisles at this year's American Library Association meeting in New York City was, for me, a sobering and disheartening experience. Were black writers suddenly incapable of writing well? Of course not, but we were perceived as no longer being able to sell well.

The talk in publishing circles has switched to book packaging, books for the preschool offspring of Yuppie parents, and the hoped-for upswing in retail stores. In the 70's black people called on publishers to exercise what then seemed to me the industry's responsibility. We demanded that the industry publish multicultural literature that reflected the society we live in.

I have changed my notion of the obligation of the book publishing industry. While it does have the responsibility to avoid the publishing of negative images of any people, I no longer feel that the industry has any more obligation to me, to my people, to my children, than does, say, a fast-food chain. It's clear to me that if any race, any religious or social group, elects to place its cultural needs in the hands of the profit makers than it had better be prepared for the inevitable disappointments.

What is there to be done? We must first acknowledge that in much of the black community reading as both a skill and as recreation is seriously undervalued. It is the urgent task of the black community to reinvest value in education and, specifically, in reading skills. If the market is created the books will come. Blacks are, arguably, the largest homogenous group in the country. We should be able to command a great share of the market and fulfill much of our needs ourselves.

If this seems unnecessarily harsh, or just not feasible, then we will simply have to wait for the next round of race riots, or the next interracial conflict, and the subsequent markets thus created. We can be sure, however, of one thing: if we continue to make black children nonpersons by excluding them from books and by degrading the black experience, and if we continue to neglect white children by not exposing them to any aspect of other racial and ethnic experiences in a meaningful way, we will have a next racial crisis. It will work, but it's a hard price for a transient market.

In the meanwhile there will be black artists recording the stuff of our lives in rich and varied hues, and they will continue to do so. We will twist and smooth and turn our lines carefully to the sun and wait, as we have done before, to offer them to new travelers who pass this way.

> Walter Dean Myers, "'I Actually Thought We Would Revolutionize the Industry'," in The New York Times Book Review, *November 9, 1986, p. 50.*

GENERAL COMMENTARY

RUDINE SIMS

[Walter Dean Myers] is a freelance writer who, in his novels, writes about what he calls "vertical living," living in the city. However, with one exception, his novels . . . are marked by a great deal of humor. Zora Neale Hurston (1958), writing about High John, the Conqueror, stated that "Heaven arms with love and laughter those it does not wish to see destroyed." Myers's work focuses on the love and laughter that is part of the Afro-American experience. Besides the novels, he has written some picture books for younger children, including some fantasy and some science fiction. His first published children's book, *Where Does the Day Go?,* focuses on differences—between day and night, between people.

Two of his picture books feature young Black boys. In *The Dancers* . . . , Michael meets ballet dancers and invites them, "uptown"; the dancers enjoy exchanging dance steps and eating soul food with Michael and his friends. In *Fly, Jimmy, Fly,* Jimmy uses his imagination to set himself flying above the city. It is Myers's unerring ear for Black speech and his

inclusion of such details as collard greens and corn bread that make the experiences memorable.

The Dragon Takes a Wife, his third picture book, is a departure—a fairy tale made contemporary, humorous, Afro-American, and controversial. Mabel Mae Jones, one of the sweetest and kindest fairies in the kingdom, tries to help Harry the Dragon win one of his battles with the Knight in Shining Armor so that Harry can win a wife. Mabel Mae is a brown-skinned, Afro-wearing beauty whose first words to Harry are "What's bugging you, baby?" Having decided that "I dig where you're coming from," she proceeds to try several rhyming incantations, such as "Fire be hotter and hotter than that. Turn Harry on so he can burn that cat." None of them work until she herself turns into a dragon and provides more direct assistance. Some Black teachers and librarians objected to the hip language and to the Geraldine/Flip Wilson-like characterization of Mabel Mae. Some whites, according to Myers, objected to a Black writer's appropriating the West European fairy tale form. . . . (pp. 92-3)

In a speech at a convention of the National Council of Teachers of English in San Francisco, Myers stated that an author writing about the urban scene must decide "where to put the exclamation points." He felt that there was pressure to emphasize the sensational, the sordid, at the expense of the rest of everybody living in the city, a pressure he resisted. Three of his four novels focus on groups of adolescents growing up, experiencing pain as well as love and laughter, but with the exclamation points behind the love and laughter. All presented in the first person, the novels have the air of adult remembrances of youthful times and youthful friends. (pp. 93-4)

[*Fast Sam, Cool Clyde, and Stuff*] is narrated by Francis/Stuff and is the story of the 116th Street Good People—the three title characters plus Gloria, Binky, Cap, Maria, and Debbie—who hang out together, support each other, and laugh and cry together. It is episodic, and the group members do deal with pain—Clyde's father is accidentally killed, Gloria's parents split up, Carnation Charlie dies—but mainly they deal with just living, learning, growing—Black urban style.

Mojo and the Russians features Dean and his gang of friends, including a white girl named Judy. While Kitty and Dean are having a bicycle race, Dean accidentally runs into Druscilla, the West Indian mojo lady, and knocks her down. She, in turn, threatens to "make his tongue split like a lizard's and his eyes to cross" and to "make his monkey ears fall off." Convinced that Druscilla has "fixed" him, Dean and his friends try to get him unfixed. . . . The situations they get into and out of are hilarious.

In *The Young Landlords,* Paul Williams and his friends from the Action Group—Gloria, Dean Bubba, Omar, and Jeannie—decide that they need to do something constructive with their lives and complain to a landlord about the condition of a tenement on Gloria's block. The landlord decides to abandon the building by selling it to Paul for $1.00. Thus, the group members become the young landlords. In carrying out their responsibilities, they have some fun and discover their own strengths. (p. 94)

The Myers humor, which is never derogatory, stems from a blend of situations, characters, and language. In *Fast Sam, Cool Clyde, and Stuff,* Sam and Clyde (dressed as Claudette) enter and win a dance contest. Another boy makes a pass at Clyde/Claudette, who takes off his wig and punches the offender. In *The Young Landlords,* Askia Ben Kenobi greets the landlords, who have come to collect rent, with "Do not speak until I have grasped the meaning of your aura!" and proceeds to chop up the bannister with karate blows.

But one of Myers's special gifts is his rendering of the style and essence of Black teenage rhetoric. Better than any of the other authors discussed [in this chapter: Lucille Clifton, Eloise Greenfield, Virginia Hamilton, and Sharon Bell Mathis], he captures many of the rhetorical qualities that Geneva Smitherman describes in *Talkin and Testifyin*—the proverbial statements, such as "Every streak of fat don't have a streak of lean"; the use of tonal semantics, such as "If you got the weight, you got to take the freight"; the image making and the hyperbole, such as "They said he had a gun and would shoot you if you sneezed wrong." He also captures the flavor of the verbal contests that boys (and apparently some girls) engage in. From *Fast Sam, Cool Clyde, and Stuff:* "If you were any uglier, they'd put your face in a museum and sell tickets to gorillas. The worst thing I could say about your mama is that you're her son. . . . If you ask me, you must be the retarded son of the Heartbreak of Psoriasis." And from the sidelines, "Hey Binky, you forgot this is national Be Nice to Ugly Week!" He also illustrates the tendency of Black teenagers to give nicknames that capture some feature of the individual—Weasel, Long Willie, Stuff, Carnation Charlie. Needless to say, he also includes a great number of specific details that bring to life the characters, their environment, and their situations.

The final novel, *It Ain't All for Nothin'*, is not at all humorous. Tippy lives with his religious grandmother until, at sixty-nine, she becomes afflicted badly with arthritis and "old age" and is taken to a nursing home. He must then go to live with his father, Lonnie, an ex-convict who has no concept of how to be a father and who has been making a living by stealing. Lonnie uses Tippy to get on welfare. At one point, Lonnie gets a job and seems about to break out of his pattern, but he is fired after a fight. He decides to pull just one final robbery and coerces Tippy into participating. One of Lonnie's friends, Bubba, is shot in the robbery, and Tippy cannot simply let him die, as Stone, the gang member with the gun, is determined to do. Tippy escapes from the house and seeks the help of a bus driver who had befriended him earlier. They call the police, and Lonnie and the gang are picked up. Even though Bubba dies and Lonnie is returned to prison, Tippy and Lonnie realize that Tippy made the right decision; he *had* to try to save Bubba and thereby save himself.

It Ain't All for Nothin' portrays a different side of city life than in other books by Myers. It is most similar to the Sharon Bell Mathis novels in its inclusion of harsh and grim realities. And, as in the Mathis books, the emphasis seems to be on the boy himself—on his strengths, on his will to save himself, and finally on his hope.

Meyers's work, then, mirrors the focus of the other four authors on some of the positive aspects of Afro-American experience— the good times, the idea that the love and the support of family, friends, and community can "prop you up on every leaning side," as a suitor promised in Zora Neale Hurston's *Jonah's Gourd Vine*. It also emphasizes the individual strengths and the inner resources that enable us to cope and to survive. (pp. 94-6)

> *Rudine Sims, "The Image-Makers," in* Shadow and Substance: Afro-American Experience in Contemporary Children's Fiction, *National Council of Teachers of English, 1982, pp. 79-102.*

THE DANCERS (1972)

A story with good potential and some humor doesn't quite come off, although it may appeal to many children because of the subject and its unusual setting. . . . [The] plot is fresh but not wholly believable. Michael goes with his father, who works at a theater, and is enthralled by ballet. His enthusiastic response prompts a ballerina, Yvonne, to talk to the small boy. He invites her to visit, she regretfully declines. But one day her car drives up to Michael's house, and she (with her partner and a violinist) perform in the street, set the children dancing, and then they all go into Michael's house for dinner, and Michael and friend Karen teach Yvonne the Chicken. Later the children see a ballet performance.

> *Zena Sutherland, in a review of "The Dancers," in* Bulletin of the Center for Children's Books, *Vol. 25, No. 11, July-August, 1972, p. 174.*

There is little material on the performing arts for the age group, but this remains a bland, disappointing attempt. . . . Nevertheless, despite the contrived action, it is encouraging to see boys dancing as well as girls and there is a friendly mixture of races. Anne Rockwell's paper doll-like drawings are colorful but add little to the very slight story.

> *Hilda Lapidus, in a review of "The Dancers," in* School Library Journal, *an appendix to* Library Journal, *September, 1972, p. 70.*

Myers at approximately six years old. From the author's collection.

THE BLACK PEARL AND THE GHOST; OR, ONE MYSTERY AFTER ANOTHER (1980)

These two static mysteries are neither well-written nor interesting. By means of a series of conversations between Detective Aramy and the inhabitants of Howloon Hotel, the theft of a black pearl is traced. In the second story, a ghost chaser named Dibble is summoned to Bleak Manor to rid it of creaking stairs, groans from the cellar, etc. By talking with Lord Bleek about the ghosts haunting the house and by consulting his ghost book, Dibble is able to drive out the spirits. No action, no suspense, and no development. Too bad that Robert Quackenbush's considerable artistic talents should be wasted on such trivia.

Janice P. Patterson, in a review of "The Black Pearl & The Ghost or One Mystery after Another," in Children's Book Review Service, *Vol. 8, No. 12, Spring, 1980, p. 113.*

Two very short, very broad spoofs in picture-book format. The first is as clunkingly obvious as "great detective" Dr. Aramy's mistakes when he is called to a resort hotel to solve the mystery of a stolen pearl. Dr. Aramy constantly interrupts the lined-up staff members' accounts of incidents surrounding the pearl's disappearance, accusing each in turn on the basis of far-fetched conclusions, until he finally hits home with the manager, the only one left. The outlandish solutions proposed by famous ghost catcher Mr. Dibble in the second story are less hollow and a bit more ingenious, but still pretty creaky. At least his contraptions—involving a silver bell on a silken cord, a one-eared black cat, chicken fat and honey on the stairs, etc.—all work, and Bleek Manor's ghost eventually packs up. Quackenbush writes some extra jokes into the pictures, but overall his illustrations are so loud that they drown out the words—a fate that the first story deserves and the second is too weak to overcome.

A review of "The Black Pearl and the Ghost or One Mystery after Another," in Kirkus Reviews, *Vol. XLVIII, No. 8, April 15, 1980, p. 514.*

The cheerfully colored, busy pictures for two short stories add nothing to creation of mood and perhaps are meant to indicate that both the detective story and the ghost story are not meant to be taken seriously. Both tales have the same format: the detective who investigates the theft of the priceless black pearl and the professional ghost catcher who investigates the ghostly noises in Bleek Manor are repeatedly and erroneously sure they've caught their prey. . . . The humor is slapstick, but it's there, and there's hardly a page without action.

Zena Sutherland, in a review of "The Black Pearl & The Ghost or One Mystery after Another, in Bulletin of the Center for Children's Books, *Vol. 33, No. 9, May, 1980, p. 180.*

THE LEGEND OF TARIK (1981)

"It came to pass" are the opening words in this book, suggesting we are in for magic and adventure, heroes and villains, with a final showdown between good and evil. Mr. Myers doesn't disappoint us. He has written what is nearly a compendium of devices used in such fiction.

Tarik has seen his father murdered by a sadistic brute who terrorizes the African countryside (historical time unspecified). Befriended by two old men, who also have scores to settle

with this same El Muerte, the boy undergoes a long period of systematic training that will prepare him to take his revenge.

The old men teach him the skills of a warrior, but more important they help him to see, hear and feel with uncommon facility, for without extraordinary qualities, as much spiritual as physical, he cannot hope to overcome an opponent who is the embodiment of evil. Tarik is given tasks to perform, and their successful completion brings him closer to manhood. While on these quests, encountering the magical and the terrifying, he learns to look at evil, to accept the truth and to use his intelligence with confidence.

Equipped with a magic sword, a powerful horse and the Crystal of Truth, Tarik sets out in the company of Stria, a girl whose passion for revenge far exceeds his own and whose portrayal is one of the book's strengths. Adventures come thick and fast. Comic relief is provided by a garrulous baker, who proves loyal in spite of his professed cowardice. The three companions move inexorably toward the final confrontation with El Muerte. The climax is, of course, predictable, as it should be in a tale of vengeance.

And as it should be in a legend, omens and prophetic dreams abound. Also conforming to the tradition of allegory, the characters are broadly drawn, some of them standing for a single quality: Faithfulness, obsession, wisdom, etc. Even so, the story does have a contemporary feeling, because moral questions of conduct are given a skeptical treatment, with a resultant ambiguity about their solutions.

In spite of a thinness of detail, particularly in descriptions of the physical setting, and a few unfortunate metaphors ("El Muerte's smile was like a white wound in the belly of a whale"), in balance it is an admirably paced novel, with plenty of action and enough about loyalty and courage to satisfy young readers who can find in parables and legends a clue to their own lives.

Malcolm Bosse, in a review of "The Legend of Tarik," in The New York Times Book Review, *July 12, 1981, p. 30.*

Frankly, I haven't encountered a line like "Men see what they want in the eyes of a woman" in more years than any of us would care to remember. Young adults today simply do not talk that way. But that's characteristic of *Legend of Tarik*. All the situational cliches are present. The hero is a brave young black boy who grows into manhood under the watchful and learned eyes of the gnarled but all knowing mentor (actually this book even has a backup mentor). . . . It's never explained, but one imagines that his quest is legendary. There is also a romantic interest. A young mysterious girl, who seems never to be on quite the same footing as the male protagonist, yet still manages to be near enough to the action for the required rescues.

Actually, this is an awful book. There is so much predictability in the shallow characters and situations that the mean spirited violence is almost welcome, but not quite. The number of beheadings, impalements and other vicious ways by which numerous individuals are dispatched could only be enjoyed by the most surfeited devotee of the current wave of horror flics. . . .

This book neither edifies nor satisfies—but why go on. Skip *Legend of Tarik,* buy a book with less pretensions and more meaning.

Alex Boyd, in a review of "The Legend of Tarik," in Voice of Youth Advocates, *Vol. 4, No. 4, October, 1981, p. 36.*

In some ways this story of medieval Africa has appeal and strength: it provides a much-needed fantasy hero who is black, it follows the classic pattern of Good triumphing over Evil, it is not overcrowded with characters or symbols or arcane terminology. It is weakened, however, by the slow start and equally slow pace, caused in part by the intermittent heaviness of the writing style. The characters are credible but drawn with little depth or nuance; this would not be an appropriate vehicle for the humor that distinguishes Myers' contemporary stories, but it could use a little lightness to offset the malevolence and violence of the book.

> *Zena Sutherland, in a review of "The Legend of Tarik," in* Bulletin of the Center for Children's Books, *Vol. 35, No. 3, November, 1981, p. 52.*

HOOPS (1981)

Skeptical of authority and afraid of emotional commitments, thanks in part to a father who abandoned him and his mother years before, 18-year-old basketball talent Lonnie Jackson is particularly suspicious of Cal Jones, former pro-ball player and sometime wino, who takes over coaching Lonnie's Harlem youth team. After a couple of run-ins, a tentative friendship develops between the two with Cal revealing to Lonnie much of his personal history and the story of his disqualification from the pros for involvement in sports betting. When gambling types put pressure on Cal again (this time to fix a tournament by keeping Lonnie benched), Lonnie's uncertainty resurfaces and their tenuous relationship is threatened. While somewhat uneven in the telling, Myers' story about trust and friendship, developed from an original screenplay by John Ballard, evolves a sharply etched image of Harlem, where sex and violence emerge naturally as part of the setting. Dialogue rings with authenticity, on-court action is colorful and well integrated into the story, and the author's dramatic conclusion is handled with poignancy and power.

> *Stephanie Zvirin, in a review of "Hoops," in* Book- list, *Vol. 78, No. 2, September 15, 1981, p. 98.*

We are almost inside Lonnie's mind, hoping and living with him, as he comes to terms with his situation as a talented young basketball player who may have an opportunity through a city-wide tournament to get out of Harlem and go someplace. (p. 442)

This is a hopeful as well as thought-provoking story, but also depressing and at times hard to get into. The language and thought processes are a black person's. The experiences drawn on are from a black perspective. There is some sex, some violence, and larceny seems to be a way of life. There is an enormous amount of soul-searching, of self-evaluation, of truth about actual situations because decisions cannot be put off until tomorrow. The only moment may be now.

You would need a mature twelve year old to get the message of promise and to overlook the larceny and some of the sex (no worse than most TV). In only one instance did the stealing demand any retribution. Also, the reader would have to be into basketball, because a fair amount of the action takes place on the court.

It is a good challenge to look at an area most of us know only through the papers. *Hoops* is hopeful and sensitive, and an experience of a seventeen-year-old's decision to become a young adult black person and not, as Cal says, a "nigger." (pp. 442-43)

> *Ruth Martin, in a review of "Hoops," in* Best Sell- ers, *Vol. 41, No. 11, February, 1982, pp. 442-43.*

This story offers the reader some fast, descriptive basketball action, a love story between Lonnie and girlfriend Mary-Ann, peer friendship problems, and gangster intrigues. Most importantly, however, it portrays the growth of a trusting and deeply caring father-son relationship between Cal and Lonnie. The story of this relationship is the best part of the book. An excellent section for booktalking is on pages 58-61 when Cal tells Lonnie about his former career with the pros.

Sometimes the theme of the urban basketball hero makes the story seem flat and predictable but there are poignant, human struggles that will appeal to any reader. Younger YAs with a strong interest in basketball will enjoy this one.

> *Patricia Berry, in a review of "Hoops," in* Voice of Youth Advocates, *Vol. 5, No. 1, April, 1982, p. 36.*

WON'T KNOW TILL I GET THERE (1982)

When Steve's middle-class Harlem parents take in Earl, a 13-year-old ex-delinquent, as a foster child, Steve's attempts to prove himself tough land him, his new brother and his two friends in the juvenile court, where the judge orders them to work the summer in an old people's home. Written in the form of Steve's journal, the novel interweaves the fight of the old people for acceptance and independence with Steve's struggle within his family to know and accept Earl on his own terms and the painful slow growth of friendship between the boys. In spite of the creaking plot, readers, as always with Myers, will love the dialogue, the fierce and funny repartee and the grotesque insults; and also the masterly control of dramatic scenes: the way in which bantering explodes into violent hostility, the move from slapstick to pathos, the sudden stabs of psychological insight. The overt didacticism is quite superfluous: excellent characterization clearly demonstrates Myers' theme that those whom we perceive in terms of labels and group stereotypes—old, Black, female, enemy, delinquent, deserting mother—turn out to be widely differing, surprising and interesting individuals when we allow ourselves to know them. (pp. 72-3)

> *Hazel Rochman, in a review of "Won't Know Till I Get There," in* School Library Journal, *Vol. 28, No. 9, May, 1982, pp. 72-3.*

The story's spark comes from Myers' special knack at making his kids seem real flesh-and-blood figures. Steve's comments throughout this diary-style recounting have an honest, down-to-earth ring that's inviting. Clear, too, are the dynamics of peer relationships; the emotional sparring between Steve and Earl and the tension that develops between Steve and best friend Hi-Note seem believable and right. The story rolls along nicely, with the increased understanding evidenced by Steve sure to be mirrored in the reader's mind.

> *Denise M. Wilms, in a review of "Won't Know Till I Get There," in* Booklist, *Vol. 78, No. 19, June 1, 1982, p. 1315.*

For the many teen-agers who perceive senior citizens to be alien and uninteresting, this novel will inspire empathy and shatter a few stereotypes. (p. 26)

Stephen's gradual rapprochement with both Earl and the senior residents is predictable, and readers will crave more details about Earl and his real mother. Also, though the residents are well differentiated as characters, they are often used to relay the book's general messages about the plight of the elderly: the stereotypical view of them as sexless, sedentary and non-productive; the loss of government benefits when they marry; discrimination against them in business.

Nevertheless, the novel is engrossing. The urban setting is skillfully evoked, and only a few adult-sounding thoughts and expressions mar the otherwise natural, youthful tone of Stephen's first-person narrative. Mr. Myers ably integrates his dual themes of complex family relationships and senior citizens' problems. And, despite the seriousness of these themes, there is ample, appropriate humor. (pp. 26-7)

> *Diane Gersoni Edelman, in a review of "Won't Know Till I Get There," in* The New York Times Book Review, *June 13, 1982, pp. 26-7.*

THE NICHOLAS FACTOR   (1983)

[Myers] explores an intriguing idea here: does an elite group have the right to impose its views on society, even if it believes its vision is right? Gerald is a college student who's asked to join the Crusade Society, a snobby campus organization. He's approached by a government agent who wants him to keep an eye on the group, heightening his already aroused suspicions about Crusader activities. After a few meetings, he's off to a Peruvian jungle with them on a do-gooder mission with an Inca tribe. But Gerald feels growing mistrust, which he shares with fellow Crusader Jennifer. Suddenly, the project is called off and the Crusaders are being hustled out of Peru, but Gerald and Jennifer discover a village filled with sick and dying Indians, caused by a Crusader "inducement" meant to accomplish their mission. The chase is on, as the leaders of the Crusaders realize what the two have found out. The reference to the Crusaders of yore is telling, for they were religious zealots who felt a holy obligation to impose their will. Myers probes and makes one think as it applies to implementing one's vision of the world. A disturbing, powerful work.

> *A review of "The Nicholas Factor," in* Publishers Weekly, *Vol. 223, No. 11, March 18, 1983, p. 70.*

One develops a deep regard for Gerald. While trying to penetrate the ominous leadership of the Society, he is also analyzing and trying to accept the relationship he had had with his father before his recent death. The book does not deliver the tension and sense of danger it tells us about, and too many arcane motives must be explained in the last chapter. But because the characters are realistically presented, the setting is exotic and the idea of the Crusader's Society is intriguing, this should be an appealing, popular adventure.

> *Lucy V. Hawley, in a review of "The Nicholas Factor," in* School Library Journal, *Vol. 30, No. 1, September, 1983, p. 138.*

There is no shortage of strange goings-on in the jungles of Peru, and Gerald's quest for information leads him on some high-speed adventures. There are some difficulties with this book, including a farfetched and not always credible plot and characters that seem stiff and distant, unlike some of the engaging characters in the author's other teen novels. Surprisingly

though, this book seems to work well as a story, and once it is begun most readers will be hooked until the end. (p. 280)

> *Becky Johnson Xavier, in a review of "The Nicholas Factor," in* Voice of Youth Advocates, *Vol. 6, No. 5, December, 1983, pp. 279-80.*

TALES OF A DEAD KING   (1983)

Rudimentary skulduggery on an Egyptian archaeological dig—for kids who take to Myers' no-frills storytelling, simple set-ups, and good sense. Teens John Robie and Karen Lacey find themselves at a seedy Aswan hotel—with only a mysterious note to explain the absence of Dr. Erich Leonhardt, John's unknown archaeologist great-uncle. Egyptian-enthusiast John, less put-out than archaeology-buff Karen, is more inclined to stick around; he also gives a thought to the family connection. But signs that "someone doesn't want us hanging around" keep stubborn smartie Karen on the spot too. The ensuing one-upmanship between the two, conveyed with a shade of self-mocking rue from John's viewpoint, is the story's strongest feature—though Myers does craftily manage a tie-in with the Tutankhamun show (supposed source of John's interest) and with some basic Egyptology: the unknown site of monotheist Akhenaton's modest burial. John guesses that the nonexistent ship *Sibuna*, mentioned in Dr. Leonhardt's letter, stands for Anubis, the Egyptian god of the underworld—meaning that somebody was after him. Karen reasons from his note-paper (never mind, flimsily, how) that the professor is still around; she remembers that "an Ahmed somebody" was said to have been helping him. . . . Dr. Leonhardt is found, the tomb properly isn't—and had it been, the professor notes, it would have held no treasure: the greedy kidnappers had nothing to gain. As for John and Karen, a little real archaeological work is in the offing. "I'd really dig that," says John—(almost) bringing down the curtain on a consciously, likably corny note. Unlike more strenuous efforts, the one grows on you by degrees.

> *A review of "Tales of a Dead King," in* Kirkus Reviews, *Juvenile Issue, Vol. LI, No. 21, November 1, 1983, p. J205.*

As usual Myers tells an entertaining story. . . . The intrigue will entice youthful readers; along the way they'll become acquainted with some Egyptian place names, and a few may develop an interest in archeology. The plot is easily followed. Unfortunately, the book does not measure up to Myers' earlier work in depth or quality. The events are improbable; the characters never rise above the level of stereotypes. Even the American teenage protagonists (a male narrator and a female who is as much foil as partner) are limited in development. Readers who enjoy watching reruns of predictable-plot shows like "Dragnet" will probably relish the book. The story will carry a reader along and thus may prove useful with reluctant readers attracted to adventure or intrigue, and it would be suitable individual reading for mystery-lovers of both sexes in grades 5-8.

> *Alan McLeod, in a review of "Tales of a Dead King," in* The ALAN Review, *Vol. 11, No. 2, Winter, 1984, p. 29.*

John's parents had read an article about a girl named Karen who'd been chosen to work on an Egyptian dig with Dr. Erich Leonhardt; since Erich was her uncle, John's mother asked if John could go also. That's how John, the narrator, found himself stranded in Aswan with a not-too-friendly peer and a note explaining that Great-uncle Erich had been called away. Question: did he just go or was he forced to go? . . . This has an interesting setting, the appeals of action and danger, and a satisfying ending, for the two do find the kidnapped archaeologist and rescue him. It's adequately written, but it's weak in characterization and unconvincing in its plot development.

Zena Sutherland, in a review of "Tales of a Dead King," in Bulletin of the Center for Children's Books, *Vol. 37, No. 5, January, 1984, p. 93.*

MOTOWN AND DIDI: A LOVE STORY (1984)

This is a tender, poignant love story set against a backdrop of junkies, threats, danger, and death. Hell-bent on getting away from the streets of Harlem by attending college across the country, Didi feels trapped by her mother's frail mental and physical health and by her brother Tony's worsening heroin habit. Motown, almost 18 and fed up with foster homes, lives in an abandoned building, takes whatever honest work he can get, and banks his money. The two come together when Motown rescues Didi from the area pusher's thugs, who attack her for trying to turn the pusher in to the police. Given his background, Motown's sensitivity is unusual, but he's been befriended by an old bookstore owner who lends him books and philosophizes about life with him. Having been emotionally bruised many times, Motown is afraid to open up to Didi, while Didi herself fights her growing attraction to Motown because he does not fit into her planned future. However, the pair cannot keep from falling in love with each other. Though the story as a whole is nondidactic, a strong, underlying anti-drug abuse message comes through. Myers obviously cares about his two main characters, and readers will, too. (p. 212)

Sally Estes, in a review of "Motown and Didi: A Love Story," in Booklist, *Vol. 81, No. 3, October 1, 1984, pp. 211-12.*

Myers at age seventeen, just home from army basic training. From the author's collection.

In spite of all the obstacles [faced by the characters] the reader is left with the feeling "love will out."

Walter Myers again takes the positive without denying the existence of the negative in his most powerful, best written novel yet. Writing about what he knows best, the inner city, Myers tells a story with a lesson for all.

C. Anne Webb, in a review of "Motown and Didi: A Love Story," in The ALAN Review, *Vol. 12, No. 2, Winter, 1985, p. 31.*

Two minor characters from *It Ain't All for Nothin'* reappear in a poignant story of a romance that blooms amidst the tough, troubled streets of Harlem. . . . The novel points out the individual and social costs of denying one's past and people and makes a potent anti-drug statement through Tony's harrowing experiences. As in *It Ain't All for Nothin'*, the author forgoes his customary levity. Instead, he humanely balances the pestilence and harshness of his characters' environment with a euphoric, improbable romance—suggesting there is good to be found and choices to be made on even the toughest streets. (pp. 186-87)

Nancy C. Hammond, in a review of "Motown and Didi: A Love Story," in The Horn Book Magazine, *Vol. LXI, No. 2, March-April, 1985, pp. 186-87.*

Self-reliant by necessity, [Motown and Didi] teach each other to trust. Each brings different strengths to the relationship, which is portrayed in a non-sexist manner.

Motown and Didi are admirable heroes in a book with many bad guys and negative images of Harlem. The dearth of positive role models makes one wonder where these two youngsters got their sense of values. Given the book's focus on some of the harsher realities of ghetto life, it's a shame that Myers didn't balance those images with some of the positives.

Still, the book is well written and fast-moving. . . . The struggle to find one's place in society while reaching for a dream will appeal to teenagers.

Judy Rogers, in a review of "Motown and Didi: A Love Story," in Interracial Books for Children Bulletin, *Vol. 15, No. 8, November-December, 1985, p. 19.*

THE OUTSIDE SHOT (1984)

In Myers' emotionally involving sequel to *Hoops,* Lonnie Jackson has found a way out of Harlem—if he can hang on to his basketball scholarship to a small Midwestern college. Totally unprepared both academically and socially for this new world, he struggles to fit in, keep out of trouble and in pocket money, please the coaches and study. The girl he is interested in, one of the few blacks on campus, thinks he's a male chauvinist. Several members of the team think he's a handy sucker for their point-fixing schemes. And Eddie, an autistic child at the local hospital where he works, thinks he's wonderful. While the games are exciting and the gambling racket suspenseful, what sets this book apart from other sports stories is Lonnie's growth in his new environment. Small moments, as when Lonnie suddenly realizes that Eddie does not want to see his bullying father humiliated in a game of one-on-one, show readers his gradual growth during this first semester. This novel should reach an even wider audience than *Hoops,* since Lonnie's college experiences will be relevant to many teenagers graduating from high school today. Altogether, this is a deeply moving, believable story of a very American rite of passage into adulthood. (pp. 135-36)

Carolyn Caywood, in a review of "The Outside Shot," in School Library Journal, *Vol. 31, No. 3, November, 1984, pp. 135-36.*

Walter Dean Myers writes about ordinary people in ordinary situations—but with concern and a sense of drama. His stories are realistic and low-key but optimistic. His *Fast Sam, Cool Clyde and Stuff,* for example, is one of the best teenage problem novels, not nearly as widely recognized as it should be.

Lonnie Jackson, who first appeared in *Hoops,* a basketball story set in Harlem, is not one of his strongest characters. Often he seems to go with the flow, letting things happen to him rather than making things happen. But in this latest book, Lonnie leaves Harlem and learns a lot about himself—and about the day-to-day problems of the college athlete and of a black youth in a predominantly white midwestern school.

Young readers who identify with the cool, resourceful but sometimes confused rookie will learn a lot, too. Sherry, the track star, teaches Lonnie to respect a woman as an equal. Eddie, the emotionally disturbed child he helps, brings out the best in Lonnie and shows him something about his own potential. Colin, his white roommate, and his family show him that there are hardships and warm family relationships outside of Harlem. Even Dr. Weiser, the sarcastic history professor who is prejudiced against all athletes, makes a point about the importance of academic regimen. And in Ray, the former college player he meets, he sees the disillusionment of the has-been athlete who doesn't make it in the pros.

The Outside Shot is more than a basketball story, but there is enough action on the court to satisfy the young reader who thinks he's going to make it to the big time with athletic skills. When Lonnie says, "I told myself that I wasn't ever going to give up. . . . If I had an outside shot I was going to take it," he's talking about more than basketball. (p. 95)

Beth Nelms, Ben Nelms, and Linda Horton, "A Brief but Troubled Season: Problems in YA Fiction," in English Journal, *Vol. 74, No. 1, January, 1985, pp. 92-5.*

[*The Outside Shot*] is a remarkable story, one that seems real and uncontrived.

YAs who like sports stories will love this one, especially older YAs who can appreciate the subtleties of relationships and Lonnie's maturation process as well as the details of the game. YAs interested in stories about black students trying to find a way to adjust to predominantly white schools will also find this story fascinating. Highly recommended for a number of reasons: the male perspective; the black perspective; the realistic view of athletics and college life; and mostly, because it is a good story about a most sympathetic character.

[Claire S. Rosser], in a review of "The Outside Shot," in Kliatt Young Adult Paperback Book Guide, *Vol. XXI, No. 3, April, 1987, p. 14.*

MR. MONKEY AND THE GOTCHA BIRD: AN ORIGINAL TALE (1984)

The celebrated novelist presents a just-for-fun tale, in rhythmic cadences that boys and girls will find infectious and will want

to imitate. "One day Monkey be thinking how he big stuff. He walking around with nose in air. Got flower in hair. He no see Gotcha Bird. . . ." So pride is nearly Monkey's downfall. Only fast thinking will save him from becoming Gotcha's dinner. In feverish sequences, the cunning captive interests the bird in other creatures as entrees. Monkey's final triumph is serving up Gotcha to the king of the jungle, through an adroit maneuver. [Leslie] Morrill's pictures in hot colors enhance the nonstop action and the atmosphere of the tropical setting. (pp. 87-8)

A review of "Mr. Monkey and the Gotcha Bird: An Original Tale," in Publishers Weekly, *Vol. 226, No. 25, December 21, 1984, pp. 87-8.*

Using rhythmic language and lots of humor in an original tale with folkloric qualities, Myers reveals how Mr. Monkey outsmarts the Gotcha Bird, who wants to eat him for supper. . . . The language, which reflects an African/Caribbean oral tradition, is wonderful when read aloud but may cause confusion among young readers: "Monkey like he live there"; "Mr. Fish love you eat he." . . . [The pages] carry just enough text to describe the activity shown. A perfect coordination of text and illustrations.

Helen E. Williams, in a review of "Mr. Monkey and the Gotcha Bird: An Original Tale," in School Library Journal, *Vol. 31, No. 5, January, 1985, p. 66.*

Myers offers an original folktale that follows traditional patterns closely enough to have a ring of authenticity. Told in a patois that lends itself very well to a storyteller's dramatization, this follows the crafty maneuverings of Monkey, who is snagged by the Gotcha Bird for supper. . . . The story's inherent humor is expanded by Morrill's vivacious illustrations. . . . (pp. 847-48)

Denise M. Wilms, in a review of "Mr. Monkey and the Gotcha Bird: An Original Tale," in Booklist, *Vol. 81, No. 12, February 15, 1985, pp. 847-48.*

ADVENTURE IN GRANADA; THE HIDDEN SHRINE (1985)

This concise, fast-paced adventure-mystery [*The Hidden Shrine*] focuses on the attempts of three teens to find and expose the thieves who are stealing antique artifacts from the temples of Hong Kong. Chris, 16, and Ken, 14, expect to be bored in Hong Kong while anthropologist/professor mom participates in a study with the father of their new friend, Won Li Hwuang, so their investigation begins as "something-to-do." It becomes more sincere as the pursuers are soon pursued, and several life-threatening near-misses occur. This slim volume with its short chapters—average six pages—hinders the full development of characters, but the suspense is well-paced and enticing.

JoAnn Butler Henry, in a review of "The Hidden Shrine," in School Library Journal, *Vol. 32, No. 6, February, 1986, p. 98.*

[*Adventure in Granada* is a] light, fast-paced adventure that might appeal to fans of "The Hardy Boys" and similar series. This brief novel features two American teenagers and their attempt to clear a Spanish friend of the suspicion that he has stolen a valuable artifact from a local church. While the story certainly moves right along, none of the characters are really developed, and the Spanish setting is not utilized at all. The story could just as easily be taking place virtually anywhere else in the world. A disappointment.

Elizabeth Mellett, in a review of "Adventure in Granada," in School Library Journal, *Vol. 32, No. 8, April, 1986, p. 91.*

Seventeen-year-old Chris and his fourteen-year-old brother Ken enjoy an enviable life-style accompanying their mother, anthropologist Dr. Carla Arrow, to exotic locations where she researches local culture. In *Adventure in Granada* the boys befriend Pedro Barcia while their mother is studying Spanish gypsies. When Pedro is accused of stealing an old cross from a local church, the boys set out to help him prove his innocence. They are followed by mysterious strangers, run off the road by a car, and Pedro's goat is kidnapped before the three satisfactorily unravel the mystery. In *The Hidden Shrine,* Dr. Arrow is working with Hwuang Ton Li at the University of Hong Kong. His son, Won Li, tells the boys that artifacts have been disappearing from several area temples. When the three begin to investigate, someone tries to ram their boat, and they know they're on the thieves' trail. In both books the adventure and intrigue gain an immediacy through Myers' skilled use of Chris as narrator. The crisp dialogue flows naturally, blending humor and sibling quips with the boys' attempts to hide their adventures from their mother. The brief texts and exciting pace will attract older reluctant readers as well as younger adventure fans to this new series.

Linda Callaghan, in a review of "Adventure in Granada" and "The Hidden Shrine," in Booklist, *Vol. 82, No. 15, April 15, 1986, p. 1226.*

SWEET ILLUSIONS (1987)

An intellectual and emotional workbook for teen-agers on the subject of pregnancy.

The author gives each of his 14 fictional characters (five unwed mothers, five fathers, four family members or other interested parties) a chapter to describe his or her response to sudden parenthood. The characters have urban, lower-middle-class backgrounds, are mostly black or Hispanic, and face the situation with varying realistic combinations of confusion, fear, anger, hope and indifference. Myers tries to be nonjudgmental, but few of the men display courage or a sense of responsibility, and the one woman who has an abortion becomes unstable. The narratives are tenuously linked together, and finished with a **"Seven Years Later"** epilogue, but plot definitely takes a back seat to didactic purpose. Each chapter ends with several blank ruled pages; readers are invited to think about what they've just read and to write (on their own paper if they're reading a library copy) a relevant letter, day-dream or essay.

There's no physical violence or drug abuse here, but these tales are nonetheless very scary, and adolescent readers will find them involving and disturbing. (pp. 228-29)

A review of "Sweet Illusions," in Kirkus Reviews, *Vol. LV, No. 3, February 1, 1987, pp. 228-29.*

This is an unusual YA novel because the readers are invited, at the end of each chapter, to participate in the story by imagining they are the narrator. . . . Reading [each character's story] brings home the truth of the tremendous responsibility a pregnancy and a baby is, and each chapter will stimulate the reader's thoughts and feelings. Helping YAs imagine themselves in this situation is not only a good way to initiate a writing project,

it also helps teenagers avoid the predicament the characters are in.

There are blank pages in the format for the reader's responses, but everywhere are notes saying that if the book is from the library, separate sheets of paper should be used. Teachers could make good use of this exercise in sex education classes or any forum for a discussion of teenage pregnancy—with teenage boys as well as girls.

[Claire S. Rosser], in a review of "Sweet Illusions," in Kliatt Young Adult Paperback Book Guide, *Vol. XXI, No. 3, April, 1987, p. 27.*

Put together by Myers under the auspices of the Teachers & Writers Collaborative of New York City, this is one of those books that might well be passed over by librarians because of its write-in format and obvious applicability as a teaching tool. That would be a shame because the book is an astute, realistic consideration of some of the problems associated with teenage pregnancy, valuable for personal reading as well as classroom discussion. It also offers excellent perspectives on teenage fathers, who are too often slighted. Though it is fiction, *Sweet Illusions* reads a lot like fact. . . . Myers' profiles are quick and clever; his characters, stubborn, confused, and vulnerable, draw substance and individuality from tough, savvy dialogue and credible backdrops. He poses hard questions, steering readers gently while encouraging them to become extensions of the people whose lives they read about by writing down their responses to thought-provoking concerns: write to Harry (whom you've met only once) that he has fathered your child; you are Gloria—speculate about what your life will be like in 10 years; imagine you are Billy and explain how you would convince a hardheaded friend to take responsibility for his son. But whether readers finally decide to supply written response or not, they will still find much to consider and discuss in Myers' unusual and important book, which can serve as an excellent, highly accessible adjunct to nonfiction materials on the subject.

Stephanie Zvirin, in a review of "Sweet Illusions," in Booklist, *Vol. 83, No. 20, June 15, 1987, p. 1591.*

CRYSTAL (1987)

Black and beautiful, sixteen-year-old Crystal had been spotted during a commercial made at her church, and now she is launched on a career as a model. Her mother is anxious to have Crystal succeed and advises her daughter to expect and accept some disadvantages; her father wants to protect his child's innocence and integrity. It is Crystal herself, however, who decides (partly because of a producer's sexual overtures, partly because of another young model's tragic end, partly because she knows she's missing a social life that's normal in adolescence) to stop modeling. The milieu is convincingly detailed, the characterization and storyline equally believable. Myers writes with an easy narrative flow that smoothly blends plot and nuances in relationships.

Zena Sutherland, in a review of "Crystal," in Bulletin of the Center for Children's Books, *Vol. 40, No. 9, May, 1987, p. 175.*

Unfortunately, the author seems uncomfortable with female sexuality, having Crystal "pretend" for photos and having her feel embarrassment at men being attracted to her, remaining unmoved by local boys and rock stars alike; and his apparent unfamiliarity with modeling leads to some awkward writing.

Still, there is enough storyline and atmosphere to make the book work for Myers fans and girls curious about modeling. And no one can complain about the moral.

A review of "Crystal," in Kirkus Reviews, *Vol. LV, No. 8, May 1, 1987, p. 723.*

The plot is sometimes awkward, and the ultimate message is heavy, but Rowena's victimization by home and career is evoked with sadness and restraint. Myers' honesty about the glamour as well as the sordid side of the modeling scene will draw teens, who will sympathize with Crystal as she resists the bright world that tries to lure her from who she is.

Hazel Rochman, in a review of "Crystal," in Booklist, *Vol. 83, No. 19, June 1, 1987, p. 1516.*

Kay (Rasmus) Nielsen

1886-1957

Danish illustrator of folk and fairy tales.

Nielsen ranks among the giants of the Golden Age of children's book illustration for the extravagant yet meticulously detailed paintings he created for deluxe gift book editions of classic tales. He is recognized as an especially original and imaginative artist who, along with illustrators Arthur Rackham and Edmund Dulac, raised illustrated books for children to new heights of sophistication. Influenced by the decorative style of Aubrey Beardsley as well as by Middle Eastern and Oriental art, Nielsen introduced children to an exotic world of fantasy and mystery which often bordered on the grotesque. Combining the technique of early Italian paintings with the ornamental detail of Persian miniatures and the asymmetry, strong lines, and large, empty spaces of Japanese woodcuts, he created pictures in watercolor and pen-and-ink which frequently incorporate decorative motifs such as stripes and circles. Characteristically dense yet stylized, these illustrations are noted for their combination of strength and delicacy and for their haunting, melancholy effect on viewers. Nielsen's slender, often slightly distorted characters strike elaborate poses before tapestried backgrounds rich with symbolism, attributes which reflect his passion for the theater and his fascination with design.

Brought up among the artistic elite of Denmark and later educated in Paris, Nielsen established his reputation primarily with four books originally published in England: *In Powder and Crinoline* (1913), a collection of retellings by Sir Arthur Quiller-Couch retitled *Twelve Dancing Princesses* in the United States; *East of the Sun and West of the Moon: Old Tales from the North* (1914), a collection of fifteen Norse folktales by Peter Christen Asbjörnsen and Jörgen Moe which contains Nielsen's most well-received illustrations; Hans Christian Andersen's *Fairy Tales* (1924); and Jacob and Wilhelm Grimm's *Hansel and Gretel and Other Stories* (1925). A fifth book, *Red Magic: A Collection of the World's Best Fairy Tales from All Countries* (1930), is a compilation by Romer Wilson of tales ranging from Charles Perrault's "Bluebeard" to modern nonsense tales. Although it is considered a brave attempt at stylistic experimentation, *Red Magic* is usually thought to lack the decoration and subtlety of Nielsen's previous works.

Nielsen began illustrating books for children when London's Leicester Galleries, impressed with his 1912 exhibition of black and white drawings for the unpublished *The Book of Death*, commissioned Nielsen to paint twenty-four watercolors as illustrations for *In Powder and Crinoline*. Pleased with the book's fine reception, Leicester Galleries then commissioned *East of the Sun and West of the Moon*, a work in which Nielsen's firsthand knowledge of Scandinavian landscape and folklore revealed itself in subject matter and feeling. After the First World War, Nielsen began to fashion sets and costumes for elaborate productions at the Danish State Theater as the collaborator of actor and producer Johannes Poulsen. Nielsen continued to illustrate books and to work with Poulsen until 1936, when the collaborators were invited to come to Hollywood. Following Poulsen's death in 1938, Nielsen began working for the Walt Disney Studios, where he designed the "Night

on Bald Mountain'' sequence for the film *Fantasia*. The post-Second World War period marked a shift in public taste from an interest in fantasy to a concentration on realism and naturalism. Nielsen never regained favor in either the United States or his native Denmark: he created four murals for California schools and libraries, but died in penniless obscurity. However, when the early 1970s brought a resurgence of interest in the illustrators of the Golden Age, especially among adult collectors, Nielsen's works were once again made accessible for study and appreciation.

Critics applaud Nielsen's creativity, extraordinary artistry, sense of design, and ability to conceptualize dreams and evoke atmosphere. They also acclaim his theatrical expertise in staging his characters like actors and producing backgrounds of exceptional beauty and balance. Although they question whether his sophistication and tendency towards the erotic is suitable for children, they agree that Nielsen's interpretation of familiar tales has made unique and memorable contributions to children's literature.

(See also *Something about the Author*, Vol. 16.)

AUTHOR'S COMMENTARY

Both my father and mother were artists. My father, Professor Martinius Nielsen, was in his youth an actor in the classical repertoire. He became the leading and managing director of the Dagmartheater in Copenhagen, which under his directorate became the modern literary stage.

My mother, Oda Nielsen, was actress to the court of the royal theater in Copenhagen. In her youth she lived in Paris and brought home the great French repertoire from the eighties. Later she joined the Dagmartheater and the repertoire thereon. Her love for the French she kept in her song (repertoire Yvette Gilbert) and she also became the interpretress of the songs of the Old Danish folklore.

In this tense atmosphere of art, I was brought up. I remember such men as Ibsen, Bjornsen, Lie, Grieg, Sinding, Brandes and many others probably unknown to the American public. Since early boyhood I have been drawing. When the Sagas were read to me I drew down the people therein. Anything I heard about I tried to put in situations on paper. I heard much and saw much concerning art, but I never really intended to be an artist myself.

When I was twelve years of age I was taken out of school and given my own teachers. I had a vague idea of being a medical man, but when I was seventeen I suddenly broke off from books and went to Paris to study art.

I lived in Paris at Montparnasse for seven years and I frequented several schools of art. First the "Académie Julien" under Jean Paul Laurence; thereafter "Collarossi" under Kristian Krog, and several others; the last was Lucien Simon. I worked and lived in the usual routine of French school life, always working from nature, but in my hours away from the school I did drawings out of my imagination. . . . Or, inspired from reading, I did drawings to Heine, Verlaine, Hans Andersen. These drawings, most of them done in black and white, became numerous and in 1910 they were seen by London people and an exhibition was offered by Dowdeswel and Dowdeswel.

In 1911 I left Paris for London. In 1912 I had my first show held by Dowdeswel and Dowdeswel, consisting of the drawings done in my Paris days. After this I worked for England entirely.

From 1918-1922 I worked on a Danish translation from the original ***Thousand Nights and a Night*** (***Arabian Nights***), unpublished, and in the same period I did a series of settings for the Royal Theater in Copenhagen: Shakespeare, *The Tempest*; Oehlenschlaeger, *Aladdin*; Sibelius, *Scaramouche*; Magnussen, *The Dream of a Poet*.

I was brought up in a classical view concerning art, but I remember I loved the Chinese drawings and carvings in my mother's room brought home from China by her father. And this love for the works of art from the East has followed me. My artistic wandering started with the early Italians over Persia, India, to China. (pp. 173-75)

Kay Nielsen, "Kay Nielsen's Own Story," in The Horn Book Magazine, *Vol. XXI, No. 3, May-June, 1945, pp. 173-75.*

GENERAL COMMENTARY

GEORGE MATHER RICHARDS

Often overloaded with a delicate tracery of beautiful design and obsessed by a grotesquery which is not kin to the imagination of a child, yet in the illustration [from ***East of the Sun and West of the Moon*** titled **"The North Wind goes over the Sea,"** Kay Nielsen] has, like Rackham, sensed the spirit of the tale. It is a very north North Wind and a very Scandinavian North Wind that he has given us. Without doubt ***East of the Sun and West of the Moon*** he is bound and a strange and dangerous and wonderful place the little princess-to-be will find it.

Here, side by side with essential feeling of the incident, there came to the artist's vision a strong, simple and highly decorative composition. As a general thing, however, Nielsen is generally moved by the decorative element primarily, with character almost entirely subordinated to æsthetic requirements, so that his appeal is more direct to the trained vision of the adult than to the mind of the child. (p. 89)

George Mather Richards, "Pen and Brush in Fairy Land," in Arts & Decoration, *Vol. XII, No. II, December 15, 1919, pp. 88-9.*

MARTIN BIRNBAUM

[Kay Nielsen has] a graceful, vigorous, graphic style which London at once recognized and applauded [at his first exhibition]. The unapproachable greatness of Aubrey Beardsley, the splendors of Dulac and Parrish, or the distinct personal charm of Rackham, did not interfere with his success in any way, for all the critics realized that Nielsen's talents were original and of a very unusual kind. The incisive line was his own, and his fairyland less sombre than Rackham's. The extremely delicate and transparent color left the drawing to take its part as a graceful woven pattern more clearly than in a drawing by Dulac. He seemed from the very beginning to be able to make an author's single phrase the pretext for delightful landscape vistas and visions of delicate beauty. Swathed in amusing fripperies, his elusive princesses, so diaphanous and light and dignified, and so far removed from the common level of mankind, are drawn in just the right spirit,—not a single element of comedy or pathos in their fragile lives having been missed. Their singular daintiness, and their artificial but attractive grace, are in astounding contrast with such a drawing as **"Shadows of Night."** Here Nielsen vindicates his right to be deemed an imaginative draughtsman of a rare order in the realm of sinister mystery and of the macabre. The drawings in a similar vein of our own Herbert Crowley are the only works we can think of by a living man, whose technique and power can be compared with Nielsen's and it will be interesting to follow his incursions into the field of satirical caricature where he is rigorous in the suppression of certain details. Several examples inspired by the Great War are powerful, and impressive, although he does not indulge in the magnificent hatreds of Raemaekers. . . . We love him best, however, as the illustrator of **Hans Christian Andersen's *Tales,*** for in these the gifts which made him a cosmopolitan favorite and celebrity are most obvious. He handles with great skill the author's most delicious impertinences. The wistful melancholy figures, which recall Heine's bitter-sweet philosophy, are bordered by fascinating filigree work, and the exquisite accessories and embroideries merely accentuate the refinement and subtle beauty of the central figures. Where a native Scandinavian accent is coupled with his naïveté and quaint humour, as in the drawings for ***East of the Sun and West of the Moon,*** Nielsen is inimitable. His most intricate inventions never seem laboured. Controlled in a measure by Norse ornamental traditions, he reaches an absolute equality with the poetical text, and it is a genuine pleasure to reach the oasis of a Kay Nielsen picture in a journey through the printed pages of the book. Sometimes the designs come into existence through all manner of borrowings, the spoils of many altars. Not infrequently he forces the note of the grotesque, or indulges too freely in amusing anachronisms and to this day there are details, like the dripping candles and drifting spangles, which have the Beardsley or the Conder savour. At the same time, he has mounted so freely and easily into a realm entirely his own that we can enthusiastically join the London and continental throngs which have long since surrendered to the intensity of conviction which we feel in these small works. (pp. 79-82)

Martin Birnbaum, "Kay Nielsen," in his Introductions: Painters, Sculptors, and Graphic Artists, *Frederic Fairchild Sherman, 1919, pp. 78-82.*

JASMINE BRITTON

Kay Nielsen arrived in New York carrying a portfolio of pictures, but with a gifted mind, skilled fingers, and an established place of twenty years' honor in the book world and libraries of America, London, and Paris. He is a perfectionist; he is exacting, meticulous; he brings rare detachment in judgment to his art. For this reason he works slowly, but with driving perseverance. He will not let go of an art problem until he gets it, in sweltering heat, midnight, Saturdays, Sundays, even on Christmas Day. He would not stop even then but for the protests and pleading of Mrs. Nielsen, eager to prepare delectable Danish food for the holidays and to enjoy good friends. On and on his ideal drives him. Intensely serious, silently looking and looking, a somber Dane, he shakes his head over the problem. Even the dogs slink by until at long last the picture comes right and one more minor crisis has been passed. When he submits a picture for the first time, he is doubtful and nervous. It is something like stage fright. Yet he has a sure sense of balance and proportion. When two students from the Otis Art Institute

"Don't drink!" cried out the little Princess, springing to her feet; "I would rather marry a gardener!" Illustration by Kay Nielsen from In Powder and Crinoline: Old Fairy Tales, *by Sir Arthur Quiller-Couch. Hodder & Stoughton, 1913. Reproduced by permission of the publisher.*

came one day, he took all the time in the world to talk over clearly and explicitly their questions on perspective and balance. Still he always insists he cannot talk and above all that he could never be a teacher.

Mrs. Nielsen smilingly says, "Kay is slow. He says he could really paint another ten years on this mural, but he plans and he is on time according to the schedule and as you can see it's good. He is always good!" (pp. 168-69)

[Many] will have an opportunity to see the Nielsen mural [, **"The First Spring,"** in Los Angeles's Central Junior High School Library]. The other day a note came from Gladys English of the Public Library which said,

> Kay Nielsen's mural has held me under its spell ever since I saw it. What a wonderful thing it is to have in Los Angeles for all the children to enjoy. I hope other schools will make annual pilgrimages to Central Junior High School to see it.
>
> (p. 170)

The students of Central Junior High School feel that [**"The First Spring"**] is completely their mural. They chose the subject. They saw it from the first sketch to the completed picture. They hung in at the open windows after school and offered suggestions and free advice. One boy begged Kay Nielsen to hurry and finish it before he graduated. Another boy now in senior high school has returned several times to see the progress made, while still another wrote from a hospital bed in France to ask about the library's new picture. Several of the young people have begged that the animals and plants they cherished be included in the painting—a starfish, a field mouse, lady bugs, and a four-leaf clover. One day a fat boy of thirteen, slow of speech and profoundly thoughtful, said, "How do you like to be an artist, Mr. Nielsen?" Kay Nielsen answered, "Well, my boy, it gives me lots of joy, but also it gives me lots of headaches," to which the fat boy contributed this bit of philosophy: "But those are the kind of headaches that give joy to other people." Another child looked with starry eyes as she said, "I've never seen such a beautiful picture. It glows; there is a fresh new light over all the earth."

The little girl, Filippa Pollia, in whose memory this mural is given, would have responded joyously and whole-heartedly to the beauty of **"The First Spring."** Her shining eyes would have discovered the small lizard and beetles among the gay wild flowers in the foreground. She would not have missed the monkey, the kangaroo, the mountain goat high up on the ledge.

There are several things which the mural is not. First of all, it is far from clanging machinery, pistons, dials, and wheels, with the taut muscles of labor. It does not depict the wartime clash of military forces. It is not California history done in the brilliant colors of Spain. But instead, it brings eternal values of the out-of-doors and growing things. It refreshes the spirit with its harmony of color and fine drawing. One of our art instructors said, "It is as supremely beautiful as the Grieg 'A-Minor Concerto.'" For Kay Nielsen it harks back to boyhood memories. He and two other boys were taken to their first concert. While Haydn's "Creation" was played, three awestruck boys listened. First there was the phrase, "The Heavens Are Telling," and next, "With Verdure Clad." The music took on meaning when the wise father smiled and pointed out to them, through the various instruments, the voices of the animals. They heard the lowing of the cattle, bird notes, and the voice of Gabriel over all, as the instruments blended in one joyous harmony. Their interest in animals made the music more meaningful. Kay Nielsen never forgot this enriching experience of his youth.

Years after, he recalled once again the charm of Haydn's music and turned to the first chapter of Genesis, the twenty-fifth verse, which reads: "And God made the beast of the earth after his kind, and cattle after their kind, and everything that creepeth upon the earth after his kind: and God saw that it was good."

As music heard long ago enriched Kay Nielsen's youth and extended its influence in widening ripples through the years to his work today, so in turn Kay Nielsen with his exquisite art, now deepened with spiritual values, has enriched the lives of the young people in Central Junior High School. It will continue down through the years to bring succeeding classes of boys and girls a greater awareness of beauty.

His work on "The First Spring" has been Kay Nielsen's opportunity to express his appreciation to this nation which has given him a welcome and freedom to paint in these tragic times. He likes to think of it as his contribution to democratic ideals in which men of goodwill in all countries believe. (pp. 170-73)

> *Jasmine Britton, "Kay Nielsen—Danish Artist," in* The Horn Book Magazine, *Vol. XXI, No. 3, May-June, 1945, pp. 168-73.*

BRIGID PEPPIN

The flavour of exoticism is . . . strong in the work of the Danish artist Kay Nielsen. . . . Nielsen had the unique ability to invoke mystery, tension and even horror with a graphic style that was almost frivolous in its elegance. Like Dulac, he studied at the Académie Julien in Paris, designed for the stage and acknowledged the profound influence on his work of oriental art. His imagery, however, had a wildness and atavism of its own, perhaps stimulated initially by the Norse sagas that had been read aloud to him in childhood by his actress mother. . . . The Russian Ballet, which took Paris by storm while Nielsen was studying there, is an influence that is strongly suggested by the vigorously patterned, exotic costumes of the figures in *East of the Sun, West of the Moon.* The earlier *In Powder and Crinoline,* however, is in the rococo style as reinterpreted by Beardsley in *The Rape of the Lock.* Nielsen frequently used symbolism to elaborate his ideas, as in the two life-size guttering candles in his illustration of '**The Lindworm**'. (p. 21)

> *Brigid Peppin, in an introduction to her* Fantasy: The Golden Age of Fantastic Illustration, *Watson-Guptill Publications, 1975, pp. 7-22.*

KEITH NICHOLSON

Nostalgia for a Golden Age, it would seem, is part of the human condition. In times of great social upheaval and stress men look to the past for solace or escape from present evils. L. P. Hartley likened the past to a foreign country, and history, indeed, is like a map where we can trace our steps and find new routes to an ideal destination. Not only objective time past but our own memorable childhood offers a territorial perspective for the rediscovery of lost innocence and joys. Hence the potency of myth, legend and fairy-tale, peopled by the exotic and the bizarre, where man's predicament is effectively symbolized. Such a world was inhabited by the Danish artist and designer Kay Nielsen. What Nielsen offers in his beautiful paintings and book illustrations is not merely an escape from the mindlessness of modern existence. His retreat into a world of childhood fantasy is no innocent indulgence; it is where, like his romantic predecessors, he finds the imagination can

conceive of infinite possibility and grasp an alternative vision where hope remains undimmed. (p. 5)

Nielsen was born in Copenhagan in 1886. . . . [In] 1904, after considering a medical career, he left for Paris to pursue his great passion for art in the schools of Montpamasse. He studied at the Académie Julienne under J. P. Laurens and subsequently at Calerossi's. It was at this time, like so many other young artists, that Nielsen became fascinated by the work of Aubrey Beardsley. As a boy Nielsen had been visually excited by the drawings his grandfather had brought back from the Far East. Beardsley was the artist par excellence who had absorbed these influences and evolved them into his own inimitable style. It was the Japanese woodcuts of Hokusai, Hiroshige and Utamaro that had such an effect upon Western art when they reached Paris in the later 19th Century. The simplified and formalized landscapes of the Japanese represented an exciting and unfamiliar perspective that was to be assimilated by artists in Vienna, Moscow (in the work of Bilibin) and New York, as well as Paris. The asymmetry of their compositions, the frequent diagonal stress, the vacant white space surrounding the figures and the high viewpoint were characteristic of these cultured, two-dimensional woodcuts. Perhaps of all the constituents that came together to form what we understand as Art Nouveau the contribution of the Japanese was the most significant. And as an exponent of this style it was Beardsley perhaps who deserved the most praise and earned the most notoriety. . . . It was the fastidiousness, the ostentation, but more particularly the unwholesome excess of the later Beardsley which most captured the imagination of the impulsive and pessimistic young Nielsen.

The Book of Death, a series of black and white drawings after Beardsley, were the principal illustrations Kay Nielsen chose to put before the public at his first exhibition after his arrival in London in 1911. These were shown at the Dowdeswell Galleries in New Bond Street in July the following year. (As these illustrations were never issued in book form—a fate which befell much of Nielsen's work—the only copies which survive are those printed with contemporary reviews of the exhibition. The originals are in private collections or have been lost.) *The Book of Death* series represented a high sense of drama in Nielsen's outlook and the exhibition was a great success. The theme—the love of Pierrot for a beautiful young maiden—as well as the sincerity of the artist's mood, largely accounted for their popularity. A sharp foreboding—some presage of imminent disaster—is ever present to the lovers. . . . In contrast to the Strindbergian morbidity of the collection, the mood of which keenly anticipates impending world events, and some equally lugubrious settings of poems by Heine, Nielsen also included designs for water colors of *Hans Andersen* and the collection *In Powder and Crinoline* that were published later.

With the publication of *In Powder and Crinoline* in 1913, Nielsen held an exhibition of the original water colors at the Leicester Galleries in November of that year. . . . With these water colors Nielsen had entered the second phase of his career, emancipated from the Beardsley tradition and indebted to the great Chinese colorists for inspiration. While the art of all young painters is bound to be derivative, Nielsen shows in his development a fancy so delicate and an outlook so original that no charge of plagiarism can be brought against him. His color work is delicate and suggestive rather than forceful. Very lovely in its faint blues and greens with tones of peach is the illustration [to the story "**Felicia; or, The Pot of Pinks,**"] where the high folly, the love birds and the blossom testify to the legacy of Japan. Properly subdued to the scheme of a purely decorative theme is the illustration to the story of *Rosanie*; yet here again and in [the illustration "**A look—a kiss—and he was gone**"] and [the illustration to "**The Twelve Dancing Princesses**"] the Beardsley tradition is evident. Inimitable as a study of character is the glimpse of the early Victorian coulisse in "**The Man Who Never Laughed**" where Nielsen has struck a pretty vein of his own. The louche, blear-eyed waiter fingering his money is a study in himself. Another illustration to this story . . . has all the grimness of Edvard Munch, and both this and the curious mixture of black and color in [the illustration for "**John and the Ghosts**"] represent Nielsen at his most menacing and grotesque.

East of the Sun and West of the Moon was published in 1914 and the exhibition of water colors took place in March the following year. These 25 illustrations represent Nielsen at his most celebrated and certainly at his most spectacular. An advance in strength and decorative feeling on his former illustrations is very marked. The great charm of these paintings lies in the artist's power of combining eerie suggestion with beautiful decorative effect. The drawings are immediately understandable and clearly convey the details of the scenes they are intended to depict so that a child can follow the incidents of a story-book in them. At the same time each drawing is conceived as a decorative composition, admirably balanced and spaced and with the masses of black, white or color arranged in harmonic unison. Among the most successful is [the illustration "**He too saw the image in the water**" from "**The Lassie and Her Godmother**"], where Nielsen's predilection for height, flow and decorative effect is noticeable. Whatever style he adopts, and this is very much determined by subject matter, his individuality is sufficiently strong to make it his own. A flavor of art nouveau is especially noticeable in the modernity of [the illustration for "**The Blue Belt**"] and in the elaborate curves of his foam-topped waves in some other drawings, but this is a diminishing influence. Above all this collection has the authenticity of felt experience—the scent of the pine forest, the ice of the polar flows, the solitary birch in the arctic waste, the creatures that inhabit the lands of fjord and midnight sun, the heroes of Lied and Saga.

Nielsen staged an exhibition of his works in New York in 1917 and then returned to Copenhagen as the war ended. This period of his life is marked by his close friendship and collaboration with the young actor and producer Johannes Poulsen, a pioneer of Danish cinema, with whom he shared great similarities of artistic feeling. In 1919 they mounted a spectacular production of *Aladdin* in the poetic version by Adam Oehlenschlaeger at the Danish State Theater, the performance extending over two evenings. Nielsen designed the sets and costumes, recreating on a Northern stage the glories and wonders of the East, with its wealth of light and color, of shadows dark and somber (an undertaking that must have been very close to his heart). From contemporary accounts we understand that he succeeded in evolving from his lurid imagination scenes of the most fantastic beauty and splendour.

In 1922 Nielsen and Poulsen mounted a similar epic production of *Scaramouche* for which Nielsen also made drawings for the published score of the music by Sibelius. Later productions included *The Poet's Dream* and Ostrovsky's *The Storm*.

Nielsen returned to London for the publication of his edition of *Hans Andersen* in 1924 and the exhibition was held in February. . . . The paintings for *Hans Andersen* are difficult to assess as some of them date from an earlier period and his work in black and white, particularly "**The Shepherdess and

the Chimney Sweeper.**" Influences of the East, in "**The Nightingale**," and a rare acknowledgement to Edmund Dulac, in "**The Hardy Tin Soldier**" are apparent. (pp. 6-10)

[Nielsen] in December 1930 was back in London for his last exhibition at Leicester Square, where the *Red Magic* drawings and the illustrations for *The Brothers Grimm* were on sale. This collection, which also included a set of drawings for Heine's *The Old Old Story*, is somewhat disappointing. It is sad to notice a considerable diminution of the artist's powers. Although it is clear Nielsen was attempting an approach akin to folk-art for these settings, the angular austerity of the designs, the absence of decoration and his usual obsessive detail, and particularly the thinness of color, suggest a decline in inspiration.

In 1936 Nielsen traveled to Hollywood with Poulsen to mount a production of *Jedermann* (based upon the early English *Everyman*) by Hugo von Hofmannsthal. Poulsen died soon after in 1938 and Nielsen settled in Los Angeles, where he worked in the wilderness that was then Hollywood, as an actor, director, set designer and muralist until his death in obscurity in 1957. (p. 10)

Kay Nielsen has passed into history. He belonged to a Golden Age of books and illustrations. But when we see his work—

The North Wind goes over the sea. Illustration by Kay Nielsen from East of the Sun and West of the Moon: Old Tales from the North, *transcribed by P. C. Asbjörnsen and Jörgen Moe. Hodder & Stoughton, 1914. Reproduced by permission of the publisher.*

time-locked and enduring—we too can share his vision and dream of more wonderful things. (p. 11)

Keith Nicholson, in an introduction to Kay Nielsen, *edited by David Larkin, a Peacock Press/Bantam Book, 1975, pp. 5-11.*

WELLERAN POLTARNEES

[*In the following excerpt, Poltarnees describes his reactions to a selected group of illustrations from Nielsen's books for children.*]

[The] exquisite revelers under the trees [in the picture titled **"The Princess on the way to the dance"** from *In Powder and Crinoline*] remind me of Fragonard. As in his paintings we have an instant of inconsequential gaiety captured and held for us, like lime blossoms still fragrant from a cannister, or a hair ribbon kept bright between the pages of a book. Nielsen, is, however, less sustained by reality. He uses only sparingly the techniques by which a painter achieves the impression of truth. He does not want us to see these trees, these stars, as those we live by and under. He wants us to know that this is a different world than ours. They are Kay Nielsen trees, shaped thus to please his designer's mind. The fall of light in the picture is not realistic. It is too bright, too uniform to have come from moon or stars. The girls glow as under a spotlight. It is as if he showed us an event occurring not in the real world, but on a stage, where the backgrounds are painted, the illumination achieved by the complex devices of stage lighting. Nielsen thinks as a stage designer, arranges his world as for an audience through a proscenium arch. His deliberate artificiality is in part the oddness proper to a fairy realm, in part the inevitable result of his temper reacting to the materials, but also, I think, it mirrors his love of the stage which later flowered into the designing he did for Copenhagen's Royal Theatre. It is not merely the lovely strange trees, or the bright scene at night, but the girls, who do not rush along, but posture attractively; not really going anywhere, but only pretending decoratively to do so, taking their positions, as the curtain rises, in a tableau of such beauty that the audience will reward it with a ripple of applause even before the action begins.

     .   .   .   .   .

[The bird in the picture titled **" 'I have had such a terrible dream,' she declared, '. . . a pretty bird swooped down, snatched it from my hands and flew away with it,' "** from *In Powder and Crinoline*] is a bird such as never was, a bird designed to fill and balance the space rather than to fly. But is it fair that we ask of a bird in a fairy story that he should be so constructed that he could be expected to fly? Certainly neither the laws of aerodynamics, nor even the subtler rules of bird flight obtain absolutely in the dream kingdom. But he should look as if his flight were genuine, and this bird, for me, seems bound to fall; seems constructed with a downward rather than an upward purpose. It is not the great feathers which trail up and over the black and white lady. I enjoy their pinkness, they draw the picture into a whole, and as they are feather-light, they could be as they are. It is his wings and his neck which both reach down as if he were wrong-side-up. I prefer to accept wonders without question, but an artist must make it easy for us to do so. The probable must be balanced with the improbable if we are to believe easily. It is one of Nielsen's traits to skate too near to unlikelihood; to set us adrift in boats which will not float, or bend a knee as knees cannot be bent, or make us birds who should not fly. It is his need to transform, to put his maker's mark everywhere, to give us everything altered by his fancy. I do not regret this, for it is at the center of his genius,

and it is a genius I admire. I only remark it because it is one of the areas in which he can fail; where he sometimes rends the fabric of fancy by attempting to stretch it too far. To understand him we must know his strengths and his weaknesses, and watch him walking on a tight rope suspended between them.

     .   .   .   .   .

The story which [Nielsen's] painting illustrates, **"The Man Who Never Laughed"**, [from *In Powder and Crinoline*] is about a young man who possesses, for a time, the best that life offers. We see him here being carried away to his life of love and power and honor on a splendid ship. He and his companions are less important than the ship. They are but pale forms precariously situated on a vessel that seems to have small room for them. It is the ship, the vehicle of the dream, on which Nielsen focuses. The sea and the sky through which it moves seem on a lesser plane of existence. Its strangely decorated form is the reality he gives us; its carved sides and glowing sails and painted decks the things he throws his net over and brings back to us from imagination's realm. It is a stylistically confused and unbalanced picture. It does not deepen our understanding of the young man whose story it decorates, and yet we cannot forget it, and will forever be glad we opened the page and let it sail out into our imaginations.

     .   .   .   .   .

The story [**"East of the Sun and West of the Moon"**] tells us how the Prince took the Princess, and all the gold, home from the castle that lay East of the Sun and West of the Moon. Nielsen has visualized this with astonishing felicity [in the picture of the same name]. They descend from the sky on an arched bridge, elaborately decorated. They come from the sun, which smokes in beautifully curling patterns. The smoke carries within itself clusters of golden cinders. The Prince's embroidered cloak spreads fifteen feet before them, its scarlet arch, in conjunction with the bridge's path, suggesting a rainbow. The guardian beast, at the castle's entrance, shows us three feet of crimson tongue. The spotted horse moves majestically despite the weight of his riders and the burden of precious metal and the force of the wind from the destroyed world. The Prince's shield is like the sun. The odd little island with its precarious tree, which fills the picture's lower right, is unexpected, but nevertheless right.

Nielsen has responded to this event by opening the wells of imagination within himself. What could have been a simple road, a gate, a horse with the two riders has become a magnificent vision. This descent is such as gods might make.

     .   .   .   .   .

The young man in the foreground [in the picture titled **"He took a long, long farewell of the princess, and when he got out of the Giant's door, there stood the wolf waiting for him"** from *East of the Sun and West of the Moon*] has six brothers. A giant has turned all six of them, and their brides, into stone. Boots, the young man, is striving to free his brothers and in this he is being aided by a Princess who is a captive of the giant and a wolf who we see here saddled and waiting.

Boots and the Princess are shown to us in most striking contrast to the stone people who fill the background of the picture. They pulse with life and color, like two flowers just come to bloom. Nielsen has made the stone figures even more lifeless than we would have anticipated. They lack not only vitality and color, but dimensionality as well. He sees them as icy lines strangely joined together so that we have a colorless frieze against a hillside.

Nielsen's genius operates here in a characteristic manner, subordinating the claims of realistic depiction to those of design. Boots and the Princess are straightforwardly represented, though their stance and occupation of space is dictated by his desire for dramatic effect rather than a realistic probability. The hillside which occupies the background of the picture delights and intrigues, but does not serve to connect us spatially, or kinesthetically with a world like ours. We are not sure where things are, or what they are. What is the blackness against which we see the frozen ones? Where does the hillside end and the stone brothers begin? What is the fall of blue in the upper left? What distances, dimensions and materials are involved? There is a rightness in not being able to answer these questions about the fairy realm.

. . . . .

One of the best things about story books is that the things in them are shapely and fully satisfying, whereas life usually offers us beauty only piecemeal. As the photographer makes the experiences of the real world more meaningful by selecting and then arresting an instant for our inspection, so the artist of the fairy realm chooses and presents a moment which is a distillation of our best hopes and imaginings. Kay Nielsen has the power to give proper form to ideals and dreams. His fairyland is both convincing and desirable and we look longingly at the pages wishing to understand all that he shows us, to remember, to enter.

This prince carrying this beautiful lady on an exquisitely apparelled horse [in the picture titled "**Then he coaxed her down and took her home**" from *East of the Sun and West of the Moon*] is an image of power because it is real, because it is beautiful and because it gives perfect form to an ideal of romance. The ground on which they move is covered with flowers and the horse with his measured steps releases their fragrance. This horse is totally satisfying, moving with grace, lending himself unresistingly to his baroque trappings, bearing his master and the lady with perfectly fused majesty and obedience. The prince is a magnificent horseman, disturbed in his balance neither by his heavy crown nor by the lady in his arms. The tools of war—the armour, the sword, the shield—are not bloody necessities, but ornaments of unforgettable beauty. The man and the woman are mythic embodiments of masculinity and femininity; the man like a sword, the woman like a crescent moon, the two together a peaceful whole. This is the land we seek in our dreams.

. . . . .

[The picture titled "**In the night the dog came again, took the princess on his back and ran with her to the soldier**" from *Fairy Tales by Hans Andersen*] is an unforgettable portrait of that dog who remains in our memory from Andersen's "**Tinder Box**," the dog with eyes as big as teacups. Andersen does not otherwise describe him, though we do know he is big enough to carry the princess on his back. Nielsen's imagination has made him first a great Pekinese, and then has made him elaborate and becurled like a queen's Pekinese just come from the hair dresser, and then has gone further and made him into a beautiful tufted and quilted bed on which a princess can repose, and then, finally, has stopped him in his flight, in a statue's pose, his leg raised, his great eyes turned wondering upon us, and at this moment has turned him into a chinaware figure

worked by master artisans and kept a perfection for us to look upon.

Nielsen's palette is here very limited, and rightly so. The soft pinks and grays and blues bring to us the deserted town through which the magic dog carries his lovely burden. The hushed colors help to drop over us the spell of that moment, the blue night, the silent church, the soaring moon.

The border is soft, and shows most clearly Nielsen's absorption of the Persian miniaturists. He understands the powerful effects to be achieved by framing; the usefulness of leading the observer's eye and mind, by slow stages, back from the central vision through the less demanding artistry of abstracted decoration to the bareness of the page, and then, with a shock, to the world itself. As an exercise, cut strips of paper and block out the borders of this or any other of Nielsen's bordered paintings. It is, so shown, still a beautiful picture, but, with its soft gray border, trailed with vines, we have a wholeness.

. . . . .

[The picture titled "**We'll mount so high that they can't catch us, and quite at the top there's a hole that leads out into the wide world**" from *Fairy Tales by Hans Andersen*] illustrates the story of a porcelain shepherdess and a porcelain chimney sweep who, in love with one another, flee from the safety of their parlor to the great world. They pass through a stove, a maze of pipes and up a chimney. Nielsen's picture is very satisfying. The movement of the two beautiful figures upward into the center of the page, their visual impact against the dark space through which they crawl, the power and promise of the night sky, the piece of tree, the waiting moon, the small sinuous inner border, the wide restful green border; all of this creates an impact of great power. Once I looked at this book in a used bookstore but failed to purchase it. For twenty years I did not see it again, and yet I remembered the black clad sweep helping upward the lovely lady in white with the embroidered underslip. I remembered the tunnel of darkness, the angle of the ladder, the peeping moon. Such is Nielsen's power over the imagination.

. . . . .

Andersen's "**Story of a Mother**", which this picture illustrates, tells of a mother's attempts to rescue her child from death. She reaches, in the end, a state of reconciliation arising from her discovery of the unfathomable complexity of the scheme of creation. Andersen tells us that death is a tall old man, and introduces him to us as God's gardener. Nielsen, out of these concepts, brings us the perfect image. Death is so lank, and his soft old clothes hang on him so rightly. His tallness is accentuated by our not being shown his whole length, his feet being concealed by the frame through which we look. His great height is emphasized by the tininess of the child he carries on his arm. The gentleness of the picture, of the figure, are in perfect accord with Andersen's concept of Death as an almost unwilling agent of necessity. He is old and tired and but serves the will which moves us all. He is in the form of a man, but is not quite a man, being at the same time a force, like the earth's turning, which brings down the leaves and puts out the sun. Nielsen does not let us see his face, but turns him from us and hides his head in a great soft hat. He is fluid, muted and sleep-stained, except for the scythe he carries in his pocket. He steps carefully, holding the child, into an innocent brightness, toward the sun.

The transformation of the bottom edge of the border into a kind of window seat, on which the mother and a pot of flowers sit, is bold and effective. We have been led, by Nielsen's use of one-dimensional borders throughout the book, to a certain expectation, and here, in the last picture of the book, he fractures that expectation. By so doing he calls attention to the artist at work behind the images, and reminds us that he, at every point, shapes the vision and can change the forms to fit his changing needs. Further, he chooses this moment for the transformation because out of his compassion he wishes to offer the grieving mother a gallantry; he wishes to make a seat for her to rest upon, and changes reality to do so. Even beyond this, Nielsen makes what was a frame into a window, for a window draws us closer, is a more human thing, and for an event of this significance, a moment so powerful and universal, he does not want to keep us out, but to invite us in.

* * * * *

Density is one of Nielsen's chief characteristics. We search his small paintings so avidly because their fullness somehow demands it. They are not merely rich in details, but complex and mysterious in their conception. We search them not only to see all that he shows, but also to understand all that we see. In this lovely painting of Catskin [titled **"She managed to slip out so slyly that the King did not see where she was gone"** from *Hansel and Gretel*] we are not only given the beauty of the young lady as she sweeps from the light filled room out into the elaborate courtyard, we are also given puzzles for the eye and mind. Why does the light follow her? What is the construction of her garments? Is the crown around her head a halo, an aura, a collar, an ornament or is she passing in front of an object which frames her? What so lights the night sky? What is the real spatial relation of the planes on which she moves, all of which Nielsen has turned at right angles to our sight? Are the black and white boxes behind her tiled panels or most unreal garden plots? Are the trees in the upper left hand corner within or without the enclosure? We do not, as we look, articulate these questions, but they are there to be asked. Our lack of full comprehension is a source of delight rather than frustration and is one of the means by which he forces to linger, to wonder, and to remember.

* * * * *

[The picture titled **"Then the fisherman went home and found his wife sitting upon a throne, and she had three great crowns upon her head"** from *Hansel and Gretel*] summarizes the complex and marvelous story of the fisherman who saves a magic fish, is granted wishes of transformation as his reward, is raised to wealth and luxury by these wishes, but is in the end brought down by his wife's insane ambitions. Nielsen, in this small compass, shows us the two central elements in the story: the fisherman asking of the fish a favor for this wife, and the fish responding with majestic impatience; and above that the wife holding court, on her throne, surrounded with guards and courtiers and wearing her king's and emperor's and pope's crowns. Like a medieval painter Nielsen obeys laws of valuation rather than those of reason or time. He gives us all the things that matter in one place, for our convenience and his. His picture is ambitious and satisfying. The sunburnt fisherman on the rock petitions the kingly fish, who floats above the waters. The sea is wild and picturesque and the wave above the fish reflects his anger by turning at right angles and threatening the fisherman. The sky in the left side of the picture is dramatic with white and black clouds and bars of light. The fisherman's wife fills the right hand portion of the frame as if she floated

in a giant bubble and her world is joined to both the sea and sky by its halo of energy. Nielsen has the matter here for several fine pictures, but he has made them one.

* * * * *

Nielsen's last book, *Red Magic* is a fascinating collection of stylistic experiments, and although it lacks the wholeness of the other books, it offers many diverse pleasures. However, its pictures do not shout "Nielsen!" at us. They are not radically unlike his others, but they do not go as far in the directions he usually takes us. It seems as if he were deliberately trying to vary his style, particularly in the drawings. "I'm a sailor-cat today," though brilliant and persuasive, seems like the work of another artist.

"St. George and the Dragon" exemplifies the difference between this book and its predecessors. Nielsen has given us the subject in a straightforward fashion, has not decorated and elaborated the subject as was his habitual wont. St. George's amour, for instance, is not the intricate kingdom that we would expect a Nielsen knight to wear. The eye does not weary exploring it. His horse is simply bridled and saddled, where ordinarily a Nielsen horse is a treasure house of beaten metals and woven cloths. Compare this horse and this knight with those in "He coaxed her down." . . . There one may feast their eyes on Nielsen intricacy. The braided horse's tail alone is the subject of a delicious scrutiny, and the rider's habiliments and the lovely sword, the shield in the form of an old man's face all let us know unmistakably that we are in the realm of fairy, and that Kay Nielsen is our guide. But St. George is not so apparelled, and belongs less to the realm of fairy than to the traditions of European representational painting. The ground on which they fight is not the beflowered fabric we would expect; there are in the background no pleasingly twisted trees, and even the dragon is a simple serpent, without the sinuosities that Nielsen would be expected to provide. The picture is effective, utilizing a clear region and sculptural simplification to achieve its impact.

Are we wrong in expecting of Nielsen that he perform according to our idea of him, that he move from known point to predictable point? Was Nielsen wrong in exercising his right to paint as his muse prompted him? (pp. 8-36)

Welleran Poltarnees, in his Kay Nielsen: An Appreciation, *The Green Tiger Press, 1976, 40 p.*

HILDEGARDE FLANNER

[Kay Nielsen's] disadvantage lay in the narrowness of his range in a day that was suspicious of fantasy—unless neurotic or Joycean—that "the Golden Age of Illustration" in which his name had been notable along with those of Morris, Beardsley, Boecklin, Pyle, Rackham, Dulac and their brotherhood had closed, and however vital his skill in decoration he had no ease in self-promotion. Only an occasional haughtiness. Both war and competition are hard on the arts and crafts as on other decencies. In other times his talent and reputation might have carried him without anxiety for the rest of his life, yet already in the forties of the century and his own middle-fifties his successes, both European and American, were all in the past and apparently out of sight. . . . (p. 10)

Kay Nielsen, being an illustrator, worked from a literary imagination. With extraordinary richness of detail, refinement and ephemeral delicacy he transformed the matter of other men's minds into his own kind of deliberate charm. He achieved personal style by slow, attentive, monkish reliance on insight

"We'll mount so high that they can't catch us, and quite at the top there's a hole that leads out into the wide world." Illustration by Kay Nielsen from Hans Andersen's Fairy Tales, *by Hans Christian Andersen. Hodder & Stoughton, 1924. Reproduced by permission of the publisher.*

into the decorator's means of giving pleasure. Though naturally conversant with the historic advance of painting in the twentieth century he remained aloof from the times in his work. Excelling in the lyrical and the poetical was the ideal that absorbed him and he made no effort to modernize the subject-matter that had governed his style. He had, perhaps as an inheritance from parents of the theater, a good stage sense of how to cross a page or stand still off center. In his early work under the shadow of Beardsley he was elegantly morbid or perverse, a thing he could manage by the droop of an eyelid or the turn of a silk ankle, and in his later work the morbidity was gone while the tension sometimes remained as an element of manner—that slight pull away from the representational, an attractive awkwardness or distortion of common forms. The unspoiled manners he practiced in social relationships were the same manners he practiced in art, special to his own person and never ambivalent. The murals in the schools contain nothing controversial, either aesthetic or social, at a time when proletarian sympathies were easily suggested by just an extra breadth to the shoulders, an added stoop to the back. They contain neither belief nor unbelief, although possibly an old fashioned trust in the civilizing powers of beauty, and that, if implied was not meant to be insisted on. His paintings could not have been moralistic. They were, in a modesty aristocratic way, utilitarian, in the sense that it is a pleasure to use anything made to be seen. The murals were made to give pleasure. (pp. 11-12)

Hildegarde Flanner, "An Elegy," in The Unknown Paintings of Kay Nielsen, *edited by David Larkin, A Peacock Press/Bantam Book, 1977, pp. 7-17.*

M. CROUCH

[*The stories in* Fairy Tales of the Brothers Grimm *were transcribed by Jakob and Wilhelm Grimm. The stories in* In Powder and Crinoline, *originally retold by Sir Arthur Quiller-Couch, were retold by Anne Carter for the 1979 edition.*]

Kay Nielsen flourished in the great age of the colour-plate book. . . .Much as these books might delight the children, they were produced with an eye firmly on the adult, and especially the collectors', market. They were books of pictures with related text rather than true illustrated books. This, I think, is true rather more of Nielsen than of his contemporaries Dulac and Rackham. Nielsen had his heart in the theatre, not the printing-house, and the exquisite colour-plates in these two characteristic books [J. and W. Grimm's *Fairy Tales of the Brothers Grimm* and A. Carter's *In Powder and Crinoline*] one from his early work, the other (Grimm) from his maturity, are full of splendid histrionic gestures. Whether portraying the elegant creatures of high society (*In Powder and Crinoline*) or Grimm's wily peasants, they pose their lay figures in stage sets of unequalled beauty. Gorgeous, and admirably reproduced in both books, "C'est magnifique, mais ce n'est pas l'illustration!"

The original English text of *In Powder and Crinoline* was by Quiller-Couch. This has now been virtually rewritten by Anne Carter, to the advantage of the modern reader. The versions of Grimm's tales belong to the rather horrid Victorian literary tradition and, like the pictures, are far from the world of the Black Forest peasants. This latter book is based mainly on one published in France in 1929 and includes not only twelve full-page plates by Nielsen—one to each story—but also some fascinating head-pieces and other decorations by Pierre Courtois. Altogether a remarkable period-piece and. . .a desirable collectors' item. Whether children will like it is entirely another matter. (p. 60)

M. Crouch, in a review of "Fairy Tales of the Brothers Grimm" and "In Powder and Crinoline," in The Junior Bookshelf, *Vol. 44, No. 2, April, 1980, pp. 59-60.*

JILL P. MAY

There is fine attention to detail and to use of space in Nielsen's illustrations. Looking at the reproductions of Nielsen's books one tends to study the detail and to wish to see the original art work. In his edition of Andersen fairy tales Nielsen depicts the characters in tableau poses, and even when they are moving they have a stationary look. His best known illustrations are found in his *East of the Sun and West of the Moon*. The book originally contained 25 color plates. The illustrations are strong on design. The story's scene was maintained, but the characters themselves stood out less as personalities and more as symbols. His first books were large art books; the illustrations were framed on the page, tipped in, and covered with lightweight paper. While this is for protection, it tends to isolate the color graphics from the text. Nielsen's work is artistic and worth studying, but it is not childlike. (p. 18)

Jill P. May, "Illustrations in Children's Books," in Children's Literature Association Quarterly, *Vol. 6, No. 4, Winter, 1981-82, pp. 17-21.*

SUSAN E. MEYER

When Kay Nielsen arrived in England in 1912, Arthur Rackham and Edmund Dulac were already famous illustrators. Although their pictures had first been published only a few years earlier, the meteoric success of Rackham and Dulac occurred precisely at the time when the vogue for the deluxe gift book was at its height. Kay Nielsen became the third great illustrator of the gift book, and was acknowledged then as an artist whose talent equaled that of Rackham and Dulac. Indeed, if he had only begun his career five years earlier he might have surpassed any illustrator of his day. But he was not so fortunate.

Kay Nielsen's reputation as an illustrator of children's books was based on only four books of fairy tales, two published before World War One and two published afterward, when the fashion for fairies, fantasy, and extravagant books had all but vanished. While Arthur Rackham's reputation was sufficiently secure to transcend the passing vogue, Kay Nielsen had not been visible long enough to withstand the vicissitudes of public taste. He abandoned England and even illustration, and by 1957 when he died, Kay Nielsen's name was almost totally forgotten. Through the years, Nielsen's books have been cherished by those who were lucky enough to encounter them, and recently interest in the illustrator has dramatically revived. Long after the publication of those four books of fairy tales, Kay Nielsen has rejoined his peers as one of the greatest illustrators of children's books.

What little is known about Kay Nielsen derives from information published now and then in catalogs and anthologies. From these, the facts are easily assembled, but the soul behind the facts is more elusive. He was not an opinionated man— on this his friends all agree—so that the hopeful biographer is hard-pressed to locate journals and documents quoting Nielsen's ideas about the world, about his painting, or about art in general. He remained detached from the upheavals of politics, eschewed publicity, and applied his most fervent energies to his work, creating an imaginary world remote from any particular time or place. (pp. 195-96)

Nielsen's second book . . . became his most famous: *East of the Sun and West of the Moon,* a collection of fifteen old tales from Norway. Twenty-five watercolors were published in the first edition, demonstrating Nielsen's extraordinary prowess as an illustrator. In these elegant paintings, he combined qualities of Oriental design with those unique features of his native Scandinavia: the melancholic mystery of a bleak Nordic twilight seemed to cast a magical spell on the images themselves. If it were not for the outbreak of war that year, there is no doubt that Nielsen would have continued to produce many more of these remarkable paintings for children, to establish him as a great master of the Northern fairy tale.

Nielsen's career was abruptly interrupted by the war. His income might have vanished completely if it were not for the recognition he had received so quickly in America. Scott & Fowles Gallery . . . . exhibited the watercolors of Kay Nielsen in 1917. The catalog for the exhibition, written by Martin Birnbaum, suggested that Nielsen was unique among his peers [see excerpt dated 1919 in General Commentary]. . . . (pp. 200, 205)

These were not good times for an illustrator of Nielsen's bent, however. The public was far too preoccupied with the travesties of the war to indulge in tales of fantasy. As the war ended, Nielsen decided to return to Copenhagen where he found himself inevitably drawn back into the familiar environment of the theater. (p. 205-06)

In an attempt to reinvigorate the market for gift books after the war, Hodder & Stoughton resumed the publishing of Kay Nielsen's books, though on a more modest scale. In 1924 they published a work that Nielsen had begun in 1912, *Hans Andersen's Fairy Tales,* including sixteen stories illustrated with twelve watercolors. Nielsen returned to London, and in 1925 his final book for Hodder & Stoughton, *Hansel and Gretel,* appeared with twelve color plates. Leicester Galleries exhibited Nielsen's illustrations simultaneously with the publication of each book.

In spite of the efforts made by publisher and gallery, the market for Nielsen's books failed to recover, and the artist returned to Copenhagen to resume his work in the theater. . . . (p. 206)

In 1930 Nielsen again returned to London for the publication of his last book, *Red Magic,* a collection of fairy tales from around the world. Published by Jonathan Cape, the book was a modest edition, containing eight color plates and fifty black-and-white illustrations. The book exhibited little of Nielsen's powers as an illustrator and received only slight attention. With the exception of the watercolors he prepared for an ambitious project of *A Thousand and One Nights*—a series of twenty paintings that was considered too costly to reproduce at the time—Nielsen never illustrated another book. (pp. 206, 209)

Nielsen's condition of poverty was known only to a circle of good friends in California. He had been forgotten by his public, and when he died in 1957 the newspapers barely took notice. Ulla Nielsen survived her husband by only a year. To her loving friends the Monhoffs she gave Nielsen's entire set of unpublished gouaches for *A Thousand and One Nights.* Hoping to establish a memorial to Kay Nielsen, the Monhoffs searched for a museum to house the collection, with no success. No museum, not even in Denmark, expressed interest in the paintings. It is our good fortune that these friends never abandoned hope; they remained confident that one day Nielsen's gifts would again be appreciated, which is precisely what happened. In 1977 the paintings were published for the first time by Peacock/Bantam Books, and the proceeds earned from the publication were applied to a fund for the benefit of promising artists, a fund established by the Monhoffs and administered by the Los Angeles County Museum of Art. Kay Nielsen is no longer an illustrator buried by changing fashions. He has returned to an adoring public, home at last. (p. 209)

> Susan E. Meyer, "Kay Nielsen," in her A Treasury of the Great Children's Book Illustrators, Harry N. Abrams, Inc., Publishers, 1983, pp. 195-209.

BRIGID PEPPIN AND LUCY MICKLETHWAIT

Though he illustrated several books abroad, Nielsen's most remarkable illustrations were for the four lavishly produced limited editions published by Hodder and Stoughton [*In Powder and Crinoline; East of the Sun, West of the Moon;* Hans Christian Andersen's *Fairy Tales;* and *Hansel and Gretel*]. Though influenced in style by the drawings of Aubrey Beardsley and by Oriental and Middle Eastern art, his work revealed above all his talent for theatrical design. His illustrations were formally dramatic in conception, the figures portrayed as actors posed against backdrops, their clothes depicted with all the elegance of costume designs. Within this essentially artificial context, he was able to introduce images that were sometimes strikingly imaginative or bizarre. He drew in pen and ink, often with watercolour washes, in a manner that was decorative, stylish and immaculate, and the gift books in which much of his work appeared were further embellished with his designs for endpapers, initial letters, friezes and other decorative motifs. (p. 216)

Brigid Peppin and Lucy Micklethwait, ''Kay Rasmus Nielsen,'' in their Book Illustrators of the Twentieth Century, *Arco Publishing, Inc., 1984, pp. 215-16.*

IN POWDER AND CRINOLINE: OLD FAIRY TALES   (1913; U.S. edition as *Twelve Dancing Princesses*)

[*The stories in* In Powder and Crinoline *were retold by Sir Arthur Quiller-Couch.*]

The publishers believe that Mr. Nielsen is the most accomplished illustrator "discovered" for many seasons past. In some of its aspects his art is reminiscent of that of the late Aubrey Beardsley, but Mr. Nielsen is strong enough and original enough to stand by himself.

A review of ''In Powder and Crinoline,'' in The Athenaeum, *No. 448, October 18, 1913, p. 438.*

[Some] old favourites are retold by Sir A. Quiller-Couch, but those which he borrows from the French are not so well known, and there is one story of his own, a whimsical effort to find an Early Victorian fairyland.... Apparently the artist chose the title and wished to illustrate fairy stories with characters *In Powder and Crinoline.* Mr. Nielsen adds to the general sumptuousness of the book with his clever, ambitious, and very decorative pictures, strongly influenced by Beardsley's style. Is it necessary to add the hard saying which, after that, must be obvious? They are wholly unsuitable for unsophisticated children. (p. 691)

''Fairy and Other Stories,'' in The Spectator, *Vol. III, No. 4453, November 1, 1913, pp. 691-92.*

The fairy tales retold by Sir Arthur Quiller-Couch and entitled *In Powder and Crinoline,* though somewhat heterogeneous, are amusing enough, and one of them, **'The Czarina's Violet,'** suggests that a corner of Hans Christian Andersen's mantle has descended upon "Q." Unfortunately the drawings by Mr. Kay Nielsen which accompany them are examples of artistic perversity. Repulsive countenances, cadaverous complexions, and distorted bodies mark the princes and princesses of the artist's imagination, and he appears to think ugliness humorous. Presumably his model is Aubrey Beardsley, but his anatomical convention is rather that of "Phiz."

A review of ''In Powder and Crinoline,'' in The Athenaeum, *No. 4495, December 20, 1913, p. 727.*

EAST OF THE SUN AND WEST OF THE MOON: OLD TALES FROM THE NORTH   (1914)

[*The stories in* East of the Sun and West of the Moon: Old Tales from the North *were transcribed by P.C. Asbjörnsen and Jörgen Moe.*]

Somewhere just hereabouts, east of Suez as far as the Ten Commandments go, is the land of *Sindbad the Sailor and Other Stories from the Arabian Nights.* This is superbly pictured by Edmund Dulac.... Somewhere in the same No Man's Land (one of the most salubrious districts of the habited globe) is situate *East of the Sun and West of the Moon.* The "exquisite bizarrerie" of which the preface speaks, is a phrase fully jus-

tified by the work of Mr. Kay Nielsen. There is a brilliant and successful strangeness about these pictures. Finely and carefully drawn, keeping subordinate to the main scheme its passion for detail and massing its main effects simply, they both arrest the delighted attention at once and disclose new beauties of study. Mr. Nielsen does not intend his settings to have the actuality of Mr. Dulac's, nor does he seem to desire that his human beings have any earthly qualities. Rather are they the amorphic creatures of the imagination which people dreams. Mr. Dulac's pictures, while by no means inferior in imaginative quality, have less of the supernatural quality and are more expressive of life and motion.... In both artists the fertility of detail appears inexhaustible. (p. 430)

Algernon Tassin, ''The Magic Carpet,'' in The Bookman, *New York, Vol. XL, December, 1914, pp. 418-35.*

This very handsome volume contains a selection of folktales from the "Norske Folkeeventyr" of Asbjörnsen and Moe. Nursery tales as they are, these old world, old wives' fables are in the broadest sense legends. "They are the romances of the childhood of nations; they are the never-failing springs of sentiment, of sensation, of heroic example, from which the primeval peoples drank their fill at will.... [No] praise can be too high for Mr. Kay Nielsen's exquisitely sensitive and imaginative illustrations, most delicately reproduced in colour. Mr. Nielsen has been able to read the "Norske Folkeeventyr" in the original, and has caught to the full the quaintness, tenderness and grotesqueness of this Northern folk-lore, with its strange blending of actuality and supernaturalism. A perfect gift-book, this, for young or old. Those who are looking for something new in stories will go far before they find any that are fresher than these old tales of the North.

A review of ''East of the Sun and West of the Moon,'' in The Bookman, *London, Vol. LXVII, No. 399, December, 1924, p. 62.*

[*A reissue of the 1914 edition of* East of the Sun and West of the Moon *was published in 1976.*]

A selection from the Norse folktales in *East of the Sun and West of the Moon* was first published in English in 1859. Since then there have been many illustrated editions but the stories are best known through this collection with its illustrations by Kay Nielsen, which was first published in 1914.

It is not that Nielsen chose unusually illuminating passages to illustrate or that he gave the heroes and heroines memorable features. Indeed, his princes and princesses and the malicious trolls all conform to familiar types. Nor can he be said to have been a fine draughtsman, coming a poor second to Beardsley whom he so admired. What is remarkable about the illustrations is the emotive power of their patterns. By piling up stripes, zigzags, spirals, checks, stars and circles, Nielsen evokes a world in which it becomes possible to believe in moons flying out of forbidden rooms and men wearing bearskins passing for real bears.

Susan Lambert, ''The Art of Illumination,'' in The Times Literary Supplement, *No. 3900, December 10, 1976, p. 1550.*

East of the Sun and West of the Moon is surely Nielsen at his best. The illustrations not only have the wonderfully inventive decoration of all his work but strength of design, a harmony of space and mass, and a fragile elegance of line. The haunting melancholy of so many of the pictures must surely reflect his own feelings and experience. (p. viii)

Kay Nielsen was a gentle man, a kind man and so much that one hears about him seems tinged with melancholy. It is partly because these qualities come across in his best work that it is so good, and will survive and be enjoyed as long as books survive. (p. x)

D. J. W., "Kay Nielsen," in East of the Sun and West of the Moon: Old Tales from the North, *1976. Reprint by Doubleday & Co., Inc., 1977, pp. vii-x.*

When I was young and attending a school for girls in the middle western city where my family lived it was my greatest pleasure to come home of an afternoon, done with arithmetic and Latin, free at last to lie on the library couch with graham crackers and a banana, wide open on my hiked-up knees the most beautiful book in our house. To me, the most beautiful book on earth [was] *East of the Sun and West of the Moon: Old tales from the North,* illustrated by the Danish artist Kay Nielsen. The stories had the elemental appeal of ancient legends and the courtliness of being told often by people who loved them, but it was the enchantment of the illustrations that I threw myself into after a day of tedious lessons. I was too ignorant to know anything about the artist or his reputation although the size of the book carried a worldly importance. In my young way I was certain that he was a creator inspired and flawlessly on fire as snow may be on fire with the northern lights. It is good when we are young to be so possessed. And through the pages moved the heavy, pale stallions, the lean and lovely women, the pure, muscular knights of the Nielsen imagination, a company whose joys and sufferings lifted me straight up from the printed page into late afternoons of heaven. It was a folk-heaven of romance and danger, of old evils and cranky virtues, of love and the marvel of proud regal gender, but no sex. Under the long, sweeping garments of Art Nouveau as within the emblazoned armor of these pictures there was no rage of the flesh.

I was brought up a religious child, but the illustrations of Bible stories showed a young man too sweetly moral to have mystery or authority, and the question sometimes asked, "Do you know Jesus?" held no interest for me. But if any one had had the insight to ask, "Do you know the Lindworm?" with what elated terror I could have cried, "I do!", and opened the book to the page where the tall serpentine prince, the redeemed and redeemer, stood in his coils and commanded a kingdom with his hard red mouth.

In almost any group of adult people today there are one or two who knew the work of Kay Nielsen when they were young. Then, they would have known him ardently and doubtless mispronounced his name. Kay is Kigh. Not he, but his young admirers might have been guilty of excess. He would have made them happy and lonely and inarticulate. Yet he had passed into obscurity, become something nostalgic, of childhood memories, not of the present.

Until in May, 1975, there occurred a publishing event that provided both pleasure and surprise to people who knew his work and had not foreseen any early renascence of interest in it beyond what the greeting card industry has been promoting on the west coast and in England. [*Kay Nielsen,* edited by David Larkin] gave back to public view forty of his most characteristic designs selected from now rarely found volumes of his career. These meticulous yet highly imaginative paintings have, in their deliberate charm and exquisite refinement, no

Six white swans were flying high in the sky. Illustration by Kay Nielsen from Hansel and Gretel and Other Stories, *transcribed by Jacob and Wilhelm Grimm. Hodder & Stoughton, 1925. Reproduced by permission of the publisher.*

relationship to contemporary tendencies or tastes. The consequent neglect through which they have survived has been, as a matter of fact, a jealous neglect maintained by his admirers who never forgot him but had the good sense to let him be, and knowing how completely out of step with our times he was, did not betray him to inevitable indifference. He belonged with many others to what has been called "the Golden Age of Illustration," an age that for more than half a century has continued to have academic respect but no enthusiastic attention. . . . There are not many people still living who knew him, and I am one of them and have a conscience about him. It is proper to set down what I remember. Proper, but not easy, because reticence and good manners such as he practised do not focus sharply, and what comes to mind is a gentle figure in soft light. (p. 7)

Since the time when I had first known the Nielsen illustrations more than a quarter of a century had passed when I was singled out by a curious destiny to be unique, not in myself unique, but by a caprice of circumstances made the recipient of odd personal fortune, so shaped by coincidence that it was hard to believe. I was married to Frederick Monhoff, an architect and artist, living in a suburban community in the foothills of southern California. These recollections begin during the second war. The old garden in which we lived was surrounded by a tall hedge of Monterey cypress. From the street it was difficult to obtain any glimpse of what was within, including ourselves. I became aware that someone, when passing, tried to peer in, and at length, in a brief scurry, I caught him at it. It was not a man, but a woman, somehow European-looking and leading two Scottie dogs, then faddish, on a double leash. There was tone about her and that double leash and the well-groomed dogs. She quickly took off down the street. On other days I heard her talking to the Scotties, but I could not make out what she said. She and the dogs were not speaking English.

Then one day, accompanied by a distinguished man, she came to call on my family. Our callers were new-comers living around the corner. They were from Denmark, and it is the courteous Danish custom, we learned, to present oneself to people established nearby. When I heard that the distinguished man was Kay Nielsen, whom I had revered for most of my life and who had, in an eerie way an influence on my mind, I was overcome by shyness and a childish feeling of unworthiness, and by the overwhelming strangeness of his having been led from the limitlessness of the earth and his native snows to the sub-tropical suburban spot where I lived as if, somehow, for my own sake. I never returned the call.

In spite of such foolishness we all became close friends. . . . (pp 7-8)

Stirred and bewildered by the luck that had made me the neighbor of Kay Nielsen I turned back to the book that had left its mark on my childhood, hoping to step again into the obsessive world he had given me, hoping to be able to find a name for whatever it had been that had gripped me, rising from these pages. I had been a believing young person and now I was an unbelieving woman, yet it was not a faith in anything with a mere tag like magic that I had grown out of, for that had never meant more than entertainment, the tune that turned the lock to let the story in and out. And magic, in any case, was only the expected melody, and not the real amazement, the intense music, the long clear tone straight from the instrument of art itself. This hypnotic sound I had known, as the paintings fulfilled the stories, and it had become a part of me and my memory, but how to define it? I opened the book, carefully and hopefully. There they were! Those people with elongated bodies, slim, majestic and with high shoulders supporting faces of diffident haughtiness. Had I been fascinated by alien character and person? Was I in love with lordly profiles? Caught by the appeal of spectral innocence, of exquisite and fateful landscapes? Had I, young and impressionable, created some of this myself, for myself? I looked and looked, much as I used to, years ago, but now with purpose added. Gradually I understood that what had moved me most had been the commandment of the artist's emotion coming vividly from his mind in the occult movement of style across the page. Now I was older and I could recognize the excitement of a first-rate imagination and the skills of design that belonged with it, and I saw them as consolation for the loss of more naive and younger enjoyments, and as consolation even for the passing and unreturning years. Fondly, respectfully, I turned the pages of the book, and they fell open to the mounted knight, one large hand holding the bridle and the other hand holding the slender girl before him on the horse. Once more, I could feel the size, the weight, the heat of that hand. And I never brought myself to tell my feelings to Kay. (pp. 8-9)

Hildegarde Flanner, "An Elegy," in The Unknown Paintings of Kay Nielsen, *edited by David Larkin, A Peacock/Bantam Book, 1977, pp. 7-17.*

HANSEL AND GRETEL AND OTHER STORIES (1925)

[Hansel and Gretel and Other Stories *was transcribed by Jakob and Wilhelm Grimm and reissued as* Fairy Tales of the Brothers Grimm *in 1979.*]

[A] gifted Dane, illustrator Kay Nielsen, is represented by a reissue of his *Fairy Tales of the Brothers Grimm*. . . . A sophisticated, elegant work, more likely to be appreciated by adults than children, Nielsen provides one jewel-like illustration per tale. Art nouveau in inspiration, his pictures convey the spirit of each story rather than illuminate the words. Once having heard the dozen tales, children, too, are likely to be entranced by Nielsen's oblique and highly stylized work.

Selma G. Lanes, in a review of "Fairy Tales of the Brothers Grimm," in The New York Times Book Review, *November 11, 1979, p. 64.*

The existence of this book of folk tales is due to the 12 watercolor paintings by Kay Nielsen. . . . [The] book is indeed a handsome edition. However, though a facsimile of a book from the "golden age," when compared to the haunting black-and-white drawings by Sendak in the 1973 edition of Grimm, Nielsen's appear more as bright decorations than extending illustrations.

George Shannon, in a review of "Fairy Tales of the Brothers Grimm," in School Library Journal, *Vol. 26, No. 4, December, 1979, p. 86.*

The tone of this handsome volume is set as much by the elegant chapter-heads and ornamental capital letters by Pierre Courtois, from the first French edition, as it is by the courtly, bland, formalised compositions of Nielsen, with their expanses of sky, their elongated human forms and carefully arranged branches, foliage or buildings. These may seem to be pictures to look at for their own sake rather than as reflections of fairytale. The triangular grouping of the figures of boy, girl and trumpet-blowing angel in **"The Goose Girl,"** surrounded by an airy deployment of clouds, branches and grazing geese, or the complicated assembling of literal details in **"The Fisherman and his Wife"** suggest, however, that in his pictures Nielsen wanted to reflect something of the tension, the magical mystery, which he saw in the tales, with their unique commentary on humanity. In this sense, his depiction of the seven dwarfs in **"Snowdrop,"** a dejected group peering into dark water from a rock, with vacuous, distorted features, is perhaps the most typical and understandable of these extraordinarily imaginative scenes.

Margery Fisher, in a review of "Fairy Tales of the Brothers Grimm," in Growing Point, *Vol. 18, No. 5, January, 1980, p. 3632.*

Still another flossy revival—of elaborate Art Deco illustrations (dating from 1925) that are moderately interesting as period-pieces and absolutely inappropriate, in settings or tenor, to Grimm. (Opening this volume, you might think you were looking at a vapid, rarefied version of *The Arabian Nights*.) There's also a lavender double-border choking the block of text on each page—a text, finally, composed of compound sentences that sometimes stretch for five or six lines. Only for comprehensive assemblages of book illustration, and more of a misfire than a model at that.

A review of "Fairy Tales of the Brothers Grimm," in Kirkus Reviews, *Vol. LXVIII, No. 2, January 15, 1980, p. 69.*

RED MAGIC: A COLLECTION OF THE WORLD'S BEST FAIRY TALES FROM ALL COUNTRIES (1930)

[Red Magic *was edited by Romer Wilson.*]

Pictures are not so important in fairy-tales. "She was the most beautiful princess in the world" can be more easily written than drawn. But in *Red Magic* the illustrations, some of them exquisitely coloured, have a quality of their own. They do not belong closely to the tales collected in this book, but are worth looking at for themselves. [Mr.] Nielsen's style is Chinese and delicately fantastic; though there is a drawing for **"The Story of the Three Bears"** of the old woman jumping out of the window with a backward look at the astonished bears which is cheeky as well as decorative. (pp. xiv, xvi)

> *"Round the Christmas Shelves," in* New Statesman, *Vol. XXXVI, No. 919, December 6, 1930, pp. xiv, xvi.*

The mantle of Andrew Lang lies cosily on Miss Romer Wilson's shoulders. . . . *Red Magic* contains a good selection from the Arabian Nights and Percy's Reliques, besides the tales of Perrault, Hawthorne, Southey and a few modern rhymes. Some of Mr. Kay Nielsen's black and white illustrations may prove themselves decoys for nightmares, but the coloured ones are all entrancing, particularly one that shows Bluebeard's beard, long and flowing as a stream of ice-cold water. (pp. 897, 899)

> *Barbara Euphan Todd, "Fairies and Animals," in* The Spectator, *Vol. 145, No. 5345, December 6, 1930, pp. 897, 899.*

THE UNKNOWN PAINTINGS OF KAY NIELSEN (1977)

[The Unknown Paintings of Kay Nielsen *was edited by David Larkin.*]

Kay Nielsen is not a household word, and it is doubtful that this large-size paperback will make him one. (p. 76)

[Biographical facts] only [serve] to introduce an artist and place him in a time frame. Even the embarrassingly maudlin "Elegy" by Hildegarde Flanner [see excerpt under title *East of the Sun and West of the Moon* (1977)], which sheds no light on the artist but considerable attention on her friendship with Nielsen and his wife, is unnecessary.

What is essential, however, are the twenty vibrant paintings which have at last seen the light of publication. They are illustrations for a never-completed edition of the *Arabian Nights,* a combination of stylized eroticism and genuine fantasy.

Each work has been labelled and described as to content. Many of the illustrations include details of interest, along with reproductions of the equally important borders. Obviously Nielsen knew something about Islamic religion, and these surreal visions merit further study by those with an interest in art. (pp. 76-7)

> *Andrew Aros, in a review of "The Unknown Paintings of Kay Nielsen," in* Best Sellers, *Vol. 37, No. 3, June, 1977, pp. 76-7.*

The illustrations for an unpublished edition of *A Thousand and One Nights* are presented in this second volume of Kay Nielsen's paintings. Each full-color picture is framed by an elaborately patterned border and followed by a close-up detail surrounded by black-and-white designs. Rich in color but subdued in tone, sensitively composed but theatrical in effect, and combining orientalism with *fin de siècle* mannerisms and posturing, the paintings are frankly erotic and reveal the artist's refined sensuality.

> *Paul Heins, in a review of "The Unknown Paintings of Kay Nielsen," in* The Horn Book Magazine, *Vol. LIII, No. 5, October, 1977, p. 551.*

Scott O'Dell

1898-

American author of fiction.

Recognized as a master of historical fiction for children and young adults, O'Dell is respected as a writer whose stories about the past successfully reveal profound truths about human nature. Acknowledged for the strong moral sensibility he brings to his works, O'Dell depicts both the positive and negative attributes of his characters while stressing the resilience of the human spirit. He is best known as the author of *Island of the Blue Dolphins* (1960), perhaps the most popular and enduring winner of the Newbery Medal. In this novel, O'Dell's first work for young people, he describes a young Native American girl who is left alone on an island after raiders expel her tribe and a wild dog kills her brother. Basing his work on the true story of the "Lost Woman of San Nicolas" who lived in isolation for eighteen years on a Pacific island off the coast of California, O'Dell explores Karana's growth in confidence and sensitivity as she forgives her human and animal adversaries and develops a deep reverence for life. O'Dell completed Karana's story in *Zia* (1976), a novel which has her niece as its central character. In *Island* and in works such as *Sarah Bishop* (1980), the story of a young American who escapes to the New York wilderness during the Revolutionary War, O'Dell extols the strengths and capabilities of women while examining the individual's conflicting desire for social acceptance and the need for solitude.

Usually composing his books in deceptively simple prose which belies their complex action and emotional depth, O'Dell addresses such themes as the battle between good and evil, the mechanisms of corruption, and the social and internal conflicts that occur when cultures collide. Placing many of his works in South and Central America, Mexico, Spain, and his native Southern California, O'Dell provides unique views of such events as the Spanish conquest of the Indians of Peru and Yucatan and the Battle of San Pasqual through the eyes of his narrators. Especially vivid examples are *The King's Fifth* (1966), the sophisticated tale of a treasure hunt in sixteenth-century Mexico which is often considered O'Dell's best book after *Island*, and the Seven Serpents trilogy—*The Captive* (1979), *The Feathered Serpent* (1981), and *The Amethyst Ring* (1983)—which chronicles the corruption and reformation of a young seminarian living in Central and South America during the 1520s. O'Dell's works are also noted for highlighting such figures as St. Francis of Assisi, William Tyndale, Sacagawea, and Pocahontas. In addition to his historical fiction, O'Dell has written three works of realistic fiction set in contemporary times which examine the issues of drug addiction, the effects of Chicano machismo, and a teenager's moral dilemma; two gothic novels about a young woman who inherits the California island where she has been kept prisoner by her wealthy father; and a travel adventure about a cruise the author took up the Pacific coast.

O'Dell is praised as a superior craftsman whose works clearly delineate a variety of time periods through a wealth of detail and exotica. Lauded for his skillful handling of first-person narration and for creating an unforgettable protagonist with Karana, he is also commended for his historical accuracy,

objectivity, and sensitivity. Although several of his books are considered minor, O'Dell is esteemed for impressing young readers with the universality and timelessness of human experience while entertaining them with compelling and affecting stories.

In 1972, O'Dell became the second American to receive the Hans Christian Andersen Medal. He received the University of Southern Mississippi Medallion in 1976 and the Regina Medal in 1978. In 1961, *Island of the Blue Dolphins* won the Newbery Medal and the Lewis Carroll Shelf Award; it was also on the International Board on Books for Young People (IBBY) Honor List in 1962 and won the Deutscher Jugend-literaturpreis from the German International Board on Books for Young People in 1963. *The King's Fifth* was selected for the latter award in 1969 and as a Newbery Honor Book in 1967. *The Black Pearl* and *Sing Down the Moon* were selected as Newbery Honor Books in 1968 and 1971 respectively. In 1981, O'Dell created the Scott O'Dell Award for Historical Fiction, a prize first given by the awards committee, comprised of the advisory committee of the *Bulletin of the Center for Children's Books*, in 1984; *Streams to the River, River to the Sea* received the award in 1986.

(See also *CLR*, Vol. 1; *Contemporary Literary Criticism*, Vol. 30; *Something about the Author*, Vol. 12; *Contemporary Au-*

thors New Revision Series, Vol. 12; *Contemporary Authors,* Vols. 61-64; and *Dictionary of Literary Biography,* Vol. 52: *American Writers for Children since 1960: Fiction.*)

AUTHOR'S COMMENTARY

[The following excerpt is from an interview by Peter Roop.]

O'Dell's books for children number nineteen and that list continues to grow as this prolific author examines the problems and people of the past and present.

"History has a very valid connection with what we are now," O'Dell emphasized. "Many of my books are set in the past but the problems of isolation, moral decisions, greed, need for love and affection are problems of today as well. I am didactic; I do want to teach through books. Not heavyhandedly but to provide a moral backdrop for readers to make their own decisions. After all, I come from a line of teachers and circuit riders going back two hundred years."

Before the publication of *Island of the Blue Dolphins* Scott O'Dell had written six adult books, most of them about his beloved native California. . . . [It] was anger and frustration which turned O'Dell to writing for children.

In the January 1968 issue of *Psychology Today* O'Dell wrote, "*Island of the Blue Dolphins* began in anger, anger at the hunters who invade the mountains where I live and who slaughter everything that creeps or walks or flies. This anger was also directed at myself, at the young man of many years ago, who thoughtlessly committed the same crimes against nature."

He expanded this statement saying, "I was angry and wished to do something about it. I considered writing a letter to the editor of the Los Angeles Times to express my anger. But I realized that such a letter would be read by only a few people and would be easily dismissed. So I wrote *Island of the Blue Dolphins* about a girl who kills animals and then learns reverence for all life." (pp. 750-51)

Historical events and places often provide O'Dell with the focus of his books. He also draws heavily from the places of his own past; San Pedro and Dead Man's Islands were favorite boyhood haunts and gave O'Dell material and memories for *Island of the Blue Dolphins;* a childhood visit to West Virginia provided information for *Journey to Jericho;* trips to Spain, Peru, England were sources for other books.

"I always visit a place I am going to write about," O'Dell said. "That gives me the true feeling of the locale, the weather, the land, the sky, the people who once lived there." (p. 751)

Children often ask Scott O'Dell where he gets his ideas. I pondered such a question but, before I could ask it, he began telling me about the lake [near his home].

"There's a cave at the head of this lake. A small place where a young woman named Sarah Bishop lived during the Revolutionary War. I became interested in this girl. I began my research, but the only information was one short paragraph about her in a newspaper of the time when she died. I took that sparse information and created *Sarah Bishop.* I put fiction and fact together to create her. Sarah Bishop lives through me and my words."

The story of Karana in *Island of the Blue Dolphins* is similar. From the sparse information about a young woman stranded on an island off the coast of California, O'Dell fashioned a story that is a consummate blend of the facts of history and the storyteller's art. "I used Karana to tell my story. She grows from an unconcerned hunter to a person who respects the gift of life."

This use of history to tell his own stories runs through many of O'Dell's books. *The King's Fifth* serves to expose the overwhelming greed of the Spanish conquistadors. Bright Morning in *Sing Down the Moon* demonstrates the will to overcome seemingly insurmountable odds during the Navajos forced evacuation of their homeland. Julian Escobar in the recent trilogy shows feet of clay when power comes within his grasp as O'Dell employs the Mayan myth of Kukulcan to help tell his story.

O'Dell states that he writes mainly for himself, focusing his books on a particular issue which concerns him or an idea he wishes to express. History serves as a background for his intellectual and emotional explorations of areas shared by children and adults alike.

When asked about the value of historical fiction for today's young readers O'Dell replied, "Historical fiction has extreme value for children. Children have a strong feeling that they sprang full-grown from the forehead of Jove. Anything of the past is old hat. But no educated person, however, can live a complete life without a knowledge of where we come from. History has a direct bearing on children's lives."

Historical accuracy is a hallmark of Scott O'Dell's books. O'Dell incorporates details that give the reader a sense of time and place.

"I know ninety percent more about the time than I can include in my books," he explained. "Too many facts overwhelm the story. I try to find certain words indicative of the time."

Many of O'Dell's main characters are young women: Karana, Bright Morning, Sarah Bishop, Kathleen. When asked why he portrayed such strong, vital women in his books O'Dell replied, "It is rather simple. I have been appalled by the status of women. Women have been treated as second-class citizens. I am didactically in favor of the women's movement. The main character of my newest book *Alexandra* is a typical young woman who does things men usually do. I am trying to show that women and men *do* have the same potential." (pp. 751-52)

When asked if writing for children was rewarding O'Dell answered, "I enjoy writing for children because I get such great response from them. Children get involved in a good story; they really care and that makes writing worth the hard work." (p. 752)

Peter Roop, "Profile: Scott O'Dell," in Language Arts, *Vol. 61, No. 7, November, 1984, pp. 750-52.*

GENERAL COMMENTARY

JOHN ROWE TOWNSEND

To readers in Britain, Scott O'Dell seems to live and write on the far western rim of the world: California, Mexico, the Pacific coast and the islands beyond it. And of his first six books for children, five are set in the past and four at least have the flavour of a West that is Indian or Spanish rather than 'American' in the present sense of the word. Their times and places are mysterious and exotic to the insular Englishman—the vague edges of an antique map where dolphins play.

The title of *Island of the Blue Dolphins,* lovely in sound and evocative in all its key words (for the 'blue' transfers itself to the ocean), sums up the attraction of the O'Dell world. But it is not a matter of settings alone; this is an admirable novel; and its successor, *The King's Fifth,* is to my mind even finer, although in Britain it is not well known. The subsequent O'Dell books, up to the time of writing, have been slighter.

Island of the Blue Dolphins accepts some severe limitations. It is the story of an Indian girl who survives for many years alone on a small and desolate island. For much of its course it has only one human character; so all that large part of the more usual story which depends on dialogue and the interaction of personality is ruled out. The heroine is uneducated, has never been beyond her own tiny territory, has no wider frame of reference; so abstract thought is almost ruled out, too, and figures of speech can only be of the simplest. There is little plot in the conventional sense; the story goes on and on with a good deal of sameness over a long period; its development is in the character of the heroine herself, and this is a theme which it is extremely difficult to make interesting for young readers.

Yet all these limitations have been converted into strengths. The fact that there is only one central character, in this remote and isolated setting, makes identification total; the reader must *be* Karana or the book is meaningless. The telling of the story has a memorable purity to which its fresh direct concreteness contributes as much as the author's excellent ear. And the long, continuous time dimension allows the story to take itself outside our clock-and-calendar system altogether, to complete the islanding of a human being's experience.

A Robinson Crusoe story has of course an appeal of its own which hardly needs to be spelled out. Survival is not an immediate problem at present for most of us in the civilized Western world, but as a theme it still touches upon our deepest inborn instincts and unconscious fears. And the details of survival, so compelling and convincing in *Robinson Crusoe* itself and in all successful Robinsonnades, are absorbing here, and clearly authentic. Last, *Island of the Blue Dolphins* shows a human being in changing relationship to animal life, about which the author obviously knows a great deal. Birds, beasts and fishes are to Karana at first, and to a great extent must continue to be, either things to be hunted or competitors for the means of subsistence; but as she grows she achieves an acceptance of them as fellow-creatures. If there is a key incident in the whole book, it is the one in which she befriends her arch-enemy, the leader of the wild dogs.

It is a story with intrinsic sadness; and not only because of the early death of small brother Ramo and the later death of Karana's only close friend, the dog Rontu. It is immensely sad to lose human company throughout the years of youth. The depth of this loss is hinted at, no more, in the brief, tentative relationship with the girl who accompanies Aleutian hunters to the island; in the tiny touch of vanity over the cormorant-feather skirt; in the girl's marking her face, on being rescued after all those years, with the sign that she is still unmarried. Karana herself is no mere cipher. She has the qualities which are implied and indeed required by her situation; she is strong, sensible, intelligent, resourceful. And while she is unsentimental she can—even in the desolating absence of other human beings—love. A sad story, yes; but the sadness of *Island of the Blue Dolphins* is of a singularly inspiring kind. Among all the Newbery Medal winners there are few better books.

The King's Fifth is a more complex novel, notable among other things for its formal structure. The hero Estaban de Sandoval is in a prison cell in Spanish Mexico, awaiting trial on a charge of having deprived the King of his lawful fifth share in a treasure found far to the north in the unknown lands of New Spain. Interspersing the story of his prison life and trial is Esteban's account, written night by night in his cell, of the events that led up to it; the stories of 'now' and 'then' move forward side by side until they merge in the last chapter, when all has been told and the verdict is handed down.

The underlying story is that of a treasure hunt, in which Estaban, a cartographer, forms one of a small band led by the daring and unscrupulous adventurer Captain Mendoza. The party includes, besides Mendoza's henchmen, a young Indian girl, who is guide and interpreter, and Father Francisco, whose concern is to save souls. As an adventure story—the story of a quest followed by a trek for survival—it does very well; but it is a moral as well as a physical exploration, and there are moral as well as physical events in it.

Treasure is sinister; that is the heart of the matter. It is not merely that treasure is often both hidden and discovered in circumstances of violence and treachery. The truth is also that the hope of great unearned gain can be one of the most corrupting ever to get men in its grip. In *The King's Fifth* there are not so much good and bad characters as the innocent and the corrupted. The guide Zia, who longs to ride a horse and to help with the mapmaker's art, is innocent; so is Father Francisco; so are those Indians to whom gold is mere dirt for which they have no use. The narrator Estaban is less simple. He is led into the quest by his yearning to map what no man has mapped before, and at first devotion to his craft protects him; but the gold which is won at last from an Indian city begins to exert its baneful influence. Mendoza dies, killed by a dog he has trained in savagery; Zia goes her way, for she sees Esteban becoming another Mendoza; and Esteban finishes in the Inferno, a hot white sandy basin where his last companion, Father Francisco, dies. And only now does he grasp the enormity of the evil burden and tip the gold, enough to make many men rich, into a deep bubbling crater of foul yellow water where it will be lost for ever.

In the parallel story of the consequences—Esteban's imprisonment and trial—the seedy majesty of Spanish law and administration is seen to be similarly corrupted. No one cares for more than the outward forms of justice, but everyone hopes to recover the treasure. Esteban refuses an offer to let him escape, and is ready to serve a three-year sentence in daunting conditions, because freedom for him can now only come through expiation.

The King's Fifth is a sombre and searching book. The two that followed it were less substantial. *The Black Pearl* is the terse, masculine story of young Ramon, who seized the Pearl of Heaven from the underwater cavern of the great Devilfish; and of Ramon's father, who donated the pearl to the statue of the Madonna in the church on the coast of Lower California, mistakenly thinking to buy divine protection against wind and water; and of the tall-talking Sevillano, who sought to steal the pearl, and fought the Devilfish when it came seeking its own, and died. At last the great pearl, purified now, is placed in the hand of the Madonna-of-the-Sea as a gift of love.

This brief, spare piece of writing . . . is something between a fable and a mystery. The greed and presumption of men are punished. Who is Ramon's father to think he can buy the favours of the Almighty, who is the Sevillano to think he can defeat and steal from the mighty Devilfish? Obviously there are symbolisms involved; for while the Madonna is to be adored the dark powers represented by the Devilfish must also be reckoned with. But what are the dark powers, and are they inside or outside the minds of men? That is part of the mystery, and a mystery does not need to have a simple solution, or indeed any solution.

The way the Devilfish dominates this story makes one think of *Moby Dick;* and it is interesting but not surprising that an obsession with that book is the core of O'Dell's next novel. The narrator of *The Dark Canoe* is Nathan Clegg, cabin boy on board the Nantucket whaler *Alert;* but the dominant character is his elder brother Caleb, part-owner of the ship, who lost his captain's licence in strange circumstances. Caleb resembles Captain Ahab in *Moby Dick,* even to the extent of being similarly scarred and lamed. He resembles Ahab in disposition, too; and there is a description of him 'with his massive head thrown back, black hair, raven black once but now streaked with grey, falling around his face, hands clenched at his sides'. Caleb is not acting the part of Ahab, even though he knows the book by heart; rather, he is 'a man tortured in body and mind who had read Ahab and in time knowingly had become Ahab'. . . . (pp. 154-58)

There is much in this short book: a surprising amount. It raises the difficult question whether a novel can depend upon another and live in its own right. I am disposed to think that an author is as much entitled to draw upon a classic novel as upon myth; and *Moby Dick* as much as any novel has the size and depth of myth; the test, as I have suggested in discussing books based on myth, is whether the author has successfully absorbed his material and made it his own. By that test it must be said that *The Dark Canoe* fails. Though relevant parts of *Moby Dick* are explained, O'Dell's book does not fully live apart from Melville's; does not make full imaginative or psychological sense without it.

Sing Down the Moon is again a short book: too short perhaps for the story it has to tell. It is concerned with the sufferings of the Navajo Indians who were driven from their homes and forced into the long, dreadful march to Fort Sumner in 1864. The story is told in the first person by a young Navajo girl, Bright Morning; and, as in *Island of the Blue Dolphins,* O'Dell shows a gift for assuming a feminine identity which is all the more remarkable in a writer whose work is generally very masculine. There is a lovely, grave simplicity in this telling; yet one feels that perhaps it has been pared down too far, that a style which was admirably suited to the lonely setting of a Pacific island is less appropriate for a story that is full of people and harsh, clashing action. With the limpid brevity of *Sing Down the Moon* goes a sense of remoteness, almost of withdrawal.

Journey to Jericho is a story for younger children about David and the jar of watermelon pickle he takes with him when he travels from West Virginia to join his father in California. The jar, carefully cherished throughout the journey, falls into proportion (and on the ground, and into fragments) when David sees his father and runs to his arms. It is a pleasant enough story, but the adjustment to a small child's eye level does not seem to come easily to this author. To write about real life for young children without being crabbed by the restricted range of a child's experience, one needs a particular lightness of touch, a gift for seeing ordinary things in a fresh, un-ordinary

way which is childlike in a good sense of the word. . . . (pp. 158-59)

John Rowe Townsend, "Scott O'Dell," in his A Sense of Story: Essays on Contemporary Writers for Children, *J. B. Lippincott Company, 1971, pp. 154-62.*

SALLY ANNE M. THOMPSON

Viewing the majority of O'Dell's work, one discovers several qualities ever present. The quality woven into the grain of his rich tapestry in his own personal philosophy. No where does he overtly share innermost feelings or beliefs. These are felt or witnessed but not verbalized. From his writings though, we appreciate the fact that O'Dell is an individual with a strong moral sense. He has spent his life intricately meshing bits of his own moral fiber into his books, and ultimately into the minds of his readers. His style is perceptive, complete with insights, as he skillfully creates depths of texture and fiber within his characters. O'Dell expresses his point of view discretely through means of symbols and imagery, as manifested in Tyndale's not allowing his life to be saved by the killing of another human being in *The Hawk That Dare Not Hunt By Day.*

The author is realistic in his approach to life. Good is not always rewarded—Esteban was sentenced to five years in prison for his part in *The King's Fifth.* Evil is not always punished—Kit Carson pillaged, looted, and killed as viewed in *Sing Down the Moon,* but became one of our nation's folk heroes. People do not always live happily ever after—Caleb Clegg remained a haunted, driven man even after finding the ship's log that proved his innocence in *The Dark Canoe.*

Woven throughout most of O'Dell's work is his kinship with the sea and his abiding love of the Southwest. (p. 340)

The best in historical fiction is consistently exemplified by O'Dell. His stories detail qualities which insure satisfaction for the reader and lasting interest in his books. Historical events, facts and characters recapture the flavor of the time, captivating the reader by allowing him to enter a world of romantic appeal, totally encompassed in authentic language and custom. Yet, the historical data does not appear as cold facts as in a documented commentary, but comes alive as warm essentials.

O'Dell's stories cause the reader to ponder the effects people have upon each other; the character, conduct, morality and ethical values; enabling one to see that human nature was the same then as now. Picturesque language, scrupulously accurate details such as a church that took three generations to build, all add dimension to the authenticity of the stories.

Readers are helped to understand the past, what the struggle of man has been and why people have acted as they have. "Children don't relate to names of battles, dates of treaties, to statistics. Like us, they relate to individuals, to emotions they can feel within themselves, to stories that arouse their curiosity," said O'Dell.

Perspective and balance are part of the lesson of history and the thoughtful reader will see this reflected in the problems and issues of each era O'Dell covers from the Civil War period to *The 290,* the whaling days of *The Dark Canoe,* the explorations of the Spanish of *The King's Fifth,* to the realization that the United States Army did march the Navajos to Fort Sumner as did Bright Morning in *Sing Down the Moon.* (p. 341)

The master weaver weaves his ideas of human relationships as evidenced in the close family bond between parents, child and grandmother in *Journey to Jericho*; man's place in the universal

scheme, witnessed in Karana's fight for survival; the oft la-
mented theme of man's inhumanity to man in the brutality and
cruelty measured out to the Indians three hundred years ago
by the Conquistadors in *The King's Fifth.*

As the reader relates to O'Dell's characters he can come to
grips with himself, gain an understanding of self. The characters such as Tom, Karana and Esteban embody the hopes
and ideals of the reader. This has appeal as a source of challenge
and enjoyment. Part of this lies in having one's imagination
stimulated. O'Dell breathes life into his characters with painstaking craftsmanship; flesh and blood personalities. Characters
that are real, that live and move in a rotating world. Characters
that are not static, but individuals that are ever growing, changing and unique in their actions. They live their lives as the
author sees them, realistically portraying the whole spectrum
of human life with no quick and easy solutions to serious
problems. The convictions of the author are so skillfully tied
into the pattern of the work that the individual fibers are taken
for granted. The author hopes that the reader is capable of
formulating a set of values and a sense of responsibility through
understanding the complexities of concepts of truth and honesty, as depicted by specific situations and vicarious experiences that give insight into the characters groping to deal with
their problems.

O'Dell, with rare talent, is able to accurately depict characters
through revealing speech and incident. He does not tell his
reader how life is, or how people are capable of behaving, he
merely creates the situations that force his characters to be
themselves.

He has not subjected his readers to stereotypes that have been
common especially in books written before the mid 1970's.
Instead, his females are respected as individuals, active participants with characteristics suitable to their roles. (pp. 341-42)

O'Dell stories entertain the reader, hold his attention and make
him care about the dilemmas of the characters. The reader can
vicariously experience the defeats and victories of each character. Perhaps this is because he writes about situations pertinent to the human condition; the constant battle between the
good and evil obvious even to the pre-adolescent reader. O'Dell
is capable of subtly and skillfully weaving this message between the written lines of his stories, much as the Navajo
weaves her rug, thread by thread, to form a complete and
beautiful expression of herself.

Child of Fire portrays the seriousness of brutality as a way of
life. But the grim details are used for a purpose; to give the
reader as accurate a picture as possible of the events taking
place in the story and of its setting. O'Dell has given the reader
what has meaning for him. . . .

Scott O'Dell has made a memorable contribution to the world
of children's literature. . . . His writings have and will stand
the test of time, because his message is so potent and accurate
that it speaks to all generations.

Thus does Scott O'Dell, master weaver, qualify for Walter de
la Mare's quote "'. . . only the rarest kind of best in anything
can be good enough for the young. (p. 342)

*Sally Anne M. Thompson, "Scott O'Dell—Weaver
of Stories," in* Catholic Library World, *Vol. 49, No.
8, March, 1978, pp. 340-42.*

ISLAND OF THE BLUE DOLPHINS (1960)

AUTHOR'S COMMENTARY

*[The following excerpt is taken from O'Dell's Newbery Award
acceptance speech given on July 11, 1961.]*

Samuel Johnson has said that a man may turn over half a library
to make a book. It is equally true that a writer may turn over
a whole lifetime to make a book. Indeed, this is what I did
when I wrote *Island of the Blue Dolphins.*

Down the corridors of memory, at the far end of that labyrinth,
I saw clearly a certain night.

I was four years old and I had awakened out of a long sleep.
The room was dark. The sea made faint sounds among the
eaves, like mice stirring. From far off came the sound of waves
breaking upon the beach. Though I listened, I heard nothing
else.

Lying there in my small bed, in the deep night, it suddenly
came to me that the house was deserted, that I was alone.
Quickly I slid to the floor and groped along the hall to my
mother's room. I felt the bed. It was empty.

At that instant I heard from a distance the sound of music. By
some strange alchemy of love and fear and memory, standing
there in the empty room, music and my mother became one.
I would find her where the music was. They would be together.

I tried to open the front door, but it was locked and the back
door was locked too. Then I noticed that the window above
the kitchen sink was open. I found a chair and climbed upon
it and thus reached the window. (To this day I can feel the
coldness of unwashed silverware on my bare feet.) I grasped
the window sill, squirmed outside, hung for a moment, fell
sprawling on the sand, and picked myself up.

Now the music was clear on the summer air. Against the sky
I could see the glow of colored lights. I ran toward it, falling
in the deep sand and getting up, running again, shirttails dragging at my ankles.

I came to a boardwalk. The walk led to a pavilion, to the source
of the glowing lights, where clusters of people moved about.
But the music was still farther, beyond them; and I went toward
it, feeling my way through a forest of legs and a sea of dresses,
to a place where couples drifted about.

There on a platform above them was the music and below the
platform, the lights shining on her, was my mother. Her back
was toward me but I knew well the golden hair. With my last
breath I ran across the floor, unaware of the eyes that must
have been turned upon me. I stretched out my arms and clutched
her dress and though she was whirling, held on. As she turned
and stared down at this apparition in a nightshirt, at her son,
I am forced to say that she was not so glad to see me as I was
to see her.

You will not find this incident in *Island of the Blue Dolphins,*
but you will find its meaning. The human heart, lonely and in
need of love, is a vessel which needs replenishing.

I saw a boy of eight, towheaded and restless, who with other
boys of his age went out on Saturday mornings in sun or rain
in search of the world.

This was a small world, but a world in microcosm. It was
bounded by the deep water and wharves and mud flats of San
Pedro Harbor. By the cliffs and reefs of Point Firmin and

Portuguese Bend. By the hills of Palos Verdes, aflame with wild mustard in spring, lion-colored in summer.

Many summer days we left the landlocked world and went to sea. How? Each of us on a separate log. The logs had been towed into the harbor in great rafts—from Oregon. They were twelve feet long or longer, rough with splinters and covered with tar. But to each of us young Magellans, they were proud canoes, dugouts fashioned by ax and fire. Graceful, fierce-prowed, the equal of any storm.

We freed them from the deep-water slips where they waited for the saw mill. Astride, paddling with our hands, we set to sea, to the breakwater and beyond. We returned hours later, the watery world encompassed.

These memories went into *Island of the Blue Dolphins*. You will find them in the book—where Karana leaves the Island in search of the country that lies to the East.

Many mornings we went into the Palos Verdes Hills. There we turned over every likely rock, looking for small monsters. We thrust our hands down every squirrel and coyote hole in our path. Commonly we found an owl. This was the prize of all prizes. It was twice the size of your fist, soft-feathered, with great yellow eyes that blinked in the sudden sun.

What did we do with this creature of the nocturnal air? We killed it, of course. We wrung its neck. We cut off its legs. For the exposed tendons of an owl's legs, when pulled in a certain way, made the tiny claws open and retract in a ghastly simulation of life.

To this day, indeed to this very minute, I remember these depredations with horror.

This horror, muted but nonetheless real, you will find in the latter part of *Island of the Blue Dolphins*. The latter part of the book, only, because my Indian girl began where youth begins. In the closed world of selfishness and cruelty where everything, whether of fur or feather, whether it creeps or walks or flies, is an object of indifferent cruelty.

Down that dark corridor of time I also saw Jack Iman.

Freckled, with black eyes alert under a bang of black hair, a Hercules in miniature, Jack hated me the moment we met. For no other reason, I am certain, than that I was a city boy, lately come to his town. I also hated him. And for no other reason except that he hated me.

In all weather, during the school week and even on Sunday, Jack pursued me. In class with his black eyes. On the school grounds with taunts. Off the school grounds with his fists. He was my nemesis. My tormentor. The embodiment to me of all evil.

Years later I read in the newspaper that Jack had become a prizefighter. Sometime later I saw him fight. I went to see him beaten. But the same Jack Iman I remembered, only with vaster muscles, was the victor. I went again and again to see him fight, each time hoping for his humiliation. Finally, after a year of fights, Jack Iman was knocked out and carried groggily from the ring. To my surprise, sitting there at ringside, I somehow felt diminished.

I went back, using the privilege of a press badge, to his dressing room. I went there to introduce myself, for I was sure he wouldn't remember me, and to quietly gloat.

Though he was just returning from another world, Jack Iman recognized me at once. Unsteadily he came towards me, put his arms around my shoulders and wept.

That too is in *Island of the Blue Dolphins*. It lies in the heart of the episode of Karana and her enemy, the Aleut girl. It also colors the climax of the book. For I believe and wished to say, with whatever power I might summon to the task, that we must forgive our enemies. Further, I believe that the hopes of civilization, unique and obscure as they are, really exist in the act of identification with our enemies. (pp. 99-102)

Places I have known, creatures I have loved are in *Island of the Blue Dolphins*. The islands—San Nicolas, Santa Cruz, San Miguel, Catalina, Anacapa, Todos Santos, San Martín, the Coronados—seen at dawn and at sunset, in all weathers over many years. Dolphin and otter playing. A mother gull pushing her grown brood from the nest, watching them plummet a hundred feet into the sea, then flying down to herd them onto their new home, a rock safe from the tide.

And finally there is Carolina, the Tarascan girl of sixteen. . . . (p. 103)

The Tarascans are a great people. They were never conquered by the Aztecs, the only tribe, incidentally, that did not fall under the Aztec yoke. Nor did the Spaniards, led by the incredibly cruel Guzman, subdue them. (pp. 103-04)

Carolina, when she first came to work for us, wore a long red skirt of closely woven wool. As a bride her mother had received the gift of sixty yards of this red cloth from her betrothed, a custom of the Tarascans. With it, by winding it around and around her waist, she made a skirt. At night she used it as a blanket for herself and her husband, and later for their children, against the fierce cold of the mountains. For each girl child she cut lengths of the cloth and this in turn became a skirt. The red skirt, the *falda roja* which Carolina wore, came to her in this fashion. She wore it proudly, as a shield against the world, in the way Karana wore the skirt of cormorant feathers. The two girls are much alike.

Through them I wanted to say to children and to all those who will listen that we have a chance to come into a new relationship to the things around us. Once, in Defoe's day, we were cunning manipulative children, living in a palace of nature. In her brief lifetime, Karana made the change from that world, where everything lived only to be exploited, to a new and more meaningful world. She learned first that we each must be an island secure unto ourselves. Then, that we must "transgress our limits," in reverence for all life. (p. 104)

Scott O'Dell, "Newbery Award Acceptance," in Newbery and Caldecott Medal Books: 1956-1965, *edited by Lee Kingman, The Horn Book, Incorporated, 1965, pp. 99-104.*

Each year, with the increase in number of children's books, it is often necessary to retreat from the volume of present publication to reexamine those works which have, for various reasons, endured to become classics. One such work is Scott O'Dell's *Island of the Blue Dolphins*. . . . (p. 442)

Although the desert island motif has been a standard fictional theme since Shakespeare's *Tempest* and Defoe's *Robinson Crusoe*, O'Dell is faced with several new problems. Because he is writing children's fiction, he must create a story in which narrative pacing is relatively fast. His specific subject matter, the lonely eighteen years spent by Karana on the Island of the Blue Dolphins, raises difficulties. . . . For a large part of her story, Karana does very little except engage in the diurnal chores of survival. How, then, has O'Dell created a story which continues to grip young readers fourteen years after its publication?

First, the story of Karana's isolation does not begin until the end of the eighth chapter, after her brother Ramo has been killed by the pack of wild dogs. By so delaying the story of her survival, O'Dell is able to create a sense of the social milieu in which she had developed, a feeling of the fear and distrust of the Aleuts, which she will harbor during her solitude, and a contrast between the activity she had known with the tribe and the desolation she faces alone. Moreover, the basic character traits she exhibits during her eighteen years of loneliness have been clearly established during the early part of the novel.

Second, O'Dell intermingles accounts of Karana's day-to-day activities with the highlights of her adventures. Thus the narrative pace is never allowed to slacken, while at the same time the reader is given a sense of her day-by-day existence. For example, Chapter Nine, which describes her first year alone, presents both her finding food and shelter and her fear of the roving dog pack; and Chapter Seventeen tells of repairing her canoe and learning to love Rontu.

These "how to" selections are rendered interesting not only because they are placed between narrative segments, but also because of the vividness with which O'Dell has presented them. Young readers have an interest in survival techniques, as is indicated by their own attempts to build tree houses and wood shelters. . . . O'Dell succeeds so well because of his deep knowledge of his subject. . . . Thus the convincing quality of his accounts renders them believable.

But the most important aspect of the story, that which has made it the classic it is, is the portrayal of the character of Karana. Prefatory to an examination of her character, we should note two aspects. First, O'Dell very wisely chooses the first person point of view. While Karana's life is interesting, her attitude to that life is much more so. Second, as attitudes are intangible, they must be given objective correlatives in order to be fictionally realized. Thus the book is developed around a series of presentations of Karana's attitudes toward her daily survival activities, inanimate objects, animals, and other people. Each of the chapters thus contains a series of symbolic episodes which illuminate aspects of Karana's character and the changes it undergoes.

Chapters One through Eight present two main character traits which are fully explored in the remainder of the novel: Karana's sociality within her family and tribe and her fear of the Aleuts. First seen gathering roots with her brother Ramu, who has been her charge since the death of their mother, Karana appears as a person fully involved in the life of the tribe. She cheerfully accepts her duties as babysitter, acquiesces to the tribal taboos which involve sexual role separation, busily contributes to the arduous task of survival on the somewhat barren island and happily bedecks herself, as does her sister Ulape, in the maiden fashions of her people. She shares the well-founded tribal suspicion of the Aleuts, the hunters who are to rob the island and kill her father and other warriors, and whose dogs mutilate her brother. Later in the story, her desire to be reunited with her people will become the motivation behind her drive for survival, and it will create a need for a substitute animal family.

Later, her hatred of the Aleuts will be seen as a character flaw she must work to overcome, as she does in her relationships with Rontu and Tutok. (pp. 442-43)

[Chapters Nine to Twenty-Nine, which deal] with Karana's psychic and physical survival and her final departure, can be divided into three major sections, each one tracing a significant phase in her character development. Chapters Nine to Fifteen deal with her early life on the island and take her to the point of her friendship with Rontu; Chapters Sixteen to Twenty-Two continue the account of her daily activities and end with her friendship with Tutok; Chapters Twenty-Three to Twenty-Nine emphasize her loneliness and conclude with the arrival of the ship which will take her to be reunited with her people. In each section and from one section to the next, there is what we may call an integrative movement, as Karana moves from a state of loneliness and/or hatred to one of community and friendship. In each section there are a series of symbolic incidents which reveal aspects of this movement.

On first finding herself alone, Karana's hope is that she will soon be rescued by a returning ship. However, after a year, her hopes are ended and she realizes that she must take definite action herself, which she does by repairing a deserted canoe with which to paddle to a new island. When, in her attempted escape, she loses sight of the island and is forced to retreat, she refers to the island as home for the first time since her lonely stay began. In her withdrawal and return by canoe, we have the second variation on the motif of ships departing from and arriving at the island. Whereas the Aleut arrival had led to Karana's loss of family, this time, her homecoming emphasizes her growing sense of self-reliance. She faces the fact that she is completely alone and devotes her energies to the problem of survival.

In the early stages of her life on the island, she has made two significant steps which have led to this position of self-reliance. First, she has turned her back on the immediate past by burning the village, knowing that painful memories cannot help her. Second, she has understood that if she is to survive and avenge her brother's death by wild dogs, she must violate the tribal taboo which forbids women to make weapons. (p. 444)

Although the chief motivating force behind her actions on the island has been her desire to kill the wild yellow-eyed Aleut dog who leads the pack, she only wounds him, refusing to let fly the fatal arrow. . . . Her decision not to kill Rontu marks the second major phase of her development. She had earlier learned self-reliance, now she comes to understand that she cannot take another life in the name of vengeance. . . . Her decision has been a wise one, for in befriending Rontu, her enforced loneliness has ended and she has made the first step toward establishing an animal society to replace the human one of which she had been deprived:

> Because of this I was not lonely. I did not know how
> lonely I had been until I had Rontu to talk to.

The second major phase of Karana's development ends with her friendship to Tutok. However, two significant events take place before the establishment of this relationship. First, the young girl engages in her long awaited struggle with the giant devil fish she had first seen in the dark sea cave. The incident nearly proves disastrous for, in attempting to free Rontu, who has become trapped in the octopus' tentacles, she is nearly dragged down herself. Her decision not to pursue it is further important, for it indicates her awareness that there are forces in nature which she cannot control. Later, the earthquake and tidal wave enforce the point more strongly.

More important is the discovery of the skeleton of her ancestors in Black Cave where she is forced to spend the night when trapped by the rising tide. Upon her escape, she tells Rontu:

> I suppose this cave once had a name . . . but I have never heard of it or heard it spoken about. We will call it Black Cave and never in all our days go there again.

Karana has faced her past and has found that to survive she must never dwell on it, for to do so would be to become engulfed in an inner darkness as great as that surrounding the figures in the cave. (pp. 444-45)

When the Aleuts arrive, Karana hides, noting that "It was the girl I was afraid of". But when she first sees her, Karana does not shoot, accounting for her reasons in terms much like those she had used when explaining why she did not kill Rontu. "Why I did not throw the spear, I do not know, for she was one of the Aleuts who had killed my people". Just as her mercy to Rontu indicated her forgiveness of the animal who had destroyed her brother, so her actions toward Tutok indicate a larger response, forgiveness of the representative of a group which had been her enemy. At the moment she puts her spear down, Rontu runs eagerly to the Aleut girl, apparently recognizing her. The point is clear: Rontu had been Tutok's dog, and she is the unidentified girl of the earlier Aleut visit. O'Dell has thus used the friendship between Karana and the dog as the preparation for the human friendship between the two girls.

For the first time in many years Karana hears another person's voice, realizing as she does how great had been her need for human companionship. . . . When, after several meetings, Karana has developed a sense of trust toward Tutok, she performs two acts which are in contrast to her earlier actions in the novel: she takes the necklace proffered by the Aleut, and reveals her secret name. Shortly after having been marooned, Karana had discovered the chest of Aleut trinkets but had refused to wear any, and when she had heard her father give the sea captain his secret name, she had been appalled, feeling that he would weaken himself. Now her sense of love and confidence in her new friend is so great that she can accept gifts and she can give a secret name knowing that Tutok will not betray her.

With the achievement of this relationship, a life alone can no longer be fulfilling for Karana. . . . Thus the final seven chapters of the book prepare us for her departure. Feeling her loneliness, she befriends the otter Mon-a-nee, makes jewelry, and watches the fledglings grow. But these activities are insufficient. . . . The extent of her loneliness is revealed in the fact that she determines not to kill any more animals because "without them the earth would be an unhappy place".

The emptiness of her existence increases. She seldom thinks of the possible arrival of the whites or Aleuts, ceases counting the months because "the passing of the moons now had come to mean little," and spends much of her time thinking of her closest friends, Tutok and [her sister] Ulape. With the death of Rontu and the lonely winter that follows, her isolation seems complete. The taming of Rontu-aru, son of Rontu, does not seem to give her the joy of her earlier animal relationshps. In fact, most of the members of her animal family have mated, leaving her the only "spinster" of the group.

The tidal wave and earthquake made evident the danger of future habitation of the island. . . . Immediately she sets about

building a new canoe and eagerly prepares to depart when she sees a ship arriving. Although it departs before she can get ready, she spends the next two years in a state of preparedness, often thinking of the voice of her would-be rescuer calling her. When at last the ship returns, she places on her face the marking of the unmarried girl, as she had done eighteen years earlier, and, in so doing, prepares for reunion with society. . . . Boarding the ship, she has rejoined humanity, completing the process which had been interrupted eighteen years before.

We see, then, how O'Dell invests the lonely, often monotonous life of a young girl with significance. He presents details with graphic realism, arranges a series of symbolic events, and, from within the mind of his principal character, tells of the courage and love she uses to survive an inner loneliness which is greater than the outer dreariness of her life and of the maturing process in which hatred and fear have been replaced by love and sociality. (pp. 445-46)

> *Jon C. Stott, "Narrative Technique and Meaning in 'Island of the Blue Dolphins'," in* Elementary English, *Vol. 52, No. 4, April, 1975, pp. 442-46.*

In its earlier forms, "survival" literature was almost entirely limited to young males pitting their skills against the wilderness or the sea. At first stylized and hackneyed, the stories gradually achieved considerable depth. As ably represented in such books as Roderick Haig-Brown's *Starbuck Valley Winter* and Farley Mowat's *Lost in the Barrens*, survival literature could offer a genuine "feel" for the physical environment, an affecting depiction of friendship, and a dramatic unfolding of plot, laced with exciting yet plausible events.

This type of straightforward yet sensitive adventure story came to a peak and in a sense to its end in 1960 with Scott O'Dell's *Island of the Blue Dolphins,* deservedly called a modern "classic" for its imagery, emotional quality, and poetic style. As a "Robinsonnade," its link to the past is obvious, but while Robinson Crusoe had his faith in his personal God to solace him, Karana, the Indian girl, is completely alone, except for her animal companions, and sustained only by her inward courage. Even so, Karana survives and we readers are never in any doubt that she will do so. Moreover her dangers only seem to add spice to the story; they do not traumatize and indeed appear to leave almost no mental or emotional residue. (p. 35)

> *Sheila A. Egoff, "Realistic Fiction," in her* Thursday's Child: Trends and Patterns in Contemporary Children's Literature, *American Library Association, 1981, pp. 31-65.*

Island of the Blue Dolphins is believable because Scott O'Dell has spent considerable time describing nature and has made it a complex antagonist. First of all, Karana's people have always lived with nature, using its bounty, conserving its offerings, and preparing for its dangers. However, when Karana is left alone, she is forced to violate the taboos accepted by the tribe in order to survive. . . . The protagonist is threatened by one element after another, each one a component of nature, the antagonist. Karana's conflict is dramatic, building up to the earthquake and its following tidal wave. . . . (p. 58)

We must be aware of the passing of time and of the seemingly endless period of Karana's isolation as she waits for rescue. If we did not see the dangers that threaten her survival on the island, we might find the story a happy, escape-to-the-wilderness tale. Instead, because of the many and vivid descriptions, *Island of the Blue Dolphins* is an account of a patient and determined young woman who struggles and survives against a powerful antagonist—nature, which brings hunger, thirst, injury, wild dogs, an earthquake, and a tidal wave. Setting, Karana's anatagonist, is vivid. We see, hear, smell, and feel it in O'Dell's descriptions. Karana is a strong protagonist; although her adversary is also powerful, Karana is not overwhelmed. (p. 89)

O'Dell carefully maintains credible first-person point of view [in *Island of the Blue Dolphins*]; at no time does Karana ever pretend to know what is in the minds of others, not her brother, the hunters, Tutok the Aleut stranger, or the animals. Karana can only draw conclusions about the feelings of Tutok from her actions. Tutok comes out from the brush quickly; Karana says, "She must have been waiting nearby." That possibility is all that Karana can know about Tutok's motives. Tutok hugs Karana when she receives the shell necklace. Karana says, "She was so pleased that I forgot how sore my fingers were." A hug—action from another character—makes Karana conclude that Tutok is pleased. Although Karana knows her dog Rontu very well, she describes only his actions, never his thoughts. Karana concludes that Rontu wishes to bark only because he always had. Rontu

> raised his ears at the sound, and I put him down, thinking that he wished to bark at [the gulls] as he always did. He raised his head and followed them with his eyes, but did not make a sound.

Had O'Dell violated the first-person point of view by telling us Rontu's feelings, we would have lost some of our concentration on Karana and the story would have been less real.

As we can see clearly from these passages, one of the strongest assets of first-person narration is its great potential for pulling the reader into what appears to be autobiographical truth. Because Karana's thoughts are interesting to us, we are sympathetic with her. She is consistently credible because she is believably limited in what she can admit to knowing. Because solitary Karana—like solitary Robinson Crusoe—tells her own realistic story, the vicarious experience of survival is a powerful reality, convincingly immediate to the reader. If the story had been filtered through an omniscient writer, the immediacy of the experience would probably have been less intense. The intervention of someone who wasn't there but who still knows and can tell it all would create an intervening omniscience between the solitary protagonist and the reader. The story would then be more remote, less immediate, and less intensely real. (p. 120)

O'Dell's formal and restrained language and simple sentence structure constitute the style suited to the setting, conflict, and character in his story *Island of the Blue Dolphins*. The protagonist, who lives a life totally dependent upon nature, says in the opening lines,

> I remember the day the Aleut ship came to our island.
> At first it seemed like a small shell afloat on the sea.
> Then it grew larger and was a gull with folded wings.
> At last in the rising sun it became what it really was—
> a red ship with two red sails.

O'Dell uses nature comparisons throughout the story. Karana's brother Ramo has eyes "half-closed like those of a lizard lying on a rock about to flick out its tongue to catch a fly." An invader's beard is combed until it "shines like a cormorant's wing." Karana says the enemy's mouth is "like the edge of a stone knife." But a swarm of friendly dolphins dives in and out "as if they were weaving a piece of cloth with their broad

snouts." The sea elephants have faces "like wet earth that has dried in the sun and cracked." Word pictures and comparisons describe characters, action, and setting, but in a style suited to this story of a protagonist who lives with her antagonist, nature. (pp. 137-38)

O'Dell in *Island of the Blue Dolphins* never condescends, never demeans Karana's life by sentimentality. Her people have always lived on a windswept island, dependent upon themselves and their own capacities to use what is provided by nature, and avoid death at nature's impersonal hands. A product of this culture, living close to the elements, Karana quietly accepts what faces her. Life is sometimes cruel; humans survive by self-control. Ramo's being killed by wild dogs does not make Karana wild in her grief; we sense instead her feeling of inevitability and of necessity for restraint.... O'Dell's tone of restraint makes us feel sympathy for and understanding of Karana in her isolation and loneliness; there is no sentimentality here. (p. 167)

> *Rebecca J. Lukens, in her* A Critical Handbook of Children's Literature, *second edition, Scott, Foresman and Company, 1982, 264 p.*

Scott O'Dell's *Island of the Blue Dolphins* is a survival tale, an animal story, and a feminist parable. It is the account of a girl's passage into adulthood and her achievement of a rare maturity and wisdom. The author based this children's novel on an historical figure, "The Lost Woman of San Nicolas," who was left behind by her tribe on an island off the coast of Santa Barbara and lived alone there between 1835 and 1853. The heroine, Karana, narrates this simple, Robinson Crusoe-like tale of her adjustment to a solitary existence on the island. The story is episodic in structure and takes on the quality of a diary: full of the details of her day-to-day survival, her frustrations and loneliness, her triumphs and joys. The immediacy and poignancy of the account make *Island of the Blue Dolphins* a compelling book for readers of all ages. Though the film version, directed by James B. Clark for Universal in 1964, suffers from the limitations of translating into film a novel whose interest lies primarily in its strongly subjective point of view, and from the poverty of the film's images compared to O'Dell's descriptions, it is nevertheless an important children's film thanks to its sensitive treatment of the relationship of people to the environment, the struggle for life amid the ever-present danger of death, and the singular experiences of a capable, sagacious young woman.

In presenting challenges to the human will and spirit, survival tales have enormous appeal. They speak to the fantasy of living in a state of complete independence, alone with nature and free of all social responsibilities. For children, this fantasy is particularly powerful because of the dependent and subordinate nature of children's relationships to parents and teachers. The presence in children's literature of so many juvenile protagonists who are orphans contributes to this mythology of facing the world alone. In *Island of the Blue Dolphins,* Karana experiences none of the social constraints children face at home and at school. She is entirely self-sufficient and free of supervision. The price which she pays for her independence is loneliness and the threat of physical danger, and this provides the compensatory aspect of the fantasy. Few of us would be able to survive physically and emotionally under such circumstances and this gives a strong element of anxiety to our interest in survival tales as well. (pp. 182-83)

The book, of course, presents Karana's activities in much greater detail and conveys a great deal of practical information about survival skills. Every challenge which Karana encounters is described as a problem to be solved. The heroine discusses her needs and each potential alternative for meeting them. Every step in the survival process is logically thought through; each success or failure is carefully evaluated. These passages in the book convey Karana's intelligence and the strength of her will. One of her most striking characteristics is her continual ability to plan ahead. In her moments of despair, she invents another project to occupy her days and test her skills: hunting a sea elephant, capturing a devilfish, sewing clothes of otter skin or cormorant feathers.

As a story of emotional survival, *Island of the Blue Dolphins* is unusual because Karana's isolation is never depicted pathetically. The character describes her loneliness and the process of mourning candidly and without self-pity. At the beginning of the story, Karana's father, chief of the tribe, and most of the men on the island are killed wantonly by a group of Russian traders who have come to the island for otter pelts. In the book, Karana describes the grief of her people:

> . . . more than the burdens which had fallen upon us all, it was the memory of those who had gone that burdened our hearts. After food had been stored in autumn and the baskets full in every house, there was more time to think about them, so that a sort of a sickness came over the village and people sat and did not speak, nor even laughed.

Such a frank and unsentimental treatment of depression is rare in children's fiction. The book also treats her feelings of anger and vengeance in response to the death of loved ones. When Karana's brother is killed by the wild dogs, she vows revenge. Planning a way to kill the dogs preoccupies her during her first days alone on the island, forcing her to take action rather than mourn passively.

A turning point in Karana's emotional adjustment to her solitude occurs when she attempts to escape from the island by canoe—a part of the narrative which does not appear in the film adaptation. She explains her motivation for taking such a risk:

> . . . whatever might befall me on the endless waters did not trouble me. It meant far less than the thought of staying on the island alone, without home or companions, pursued by wild dogs, where everything reminded me of those who were dead and those who had gone away.

After three days on the ocean, the canoe begins to leak dangerously and Karana, exhausted and heavyhearted, decides she must turn back. The following morning, she realizes that she has achieved on the journey a new acceptance of her situation. . . . Reconciled to life on the island, she begins building her new home. Her love for and appreciation of nature make her life a joyful one. While Karana misses her family and her people, living alone is not a tragedy for her.

In the film adaptation of *Island of the Blue Dolphins*, Karana's solitude is treated more conventionally and sentimentally. The film character seems younger and less mature than the narrative voice in the book. . . . [When her dog, Rontu,] leaves her to return to the pack, she reacts bitterly. After repeatedly calling the dog and begging him to return, she says aloud, "All right, go with them. You stay with them! You dare come back now and I will throw stones at you. I don't need anybody." The immaturity of this outburst stands in striking contrast to the even temperament of the book's character. (pp. 183-85)

When the dog Rontu dies in the film, Karana falls sobbing over his body. Author Scott O'Dell, however, treats the dog's death matter-of-factly:

> I buried him on the headland, digging for two days from dawn until the going down of the sun, and put him there with some sand flowers and a stick he liked to chase when I threw it, and covered him with pebbles of many colors that I gathered on the shore.

In the film we see Karana standing at the grave; the emphasis is on her emotional reaction. It is the same place where her brother, Ramo, is buried, and she says aloud by way of eulogy: "If you had known him, Ramo, you would have loved him, too."

The film version of *Island of the Blue Dolphins* is a more straightforward animal story than the book. Karana's relationship to Rontu is the main narrative interest in the film; it takes up only a fraction of the book's plot. (pp. 185-86)

The animal story in O'Dell's *Island of the Blue Dolphins* is more than just an account of the companionship between a child and a dog, however. The relationship of Karana to Rontu functions as a metaphor for the human capacity to accept, appreciate and live in harmony with nature. When the wild dogs kill Karana's younger brother, she develops a fierce hatred for them and promises to kill them. She succeeds in injuring the leader (Rontu) with her bow and arrow. When she discovers the dog later, wounded and near death, she inexplicably begins to help him. At considerable risk, she approaches the dog, removes the arrow, treats the wound with herbs, leaves food and water for the dog and finally takes him into her home. In the beginning the two are extremely wary of each other, but they gradually develop a strong bond of trust and affection. Karana learns through her relationship with Rontu to appreciate the fellowship animals can provide, and she comes to realize the senselessness of violence against them. When Karana forgives Rontu and nurses him back to health, she begins to live more harmoniously with her whole environment.

In the course of the film, she befriends not only Rontu but also Rontu's puppy, a pair of birds and a young otter. Rontu is the only animal we see Karana hunt in the film. In the book, however, Karana initially has no qualms about killing animals and hunts many of them. Eventually, her relationships with animals bring her to the decision never to kill any kind of animal again. She comments on how strange this resolution would seem to her family:

> Yet this is the way I felt about the animals who had become my friends and those who were not, but in time would be. If . . . all the others had come back and laughed, still I would have felt the same way for animals and birds are like people, too, though they do not talk the same or do the same things. Without them the earth would be an unhappy place.

The reasoning behind her decision is compelling in its simplicity and its compassion. Karana's respect for nature gives *Island of the Blue Dolphins* a powerful ecological message.

The most unique aspect of *Island of the Blue Dolphins* is its strength as a kind of feminist parable. The novel's diary-like quality is significant since diaries have traditionally been one of the primary forms for women's self-expression. As a courageous, capable and stalwart character, Karana offers an exceptionally positive role model for girls. A new range of possibilities open up to Karana when she is left alone on the island. Existing outside of traditional social and familial roles, her ego, identity and world view develop in an unusually individual way. Ramo's death has left her in solitude but it has also freed her from the duty of her maternalistic, big sister role.

In both the book and the film the change in Karana's character after her little brother's death are obvious. In the beginning, Karana is more subdued and restricted. She always has Ramo with her, and is constantly busy taking care of him or worrying about him. Her feeling of responsibility for Ramo is epitomized when, having sailed away from the island with her people, she realizes that Ramo has been left behind, dives into the water, and swims back to the island. Karana's isolation is also her liberation, allowing her to create her own world, concentrate on herself, and discover the power of her own self-reliance.

Karana re-creates her environment on the island and adapts the culture she has learned as a child to suit her own purposes. She burns the circle of huts which constitute the village she was reared in and builds her own home high on the rocks, from which she has a view of the entire island. When Karana meets each of her animal friends the first thing she does is name them. The process of naming takes on great significance for her; it is her way of understanding and claiming the world around her. . . . She carefully chooses the names for her dogs, birds and otter. When she tells Tutok, the girl working for the traders, her secret name, it is her greatest token of friendship. Inventing language and naming things in the physical world are Karana's means of creating her own culture.

Island of the Blue Dolphins has an explicitly feminist message about restrictions on female activity. Karana faces a serious problem in reconciling her cultural heritage with her immediate needs on the island: it is traditionally forbidden for women to make or use weapons. . . . In the book, Karana discusses her fear of breaking the taboo; she has been repeatedly told that weapons will always fail in the hands of women at the crucial moment. Recognizing the necessity of weapons, Karana does not let the taboo intimidate her. In making the spears and the bow and arrow, she must remember what she has observed but never been taught. Karana takes over such ''man's work'' easily and naturally. Having mastered these skills, she has the wisdom to avoid anything which she sees as harmful to the environment or an unnecessary waste of life. The book offers a rare vision of feminine understanding and love of nature. Its theme is very different from the man *against* nature motif found so often in literature. Instead, we are shown a woman in peaceful, harmonious coexistence with the environment. Karana feels no need to ''conquer'' the environment.

Karana's physical strength is underplayed in the film, which tends to rely on more conventional and more sexist representations. When swimming back to the island to join Ramo, Karana is shown in a series of shots gasping and weakly stroking the water as though she is nearly drowning. In the book the same incident is described this way: ''I could barely see the two rocks that guarded the entrance to Coral Cove, but I was not fearful. Many times I had swum farther than this, although not in a storm.'' The film turns a scene in which Karana sprains her leg while hunting into an accident in which she simply drops the canoe on her foot. . . . In the comparable scene in the book, the pack of dogs attacks Rontu, and Karana stands by, ready to intervene with her bow and arrow to save the dog.

Adapting *Island of the Blue Dolphins* to film must have been a difficult task. The screen has no devices other than voice-over for conveying the interior first-person narration, and since this technique is not used here, Karana is left talking aloud to herself or the animals. The language of the novel is spare and formal; the simplicity of its style is perfectly suited to the episodic story. The film translates this into visual simplicity—compositions and camera angles are unobtrusive to a tedious degree. . . . The physical distance of the camera from the actress throughout the film and the tendency to shoot her from high angles breaks our identification with her and diminishes her character. The film does nothing to replicate the sense of intimacy with Karana developed in the book. . . . Reading the novel, one imagines a visually richer world than what we actually see in the film—shot on location in California. (pp. 186-90)

However, the film version of *Island of the Blue Dolphins* does have some powerful moments. The killing of Karana's tribesmen by the fur traders is more shocking on the screen than in the book. The opening sequences are unusual for a children's film in their portrayal of the exploitation of the Native Americans by the white traders. At the end of the film, Karana walks down the cliff at sunset to meet the missionary priest and the men who have finally come to rescue her. The final shot shows Karana walking in silhouette toward the water. She is dressed in her cape of cormorant feathers, carries her bird cage in hand, and walks with her dog at her side. The image conveys a sense of a world lost as much as the narrative resolution accomplished by Karana's rescue. (p. 190)

> *Ellen E. Seiter, ''Survival Tale and Feminist Parable,'' in* Children's Novels and the Movies, *edited by Douglas Street, Frederick Ungar Publishing Co., 1983, pp. 182-90.*

CHILD OF FIRE   (1974)

A probation officer wouldn't seem to be a very promising narrator for a story about Chicano youth, but in this case he turns out to be the right kind of concerned but neutral observer, one distanced enough to reduce the character of young gang leader Manuel Castillo to a series of dramatic, highly symbolic gestures. We first meet Manuel in the bullring, where he leaps from the stands to confront a charging bull and, hopefully, demonstrate his machismo to a young lady; he is last seen throwing himself under a mechanical grape picker in a desperate gesture of defiance against the automation of the local vineyard. In between, Manuel's naive but fiery idealism pits him against Ernie Sierra—a smooth operator and leader of the rival Owls who turns out to be smuggling heroin from Mexico via homing pigeons. Like the bull and cock fights that apotheosize the action, Manuel's nobility can best be appreciated as an aesthetic abstraction; O'Dell tells the tale—and it's a compelling one—with enough laconic conviction to make this possible, while at the same time using the skeptical comments of the officer's pragmatic minded wife Alice as a foil. And when we question whether the officer really sees the truth about Manuel, then we remember that his reactions are filtered through his own frequently expressed sense of futility and uninvolvement. Contemporary parables are a tricky business; O'Dell invests this one with a self-contained dignity, and it can be read as a psychological thriller even while one is pondering just how deep the vein of fatalism really runs.

> *A review of ''Child of Fire,'' in* Kirkus Reviews, *Vol. XLII, No. 15, August 1, 1974, p. 810.*

Through the carefully bland Delaney who is secretly respectful of Manuel and his Spanish culture, O'Dell allows readers to judge the ambiguities in the boy's behavior which can be seen

O'Dell on the fly deck of The Artic Star *in Tracy Arm, Alaska, in 1972. Photograph by Elizabeth Hall. Courtesy of Scott O'Dell.*

as a course toward self-destruction, or as an ultimately successful search for a statement of himself and his worth. In dealing with such difficult yet basic themes in a direct style and involving story this moves closer to elemental truths about human nature than the shock value "realism" of many current junior novels. (p. 110)

> *Margaret A. Dorsey, in a review of "Child of Fire," in* School Library Journal *an appendix to* Library Journal, *Vol. 21, No. 1, September, 1974, pp. 109-10.*

In **Child of Fire,** Scott O'Dell grabs the reader with a flamboyant presentation of fact and fiction relating to bull fights, Chicanos, Mexicans, Tijuana and the law. He has crafted a fast-paced adventure story and seasoned it heavily with exotic cultural elements.

Unfortunately, his interpretation of Chicano culture ranges from being on-target to being so fictional that a Chicano reader would either disbelieve it or be totally confused. O'Dell's descriptions and definitions of the terms *bato loco,* Chicano, *ocho, macho* and *Mexicano* are, at best, regional and, at worst, offensive to the young Chicano reader. The use of horses as a primary means of transportation in the Tijuana/San Diego area might be acceptable to the uninformed, but young Chicanos would definitely find this bewildering.

Furthermore, few Chicanos would identify with the very Hispanic hero, Manuel, whose lineage is given as being directly traceable to Spain. Indio heritage is completely lost—an offense to Chicanos who value that heritage.

The book's leading female character is highly stereotyped. She is a sexy, "older woman" type who captivates and manipulates Manuel and a villainous character named Ernie. Blind to her deviousness, Manuel is finally saved through the intervention of your usual benevolent, patronizing *gringo* deliverer in the form of a gang-busting probation officer.

Gringo Delaney is just too good to be true, and I doubt that many people—Chicano or otherwise—would be convinced by this larger-than-life portrayal. He is sensitive (as only a culturally superior individual can be), informed, concerned, involved, tolerant—he hates bull and cock fights but, of course, "accepts" them. He makes life better for everyone except our hero. Thank heaven Manuel is too wild, bright, inquisitive, romantic and charismatic to be "helped".

The interweaving of the farmworkers' struggle (Cesar Chavez makes an appearance), urban problems (Manuel) and the law (in the person of Delaney) represents an attempt by a skillful craftsman to capture the texture of Chicano life. Notwithstanding that effort, **Child of Fire** reads like science fiction. Given its misrepresentation of crucial elements of Chicano existence and projection of inaccurate images of La Raza, the book would more than likely alienate those who know and misinform those who don't.

Uvaldo Palomares, in a review of "Child of Fire", in Interracial Books for Children Bulletin, Vol. 5, No. 7-8, October-December, 1975, p. 17.

___

THE HAWK THAT DARE NOT HUNT BY DAY (1975)

Bible smuggling in the days of Henry VIII is the topic of this reticent though admirably researched demi-adventure. Tom Barton, who is given reason to expect that he is the rightful owner of his Uncle Jack's ship *The Black Pearl*, is drawn into a plan to smuggle William Tyndale's English translation of the New Testament. After Uncle Jack is arrested and thrown into Clink where he dies of the Black Plague (the enigma of his personality still unresolved), Tom finds himself forced into accepting a business partnership with ratlike Herbert Belsey and fanatical Henry Phillips, two of Tyndale's most determined enemies. Most of the characters (though not the Bartons) are historical; however the appearance of Juan de Palos, Christopher Columbus' pilot, on the *Black Pearl*'s roster stretches plausibility a bit far. And the period background is full-bodied—right down to the pubs, populated appropriately by "gixies, fustylegs and drunken sailors." Certainly O'Dell writes well enough to integrate the non-violent flight and martyrdom of the saintly Tyndale with the original mood of raffish action/ entertainment. Yet readers drawn by the adventure might balk at the more reflective turn of events after Tom fails to save his friend Tyndale, his involvement with Belsey peters out, and he eventually forgives the much chastened Phillips. Worthwhile, though the parts are more interesting than the whole.

A review of "The Hawk That Dare Not Hunt by Day," in Kirkus Reviews, Vol. 43, No. 19, October 1, 1975, p. 1139.

O'Dell's latest is a fairly interesting, occasionally exciting historical novel that centers on the intrigue involved in the printing and distribution of the first English translation of the New Testament. . . . The religious and political turmoil of the time is presented with clarity, and in addition to Tyndale himself, King Henry VIII and printer Peter Quentel play their real-life roles. It's a well-guided journey into the past for young teens with some interest in the era; however, it lacks the vitality and the basic situational appeal of some of O'Dell's previous novels. (pp. 60-1)

Margaret A. Dorsey, in a review of "The Hawk That Dare Not Hunt by Day," in School Library Journal, Vol. 22, No. 4, December, 1975, pp. 60-1.

Since good story ideas do not come along like streetcars even to master storytellers, it is a happy day when a compelling writer like Scott O'Dell meets a compelling subject like William Tyndale. . . . An unlikely subject, one may think, for the author of *Island of the Blue Dolphins, The King's Fifth,* and other books set on the Pacific Coast. Yet Mr. O'Dell seems completely at home in Europe in a conniving, turbulent age, and his subject gives him scope to examine a theme that has obviously haunted him for some time.

Writing books, Scott O'Dell once said, is "an attempt . . . to work out through a form of self analysis a needed and desired personal development." That this new story has some symbolic relation for him with his past books is apparent as soon as one

sees that the name of Tom Barton's ship is the same as one of Scott O'Dell's earlier books—*The Black Pearl*. Why *The Black Pearl*?

Before finding the answer, one must ship aboard with young Tom Barton, the narrator, and take part in the dangerous adventures that await anyone smuggling into England the new English Bible. . . . It is a race against time—for William Tyndale a race to get his Bible off European presses before his enemies, the heretic-hunters, stop him; for Tom Barton, Tyndale's friend, a race to avoid having to take on two of these very enemies as his partners.

Who wins the race? The enemies, it would appear, for William Tyndale, betrayed by one who has posed as his friend, is strangled and burned at the stake. That is the way Tom saw it, for he went, armed, to kill the traitor. Yet he does not kill because he remembers that Tyndale, who had himself (like Esteban in *The King's Fifth*) refused escape when given the chance, would not have condoned murder. So it becomes clear that Tom along with Tyndale and along with Ramon of the earlier book, *The Black Pearl*, are the real winners. Not evil but love overcomes evil.

Jean Fritz, in a review of "The Hawk That Dare Not Hunt by Day," in The New York Times Book Review, February 22, 1976, p. 18.

___

ZIA (1976)

Karana, the Indian girl left to survive alone for 18 years on the Island of the Blue Dolphins, was a one-in-a-million child protagonist—a loner free to work her destiny totally without interference from adults . . . [Karana's story] has since become almost an instant classic, as popular with children as it was with the critics.

The jacket copy of Scott O'Dell's new book, *Zia,* notes that O'Dell has received many requests to tell what happened to Karana, and one can see in this novel some of the tension between the pressure to produce a good storyteller's sequel and the author's reluctance to violate an essentially self-contained episode, based on fact, with a fictional post script.

Thus the heroine of this story is not Karana, who reappears only briefly and tragically later on, but her niece Zia. Zia and her brother Mando are apparently the only other survivors of their tribe, and they live and work under the padres of the Santa Barbara mission where they conform despite a passive, impersonal resistance to their Spanish overlords.

When we first meet Zia she has discovered a whaler's boat washed ashore and she conceives a daring plan: with her younger brother as crew she will sail to rescue the aunt she has heard about and bring her back to the mainland. From the moment Zia and Mando set out we are under the spell that O'Dell creates so effectively. The mood is portentous, and the journey is not destined to end well. . . .

Having failed in her first plan, Zia persuades the friendly Captain Nidever to go looking for Karana and Nidever takes Father Vicente, the most sympathetic of the priests, along to win Karana's confidence. But while Nidever is gone there is a revolt at the mission; the other Indians, led by a man aptly named Stone Hands, slip off in the middle of the night and Zia, who has stolen a key to help the plotters, is thrown in jail for refusing to tell where they have gone.

Zia is released from jail by Father Vicente when he returns triumphantly with Karana. Karana is at first ecstatic over her new experiences—the taste of melons, the sight of wild horses, learning to weave at the loom—but the mainland soon becomes another kind of prison. She is unable to communicate with anyone; even Zia has forgotten her native tongue and the other Indians regard her as crazy.

In the end Karana runs away to live in a cave on the beach and dies there while Zia, with nothing left to tie her to the mission, simply walks away to find her tribe's old abandoned home in the north. As much as one wants Zia to be free, her leaving has its troubling side. California is not an island, and one knows, historically that there was no escape for the Zias whose way of life was obliterated by the coming of the Spanish.

Nor does Zia's streak of detachment make for high adventure in the traditional sense. "I like you but this is not my home," Zia tells Father Malatesta calmly as she prepares to leave the mission once and for all. This kind of resigned statement is not what one expects from a child heroine. And though lots of exciting, even dangerous things happen to Zia—besides the boat trip and being thrown into jail, she is nearly caught in a brush fire set by one of Stone Hands' followers—the physical action is downplayed. O'Dell is not the arm-waving sort.

What draws one into this book, and probably accounts for the popularity of *Island of the Blue Dolphins* as well, is O'Dell's short, loaded sentences which force the reader to participate. When Zia says, soberly, that she is scared—"I was afraid all over—in my stomach and in my head"—her emotional reactions are not spelled out to the last detail. Adults of course are so familiar with this style of writing that it hardly bears commenting upon, but young readers are rarely given this much leeway.

Once, when Zia is visiting Karana in her cave retreat, the older woman points out a fossilized "giant bird" visible in the cave wall.

> We watched the giant bird with the firelight casting shadows on it. And the skeleton came alive as I watched and as the shadows changed and became feathers, each feather heavier than a strong man could lift, and I saw an eye larger than the table. It was the color of amber. When you looked at it, the eye moved away, but when you were not looking you knew it was watching you.

And for the moment O'Dell does give us the power to imagine the thing alive; just as he enables us to pin our personal hopes on Zia's gallant bid for liberty.

At times like these one decides to forgive *Zia* for not being another *Island of the Blue Dolphins*. Stood side by side the two books seem to prove that truth is not only stranger but, well, truer. Zia is not the kind of archetypal heroine who will win a devoted following, but she has a self-contained strength of her own.

> *Joyce Milton, "Beyond the Blue Dolphins," in* Book World—The Washington Post, *May 2, 1976, p. L2.*

[*Island of the Blue Dolphins*] had all the ingredients of a classic: a strong heroine, suspenseful narrative, and language as clean and taut as a drawn bow.

Now, 15 years later, O'Dell has written a follow-up to the original book—and it is a brave endeavor. . . .

It would be easy for the reviewer to compare this book to the earlier one and bemoan the fact that sequels are risky. But the truth is that *Zia* is a completely fresh creation, rich in character and action. The ending of the story, in which Karana gives her niece the courage to leave the Mission and rediscover her tribal heritage, is both surprising and correct—as it always is in good fiction. Once again Scott O'Dell has used history as the mainspring for revealing the truth about human beings: their passion, their grief.

> *Barbara Wersba, in a review of "Zia," in* The New York Times Book Review, *May 2, 1976, p. 38.*

[The] plot is thick and busy. But the writing looks simple: short sentences, few opinions, little theorizing. Like the mission fathers, one is sometimes a little baffled by Indian ideas; like Zia, at times confused by theirs. Spanish certainties weigh lightly on Indian impassiveness; Zia accepts most things; and the magnificent Pacific shimmers, the breakers crash: with little description, one sees and feels her surroundings, the enormity and beauty of nature in those parts. *Zia* is not quite a sequel but an independent offshoot of *The Island of the Blue Dolphins*. Its main skill and originality lies in using, as American teenage novels often do, the haphazardness of life, apparently random moments picked from a rich choice, a mixture of cultures, oddities of life-style. Nothing runs true to form—in other words, to fictional cliché. Good and bad are not wholly so, the mission is not quite right or quite wrong, people grumble rather than revolt and if loss of home can kill an Indian as surely as illness can, what about those displaced Californian Spaniards? It is a book that, without quite asking them, suggests such questions and, while the action seems unplanned and often, like life, surprising, the form is clear and satisfying.

> *Isabel Quigly, "Child of the Sun," in* The Times Literary Supplement, *No. 3931, July 15, 1977, p. 860.*

THE 290 (1976)

A minor effort from O'Dell but still a deftly written one. Teen-aged James Lynne, apprenticed to a British shipbuilder in 1862, aids in the construction of the Confederate sea raider, *The Alabama*, known as *The 290*. Motivated by his love of the ship Lynne sails with Captain Raphael Semmes whose exploits in sinking most of the Union merchant fleet without taking a life is adventure enough for one story. Unfortunately, O'Dell tries to tell two stories that are only tenuously connected when, a third of the way through, he has Lynne sail to the Caribbean and while in port undertake to free slaves owned by his father. The novel rambles too much to be completely satisfying, and Semmes remains faceless. Still, although O'Dell is not at his best here, he never wastes a word and once again he is able to refract universal themes of liberty and self-awareness through history's prism.

> *Michael T. Carollo, in a review of "The 290," in* School Library Journal, *Vol. 23, No. 5, January, 1977, p. 95.*

The 290 seems set fair to be a roistering yarn about a young seaman aboard a Confederate raider. The foreword gives the clue to the disappointment of the book, however: the story is based very firmly on historical fact. As a result, the novel is almost a documentary, since one episode does not precipitate another in the patterned way we expect of narrative.

The painstaking research becomes a straitjacket. A sailor is taken on board, leads a mutiny and is dismissed, never to be seen again. It does not matter to a reader that this actually happened historically—he is left wondering what the point of the incident is *in the story*. The book would be thoroughly useful background reading in a history project on the American Civil War, but is a succession of anti-climaxes as a novel.

> Geoff Fox, *"Moments of Truth,"* in The Times Educational Supplement, *No. 3269, February 3, 1978, p. 36.*

This is a short novel which would serve most usefully to support a Civil War project for older juniors and younger secondary children although, even here, a more exploratory approach to some of the related issues could have added substance.

As a story, *The 290* reads more like a first draft, lacking realisation of action or character—particularly surprising from this author. . . . (pp. 263-64)

> Gordon Parsons, in a review of *"The 290,"* in The School Librarian, *Vol. 26, No. 3, September, 1978, pp. 263-64.*

CARLOTA   (1977; British edition as *The Daughter of Don Saturnino*)

Carlota de Zubarán makes an interesting heroine for O'Dell's evocation of mid-nineteenth-century California society. She's 16 and has been raised by her father to take the place of a son killed in an Indian raid. So, despite her steely grandmother's disapproval, Carlota rides her stallion Tiburón astride, bests the young men in a horse race at her sister's wedding, and, when war comes, accompanies her father and his militia group to confront the hated gringos. Carlota's innate forthrightness and clear thinking lead inevitably to some independent stands. . . . [Later] after Señor de Zubarán's death, it's no surprise to see her firmly assert herself in operating the ranch. At the story's end, though, the future is entirely uncertain. The effects of American occupation remain threatening, and though Carlota is fully determined, there is the foreboding that forces stronger than she may bode ill for the de Zubaráns. O'Dell's laconic style lends dignity to the telling and, but for a conclusion that seems underdeveloped even in terms of its deliberately unsettled state, the plot is sustaining.

> Denise M. Wilms, in a review of *"Carlota,"* in Booklist, *Vol. 74, No. 3, October 1, 1977, p. 300.*

Occasionally, a seemingly minor incident has a symbolic importance belied by the proportion of space it is allotted in the annals of history. Such an incident occurred in California at the end of the war between Mexico and the United States when a small, badly outnumbered, quixotic contingent of Spanish landowners, armed only with lances and pride, defeated General Kearney's Army of the West. Known as the Battle of San Pasqual, it is the climax of an economically told story which, in its delineation of a strong-minded, independent heroine, recalls the author's memorable *Island of the Blue Dolphins.* The spare, well-honed style is artistically suited to the first person narrative. Carlota de Zubarán—a fictional counterpart of Luisa de Montero who lived in Southern California during the early nineteenth century—indicates the changing political and social climate which caused the passing of a distinctive but insular culture caught between the territorial imperatives of the warring nations. Encouraged by her father to be as self-

sufficient as the son he had lost, Carlota defies the conventions of ladylike behavior valued by her matriarchal grandmother and is the only member of the immediate family able to cope with catastrophe after the Spaniards' Pyrrhic victory. . . . The principal characters are realistically portrayed as unique individuals and as universal figures in an allegorical drama. Multidimensional, masterfully crafted, the novel is compelling in its powerful yet restrained emotional intensity.

> Mary M. Burns, in a review of *"Carlota,"* in The Horn Book Magazine, *Vol. LIII, No. 6, December, 1977, p. 670.*

O'Dell creates memorable incidents rather than characters, such as Carlota's near-fatal encounter with a burro clam at Blue Beach, her carryings-on at her sister's wedding, and the bloody encounter at the Battle of San Pasqual, with each violent happening building up to the book's climax. Animals play an important role. They figure in the plot; they mirror Carlota's change of attitude toward herself as she changes towards them; they set the tone of the story, with O'Dell's language racing to the stallion's canter, or beating a staccato to the gelding's trot. A lengthy anti-climax and indeterminate conclusion left me unsatisfied after the hectic pace of preceding chapters. Based in part on the life of real people, the story casts light on a relatively unknown segment of an unpopular war and its effect on some of those who were involved. Spanish expressions lend a note of exotic authenticity.

> Ruth M. Stein, in a review of *"Carlota,"* in Language Arts, *Vol. 55, No. 4, April, 1978, p. 523.*

KATHLEEN, PLEASE COME HOME   (1978)

The diary of a runaway girl, whose dismal experiences are attributed largely to "going along" with a bad companion. Early on, Kathleen, just 15, becomes engaged to a young wetback who warns her against the drugs friend Sybil is so free with. But Ramon is arrested and later killed in a raid, and when Kathleen realizes that it was her concerned, English-teacher mother who turned him in, she accepts Sybil's invitation to take off for Mexico. There life is a series of ups, downs, bags of horse, and angel dust. The two girls split when Kathleen learns that she's pregnant by Ramon, but get together again in time for an auto accident that is fatal to both Sybil and Kathleen's unborn baby. (That makes two too many convenient disasters, both of which free Kathleen from commitments.) The end sees Kathleen and Joy, another convalescent druggie, throwing away Sybil's valuable stash of heroin and heading into a straight future. O'Dell undoubtedly knows the scene better than many writers who would warn YAs on drugs, but still his social worker's presence can be felt at nearly every turn. Of course this sort of material has an enduring fascination for daydreaming stay-at-homes. (pp. 311-12)

> A review of *"Kathleen, Please Come Home,"* in Kirkus Reviews, *Vol. XLVI, No. 6, March 15, 1978, pp. 311-12.*

Scott O'Dell's *Kathleen Please Come Home*, is a sympathetic portrait of a 15-year-old from a happy middle-class home who runs away. Mr. O'Dell . . . can weave a suspenseful tale, and he has done so in his latest novel, which is in large part a young woman's diary. . . .

There is a moving section in the book in which Kathleen's mother, Sara, writes down in *her* diary her reactions after she realizes that her daughter has run away. She finds it difficult to understand how her daughter could "continue to doubt that what I did was done only for her health, her happiness, all the days of her future." When Kathleen finally returns home months later, she finds her mother has sold her house and is "somewhere" in the East, following tips from the police as to the whereabouts of her daughter.

Kathleen, Please Come Home is unsettling in a number of ways. A fast-paced story chock-full of adventures and "colorful" characters, it seems to have all the trappings of a made-for-television movie. There are the unsavory types in San Diego (Kathleen's hometown) who prey on illegal Mexican aliens and the parents of runaways. Sybil is an inveterate drug user and would-be heroin pusher. She uses—in order of appearance—marijuana, hashish, PCP, uppers and downers, heroin and angel dust. Curiously, Mr. O'Dell has chosen to present every one of the drugs as having favorable effects on Kathleen. What she got from her first taste—literally—of PCP was "a heavenly moment that seemed to last a million, million years" and a headache afterward. . . .

Mr. O'Dell's book offers few insights on the subject of runaways. Kids in flight seem merely a vehicle for a readable book.

Margarett Loke, "Splitting Is Hard," in The New York Times Book Review, April 30, 1978, p. 53.

Readers who pick up Scott O'Dell's *Kathleen, Please Come Home* expecting another visit back into California history will be momentarily disoriented. The landscape is no surprise, for the action ranges from San Diego to the tip of Baja, but the story takes place now, not yesterday, and the issues are contemporary indeed.

Through entries in her journal we meet Kathleen, a naive fifteen-year-old whose response to the world around her is typified by "Wow!" The loss of this naivete is the theme of the book. (p. 74)

[When Kathleen runs away from home] the novel switches to the mother's journal. With the sureness of a master craftsman, O'Dell gives us the fear, the helplessness, the total aloneness she feels as she discovers that her daughter has run away across the border into Baja and is not going to come back. . . . [Kathleen's] journey back from La Paz becomes a journey into self control and maturity. The fight is lonely and hard and not glamorous, and the outcome is honest. Though she does finally break the addiction, she is not back to where she was, for she can never be that pampered, naive girl again, and things have happened that can never be undone. Like Thomas Wolfe, she can't go home again.

There are some weaknesses in the book but one has to strain to find them. The loss of the unborn child in a car accident is perhaps too convenient, for example. Nevertheless, once having read the first few pages, one cannot put the book down. Its appeal comes not only from a structured plot, but from its truth. With a sensitivity that makes us live the experience intensely, O'Dell portrays the euphoria and total commitment of first love. The journal technique allows him to reveal the dawning insights as they come to Kathleen, and so we experience her temptations and her growth as she does.

Kathleen, Please Come Home is the story of change, an honest rendition of the struggle and hardships involved in the growth from innocence to maturity. On this level, the novel is arche-

typal, deeply moving and profound. With this book, O'Dell has moved to a new level. (pp. 74-5)

Sally Rumbaugh, in a review of "Kathleen, Please Come Home," in The World of Children's Books, Vol. III, No. 2, 1978, pp. 74-5.

THE CAPTIVE (1979)

A superbly written novel, rich in plot and historical detail, that explores Spanish penetration into the Americas in the early 16th Century. A follower of Bartolomé de las Casas, an anti-slavery priest, 16-year-old Julián Escobar is yanked from his studies at the seminary in Seville for a journey to the island of Buenaaventura in the New World. When the ship lands and the Spaniards discover gold, Julián witnesses acts of brutality against the peaceful inhabitants that sicken him and is afraid to speak out. A hurricane sinks the ship and Julián believes he and the horse Bravo are the only survivors in an uninhabited land. He leads a Robinson Crusoe existence until he finds a hideous idol, from which he deduces there must be others nearby. Ceela, a young Mayan girl, leaves him fire and food and, in exchange for rides on Bravo, teaches him her language and customs and tells him about the great city of the Seven Serpents. She is uninterested in Christianity and, with some explosives salvaged from the ship, he blows up the idol. The next day, he is visited by a delegation from the City led by a Spaniard, a crafty dwarf named Guillermo Cantú, who tells Julián the Mayan legend of the god Kukulcán: how he disappeared and promised to return as a young, blond man. Despite himself, Julián is drawn into Cantú's plot to pass him off as the god. The book—"the first part of a story to be called *City of the Seven Serpents*," according to an author's note—ends with Julián, standing atop a pyramid, accepted as Kukulcán and already seduced by the glory that will be his. Characterizations are all finely drawn, and Julián's transformation from insecure, humane seminarian to pretend god is remarkable in its honest development.

Nancy Berkowitz, in a review of "The Captive," in School Library Journal, Vol. 26, No. 3, November, 1979, p. 92.

This brilliant first volume in a projected sequence begins when Julian Escobar, an idealistic 16-year-old seminarian in early 16th-century Spain, is part bullied, part lured by the promise of savage souls and a future Bishopric, to accompany imperious young Don Luis to the nobleman's New World island. . . . We leave Julian, arrayed as the god, surveying his newly acquired domain—sickened by the human sacrifices being made in his honor, but stirred moments later by visions of empire. And O'Dell leaves readers impatient for further developments. It is a measure of his seriousness and his skill that the suspense focuses not on events, which have so far been swift and stunning, inevitable and unexpected, or on the artfully foreshadowed intrigue, confrontations, and dangers that are sure to follow, but on Julian's moral choices and on what he will make of his false, exalted position.

A review of "The Captive," in Kirkus Reviews, Vol. XLVIII, No. 2, January 15, 1980, p. 71.

This novel is, apparently, only the first part of a longer work, promised for future publication. Whether or not it will gain enormously by subsequent revelations can be no real concern of the reviewer, or, for that matter, of the purchaser and the reader. It must stand or fall by itself. One does not, after all, buy an automobile on the understanding that the engine will follow in a year or so.

Scott O'Dell is a much-honored author, a real general of children's literature who comes with as many medals as a prize-winning Swiss chocolate. Therefore he must be judged by the highest standards as one's expectations are keenly aroused. Alas, they are not fulfilled. We all understand what is meant by a good bad book. It is a book that is thoroughly reprehensible and lacking in all the higher qualities of literature, such as moral values, philosophy, construction, character-drawing and general credibility, and yet contrives to be thoroughly readable. Such a book as, say, *The Scarlet Pimpernel*. Well, *The Captive* is what I can only describe as a bad good book. It is good inasmuch as it is well constructed, well researched, contains many interesting items of unfamiliar knowledge, and displays unimpeachable moral worth (Mr. O'Dell comes out very strongly against Slavery, Murder and Human Sacrifice; he doesn't hold with them for a moment!); but it is not very readable. It is inclined to be ponderous, and the prose style reminds one of a careful translation.

The story, told in the first person, is of Julián Escobar, a young seminarian who embarks with the conquistadors for the New World, where he witnesses the monstrous behavior of those who seek for gold. He is, naturally, horrified and repelled; and yet his own course proves to be not entirely beyond reproach. In his zeal to do good, Julián falls victim to the sin of spiritual pride and an apt parallel is drawn with Christ's Temptation in the wilderness.

It is a strong theme and might have been a gripping tale . . . but for the author's refusal to become involved in it. The very reference at the end to the Temptation in the wilderness is thought of as "the scene where Satan took Christ unto an exceeding high mountain." The *scene*. Surely no Spanish seminarian would think of Holy Writ in such theatrical terms! And so it is throughout. There is no immediacy. One gets the impression that the author is looking at a series of pictures and carefully describing them. At no time are we really with the hero. We receive no impression of his sensations. There are none of those touches that enliven the imagination. When our hero's hands are bound behind his back, there seems to be no reaction, no sense of helplessness, of indignity.

I looked into a copy of *Don Quixote*, thinking that, perhaps, O'Dell was modeling his own refusal to be perturbed, or even interested in what was going on, after the manner of a 16th-century Spanish author. I found a passage where a man was in chains. The character, explaining what it was like, remarked that, in order to pass the time, he and his fellow prisoners amused themselves by seeing how far they could jump in their chains. It is just that sort of shaft of imagination that *The Captive* lacks, that shaft of imagination that illuminates the narrative and makes it live.

It may be that I am being unjust, and that future developments will illuminate all and justify what has gone before. I hope so, for I would not like to think that so admirable an author as Scott O'Dell (*The Island of the Blue Dolphins* was a splendid book) has fallen so far from his own high standards. As it is, I can only recommend the present book to those with a passionate desire to know more about the history and culture of the Mayan Indians.

Leon Garfield, "Young Man among the Mayans," in Book World—The Washington Post, *March 9, 1980, p. 7.*

SARAH BISHOP (1980)

Writers may choose their subjects, but good writers have less to say about their themes, which are apt to rise, bidden or unbidden, from the raw material of their deepest preoccupations. Never does Scott O'Dell play better music than when he introduces what seems to be his favorite motif: the pull between the individual's need for solitude and the need for society.

Identified primarily with Western subjects, Mr. O'Dell has set his new book in Westchester County during the Revolutionary War. After losing her father at the hands of the rebels and her brother at the hands of the King's men, Sarah Bishop, in fear of both parties, hides in a cave, gradually learning to take a fierce joy in her hard-won self-reliance. And when at the end of the book it is clear that Sarah will move back to town, the reader understands that Sarah is under no illusion that living with people will be easier than living alone.

Mr. O'Dell has always been a master at lighting up an era with details that seem to have been learned on the spot. ("Don't forget to return the sack," the miller calls to Sarah. "It's muslin.") So this book is a vivid reflection of life in Revolutionary New York, and Scott O'Dell is obviously very much at home. First and foremost, however, this is the story of Sarah Bishop, a stout-hearted heroine who, although caught in the conflicts of her own age, might have lived anywhere at any time.

Jean Fritz, in a review of "Sarah Bishop," in The New York Times Book Review, *May 4, 1980, p. 26.*

Despite a series of highly dramatic incidents, the story line is basically sharp and clear; O'Dell's messages about the bitterness and folly of war, the dangers of superstition, and the courage of the human spirit are smoothly woven into the story, as are the telling details of period and place. To many readers, the primary appeal of the book may be the way in which Sarah, like the heroine of *Island of the Blue Dolphins,* like Robinson Crusoe, makes a comfortable life in the isolation of the wilderness.

Zena Sutherland, in a review of "Sarah Bishop," in Bulletin of the Center for Children's Books, *Vol. 33, No. 10, June, 1980, p. 198.*

Once again Scott O'Dell has taken a figure from history, brought that person and her times vividly alive, and shown us something profound about ourselves. *Sarah Bishop* is an exciting, moving book that deserves awards.

The real Sarah Bishop came from England to Long Island just before the American Revolution. As O'Dell tells it, Sarah's widowed father is a sternly religious Christian and a staunch Tory. Faced with hostility from vehement patriots, he tries to teach Sarah the Christian concept of forgiveness. However, the patriots tar and feather him, and he dies. Sarah goes off to search for her only brother, a patriot soldier, only to find he has died on a cruelly-run British prison ship. Tearing from her Bible the passage "Love your enemies . . . ," Sarah turns to the Old Testament stories of revenge. And yet, revenge against whom? Both sides have murdered members of her family.

O'Dell's theme is the age-old conflict between the desire for revenge and the need for inner peace. From this moment, the book does not slow down, for Sarah herself is wanted by the British; the story is taunt with tension right to the end. Despite all the action and suspense, O'Dell manages to keep the focus on his theme, the inner growth of his protagonist. The novel is a masterful study of the process of grief. At first Sarah wants to lash out, then her anger cools to a deadly chill. Trusting only her musket, she rejects the human race, hiding alone in the wilderness all winter. In the beauty of the woods she finds peace. When she finally makes friends with a tiny bat, the healing process begins, and it grows almost imperceptively as the winter thaws until she tentatively starts a friendship with a young Quaker. We feel her healing will continue.

A self-reliant heroine with strong emotions has been caught in a world where suspicions and hatreds explode into violence. Out of the tensions of a country at war, O'Dell has raised significant questions relevant today. What happens inside a person who is a victim of brutality? How does one survive, not only physically, but emotionally and spiritually, in a violent world? In his gentle and understanding treatment of Sarah Bishop, O'Dell reassures us that the human spirit has within itself the capacity to survive and become whole again. (pp. 86-7)

> *Sally Rumbaugh, in a review of "Sarah Bishop," in* The World of Children's Books, *Vol. VI, 1981, pp. 86-7.*

THE FEATHERED SERPENT   (1981)

AUTHOR'S COMMENTARY

Years ago, after *Island of the Blue Dolphins* came out, I went to work on a story called *The King's Fifth* based in part upon the premise that one-fifth of all treasure—slaves, silver, gold, whatever—belonged to the King of Spain and must be delivered to him on pain of death. The background for the story was Coronado's legendary search for the Seven Cities of Cibola, where the doorknobs were made of gold, even the streets were paved with gold, and gold was so common that the snobbish nobles chose to eat only on wooden plates.

I had an ambitious, overly ambitious, theme. Each of the golden cities represented a vice—avarice, sloth, cruelty, and so forth— and as my hero journeyed from one city to another, he was caught in these snares. One midnight, having worked on the story for some three months, I awoke to the horrible realization that I was in a head-on competition with Dante Alighieri. To my credit, by the dawn's early light I tossed the manuscript into the fire and started over again on a more modest scale.

After I had written *The Captive,* the first book of the trilogy, I encountered an equally large, if dissimilar, problem. It lasted for weeks and ended with sixty pages consigned to ashes.

Offhand the problem seemed simple enough. *The Captive* was complete in itself. The second book, *The Feathered Serpent,* should also be complete, an entity not dependent upon the first book. In other words, a reader taking up *The Feathered Serpent* must be given as painlessly as possible all the information contained in *The Captive* which is vital to the second book, and at the same time not be subjected to a double helping of what he already knows. It all sounds simple, but for me it was not. I went to the shelves, hoping here to discover how best to handle the difficulty. Ford Madox Ford, Dickens, Scott, Balzac, Calderon. (We all stand on the backs of our betters.) I found no answer to the problem. The solution, if indeed it is a solution, is my own.

For me stories are always replete with problems. In other activities I seem to find more or less satisfactory answers as I go along. But not with writing. Each new book is as difficult as the last, if not more so. Take the matter of local color. What goes in? and what do you leave out?

I am just back from Peru, the scene of Pizarro's monstrous deeds, and I can hardly wait to find an excuse to describe him as he lies in his crystal coffin—a small bundle of bones and the tiny face of a marmoset—the man who fought a hundred fights, who conquered a continent. (pp. 140-41)

Furthermore, in the matter of how much local color should go into this third volume of the Maya-Aztec-Inca story and, lest I be accused of showing off, how much should be left out, what can I do with the llamas—those trim little beasts with eyelashes four inches long, under which they regard you with bored curiosity, who only consent to work at an elevation of ten thousand feet or more and who, if you put one ounce in excess of eighty pounds on their backs, will lie down? And with the fact that the mighty Amazon at its headwaters near Iquitos in Peru is barely fifteen feet above sea level at Santa Margarita de Belém, thousands of miles away on the Atlantic Ocean? And also with the fact that the Maya invented the zero for themselves—the Greeks and Romans and Egyptians did not—without which it is virtually impossible to be mathematically serious? That using stone markers, the Maya foretold the movement of heavenly bodies within seconds of our own predictions, which were arrived at by sophisticated instruments?

Besides the problem of what to put in and what to leave out, of how to connect the freight cars to the locomotive so that the train moves off without a jolt, there's the difficulty of how best to show the stages by which your protagonist—who in this case is a seminarian, a disciple of Christ, a follower of the meek St. Francis—becomes corrupted, somewhat of a villain, if not a monster. And to ask your reader, while you are doing all this, to look upon him with Christian forbearance, a gift rarely granted to us, especially to the young.

There is also the problem of sex. I have recently been taken to task by a reviewer for a lack of it in my chronicle [see excerpt dated January 10, 1982]. Apparently he hadn't read *The Captive,* had read only parts of *The Feathered Serpent,* and consequently didn't know that Julián Escobar was a seminarian living in an age whose energies were not absorbed by sex, in contrast to the present when the phenomena dependent upon the differences between the male and the female are presented to us on a twenty-four-hour schedule, a bacchanalia beginning with children as they eat their Wheaties and ending only with those who cannot sleep.

I was tempted in *The Captive* to have Julián fall in love with the young Mayan girl. But only tempted. In *The Feathered Serpent* I was also tempted. In the third book of the chronicle [*The Amethyst Ring*] I may be tempted again. If so, since I am a product of my age, who can say what will happen?

As a sidelight on story construction, the handling of Ceela, the Mayan girl, may be of interest; at least, it shatters a precedent. Ceela played a prominent role in *The Captive.* In my first version of *The Feathered Serpent* her role was slighted—a fault which I corrected by having her appear late in the story as Marina, the interpreter for Hernán Cortés. This rather high-handed transition I justified by the fact that Marina's origins were not known, only guessed at. That she was born a Maya on the Island of the Seven Serpents is as good a solution as any, and better than most, and it eased me out of a fix.

There is still the final problem. A historical trilogy for the young is a well-nigh untameable beast. The momentum gained in the first book tends to be progressively lost as the story moves on into the second book and then into the third.

And yet, the historical novel, whether in three parts or one, despite all of its technical difficulties and in the face of neglect from young readers, is still worth the writer's best. (pp. 142-44)

For children, who believe that nothing much has happened before they appeared and that little of the past they do perceive has any possible bearing upon their lives, the historical novel can be an entertaining corrective, a signpost between the fixed, always relevant, past and the changing present. (p. 144)

> *Scott O'Dell, "The Tribulations of a Trilogy," in* The Horn Book Magazine, *Vol. LVIII, No. 2, April, 1982, pp. 137-44.*

[*The Feathered Serpent* continues] the story, begun in *The Captive,* of the idealistic young Spanish student, Julián Escobar, cast away among the Maya in 16th-Century Mexico and mistaken for the returning god, Kukulcán. Corrupted by his power, and with a driving ambition to restore the decaying Mayan civilization to its former splendor, Julián establishes himself as god and ruler. He journeys to the powerful Aztec empire to learn how to conquer and rule and is caught up in Moctezuma's tragic encounter with the conquistador, Cortés. O'Dell recreates the conflicting cultures in a fast-moving narrative, describing the widespread brutality with quiet control. Moctezuma, seen through Julian's eyes, is glorious, enigmatic, and finally—as he accepts the inevitability of Cortés's conquest—resigned and helpless. Cortés is ambitious, ruthless, fearless; his cruelty is as evident in the individual act of ordering envoys' hands hacked off as in the destruction of populations. As in the first book, the central character interest and moral complexity lie in Julián, whose first-person narrative is used by O'Dell with powerful irony.

> *Hazel Rochman, in a review of "The Feathered Serpent," in* School Library Journal, *Vol. 28, No. 2, October, 1981, p. 152.*

The one thing a novel about the Aztec is bound to have is exotica. What with tombs lined with gold, hearts torn palpitating from sacrificial victims, feather banners, temples and palaces, it is hard to imagine an Aztec book that is dull. And Scott O'Dell's latest book is not dull.

As a character, Julián has more insight than many conquistadors, actual and fictional. He understands, for example, that Cortés threatens the Mayas, who trust him (Kukulcán) to protect them, with both death and demoralization. At the same time, he displays odd vacancies of personality. He seems to have little emotional life, no real curiosity about an alien society and (strangest of all) an implausible lack of awareness of the opposite sex. The result is that, while the book is not dull, neither is it deep or gripping.

> *Georgess McHargue, in a review of "The Feathered Serpent," in* The New York Times Book Review, *January 10, 1982, p. 26.*

In the course of the story Julián makes the following point to his companion, " 'We are not fighting *against* the Azteca. Nor are we fighting *for* Cortés and his Spaniards' "; for he is morally repelled both by the bloody human sacrifices and by the Spanish lust for gold. Further narration of his adventures can be the only possible key to the ultimate meaning of his ambiguous position: his feeling of power as Kukulcán and his desire to convert the Indians. The episodic novel recounts the excitement of battles, the horrors of human sacrifice, and the wonders of ancient civilizations; but more moving than these are the subtly hinted inconsistencies of character and the uncanny suggestions of violent events. (pp. 54-5)

> *Paul Heins, in a review of "The Feathered Serpent," in* The Horn Book Magazine, *Vol. LVIII, No. 1, February, 1982, pp. 54-5.*

THE SPANISH SMILE   (1982)

The setting of his latest novel, an island off the coast of California, and the central figure of a young girl held prisoner recall Scott O'Dell's classic *Island of the Blue Dolphins.* These are the only resemblances between the two novels, however. The heroine of *The Spanish Smile*, Lucinda de Cabrillo y Benvides, is the sheltered only daughter of the proud descendant of Spanish conquistadors, Don Enrique. Cloistered away in a gloomy castle, Lucinda is allowed no radio, television, newspapers or even any book written in the 20th Century. Her father pursues a deranged dream of restoring Spanish rule to California. All of the gothic machinery is in place in this story; the castle with its mysterious crypt guarded by deadly serpents, the young girl in distress and the charming young man who comes to her aid; and O'Dell's fluid style moves it along crisply. Readers who are put off by a plethora of literary and historical references may get bogged down in a few spots. There are times also when credulity is stretched almost to the breaking point, even for a gothic. In spite of overwhelming evidence, it takes two thirds of the book for Lucinda to realize the depth of her father's madness and to begin to assert herself. Still, O'Dell has written a story that is several cuts above others in the genre.

> *David N. Pauli, in a review of "The Spanish Smile," in* School Library Journal, *Vol. 29, No. 2, October, 1982, p. 163.*

Readers looking for pure escapism will find an ample portion of it in this novel about a young girl growing into adulthood. . . . Scott O'Dell has not created an ordinary young girl as heroine of the latest of his impressive (*Island of the Blue Dolphins, Sarah Bishop*) children's books.

The novel features a wide diversity of characters, some innocent and admirable, others entirely corrupted. This diversity adds interest and color to this exotic story. Although improbable and unrealistic, this book will provide enjoyable, though largely frivolous, reading.

> *Margaret Parente, in a review of "The Spanish Smile," in* Best Sellers, *Vol. 42, No. 9, December, 1982, p. 366.*

[*The Spanish Smile*] is the kind of young adult book that really excites the imagination. . . . *Smile* contains only one pure fantasy element, but it's a great one; an island, just off the coast of California, run almost as an independent kingdom by Don Enrique, who lives there with his daughter, Lucinda. . . . The book is told from Lucinda's point of view, and she sees everything colored by the books she has read, one minute looking at romance as she might look at Heathcliff in *Wuthering Heights* the next minute interpreting her father's actions with a horror straight out of Edgar Allan Poe.

And O'Dell's book gives Lucinda a lot to look at. *The Spanish Smile* is filled with mad plots to take over California, giant bushmasters (the largest poisonous snakes in the world), huge mausoleums filled with ornate coffins, and hastily constructed walls that may hide the remains of one or more bodies. And, because all these fantastic things are told from Lucinda's 19th-century romantic point of view, O'Dell not only gets them to work, he turns the novel into a headlong romp, something I couldn't put down as I waited for the next wonderfully unbelievable thing to happen. (p. 11)

> *Craig Shaw Gardner, "Fantasy to Cut Your Teeth On," in* Book World—The Washington Post, *January 9, 1983, pp. 11, 13.*

THE AMETHYST RING   (1983)

In a sequel to *The Captive* and *The Feathered Serpent,* O'Dell continues the stirring story of the young Spanish seminarian, Julian Escobar, who had been shipwrecked in the New World and become a god/ruler to the Mayan people. As this fine historical novel starts, Escobar has escaped from a vengeful Cortes after the death of Moctezuma. Now he is back in his city, on the island he hopes to defend against the ruthless Cortes, and he finds his people have a hostage, a bishop who is wearing the amethyst ring that shows his status. Escobar lets his people kill the bishop and thereafter wears his ring, an error he regrets when he is later hounded by the Spanish explorers. In the end, after many adventures, Escobar returns to Spain, refuses the chance of being wealthy, and joins the Brothers of the Poor. This is both an exciting adventure story of a man corrupted by power, and a vivid account of the conquistadores who ravaged an ancient civilization, and it is notable for its structure and characterization as well as for the research that colors but does not clog the narrative. (pp. 131-32)

> *Zena Sutherland, in a review of "The Amethyst Ring," in* Bulletin of the Center for Children's Books, *Vol. 36, No. 7, March, 1983, pp. 131-32.*

Here concludes O'Dell's dazzling drama of the temptation, fall, and redemption of Julian Escobar. . . . Julian has come to sympathize wholly with the Indian victims against the Spanish conquerors and their priests, but he never gives up his Spanish religion. Dispirited, he returns to Spain to find [his dwarf companion] ensconced as the Marquis of Santa Cruz and the Seven Cities. "You always had a heavy conscience," observes the dwarf, as Julian gives up both his dream of priesthood and his share of the dwarf's gold to join a lay order, the Brothers of the Poor—a weary renunciation that could come only after the once-untried idealist had won and lost and soured on power and glory. This evolution, and the small choices Julian makes along the way, have remained the compelling focus of a trilogy crackling with intrigue, historical spectacle, and the conflict of cultures that confounds his loyalties.

> *A review of "The Amethyst Ring," in* Kirkus Reviews, *Vol. LI, No. 8, April 15, 1983, p. 462.*

In completing the trilogy which began with *The Captive* and *The Feathered Serpent,* the author has carried to a logical conclusion the adventures and experiences of Juliàn Escobar. . . . A historical novel in the sense that the splendors and the horrors of the ancient Indian cultures of America are understandingly

portrayed, the narrative related by the unhappy, unheroic protagonist is not merely an account of random adventures. The author has eschewed the grand scale and the melodramatic in his telling but has been both sensitive and objectively perceptive of the memorable moments that reveal the depths of human experience "in this world of pain and beauty."

> *Paul Heins, in a review of "The Amethyst Ring," in* The Horn Book Magazine, *Vol. LIX, No. 3, June, 1983, p. 315.*

THE CASTLE IN THE SEA   (1983)

O'Dell reworks the Gothic horror elements of *The Spanish Smile* in a thinly plotted, imitative sequel that continues the bizarre story of the beautiful young heiress, Lucinda de Cabrillo y Benivides, who discovers that her father's machinations seem to extend from the grave to hold her in thrall on the Isla de Oro. Replacing her father as villain is the equally mad Ricardo Villaverde, former servant, now Luncinda's guardian, who, dressed in her father's Spanish *grandee* clothes, is determined to carry out her father's plans for her. Even the arrival from Spain of her aristocratic financé, Porfirio de Puertoblanco, does not free her; instead, both she and Porfirio become victims of several "accidents," and it suddenly occurs to Lucinda that someone is out to either drive her mad or murder her. The deadly snake that killed her father pops up again, this time in Luncinda's bed where she lies still all night so as not to incite the snake to strike. Perhaps offered tongue in cheek, the tale would have been more successful; nevertheless, readers caught up by the first book may get a charge out of this one for all its melodrama.

> *Sally Estes, in a review of "The Castle in the Sea," in* Booklist, *Vol. 80, No. 2, September 15, 1983, p. 160.*

Disappointing best describes this novel. The characters are shallow and easily confused. The story line is difficult to follow with events left vague and unexplained. O'Dell's free use of Spanish words and phrases only muddles things more. The reader is not endeared to any character and is left indifferent to the ending. Unfortunately, attention will be drawn to this novel due to O'Dell's previous award winning works.

> *Patty S. Harber, in a review of "The Castle in the Sea," in* Voice of Youth Advocates, *Vol. 7, No. 1, April, 1984, p. 34.*

ALEXANDRA   (1984)

Alexandra Dimitrios' grandfather was one of the first sponge divers from the Greek island of Kalymnos to come to Tarpon Springs, Florida, the "sponge capital" of the world. Now Grandfather Stefanos is partly crippled from many years of diving, but when Alexandra's father is fatally stricken with the bends, Grandfather stubbornly determines to carry on the family business and teach the willing Alexandra to dive in her father's place. The idea of a female sponge diver is repellent to many, including Alexandra's mother and sister, but her first good haul brings in an awesome sum of money. Alexandra, now a local celebrity, is quietly pleased with her diving success, though she is uneasy about her attraction to her sister's fiancé. Gradually, however, Alexandra realizes that their small sponging operation is being used by cocaine smugglers, a discovery that snares her and Grandfather Stefanos on the horns of a moral dilemma. Although O'Dell's meticulously detailed setting and insightful depiction of the Greek-American community of sponge divers is in itself fascinating, the story line is nearly overwhelmed by the proliferation of local color. Alexandra never comes fully to life, and her feelings about her father's sudden death, her glamorous older sister, and her diving career are strangely unarticulated. Readers able to lose themselves in Alexandra's well-realized world will find this an enriching contemporary novel, but others who demand more vigorous character and plot development will be less than satisfied. (pp. 1345-46)

> *Karen Stang Hanley, in a review of "Alexandra,"*
> *in* Booklist, *Vol. 80, No. 18, May 15, 1984, pp.*
> *1345-46.*

Even before the smuggling is revealed, this is a suspenseful contemporary adventure story. The dangers inherent in [the little-known occupation of sponge fishing] including sharks, a possibly dangerous sea turtle, the "bends" and the constant threat of hurricanes add interest. At the conclusion, readers know what Alexandra's decision is, but the story ends before they learn the outcome of her decision. A sequel may follow, but in the meantime, the ending is unsatisfying. In spite of this drawback, Alexandra is a self-reliant and appealing young woman. Her interactions with her stubborn grandfather, her worried mother and older sister are believable and will cause readers to think seriously about the consequences of her choice. (p. 86)

> *Barbara Chatton, in a review of "Alexandra," in*
> School Library Journal, *Vol. 30, No. 10, August,*
> *1984, pp. 85-6.*

[*Alexandra*] is not simply another tale of adventures at sea, spiced with visions of romance. It also chronicles a young woman's discovery of something more dreadful at sea than sharks and hurricanes—a man's greed and callous manipulation of others. Her secret knowledge creates a complicated moral dilemma that only she can resolve. "The deepest waters," her grandfather tells her, "are not out in the Gulf but somewhere deep inside you."

Once more Scott O'Dell offers junior high school readers a charming tale. His portrait of the grandfather is especially well-drawn. And although the character Alexandra is not portrayed with enough depth of emotion to make her dilemma a compelling one, the story moves swiftly to her conflict and does provide some suspense on how she will resolve it. Good entertainment.

> *Jane Yarbrough, in a review of "Alexandra," in* The
> ALAN Review, *Vol. 12, No. 1, Fall, 1984, p. 23.*

THE ROAD TO DAMIETTA (1985)

[O'Dell] has written what may be his finest novel. He notes that his book "leans heavily upon" *Francis of Assisi* by Arnaldo Fortini, translated by Helen Moak, who also added valuable findings of her own. The Fortini biography is deemed the best of countless histories of the saint, but O'Dell's novel is unsurpassed at recreating the human beings in the orbit of St. Francis and the places where the great events of his life occured.

The narrator is Cecilia Graziella Beatrice Angelica Rosanna di Montaro (based on Angelica di Rimini, a contemporary of Francis). Called "Ricca," the girl is 13, secretly burning with love for Francis Bernardone. The foppish, pleasure-bent youth

is scorned by other men in Assisi, but adored by most women, including Ricca's slightly older friend, Clare di Scifi, whose family demands that she wed "advantageously," which is the aim of the di Montaros for Ricca. Transfixed by Francis, the girls witness his public disavowal of his rich father when the scapegrace strips off his clothes and declares himself a mendicant for Christ. This is the beginning of the wanderings that take Francis and his band to Damietta where men of the Fifth Crusade slaughter the Saracens, in the name of Christianity.

Ricca follows Francis and, through her words, we experience the horrors and the loss of hope when the saint's rapport with Sultan Malikal-Kamil fails to bring peace. Bishop Pelagius, leading the crusade, drives his soldiers to further brutalities while the sultan shows the mercy expected from followers of the Nazarene.

Back in Italy, Ricca is with Clare—now founder of the Poor Clares who imitate Francis's brotherly band—when the saint dies. It will be a long time before readers cease to feel the impact of O'Dell's drama and the influence of the saint who urged us to love each other and "all things great and small."

> *A review of "The Road to Damietta," in* Publishers
> Weekly, *Vol. 228, No. 18, November 1, 1985, p.*
> *66.*

O'Dell has a compelling style, and there is much of historical interest in Ricca's story, but it is often difficult to see where fact ends and fiction begins. The description of Damietta, besieged by Crusaders and starved into submission, is vivid, as is the description of the pathetic outcome of the Children's Crusade. When Ricca finally is convinced that Francis will never return her earthly love, the story moves, shifting rather abruptly, to a faster pace to wind up the action. In sum, competent writing of historical fiction is marred by a scope so ambitious that it weakens the cohesion of the narrative.

> *A review of "The Road to Damietta," in* Bulletin of
> the Center for Children's Books, *Vol. 39, No. 4,*
> *December, 1985, p. 74.*

The sights, smells and biases of 13th-Century life are vividly and realistically portrayed. Although the strong, willful character of Ricca is believable, Francis remains elusive and underdeveloped. Much of Francis' dialogue includes quotes from his poetry. While they do reflect his philosophy, they are not sufficient for solid character development. However, Ricca's strength and the rich historical background make this an enjoyable reading experience.

> *Cynthia M. Sturgis, in a review of "The Road to*
> *Damietta," in* School Library Journal, *Vol. 32, No.*
> *4, December, 1985, p. 104.*

STREAMS TO THE RIVER, RIVER TO THE SEA: A NOVEL OF SACAGAWEA (1986)

O'Dell returns here to his most effective voice, a simple first-person narration of historical journey. The story begins with Sacagawea's capture, along with her Shoshone cousin, by Minnetaree warriors. Her adjustment to life with that tribe, escape from a hostile neighboring chief, and marriage to a French trader after her owner's gambling loss all test the courage and strength she will need to survive the hardships of the Lewis and Clark expedition to the Pacific—which she makes with a baby strapped to her back. This is action-packed drama, believably revealed by a stoic heroine who maintains her self-worth despite vagaries of fortune in which she's a pawn of men and natural forces. Although the return eastward telescopes into almost a catalogue of tribes and perils overcome, the book retains its grip on the reader to a fine-honed finish, when Sacagawea abandons her romantic feelings for Clark and returns to her people. An informative and involving choice for American history students and pioneer-adventure readers.

A review of "Streams to the River, River to the Sea: A Novel of Sacagawea," in Bulletin of the Center for Children's Books, *Vol. 39, No. 8, April, 1986, p. 155.*

Those familiar with what is known of Sacagawea from mentions of her in the journals of Lewis and Clark may be troubled by O'Dell's liberal fictionalizing of the known incidents in which she figured. But translating brief, expository statements into narrative scenes and dialogue necessarily requires invention of conversations, probable motives and likely actions—and O'Dell uses all of these to move this novel along. His account centers on the period of Bird Woman's involvement with the Lewis and Clark expedition. It is a suspenseful, well-paced retelling of this remarkable, true-life adventure from 1804 to 1806. (p. 107)

George Gleason, in a review of "Streams to the River, River to the Sea: A Novel of Sacagawea," in School Library Journal, *Vol. 32, No. 9, May, 1986, pp. 107-08.*

There is probably no more enigmatic or fascinating a figure in the history of the United States than Sacagawea.... Scott O'Dell combines the historical record with the novelist's speculation to create a vital human being as vigorous and appealing as Karana in *Island of the Blue Dolphins* or Bright Morning in *Sing Down the Moon.* He seems to have a particular empathy for and interest in those who are caught between two cultures and who, at times, are torn between conflicting loyalties. Beginning with Sacagawea's capture, at thirteen, by a tribe hostile to the Shoshones, he effectively builds tension through the skillful re-creation of the Lewis and Clark entourage. The magnitude of that undertaking—four thousand miles "on foot, on horseback, by canoe ... on a journey that ranks in courage and danger with any journey of recorded history"—is clearly delineated through the narrative, written as if composed by Sacagawea herself. This perspective allows the author to develop the relationship between the Indian girl and William Clark more fully than the journal references indicate. However, O'Dell, while indicating Clark's obvious affection for her, avoids an overly romantic interpretation of their relationship by indicating that, to Clark, she is a "beautiful Indian child." Certainly, that interpretation is a plausible speculation which gives the novel its touching conclusion as Sacagawea parts from the explorers at the Mandan Village on the Missouri River where their journey began. Although she has existed in the shadows of legend, she becomes something more—the central character in a fascinating and poignant drama.

Mary M. Burns, in a review of "Streams to the River, River to the Sea: A Novel of Sacagawea," in The Horn Book Magazine, *Vol. LXII, No. 5, September-October, 1986, p. 599.*

THE SERPENT NEVER SLEEPS: A NOVEL OF JAMESTOWN AND POCAHONTAS (1987)

Although she meets King James of England and is invited to come and write letters at court because of her fair penmanship,

Serena Lynn takes a ship for the New World, following the fortunes of Anthony Foxcroft, hot-blooded son of the Countess who had employed her. She wears a serpent ring given her by King James; he told her it would protect her. The ship wrecks off Bermuda; although there is ample to eat, there is faction and dispute among the survivors. Foxcroft then sets out on a small vessel constructed from the wreckage, but only bits of it are ever seen again. Finally, in a larger ship, the colonists reach Jamestown, finding the settlers there decimated.

Aware of the story of John Smith and Pocahontas, Serena decides to find the Indian maiden and beg assistance of her to help the starving colonists. She becomes part of a plot to kidnap Pocahontas, and is instrumental in the romance between her and John Rolfe. Serena marries; she and her husband protect Pocahontas in a stand-off with the Indian; their cabin burns but all survive. Pocahontas notes that Serena is calm, while Pocahontas will soon be dead, and that the ring makes her calm. Serena throws the ring into the fireplace with vague regret. Later, news of Pocahontas' death in England comes to the colony.

This historical tale is at times confused—as with the factions in Bermuda—and at times disjointed. Pocahontas is right: Serena is too calm, and so dispassionate that we cannot really identify with her. Young readers might do better with Frances Mossiker or Jean Fritz as biographers.

A review of "The Serpent Never Sleeps: A Novel of Jamestown and Pocahontas," in Kirkus Reviews, *Vol. LV, No. 12, July 1, 1987, p. 998.*

Although Serena appears to be a fictional character, other characters and events are historically factual. O'Dell creates a vividly detailed picture of the time period, including the many political power struggles. However, the picture, stretching from England to Bermuda to Jamestown, is very much a panorama. There are so many events and characters portrayed that it will be difficult for readers to feel any sense of involvement with or understanding of the characters. Even Serena's motivations aren't fully examined. It is never clear why she is so taken with the self-absorbed Anthony or why she feels such an affinity for Pocahontas. Despite the lack of focus and the emotional texture found in O'Dell's earlier works, this book is worth reading for the fascinating story and would be a fine supplement to a colonial history lesson.

Heide Piehler, in a review of "The Serpent Never Sleeps: A Novel of Jamestown and Pocahontas," in School Library Journal, *Vol. 34, No. 1, September, 1987, p. 198.*

The credibility of this novel lies not in the heroine, and far less in the immature hero, handsome Anthony Foxcroft, but rather in the stark grim reality of sheer survival in the inhospitable Jamestown wilderness. O'Dell's portrayal relates the privations and dangers of every side—from within—power struggles to the death if need be, and the swift and brutal justice of martial law—and from without—the elements and the Indians. The fictional character development is weak; it is the historical characters and incidents that drive the plot forward. Purchase where necessary for curriculum-related tie-ins.

Phillis Wilson, in a review of "The Serpent Never Sleeps: A Novel of Jamestown and Pocahontas," in Booklist, *Vol. 84, No. 5, November 1, 1987, p. 483.*

Reginald (Leslie) Ottley

1909-1985

English-born Australian author of fiction.

Acknowledged as one of Australia's leading authors for children and young adults, Ottley is renowned for his unsentimental depictions of the land and its people. His books are considered starkly honest accounts of the struggle for survival and the mutual dependence of all living creatures amid nature's most formidable elements. Ottley characteristically based his stories on the places he lived, his own experiences, and those of the people he met in his extensive travels. Acclaimed for his ability to evoke atmosphere in a style that ranges from strongly descriptive to deliberate and low-key, Ottley stresses the positive virtues necessary to transcend the often hostile circumstances of daily life without sparing young readers the grim details of the brutal Australian environment. Addressing a wide range of subjects and settings, such as nomadic cattle-drovers, sheep stealing in the Snowy Mountains, street life in Depression-era Sydney, and subsistence on a South Pacific island, he describes the enduring friendships and familial bonds that can result from individuals cooperating in times of difficulty. Many of his works share common themes: loyalty among people; profound affection and respect for animals; and the necessity for personal strength and skill in overcoming the rigors of the harsh landscape.

Ottley is best known for his Yamboorah trilogy—*By the Sandhills of Yamboorah* (1965), published in the United States as *Boy Alone; The Roan Colt of Yamboorah* (1966), published in the United States as *The Roan Colt;* and *Rain Comes to Yamboorah* (1967). In these books, which fictionalize his boyhood experiences doing odd jobs for cattlemen, Ottley portrays a nameless youth's maturation on a vast, isolated cattle ranch against a background of loneliness, heat, bushfire, and storm. As the trilogy progresses, the boy learns to identify love in its many forms through his evolving relationships with others and his devotion to animals. Although it also deals with coming of age, Ottley's next work, *Giselle* (1968), was written as a tribute to the people of New Caledonia. Differing from his other works in structure, characterization, and locale, it is recognized as a sensitive portrayal of a fourteen-year-old French girl who seeks help for her crippled uncle. Ottley's continued adventures—wandering the outback, working on cattle stations and sheep farms, and serving with the Australian Remount Squadron—provided him with material for two collections of tales, *Brumbie Dust: A Selection of Stories* (1969) and *A Word about Horses* (1973), and a book about a family of itinerant cattle-herders, *The Bates Family* (1969). In his bleakest book, *No More Tomorrow* (1972), the desolate outback proves an insurmountable obstacle for an old man and his dog, despite their mutual courage and dedication. Ottley also wrote several fast-moving novels about runaways, street gangs, and horsebreakers which convey a sense of time and place as well as a strong feeling for the Australian lifestyle.

Critics praise Ottley for his narrative skill, unromanticized characters, compelling themes, and the memorable quality of his settings. They also admire the dignity with which he treats both his subjects and his audience in works which honor his adopted land. Although some reviewers complain of weak plots

and lack of textual unity, most agree that Ottley entertains his audience with authoritative, informative introductions to a fascinating land and people.

Ottley won several awards for his books. *Boy Alone* was the runner-up for the Australian Children's Book Council's Best Book of the Year in 1966 and won the Lewis Carroll Shelf Award in 1971. *The Bates Family* was the runner-up for the Australian Children's Book Council's Best Book of the Year Award in 1970.

(See also *Something about the Author*, Vol. 26 and *Contemporary Authors*, Vols. 93-96).

AUTHOR'S COMMENTARY

Story-telling is as old as the human race—or at least, as old as the human language. It is only through story-telling that one generation has been able to grasp what happened previously to other generations—and what life was like in countries other than their own.

I once asked an Editor of top standing in London, "What makes a writer? How does he come about?"

His reply was "re-incarnation" and, referring to me, added, "Some of your ancestors probably squatted around their campfires, telling yarns about the day's hunt, or about the past, when their fore-fathers killed a mammoth, or wrestled with sabre-toothed tigers in dark caverns.

One can imagine the horror of cruel teeth, and the puniness of man against a giant strength. Yet man prevailed, and passed on his story.

The re-incarnation theory may be right, or it may be wrong. No-one can say "yes" or "no". But I'm sure you have looked up with pleasure when a teacher has said, "We have half an hour to fill, so I'll tell you about something I read."

In my own school—a small Church of England one—we had two teachers who were good "yarn spinners". One was Mr. Carling, an elderly man whose silvery hair fell forward over one eye when he became excited, and whose face was as fresh and unlined as that of a man who had absorbed continuous youth. He used to walk up and down, whacking himself on the head with his ruler, while he told us a story. In our awed silence, we used to imagine he was driving his imagination to greater efforts.

Our other story-telling teacher was Mr. Borer. A bigger, more youngish man, with a seamed craggy face, who, unlike Mr. Carling, sat still while he was talking. His voice was deep and we had to lean forward to hear every word he said. He was a man with a withdrawn quality about him that we liked. He had been wounded during the First World War, and sometimes sat for long moments with his head bowed in his hands. Any boy who broke the enforced silence was dealt with by the rest of us afterward. It was a principle adhered to by each succeeding class.

The stories each told were differing. Mr. Carling's were classical—mostly of ancient Rome or Greece. He had written and studied much on that time and era. We liked best to hear of Gladiators and their dedication; men who cried, "Hail, Caesar. Those about to die salute thee." There was a grandeur in the words that moved us deeply. We lived in the courage of those brave, but destined men.

Mr. Borer told of other lands and other lives; of people trapped by War, or shattered by its utter misery. Sometimes he would leave his desk and draw on the blackboard—pictures in chalk to add to what he had said. Often the chalk crumbled—broken by the memories he held in his hand.

We were rich, for boys who had little money, in that we had two such teachers. We saw in them both, the men we would some day like to be.

Since school, I have heard men telling yarns in ships' foc's'les, and around campfires in the great Outback. I have listened to the old men in the Islands—in Fiji, New Caledonia and The Solomons—telling their tales of the past; of their own lore, and of a time when the white man first came to their islands; a time of great full-winged ships heaving at anchor in the bays, or rotting, gutted, on uncharted reefs.

Stories are part of man's very existence. They are as necessary to him as the food he eats.

In his Radio interview in Sydney a week or so ago, Sir William Collins—Head of the far-flung House of Collins, Publishers—was asked, "Is plot more important in a novel than characterization?"

Sir William's reply—from a vast knowledge of the world of books—was that characters and characterization were the most important. One wanted to become involved, or identified with the people in a story; live with them, and listen to them until one is part of their lives.

A play is a story being lived out in front of you; so, too, is a film. The actors, for the moment, are the characters they portray. You, as the audience, become part of the lives being unfolded before you; lives which stemmed from the pen of a story-teller. The whole—for good or ill—is the reality of his imagination.

Readers have asked me . . . "Is this, or that person real? Have you really known such people, or do they stem from imagination?"

I can only say, most of my characters are imaginary, yet based on the real. And, once created, they become, in their own right, people. I have little to do with moulding their story. They mould it themselves, as each day progresses. Sometimes, if I put the wrong words into a character's mouth, or the wrong actions into his movements, the story "sticks". It will not move. There is a complete deadlock until I rip up the sheet and return the character to his true personality. He is in context then, and continues on his course. I know that what I am writing will ultimately live—come to life in a story which others will read; people such as you.

Yet, strangely, and conversely, if a writer is honest, he does not write essentially for others. He cannot. He must follow the course of his characters. They may be in his memories, or centered around the life he is living, or has lived, or in a fragment of thought dissected elsewhere. They come vividly, bringing a story which has to be told.

Each writer is a channel through which flows his own media. We are all part of our parents, but a writer is also part of his characters. He has to be. It could be that they create him—not he create them.

And this could bring me back to my friend, the Editor, and his theory of re-incarnation—a theory of thought which takes me full circle. (pp. 279-80)

Reginald Ottley, "On Storytelling," in Elementary English, *Vol. XLIX, No. 2, February, 1972, pp. 279-80.*

GENERAL COMMENTARY

THE KIRKUS SERVICE

In contrast to a series, which is superficially sequential, a trilogy, with a sustained theme and a preconceived conclusion, is a dubious offering for children, who tend to take each volume as it comes and to expect from each a satisfying reading experience. In the case of *Boy Alone, The Roan Colt* and *Rain Comes to Yamboorah,* only the first, establishing the entente between boy and dog and man, is both artistically whole and consistently involving; the second extends the situation redundantly with little dramatic interest until the advent of the colt half way through; the third recapitulates awkwardly, with only cursory attention to the colt, until the compelling last scene in which boy saves man, thus repaying the other for his continuing concern. Read together, the boy's growth is evident and so is the author's purpose, but long stretches of introspection, in which the boy talks to himself or to the animals, become especially disconcerting in the last, and especially in the absence of action. The two aborigine girls, Alici and Maheena, figure significantly, adding vitality and an engaging versimilitude;

they're the best thing in a book which doesn't work by itself in a trilogy which might have succeeded as a single, more concise volume. Fortunately, none of this detracts from the force of *Boy Alone.*

A review of "Rain Comes to Yamboorah," in Kirkus Service, *Vol. XXXVI, No. 2, January 15, 1968, p. 58.*

BY THE SANDHILLS OF YAMBOORAH (1965; U.S. edition as *Boy Alone*)

The Australian desert and its fringes are not pleasant places, especially for a boy without family or friends, working as odd-jobber on a cattle-station. His life is hard, made harder by the aboriginal Kanga's hard-heartedness over the dog and puppy who give the boy some companionship and warmth. Yet the boy is neither made timid by his circumstances nor lacking in resource and courage. The ordeals he endures and the expedients to which he is forced, are not only episodes in his development but aspects of life in a harsh land among people where friends must be won, not merely acquired. Mr. Ottley's landscape and figures are neither romantic nor sentimental, but both seem very real. This is not a story to be skimmed or to be lightly dismissed as exaggerated. The author has known the loneliness of which he writes; the reader must feel it too.

A review of "By the Sandhills of Yamboorah," in The Junior Bookshelf, *Vol. 29, No. 2, April, 1965, p. 99.*

The plot is simple; it concerns a boy's relationship with his dog, or rather, the dog that he wishes passionately were his. In the end, terrified that it will be taken from him to be trained as leader of the cattle-station's dog pack (he has seen the puppy's mother pine and die in this pack), he runs away into the sandhills that surround the station. They find him and fetch him back when he is at the point of collapse, the puppy is given over to him, and he discovers to his surprise that the men of the station, among whom he has felt so insignificant, have in fact noticed his absence and are glad to see him safe. It is a moving book, written with economy; never maudlin. The author is not noticeably writing for children, he does not expound or moralize. . . . He presents the story and the characters with no apparent modification for children, no didactic explanation; a note at the end describing the organization of a cattle-station tells one all that is needed. The book conveys powerfully the feel of Australia and the feeling of adolescence. This is a notable addition to Australian children's literature.

Pioneers: Boys Learning Independence," in The Times Literary Supplement, *No. 3303, June 17, 1965, p. 505.*

[Children] are seldom ashamed to own to strong feelings where pets are concerned. The whole of life, indeed, may centre round them—as it does in the fascinating story, **By the sandhills of Yamboorah**. . . . From danger to happiness, inevitably—but if this kind of story has been often told in different settings, this particular version has real distinction. The author is writing of a boyhood like his own, and about a harsh, beautiful country he knows well. His book has a logical sequence of event, and its mood of loneliness and effort is intensified by the way he places the character of Mrs. Jones the housekeeper, a woman homesick for the city who sees from a not very happy distance what the boy is experiencing directly.

Margery Fisher, in a review of "By the Sandhills of Yamboorah," in Growing Point, *Vol. 4, No. 5, November, 1965, p. 597.*

Many fine books have come from Australia in recent years, but *Boy Alone,* a chronicle of life on an isolated cattle station, discloses a new writer of notable talent. Strongly autobiographical in flavor (the boy, significantly, is given no name and appears to have no past, no parents), it is a portrait of a remarkably good-hearted and appealing youngster in a world of hard-working, taciturn cattlemen. The theme, handled with great sensitivity, is a lonely boy's affection for two beautiful and devoted dogs belonging to the aged and hard-bitten dogman, Kanga, whose job it is to roam the plains exterminating the rabbits and dingoes. The boy knows with melancholy certainty that he must yield his companions in the end to their rightful place in Kanga's pack, yet for the time they are his to tend, admire and furtively love.

The unrelenting Kanga is the source both of sorrow and comfort for the boy, who instinctively seeks the rock-like stability provided by the old man. His earnest attempts to reconcile the conflicting feelings caused by this curious yet deeply truthful relationship supply an emotional undercurrent to the story which subtly colors the whole.

It is a story woven of daily events, generally mundane, occasionally dramatic. Whether it is the boy's first encounter with the gory mess of slaughtering sheep, the turmoil and stench of branding cattle, or simply the quiet companionship of shoeing a horse in the barn while dawn lightens the sky, each episode is unfolded with a constant sense of forward propulsion and an easy vividness which is impressive. It is some measure of Mr. Ottley's creative powers that one comes away from this book remembering not only the big scenes, such as the fury of a dust storm or the boy's desperate wanderings among the sand dunes, but also the multitude of minor perceptions: cold, stiff boots in the early morning and cobwebs in the rafters over the bunk; or a scarlet dawn in the empty hills with, later, the brassy-blue haze of the horizon seen from atop a windmill.

One comes to live fully in this boy's world, and the setting, with its strenuous round of activities, the ever-present dust and heat and the cheerful haven of the kitchen where Mrs. Jones, the lone woman, presides, is powerfully real. The adults who share the story and from whom the boy unconsciously draws strength and wisdom will linger in the memory. Muscular, indefatigable and decent, they surround the boy with unspoken sympathy, yet consistently refuse to make the sentimental gestures which would relieve him of the obligation to come to terms with life as circumstances require it to be lived. Their uncondescending benevolence thus suggests, paradoxically, that the boy is alone and yet never truly alone. A book of unflagging vitality, authentic and sometimes grim, yet compassionate and unexpectedly comforting.

Houston L. Maples, in a review of "Boy Alone," in Book Week—The Washington Post, *May 8, 1966, p. 2*

THE ROAN COLT OF YAMBOORAH (1966; U.S. edition as *The Roan Colt*)

The Roan Colt of Yamboorah conveys the feel of Australia better than [Ivan Southall's *Ash Road* and Colin Thiele's *February Dragon*], possibly because the author is reliving his own boyhood. Memory has inspired a wonderful picture of a cattle-station in the '30's, and of the wood and water joey (first met in *By the Sandhills of Yamboorah*) who leads a hard but contented life there. The boy's feelings, and the story, are concentrated on a lame colt, destined to be shot, stolen and hidden away by the boy, helped by two aboriginal maids. The bush fire precipitates the solution of the problem; in trying to save the colt from a gully where it has been penned, the boy shows his courage and wins his desire. This is a book of heat and effort and hard slogging work; it is not a book solely for children but for anyone, its events recalled and put down on the page eagerly, with feeling and strength. . . . [This] book is the real thing.

> *Margery Fisher, in a review of "The Roan Colt of Yamboorah," in* Growing Point, *Vol. 4, No. 9, April, 1966, p. 684.*

In *The Roan Colt,* Mr. Ottley continues the story of [a] boy on a cattle-station in Australia. He is no longer a "Boy Alone." His actions now mesh with the actions of the other people (and with the animals) on this lonely outpost, always hot under a brassy sky. For this reviewer, the boy's loss of loneliness is a loss of the poignancy that made the first story about him such a moving reading experience. But those who first met him in that first story, who shared in his fears and rejoiced in his triumphs, will be eager to know how he's making out. And they won't be disappointed—he's doing fine.

> *A review of "The Roan Colt of Yamboorah," in* Publishers Weekly, *Vol. 191, No. 14, April 3, 1967, p. 56.*

In this fine sequel to his award-winning *Boy Alone,* Mr. Ottley demonstrates the alchemy a skilled writer can work upon a very commonplace theme. The young hero, a "wood and water joey" at an Australian cattle-station, becomes attached to a roan colt which must be shot. . . .

The boy is allowed to keep the colt, but it is not a sentimental victory; the reader sees in his simple joy what a generous exception this must be in a responsible relationship between men and animals. The ranchmen and women, in the midst of their physically harsh life, show a touching concern for the boy's growing up that is a realistic relief from the falsely posited child-adult antagonism of many poor juvenile books on a similar theme.

The only seriously distracting fault in this book lies in the elliptic references to the previous novel. But that furnishes a reason to buy *Boy Alone* and present it with this new one to a deserving young reader.

> *Michele Caraher, in a review of "The Roan Colt of Yamboorah," in* The New York Times Book Review, *May 7, 1967, p. 39.*

RAIN COMES TO YAMBOORAH   (1967)

This third book about the nameless boy on a thousand-acre cattle ranch in Australia shares the qualities of its predecessors, with the boy still puzzling out the ways of the world about him with little or no help from anyone. His isolation and inexperience seem over-extreme and his acceptance of them almost unnatural, but there is authentic feeling in all the books for the setting itself, and the boy's unspoken admiration for everyone around him, like their equally unspoken recognition of his good qualities are given some plausibility by the setting. The two

aboriginal girls introduced in the second book give the boy his only real chance to converse, for with adults he is self-conscious—nor do they set him any example, and only the cook gives him any sampling of the softness of which he is so wary. He takes pleasure in the natural world, in his interest in the work on the ranch and in doing his own part well, and during the drought period he has several excitements and stops a pair of runaway horses. The book closes just as the drought has ended at last and the stern old dog-man Kanga has been found in the first rain with a broken leg. The author obviously has great respect for the old man, but leaves the reader wondering if he feels the same Ishmaelitic life would make a satisfactory future for the boy who is given so little direct experience of humanity and is so eager to make the most of the few crumbs thrown in his direction. As these stories are based on Mr. Ottley's own experiences, it is to be hoped he will continue the series long enough to show us how such a humble unrebellious boy came to break away from Yamboorah—perhaps it was when he was given a name and stopped being an anonymous bit of ranch life. The Australian background gives these "Westerns" a special flavour—there is a fascinating glimpse of emus—and the books can be specially recommended to any youngster keen on ranch stories, but others may well be chilled by this ultra-masculine world in which human qualities are suspect and often a handicap and cultural qualities non-existent.

> *A review of "Rain Comes to Yamboorah," in* The Junior Bookshelf, *Vol. 31, No. 4, August, 1967, p. 257.*

Reginald Ottley always draws a strong and fascinating picture of the cattle country he knows from personal experience, and *Rain comes to Yamboorah* has its share of excitements—a buggy ride with an unbroken colt, an encounter with a snake, the rescue of old Kanga from the dry plains. All the same, the book goes less smoothly than the earliest two. There is a heavy, affected use of adverbial phrase, a constant padding with 'thoughts' and 'reflections' rather awkwardly expressed in the midst of action, and a feeling of effort that suggests that the author may be using up his material. Though the drought provides a theme, the book seems to lack real unity. Ottley's books reflect an Australia of many years ago but link themselves with the present because an outback station is still not unlike it was in early days.

> *Margery Fisher, in a review of "Rain Comes to Yamboorah," in* Growing Point, *Vol. 6, No. 4, October, 1967, p. 976.*

Ottley's top-drawer writing stays right up there in this last book of the Yamboorah trilogy. . . . As in the other Yamboorah tales, there are information-filled events—emu egg hunt, lightning fires, and aborigine "walkabouts"—but reader sympathy will be focused on a kid growing up and itching for a responsibility that is usually given to older men. And to cap it off nicely, Ottley gives his readers the supreme satisfaction of having a boy save the life of an able-bodied, tough-minded adult.

> *Susan Roth, in a review of "Rain Comes to Yamboorah," in* School Library Journal, *an appendix to* Library Journal, *Vol. 14, No. 6, February, 1968, p. 82.*

GISELLE   (1968)

With the measured quietude of an Old Wave French film, a *symphonie pastorale* unfolds . . . in the tangled scrub, on the gleaming beaches of New Caledonia. The core of colonial life is French but the integument is tropical. Some—like fourteen-year-old Giselle, like her uncle Pierre Marcel before his body was wasted by disease—glory in the island; others, like her mother, "see sickness in the miasma creeping in from the sea." Those who have blended into the land, like Giselle's father, face another conflict—with the Australians and English and Americans who own most of it. Everything that impels Giselle to shed her innocence for early wisdom reflects these strains, but there is, in the conventional sense, very little plot and no conclusion: enough money is scrounged, saved, contributed (from Giselle's father's poaching) to send Uncle Pierre where he (only) believes he will be cured—Lourdes; Giselle's comrade Edouard, an inspired fisherman, is drowned on his last happy outing before leaving to become a priest. The sense that Giselle will keep her freshness and integrity, that she can knowingly separate self from circumstance, is the only approach to a palpable outcome. For the responsive few, a closely-felt setting and sudden shafts of understanding. (pp. 650-51)

> *A review of "Giselle," in* Kirkus Service, *Vol. XXXVI, No. 12, June 15, 1968, pp. 650-51.*

The problems of *Giselle* are far less ordinary but also far less real [than Yoshiko Uchida's *In-between Miya*.], for somehow the author's ambling narrative lacks direction, and his plot and atmosphere seem imposed on the story without much feeling. . . . The author seems mainly interested in showing a cross-section of life in a little-known part of the world and perhaps his material would have shown up better in an autobiographical piece rather than in a story which never attains real unity.

> *Margery Fisher, in a review of "Giselle," in* Growing Point, *Vol. 7, No. 4, October, 1968, p. 1183.*

Giselle is an affectionate and penetrating portrait of a figure in a landscape, a thoughtful and thought-provoking novel, infused with a humanity Reginald Ottley has sometimes been accused of lacking in his other books.

The setting, New Caledonia, is unusual; a south-sea island, but how different from one's preconceptions. The palm-fringed sandy shore and grass-skirted hula-hula girls may be there, but if so they are unseen. The Melanesian natives, Giselle's *indigènes*, form the labouring class and are regarded by her with the kind of affection she might bestow on a farm horse. Most of the characters belong to the dominant group in the population, descendants of French settlers. As in most former French colonies, they have not kept themselves aloof from manual work as the British did, and most of them are of peasant stock and outlook. Many of the men, including Giselle's father, are away from home all week working in the nickel mines. The professional class is staffed largely by expatriates.

The physical scene, too, with its mangrove-covered black mud coming down to the water's edge, distant views of mine-scarred mountains, and the stock company's fenced scrubland, is very different from what the words south-sea island usually evoke. But like the social background, it is very vividly, though incidentally, described, giving an intimate and three-dimensional picture of the island.

The story is quiet and contemplative, despite some exciting incidents, and character and atmosphere are more important than events. Giselle herself is a study in depth, everything is seen through her eyes, and the reader gets to know her through and through. Though she never utters—or even hints that she

thinks—a single critical word of her elders, they are shown as the complex, faulty creatures that all human beings are.

She has left school, but although she does not appear to have anything particular to do or any career to look forward to, she seems quite content with her lot. She leaves her querulous mother at home alone all day, and wanders on the beach, trespasses on the stock company's preserves, visits the village shops or her invalid uncle.

This uncle is a strange character. Bed-ridden and racked with arthritis, he is full of self-pity, constantly looking back to his athletic past or dreaming of a Lourdes-cured future. Devotion to Uncle Pierre is an essential part of the story, and is shown not only by Giselle and her family, but by all who know him.

About his housekeeper there is said to be a mystery, but of what kind is not explained or even suggested, nor is the nature of the relationship between her and her employer, and she is not an entirely successful character. Another enigma concerns Edouard, a friend who, like Giselle, has left school and seems to have no other occupation. Does he want to be a priest though his parents are reluctant to let him? Or do the parents want to make the reluctant boy a priest?

At first the story seems episodic and the incidents unconnected, but looking back on them afterwards one can see that they are linked together by the part they play in developing the portrayal of Giselle's character. Unfortunately the incident which closes the book seems out of balance with the rest.

This is, nevertheless, a novel to be commended, both for the insight it gives into an unfamiliar society and more especially for the wider implications it has as a character study of great depth and sympathy.

> *"In Other Lands: South Sea Story," in* The Times Literary Supplement, *No. 3475, October 3, 1968, p. 1118.*

BRUMBIE DUST: A SELECTION OF STORIES (1969)

A fine collection of nine stories. . . . Again using the arid Australian outback as background, Mr. Ottley here presents first-person narratives of catching and driving bulls, cows, brumbies (wild horses), and camels; of branding; of pub brawls; of breaking horses. The setting is as important as the characters, who include a powerful, unbreakable horse, Jones'y, a lonely swagman, Yacka, a tough old horseman, and Momba, a conniving old horse trader. A fastmoving horse round-up is the centerpiece of the book, but the overall tone is not one of action. The tough men who perform the tough occupations of the backlands are depicted in an understated manner, making these selections stylistically superior to the typical horsey and shoot-'em-up cowboy stories.

> *Susan M. Budd, in a review of "Brumbie Dust," in* School Library Journal, *an appendix to* Library Journal, *Vol. 15, No. 7, March, 1969, p. 167.*

Twenty years ago *Brumbie Dust* would certainly not have found its way on to a publisher's children's list. It is a collection of stories which would have fitted comfortably into the pages of the old *Blackwood's Magazine*, stories for armchair travellers of a rougher, tougher life than they would ever actually know. But the changing climate in the children's book world and the fact that Mr. Ottley's previous books have involved children . . . together place *Brumbie Dust* rather uncomfortably as a children's book. It is a book for anyone who likes a good yarn. Certainly a lot of young people will enjoy it and it would make a good addition to Aidan Chambers's list of Five Star Books at the back of his *The Reluctant Reader*. Extremely easy to read, with its short sentences and paragraphs and racy style, there is never any question of talking down. It is straight from the shoulder, slice-of-life stuff, with the writer himself in the midst of it. No outsider or observer, he is writing, one feels, not just from the sort of personal experience a journalist might claim from a few weeks' visit to the Back Country but from a lifetime's involvement with brumbie horses, camels and cattle, and with the hard-drinking, hard riding drovers, horse-breakers and prospectors.

Mr. Ottley records some fearful fights between man and horse, man and camel, man and man; but the overwhelming impression of the book is not of violence but of the rewards and satisfactions of strength, cooperation, freedom and skill. For all the flies and heat, thirst and sweat—and Mr. Ottley never romanticizes—this book should make a lot of boys want more from life than an office desk or factory floor.

> *"Away from It All," in* The Times Literary Supplement, *No. 3536, December 4, 1969, p. 1394.*

This collection of short stories by the author of *Giselle* has the same subtle and amazing power of appeal to the senses. In some ways, Reginald Ottley seems on surer ground writing a man's book about the Australian bushdrovers' life, their special relationship with their horses, the matter-of-fact approach to danger, the sharp appreciation of solitary beauty, and also of good food when it can be found. The stories give a wonderful picture of the men encountered by the narrator. The primitive streak they have in common makes them appreciate a bout of fisticuffs or a simple joke, but also to endure the heat, the boredom, the perils of treacherous 'bad country' or 'brumbie' stallion or bull, and the ever-present lack of water. . . . The courage and endurance, rough loyalty and comradeship, and moments of terror like the cattle stampede or the account of brumbie-running, are unforgettable, as are the colours of the bush seen at sunrise from a sandstone escarpment. This is altogether an outstanding piece of writing.

> *A review of "Brumbie Dust: A Selection of Stories," in* The Junior Bookshelf, *Vol. 34, No. 1, February, 1970, p. 41.*

THE BATES FAMILY (1969)

Loneliness, drudgery, poverty and the virtues such conditions demand if life is to continue—courage, cheerfulness, stoicism, an undemanding acceptance of inevitable deprivation—lift this book from a simple adventure yarn of the Australian outback into a poignant study of family relationships in exceptional circumstances.

The Bates family is a closely-knit group. Isolated by drought, father and children together concentrate their energies on saving their horses; cattle are trapped in mud, some have to be propped up with logs, many die. When the drought switches dramatically to rain, floods threaten.

Such harsh conditions breed opportunities for danger: Linda is swept away by a torrent of swirling water; Mr. Bates fights his way across a swollen river; Albie is almost drowned; Mervyn is lost and injured; a horseman is thrown and badly hurt in a round-up of wild brumbies; the herd of horses commits suicide as it plunges into a steep-sided chasm.

Even the end of the story is realistic. The next camp lies somewhere ahead for the Bates family and young Albie's damaged hip still nags him with pain: he struggles with it through the book but neither he nor the reader expects a miracle cure or even a hospital bed.

"It's a rough way to live," Mrs. Bates admits; it is indeed—but it provides powerful material for an unusual story. (pp. 188-89)

> *A review of "The Bates Family," in* The Junior Bookshelf, *Vol. 33, No. 3, June, 1969, pp. 188-89.*

There are eight children in the Bates family and although the story is really that of the seventeen-year-old twins, Albie and Linda, and some of the other children are hardly differentiated, it is the family that counts. The Bateses are drovers, spending their nights under canvas and their days with the cattle, often moving them for hundreds of miles. Horses are an essential part of their lives. The jacket, with its attractive picture of two blonde youngsters on horseback, might mislead some devotees of the Pony Club but the first sentence will show them that these are horses in a different country. The book starts with the death of one horse and ends with the deaths of a whole herd of brumbies. It is a harsh world where children are spared little. "It's a fight, all along the line. If it ain't drought, fire or flood, it's pests."

These Australians are the most alien of any in these books [which also include *Baker's Dozen* by Celia Syred, *They Drowned a Valley* by Margaret Paice, *Over the Bridge* by Deirdre Hill, *Peter and Butch* by Joan Phipson, and *The Gold Dog* by Anne de Roo]. They certainly don't play cricket, and they eat fried bully beef and damper rather than cornflakes. Even some of their names are strange, such as Bub and Snow. Their language is occasionally unintelligible ("I reckon the track will be crook. Some of them billabongs'll be runnin' a banker") and at all times off-puttingly full of dropped letters, but it will be a pity if children are put off. It's a moving and convincing story of the interdependence of the members of a family. Children who grumble about making their beds or clearing the table may be shaken into an awareness of what helping can mean. (p. 692)

> *"Faraway Places," in* The Times Literary Supplement, *No. 3513, June 26, 1969, pp. 692-93.*

The author's *Brumbie Dust* paints a much more graphic picture of life in the Australian outback than does this flat story about the nomadic, cattle and sheep herding Bates family. Resignation to whatever comes, be it drought, flood, personal injury, or even plenty, and strong family ties, help the Bateses to survive in their harsh land. Mr. and Mrs. Bates are the family philosophers with terse comments for all occasions—good or bad; only two of their eight children are individualized characters. Particularly sympathetic is 17-year-old Albie, whose crippled hip causes him constant physical pain that prevents him from doing things his robust twin Linda does with ease (Linda has no real personality divisible from her brother's, and their closeness is strongly, repetitiously stressed). Merv is the "different" child—the kind who almost breaks his arm trying to reach a bird's nest in a hollow tree, in an action completely unintelligible to the rest of the family. The high point of the book is the attempted capture of hundreds of brumbies, which ends in disaster with the horses' fatal leap into a chasm. But the excitement of this episode can't redeem the mediocrity of the book.

Susan M. Budd, in a review of "The Bates Family," in School Library Journal, *an appendix to* Library Journal, *Vol. 16, No. 2, October, 1969, p. 142.*

JIM GREY OF MOONBAH   (1970)

A big disappointment for Ottley fans. No one can be as gullible and naive as 15-year-old Jim Grey. Jim, restless after his father dies, is the only person around to help his mother on their Moonbah sheep station. He eagerly accepts the friendship of Russ Medway, who works at the station for a few days. When Russ goes off briefly, then reappears, Jim accepts his story that Russ, who knows nothing about sheep, has been put in charge of the large mob pastured on the government land next to Moonbah. Jim helps Russ fool the owners by driving sheep into the holding pens, but when a truck carrying the animals is caught, the boy realizes he is an accessory to sheep stealing. Horrified, and ashamed to tell his mother, he runs away with Russ. In Sydney, Jim escapes and heads for home when Russ tries to involve him in robbing the safe in a timber yard. All kinds of good Samaritans help Jim get home, where he redeems himself by pulling a truck driver from his burning truck. All the characters are stereotyped; Jim's crying and wallowing in self-pity will turn readers off.

Susan M. Budd, in a review of "Jim Grey of Moonbah," in School Library Journal, *an appendix to* Library Journal, *Vol. 17, No. 1, September 1970, p. 120.*

[It] is rather a relief that Reginald Ottley's new story is set in a more temperate region than he usually chooses. It is sometimes difficult, reading Australian children's books, not to believe that the whole country is arid and dust-choked. . . . But Moonbah is in the Snowy Mountain region, a lush green sheep station run by Jim Grey and his mother. . . .

[This] highly moral tale demonstrates how easy it is to get into bad company and how difficult to extricate oneself. The plot is fast-moving; the telling as laconic as the speech of Jim and Russ. Much more conventional than *The Bates Family* or Mr. Ottley's short stories, some boys will undoubtedly enjoy it more. (p. 1267)

"Enduring All Things," in The Times Literary Supplement, *No 3583, October 30, 1970, pp. 1266-67.*

Jim Grey of Moonbah gives a vivid picture of a sheep-run in the Snowy Mountains. There is plenty to convince the reader in young Jim's involvement in the illegal schemes of Russ Medway, since the lad meets this plausible rogue not long after his father has died and while responsibility is weighing heavily on him. Unfortunately the emotional aspect of the story is quickly dealt with so that its pace can match the pace of an active sheep-stealing plot. Since feelings are slower to develop than deeds, the final impression is of a superficial snatch at an important theme. It looks as though Ottley's earlier descriptive chronicles provided a better form for him than the more recent stories in which he attempts a "plot" as understood in adventure stories.

Margery Fisher, in a review of "Jim Grey of Moonbah," in Growing Point, *Vol. 9, No. 5, November, 1970, p. 1622.*

THE WAR ON WILLIAM STREET   (1971)

In theory **The war on William Street** has a serious theme: in practice the book seems remarkably flavourless and unimpressive. The scene is Sydney in the '30's, the Depression years; the "War" of the title is a territorial conflict between old Gran and miserly Jonesey, whose newspaper circuits adjoin. Old Gran treats her grandson Spud with the bitter unconcern and sporadic hostility she shows to everyone and the lad relies for affection, and often for food, on Corro, a half-aboriginal boy whose home is poor but secure, and Snow, whose family is well-to-do. In so far as the story has a plan, it is built round the street edginess that finally erupts into violence and lands the accident-prone Spud in hospital, but an extensive, and rather intrusive, sub-plot, an encounter with a shark at Manly, brings a rescuer into the boys' lives, a tycoon whose gratitude for his daughter's rescue looks like improving their rather drab circumstances. This is a well-intentioned book but the story-line is so slack, there is so much padding of author's comment, and the boyish chatter is so forced and improbable, that you feel the author has had to squeeze every word out of a tired mind. In terms of action, the three boys are genuinely involved in a conflict of adult interests: emotionally, this aspect of the book is never achieved.

Margery Fisher, in a review of "The War on William Street," in Growing Point, *Vol. 11, No. 1, May, 1972, p. 1944.*

The Australian author shows a vivid sense of atmosphere, but through all the book it is the loyalty and understanding of the three boys which stand out. When Spud's guardian, old Gran, threatens to starve and beat him the other two rise before 6 a.m. each day to help sell papers on her pitch in the city centre to placate her. Unwittingly, they are drawn into the gang warfare and protection rackets that exist between old Gran and her great rival, Greasy.

Although the book is exciting and the author catches the dialogue of the three boys with great accuracy there are times when the pictures are over-stressed and the loyalties and comradeship are spelt out to an agonising degree. One boy who read this book described it as "wet", and this is a fair opinion from a teenager of today who is used to seeing his gang warfare in colour on the small screen. (p. 188)

J. Russell, in a review of "The War on William Street," in The Junior Bookshelf, *Vol. 36, No. 3, June, 1972, pp. 187-88.*

[The War on William Street] is a rather clumsily plotted book, sometimes stilted and awkward in the conversations, but it somehow conveys the desperate importance of hero-worship and group loyalty, the strangled emotions and embarrassments of intense friendship. There is an honorable attempt to play fair with hardship, pain, and hopeless poverty; the hard-luck child has hard luck to the end and we finish with no more than a faint hope of good will from an adult benefactor who descends, like Jove, for brief visits between business trips. Sentimentality and all, this one sticks in the mind. (p. 228)

Barbara Rosen, in a review of "The War on William Street," in Children's Literature: Journal of the Modern Language Association Seminar on Children's Literature and The Children's Literature Association, *1973, pp. 227-28.*

NO MORE TOMORROW (1972)

The simple story: an aging wanderer and his dog Blue make their way across the desolate outback, walking from today to tomorrow, completely dependent upon one another. They walk, eat, sleep: occasionally the old man remembers a bit of some brighter yesterday. When an accident separates them, both man and beast nearly die of being apart. We leave them reunited beside a dwindling campfire. Asleep? Dead? Nothing is certain. And that's all.

And what material for squishy sentimentality . . . arf, said Bowser, licking a tear from his master's weathered cheek— but there is none. Instead, a great sense of peace, of dignity, gentleness and shared strength in a harsh land. The book would have benefited from a small glossary to ease readers through its Waltzing Matilda vocabulary of swagmen and tuckerbags; but, that quibble aside, it's a beauty. (pp. 12, 14)

> *Robert Berkvist, "Wombats in the Outback," in* The New York Times Book Review, *May 2, 1971, pp. 12, 14.*

Perhaps laughter would be out of place in *No More Tomorrow,* but it is missed. The heavy mood settles like dust and finally covers everything, even the depth of feeling between man and beast.

Reginald Ottley's tale is convincingly, sometimes beautifully told, largely in dialect. But the weather-beaten characters who people this solitary land do nothing to relieve the grimness. Though one feels pleasure in the protagonists' many escapes from impending danger and is concerned when they are separated, there is no hope for the future. The old man relives the past until the present ceases to be.

> *David K. Willis, "What Sarah Says," in* The Christian Science Monitor, *May 6, 1971, p. B2.*

A tough old man and his proud beautiful dog, Blue, walk the dusty trails of the Australian outback. . . . The old man talks a lot to the dog, mostly tales of disappointments and disasters. You know he's doomed. The book reminds me a little of Hemingway's *The Old Man and the Sea,* but the climax is low-keyed, lacking the face-to-face drama that a plain tale needs. To be totally involved you would need to be passionately devoted to dogs and the outback. With only one of these interests I still found it rewarding.

> *Alex McLeod, in a review of "No More Tomorrow,"* in The School Librarian, *Vol. 20, No. 4, December, 1972, p. 349.*

A WORD ABOUT HORSES (1973)

Like Grey Owl, Reginald Ottley . . . tells of his life in a wild country—the Australian outback: drawing on his memories as a wandering stockman, he treats his incidents as fiction and his simple, vivid language draws the reader directly into the action. Unlike Grey Owl who describes his Canadian landscape, this author gives no specific descriptions: the desert, the heat, the work, the men and the horses are all fused into a solid Australian essence, which is powerful and without false glamour. He releases a wide range of emotion—from tenderness for a wild budgerigar chased by a hawk and laughter over cricket and kangaroos, to pathos when he meets a crazed "hatter", and fear as he fights bush and scrub fires. But the overriding feeling is love for horses. And what horses they are,

and how Reg Ottley and his mates enjoy their working relationship with them! (There is a valuable central non-fiction chapter on different . . . working horses which subject cataloguers may like to note as this information is probably not to be found elsewhere.) And always hovering beyond reach are the desirable wild brumbies, necks clothed with thunder, the poetry of Horse. We can envy Mr. Ottley the organic unselfconscious culture of which he is a part and which he portrays so tellingly for children.

> *"Natural Adventures," in* The Times Literary Supplement, *No. 3709, April 6, 1973, p. 378.*

This collection of anecdotes is about real horses who, wild or tamed to man's service, are the essential partner of those who work the Australian outback. How they will be received by the pony-loving sorority in this small island is difficult to say. For us, the horse is a lovable pet to be jumped, raced or carried by horse trailer from show to show. Such cossetted creatures would surely have an attack of the vapours if faced with a herd of "brumbies", as the wild horses are called, or required to survive and work in the harsh climate and terrain down-under. It is a chatty book, conveying a credible atmosphere and using a nice turn of phrase. To read of "one hot November morning" does more for the geographical sense than a bald textbook statement, and indeed the whole book says more about the interior of that distant continent than a dozen blackboard expositions. (pp. 203-04)

> *D. A. Young, in a review of "A Word about Horses," in* The Junior Bookshelf, *Vol. 37, No. 3, June, 1973, pp. 203-04.*

A word about horses is a collection of anecdotes, reminiscences of [Reginald Ottley's] own experience, stories he has heard here and there, told in an easy, rambling fireside style. There are moments of drama—the escape of a stallion from new quarters, danger in a flooded river, bush fires, a fantastic leap with which a wild horse eludes its pursuers. The flexible form of the book allows plenty of room for the author's characteristic shrewdness about people and horses and his power to evoke the Australian bush, plains and townships.

> *Margery Fisher, in a review of "A Word about Horses," in* Growing Point, *Vol. 12, No. 2, July, 1973, p. 2183.*

MUM'S PLACE (1974)

When eight-year-old Kim loses his mother, he is forced to leave their rickety chicken and pumpkin farm in the Australian outback. His mother's only true friend, Harry Muhler, an itinerant horsebreaker, takes the boy to share his footloose life. The resulting partnership proves a strain for both: Kim realises that Harry finds the duties of assumed parenthood restricting, Harry discovers that the responsibility of a small boy makes his work seem foolishly self-destructive. Kim is tempted to dishonesty when he finds the cached savings of the Chinese cook at Bawon Station where Harry is working—it is only his knowledge of Harry's fierce independence that prevents him taking it so he can buy his mother's farm. Harry allows a horse to kill itself rather than risk an injury that would interfere with his guardianship. For both a sanctuary would seem to exist in the farm they think of as 'Mum's Place' and to which they are determined to return.

The book bears Mr. Ottley's stamp—the harsh Australian setting of dusty landscapes and board buildings, the smell of horse-sweat and tired clothes, the difficulties of human relationships in an unyielding environment. It has the characterisation and narrative skill that one has come to expect. My only reservation concerns its audience; children young enough to identify with Kim are too young to read the book. There seems no point of direct entry for the adolescent who could benefit from reliving the experience. But there is skilful storytelling and the appeal of the exotic background.

> *C.E.J. Smith, in a review of "Mum's Place," in* Children's Book Review, *Vol. IV, No. 2, Summer, 1974, p. 66.*

Reg Ottley's latest Australian story is rather thin and disappointing. The book is marred throughout by the repetition of the child's grief at his mother's death—this may be perfectly true to life but in the book it comes through as monotonous sentiment. The glory of the horses is still there, though.

> *"Underground Resistance," in* The Times Literary Supplement, *No. 3774, July 5, 1974, p. 715.*

To bring alive the Australian scene is Reginald Ottley's forte. His vignettes of the outback in *A Word About Horses* had an authenticity which made them remarkable. He brings to *Mum's Place* the same feeling for the land, its people and their way of life. Kim at eight is orphaned, and it is his efforts to establish himself once more on his original homestead with the help of a not too confident adult which make the bones of this book. Fleshed out with the detail of a tired rural community, its conflicts and misunderstandings, the story moves at a fast pace to the conclusion sought by both Kim and the reader. Mum's place is once more to be worked by its rightful heir.

> *D. A. Young, in a review of "Mum's Place," in* The Junior Bookshelf, *Vol. 38, No. 4, August, 1974, p. 234.*

Piero (Luigi) Ventura

1937-

Italian author/illustrator of nonfiction and fiction.

Ventura is recognized for his inventive and captivating approaches to history and for creating adept illustrations distinguished by their impressive panoramic bird's-eye views, intricately detailed structures, and engaging miniature people and animals. Characteristically using line drawings of pen-and-ink with watercolor washes on a large double-page format, he is also credited for his precise and skillful use of white space, a feature for which he is often compared to Mitsumasa Anno. Ventura's nonfiction, usually appropriate for all ages, includes biographies of popular figures, famous archaeologists and their discoveries, and cultural or historical looks at cities, architecture, and Western civilization. Ventura gained immediate attention with his first book, _Piero Ventura's Book of Cities_ (1975), which presents an international selection of well-known cities and towns. Perhaps his most unusual factual works are _I grandi pittori_ (_Great Painters_; 1983) and _L'uomo a cavallo_ (_Man and the Horse_; 1980). The latter is an overview of world history through evolving uses of the domesticated horse. _Great Painters_ looks chronologically at the development of art and the lives of famous artists through page layouts which add small reproductions of the masterpieces within natural backgrounds along with the artists at work. Ventura has also illustrated several well-received books by Gian Paolo Ceserani, such as _Il viaggio di Marco Polo_ (_Marco Polo_; 1977) _Il viaggio di Colombo_ (_Christopher Columbus_; 1977), and _Le grandi costruzioni_ (_Grand Constructions_; 1981). Ventura's fiction consists of two picture books directed to an elementary school audience: _The Magic Well_ (1976), a fantasy set in a medieval village, and _The Painter's Trick_ (1977), a comic tale about vanity and greed which Ventura created with his wife Marisa.

Most critics focus on Ventura's talent as an illustrator who deftly applies meticulous details to bright, colorful scenes which come to life with activity; he is also esteemed for offering lighthearted humor and historical validity in both text and art. Critics occasionally complain that the thrust of Ventura's works is predominantly male and that his topics sometimes try to cover too much material. However, most observers praise Ventura for creating books which arouse the imagination and, by humanizing their subjects through an emphasis on daily activities, make often formidable topics accessible to his readers.

Ventura has won several international awards for his illustrations.

(See also _Something about the Author_, Vol. 43 and _Contemporary Authors_, Vol. 103.)

GENERAL COMMENTARY

CARLA POESIO

It is often said of artists that they have invented a personal style. In the case of Piero Ventura, one could more aptly say that he has invented a new language, a language that is both informational and narrative, that blends knowledge and ideas with feelings and emotions.

Courtesy of Piero Ventura

Ventura has deliberately *chosen* his subjects for illustrating: fascinating nonfiction texts that aim to reconstruct the most important stages in the history of mankind. The settings are already eloquently described in the titles of his books: *The voyage of Marco Polo* and *The voyage of Livingstone* are two examples from a series "The great voyages" and *Crete, Pompeii* and *Tutankamon* are major titles in the series "The adventures of the world." One of his most remarkable books, *Grand Constructions,* traces great architectural manifestations ranging from Stonehenge to the Sidney Opera House, and *The Great Painters* is an original interpretation of the lives and works of ingenious artists from Giotto to Picasso.

What then are the main features of Ventura's pictorial tales? His illustrations usually cover entire pages, sometimes even two consecutive pages. He uses the large surfaces like stage settings where action takes place in a type of composition reminiscent of the great Renaissance frescoes. Landscapes, architectural elements and various objects are reproduced with extreme accuracy, never leaving anything to chance, never creating a detail devoid of historical fidelity. His "figurative storytelling" is at its best in the representations of the past. It can be compared to the lucky discoveries of an archeologist bringing to light, almost untouched, buildings, apparell, objects and human bodies: an entire world resuming life as though there had been no passing of time.

What might appear as cold reproduction is actually artistic invention, fancy, brilliant creativeness filling the illustrations with genuine life. An incredible number of figures populate these illustrations, and thus they have been called "gli amini di Ventura", which means Ventura's little men. They look like speedy sketches in the journal of a writer, made to fix some ideas. They are *not* speedy signs or improvised notes, however. The decisiveness with which the characters' action is represented, the accuracy with which their dresses or hairstyles are reproduced or the attention given to some detail (a gesture or other reference to the central scene)—all of this clearly shows that they are all important and are characterized as a gallery of co-starring heroes.

At times a touch of humour emerges from these little men, especially when Piero Ventura allows us a glimpse into the privacy of their everyday lives. Such subtle humour, such private glimpses make the great flow of history more credible, more understandable and more human.

The best of Ventura can be found in the reproductions of great buildings, especially such great architectural constructions as a fortress or a medieval village, for instance. Ventura likes to represent these as seen from above, as though the viewer were passing over in a helicopter from where he has a general as well as a detailed view of the construction, penetrating what is closed and insurmountable.

The architectural element, the solid mass, is frequent in Ventura's illustrations. This may be merely a wall or the side of a mountain or the shape of a ship parting the waves with the solidity of a stone building. The presence of this solid mass breaking the open spaces creates a composite equilibrium by means of contrast.

The harmony of composition is one of Ventura's outstanding artistic qualities. The large illustration allows him to create a fascinating play of open and empty spaces. His scenes are often crowded, but never confused; they are ruled by remarkable "stage direction."

Usually one finds one main colour in Ventura's illustrations: the grey of the buildings, the yellowish rose colours of some stories illumined by the sun, the white of great snow-covered surfaces, the green of uninterrupted woods or the blue of the expanse of the sea. The dominance of one colour has the main function of avoiding the dispersion and the confusion which might otherwise arise from the many aspects of the world and the human activity filling the scenes. It also serves as a sort of "echo" from one point of the illustration to another, as a connection between the left and the right, the top and the bottom or two points at opposite ends of a diagonal line. This is not mere decoration but an evidence of the solidity of the pictorial creation.

Ventura's accurate and impeccable technique (he generally uses ink and watercolours) and his use of composite space lets him be termed a highly talented graphic artist, thus reviving a question that is often discussed today: that of the close connection between graphics and illustration.

The many readers of the books illustrated by Ventura greatly appreciate the dynamism of his work. Nothing in his pictures is static; on the contrary, movement and continuous flow of action are constant features in his figurative narration.

Finally, it must be underlined that Ventura's illustrations are "open illustrations"; they overcome the limits of the page, suggesting something more than has been shown. The illus-trations thus provide stimuli for the imagination and the reader's own creative interpretation. (pp. 59-62)

Carla Poesio, "Piero Ventura," in Bookbird, *No. 2, June 15, 1986, pp. 59-62.*

PIERO VENTURA'S BOOK OF CITIES (1975)

AUTHOR'S COMMENTARY

In recreating scenes from cities that I have visited and tried to describe to my sons in words and sketches, I should like to ask a certain artist's license. These illustrations are not exact reproductions—a camera could do that better than I! They are instead an attempt to combine the special elements and colorful impressions that made each city a unique experience for me.

Piero Ventura, in a note in his Piero Ventura's Book of Cities, *Random House, 1975.*

The prospect of brightly colored oversized picture books about city life is enough to make one's heart sink. But the recent publication of two just such books [*The Big City Book* by Annie Ingle and *Piero Ventura's Book of Cities*] shows that it is still possible to take an insouciant view of the subject. . . .

It takes a little willing suspension of disbelief to appreciate *Piero Ventura's Book of Cities*, which could well be subtitled "Urbanization Without Tears." But once the reader accepts the artist's pristine point of view, there are pages of delicate drawings to enjoy. The generous picture-book format is given over to scenes from many cities (done with what looks like rapiograph and wash), all arranged rather loosely into categories called Living, Getting Around, Working and Having Fun. Almost every picture, each one a double-spread, would be nice to describe and the temptation is to try; but since such a list would risk jet lag, only a few examples follow.

There is fire fighting in Stockholm: a *sumo* match in Japan; "Aïda" at La Scala; the Los Angeles freeway system; the canal-crossed city of Venice; a bird's eye view of a New York subway station so clean and airy that no New Yorkers would recognize it. Nearly all the illustrations have lots of people in them—working, playing, stumbling off at bus stops, running into each other with arms full of packages, browsing in bookstalls by the Seine, and even buying azaleas. The overall effect of so many city sights and people, even if rose-colored, is exhilarating. An easy book to recommend, especially to would-be city planners.

Sidney Long, in a review of "Piero Ventura's Book of Cities," in The New York Times Book Review, *February 8, 1976, p. 16.*

The undistinguished text discusses transportation, recreation, and types of work in various cities. But the colorful illustrations of these places . . . are replete with fascinating detail and humorous activities; the drawings capture the feeling of the different locales. A national bias does seem to emerge from the text; for although judgments about the city are normally not given, the author does say that Venice is "one of the loveliest places in the world" and that Roman citizens are "among the friendliest people in the world." But the appeal of the book is universal, since it celebrates the diversity and multiplicity of the world's great cities. (pp. 167-68)

From Grand Constructions, *written by Gian Paolo Ceserani. Illustrated by Piero Ventura. G. P. Putnam's Sons, 1983. Copyright © 1983 by Arnoldo Mondadori Editore S.p.A., Milano. English translation copyright © 1983 by Arnoldo Mondadori Editore S.p.A., Milano. All rights reserved. Reprinted by permission of The Putnam Publishing Group.*

Anita Silvey, in a review of "Piero Ventura's Book of Cities," in The Horn Book Magazine, *Vol. LII, No. 2, April, 1976, pp. 167-68.*

The author/illustrator responsible for this book tells us that in re-creating scenes from cities he has visited, he was seeking to "combine the special elements and colorful impressions that made each city a unique experience. While he succeeds in fulfilling his own aims, he fails to fulfill the publisher's promise of showing "how people live, work, travel and have fun in cities around the world."

The contrast between the text and drawings is curious. Although the drawings are the focus of the book, it is the text which has the greatest strengths—good description, sound observations, good detail and liveliness. In the drawings, charming and colorful though they are, Ventura fails to capture the very quality of the cities which makes them cities. Indeed, the *reality* of a city seems to have been lost in the process of abstracting those "unique and special elements" from their surroundings.

The whole emphasis, in drawing after drawing, seems to be on fairy-tale qualities. A garden in Kyoto, St. Basil's Cathedral in Moscow, the Spanish Steps in Rome—each of these subjects

looks like a ballet set prettily drawn, centered in a large white space. But the *feel* of the city—the busy streets, the pace, the crowds, the constant activity, and—above all—the glorious variety of the city's population—is largely missing. All right, if one wants to show a certain homogeneity in Copenhagen, fine. But in London's Hyde Park?! In New York's Central Park?! In Washington, D.C.?! In Rome, all of the 200-odd people so painstakingly drawn look as if they were born of the same mother and father. Thank God for Hong Kong, Baghdad and Tokyo!

The most successful blend of text and illustration is in the section on "Transportation." Here, one gets the feel of a traffic jam in London; of the complexity of New York's subway system with its maze of stairs, exits, tracks, escalators; of the freeway in Los Angeles (although, again, abstracted from its surroundings, it looks more like New York's little old Major Deegan).

The chapters on "Work" and on "Fun" are well written and include scenes full of detail that will absorb children for hours on end. Hamburg, with its lakes, rivers, canals and railroad, is a fascinating harbor and wonderfully executed. There are also good scenes of the Baghdad markets, Stockholm's Fire

Department, Venice's gondolas filled with vegetables, a wrestling exhibit in Tokyo and an exciting production of *Aida* at the La Scala Opera.

The *Au Printemps* store in Paris, however, seems strangely bare and sterile. And although it "sells everything from neckties to sailboats," only one woman—a mother with her young son—is shown among a sea of French*men* in the sports department. *Women* are depicted buying clothes (mutilating each other at a sales counter), perfume, wines and *Paris Match.* Voila! La liberation des femmes.

Mr. Ventura has a sense of humor, a gifted palette and is an enthusiastic and skilled observer. Since this is the first in a projected series of journeys, it will be interesting to see what happens when he travels again. I would like to see the "unique impressions" a unique city like Nairobi would make on Mr. Ventura. (pp. 38-9)

> *A review of "Piero Ventura's Book of Cities," in* Human—and Anti-Human—Values in Children's Books, *CIBC Racism and Sexism Resource Center for Educators, 1976, pp. 38-9.*

THE MAGIC WELL   (1976)

Precision plus imagination (to say nothing of an acute sense of color) are the hallmarks of Ventura's works. Here he offers an astonishingly beautiful and intriguing book which could be a first: an SF picture book! The village of Pozzo is peaceful; life there goes along like a song, some say because the well in the village square has magical water. But trouble comes to Pozzo when huge yellow balls come charging out of the well and inundate the place. The leading citizens, including Mimi—a dragon—try to get to the bottom of the mystery. They think they've licked the problem when they get help from technicians in the city of Mechanics. But the situation worsens when the neighbors, computer types, take over. It gets better and better for the readers, though, as the spoof of "modernity" continues.

> *A review of "The Magic Well," in* Publishers Weekly, *Vol. 210, No. 20, November 15, 1976, p. 75.*

The imagination evident in this science-fiction-like picture book, and the detailed, full-color illustrations are definite strong points; however, the story is too rambling and diffuse to sustain interest. Children might enjoy perusing scenes of robot houses powered by golden balls emitted from the magic well, and then construct their own tales.

> *Jody Berge, in a review of "The Magic Well," in* Children's Book Review Service, *Vol. 5, No. 6, Winter, 1977, p. 52.*

[Piero Ventura] has produced a marvelously comic fantasy in picture-book form. . . . The story is imbued with typically European satire, but the humor is direct and lighthearted. Full-color illustrations—some of them ample double-page spreads and others framed in small boxes or strips—bubble with activity and are replete with minute, engrossing details.

> *Ethel L. Heins, in a review of "The Magic Well," in* The Horn Book Magazine, *Vol. LIII, No. 1, February, 1977, p. 42.*

THE PAINTER'S TRICK   (with Marisa Ventura, 1977)

One morning an itinerant painter stops at a monastery, hoping to exchange one of his paintings for some food. He agrees to decorate a wall with a painting of St. George in return for food, but finds that the soup the Brothers provide tastes terrible. He tricks each brother in turn into giving him better food by telling each one that he will use his face for St. George. How he in turn is tricked by the brothers provides an amusing conclusion. Unfortunately for the story, the illustrations detract: because of the cartoon-like style, all the brothers look alike. The book also seems to be promoting a kind of sneakiness which the moral ending does not entirely obliterate.

> *Anne Devereaux Jordan, in a review of "The Painter's Trick," in* Children's Book Review Service, *Vol. 5, No. 13, July, 1977, p. 124.*

When the monks eagerly unveil the fresco, they discover that the painting is magnificent, indeed, but that the face of the St. George is "the face of the rascal painter!" Chastened, they treat the painter to a trick of their own; and although their revenge falls rather flat, the characters of the gullible monks and of the raffish painter are amusingly cartooned. The illustrations, which carry the sharp outlines and soft tones characteristic of frescoes, are always placed above the lines of text. An entertaining tale but less engaging in format and coloring than *The Magic Well* or *Piero Ventura's Book of Cities.*

> *Charlotte W. Draper, in a review of "The Painter's Trick," in* The Horn Book Magazine, *Vol. LIII, No. 5, October, 1977, p. 526.*

Last number, we selected Piero Ventura's *The Magic Well* as one of our baker's dozen. We now offer another of his books, *The Painter's Trick,* a work on which his wife Marisa collaborated. The vanity and greed of human nature are the subjects of this tale, set in a mediaeval [monastery]. . . . It is the cleverness of the plot, as it shows the intricacy of deceit and counter deceit, that raises the story above a platitudinous fable; it is the excellence of the illustrations which make this a first rate picture book. Using the style of mediaeval fresco paintings, [the illustrations are] accurate in both detail and mood in depiction of mediaeval life. The cartoon like faces capture character, and the added element of a duck who is an onlooker in nearly every picture seems to express the animal's wonderment over the strange ways of humankind. (pp. 13-14)

> *Jon C. Stott, in a review of "The Painter's Trick," in* The World of Children's Books, *Vol. II, No. 2, 1977, pp. 13-14.*

IL VIAGGIO DI COLOMBO [CHRISTOPHER COLUMBUS] (1977; British edition as The Travels of Columbus)

[Il Viaggio di Colombo *was written by Gian Paolo Ceserani.*]

We may yawn, now that we've been to the moon, but it was probably no easy job for Columbus to get those three tiny ships across the Atlantic. Now Piero Ventura wants to tell us all about it. In a series of exceedingly detailed and brightly colored aerial views, he first displays the busy, bustling world the admiral left behind—Genoa, with its cannon, cloisters and churches; the Spanish port of Palos with its fishing fleet, idlers and little knot of important citizens come to see three ships off on a very doubtful venture. Then comes a cross-section of the Santa Maria, showing how every foot of her little hull (less than one-tenth the length of a modern liner's) was crammed

Canaletto has just finished The Grand Canal and the Bembo Palace, a scene from mid-18th-century Venice.

112

From Great Painters, *written and illustrated by Piero Ventura. G. P. Putnam's Sons, 1984. Copyright © 1984 by Arnoldo Mondadori Editore S.p.A., Milano. English translation copyright © 1984 by Arnoldo Mondadori Editore S.p.A., Milano. All rights reserved. Reprinted by permission of The Putnam Publishing Group.*

with supplies and equipment, so much so that the sailors had to sleep in odd corners because there were no regular berths below. There is even a group portrait of the Santa Maria's crew of 40 or 39, (depending on whether you look at the text or the picture), from Columbus down through the captain and pilot, the two royal officials, the interpreter (head perhaps buzzing with fragments of Hindi), and the rest of the standard ship's complement.

Mr. Ventura's account of the voyage and arrival in the New World is succinct and unsensational, emphasizing Columbus's contributions to oceanography and ethnobotany rather than the old fall-off-the-edge-of-the-world nonsense. More aerial panoramas open out across the pages, showing the green and soupy Sargasso, the magnificent seagoing dugouts of the Arawak (carrying more men than the Santa Maria), or a comfortably thatched and palisaded Cuban village as full of activity as faraway Genoa. The book covers only the first voyage in detail, but what there is is fresh and informative.

> Georgess McHargue, "In 1492 and 550 A.D.," in The New York Times Book Review, *April 29, 1979, p. 30.*

Ventura's hand shows a steadfast penchant for detail, bright color, and good humor. Panoramic scenes, gay-looking and astutely composed against large expanses of white space, overflow with eye-tickling line and animation. Even instructional illustrations like the cross-sectional view of one of Columbus' loaded ships, have a humor that belies the book's nonfictional label.

> Denise M. Wilms, in a review of "Christopher Columbus," in Booklist, *Vol. 75, No. 18, May 15, 1979, p. 1437.*

IL VIAGGIO DI MARCO POLO [TRAVELS OF MARCO POLO] (1977; U.S. edition as *Marco Polo*)

[Il Viaggio di Marco Polo *was written by Gian Paolo Ceserani.*]

A thorough and readable account of Marco Polo's travels to, from and in China. . . . The colorful, uncluttered pictures present a myriad of details that greatly complement the text, details that depict the architecture, people and everyday activities encountered by Polo on his adventures. The overall layout is spacious and immediately attractive. Endpaper maps are exact and readily understood. The accessible factual material and striking illustrations make this one of the better Polo books available. It fills the gap between Demi's simpler *Adventures of Marco Polo* and the more complex *Marco Polo* by Preston and *Marco Polo* by Graves.

> Peter Roop, in a review of "Marco Polo," in School Library Journal, *Vol. 28, No. 9, May, 1982, p. 50.*

A clear, uncomplicated account of the life and travels of Marco Polo is presented in picture-book format. . . . The full-color, carefully detailed line drawings depict panoramic scenes of European and Asiatic communities, suggest the emptiness of the Gobi desert, limn the features of a gigantic stone Buddha, and embody the formalities of Chinese court life. Each scene pictures people in their daily activities; the effect is Lilliputian yet full of life and bustle. (pp. 304-05)

> *Paul Heins, in a review of "Marco Polo," in* The Horn Book Magazine, *Vol. LVIII, No. 3, June, 1982, pp. 304-05.*

The fields of paddy rice stretch to the horizon, some green with the crop, others sheets of water mirroring the sky. Across the two-page spread the small bright procession follows the wide road across an arching bridge over the canal. The open countryside is evoked nicely by the painter, who works in convincing detail yet leaves most of the page paper white. You cannot miss the central actor; it is young Marco Polo, riding on the Great Khan's business in a closed crimson sedan chair borne by 16 coolies. (p. 41)

There in front of the cathedral a little group is retelling Marco's travels with the aid of a drum and pictures spread out on a board, a 13th-century version of what the author and the illustrator have done for young readers today. . . .Their book of 32 pages of paintings with its crisp and specific text conveys the sense of the great traveler's classic: the crowded ports of the Levant, the dusty wastes of the fearful Gobi, the enormous Buddha image and the nomad's yurt, and at last the colorful symmetries of the temples and the cultivated simplicities of the evergreen gardens of Khanbaliq. Paper money and a black stone that burns, printed books, fireworks, the compass and above all the lavish scale of Kublai's China are here drawn or described. (pp. 41-2)

> *Philip Morrison and Phylis Morrison, in a review of "Marco Polo," in* Scientific American, *Vol. 247, No. 6, December, 1982, pp. 41-2.*

L'UOMO A CAVALLO [*MAN AND THE HORSE*]   (1980)

Ventura's once-over on humankind's use of the horse down through time gets its spark from the artist's crisp, fine-lined drawings. These are sometimes sprawling, airy spreads and other times bold, single portraits, but either way they keep the reader attuned to the commentary. The narrative reports on how the horse was involved alongside developing civilization (presumably not just man), "sometimes for the better and sometimes not," as it aided in farming, hunting, traveling, migration, exploring, trading, and war making. While the text is straightforward, there are both humorous and sobering elements in the art. There is no index or table of contents, but this is a relatively brief work. It will be of chief interest to browsers or students needing light background on the subject.

> *Denise M. Wilms, in a review of "Man and the Horse," in* Booklist, *Vol. 79, No. 2, September 15, 1982, p. 120.*

Piero Ventura's attempt to give insight into history by following the single theme of the horse is imaginative, and his cross-cultural perspective (bringing Eastern and Western history together) is splendid. But while the easygoing text that accompanies his full-color pictures occasionally notes that horses have been important in commerce, agriculture and as the original

"horsepower" engines, it is upsetting that the horse's use in warfare dominates the book.

And what about women? Every now and again there's a tiny background picture of a creature who seems to be female, but the overall suggestion is that women hardly exist. From its unfortunate title on, **Man and the Horse** seems wrongheaded in this regard—historically old-fashioned.

> *Elaine Edelman, in a review of "Man and the Horse," in* The New York Times Book Review, *October 10, 1982, p. 24.*

Tiny watercolor figures, outlined in pen and ink, invite scrutiny as they draw readers into different landscapes with each turned page. Readers may question that "the knight's shield was made of iron covered with wood" and may want to see the cowboy described in the text but missing from the cowhorse's saddle. The final sampling of breed drawings does not distinguish one from another. The oversize, full-color book has no index, but it would make a handsome browsing addition for medium and large collections.

> *Pat Harrington, in a review of "Man and the Horse," in* School Library Journal, *Vol. 29, No. 5, January, 1983, p. 68.*

LE GRANDI COSTRUZIONI [*GRAND CONSTRUCTIONS*]   (1981)

[*Le Grandi Costruzioni was written by Gian Paolo Ceserani.*]

Grand Constructions is itself grand, page after page of Piero Ventura's fine detailed pen drawings washed in exquisite watercolors. The drawings do justice to the vertiginous steepness of a Mayan pyramid, the busyness of a baroque facade and the monumental beauty of the Capitol. He makes full use of the wide open spaces in this generously large book (a two-page spread stretches 20 inches), sometimes even cropping the drawings in ways that make you imagine the tower or dome or whatnot that is just off the page. . . .

Ceserani and Ventura devote many pages to their native land, as is fitting. The rest of the West gets less consistent attention, but for so short a book there is a good taste of its diversity: from the ruins of Machu Picchu to the splendors of Versailles to Frank Lloyd Wright's Guggenheim Museum. Ceserani discusses the influence of Palladio on American architecture, but nowhere does he mention the sacred name of Jefferson.

The story of architecture is of course inextricable from the story of man and the story of art. For the young reader, and even for this not-so-young one, a good many seeds are scattered throughout this book, waiting to be planted. Read more of Stephens and Catherwood, the Americans who rediscovered the Mayans; read more about Christopher Wren; about Bernini; about Versailles; about the Aztecs; about Le Corbusier. And then let these drawings seduce you back into **Grand Constructions**.

> *Robert Wilson, "From Stonehenge to Skyscrapers," in* Book World—The Washington Post, *March 13, 1983, p. 8.*

An oversize book offers good scope for Ventura's impressively detailed and colorful examples of architectural landmarks and some examples of famous sites (rather than buildings) like the gardens at Versailles or typical architectural structures like the imperial hall of the episcopal palace at Würzburg. Ventura does not give the sort of diagrammed details that David Macaulay provides; his paintings have the combined design and sweep of Anno's architectural drawings, especially in their use of perspective. Each page, or double-page picture, has an accompanying text that provides background information as well as some facts about the structure that is illustrated. This should also appeal, visually, to readers for whom the text may be too difficult.

Zena Sutherland, in a review of ''Grand Constructions,'' in Bulletin of the Center for Children's Books, *Vol. 36, No. 8, April, 1983, p. 145.*

What do Aztec pyramids, scaffolding in the Sistine Chapel (with a painter on top) and a mosque in Isfahan have in common? All are imposing manmade structures included in **Grand Constructions**, a chronicle of architectural achievements through the ages. The book ranges from a Roman aqueduct, a medieval village and a Renaissance villa to the United States Capitol, Brasilia and the World Trade Center.

The widely varied works shown are given a unity by the exquisite ink and watercolor illustrations of Piero Ventura, most of which exuberantly fill the pages. In some, the artist uses great economy of line and with just a few washes conveys the elegance of a Maillart bridge spanning the gorgeous Alps or the mystery of Machu Picchu in its dramatic setting in Peru. Elsewhere, Mr. Ventura lovingly details every brick, shingle and rafter, and relishes the excesses of a Baroque interior.

From There Once Was a Time, *written and illustrated by Piero Ventura. G. P. Putnam's Sons, 1987. Copyright © 1986 by Arnoldo Mondadori Editore S.p.A., Milano. English translation copyright © 1987 by Arnoldo Mondadori Editore S.p.A., Milano. All rights reserved. Reprinted by permission of The Putnam Publishing Group.*

What is special fun are the tiny people who give scale to the illustrations as they feed pigeons, beg, empty chamber pots out windows or drop brushes from the scaffolding. All wear the dress of the place and time—except for the citizens of the paleolithic village, who wear practically nothing at all. (p. 24)

Though much can be learned from reading **Grand Constructions** thoroughly, this beautiful book can be enjoyed by the casual browser of any age. (p. 26)

Rolf Myller, in a review of ''Grand Constructions,'' in The New York Times Book Review, *May 15, 1983, pp. 24, 26.*

POMPEI [IN SEARCH OF POMPEII] **(with Gian Paolo Ceserani, 1982);** *CRETA [IN SEARCH OF ANCIENT CRETE]; TROIA [IN SEARCH OF TROY]; TUTANKHAMON [IN SEARCH OF TUTANKHAMUN]* **(with Gian Paolo Ceserani, 1985)**

[*In Search of Troy* and *In Search of Pompeii*] are large, bright books, attractive to look at, with whole pages of clear, coloured drawings. They are not quite the exciting and gripping adventure stories promised on the back cover, but rather concise, simply written accounts of archaeological discoveries. *Troy* gives over half of its space to the life of Heinrich Schliemann before retelling Homer's *Iliad* and describing the life-style of the early Greeks; and ends with Virgil's account of the wooden horse.

Pompeii starts with the haphazard discoveries made in 1748 and goes on to modern times, explaining the problems the early archaeologists had to face; then gives the history of the city itself from 400 BC. The drawings show Pompeii as it was, reconstructed with complete houses and swarming with perky citizens; then modern ruins, full of tourists. The plan of a wealthy Roman's house shows how the family lived, what they ate, their furniture and lamps. Other pictures show how bread was baked and textiles woven. The facts are made interesting: 'Roman baths were rather like a modern sports centre'; and 'Not until the twentieth century were so many people able to read as in Ancient Rome.' The book ends suitably with Pliny and the eruption of Vesuvius.

Margaret Campbell, in a review of ''In Search of Troy'' and ''In Search of Pompeii,'' in The School Librarian, *Vol. 33, No. 2, June, 1985, p. 172.*

A colorful format includes numerous detailed pen-and-watercolor drawings characteristic of other Ventura/Ceserani books. Although the accounts appear to be accurate, with conjectural matter clearly stated as such, there are no acknowledged sources and no bibliographies or indexes. The publisher does acknowledge that the books have been adapted, which may account for the often choppy, wooden tone of the text. Shiny paper-over-board covers detract from the attractive layout in each book. Despite the monotonous writing style, the books successfully synthesize elements of biography, history, the principles of development of archaeology, and the excitement and enormously hard work of these truly fabulous discoveries.

Margaret A. Bush, in a review of ''In Search of Ancient Crete,'' ''In Search of Troy,'' and ''In Search of Tutenkhamun,'' in The Horn Book Magazine, *Vol. LXII, No. 4, July-August, 1986, p. 465.*

I GRANDI PITTORI [GREAT PAINTERS]   1983)

This informal and unconventional history of Western painting highlights the great painters from Giotto to Picasso and reveals details of techniques and styles as it does so. A wealth of accurate material is presented in a readable and spirited style, but browsers can also enjoy the illustrations without the text. Each artist's life and selected works are given an unusual dimension as Ventura combines reproductions of the paintings he discusses with his softly hued watercolor backgrounds of the artists, their surroundings or their audiences. These panoramas vibrate with interest, as in the section on Impressionism, in which Manet's then-controversial painting *Olympia* is shown in an imaginary gallery while viewers quarrel below. These scenes and the text succeed as did Ceserani's **Grand Constructions** which Ventura illustrated in a similar style. Included at the end of the book are 73 mini-biographies; an index of selected names; a description of styles and periods; and a list of illustrations. While the book might be criticized because of its inclusion of so many minor Italian painters and the abrupt conclusion that might imply to children that art history ends with Picasso, children, particularly those who enjoyed Goffstein's *Lives of the Artists* for its distinctive approach, will appreciate this large format introduction to art history and appreciation.

> *Lorraine Douglas, in a review of "Great Painters,"* in School Library Journal, *Vol. 31, No. 6, February, 1985, p. 88.*

Some of the information is lively and includes interesting details in much the same way the illustrations do. One learns that 15th-century Flemish artists rediscovered the lost formula for combining pigments with oil paint. When Antonello da Messina, a Sicilian who was painting in Flanders, ran off to Italy with this knowledge, the Flemish painters hired a killer to pursue him. Fortunately for Italian artists and the late Renaissance, he got home unscathed. A young student of portraiture can judge the ways in which Raphael's portrait ''La Muta'' resembles Leonardo's ''Mona Lisa,'' and learn that the great portrait painter, Hans Holbein, earned 30 pounds a year at the court of Henry VIII, less a 3-pound annual tax.

The works of 72 painters from Cimabue to Picasso crowd these well-reproduced pages. In part because of the range and complexity of the material, it proves unwieldy. If the prose had been edited more skillfully, it would have the comprehensiveness and clarity necessary to such an introductory work. As it is, great schools and movements are often reduced to a shorthand of names and dry facts: ''Andrea Mantegna's wife, Nicolosia, was the sister of Giovanni Bellini, another great painter. Giovanni Bellini and his brother Gentile both worked as artists in Venice.'' This is not the kind of data likely to be illuminating to a 12-year-old unfamiliar with Mantegna, Bellini and Venice. An adult seated nearby and capable of enlivening such passages would be a welcome guide—one who could untangle descriptions as opaque as this one of Renoir's ''Dance at the Moulin de la Galette'': ''The figures were no longer physical objects in a set of surroundings, but apparitions generated by the atmosphere of those surroundings.''

The history of painting is perpetually exciting. These reproductions and the sketches framing and extending them make some of that excitement palpable. The explanatory prose should have told the same story with equal precision and vitality.

> *Karla Kuskin, in a review of "Great Painters," in* The New York Times Book Review, *March 3, 1985, p. 28.*

Using the same lively, animated style that distinguished **Grand Construction,** the Italian illustrator has chronicled in brief form the lives of over seventy painters. . . . Often one canvas is shown while figures that appear in other famous canvases of the artist are shown posing in the drawing by Ventura. Frequently this technique leads to marvelous juxtaposition; one double-page spread shows Canaletto's *The Grand Canal and the Bembo Palace* and Ventura's rendition of the same scene. Although the text is appropriately reverent, the illustrations are often sly and humorous. Artists scratch their heads over the problems of perspective and sit dejected in front of sketches of masterpieces. These wonderful, homey, familiar touches do humanize the great painters and make them more understandable for young readers in the same way that Jean Fritz's books have made historical figures accessible. But it is terribly disconcerting when these cozy figures are posed with strong pieces of art in front of them: Seeing Goya's *The Third of May, 1808* and Picasso's *Guernica* comfortably tucked inside a studio takes away from their power. The book, however, is a delightful, funny, and beguiling glance into the lives of some of our distinguished painters. (pp. 198-99)

> *Anita Silvey, in a review of "Great Painters," in* The Horn Book Magazine, *Vol. LXI, No. 2, March-April, 1985, pp. 198-99.*

COM'ERA UNA VOLTA [THERE ONCE WAS A TIME]   (1987)

The irregular use of double columns of print, broken by illustrations or captions, makes many of the pages of this oversize book seem cluttered and at times confusing. Ventura's approach is one that brings history to an accessible view: not kings and battles and place names, but information about how people lived and worked and dressed in a series of historical periods. Most of the text is briskly and informally informative, but because it covers so broad a span there are frequently abrupt jumps or awkward juxtapositions of details. The illustrations are remarkably deft and detailed, as handsome as they are useful. Additional information is provided by appended notes.

> *Zena Sutherland, in a review of "There Once Was a Time," in* Bulletin of the Center for Children's Books, *Vol. 41, No. 1, September, 1987, p. 19.*

Ventura blithely takes on the job of explaining the history of Western civilization in 150 heavily illustrated pages. Seemingly undaunted by the enormity of the job, he organizes his material into eight eras, with nine color-coded sections in each (agriculture, dress, inventions, society, houses, crafts, trade, transportation, warfare) so that readers can survey one subject chronologically if desired. The only form of index is a one-page guide to the topics and periods discussed. While one's ability to locate information is limited, finding specific facts seems almost beside the point. This lively look at social history provides a feast for the eyes, though time passes by with somewhat bewildering speed. While many broad concepts and interesting tidbits of information are to be found in the text, the visual panorama of changing times is the book's strength. Ventura's bright, detailed watercolors are delightful, lending a lively touch of humanity to a whirlwind tour of the ages, from ancient Egypt to pre-World War II Europe and America. (pp. 74-5)

Carolyn Phelan, in a review of "There Once Was a Time," in Booklist, *Vol. 84, No. 1, September 1, 1987, pp. 74-5.*

A fascinating social history of Western civilization. . . . Each time period is broken down into nine sections that examine society and government, housing, agriculture, arts and trade, economy, fashion, transportation, inventions and technology, and warfare. Such an overview illustrates the synchronization of history. It shows how present-day farming emerged from advances made throughout the centuries, beginning with the invention of the plow by prehistoric man, crop rotation and irrigation systems introduced by the Romans, the development of family farms during the Middle Ages, to steam-powered farm machinery invented in the 1800s. Additional information to the chapters is appended, but the most interesting information is offered in Ventura's well-captioned watercolor illustrations. A page and a half of well-drawn, appropriately colored, richly-detailed illustrations accompany each half page of text. . . . The broad scope prevents much detail about any given society, and there is no index, making this an unlikely choice for assignments, but it is well-conceived, accurate, and excellent for browsing or recreational reading.

Karen K. Radtke, in a review of "There Once Was a Time," in School Library Journal, *Vol. 34, No. 2, October, 1987, p. 136.*

Rosemary Wells

1943-

American author/illustrator and illustrator of picture books and fiction.

Wells is a popular and versatile writer noted for the realism, perception, and humor of her picture books and young adult novels. Spotlighting personal relationships with a sensitive eye, she conveys recognized values with understanding and wisdom. Wells's nonsexist texts occasionally combine fantasy with reality, contain elements of slapstick, irony, and astringent wit, and often conclude with unconventional or surprise endings. Her picture books, for which she is best known, are sometimes written in verse and generally feature a variety of engaging anthropomorphic animals caught in comic predicaments and universal childhood dilemmas. Usually focusing on sibling rivalry, Wells examines such concerns as bullies, bedtime fears, and inattentive parents while also producing spoofs on more controversial topics like evolution and natural history. Several of these works, including some of her board books about Max, a charming white bunny who innocently upstages his older sister, grew out of the author's observations of her two children. Drawn in pencil or pen and ink and washed with watercolors, Wells's uncluttered, whimsical illustrations characteristically outline deceptively simple, stumpy figures with expressive eyes and body language. Her novels, which include realistic fiction, mysteries, and psychological thrillers, explore difficult ethical situations such as premarital sex, betrayal of trust, and stealing without offering easy answers, and often draw on incidents and details from her own youth and that of her teenage friends. Utilizing a nonjudgmental tone, honesty, insight, and her usual sense of humor, Wells allows her protagonists to find their inner strength and make their own choices.

Reviewers consider Wells an original writer and able illustrator whose delightful picture books, amusingly wry drawings, and candid novels capture the essence of child and adolescent behavior. Admiring the range of her comic sense and her ability to create strong and endearing characters, most critics regard Wells as a multi-talented author/illustrator whose percipient probings into the human condition are both compelling and lighthearted.

Wells has received numerous adult- and child-selected awards for her works.

(See also *Contemporary Literary Criticism*, Vol. 12; *Something about the Author Autobiography Series*, Vol. 1; *Something about the Author*, Vol. 18; and *Contemporary Authors*, Vols. 85-88.)

AUTHOR'S COMMENTARY

[I was born] with two small lights—like tiny Italian Christmas bulbs, as I picture them—inside my brain. They are drawing and writing. I did not know about the writing light until I was long grown up. People ask all authors, "Where do you get your ideas?" The answer is, "They come to the lights like moths. Then I can see them."

Courtesy of Dial Books

I work in a spare bedroom rigged up as a studio. One side of the room has a couple of drawing boards and many shelves stacked with school trip permission slips, published and unpublished artwork, dried up ink bottles, unanswered mail, ten-year-old royalty statements, unpaid bills, antihistamines from 1975, and items which need sorting at all times, even if they have just been organized.

When I am drawing, I listen to one of four classical music stations on an old radio. I constantly change stations in quest of music written before 1810. The two dogs, West Highland white terriers, stay with me. I am restless while drawing, constantly aware of my technical limitations. I make coffee I don't drink. I call Susan Jeffers, and we gossip about our children, friends, vitamins, and so forth. I stare out the window. I think about the car-pool in one school and the Substance Abuse Committee in the other school.

Many of the stories in my books come from our two children, Victoria and Beezoo. Ruby and Max are Victoria and Beezoo. They appeared on my drawing board in the summer of 1977. Victoria was then five and Beezoo nine months. Victoria had taken it upon herself to teach her baby sister about the world and dragged her, like a sack of flour, because she was too heavy to really carry, from object to object shouting, "Table, Beezoo! say table. TA-BLE!" Beezoo did not cooperate at all and was always off in a world of her own.

Victoria tried to teach Beezoo how to get dressed—another complete failure, as Beezoo preferred to be undressed at all times. Victoria attempted to instruct vocabularyless Beezoo to share and not to take toys that didn't belong to her. This was like talking to the wind. Victoria took pride in wheeling Beezoo's stroller along the boardwalk. Beezoo had to be harnessed into it, with the zipper put on backward and pinned in four places, or she would immediately escape and crawl like a racing crab right into the ocean or the traffic or wherever danger lay.

These simple incidents from childhood are universal. The dynamics between older and younger sibling are also common to all families. What is funny is not the events but Victoria's dogged insistence on leading Beezoo in the paths of righteousness and Beezoo's complete insouciance in the face of slightly skewed authority.

I could say that I did the board books because there were no funny books around for very young children at that time, that I saw a great black hole in the marketplace. But this is not true. I did the Max and Ruby books because the characters materialized on paper in front of me, under my hand, so to speak. The characters were alive. The stories were going on all around me. I submitted them to my editor, Phyllis Fogelman, hesitantly because there had never been any books like them. Phyllis did not take them hesitantly.

Other books come from other episodes in my life, in the children's lives. Victoria, in first grade, came home the day of the Christmas concert in bitter tears. It took me three hours to get out of her what was wrong. At last the truth spilled on the damp pillow. She had selected a blouse and kilt to wear that morning. Someone in the class had noticed. "You're supposed to wear a dress to the Christmas concert, not an old kilt," little Audrey had whined, crushing Victoria. We patched up the day with conventional wisdom, but Audrey's remark stuck in my mind long after it had dissolved in Victoria's. It became *Timothy Goes to School*. Audrey is still there in Victoria's eighth grade, still making trouble. It amuses Victoria and me that since *Timothy* was a successful book, we made a pretty penny on Audrey, and she and her mother will never know.

When Beezoo was in second grade, she wanted more than anything to take in her favorite stuffed animal for show and tell. She decided at the last minute against it, however, because, as she put it, "The boys would rip it up." There was *Hazel's Amazing Mother* right in front of me. I, like all writers, take many small fragments and run them through to their logical conclusions in my mind, like a film on fast forward.

Benjamin and Tulip was written, on the other hand, before we had any children. It is partly a story of my best friend and me wheeling our bicycles up a steep hill every day after school and being regularly ambushed by Norman Buck and his brothers who lived at the top of the hill. This happened many times. Any mother who called Mrs. Buck to complain was met with shouts of "I can't hear you," because Norman and his brothers made so much background noise. Norman did not fit well in the story, so I got rid of his brothers and changed him into Patty Lombardi, queen of the second grade at five foot six and one hundred thirty pounds, who was heard to say only two things in her career: "I'm captain" and "I'm gonna beat you up."

Once the story is there, the drawings just appear. I feel the emotion I want to show; then I let it run down my arm from my face, and it goes out the pencil. My drawings look as if they are done quickly. They are not. First they are sketched in light pencil, then nearly rubbed out, then drawn again in heavier pencil. What appears to be a confident, thick ink line is really a series of layers of tiny ink lines intensifying all day until the drawing is ready for color.

Most of my books use animals rather than children as characters. People always ask why. There are many reasons. First, I draw animals more easily and amusingly than I do children. Animals are broader in range—age, race, time, and place—than children are. They also can do things in pictures that children cannot. They can be slapstick and still real, rough and still funny, maudlin and still touching. In *Benjamin and Tulip*, Tulip falls out of a tree and mashes Benjamin in the mud. If these pictures were of children, they would be too close to violent reality for comfort, and all the humor would be lost. All of my stories are written with deeply felt emotional content. Animals express this best most of the time for the same reason that a harpsichord expresses certain concertos better than an organ does.

At the end of a day my hand hurts. I run it under the hot tap. My glasses need strengthening. I put off the appointment with the optometrist, who keeps sending me little reminders. I hear the school bus deliver Beezoo. I jump up.

Another side of my studio is for writing. It contains a word processor which will be obsolete in three years. I slip in the discs to start it up. I am not aware of writing. I sink myself in the screen as if I were hovering over a coral reef with a snorkel mask in the warm Caribbean. I am not aware of time passing. It is a nuisance to get hungry and break my concentration. I do not feel that I get ideas. Books come up on the screen from outer space. Beezoo comes home from school. She drops her bag and opens the cookie cabinet. I do not jump up. I say, "I'll be right there, Sweetie!" Fortunately, she is a patient child who knows I love her anyway. Victoria bangs on the door two hours later. By that time I can't write anymore. I stand up with a crick in my neck and write *swim* on the calendar for the next day. (pp. 163-68)

I am glad I am not starting out now. It would be harder for me. It took me ten books to get going, ten books and five years even to learn what writing for children was about. I am glad that I got my start in this profession at a time when it would have been rightfully considered a laughable heresy to retell or reillustrate Beatrix Potter or any other book that is as perfect now as it was many years ago. I am glad I got my start in 1968 when [my editors] said to me again and again, "Stop rooting around in the public domain. Write your own stuff."

This was good advice. Children's books have refried the past enough now. . . .

Instead of resurrecting every last fairy tale and Mother Goose verse, we must encourage literary originality and let the past flower in the natural flow of time. We must imitate nothing and be true to ourselves. (p. 170)

Rosemary Wells, "The Artist at Work: The Writer at Work," in The Horn Book Magazine, *Vol. LXIII, No. 2, March-April, 1987, pp. 163-70.*

GENERAL COMMENTARY

JENNIFER FARLEY SMITH

Miss Wells's stories are sweet but never saccharine, her humor a marvelous mixture of slapstick and delicate irony. Her pictures and text are spare, and yet in a few lines and pale colors artist Wells can speak volumes to her young audience. Her small, fist-sized books strike a gentle blow against the tyranny of older brothers, baby sisters, bullies, and too-busy parents. . . .

[Rosemary Wells] is one of the most gifted picture-book illustrators in the United States today.

Jennifer Farley Smith, "Animals Are Enduring Heroes," in The Christian Science Monitor, *March 6, 1974, p. F2.*

MYRA POLLACK SADKER AND DAVID MILLER SADKER

[*Noisy Nora*] depicts a child in a family that is loving and affectionate, but the parents do not have quite enough time for all the children.

> Jack had dinner early,
> Father played with Kate,
> Jack needed burping,
> So Nora had to wait. . . .

Nora is the middle child in a busy family and she goes to great lengths to get her parents to pay attention to her. Her characteristic banging windows, slamming doors, and knocking over lamps and chairs is simply background noise to which the family has become accustomed. However, when she temporarily runs away, she learns how important she is to her family. The verse and illustrations of the mouse family convey, with humor and understanding, how frustrating it is to be the child who always has to wait. . . . (p. 17)

[In Norma Klein's *It's Not What You Expect* and *Mom, the Wolf Man and Me*] the condemnation usually associated with premarital sexual relations, illegitimacy, and abortion [is] absent. However, the challenging of conventional morality is somewhat distant and removed. In both books it has taken place long before the story begins, and in both cases involves not the central character but her mother instead. Rosemary Wells's fine recent novel *None of the Above* offers a more immediate and a more dramatic challenge to traditional sexual mores.

None of the Above describes the gradual change in Marcia, an unambitious, submissive girl who, when her father remarries, finds herself in an alien environment—one that is, both intellectually and socially, far tenser and more demanding than any she has ever known. Used to reading movie magazines, watching the dating game on television, and giving a half-hearted effort to the general course in high school, she finds her new siblings busy with skiing, horseback riding, and intensive studying, their goals set on the most demanding and prestigious colleges. Marcia changes, succumbs to the driving nature of the household, and leaves the general course for the college track, where she achieves an outstanding record.

Although Marcia succumbs to the intellectual pressure, socially she defies the expectations of her new home. She begins dating Raymond Siroken, who looks like Robert Redford and is one of the high school's most popular and reputedly fastest boys. Raymond takes her to a party and then as a matter of course leads her to an upstairs bedroom. Afraid to say anything foolish, Marcia remains quiet while he lies on top of her and takes a foil package out of his pocket telling her that they are going to go all the way. She is completely unaroused, almost repelled, and Raymond, angry and frustrated, stops. Marcia continues to date Raymond and to submit to the rough violent bedroom sessions, although Raymond never again takes out the foil packet. As their relationship develops, Raymond and Marcia

become more compassionate toward one another, and she understands the problem with their lovemaking:

> "It's . . . me," he said, "I'm . . . it's my . . . fault. I can't."
>
> "You . . . can't what?"
>
> "Look . . . I'm not . . . I'm not a real man, I . . ." but he couldn't explain. . . .
>
> "There's a word for . . . what I am. I know very well what it is. I can't say it. . . .''
>
> "It'll get better, Raymie. I know it will." He said nothing.
>
> "We'll work it out, you'll see," she said, looking questioningly at the cowlick in his hair. "And I won't leave," she added.

Their lovemaking becomes more tender and sensual, and, as Marcia promises, they do work things out, Marcia using the pill to protect herself from becoming pregnant. By the novel's conclusion Marcia must choose between Sarah Lawrence or an early marriage to Raymond. Although one may question the wisdom of Marcia's choice, or indeed the appropriateness of either of her choices, one senses no condemnation of her behavior. There is no premarital pregnancy, no ostracism, no forced early marriage. Quite simply Marcia chooses her own course of sexual behavior, and she uses a contemporary form of birth control to avoid pregnancy. . . . (pp. 66-7)

Myra Pollack Sadker and David Miller Sadker, "Family Matters" and "Sex in Fact and Fiction," in their Now Upon a Time: A Contemporary View of Children's Literature, *Harper & Row, Publishers, 1977, pp. 13-47, 48-70.*

JEAN F. MERCIER

Within the first few minutes of meeting Rosemary Wells, it is evident that interviewing her will be pleasant and uncomplicated. In conversation, Wells is eloquent and witty, just as she is in the books she creates for young readers. Published by Dial Press, these range from such picture books as *Noisy Nora, Don't Spill It Again, James,* [and] *Stanley and Rhoda* to sophisticated novels for teenagers—winners, all, of a string of honors.

Once past the mandatory first questions ("How did you get started in children's books?" etc.), Wells requires little prompting. The tall, dark-haired, handsome woman . . . vibrates with energy. One suspects she could triple her contributions to the several roles she plays (author, architect's wife and mother of two small daughters) and still have vigor and enthusiasm to spare.

Keeping busy is a Wells habit. "As far back as I can remember, I did nothing but draw," she says. "I parlayed this into the sham of a school career. I discovered very early that making a picture of anything meant people saying, 'Look at that!' and how else could I get that kind of attention?"

The author makes no bones about being a "very poor student." After skinning through high school in her hometown, near Red Bank, N.J., she attended a prestigious art school in Boston, but not for long. "I hated it. I quit to get married at 19 and was delighted at the chance to say goodbye to my teacher, who said it was no loss. I was nothing but an illustrator, anyway. Pretty snobbish, eh?" She gave out with one of the uninhibited laughs that punctuate the meeting, signs of the lively appreciation of the ridiculous that sparks her stories and pictures. (p. 72)

[Wells] acknowledges debts to her six-year-old Victoria (Vicky) and two-year-old Margaret (Meg) for ideas they provide for picture books, including her latest. Called Very First Readers, these four board books dramatize the efforts of an older child, Ruby, to make a baby brother, Max, shape up. Wells says that **Max's First Word** and its three sequels grew out of officious Vicky's impatience with Meg's progress and her efforts to push little sister into speaking, counting and, in general, moving faster toward being grownup—"like herself, of course," says her mother.

> Watching their daily skirmishes, I began to think of how books for children in their early years could be more inviting. I had always read to the girls; we never allow them to watch any television, so the story hours were their main entertainment. And, as everyone knows, children want to hear the same story, over and over. I found little for their age that wasn't dull, unexciting. So I began to figure out how to invent some extremely simple stories that wouldn't drive parents up the wall when they had to repeat them over and over. I wanted to give children adventures they could understand and include jokes parents would recognize. To do what such books should: teach, yes, but offer a story, something to giggle at—shapes, color and movement. Not just static words and pictures of a ball, dog, cat—page after page.

The Very First Books are doing the trick, from all reports.

We ask Wells to fill us in on the genesis of the three novels, so different from her picture books that even some professionals in publishing don't realize they are written by the same Rosemary Wells. The novels, we learn, are also rooted in her childhood. "When I wasn't drawing, I used to write stories, but only for myself. How are you going to get instant attention for something you write, the way you do with pictures? And what have you got to write *about*, when you're a kid? Nobody should write until after age 30!"

Wells was "after 30" when Dial published her first novel, **The Fog Comes on Little Pig Feet,** a serious but bitingly comic story of a disaffected college dropout. The book won raves, with most reviewers impressed by the real-life feel of the chief character. ("Me," Wells confirmed.)

The author's second was **None of the Above,** concerning a passive, not overly bright girl "taken in hand" by well-meaning people who push her to do what they regard as right for her. In the end, the girl opts for what will almost certainly be a bleak future, a denouement that dismayed some critics.

To Wells, these responses were as welcome as the generally favorable notices. "It showed they cared about her," she believes. "And later, when the angry ones thought about it, they did understand the point I was trying to put across. No matter what the girl decided, it was her *own* choice, her first choice, the beginning of independence."

Leave Well Enough Alone, Wells's third novel, was a powerful psychological thriller, based on the young heroine's need to solve a tricky ethical dilemma. This story coaxed superlatives out of the toughest critics. But Wells regards the remarks of one reviewer, in particular, her greatest compliment. "The piece stated that the author had indisputably drawn on her Irish-Catholic background, her intimacy with nuns as teachers especially, in creating the heroine. And then she found out I was a damn WASP!"

After another good laugh, Wells adds,

> Actually, I did draw on such a background, but it isn't mine. One of my best friends, a girl I grew up with in Red Bank, was Irish-Catholic, and I learned about her religion, her experiences in parochial school, from her. I think I could write as convincingly about a character from a Jewish family. Our neighborhood was quite mixed, and I was in and out of everybody's house all the time. I got to know a lot about religious and ethnic observances, family customs.

What, *PW* wondered, after our session with her, is now germinating in Wells's fertile imagination? Even Phyllis Fogelman couldn't tell us that. She did tell us about a recent phone call from Wells that jetted off: "I'm trying to make up my mind about these three projects. I want to get started right away, so I'd like to know what you think would be best to tackle first, before I get on with the other two. Here's the idea. . . ." (pp. 72-3)

Jean F. Mercier, in an interview with Rosemary Wells, in Publishers Weekly, *Vol. 217, No. 8, February 29, 1980, pp. 72-3.*

ZENA SUTHERLAND, DIANNE L. MONSON, AND MAY HILL ARBUTHNOT

Although she has written several stories for older children, Rosemary Wells is primarily known for the picture books she writes and illustrates. Picture story books like **Morris' Disappearing Bag** and **Don't Spill It Again, James** have a sense of wry comedy that pervades the illustrations as well as the text. The stumpy little animal children of her deft drawings appeal both because they capture the essence of children's behavior and because they have marvelously expressive faces. In **Benjamin and Tulip,** for example, much of the humor comes not from what the two do, but from how they look: Benjamin astounded and Tulip smugly victorious when she outwits him yet again. Text and pictures are smoothly complementary, and never more so than in the series of stories about Max; on heavy board pages Wells uses a minimal text, as Max—in **Max's First Word** blandly comes out with a polysyllabic answer when his sister is urging him to say a simple word. In **Max's Ride** the pictures are full of action as Max rides in a baby carriage careening downhill; the book also stresses concepts of direction, as he goes *over* a laundry basket, tumbles *out*, and is bounced *up* in the air, *between* two trees. (p. 149)

Zena Sutherland, Dianne L. Monson, and May Hill Arbuthnot, "Artists and Children's Books," in their Children and Books, *sixth edition, Scott, Foresman and Company, 1981, pp. 124-55.*

ZENA SUTHERLAND

[**Max's Christmas**] should win new fans and delight those who are already addicted to stories about Max, the small rabbit who is cared for by his patient older sibling Ruby. What makes this series of books by Rosemary Wells so successful is the ingenious quality of the writing (and the pictures) so skillfully pruned by the author to the essentials of the story. Too, Max is the Great Success of the preschool set, appearing shy and baffled but always, at the close, surprising Ruby with a turnabout ending.

Zena Sutherland, in a review of "Max's Christmas," in Bulletin of the Center for Children's Books, *Vol. 40, No. 3, November, 1986, p. 59.*

Wells, approximately two years old, at her grandmother's house. Courtesy of Rosemary Wells.

JOHN AND THE RAREY (1969)

It took no perception to spot Rosemary Wells as a fresh new talent in children's books. All that was necessary was to look at the W. S. Gilbert lyrics she illustrated for Macmillan, *A Song to Sing O!* and *The Duke of Plaza Toro.* Now she has written her own lyrics and illustrated them in this witty story of a boy who doesn't want to be an airplane pilot like his father, who does want a pet. She has arranged a happy ending. He does go off into the wild blue yonder, not in a plane but on the back of his wild pet. So everybody, including the readers, is happy.

> *A review of "John and the Rarey," in* Publishers Weekly, *Vol. 195, No. 16, April 21, 1969, p. 64.*

[The] fantasy-nonsense that ensues when John takes the little blue-eyed creature home will appeal to all children who have been faced with a frustrating family situation. While the subdued orange and lavender pages may not be to every taste, the drawings pull the reader from page to page and give a feeling of character and action. (p. 400)

> *Sidney D. Long, in a review of "John and the Rarey," in* The Horn Book Magazine, *Vol. XLV, No. 4, August, 1969, pp. 399-400.*

MICHAEL AND THE MITTEN TEST (1969)

"Do they fly off your hands?" Michael's mother asked when he lost the eighth pair in a year, and she pinned a pair of his brother's mittens to Michael's sleeves. He was to sit in a chair, she said, and see what happened. Nothing happened. Then they tried it without the pins, and Michael passed that test, too—but when his mother went off to answer the telephone, he went outside. The last double-page spread announces, "It was spring," and there is Michael, who has shed not only his mittens, but half of the rest of his clothing. The story has a raffish humor, and the appeal of an all-too-familiar situation, but the ending is abrupt and disappointing.

> *Zena Sutherland, in a review of "Michael and the Mitten Test," in* Bulletin of the Center for Children's Books, *Vol. 23, No. 9, May, 1970, p. 154.*

MARTHA'S BIRTHDAY (1970)

Martha's Birthday is a perfect birthday present for any small girl with a sense of humor. For Rosemary Wells, who wrote and illustrated this witty account of the choices a girl must make, has a wry astringent humor herself. And Heaven knows, and so do all of us whose job it is to read all the new juveniles, humor, especially wry, astringent humor, *is,* in current children's books, rarer than hen's teeth.

> *A review of "Martha's Birthday," in* Publishers Weekly, *Vol. 197, No. 16, April 20, 1970, p. 62.*

A funny, modern parallel to the *Little Red Riding Hood* story. When Martha receives a pair of homemade argyle socks from Aunt Elizabeth for her birthday, her mother sends her across town (carrying a pie and wearing the socks) to thank her aunt personally. Martha's attempt to hide the hated socks from sight will be familiar to most readers, and the expressions on her face will captivate them. In her humorous pictures, Miss Wells conveys to perfection the child's dilemma in trying to avoid both being laughed at and hurting her aunt's feelings. Fortunately for Martha, the socks were meant for her father (though argyle socks have been out for years and he probably won't want them either!) and Aunt Elizabeth has a more appealing gift for her—a baby skunk.

> *Alice D. Ehlert, in a review of "Martha's Birthday," in* Library Journal, *Vol. 95, No. 13, July, 1970, p. 2530.*

THE FIRST CHILD (1970)

Rosemary Wells is a wild woman: her ideas are so unfamiliar that we have to fly into the wild blue yonder to catch up with her. She makes it well worth the flight because her laconic style of writing and illustration, as in this brilliant story of the dangerous voyage the first child made from protoplasm to man, shows the discipline of true talent.

> *A review of "The First Child," in* Publishers Weekly, *Vol. 198, No. 15, October 12, 1970, p. 55.*

A fanciful story of human evolution, the illustrations (less harsh than most of the author-artist's previous work) showing all the proper life forms of the era save for one preposterous creature. . . . Although sophisticated in concept, this is delightfully silly, written with dry humor and deftly concluded.

A review of "The First Child," in Bulletin of the Center for Children's Books, *Vol. 24, No. 5, January, 1971, p. 83.*

MIRANDA'S PILGRIMS   (1970)

Another of those intriguing fugitive presences that disintegrates when you try to pin it down. Wrongly blamed for filling brother George with fear of beasts under his bed, Miranda is met by her nighttime nemesis, a pack of Pilgrims who put her to work that never gets done; when she calls them *mean* (for killing a butterfly), they shrink and flee, and she offers to change beds and "take care of the lions and tigers for tonight." From this one can conclude variously that (1) honesty and hard work go unrewarded; (2) the Puritan ethic is a greater menace than the wildest nature. There's something to it, but what does a youngster get from it? Especially if Pilgrims mean only Thanksgiving bounty to him.

A review of "Miranda's Pilgrims," in Kirkus Reviews, *Vol. XXXVIII, No. 22, November 15, 1970, p. 1245.*

The astringent wit of Rosemary Wells, in words and illustrations, is as welcome as a very dry martini after a series of Pink Ladys. This time she points her rapier at the Pilgrim Fathers. . . . She routs them and their rigid influence forever, thus diminishing the income of the headshrinkers and increasing the pleasure of her readers.

A review of "Miranda's Pilgrims," in Publishers Weekly, *Vol. 198, No. 24, December 14, 1970, p. 39.*

UNFORTUNATELY HARRIET   (1972)

What can you do if you spill varnish on a new rug? Author/artist Rosemary Wells has several suggestions, all of them highly amusing and guaranteed to bring a chorus of giggles from small children who have found themselves in similar predicaments. If you happen to be the unfortunate Harriet of this story, you can try to clean the spot with a sponge or dustpan, or shout at it to magically disappear, or pile furniture on the spot to cover it, or in final desperation, run away. Whatever your solution, Rosemary Wells has aptly captured the frustration of a child's world.

A review of "Unfortunately Harriet," in Publishers Weekly, *Vol. 201, No. 5, January 31, 1972, p. 247.*

Wells's pencil drawings with orange, brown, and purple watercolor aptly capture the reactions of the unfortunate protagonist but are better than this slight story. . . . The surprise ending might appeal to children who fear parental reprisals for real or imaginary destructive accidents, and the book could conceivably be used as a basis for discussion of such matters. However, most thoughtful mothers would not likely give a young child access to a product as dangerous as varnish since the outcome could be much more serious than a spot on a rug. (pp. 71-2)

Linda Lawson Clark, in a review of "Unfortunately Harriet," in School Library Journal, *Vol. 18, No. 9, May, 1972, pp. 71-2.*

THE FOG COMES ON LITTLE PIG FEET   (1972)

Young teens will devour this fast-paced, adequately written entertainment. Rachel Sasakian, 13 years old, is from a middle-class Brooklyn family and here tells her story in diary form. She would rather go to Music and Art High School and become a concert pianist, but her electrician father and social-climbing mother have been saving for years to pay the $4,000 tuition at North Place, an elite boarding school. "'We want you to have better than us.'" her mother says. During the first hateful week, Rachel becomes embroiled in a series of lies invented as a defense against conformity and to protect an upper classman, Carlisle Daggett, who is allegedly mentally unbalanced and who has run away to a Greenwich Village commune. Brought up before Honor Court, Rachel continues her fabrications, and then, in desperation, involves her parents by asking them to invent a family emergency so that she can come home for the weekend. Once there, she sneaks into the Village to see Carlisle who admits having tried suicide. Shocked and confused, Rachel goes back to North Place and a second confrontation with Honor Court only to discover that her diary has been found. Faced with exposure, she rats on Carlisle—then is told that her parents have decided to let her go to public high school. Although the characters—particularly the North Place girls, the headmistress, and Rachel's parents—are stereotyped and one minor character never develops as expected, Wells does successfully portray the beginnings of puberty and an adolescent's need for privacy. Rachel's obsession about getting her period, counting her pubic hairs (she has 37) and examining her chest for signs of developing breasts are related with humor and understanding. Well's black-and-white line drawings, unfortunately, do not match the mood of the story.

Alice Miller Bregman, in a review of "The Fog Comes on Little Pig Feet," in School Library Journal, *Vol. 18, No. 9, May, 1972, p. 89.*

To start with, Rachel's snobbish working-class mother . . . is just unreal. She's a type rather than an individual but she isn't true to any type, and Ms. Wells' unsympathetic treatment of her indicates a little snobbery on her own part: "It will reflect on Daddy and I if you don't speak properly." The initial picture of the rigid repressive school gives a similar impression of garbled sociology, even to the expensive, out-of-season asparagus served at dinner. Once we're into the story, though, certain recognizable absurdities are given properly incidental notice (any infringement of the rules invites demerits, but you can work them off by writing out Gettysburg Addresses—five Gettysburgs for every chit), and the quirky humor that has always been evident in Ms. Wells' pictures assumes some happy verbal manifestations here. And Rachel herself, a reluctant nonconformist who hates the school because it allows her no time to practice piano or just be alone, is quietly convincing all along. . . . The story too grows up as it goes along.

A review of "The Fog Comes on Little Pig Feet," in Kirkus Reviews, *Vol. XL, No. 10, May 15, 1972, p. 581.*

Scattered through this glimpse into adolescence are priceless vignettes, some caustic, others poignant, and still others hilarious. Picture Carlisle's living anatomy lesson—she painted all the organs illustrated in the foldover encyclopedia pages on her own body, in living color, and then marched down the hall. Or suffer, vicariously, the two-way tug of wanting, and fearing, physical contact with people. Again, observe the brittle philosophy of "rich is right" enacted at the introductory Dean's Tea.

In this first novel, Miss Wells brilliantly demonstrates her writing abilities are an easy match for her already famous artistic talents. Highly recommended for ages 11-16.

> *Mrs. John G. Gray, in a review of "The Fog Comes on Little Pig Feet," in* Best Sellers, *Vol. 32, No. 8, July 15, 1972, p. 200.*

NOISY NORA (1973)

Nora's noisy bids for attention are ignored by her preoccupied parents but won't escape the notice of preschoolers. Competing with a demanding baby and an accomplished older sister who overshadows her, Nora the mouse turns into a dynamo of domestic destruction. When slammed doors and overturned furniture fail to turn the tables, she threatens to split—" 'And I'm never coming back.' " The sudden silence after her pretended departure is heard by all, and a search of house and environs is initiated. Nora's emergence from the broom closet (upsetting mop, bucket, and scrubbing brush "With a monumental crash") finally elicits the proper response from her family and provides a satisfying end. Told in engaging verse with pen-and-ink drawings which humorously depict Nora's subtler ploys—e.g., crowning herself with an upturned bowl; surreptitiously poking her sister with a pencil—Wells' story never condescends to the situation of kids who sometimes have to wreck their way to stage-center.

> *Pamela D. Pollock, in a review of "Noisy Nora," in* School Library Journal, *an appendix to* Library Journal, *Vol. 98, No. 10, May, 1973, p. 68.*

A small book with rhymed verses and anthropomorphic mice has been illustrated with buoyant pastel drawings that add humorous details to the story—father mouse playing chess, Nora throwing items helter-skelter, and father mouse unrolling Jack from a towel. The universal emotion of a child's feeling slighted because of its siblings has been given life in a simple book.

> *Anita Silvey, in a review of "Noisy Nora," in* The Horn Book Magazine, *Vol. XLIX, No. 3, June, 1973, p. 263.*

It would be ungrateful to resent the moral so wittily concealed behind the disasters of *Noisy Nora.* Incidents and domestic interiors will be equally recognisable to small children as they follow the anarchic behaviour of Nora. . . . I am not sure whether this miniature drama is supposed actually to make it easier for middle children to accept the small pricks of family life but I *am* sure that what any young reader or listener will enjoy is Nora's calculated naughtiness, expressed in simple sentences under illustrations, black and white with overlaid pinks and yellows, which are delicate, funny and felicitously explicit.

> *Margery Fisher, in a review of "Noisy Nora," in* Growing Point, *Vol. 15, No. 4, October, 1976, p. 2965.*

BENJAMIN AND TULIP (1973)

This mildly pleasant story revolves around a not-so-pleasant situation. Tulip, the bully, and Benjamin, the victim, have a perfect sado-masochistic relationship: she beats him up everytime he passes her tree, and he keeps on taking it, along with the injustice of being thought the aggressor by his Aunt Fern.

As can be expected, the worm turns—Tulip chases Benjamin up a tree, and they both fall off. He lands on top of her, and the reversal of positions causes a reversal of roles as well. Courageously, Benjamin smashes her with the piece of watermelon he was carrying. Now Tulip is properly cowed, and they both sit eating watermelon, spitting pits at each other. The amiable cartoons of dressed-up raccoons and the humorously natural dialogue (" 'This is my brand-new suit,' said Benjamin. 'I'm gonna mess it up!' said Tulip.") take all the punch out of the aggression that the story is supposed to be about. What's left is a confusingly half-hearted little book that will undoubtedly amuse some but which has absolutely no impact.

> *Marilyn R. Singer, in a review of "Benjamin and Tulip," in* School Library Journal, *Vol. 20, No. 4, November, 1973, p. 44.*

How the victim vanquishes the victor is the satisfying conclusion to a piquant picture story featuring an engaging pair of raccoons. The brief text, interpreted in delicately amusing pastel and pen-and-ink drawings, is appropriate to the size of the book, comfortably scaled for small hands. An anthropomorphized version of the Charlie Brown-Lucy confrontation for pre-Peanuts fans.

> *Mary M. Burns, "Stocking Gift," in* The Horn Book Magazine, *Vol. XLIX, No. 6, December, 1973, p. 584.*

Here is an inconsequential but amusing little book about two small hairy animals (I was unable to identify the species but this is unimportant). . . .

The small format, simple but evocative illustrations and brief text will appeal to most young children. Small boys and girls will be able to identify, sympathising with the character closest to their own experience of the earliest rounds in the battle of the sexes!

> *M. R. Hewitt, in a review of "Benjamin and Tulip," in* The Junior Bookshelf, *Vol. 41, No. 6, December, 1977, p. 330.*

NONE OF THE ABOVE (1974)

When her father remarries, doltish Marcia who likes day-glo pink angora sweaters, watching TV, and movie magazines, finds herself out of place with her sophisticated stepmother and her whiz-kid stepsister Chris. In the five years that the novel spans, Marcia becomes more acceptable to her new family (she switches into college preparatory classes and is accepted at Sarah Lawrence) but in so doing seems to lose herself. Her growing involvement with Raymond, a hoody high school hero who is impotent until his relationship with Marcia, forces her to choose the direction of her life—and Wells refuses to provide any "happily ever after" solution to Marcia's problems. An unusual and oddly affecting heroine, Marcia seems, at times, to be sleepwalking through the events of her life. The author skillfully captures the girl's confusion in this timely, realistic and moving novel which should reach a wide audience.

> *Joni Bodart, in a review of "None of the Above," in* School Library Journal, *an appendix to* Library Journal, *Vol. 21, No. 3, November, 1974, p. 69.*

The characterization is strong and consistent, and the complexities of relationships within the family are beautifully de-

Wells holding her daughter Victoria in 1973. Courtesy of Rosemary Wells.

veloped. Wells is particularly adept at dialogue, using it adroitly to develop both the story line and the characters in a story that is sensitive and candid.

Zena Sutherland, in a review of "None of the Above,"
in Bulletin of the Center for Children's Books, Vol.
28, No. 8, April, 1975, p. 139.

Robert Cormier's *The Chocolate War* was not the only novel of despair for young adults to appear in 1974. There was William Sleator's *House of Stairs* and also Rosemary Wells's *None of the Above.* But where the first two are despairing on the grand scale—abstracted darkness—*None of the Above* is firmly rooted in a dreary, ordinary world, its bitterness arising from the most common details, situations, and choices faced by young adults in 1974 and today.

Wells sets the caustic tone with the first sentence: "'Marcia Mill is a big fat pill,' said Christina Van Dam in not a particularly low voice.'' Marcia and Chrissy are new stepsisters, Marcia's father and Chrissy's mother having remarried after their former spouses died (a rare detail, unlike the more common disposition by divorce). (p. 368)

While Marcia is the protagonist, we can see why Chrissy calls her a pill. Marcia is dull and mopey, wears tight, cheap clothing, and has no intellectual interest whatsoever. Along with believing that blue cheese dressing can kill you, Marcia thinks that *The Lion in Winter* is a wildlife movie; she would rather go see *Hello, Dolly!*

There's a shared expectation between reader and author: they both know better than Marcia; she will not fulfill the conventional function of a young-adult protagonist as guide or lens. We are not expected to identify with her. We feel instead that we are looking down on Marcia, not with contempt but simply with the knowledge that we know more about her than she does. How can a reader identify with a heroine who doesn't like to read? *Heroine* is probably not the right word, for it implies more energy and will than Marcia seems to possess. How are we supposed to feel about Marcia? Where do the author's sympathies lie? We get very few clues. Wells keeps herself out of the story, employing neither direct authorial comment nor the device of a mouthpiece in the form of a sympathetic character upon whose perceptions the reader can rely. She spares no one. Marcia's sister Sharon is blowzy and ignorant and becomes pregnant while her husband is in Vietnam. Chrissy is irritating, and her mother is given to such profundities as "'We wouldn't have disagreements if everybody agreed on the same things.'' Excepting an occasional, feeble defense of his daughters, Marcia's father is voiceless and faceless. While characters do make tentative attempts to reach one another, their motives often seem ambiguous, and their efforts are almost invariably misunderstood. All of the characters have extremely limited imaginations.

The book has much in common with today's adult fiction, in particular with short story writers like Bobbie Ann Mason and Ann Beattie: the attention to precise, tacky detail—"Marcia spent most of her money on a day-glo pink angora sweater and a Bambi pin''; disjointed, distracted conversation; a passive protagonist; the flat, ironic style. The brief first chapter of *None of the Above,* ending with Mr. Mill and Mother showing slides of their honeymoon, could stand alone as a *New Yorker* short story.

Various people have ambitions for Marcia, who herself only vaguely dreams of meeting David Cassidy or becoming a stewardess. Sharon wants Marcia to move down to her mobile home in Florida; an English teacher thinks Marcia is college prep material. So does Mother, who believes Marcia would do well at the University of Massachusetts—her own daughter is going to Yale. Carla, stepbrother John's Bohemian girlfriend, pushes Kahlil Gibran and Joseph Conrad on Marcia and takes her to foreign films. "She wished it were at least in color. Everything was twice as serious in black and white." In what is clearly as much a rivalry with Mrs. Mill as a concern for Marcia, Carla also talks her into applying to Sarah Lawrence.

Marcia tries. She moves into the College Prep track and works hard but loathes it. "This book, Marcia decided, had bored many people." The only thing Marcia genuinely enjoys is her summer job as a diner waitress, where, in a rare moment of assertion, she tells everyone her name is Kimberly. "She liked being called Kim. She enjoyed being good and being liked."

These are also the qualities that sustain Marcia in her relationship with Raymond, the school "hunk," who masks his sexual inadequacy with bragging stories and a motorcycle. While he constantly tells her she thinks too much or talks too much (neither of which could Marcia be accused of overdoing), he desperately needs her, and for Marcia, that is enough. As Marcia grows . . . she gradually "notices" the emotional neediness of those around her: the way her stepmother reaches for her husband's hand; how frightened Chrissy is of boys. She notices, often acutely, but she does not know what to do with what she sees.

In the last chapter, Marcia, after an incomprehensible exam on Browning's "My Last Duchess," faces a choice. She has been accepted at both the University of Massachusetts and Sarah Lawrence, and Raymond has asked her to marry him. Which will it be? "Never, never in her whole life did she want to read a book again. Fourteen minutes to nine. Raymond would be waiting." She puts on her engagement ring, goes outside, and starts walking toward Raymond's car. She hopes he sees the diamond on her finger reflected in his headlights, but Raymond is absorbed in *Car and Driver.*

> Marcia started to run. She could already hear the voices, Mother's and even Carla's, through the floor.
>
> "Why? why? why did she do it? She could have gone to Sarah Lawrence. Anywhere! Even the University of Massachusetts wouldn't have been so bad. She had everything ahead of her."
>
> "Don't ask me. She talked to you a lot more than she talked to me. Didn't she say anything? Didn't she at least give some reason for getting married? You could talk to her. You could make sense of her."
>
> Marcia felt a tug in her stomach. The deep silent pool inside, she thought. It's nothing but a stomach full of ulcers! She ran downstairs in her imagination.
>
> "Because," she said right out to them. "Because we're in love. Isn't that enough?"
>
> The familiar pain engulfed her for a moment, but she kept on running as if it were not there at all.

The conclusion caused some confusion for reviewers, who could not decide if the ending was happy, pessimistic, or ambiguous. It was not even clear that Marcia had actually left the house. The key is found earlier in the book when Marcia makes a remark to Carla: "Through the walls, through the floor, through the roof! Sometimes I even hear things I don't hear. Sometimes I even hear them talking when I'm miles away from the house." Marcia is running, but it is not so much an act of assertion as one of desperation, and we know she is merely exchanging one set of people's expectations for another. Life with Raymond holds no promise of satisfaction. Despite what Marcia imagines telling Carla and Mother, she doesn't love Raymond; she only knows that Raymond loves her. That quiet place inside her, a haven she seeks throughout the book, is an ulcer, and as she runs, the pain continues.

Marcia has had daydreams, fantasies, and false reassurances, but she has never been able to exert herself to any real possibilities beyond the ones presented to her. This may indicate the limits of Marcia's imagination, but even more grim, it may indicate the limits of Marcia's banal world. There are no other choices. What can we say—that she would have made an excellent waitress? And how can we say even that without becoming just another of those thundering voices? (pp. 368-71)

Roger Sutton, "A Second Look: 'None of the Above'," in The Horn Book Magazine, *Vol. LXIII, No. 3, May-June, 1987, pp. 368-71.*

ABDUL (1975)

The setting for Wells' latest picture book is the Sahara—more or less. Gilda the camel has given birth to Abdul, an offspring of such peculiar proportions that she hides him. However, since the oasis has just dried up, Gilda, her master Feisal, and Abdul have to move out with everyone else. Readers will see that Abdul is a horse, but Feisal's ignorant fellow-travelers think he is a devil and abandon him. A windstorm blows Abdul into "a nice new oasis" where faithful Gilda and Feisal find him surrounded by lots of other horses. They all settle down happily although "none of Abdul's new friends had ever seen a horse as funny as Gilda." Although this gambit in unnatural history may confuse some among its intended audience, the text is clever and the illustrations at Wells' droll best.

Janet French, in a review of "Abdul," in School Library Journal, *Vol. 21, No. 9, May, 1975, p. 51.*

The sands of the Arabian desert—minus oil derricks—form the background of a picture book that comically explores how aberration is in the eye of the beholder. . . . The artist's sense of humor has created a tour de force; wonderfully ridiculous characters, their faces always contorted into amusing expressions, contrast beautifully with the stoic beasts of burden; and the pure backgrounds of blue sky and yellow sand accentuate the activities of the figures placed against them. However, the outrageous caricaturing may be offensive to some people. (pp. 258-59)

Anita Silvey, in a review of "Abdul," in The Horn Book Magazine, *Vol. LI, No. 3, June, 1975, pp. 258-59.*

MORRIS'S DISAPPEARING BAG: A CHRISTMAS STORY (1975)

If you missed this book this past Christmas, it is a must for next year. Rosemary Wells presents us with more endearing animals—this time a family of rabbits. On Christmas morning when they opened their presents, Victor got a hockey outfit, Rose a beauty kit, Betty a chemistry set, and Morris a bear. The three older children spent the day enjoying each other's gifts, but they told Morris he was too young to play with chemicals, too little to play hockey, and too silly to use the beauty kit—and no one wanted to play with his bear. It wasn't until all the rest of the family was eating dinner that Morris noticed one more package. Inside he found a disappearing bag. How he used this magical gift to bring him the attention he wanted from his older siblings is amusingly related in the conclusion. As usual, Wells's colorful illustrations are delightful, with Morris especially lovable, clad in holly-print pants. A warmly satisfying story for children of all ages. (pp. 404-05)

> *Barbara Dill, in a review of "Morris's Disappearing Bag: A Christmas Story," in* Wilson Library Bulletin, *Vol. 50, No. 5, January, 1976, pp. 404-05.*

Perhaps the best way of conveying the quality of Rosemary Wells's very short new Christmas story, **Morris's disappearing bag** is to say that it stands comparison with [Kenneth] Grahame. As in the works of the master, there is nothing annoying about Morris being a rabbit instead of a person, and the deceptively simple pictures carry a great deal of very human character and feelings.

> *Virginia Makins, "Post Early . . . ," in* The Times Educational Supplement, *No. 3255, October 28, 1977, p. 23.*

You can tell it's a Christmas story because Morris's overalls have holly on them. . . . The one-last-package-under-the-tree that solves the problem of getting ignored at holidays is ingeniously creative. This is a hilarious book, drawn and written by a master, for deserving 3- to 7-year-olds.

> *Janet Domowitz, in a review of "Morris's Disappearing Bag: A Christmas Story," in* The Christian Science Monitor, *December 4, 1978, p. B19.*

LEAVE WELL ENOUGH ALONE (1977)

Sophomore at Sacred Heart Academy and youngest daughter of a Newburgh, New York policeman, 14-year-old Dorothy has been raised to believe in the bedrock of right and wrong. Yet as mother's helper to the high-living Hoades, she suddenly finds that her absolute standards don't apply. The Hoade's world of lavish parties, swimming pools, horseback riding is both alluring and unsettling, bound up as it is in lies and half-truths. Mr. Hoade with his vague career in "public relations" is mixed up with a shady union leader; Mrs. Hoade deceives her daughters about their infant sister (a mongoloid); and above all Dorothy comes to suspect something fishy is going on in the off-limits cottage where the baby is supposedly kept. Against warnings from friends and family to *Leave Well Enough Alone,* she snoops around until she discovers the family secret—Mrs. Hoades' terminally ill grandmother had been kept prisoner so she would sign over a new will. Dorothy is then left on her own to decide the most moral course of action. Although the mystery is contrived and confusing at times with too many false or oblique clues, the characterizations are superb, especially Dorothy's "martyred" older sister who, at 20, is saddled with a baby and bunions; and, of course, Dorothy, herself, caught squarely between her Catholic conscience and ambitious nature. Wells' finest novel yet, this raises thorny ethical questions and discusses them compellingly and with great humor.

> *Jane Abramson, in a review of "Leave Well Enough Alone," in* School Library Journal, *Vol. 23, No. 9, May, 1977, p. 73.*

I began this book laughing with delight at Rosemary Wells's marvelous re-creation of fourteenness—the fervid rejoicing over a mistake not made, the strain of drinking a Coke noiselessly in the presence of an adult one is struggling to impress, furtively removing and disposing of one's ruined stockings, only to have them returned by a smiling porter. And for those of us who grew up pious in the '40s and '50s there is that ever losing battle for goodness—the feverish yielding to the very temptation one has seconds before praised God for the power to overcome.

I began the book laughing. I ended it in goosebumps. In between I had gobbled up red herrings like gum drops.

To say that Wells deceived me right up until the next to the last page is to acknowledge her ability as a writer of suspense, but it is the shimmering threads of humor and human insight with which she has spun her tale that completely entrap the reader.

> *Katherine Paterson, "The Case of the Curious Babysitter," in* Book World—The Washington Post, *May 1, 1977, p. E4.*

Not since Dorothy was whisked off to Oz have I encountered a Dorothy as impressionable and thoroughly sympathetic as the heroine of Rosemary Wells's **Leave Well Enough Alone**. (p. 20)

As Dorothy pursues clue after clue in her search for truth and in a desire to gain personal recognition, she also begins to discover that the world is a very complex place with a gray area between right and wrong where even a person of conscience cannot easily cope. Despite the aura this serious issue gives to the novel, Mrs. Wells has not lost her touch for writing funny dialogue or her ability to develop believable characters. In fact, the Hoade girls' mother, Maria, is so pathetically real and zany—she wears her homemade sweater inside-out because she knitted the initials from the manual into it instead of her own—she sometimes threatens to steal the whole show from Dorothy.

All in all, this is a well-written book full of humor and suspense. It does, however, have the added plus of leaving the reader to wrestle with the question of whether "leaving well enough alone" *is* the right solution to a complicated moral dilemma. (p. 21)

> *Susan Terris, in a review of "Leave Well Enough Alone," in* The New York Times Book Review, *July 10, 1977, pp. 20-1.*

DON'T SPILL IT AGAIN, JAMES (1977)

Popular, talented Wells again features the furry little foxes that critics and readers hailed in *Noisy Nora* and other picture books. Here are three short tales, told in rhyme, all depicting the deep but sorely tried love of two brothers. James's older brother expresses his exasperation at the tiny boy while they're struggling home through the rain. James is carrying a big bag of groceries and drops it, breaking a ketchup bottle and making a general mess. Big Brother scolds the child but his attitude softens and they become friends again. In the last story, **"Goodnight, Sweet Prince,"** the bigger boy tenderly tucks the baby into bed, a scene hard to beat for pure enchantment. The book is a blessing to little brothers everywhere and a lesson to older ones.

> A review of "Don't Spill It Again, James," in Publishers Weekly, Vol. 212, No. 9, August 29, 1977, p. 366.

Small children will not need the text to follow the plot since a full-color drawing on every page provides ample clues to the story line. The book, in fact, works better without the limping lines of verse which wander further from the illustrated action in each succeeding tale. Forget the rhymes and enjoy the pictures—just what the children will do. (p. 46)

> Janet French, in a review of "Don't Spill It Again, James," in School Library Journal, Vol. 24, No. 4, December, 1977, pp. 45-6.

Whether picking up groceries in the rain, suffering a smoker in a train, or being put to bed, James—and the reader—benefit from skillful rhyme to suit each occasion and expressive colored pictures to perpetuate the smiles which the writing engenders. A humdinger of a book, humming with action at the beginning, then tapering off to a lullabye full of soothing imagery. A real treat for the primary grades.

> Ruth M. Stein, in a review of "Don't Spill It Again, James," in Language Arts, Vol. 55, No. 5, May, 1978, p. 617.

STANLEY AND RHODA (1978)

An author of prize-winning novels for teenagers, gifted Wells has also contributed incomparable picture books, to the joy of the tinies, and this is another jewel, starring a mouse family. Wells accompanies three stories with bravely hued, imaginatively conceived scenes of Stanley, Rhoda and their mom. The clothing, house furnishings and every detail in the book are deliciously quaint visuals. Stanley, an exemplary older brother, is exploited sometimes by his persnickety sister Rhoda. In the first story, mom asks Stanley to show Rhoda how to neaten her messy room. The tyke devotes herself to a trivial task while Stanley "shows" her how to fold her clothes, make the bed, etc. Mother is pleased; "Stanley helped," says Rhoda. But in the next two stories, Stanley practices a bit of oneupmanship on his small sibling.

> A review of "Stanley and Rhoda," in Publishers Weekly, Vol. 214, No. 15, October 9, 1978, p. 76.

Welcome to yet another household full of children's paraphernalia and zany antics in Rosemary Wells's *Stanley and Rhoda,* a thoroughly delightful collection of three stories about Rhoda and her clever big brother Stanley. These stories present common childhood dilemmas: cleaning up one's room, suffering a bee sting, dealing with the new babysitter. In each, little Rhoda merrily does what she wishes, coyly influencing Stanley, a self-possessed and ingenious older brother dedicated to keeping the peace.

Rhoda is always caught up in her own world and does not always pay attention to what Stanley is saying. When she is obsessed with her bunny berries, nothing else matters. Her bee sting hurts only as long as it is in her interest for it to hurt. And she hates the new sitter only until he comes down to her level. Stanley instinctively knows how to handle his little sister: he always draws from her the desired comment, the appropriate

reaction. The overall effect is one of warm, funny harmony. It is impossible not to love each of them.

Rosemary Wells matches the wit of her pen with the wit of her drawings. Stanley and Rhoda accomplish much in very few words; the language is unadorned, yet rich by its very conciseness. The physical portrayal of the two is equally easy to decipher: we know exactly what is going on in the minds of these two children. And although we expect what will happen, we are nonetheless taken by surprise through the superb manipulation of facial expressions.

Rhoda is no more the selfish little sister than Stanley is the goody-goody brother. After all, Rhoda does not always get her way, and Stanley derives great satisfaction from sneaking back into Rhoda's freshly-straightened room to spill her bunny berries. They are two children who thoroughly understand each other and who have developed their own little mutually-satisfying outlook on how to get along. In this way, *Stanley and Rhoda* leaves us feeling that everything is going smoothly. . . . (pp. B3, B11)

> Dana G. Clinton "Sibling Rivalry Comes to a Happy Truce," in The Christian Science Monitor, October 23, 1978, pp. B3, B11.

Three vignettes of a sibling relationship are illustrated with pictures of an animal (vaguely hamsterish) family; the pictures add touches of sly humor to the text, complementing and extending it. The three episodes consist primarily of dialogue, and Wells has a marvelous ear for speech patterns as well as an appreciation of the wiles of the young. . . .[The last episode] ends with a nice twist. An entertaining story that invites children to laugh at their own foibles, this is one of those unusual books that can also beguile adult readers-aloud.

> Zena Sutherland, in a review of "Stanley and Rhoda," in Bulletin of the Center for Children's Books, Vol. 32, No. 6, February, 1979, p. 108.

MAX'S FIRST WORD; MAX'S NEW SUIT; MAX'S RIDE; MAX'S TOYS: A COUNTING BOOK (VERY FIRST BOOKS) (1979)

You'd expect Wells' first foray into board books to outclass the competition, and as far as the art goes, you'd be right. Unfortunately, the art doesn't go far enough.

The tailor-made nursery topic of getting dressed alone gives *Max's New Suit* just the right fit, and the humor will wear well. Ruby tugs sibling Max—comically bulky and balky—into a three-piece outfit he promptly sheds in order to do the honors himself: "Max put his jacket on, one ear at a time, and . . .".

Max is a boy of few words—one, in fact—and, to the frustration of big sister Ruby, no matter what she shows him, *Max's First Word*—"BANG"—is the only thing he'll utter. So far, so good. But the punch line—Ruby prompts "YUM YUM," Max parries "DELICIOUS!"—knocks this one way out of range. If you're young enough not to know the words introduced, you're too young to get the joke.

Max's Ride—via runaway carriage—is as precipitious as it is prepositionous. With Max tumbling ground-ward when he's "BETWEEN" and his buggy rolling downhill when he's dropping "INTO" it, two year olds won't know which way is up.

Max's Toys in toto is Ruby's asking—and getting—price for her one doll. Toting up Max's intermediate offers is the nominal point of our boy's bad (albeit nonsexist) bargain. But the toy chest negotiations are tough to buy and the skills imparted shaky. The unlikely assumption that a stuffed chicken, moose, giraffe, and snake will be seen as "4 ANIMALS" count this concept book out as a classic case of "too much, too soon."

Wells is so talented it's a shame she didn't dip into Gesell before tackling the under-three set.

> *Pamela D. Pollack, in a review of "Max's First Word" and others," in* School Library Journal, *Vol. 26, No. 2, October, 1979, p. 146.*

Someone no less than Rosemary Wells has done it: she has developed a set of durable cardboard books that drive a real wedge into the existing block of unnotable, overcute, didactic baby-toddler tomes. Rabbity Max and sister Ruby give off authentic airs of the pre-pre- and preschool society. Most remarkable is the special blending of concept exploration and story: though Max himself can't count, he covets Ruby's *one* favorite doll house while shunning his own *two* soldiers, house with *three* windows, etc. In the process of trying to teach her brother words beyond "bang," Ruby identifies for us a host of familiar items. Max also demonstrates his toddler rights to put on clothes with illogical logic and takes a wild buggy ride *down*, *over*, *up*, and *under*. More to the audience's point: Max is just where he ought to be—in the center of his universe in these four 10-page, gay-colored, rip-proof books. Ages 1½-3, older for jealous siblings.

> *Judith Goldberger, in a review of "Max's First Word" and others, in* Booklist, *Vol. 76, No. 4, October 15, 1979, p. 359.*

[There] is a small—but fortunately growing—number of ["first"] books that appealed to me at least as much as to my child. . . .

At the top of the pile comes a book called ***Max's First Word***. Readers familiar with ***When No One Was Looking*** or ***Leave Well Enough Alone*** may be surprised to hear that its creator (author-illustrator) is Rosemary Wells. Not only does it have a text: it has a *plot*! The characters (here, and in 3 other "Max" books) are two small, dumpy, but endearing rabbits, drawn in a style that, although little more developed than a cartoon, allows them a wide range of easily readable, yet still subtle, expressions. Ruby, elder sister of the eponymous hero, is trying to prod Max into speech. But "Max's one word was BANG! No, Max, said his sister Ruby. Say CUP. Bang, said Max. POT, Max, said Ruby. Bang, said Max." After half-a-dozen similar attempts the now exasperated Ruby hauls Max to his highchair and falls back on the tactics of Eve: "Say APPLE, Max," proffering a tempting one, "YUM, YUM, Max, say YUM YUM. DELICIOUS! said Max." I enjoyed this mild joke almost endlessly (after several months with a tiny infant one does not despise even modest helpings of humor); my son, who no doubt missed the finer points of the story, nevertheless laughed most gratifyingly every time I said "BANG!" Soon we were able to perform the dialogue together: I would pause in the appropriate place for him to shout "BANG!" delightedly. He was, in a real sense, a partaker of the book; it had drawn him in and made him an active participant before he was quite a year old. No other book had elicited this active engagement because there was (and to my knowledge still is) no other book for this age with any amount of dialogue (virtually all of ***Max's First Word*** is dialogue.) (p. 114)

From Benjamin & Tulip, *written and illustrated by Rosemary Wells. The Dial Press, 1973. Copyright © 1973 by Rosemary Wells. All rights reserved. Reproduced by permission of the publisher, Dial Books for Young Readers.*

Patricia Dooley, "'First Books': From Schlock to Sophistication," in Children and Their Literature: A Readings Book, *edited by Jill P. May, ChLA Publications, 1983, pp. 112-16.*

WHEN NO ONE WAS LOOKING (1980)

Starting ostensibly as a story of athletic prowess, the novel gradually develops as a series of moral issues that take on tragic overtones. At fourteen Kathy Bardy was an excellent tennis player, hoping to become a professional and anticipating success in the New England Championship competition at Newport. Although she had the encouragement and full financial support of her father and mother, the girl felt the force of many pressures. In addition to the parents' emphasis on her achieving her goals in tennis, her need for extra study in algebra, and the antagonism of her brilliant twelve-year-old sister Jody, Kathy's consciousness of the social and cultural gap between herself and her schoolmate Julia were all exacerbated by a naturally violent temper, which was coupled with a strict code of honor. Her one failure at tennis was caused by the sudden arrival of Ruth Gumm, a morose but powerful antagonist, who shortly afterward was unaccountably drowned in a swimming pool later discovered to be overchlorinated. Kathy had not only to clear herself of the suspicions of others but to live with her own agonizing suspicions—about the possible relationship between her family and supporters and the death of her formidable rival. With a judicious use of tennis terms, with just the right amount of adult and teenage persiflage, and with satirical glances at American suburban mores, the author has created a heroine with a New England conscience—one who ultimately becomes aware of the tragically ambiguous ironies that beset human beings. (pp. 529-30)

Paul Heins, in a review of "When No One Was Looking," in The Horn Book Magazine, *Vol. LVI, No. 5, October, 1980, pp. 529-30.*

[**When No One Was Looking** is] a highly absorbing story of a girl with lots of potential, pressure and problems. Among the problems are two well-meaning but asinine parents who push Kathy to the limit and are mortgaging everything to see her a winner; a jealous sister; heaps of self-doubt; and the awful fear that one of her friends or relatives may have contributed to the death of the drowned girl. There is also a nicely presented friend, a wealthy girl who is good at drawing Kathy out from under her "Yankee" shell. Wells' style is to complete her characterizations with plenty of detail, but it is never heavy or overdone. Kathy alone remains hazy for most of the novel: she seems too fragile to be a future champion. There is a lot to this novel and most of it is excellent; it is as good, if not better, than any of Wells' earlier books.

Robert Unsworth, in a review of "When No One Was Looking," in School Library Journal, *Vol. 27, No. 2, October, 1980, p. 159.*

You don't have to be a tennis fan to enjoy this brisk, breezy story about a teen-age tennis prodigy trying to deal with the pressures of competition. . . .

Luckily, this isn't just a murder mystery. Rosemary Wells . . . is more deeply concerned about the strains placed upon a child by over-ambitious adults. Kathy herself is refreshingly unassuming, and she has one of the most down-to-earth, sharp-sighted young sisters you could hope to find. ("Do you understand the meaning of this?" Kathy's father exults after a

victory, and Kathy's sister says, "it means she has to do it again.") The mother seems a little one-dimensional—she must possess *some* quality other than pushiness—and I had trouble believing in the mystery's solution. But **When No One Was Looking** has energy and style, and it ought to rivet the most restless young reader.

Anne Tyler, in a review of "When No One Was Looking," in The New York Times Book Review, *February 1, 1981, p. 28.*

TIMOTHY GOES TO SCHOOL (1981)

Timothy and the other bouncy little animals are as engaging because of their wonderfully expressive faces in brisk, bright illustrations as because of their universally childlike qualities, in a brief story that is both touching and funny. Timothy's first few days at school are marred by the obnoxious and critical Claude; each day Timothy hopes some disaster will befall Claude, but to no avail. Then another classmate, Violet, complains about Grace. "I can't stand it anymore. She sings. She dances. She counts up to a thousand and she sits next to me!" Well, what greater bond is there than the pangs of frustrated envy? Timothy and Violet immediately form a bond, and the story ends with "Will you come home and have cookies with me after school?" It's clear that school is going to be a joy thenceforward.

Zena Sutherland, in a review of "Timothy Goes to School," in Bulletin of the Center for Children's Books, *Vol. 34, No. 11, July-August, 1981, p. 222.*

Timothy and his *bête noir* Claude are raccoon children, and it is amazing that the illustrator can show so much emotion—Timothy's misery, his mother's anxiety, and Claude's scorn—in their beady little eyes. In a small gem of a book the outcome inspires the reader with a sense of jubilation: "On the way home Timothy and Violet laughed so much about Claude and Grace that they both got the hiccups."

Ann A. Flowers, in a review of "Timothy Goes to School," in The Horn Book Magazine, *Vol. LVII, No. 4, August, 1981, p. 418.*

GOOD NIGHT, FRED (1981)

Fred, a toddler, bounces off the sofa and breaks the telephone. Big brother Arthur calmly dismantles the phone while Fred pesters him: "Are you sure Grandma's not in there?" At last, Fred goes to bed, waking to a silent house. He traipses downstairs, in pajamas, to begin a fantasy romp with a tiny Grandma who has come out of the ringing phone. The only trace of the adventure when Arthur returns (from the garage) is a suddenly intact phone. The realistic and warm sibling relationship portrayed between the boys supports the fantasy element nicely, and the drawings in muted tones are whimsical, yet apt. . . . **Fred** is enjoyable to read alone or to small groups.

Carolyn Noah, in a review of "Good Night, Fred," in School Library Journal, *Vol. 28, No. 4, December, 1981, p. 58.*

[**Good Night, Fred** is a] pleasant little story in soft pastel watercolors. . . . It's undemanding and easily read, but the fantasy element jars a bit since the audience has not been prepared for it through a credible transition. Wells' subjects seem stiffer than usual, but the sight of a tiny grandmother dancing on the piano will no doubt amuse.

> Ilene Cooper, in a review of "Good Night, Fred," in Booklist, Vol. 78, No. 7, December 1, 1981, p. 504.

A LION FOR LEWIS (1982)

Playing in the attic one day, Sophie and George agree—when their little brother Lewis pleads for inclusion in their "let's pretend" games—that he can take part, but Lewis gets tired of being assigned minor roles. He never gets to be the doctor or nurse, he's just the patient; he never gets to play mother or father, he's only the baby. But revenge comes (and it *is* sweet) when Lewis spots a lion costume into which he zips himself. Any child who's ever felt thwarted by being treated as an inferior should enjoy the story, which also shows the intensity of children's imaginative play. The soft pastel pictures are not as funny as most of Wells' animal illustrations, but they are funny, and the story is told with empathetic zest. (p. 219)

> Zena Sutherland, in a review of "A Lion for Lewis," in Bulletin of the Center for Children's Books, Vol. 35, No. 11, July-August, 1982, pp. 218-19.

As in many of her picture books, the author-artist in words and images is uncannily sensitive to the feelings and predicaments of young children. Her soft watercolors are perfect storytelling tableaux first showing the hapless Lewis and the rather smug older children and later, the little boy triumphantly turning the tables with his outrageous antics.

> Ethel L. Heins, in a review of "A Lion for Lewis," in The Horn Book Magazine, Vol. LVIII, No. 6, December, 1982, p. 644.

PEABODY (1983)

[*Peabody*] stirs remembrances of bears past. Like Pooh and Paddington, Peabody has some sweet childlike qualities. He belongs to Annie, and the emergence of a rival doll fills him with despair: "Without Annie's love Peabody did not feel real." This replaying of the theme from *The Velveteen Rabbit* and some similar sentimentalities mar the fresh, direct prose. Playful watercolors dramatize light and shadow, clouds and sea, with skill. If the children's heads had been sketched with the same ease, they would look less adult.

> Karla Kuskin, "Picture a Ghost, a Moose or a Tin Soldier," in The New York Times Book Review, November 13, 1983, p. 55.

Still another sibling rivalry book from Wells—but still a new twist. This time there is a story line within the story so that the children's sibling rivalry parallels that of the toys. Robert (who so closely resembles Lewis or Fred of previous books) is jealous of Annie's birthday toys. First he is enamored of Peabody the bear, who conveys the most wonderful expressions with a mere dot of the eye or curl of the lip. Then Peabody gets put on the shelf and is replaced by Rita the dancing, talking, glitzy doll. Peabody is jealous, Robert is miserable and Rita gets her comeupance when Robert gives her a bath. Many of Wells' soft watercolor illustrations make the book aesthetically pleasing but poor Robert never does find happiness: he is left with a broken doll who resembles the corpse of a dead child. It is only charming Peabody, who wins back

Annie's heart, that provides a questionable element of hope, an element that is so essential in a children's book.

> Roslyn Beitler, in a review of "Peabody," in School Library Journal, Vol. 30, No. 4, December, 1983, p. 62.

Wells uses the concept of toys becoming real if they're loved, of feelings of dethronement, and of sibling jealousy in so deft and light a way that they never obtrude on the story. The illustrations, in which the animals have vitality while the children seem lifeless, are bright and lively, with a humor that is echoed by the story, and the humor is spiced by some touching moments when Peabody, a toy bear, is rejected in favor of a newer toy, a doll.

> Zena Sutherland, in a review of "Peabody," in Bulletin of the Center for Children's Books, Vol. 37, No. 5, January, 1984, p. 99.

THE MAN IN THE WOODS (1984)

Fourteen-year-old Helen Curragh witnesses the Punk Rock Thrower flee after he caused another accident by throwing a rock at a car. Although Helen cannot identify the boy she saw, she is positive it isn't the boy the police eventually arrest. No one except Pinky Levy, a fellow misfit at school, believes her story. The only clue the two have to go on is an anonymous note typed on a rare antique typewriter. To find the culprit the teens must find the typewriter. Their search leads them into the tragic history of one of the town's most prominent families. And as their search becomes more desperate, they learn that drug dealing is also involved. Although the story is too long and has a final solution that is not completely convincing, the historical mystery-within-a-mystery is cleverly conceived and makes for a fascinating subplot. The book also boasts any array of interesting characters, deftly brought to life, which further ensures it a place on the shelf.

> Drew Stevenson, in a review of "The Man in the Woods," in School Library Journal, Vol. 30, No. 9, May, 1984, p. 104.

[As a mystery] this doesn't quite measure up to Wells' very best (e.g., *Leave Well Enough Alone*). But motherless Helen is an appealing, frizzy-haired, plucky but not *too* plucky heroine—with a very credible Irish father and Irish aunt at home. (They argue about the Queen and Ted Kennedy.) The high-school atmospheres are amusingly sketched. And an underlying theme of journalistic decency—Helen has to decide whether to write up the whole story or respect some innocent people's privacy—adds extra texture to a warm, layered blend of suspense, charm, and character.

> A review of "The Man in the Woods," in Kirkus Reviews, Juvenile Issue, Vol. LII, Nos. 6-9, May 1, 1984, p. J54.

In current open-ended realistic fiction for teenagers, one all too rarely meets a riveting contemporary tale of emotion, mystery, and suspense. Such a one is the author's new novel, which actually contains two mysteries—indissolubly linked yet separated by more than a hundred years.... In a complex, dexterously handled story Helen and Pinky, dissatisfied with the official investigation, are determined to identify the real malefactor.... As the criss-crossing clues inexorably lead Helen and Pinky in their research back to the Civil War era of New Bedford, the two friends . . . not only prove themselves successful detectives but lay bare an astonishing secret from the city's past. With great ingenuity the author has constructed a story contemporary in subject matter but supported by historical connections. Full of fascinating, but never gratuitous, detail, the book gains added vigor and interest from a wealth of vivid characters. (pp. 601-02)

> *Ethel L. Heins, in a review of "The Man in the Woods," in* The Horn Book Magazine, *Vol. LX, No. 5, September-October, 1984, pp. 601-02.*

MAX'S BATH; MAX'S BEDTIME; MAX'S BIRTHDAY; MAX'S BREAKFAST (VERY FIRST BOOKS) (1985)

A four-star performance from Wells. The new titles in this board book series for youngest listeners feature Max, a toddler rabbit, and his patronizingly patient older sister Ruby. Each story portrays a typical preschool trauma resolved with humor and understanding. In the first, Ruby tries to bathe a multi-colored Max (the result of jam, orange sherbet and grape juice). Each attempt produces a dirtier hare, but in the end, Max is finally clean. Ruby isn't. "Dirty," says Max, as he points at her. *Max's Bedtime* is disrupted by a beloved missing red elephant. A helpful Ruby gives him her toys, but none will do. Children will immediately spot the red tail showing under the bed, and will hold their breath until the toy is found. On *Max's Birthday,* Ruby gives him a wind-up dragon which frightens him. Ruby takes it *away,* it goes *around and around, through* Ruby's legs, etc. There's a tense moment for Ruby at the end, but all ends well as the dragon lands *on top of* Max. "Again," he says. From his expressions, every child will know that *Max's Breakfast,* a fried egg, disgusts him. But luck is with Max, and in Ruby's enthusiasm for convincing him of the egg's goodness, she eats it. "All gone," says a grinning (and all-knowing) Max. The pages are vivid and vibrant, uncluttered but full of amusing detail. There is not a wasted stroke in these deceptively simple illustrations. Max and Ruby's expressions differ on each page, from glee (his), to exasperation (hers) to disgust (both). An engaging duo in books that are fun, funny and bound to be early childhood favorites. (pp. 159-60)

> *Trev Jones, in a review of "Max's Bath" and others, in* School Library Journal, *Vol. 31, No. 7, March, 1985, pp. 159-60.*

Wells does it again; like the first four books about Max (a very young rabbit) [*Max's Bath*] is realistic, funny, beguiling, and as deft in its minimal text as in its simple and expressive pictures. . . . His bedtime, his birthday, and his breakfast are the subject of three other new books about Max. They're equally delectable, and they should be as useful for very young children as they are appealing.

> *Zena Sutherland, in a review of "Max's Bath," in* Bulletin of the Center for Children's Books, *Vol. 38, No. 8, April, 1985, p. 157.*

Max and his older sister Ruby, those fine stout rabbits with forceful personalities, have returned in four excellent examples of very early books. Max never utters more than one or, at most, two words; the plots or, rather, episodes—told in ten board-pages—must be considered thin, but both parents and children can enjoy endless repetition of these simple, extremely funny stories. . . . There is no doubt that Rosemary Wells's absolute mastery of the dubious eye and the passively resisting body add immeasurably to these small sagas of every day life. First-class stories for very young listeners. (pp. 446-47)

> *Ann A. Flowers, in a review of "Max's Bath," and others, in* The Horn Book Magazine, *Vol. LXI, No. 4, July-August, 1985, pp. 446-47.*

HAZEL'S AMAZING MOTHER (1985)

The power of maternal love fuels this fantasy. Hazel, a whimsical badger who wears a girl's wide-brimmed hat, blouse and skirt, strolls her doll around town. On the way home, she becomes lost. She is set upon by buck-toothed beaver Doris and her two friends, who unstuff her doll and throw her carriage into the lake. Just in time, a gust of wind blows mother into the tree under which Hazel stands (attributed to the power of love), and the bullies are ordered to repair the doll and retrieve her carriage. Large-format black-ink drawings with comic detail are solidly filled in with cheerful bright watercolors. Hazel's almost illuminant yellow blouse focuses attention on her on each page. A well-crafted fantasy with quality illustrations that relates to many story time themes, this deserves first purchase consideration. When reading the book aloud, though, please warn children that they, unlike Hazel, should not be taking shelter under a tree during a lightning storm.

> *Jean Gaffney, in a review of "Hazel's Amazing Mother," in* School Library Journal, *Vol. 32, No. 3, November, 1985, p. 78.*

Wells presents some audacious plotting that works because of its very craziness and its oh-so-satisfying turn-of-events as far as the villains are concerned. . . . Rich, full-color watercolor paintings illustrate the story. Colors are intense, sometimes almost jewellike, and the various animal figures, be they friend or foe, are distinctly personified, often with a good deal of humor. A beguiling book with a nonsensical streak that will make children look again and laugh.

> *Denise M. Wilms, in a review of "Hazel's Amazing Mother," in* Booklist, *Vol. 82, No. 5, November 1, 1985, p. 415.*

Certainly the annals of motherhood can show no more devoted a mother than Hazel's. . . . This rather offbeat story does raise at least one question. Although it is very satisfactory that Hazel's problem has a happy ending, the deus ex machina resolution may raise expectations in young readers that cannot be so conveniently satisfied, bullies being so prevalent and magical mothers so rare. Rosemary Wells exhibits her usual sure touch in the illustrations—Hazel and her mother, presumably badgers, show a glossy self-satisfaction that is quite disarming, and Hazel's mother's glare at the malefactors is daunting, indeed. And the natural bond of affection between mother and child could not be more clearly presented.

> *Ann A. Flowers, in a review of "Hazel's Amazing Mother," in* The Horn Book Magazine, *Vol. LXI, No. 6, November-December, 1985, p. 734.*

MAX'S CHRISTMAS (1986)

Glad tidings for Max fans—the bunny of board-book fame now stars in his first picture book. Sister Ruby has to drag Max up the steps, scrub his face with a washcloth and remind him to "Spit, Max," as he brushes his teeth. It's Christmas Eve, and Max has a lot of questions about Santa Claus—questions Ruby answers with a "Because!" Not satisfied, the curious bunny sneaks downstairs to wait for the man in red. A bunny-angel at the top of the tree looks on as Santa himself answers some of Max's questions. But he, too, resorts to a "Because!" and Max falls asleep. The next day, Ruby has queries of her own when she finds Max on the couch with a lap full of Christmas presents. Max's main answer? "Because!" Young readers will want to join resoundingly in that last line—one of the adult world's most ungratifying responses. Wells's understated story will inspire year-round cravings for candy canes and early yearnings for yule logs.

> *A review of "Max's Christmas," in* Publishers Weekly, *Vol. 230, No. 4, July 25, 1986, p. 185.*

Children won't be able to resist Max, that epitome of the small child in rabbit guise. Wells has an extraordinary talent for capturing a welter of thoughts and emotions with the placement of an eye or a turn of a smile. . . . This is an absolutely delightful book—BECAUSE!

> *Judith Gloyer, in a review of "Max's Christmas," in* School Library Journal, *Vol. 33, No. 2, October, 1986, p. 112.*

Fans of the inimitable Max, that Shirley Temple of rabbits, will not be surprised to hear that once again he has the final word—literally—in **Max's Christmas**. After eight captivating appearances in board books, Max and bossy Ruby now star in a larger and longer picture book. . . . Full-color artwork, consisting of black-line drawings and color washes, chronicles the events, including the entertaining Max versus Santa Claus encounter. Despite the book's longer format, an uncanny perceptive simplicity, both in line and in word, is still Wells's most effective tool. Once again plump Max, with his wide, thin smile and expressive eyes, is irresistible. (p. 726)

> *Karen Jameyson, "Christmas Books," in* The Horn Book Mazagine, *Vol. LXII, No. 6, November-December, 1986, pp. 725-28.*

THROUGH THE HIDDEN DOOR   (1987)

Needing a place to hide from a group of vicious classmates, Barney Pennimen joins secretive Snowy Cobb to explore a hidden cave in which a small, identified bone was found. The boys find traces of a miniature village—but are not sure whether it is a model of a community or the actual remains of a 100,000-year-old civilization. Wells tells two stories here: Barney's victimization and growing strength of character, and the boy's discovery and protection of the ancient civilization. Both are suspenseful and remarkably well integrated into the novel. Ob-

sessively private Snowy, who has emotional problems, and Barney, an intelligent boy whose past submission to peer pressure has gotten him into trouble, are both fully realized characters. These two will engage readers' interest, which will be sustained throughout by the brutal reality of Barney's school experiences and the appealing fantasy of the boys' remarkable findings. The wish fulfillment associated with that discovery will more than compensate for the minimal or non-existence scientific and historic groundings of the civilization and its unearthing (a society of six-inch humans does not fit in with evolutionary theory; the achievements of their civilization does not match cultural history; it is implausible that two boys could have the archaeological know-how to uncover the village without harming it). An absorbing school story with a twist, this one is sure to fill readers with a sense of wonder.

> *David Gale, in a review of "Through the Hidden Door," in* School Library Journal, *Vol. 33, No. 7, April, 1987, p. 114.*

[Wells] has written a riveting psychological thriller that's a cross between Robert Cormier's *The Chocolate War* and an Indiana Jones archaeological quest. . . . That Wells makes all this work is a feat in itself (though it does take some suspension of disbelief to accept the idea of Lilliputian native Americans). But the story is more than just a smoothly crafted adventure. It is a deft portrayal of individual and group psyches that explores the complex relationship between adults and children, members of peer groups, outsiders and insiders. Wells unfolds her story in ways sure to get readers thinking. Teachers who want to read this aloud chapter by chapter should be warned—kids won't want to wait for the next day's installment.

> *Ilene Cooper, in a review of "Through the Hidden Door," in* Booklist, *Vol. 83, No. 16, April 15, 1987, p. 1296.*

Like the meshed cogs of two wheels, the small but important element of fantasy and the larger one of reality together spin smoothly to create a story that has pace and suspense, strong relationships, and a sturdy structure. That such an adventure tale should have depth and nuance and compelling style, as well, means that this is one of the best stories Rosemary Wells has written. . . . This is a story about friendship, power, ethical concepts, and courage. All that, and a page-turner, too.

> *Zena Sutherland, in a review of "Through the Hidden Door," in* Bulletin of the Center for Children's Books, *Vol. 40, No. 11, July-August, 1987, p. 220.*

Appendix

The following is a listing of all sources used in Volume 16 of *Children's Literature Review*. Included in this list are all copyright and reprint rights and acknowledgments for those essays for which permission was obtained. Every effort has been made to trace copyright, but if omissions have been made, please let us know.

THE EXCERPTS IN CLR, VOLUME 16, WERE REPRINTED FROM THE FOLLOWING PERIODICALS:

The ALAN Review, v. 11, Winter, 1984; v. 12, Fall, 1984; v. 12, Winter, 1985. All reprinted by permission of the publisher.

American Imago, v. 14, Summer, 1957.

Appraisal: Children's Science Books, v. 1, Winter, 1967; v. 1, Fall, 1968; v. 2, Winter, 1969; v. 4, Winter, 1971; v. 7, Winter, 1974; v. 12, Spring, 1979; v. 14, Fall, 1981; v. 16, Winter, 1983; v. 19, Spring, 1986; v. 20, Fall, 1987; v. 21, Winter, 1988. Copyright © 1967, 1968, 1969, 1971, 1974, 1979, 1981, 1983, 1986, 1987, 1988 by the Children's Science Book Review Committee. All reprinted by permission of the publisher.

Arts & Decoration, v. XII, December 15, 1919.

The Athenaeum, n. 4385, November 11, 1911; n. 448, October 18, 1913; n. 4495, December 20, 1913.

Best Sellers, v. 32, July 15, 1972. Copyright 1972, by the University of Scranton. Reprinted by permission of the publisher./ v. 37, June, 1977; v. 41, February, 1982; v. 42, December, 1982; v. 43, December, 1983; v. 45, October, 1985. Copyright © 1977, 1982, 1983, 1985 Helen Dwight Reid Educational Foundation. All reprinted by permission of the publisher.

Book Week—The Washington Post, May 8, 1966. © 1966, *The Washington Post.* Reprinted by permission of the publisher.

Book World—The Washington Post, May 2, 1976; May 1, 1977; July 10, 1977; May 14, 1978; May 13, 1979; March 9, 1980; January 9, 1983; March 13, 1983; May 8, 1983. © 1976, 1977, 1978, 1979, 1980, 1983, *The Washington Post.* All reprinted by permission of the publisher.

Bookbird, n. 2, June 15, 1986. Reprinted by permission of the publisher.

Booklist, v. 73, December 15, 1976; v. 74, October 1, 1977; v. 74, June 15, 1978; v. 75, November 15, 1978; v. 75, December 15, 1978; v. 75, January 1, 1979; v. 75, May 15, 1979; v. 76, October 15, 1979; v. 76, May 15, 1980; v. 77, November 1, 1980; v. 77, April 15, 1981; v. 78, September 15, 1981; v. 78, December 1, 1981; v. 78, May 1, 1982; v. 78, June 1, 1982; v. 79, September 15, 1982; v. 79, November 1, 1982; v. 79, January 15, 1983; v. 79, June 15, 1983; v. 80, September 15, 1983; v. 80, May 15, 1984; v. 80, June 15, 1984; v. 81, October 1, 1984; v. 81, October 15, 1984; v. 81, December 1, 1984; v. 81, February 15, 1985; v. 81, June 1, 1985; v. 82, October 1, 1985; v. 82, November 1, 1985; v. 82, April 15, 1986; v. 83, October 1, 1986; v. 83, December 15, 1986; v. 83, March 15, 1987; v. 83, April 15, 1987; v. 83, June 1, 1987; v. 83, June 15, 1987; v. 84, September 1, 1987; v. 84, November 1, 1987; v. 84, April 15, 1988. Copyright © 1976, 1977, 1978, 1979, 1980, 1981, 1982, 1983, 1984, 1985, 1986, 1987, 1988 by the American Library Association. All reprinted by permission of the publisher.

The Booklist, v. 69, April 1, 1973; v. 70, November 15, 1973; v. 71, January 1, 1975; v. 71, February 15, 1975; v. 72, October 1, 1975. Copyright © 1973, 1975 by the American Library Association. All reprinted by permission of the publisher.

LVII, August, 1981; v. LVIII, February, 1982; v. LVIII, June, 1982; v. LVIII, December, 1982; v. LIX, June, 1983; v. LX, September-October, 1984; v. LXI, March-April, 1985; v. LXI, May-June, 1985; v. LXI, July-August, 1985; v. LXI, November-December, 1985; v. LXII, July-August, 1986; v. LXII, September-October, 1986; v. LXII, November-December, 1986; v. LXII, January-February, 1987; v. LXIII, March-April, 1987; v. LXIII, May-June, 1987; v. LXIII, November-December, 1987; v. LXIV, January-February, 1988; v. LXIV, March-April, 1988. Copyright, 1961, 1964, 1965, 1969, 1970, 1973, 1974, 1975, 1976, 1977, 1979, 1980, 1981, 1982, 1983, 1984, 1985, 1986, 1987, 1988, by The Horn Book, Inc., Boston. All rights reserved. All reprinted by permission of the publisher./ v. XIX, May- June, 1943; v. XXI, May-June, 1945; v. XXVI, September-October, 1950; v. XXVIII, June, 1952; v. XXIX, August, 1953; v. XXX, October, 1954; v. XXXI, June, 1955; v. XXXIII, October, 1957; v. XXXV, October, 1959. Copyright, 1943, renewed 1970; copyright, 1945, renewed 1972; copyright, 1950, renewed 1977; copyright, 1952, renewed 1980; copyright 1953, renewed 1981; copyright, 1954, renewed 1982; copyright, 1955, renewed 1983; copyright, 1957, renewed 1985; copyright 1959, renewed 1987, by The Horn Book, Inc., Boston. All rights reserved. All reprinted by permission of the publisher.

The Illustrated London News, v. CXXVI, January 7, 1905.

In Review: Canadian Books for Children, v. 1, Autumn, 1967. Reprinted by permission of the publisher.

Interracial Books for Children Bulletin, v. 5, October-December, 1975; v. 13, 1982; v. 15, November-December, 1985. All reprinted by permission of the Council on Interracial Books for Children, 1841 Broadway, New York, NY 10023.

The Junior Bookshelf, v. I, July, 1937./ v. 24, November, 1960; v. 25, November, 1961; v. 26, July, 1962; v. 27, July, 1963; v. 29, April, 1965; v. 29, August, 1965; v. 29, October, 1965; v. 31, February, 1967; v. 31, August, 1967; v. 33, June, 1969; v. 34, February, 1970; v. 34, October, 1970; v. 34, December, 1970; v. 35, August, 1971; v. 36, February, 1972; v. 36, June, 1972; v. 37, June, 1973; v. 38, June, 1974; v. 38, August, 1974; v. 39, February, 1975; v. 40, February, 1976; v. 40, October, 1976; v. 41, October, 1977; v. 41, December, 1977; v. 42, October, 1978; v. 44, April, 1980; v. 46, October, 1982; v. 51, August, 1987. All reprinted by permission of the publisher.

Junior Libraries, v. 2, September 15, 1955; v. 2, April 15, 1956; v. 3, January 15, 1957; v. 4, December, 1957; v. 4, April 15, 1958; v. 4, May 15, 1958./ v. 6, March, 1960. Copyright © 1960. Reprinted from *Junior Libraries,* published by R. R. Bowker Co./ A Xerox Corporation, by permission.

Kirkus Reviews, v. XXXII, September 15, 1969; v. XXXVIII, May 15, 1970; v. XXXVIII, August 1, 1970; v. XXXVIII, November 15, 1970; v. XL, May 15, 1972; v. XL, October 1, 1972; v. XL, November 15, 1972; v. XLI, September 1, 1973; v. XLII, August 1, 1974; v. XLII, August 15, 1974; v. XLII, November 15, 1974; v. XLII, January 15, 1975; v. XLIII, February 1, 1975; v. XLIII, October 1, 1975; v. XLIV, April 1, 1976; v. XLIV, August 15, 1976; v. XLIV, October 15, 1976; v. XLVI, March 15, 1978; v. XLVII, May 15, 1979; v. XLVIII, January 15, 1980; v. XLVIII, April 15, 1980; v. XLIX, January 1, 1981; v. XLIX, March 15, 1981; v. XLIX, November 15, 1981; v. L, May 15, 1982; v. L, August 15, 1982; v. LI, March 15, 1983; v. LI, April 15, 1983; v. LIII, May 15, 1985; v. LIII, September 15, 1985; v. LIV, July 15, 1986; v. LIV, October 1, 1986; v. LV, February 1, 1987; v. LV, May 1, 1987; v. LV, July 1, 1987; v. LVI, March 15, 1988. Copyright © 1969, 1970, 1972, 1973, 1974, 1975, 1976, 1978, 1979, 1980, 1981, 1982, 1983, 1985, 1986, 1987, 1988 The Kirkus Service, Inc. All rights reserved. All reprinted by permission of the publisher.

Kirkus Reviews, Juvenile Issue, v. LI, November 1, 1983; v. LII, May 1, 1984; v. LIII, May 15, 1985. Copyright © 1983, 1984, 1985 The Kirkus Service, Inc. All rights reserved. All reprinted by permission of the publisher.

Kirkus Service, v. XXXV, September 1, 1967; v. XXXVI, January 15, 1968; v. XXXVI, June 15, 1968; v. XXXVI, October 1, 1968. Copyright © 1967, 1968 The Kirkus Service, Inc. All reprinted by permission of the publisher.

Kliatt Young Adult Paperback Book Guide, v. XXI, April, 1987. Copyright © Kliatt Paperback Book Guide. Both reprinted by permission of the publisher.

Language Arts, v. 55, April, 1978 for a review of "Carlota" by Ruth M. Stein; v. 55, May, 1978 for a review of "Don't Spill It Again, James" by Ruth M. Stein; v. 57, March, 1980 for "Betsy Byars—Writer for Today's Child" by Ina Robertson; v. 60, September, 1983 for a review of "The Turtle and the Monkey: A Philippine Tale" by Ronald A. Jobe; v. 61, November, 1984 for "Profile: Scott O'Dell" by Peter Roop; v. 63, February, 1986 for a review of "Cat Goes Fiddle-I-Fee" by Janet Hickman. Copyright © 1978, 1980, 1983, 1984, 1986 by the National Council of Teachers of English. All reprinted by permission of the publisher and the respective authors.

Library Journal, v. 77, May 1, 1952; v. 78, March 15, 1953; v. 80, June 15, 1955; v. 82, June 15, 1957./ v. 87, July, 1962. Copyright © 1962 by Reed Publishing, USA, Division of Reed Holdings, Inc. Reprinted from *Library Journal,* published by R. R. Bowker, Co., Division of Reed Publishing, USA, by permission of the publisher./ v. 93, June 15, 1968 for a review of "Summer Is for Growing" by Jean Pretorius; v. 95, February 15, 1970 for a review of "Along Sandy Trails" by Evelyn R. Downum; v. 95, July, 1970 for a review of "Martha's Birthday" by Alice D. Ehlert; v. 98, June 15, 1973 for a review of "The Moving Adventures of Old Dame Trot and Her Comical Cat" by Alice Ehlert. Copyright © 1968, 1970, 1973 by Reed Publishing, USA, Division of Reed Holdings, Inc. All reprinted from *Library Journal,* published by R. R. Bowker, Co., Division of Reed Publishing, USA, by permission of the publisher and the respective authors.

The Lion and the Unicorn, v. 3, Spring, 1979; v. 6, 1982. Copyright © 1979, 1982 *The Lion and the Unicorn.* Both reprinted by permission of the publisher.

Literary Digest, New York, v. 43, November 11, 1911.

The Nation, London, v. X, November 18, 1911.

New Statesman, v. XXXVI, December 6, 1930; v. LIV, December 28, 1957.

New York Herald Tribune Book Review, May 11, 1952; May 15, 1955; September 23, 1956; November 17, 1957; May 11, 1958; November 1, 1959.

New York Herald Tribune Books, May 11, 1941.

New York Herald Tribune Weekly Book Review, April 4, 1943.

The New York Review of Books, v. XXII, February 6, 1975. Copyright © 1975 Nyrev, Inc. Reprinted with permission from *The New York Review of Books.*

The New York Times, October 22, 1911./ April 19, 1959. Copyright © 1959 by The New York Times Company. Reprinted by permission of the publisher.

The New York Times Book Review, May 4, 1941; May 16, 1943; October 10, 1954. Copyright 1941, 1943, 1954 by The New York Times Company. All reprinted by permission of the publisher./ November 13, 1955; November 18, 1956; December 30, 1956; November 10, 1957; November 17, 1957; April 26, 1959; July 10, 1960; November 5, 1961; May 12, 1963; May 7, 1967; March 17, 1968; May 5, 1968; September 14, 1969; May 24, 1970; June 21, 1970; May 2, 1971; August 12, 1973; January 6, 1974; November 17, 1974; December 15, 1974; February 8, 1976; February 22, 1976; May 2, 1976; July 10, 1977; April 30, 1978; April 29, 1979; November 11, 1979; December 2, 1979; May 4, 1980; February 1, 1981; July 12, 1981; July 19, 1981; September 13, 1981; January 10, 1982; June 13, 1982; October 10, 1982; November 28, 1982; May 15, 1983; November 13, 1983; November 27, 1983; March 3, 1985; August 4, 1985; June 15, 1986; November 9, 1986; November 29, 1987. Copyright © 1955, 1956, 1957, 1959, 1960, 1961, 1963, 1967, 1968, 1969, 1970, 1971, 1973, 1974, 1976, 1977, 1978, 1979, 1980, 1981, 1982, 1983, 1985, 1986, 1987 by The New York Times Company. All reprinted by permission of the publisher.

The Outlook, v. 81, November 18, 1905.

Proceedings of the Ninth Annual Conference of the Children's Literature Association, 1982. Copyright © 1982 by The Children's Literature Association. Reprinted by permission of the publisher.

The Psychoanalytic Review, v. 43, January, 1956.

Publishers Weekly, v. 177, April 4, 1960; v. 191, April 3, 1967. Copyright © 1960, 1967 by R. R. Bowker Company. Both reprinted from *Publishers Weekly,* published by R. R. Bowker Company, by permission./ v. 194, September 16, 1968; v. 195, April 21, 1969; v. 197, April 20, 1970; v. 198, October 12, 1970; v. 198, December 14, 1970; v. 201, January 31, 1972; v. 203, May 21, 1973; v. 205, March 18, 1974; v. 206, November 25, 1974; v. 208, September 15, 1975; v. 210, November 15, 1976; v. 212, August 29, 1977; v. 214, October 9, 1978; v. 214, November 20, 1978; v. 215, June 25, 1979; v. 217, February 29, 1980; v. 220, October 23, 1981; v. 223, March 18, 1983; v. 225, June 29, 1984; v. 226, December 21, 1984; v. 227, January 11, 1985; v. 227, May 17, 1985. Copyright © 1968, 1969, 1970, 1972, 1973, 1974, 1975, 1976, 1977, 1978, 1979, 1980, 1981, 1983, 1984, 1985 by Xerox Corporation. All reprinted from *Publishers Weekly,* published by R. R. Bowker Company, a Xerox company, by permission./ v. 228, November 1, 1985; v. 229, June 27, 1986; v. 230, July 25, 1986; v. 233, January 29, 1988; v. 233, April 8, 1988. Copyright 1985, 1986, 1988 by Reed Publishing USA. All reprinted from *Publishers Weekly,* published by the Bowker Magazine Group of Cahners Publishing Co., a division of Reed Publishing USA.

Research Studies, v. 42, March, 1974 for "The Many Mothers of Peter Pan: An Explanation and Lamentation" by Penelope Scambly Schott. Reprinted by permission of the author.

The Saturday Review, London, v. 99, January 7, 1905.

The School Librarian, v. 20, December, 1972; v. 26, September, 1978; v. 29, March, 1981; v. 33, June, 1985; v. 34, March, 1986. All reprinted by permission of the publisher.

The School Librarian and School Library Review, v. 12, March, 1964. Reprinted by permission of the publisher.

School Library Journal, v. 8, October 15, 1961; v. 8, May, 1962; v. 12, September, 1965; v. 13, January, 1967; v. 14, February, 1968; v. 15, November, 1968; v. 15, March, 1969; v. 16, October, 1969; v. 16, January, 1970; v. 16, February, 1970; v. 17, September, 1970; v. 17, October, 1970; v. 17, November 15, 1970; v. 17, January, 1971; v. 17, June 15, 1971; v. 18, October, 1971; v. 18, December, 1971; v. 18, March, 1972; v. 18, April, 1972; v. 18, May, 1972; v. 18, September, 1972; v. 19, May, 1973; v. 20, September, 1973; v. 20, November, 1973; v. 21, September, 1974; v. 21, November, 1974. v. 21, March, 1975; v. 21, May, 1975; v. 22, September, 1975; v. 22, November, 1975; v. 22, December, 1975; v. 23, September, 1976; v. 23, November, 1976; v. 23, December, 1976; v. 23, January, 1977; v. 23, February, 1977; v. 23, May, 1977; v. 24, December, 1977; v. 25, October, 1978; v. 25, November, 1978; v. 25, December, 1978; v. 26, October, 1979; v. 26, November, 1979; v. 26, December, 1979; v. 26, May, 1980; v. 27, October, 1980; v. 27, April, 1981; v. 28, October, 1981; v. 28, December, 1981; v. 28, May, 1982; v. 28, August, 1982; v. 29, October, 1982; v. 29, January, 1983; v. 30, September, 1983; v. 30, December, 1983; v. 30, May, 1984; v. 30, August, 1984; v. 31, October, 1984; v. 31, November, 1984; v. 31, January, 1985; v. 31, February, 1985; v. 31, March, 1985; v. 32, November, 1985; v. 32, December, 1985; v. 32, February, 1986; v. 32, April, 1986; v. 32, May, 1986; v. 33, October, 1986; v. 33, November, 1986; v. 33, February, 1987; v. 33, April, 1987; v. 33, May, 1987; v. 33, June-July, 1987; v. 34, September, 1987; v. 34, October, 1987; v. 34, January, 1988; v. 34, March, 1988. Copyright (c) 1961, 1962, 1965, 1967, 1968, 1969, 1970, 1971, 1972, 1973, 1975, 1976, 1977, 1978, 1979, 1980, 1981, 1982, 1983, 1984, 1985, 1986, 1987, 1988. All reprinted from *School Library Journal,* a Cahners/R. R. Bowker Publication, by permission. *Science Books & Films,* v. XI, May, 1975; v. XIII, May, 1977; v. XV, September, 1979; v. 21, November-December, 1985; v. 23, January-February, 1988. Copyright 1975, 1977, 1979, 1985, 1988 by AAAS. All reprinted by permission of the publisher.

Science Books: A Quarterly Review, v. 1, December, 1965; v. 2, March, 1967; v. 8, May, 1972; v. 8, March, 1973. Copyright 1965, 1967, 1972, 1973 by AAAS. All reprinted by permission of the publisher.

Scientific American, v. 217, December, 1967; v. 247, December, 1982. Copyright © 1967, 1982 by Scientific American, Inc. All rights reserved. Both reprinted by permission of the publisher.

Signal, January, 1982 for "Fly Away, Peter" by Nicholas Tucker. Copyright © 1982 The Thimble Press. Reprinted by permission of the author. *The Spectator,* v. III, November 1, 1913; v. 145, December 6, 1930.

Teacher, v. 90, November, 1972 for a review of "Trouble River" by Judith Higgins; v. 90, February, 1973 for a review of "Guy Lenny" by Judith Higgins. Copyright © 1972, 1973 by Macmillan Professional Magazines, Inc. Both reprinted by permission of the author.

The Times Educational Supplement, n. 3255, October 28, 1977; n. 3269, February 3, 1978; n. 3308, November 24, 1978; n. 3311, November 23, 1979; n. 3340, June 20, 1980; n. 3466, December 12, 1982; n. 3526, January 27, 1984. © Times Newpapers Ltd. (London) 1977, 1978, 1979, 1980, 1982, 1984. All reproduced from *The Times Educational Supplement by permission.*

The Times Literary Supplement, n. 3303, June 17, 1965; n. 3404, May 25, 1967; n. 3475, October 3, 1968; n. 3513, June 26, 1969; n. 3536, December 4, 1969; n. 3583, October 30, 1970; n. 3709, April 6, 1973; n. 3719, June 15, 1973; n. 3774, July 5, 1974; n. 3879, July 16, 1976; n. 3900, December 10, 1976; n. 3931, July 15, 1977; n. 3943, October 21, 1977; n. 4034, July 18, 1980; n. 4138, July 23, 1982; n. 4270, February 1, 1985; n. 4342, June 20, 1986; n. 4365, November 28, 1986. © Times Newspapers Ltd. (London) 1965, 1967, 1968, 1969, 1970, 1973, 1974, 1976, 1977, 1980, 1982, 1985, 1986. All reproduced from *The Times Literary Supplement* by permission.

Virginia Kirkus' Bookshop Service, v. XVIII, August 15, 1950; v. XX, February 1, 1952; v. XX, February 15, 1952; v. XXII, July 15, 1954.

Virginia Kirkus' Service, v. XXIV, March 1, 1956; v. XXIV, May 15, 1957; v. XXV, August 1, 1957; v. XXVI, May 1, 1958; v. XXVI, October 1, 1958; v. XXVII, June 15, 1959; v. XXVII, July 1, 1959./ v. XXVIII, January 15, 1960; v. XXIX, October 1, 1961; v. XXXI, March 1, 1963; v. XXXIII, July 15, 1965; v. XXXIV, October 15, 1966. Copyright © 1960, 1961, 1963, 1965, 1966 Virginia Kirkus' Service, Inc. All reprinted by permission of the publisher.

Voice of Youth Advocates, v. 4, October, 1981; v. 5, April, 1982; v. February, 1983; v. 6, December, 1983; v. 7, April, 1984; v. 8, August, 1985; v. 10, December, 1987. Copyrighted 1981, 1982, 1983, 1984, 1985, 1987 by *Voice of Youth Advocates.* All reprinted by permission of the publisher. *Wilson Library Bulletin,* v. 50, January, 1976; v. 62, November, 1987. Copyright © 1976, 1987 by the H. W. Wilson Company. Both reprinted by permission of the publisher.

The World of Children's Books, v. II, 1977; v. III, 1978; v. VI, 1981. © 1977, 1978, 1981 by Jon C. Stott. All reprinted by permission of the publisher.

From a review of "Piero Ventura's Book of Cities," in *Human - and Anti-Human - Values in Children's Books*. CIBC Racism and Sexism Resource Center for Educators, 1976. Copyright © 1976 by the Council on Interracial Books for Children, Inc. All rights reserved. Reprinted by permission of the publisher.

Hürlimann, Bettina. From *Picture-Book World*. Translated and edited by Brian W. Alderson. Oxford University Press, London, 1968. English translated © Oxford University Press 1968. Reprinted by permission of Oxford University Press.

Lass-Woodfin, Mary Jo. From a review of "Circle of Seasons," in *Books on American Indians and Eskimos: A Selection Guide for Children and Young Adults*. Edited by Mary Jo Lass-Woodfin. American Library Association, 1978. Copyright © 1978 by the American Library Association. All rights reserved. Reprinted by permission of the publisher.

Lonsdale, Bernard J., and Helen K. Mackintosh. From *Children Experience Literature*. Random House, 1973. Copyright © 1973 Random House, Inc. All rights reserved. Reprinted by permission of the publisher.

Lorenz, Konrad. From a foreword to *The Story of Dogs*. By Patricia Lauber. Random House, 1966. © Copyright, 1966, by Patricia Lauber. All rights reserved. Reprinted by permission of Random House, Inc.

Lukens, Rebecca J. From *A Critical Handbook of Children's Literature*. Second edition. Scott, Foresman, 1982. Copyright © 1982, 1976 Scott, Foresman and Company. All rights reserved. Reprinted by permission of the publisher.

Mackail, Denis. From *Barrie: The Story of J. M. B.* Charles Scribner's Sons, 1941.

Mazer, Harry. From an excerpt from *Literature for Today's Young Adults*. Edited by Alleen Pace Nilsen and Kenneth L. Donelson. Second edition. Scott, Foresman, 1985. Copyright © 1985, 1980 Scott, Foresman and Company. All rights reserved. Reprinted by permission of the publisher.

Meyer, Susan E. From *A Treasury of the Great Children's Book Illustrators*. Harry N. Abrams, Inc., Publishers, 1983. Illustrations © 1983 Harry N. Abrams, Inc., New York. All rights reserved. Reprinted by permission of the publisher.

Nathan, George Jean. From *The Theatre Book of the Year, 1949- 1950: A Record and an Interpretation*. Knopf, 1950. Copyright 1950 by George Jean Nathan. Renewed 1977 by Mrs. George Jean Nathan. Reprinted by permission of Associated University Presses, Inc., for the Estate of George Jean Nathan.

Nicholson, Keith. From an introduction to *Kay Nielsen*. Edited by David Larkin. A Peacock Press/Bantam Book, 1975. Copyright 1975 by Bantam Books, Inc. All rights reserved. Reprinted by permission of the publisher.

O'Dell, Scott. From "Newbery Award Acceptance" in *Newbery and Caldecott Medal Books: 1956-1965*. Edited by Lee Kingman. Horn Book, 1965. Copyright © 1965 by The Horn Book, Inc. All rights reserved. Reprinted by permission of the publisher.

Peppin, Brigid, and Lucy Micklethwait. From *Book Illustrators of the Twentieth Century*. Arco, 1984. Copyright © 1984 Cameron Books Ltd. All rights reserved. Reprinted by permission of Arco Publishing, Inc., a division of Simon & Schuster, Inc.

Peppin, Brigid. From *Fantasy: The Golden Age of Fantastic Illustration*. Watson-Guptill Publications, 1975. Copyright © 1975 by Carter Nash Cameron Limited. All rights reserved. Reprinted by permission of the publisher.

Peterson, Linda Kauffman. From a review of "Anatole" and a review of "In My Mother's House," in *Newbery and Caldecott Medal and Honor Books: An Annotated Bibliography*. By Linda Kauffman Peterson and Marilyn Leathers Solt. Hall, 1982. Copyright © 1982 by Marilyn Solt and Linda Peterson. Reprinted by permission of Linda Kauffman Peterson.

Phelps, William Lyon. From *Essays on Modern Dramatists*. The Macmillan Company, 1921.

Poltarnees, Welleran. From *Kay Nielsen: An Appreciation*. Green Tiger Press, 1976. Copyright 1976 by The Green TIger Press. All rights reserved. Reprinted by permission of the publisher.

Rees, David. From *Painted Desert, Green Shade: Essays on Contemporary Writers of Fiction for Children and Young Adults*. The Horn Book Inc., 1984. Copyright © 1980, 1981, 1983, 1984 by David Rees. All rights reserved. Reprinted by permission of the publisher.

Rose, Jacqueline. From *The Case of Peter Pan; or, The Impossibility of Children's Fiction*. Salem House, 1985. © Jacqueline Rose 1984. All rights reserved. Reprinted by permission of Salem House Publishers, Topsfield, Mass.

Roy, James A. From *James Matthew Barrie: An Appreciation*. Charles Scribner's Sons, 1938. Copyright, 1938, renewed 1965 by James A. Roy. All rights reserved. Reprinted with the permission of Charles Scribner's Sons, an imprint of Macmillan Publishing Company.

Sadker, Myra Pollack, and David Miller Sadker. From *Now Upon a Time: A Contemporary View of Children's Literature*. Harper & Row, 1977. Copyright © 1977 by Myra Pollack Sadker and David Miller Sadker. All rights reserved. Reprinted by permission of Harper & Row, Publishers, Inc.

Schon, Isabel. From *A Bicultural Heritage: Themes for the Exploration of Mexican and Mexican-American Culture in Books for Children and Adolescents*. The Scarecrow Press, Inc., 1978. Copyright © 1978 by Isabel Schon. Reprinted by permission of the publisher.

Seiter, Ellen E. From "Survival Tale and Feminist Parable," in *Children's Novels and the Movies*. Edited by Douglas Street. Frederick Ungar Publishing Co., 1983. Copyright © 1983 by The Ungar Publishing Company. Reprinted by permission of the publisher.

Sherrard-Smith, Barbara. From *Children's Books of the Year: 1982*. Julia MacRae Books, 1983. © Barbara Sherrard-Smith 1983. All rights reserved. Reprinted by permission of the publisher.

Sims, Rudine. From *Shadow and Substance: Afro-American Experience in Contemporary Children's Fiction*. National Council of Teachers of English, 1982. © 1982 by the National Council of Teachers of English. All rights reserved. Reprinted by permission of the publisher and the author.

Sutherland, Zena, and May Hill Arbuthnot. From *Children and Books*. Seventh edition. Scott, Foresman, 1986. Copyright © 1986, 1981, 1977, 1972, 1964, 1957, 1947 Scott, Foresman and Company. All rights reserved. Reprinted by permission of the publisher.

Swinnerton, Frank. From *The Georgian Scene: A Literary Panorama*. Farrar & Rinehart, 1934. Copyright 1934, © 1962 by Frank Swinnerton. All rights reserved. Reprinted by permission of Tessa Sayle Agency.

Townsend, John Rowe. From *A Sense of Story: Essays on Contemporary Writers for Children*. J. B. Lippincott Company, 1971. Copyright © 1971 by John Rowe Townsend. All rights reserved. Reprinted by permission of Harper & Row, Publishers, Inc.

Townsend, John Rowe. From *Written for Children: An Outline of English-Language Children;s Literature*. Second revised edition. J. B. Lippincott, 1983, Penguin Books, 1983. Copyright © 1965, 1974, 1983 by John Rowe Townsend. All rights reserved. Reprinted by permission of Harper & Row, Publishers, Inc. In Canada by Penguin Books Ltd.

Ventura, Piero. From *Piero Ventura's Book of Cities*. Random House, 1975. Copyright © 1975 by Piero Ventura. All rights reserved. Reprinted by permission of Random House, Inc.

Walkley, A. B. From *Drama and Life*. Methuen & Co., 1907.

Wilkin, Binnie Tate. From *Survival Themes in Fiction for Children and Young People*. The Scarecrow Press, Inc., 1978. Copyright © 1978 by Binnie Tate Wilkin. Reprinted by permission of the publisher.

CUMULATIVE INDEX TO AUTHORS

This index lists all author entries in *Children's Literature Review* and includes cross-references to them in other Gale sources. References in the index are identified as follows:

AITN:	*Authors in the News,* Volumes 1-2
CA:	*Contemporary Authors* (original series), Volumes 1-124
CANR:	*Contemporary Authors New Revision Series,* Volumes 1-24
CAP:	*Contemporary Authors Permanent Series,* Volumes 1-2
CA-R:	*Contemporary Authors* (revised editions), Volumes 1-44
CDALB:	*Concise Dictionary of American Literary Biography,* Volumes 1-3
CLC:	*Contemporary Literary Criticism,* Volumes 1-50
CLR:	*Children's Literature Review,* Volumes 1-16
DLB:	*Dictionary of Literary Biography,* Volumes 1-70
DLB-DS:	*Dictionary of Literary Biography Documentary Series,* Volumes 1-5
DLB-Y:	*Dictionary of Literary Biography Yearbook,* Volumes 1980-1987
NCLC:	*Nineteenth-Century Literature Criticism,* Volumes 1-19
SAAS:	*Something about the Author Autobiography Series,* Volume 1-6
SATA:	*Something about the Author,* Volumes 1-52
TCLC:	*Twentieth-Century Literary Criticism,* Volumes 1-27
YABC:	*Yesterday's Authors of Books for Children,* Volumes 1-2

Author Index

Author Index

CUMULATIVE INDEX TO NATIONALITIES

AMERICAN

CUMULATIVE INDEX TO TITLES

Title Index

Title Index

Title Index

Title Index